# THE POSTCOLONIAL
# AND THE GLOBAL

# THE POSTCOLONIAL
# AND THE GLOBAL

Revathi Krishnaswamy and John C. Hawley, Editors

University of Minnesota Press
Minneapolis • London

Published by the University of Minnesota Press
111 Third Avenue South, Suite 290
Minneapolis, MN 55401-2520
http://www.upress.umn.edu

Library of Congress Cataloging-in-Publication Data

The postcolonial and the global / Revathi Krishnaswamy and John C. Hawley, editors.
    p. cm.
Includes bibliographical references and index.
ISBN: 978-0-8166-4608-1 (hc : alk. paper)
ISBN-10: 0-8166-4608-2 (hc : alk. paper)
ISBN: 978-0-8166-4609-8 (pb : alk. paper)
ISBN-10: 0-8166-4609-0 (pb : alk. paper)
1. Postcolonialism. 2. Internationalism. 3. Globalization.
I. Krishnaswamy, Revathi, 1960– II. Hawley, John C. (John Charles),
1947–
JV51.P64 2007
325'.3—dc22
2007018258

Printed in the United States of America on acid-free paper

The University of Minnesota is an equal-opportunity educator and employer.

15 14 13 12 11 10 09 08                    10 9 8 7 6 5 4 3 2 1

In memory of Edward W. Said

# CONTENTS

# ACKNOWLEDGMENTS

We would like to thank individuals at our home institutions: Ari Jones at San Jose State University for helping us prepare the manuscript, and Don Dodson, Senior Vice Provost at Santa Clara University, for providing a generous grant to bring the project to completion.

# INTRODUCTION

*At the Crossroads of Postcolonial
and Globalization Studies*

# POSTCOLONIAL AND GLOBALIZATION STUDIES:
## CONNECTIONS, CONFLICTS, COMPLICITIES

*Revathi Krishnaswamy*

Postcolonial studies and globalization theory are not monolithic or homogeneous academic fields, but they do represent two dominant discursive formations that regulate contemporary knowledge production in the humanities and social sciences. Yet, unlike the confrontations that took place between postcolonialism and postmodernism, "the twin peaks of '80s theoretical thinking" (Bhabha 2003, 3), so far there have been few systematic or broad-based attempts to scrutinize the links between postcolonialism and globalization theory.[1] In fact, the two fields appear to have developed relatively apart and maintained quite different disciplinary affiliations even when their historical or geopolitical points of reference have converged. Thus, postcolonialism evolved mainly in the humanities, whereas globalization theory evolved mainly in the social sciences. Postcolonialism focuses largely on a Eurocentric colonial past and examines how subaltern practices and productions in the non-Western peripheries responded to Western domination. Globalization theory concentrates largely on a post/neocolonial present and examines how contemporary Western practices and productions affect the rest of the world. Methodologically, postcolonial studies tend to be hermeneutic or deconstructive, problematizing the issue of representation, whereas globalization theory tends to be more brazenly positivistic, taking its representational ability for granted (Radhakrishnan 2001 and this volume). Despite the professed interest in geopolitics, much of the work on globalization produced in the social sciences references the postcolonial only rarely and then rather simplistically or reductively.[2] By contrast, scholars within postcolonial studies have been more willing to recognize that "neo-colonial imbalances in the contemporary world order . . . have in fact not been engaged with enough by postcolonial critics who grapple with the shades of the colonial past much more than with the difficulties of the postcolonial present. If the discipline of postcolonial studies is to survive in any meaningful way, it needs to absorb itself far more deeply with the contemporary world, and with the local circumstances within which colonial institutions and ideas are being moulded into the disparate cultural and socioeconomic practices which define our contemporary 'globality'" (Loomba 1998, 256–57). Still, the question of *how* postcolonialism should engage globalization, on what terms and to what ends, remains unclear.[3]

Meanwhile, in tandem with the absence of explicit cross-referencing and acknowledgments, a silent proliferation of theoretical concepts and terminology has been taking place, leading to certain ideological convergences between postcolonialism and globalization theory, and muddying older distinctions between right- and left-critiques (Brennan, this volume). So whether globalization is a relatively new phenomenon (Giddens 1990) or a relatively old one (Robertson 1992), what seems relatively new about current globalization theory is its postcolonial content (Gikandi 2001; Krishnaswamy 2002): the vocabulary of deterritorialization, migrancy, difference, hybridity and cosmopolitanism, and the use of certain cultural productions designated as "postcolonial" as evidence and exemplars of globalization (Salman Rushdie's novels or Indian cricket, for example). The terms of globalization theory—universal and particular, global and local, homogeneity and heterogeneity—derive from a decidedly postcolonial grammar, especially the Homi Bhabha brand. Postcolonial conceptions of difference, migrancy, hybridity, and cosmopolitanism serve to harmonize the universal and the particular in ways that appear to open up the global to a multiplicity of cultural relationships unheard of in the age of imperialism. In many theoretical formulations, postcolonial cosmopolitanism appears to work against all forms of totalization and homogenization, be it modernization, Westernization or Americanization, capitalism, or nationalism. Welded with poststructuralist ideas of difference and decentering, and yoked to postmodernist notions of fragmentation and multiplicity, this postcolonial content is often strategically marshaled to represent the emerging global order as a deeply disruptive yet ultimately enabling condition that unleashes subaltern resistance and enables creative adaptations in the margins. In such theorizations, the earlier hostility between postcolonialism and postmodernism appears to have given way to a much cozier fit between the postcolonial and the global. Indeed, the two seem to have become one and the same so that to be global is first and foremost to be postcolonial and to be postcolonial is always already to be global (Krishnaswamy 2003, 2005). What exactly does such historical and ideological convergence mean (McMurtry, this volume; Trivedi, this volume)? And what does it portend for the future of postcolonial studies?

Simon During, who believes the category of globalization has superceded that of postcolonialism, posits a dialectical relationship between the two and argues that postcolonialism should be seen not simply as the enemy but also as the effect of globalization (During 1998, 2000). More intriguing is Lawrence Grossberg's suggestion that "globalization has replaced 'postmodernity' as the preferred concept through which to think the specificity of the contemporary formation, perhaps because it is (wrongly) assumed that the move itself is sufficient to avoid the [postcolonial] charge of Euro- or ethnocentrism" (Grossberg 1999, 11). Is globalization theory then just a strategically recast version of postmodernism—one that effectively blunts the critical edge of postcolonialism through a spatiotemporal leveling of differences? And if it is, can postcolonial studies survive its rapid assimilation into globalization theory and still manage to stake out a separate, meaningful future for itself?

Beyond the "shared cultural grammar" of hybridity, difference, and cosmopolitanism, however, the relationship between the postcolonial and the global is not very clear (Gikandi 2001, 628). It is unclear, for instance, whether contemporary globalization has been made possible by the postcolonial challenge to older Eurocentric forms of globalization premised on the centrality of the nation and narrated in terms of modernization or whether postcoloniality itself is the consequence of a globalization premised on the marginalization of the nation in the economic and cultural domains. It is unclear whether the postcolonial precedes and provides the foundations for the global and hence for transnational cultural studies (Eng and Stratton 1996), or whether globalization has created the historical and material conditions that have both enabled the production of postcolonialism and eroded its political purchase through incorporation and domestication (Hardt and Negri 2000). It is unclear whether postcolonialism has become complicit with the forces of neoliberal globalism (Ahmad 1992) or whether it has provided fertile breeding ground for uninformed anticapitalist, antiglobalist sentiments (Bhagwati 2004, 15–18). Is globalization opening up unforeseen opportunities for oppressed masses or is it merely euphemizing corporatization and imperial expansion (Brennan, this volume)? Is globalization giving postcolonial subjects a chance to enter and exit modernity on their own terms, or even allowing them to transcend modernity altogether (García Canclini 1995; Appadurai 1996; Hall 2000; Gikandi 2001)? What is the time-space of the postcolonial in the emerging dispensation? Are we witnessing the advancement and apotheosis of postcolonial hybridity or its assimilation and demise? What kind of world order is emerging in the wake of 9/11 and whose interests will it serve (San Juan, Majid, Rodriquez, all this volume)? Are we on the brink of a brave new "flat world" (Friedman 2005) brimming with opportunities for all, or are we hurtling toward a permanent state of war and planetary scarcity? Are we witnessing an intensification of American imperialism, or have we gone beyond imperialism altogether and entered "Empire," the centerless space of capital destined to be shattered by a surging multitude (Hardt and Negri 2000)? What would it mean to rethink the postcolonial in terms of "planetarity" rather than globality (Spivak 2003, chapter 3; Gilroy 2005, xv)? These are serious questions and they deserve the serious attention they are given in this volume.

## COMPARATIVITY

The project undertaken in this volume is inevitably comparativist, although it is not comparative in any received sense of the term. The older comparativist framework, conceived with the nation-state as its dominant referent, has, of course, fallen into disrepute because the terms that previously constituted the grammar of comparison have been deconstructed and shown to be nothing more than Eurocentric provincialisms pretending to be universals. Unfortunately, the valuable recognition that specific epistemologies of comparison, whether associated with modernization, developmental theory, or orthodox Marxism, are flawed and limited has often resulted in an uncritical abandonment of all comparison and an unmindful embrace of all forms of heterogeneity, multiplicity, diversity, and difference, often with little or no reference to specific historical or material contexts (Spivak 2003).[4] Although postcolonial cultural studies promised to produce a viable alternative agenda for comparison by turning to referents that exceed the boundaries of the nation-state, many of the interpretive models that have emerged from this approach appear to unwittingly replicate the aporias of the older approaches they desire to displace. Thus, for instance, the desire to overcome Eurocentrism has in some instances led postcolonial theorists to posit an indigenous realm of pure externality, a simple outside to Western/capitalist modernity, variously represented as inner spirituality, untranslatable alterity, incommensurable difference, and radical singularity (Chakrabarty 1993, 1997; Chatterjee 1993). In other instances, the desire to dismantle dominant (epistemic) regimes and schemas has led theorists to produce counterregimes in which a dehistoricized hybridity assumes an equally rigid and axiomatic hold on cultural studies as did the older purities of imperialism and nationalism.[5] Howsoever alluring in theory, these gestures have in effect opened the door to an "empirical pluralism" (Anderson 1980, 78) that provides grist for the multiculturalism mill, and alibi for global capitalism (Shohat and Stam, this volume).

Within the pages of this volume, the limitations and shortcomings in postcolonial conceptions of comparison are taken up sympathetically, if also critically, as provocations to rethink the possibilities of comparativity. The two main assumptions underlying this collection may now be articulated as follows: first, because thinking the global necessitates some form of relational thinking, the task before us, in the wake of the contemporary crisis in comparison, is not to repudiate but to reinvent a critical comparative studies; second, a productive confrontation between postcolonial and globalization studies is indispensable for such a revisioning of comparativity. Motivated by these assumptions, several essays in this volume seek to grapple, explicitly or implicitly, with the problematics of comparison and incomparativity in relation to theory, disciplinarity, identity, and geotemporal location (Mignolo and

Tlostanova; Buchanan and Pahuja; Pheng Cheah; Shohat and Stam, for example). These essays engage in active disciplinary border crossings, opening up new horizons of comparativity and novel possibilities for thinking globality. Other essays, perhaps reflecting the segregated state of scholarship alluded to earlier in this chapter exhibit a more marked disciplinary or ideological affiliation, even when it is evident that they have much broader applications (McMurtry, Radhakrishnan, San Juan, Sklair, for example). But by bringing these essays together and by juxtaposing them against each other, we have tried to generate an implicit dialog (as well as a pedagogical context) about thinking comparatively and about theorizing postcolonial planetarity. So by way of opening up rather than summarizing the rich and complex debates that follow, I discuss here some salient connections, conflicts, and complicities between postcolonial studies and globalization theory. Trying to think relationally, I have found it useful to cluster my thoughts around four issues that seem central to both fields: modernity, mobility, imperiality, and resistance.

## MODERNITY

The category of modernity represents a critical point of reference for both postcolonial and globalization studies. Modernity is widely regarded as a culturalist/chronocentric concept that posits a linear, teleological line of "development" beginning with ancient Greece and culminating in eighteenth-century Europe ("Western Civilization"). In the social sciences, modernity is assumed to be a fairly transparent category that lies at the heart of globalization. Because the spread of (Western, capitalist) modernity is seen to be the main motor driving globalization, the crisis of globalization becomes the result of the narrative of modernity, its success or failure (Giddens 1991; Bauman 1995). From this perspective "postmodernity" is understood both as a historical process in which modernity encountered its limits, as well as a critical discourse that deconstructs modernity (Jameson 2003). But even where the global is figured in terms of the postmodern rather than the modern, globalization frequently represents an intensification of modernity rather than a break with it (Brennan, this volume). Postmodern globalization therefore becomes Western modernity without labels or pretensions, mere ubiquity:

> Modernity once deemed itself universal. Now it thinks of itself as global. Behind the change of term hides a watershed in the history of modern self-awareness and self-confidence. Universal was to be the rule of reason—the order of things that would replace the slavery to passions with the autonomy of rational beings, superstition and ignorance with truth, tribulations of the drifting plankton with self-made and thoroughly monitored history-by-design. 'Globality,' in contrast, means merely that everyone everywhere may feed on McDonald's hamburgers and watch the latest made-for-TV docudrama. Universality was a proud project, a Herculean mission to perform. Globality in contrast, is *a meek acquiescence to what is happening 'out there'.* . . (Bauman 1995, 24, emphasis added)

But if "meek acquiescence" is all that's left, what happens to the postcolonial project of dismantling or transcending modernity?

Modernity, identified with Western domination, is, of course, a thorn in the side of postcolonialism. Following the Peruvian sociologist Anibal Quijano, Latin American scholarship has elaborated the notion of "coloniality" or "coloniality of power" to represent the darker side of modernity (Quijano 1997, 2000). Coloniality refers to a power grid or a matrix that links modernity, colonialism, capitalism, and racism. The concept of coloniality "moves back the ❦ clock of modern history" to the foundation of colonialism/capitalism during the sixteenth century in the Atlantic world (Mignolo and Tlostanova, this volume). It also expands the critique of capitalism by emphasizing the constitutive role of race (and gender to a lesser extent) in shaping the modern world-system. Like the "modern world-system" developed by Emmanuel Wallerstein, Samir Amin, and Giovanni Arrighi, the Latin American conceptualization of coloniality/modernity draws on dependency theory and emphasizes not a culturalistic/chronocentric but an economistic/spatial articulation of power. From this perspective, modernity is a structural relationship not a substantive content. But unlike the modern world-system, which brings colonialism into the picture "as a derivative rather than a constitutive component of modernity," the Latin American critique makes coloniality constitutive of capitalist modernity (Mignolo 2001). It may therefore be seen either as a complement or an alternative to postmodern (Eurocentric) criticisms of modernity on the one hand and to ("mainstream") postcolonial studies on the other (Mignolo and Tlostanova, this volume).

Critiques of modernity in ("mainstream") postcolonial studies have oscillated between rejection and negotiation. Those who reject the culture of modernity as Western, imperialist, ruthless, and alienating try to recover multiple forms of premodern or precolonial indigenous traditions, knowledges, and communities (Nandy 1988). The South Asian Subaltern Studies historians have been especially influential in elaborating this approach. Contending that the modular account of modernity articulated by Benedict Anderson (1983) is Eurocentric because it reduces all others to mere "consumers of [Western] modernity" (Chatterjee 1993, 5), each of the major Subaltern historians have variously sought to recover a subjectivity that has somehow eluded the tentacles of colonial modernity. For Guha the privileged resistant subject is the subaltern, "the people" expelled from history and marginalized not only by colonialism but also by elite forms of nationalism (liberal as well as communist). Guha's subaltern thus exists "at the very limits of translatability of Western codes," or at "the historic threshold that the so-called universalism of a Eurocentric reason and its engine of global expansion – capital – failed to cross in the age of colonialism" (1997, xx). For Chatterjee, the sphere of the spiritual, from which Indian nationalism supposedly emerged, constitutes an autonomous domain untrammeled by Western modernity (1993). For Chakrabarty, who takes aim at Marxist narratives of development, it is "insufficiently abstracted" labor that represents the limits of colonial capitalist modernity. Concrete real labor (History 2) "belongs," "dwells," and stubbornly refuses differentiation. It lives tenaciously against the developmentalist grain of the logic of abstract labor (History 1; Chakrabarty 2000). Although Spivak too has articulated a subalternist critique of Marx's developmentalism and his idea of "the Asiatic mode of production," she has, in a scrupulously deconstructive gesture, refused to posit an alternative autonomous domain or to fabricate a resistant world-historical subject (Spivak 1999).

Other important postcolonial theorists too have turned away from conjunctural accounts of modernity and offered their own disjunctural analyses.[6] Arjun Appadurai's *Modernity at Large* (along with *Public Culture*) has been extremely influential in articulating a more negotiated approach to modernity. Contending that globalization entails a certain "disjuncture" between the economic, the political, and the cultural, Appadurai represents the consumption of modernity in the margins as an active process through which postcolonial subaltern subjects construct their own hybrid modernities. Downgrading Western modernity to a contested if crucial point of origin/reference, and challenging both its homogenizing claim and teleological imperative, Appadurai argues that "different societies appropriate the materials of modernity differently" to produce multiple, hybrid, or alternative modernities (Appadurai 1996, 17; see also Gaonkar 2001). Appadurai thus makes a crucial distinction between older forms of modernity, whose goal was an instrumental rationalization of the world in Weberian terms, and the symbolic economy of a new global culture routed through reciprocity rather than in hierarchy. From this perspective, globalization represents a proliferation of modernities, each with its own historical trajectory rather than the universalization of a single Western modernity. The result is that the classic Enlightenment binary between traditionalism and modernity is displaced by a disseminated set of "vernacular modernities" that enable non-Western societies, to "enter 'modernity', acquire the fruits of its technologies, and yet do so to some extent on their terms" (Hall 2000, 215–16).

By deconstructing the dominant narrative of modernization and by questioning the implicit identification of the West as the beginning and end of modernity, postcolonial artic-ulations of "alternative" and "vernacular" modernities have tried to empower those marginal-ized by modernity. The problem, however, is that in doing so, they have often elided the fact that the question of modernity is subject to intense internal debate even within the cultural, civilizational, national, or ethnic spaces they take as their units of analysis. As I have argued elsewhere, claims about the alternative modernity of Indian cricket or secularism, for instance, can be sustained only by occluding their highly gendered or casteist character (Krishnaswamy 2003, 2005). The culturalist logic underlying notions of multiple moderni-ties can be problematic as well because it frequently misrepresents forms of unevenness or spatiotemporal differences as "historical residuals" of an anterior time-space rather than as "actively reconstituted features" continually produced by the internal contradictions of capitalism (Harvey 1982, 416, 1989).

Harry Harootunian argues that the proliferation of the sties of modernity in postcolonial theory (which he sees as resulting from postcolonialism's preoccupation with the spatial at the cost of the temporal) is not only reminiscent of a Weberian tendency to privilege the cultur-al (modernity) over the economic (capitalism), it also reinscribes a unified "Europe" or "West" as the privileged place of an original modernity and thus leaves the basic conceptual schema of modernization theory intact (Harootunian 2005). Harootunian's critique further alerts us to the ways in which many claims for alternative or multiple modernities continue to implicitly recuperate the binary logic they appear to repudiate. Thus in "Two Theories of Modernity," Charles Taylor suggests that instead of seeing modernity as universal or universable, it would be better to see it as taking different forms in different cultures because this would help us grasp not only what is divergent in non-Western modernities but also what is most original or unique to Western modernity (Taylor 2001). But, as Gaurav Desai points out, Taylor's argument comes up short when confronting the question of normativity. Acknowledging that modernity is not simply about successful adaptations to change but also about normative values (individualism, democracy, reason, etc.), Taylor asks in an important footnote, "Can we create a normatively superior alternative modernity?" His answer: "Not every mode of cultural distinctness is thereby justified and good." As Desai caustically com-ments, "therein lies the rub" (Desai 2006). Even such an astute critic as Fredric Jameson is not immune to this kind of culturalist ethnocentrism. "Americans," writes Jameson, "always find it shocking when foreigners suggest that human rights, feminist values, and even parlia-mentary democracy are not necessarily to be seen as universals, but rather merely local American cultural characteristics that have been exported as practices valid for all peoples in the world. That kind of shock is good for us, I want to say" (Jameson 1998, 64). What this sincere and well-intentioned exposé of American provincialism (notice the locus of enuncia-tion shifting between Americans, us, I) does in the final analysis is patent human rights, feminist values, and democratic processes in the name of America.[7]

What then is the alternative to "alterative modernities"? Is it a wholesale endorsement of the West's exclusive claim to modernity? Simon Gikandi has recently contended that what postcolonial subjects really want is neither "cultural hybridity nor ontological difference" but "a modern life in the European sense of the word." Insisting on the material rather than the ethical nature of postcolonial desire for Europe, Gikandi argues as follows: "Unsure how to respond to the failure of the nationalist mandate, which promised modernization outside the tutelage of colonialism, citizens of the postcolony are more likely to seek their global identity by invoking the very logic of Enlightenment that postcolonial theory was supposed to deconstruct" (Gikandi 2001, 630). Although Gikandi's attempt to restore the importance of modernity to postcoloniality represents an important corrective intervention in postcolonial theory, we may need to be more cautious when generalizing about diverse postcolonial contexts. In a recent essay on caste politics in India, I have shown how the very invocation of the Enlightenment by anticaste movements in India presses against the logic of reinscribing Europe as the sole site of Reason (Krishnaswamy 2005). For example, Dalit nationalist leader Dr. Ambedkar sought to strategically infuse the ideals of the French Revolution with those of another Enlightenment—the Enlightenment of the Buddha—in order to articulate a less instrumentalized, less managerial notion of reason he believed would be truly anti-imperialistic and liberatory (Ambedkar 1987). Ambedkar's stance cannot be simply categorized as outright assimilation, rejection, or negotiation. Rather, it represents a bold and imaginative attempt to re-vision Reason itself as a common human heritage to which different peoples contribute differently. Although drawing on the legacies of earlier colonialisms, Argentinian philosopher Enrique Dussel's (1998) concept of "transmodernity" also posits that modernity is not strictly European but a planetary phenomenon to which "excluded barbarians" have contributed, although their contribution has not been acknowledged. Similarly, Portuguese sociologist Boaventura de Sousa Santos (1998) has argued for "a new common sense" to designate a shared human rationality. These projects, I believe, go beyond a greater acknowledgment of the "antagonistic indebtedness" (Gilroy 1993) postcolonials have to (Western expressions of) modernity toward a more sustained recognition of the contributions of non-Western peoples to the unfinished, ongoing project of planetary transmodernity.[8]

## MOBILITY

Postcolonialism and globalization theory may be divided over the issue of modernity, but they share a strong antagonism toward one of modernity's prime manifestations, the nation-state. Rejecting all forms of national belonging as parochial and tyrannical, dominant strands in both fields embrace cosmopolitanism as the proper ethical basis of global identity. Despite contradictory evidence—witness the proliferation of nation-states after the collapse of the Soviet Union; the rise of ethnic as well as economic or white-collar nationalisms in many parts of the world; the recent rejection of the EU constitution by the French and the Dutch; the consolidation of the militarized nation-state post-9/11—and despite challenges from some scholars, the global has been theorized primarily in opposition to the national, with the former seen to be gaining at the expense of the latter.[9] A vast literature has emerged that documents the rise of a "post-Fordist" regime of flexible accumulation and flexible labor markets. According to this literature, new forms of production and consumption made possible by new technologies associated with global communication combine with new forms of global finance and speculation to create instantaneous currency flows that render the fiscal and monetary policies of even the most powerful nation-states virtually powerless. Whereas the social sciences have focused on the rise of transnational economic/financial policy-making institutions (WTO, IMF, World Bank), regional trading blocs (NAFTA, OPEC, EU), military blocs (NATO), and organizations of global governance (UN), postcolonial theorists of globalization have linked the weakening of the nation-state to the rise of global culture.

Drawing on James Clifford's notion of "traveling cultures," Appadurai has approached globalization as a dual function of increased migration and the rise of new electronic media. For Appadurai (1996, 15), globalization's profound potential to weaken the nation-state, based on primordial myths of ethnicity that articulate and naturalize boundaries of difference, is positive, even empowering because it enables "culturalism," or the instrumental construction of transnational group identities. From this perspective, the Indian IT industry, which has enabled a skilled English-speaking labor force to successfully "take away American jobs," the instrumentalized performance of American-ness by Indian call-center workers to suit their own ends, the exuberant appropriation of "the American dream" by upwardly mobile middle-class Indian consumers, the heady enjoyment of new personal freedoms by Indian youth, must all seem enormously satisfying indeed. But salutary as they are, it is difficult to see how these transformations will fundamentally alter the organization of power on a large scale or challenge capitalism globally. And thinking in terms of planetary sustainability, the prospect of billions more people chasing after the American dream is somewhat terrifying!

The rise of postcolonialism (alongside postmodernism), as many have noted, coincided with an important shift in the social sciences from a politico-economic orientation toward a more culturalist position, even though that concept of culture still seems more tied to anthropological and positivistic models than deconstructive or hermeneutic ones.[10] Thus world-system theory, which combined the traditional Marxist view of economic base-cultural superstructure with dependency theory, was challenged by Roland Robertson, John Tomlinson, and others who sought to establish culture as a relatively autonomous, even privileged, domain for the study of global relations. As a result, world-system theory itself gradually turned toward culture, although Robertson (1992, 66–67) contends the category remained unproductively anchored to Marxist conceptions of ideology. Contending that dependency theory was ineffectual because it paid excessive attention to economic and political forms of domination but failed to address the cultural dimensions of domination, Vincent Tucker (1999, 12) suggested that the social sciences should learn from the more critical, culturalist positions of postcolonial theory whose multiple logics offer alternatives to the Enlightenment rationality on which the concept of development is based. So arguing by analogy many theorists began to equate the conceptual language of cultural globalization with select aspects of the political economy—commodification, financial flows, capital transfers, flexible accumulation—that seem to resonate with the semiotic vocabulary of cultural studies. Elements of the global economy or polity that can be read under the sign of semiotic "circulation" were mobilized for a wider political and ethical argument against all forms of belonging and dwelling, irrespective of race, class, gender, and other material variables. The world market, seen as a bricolage of borderless bazaars, was hailed as the destroyer of the imperial cartography that defined global relations since the early modern period. Amidst growing "endist" euphoria (Lazarus 1999, 41–51), proclamations about the end of geography and history, prophesies about the arrival of a "flat world," continue to percolate as much on the left as on the right.[11]

Mobility—real or virtual—is seen to facilitate the emergence of a whole immense range of hitherto excluded groups, races, genders, and ethnicities into the speech of the public sphere.[12] Even Hardt and Negri, who contend that postcolonialism (along with postmodernism) has been rendered toothless by global capitalism's appropriation of hybridity, nevertheless recuperate postcolonialism's central trope of migrancy as the critical terrain on which the global is at once produced and resisted. Claiming that "nomadism and miscegenation" are "figures of virtue, the first ethical practices on the terrain of Empire" (2000, 8), they declare that "the real heroes of the liberation of the third world may really have been the emigrants and the flows of population that have destroyed old and new boundaries" (2000, 362–63). Rejecting "the slavery of belonging to a nation, an identity and a people" (2000, 8), Hardt and Negri demand that all restrictions on the mobility of labor be lifted so that people may move anywhere and acquire full citizenship in whichever country they live and work (2000, 400). In such formulations, proletarian migrancy or nomad labor, which Marx had seen as symptomatic of the power of capital, are made to appear actively agential partly by occluding practices such as outsourcing, which are rapidly rendering the movement of labor irrelevant if not obsolete.[13]

Is it proper to analyze the phenomenon of "time-space compression" (Harvey 1989, 240–41) that facilitates global mobility separately from the power relations that produce different forms of temporal and spatial mobility? We cannot, for instance, fail to note that America's recent retreat into economic nationalism, evidenced in the outbursts against immigration and IT outsourcing in major print and media outlets, reveals how American national identity continues to be strongly tied to a strategic and privileged conception of mobility that imagines the United States as the ultimate dream destination of global labor but refuses to seriously imagine the possibility of an American labor diaspora (Hashimi 2006). The notion of "transformational mobility," so central to American cultural identity (Bruce-Novoa 2003, 110), is always premised on the accessibility of free and self-willed movement, never on the possibility of forced movement, especially beyond the borders of the United States. How then can we ignore the fact that the transnational capitalist class controls the process of time-space compression and is capable of modifying it to suit its needs (Sklair, this volume), whereas the subordinated classes (migrant workers and refugees), even though they effect a great number of transborder movements, have little or no control over the time-space compression? Although some forms of forced mobility can be productive of empowering knowledge and agency for some subjects even in adverse conditions (Indian IT workers in the United States, for instance; see Sivakumar 2004; Chakrabarty 2005), the interpenetration of mobility and forcible displacement in the era of globalization is turning vast numbers of people into refugees, often in their "own" territories (Bauman 1995). As a result, the refugee camp is fast becoming a zone of normality rather than a zone of exception (Agamben 2005). Even such an arch theorist of transnationalism and migrancy as Homi Bhabha has faulted Hardt and Negri for claiming "too much too soon," for neglecting "to confront the fact that migrants, refugees, and nomads don't merely circulate. They need to settle, claim asylum or nationality, demand housing and education, assert their economic and cultural rights, and come to be legally represented" (2003, 5). Yet how can they be represented if the nation-state is dismantled? The nation-state can be repressive but it can also offer protection against imperialism.[14] Limiting state sovereignty therefore mainly deprives less powerful states of the chance to resist globally mandated measures that compromise the welfare of their citizens.[15] Although all nation-states are becoming more porous to finance capital, not all nation-states are being similarly restructured or equally eroded; it is the weaker nation-states that are being remade to suit the interests of the more powerful.[16]

On a different level, the "war on terror" is being used by nation-states everywhere to shore up and even increase their repressive powers. Deliberately muddying the distinction between legitimate concern and illegitimate fear, between military/terrorist threat and economic insecurity, even supposedly democratic states have appropriated to themselves enormous authority, often at the expense of "their own" citizens, particularly those already disadvantaged and marginalized. The United States has provided the lead in this regard, manufacturing a whole new set of practices and spawning a whole new vocabulary around the "war on terror" in order to bolster its dominance internally as well as externally. Rapidly transmitted/translated into local idioms across the world, these novel practices and vocabularies are being strategically hybridized and differentially deployed by various nation-states against varied local populations.[17] If the nation-state was indeed dying, the war on terror appears to have given it a new lease on life.

## IMPERIALITY

Is globalization simply a continuation of the West's (neo)imperial project or is it really altering the balance of world power? Is the twenty-first century destined to be another American century? What is the impact of 9/11 on the emerging global (dis)order? There is a widespread belief among theorists today that globalization is no longer synonymous with (gloomy Marxist notions of) Westernization or American imperialism. Many believe globalization is diminishing rather than increasing American power (especially in the economic but also in the political sphere), with rivals such as EU and China growing more powerful. Appadurai, for instance, rejects the idea that globalization is synonymous with homogenization or Westernization (1996, 17; see also interview in this volume where he compares the United States to Gulliver tied down by Lilliputian ropes). John Tomlinson goes further and rejects the very concept of "Westernization" as too broad.[18] "The West," Tomlinson notes, is not a homogenous indivisible package but a whole range of things including capitalist consumer culture (with such familiar icons as Coca-Cola, McDonald's, Levi Jeans), European languages (especially English), styles of dress, architecture, music, cultural values, and attitudes about personal liberty, sexuality and gender, human rights, the political process, religion, scientific and technological rationality, and so on that are chopped up and either consumed or resisted separately and differently in different locations. Arguing that Islamic societies accept Western technology while vigorously rejecting the West's sexual permissiveness, Tomlinson contends that a careful discrimination between various aspects of what is often crudely totalized as "Westernization" reveals a more complex picture (1999, 23). For Appadurai, Tomlinson, and others who stress the idea of subversive consumption, culture simply does not transfer in a unilinear way, because movement between cultural/geographical areas always involves selection, interpretation, translation, mutation, and adaptation—processes designated by terms such as *indigenization* and *vernacularization*—with the receiving culture bringing its own cultural resources to bear, in dialectical fashion, upon cultural imports. What goes unnoticed in these celebratory theories of globalization, however, is the fact that exchanges across geographic and cultural borders, which have been taking place for a long time, are almost always uneven and their impact unequal.

Increasingly, though, it is not only culturalist critics such as Tomlinson and Appadurai who believe that globalization is weakening Western hegemony. Anthony Giddens, one of the leading theorists of globalization and well known for his economism, has also powerfully linked globalization with the decline rather than the triumph of the West. Giddens writes of the "gradual decline in European or Western global hegemony, the other side of which is the increasing expansion of modern influences worldwide," of "the declining grip of the West over the rest of the world" or of "the evaporating of the privileged position of the West" (1990, 51–53). Pointing to the rise of the so-called "Asian Tiger" economies and to the crisis within the Western discipline of anthropology as two instances that attest to the loss of Western privilege, Giddens argues that "globalization today can no longer be spoken of only as a matter of one-way imperialism . . . increasingly there is no obvious 'direction' to globalization at all and its ramifications are more or less ever present. The current phase of globalization, then, should not be confused with the preceding one, whose structures it acts increasingly to subvert" (1990, 96). Basically, Giddens's argument is that though the process of "globalizing modernity" may have begun in the extension of Western institutions, the very fact of the current global ubiquity of these institutions (capitalism, industrialism, etc.)—in a sense the West's "success" in disseminating its institutional forms—also represents a decline in the differentials between it and the rest of the world, thus a loss of the West's (once unique) social/cultural edge. What is striking about this argument is the way in which the very ubiquitousness of modernity does the ideological work of transforming hegemony and homogeneity into a net gain. It seems as though the West is going global in a fit of absence of mind much like the way the British supposedly acquired their empire.

Although different from Giddens's account in important respects, Hardt and Negri's influential and polemical theorization of globalization paints a paradoxically similar picture of a "runaway world" without center, subject, or direction. In Foucauldian vein, Empire places sovereign power in multiple locations and multiple registers, minimizing the hegemonic role of the West in general and the United States in particular. As conceived by Hardt and Negri, Empire is not imperialism, it is what comes after imperialism. In contrast to imperialism (historically identified with Europe), "Empire establishes no territorial center of power and does not rely on fixed boundaries or barriers. It is a decentered and deterritorializing apparatus of rule that progressively incorporates the entire global realm within its open, expanding frontiers. Empire manages hybrid identities, flexible hierarchies, and plural exchanges through modulating networks of command." (2000, xii–xiii). Hardt and Negri acknowledge that the United States occupies a privileged place in their centerless Empire, yet its privilege, they contend, derives not from its similarities to the old European empires, but from its difference (2000, xiii–xiv). This difference, for Hardt and Negri, was brought out clearly during the Gulf War, when the United States emerged as the only power that could disburse international justice "not as a function of its own national motives but in the name of a global right. . . . The U.S. world police acts not in imperialist interest but in imperial interest." (2000, 180). But in fact this merger of the imperialist with the imperial, of the sovereign with sovereignty, of U.S. law with "international law" is precisely what is enabling the United States to universalize its national interest as the interest of the international community itself (those who disagree are by definition not part of this international community). In other words, the United States is at once a sovereign nation-state among other sovereign nation-states (albeit first among equals) as well as the embodiment of sovereignty as such (Buchanan and Pahuja, this volume). Sovereignty is indeed being redefined, as Hardt and Negri contend, but it is being redefined by the powerful in the interests of the powerful.[19]

"We are all Americans now," declared German Chancellor Gerhard Schroeder shortly after 9/11. Schroeder would have been more accurate if he had said "we are all American subjects now" — although that does not mean we are all equally subjected. The merger of the American nation-state with the state of the globe is among the most significant aspects of globalization 911 or "imperiality," as I propose to call it. I use the term imperiality (rather than "new," "informal," or "superimperialism") for two reasons: first, to suggest both a break as well as a continuity with older forms of formal imperialism; second, to establish a theoretical affiliation with the notion of coloniality. Unlike (Hardt and Negri's) Empire, imperiality continues to operate in terms of hierarchy and dependency (now euphemistically known as interdependence and globalization), although the nineteenth-century center/periphery dichotomy is indeed being altered in important ways (as "first worlds" appear inside the "third" and "third worlds" inside the "first," as the "second world" disappears and "fourth worlds" rise). Imperiality is also not about "the end of geography" but about the production of new geographies (Harvey 2003; Sassen, this volume). Étienne Balibar has drawn attention to the "violence of the border" in Europe where apartheid, officially dismantled in Africa, is being actively reproduced in the form of structures of discrimination that command uneven access to (European) citizenship (Balibar 2001). Cartographies of global violence reveal a grim line between death zones and life zones (Majid, Rodriquez, this volume). It is clear that global power has not deserted the bastions of binary thinking either. In the United States, an imperialistic (racist, masculinist) moral rhetoric of "us versus them," "good versus evil," "Christian, liberal West versus righteous fundamentalist Islam" has been given a new lease on life after 9/11 (Marable 2003; Willis 2003). And it is not confined to the (American) far right either. Even those who believe the old polarity between East and West or North and South has disappeared rely on (neoliberal) global boundaries, such as the one Thomas Friedman draws between the "World of Order" (United States, EU, Russia, India, and China) and the "World of Disorder" (failed states such as Liberia; rogue states such as Iraq and North Korea; messy states such as Pakistan and Indonesia).[20]

Yet imperiality is not simply imperialism without territory. It is distinguished by freedom from interimperialist rivalry and dependence on free-market competition. From this perspective, (Germany-led) Europe and (China/India-led) Asia appear as competitors (mainly in the economic and to a much lesser degree in the political sphere) rather than rivals (Ahmad 2004). As competitors they can grab larger shares of the capitalist cake but cannot overcome or defeat the United States, which monopolizes military power and dominates global politics to a great extent. Imperiality is also post-Communist, post–Cold War, postmodern, and, above all, postcolonial (but not postcapitalist, postpatriarchal, or postracist). It is postcolonial in the sense that it is "not only free of colonial rule but antithetical to it" (Ahmad 2004, 233). Blurring distinctions between wars of liberation, civil wars, interstate wars, racial genocide, ethnic cleansing, communal rioting, and "natural" catastrophes (famine, poverty) that are actually socially overdetermined, imperiality speaks in tongues about freedom, diversity, liberation, democracy, human rights, and just wars. At the same time, imperiality is anti-postcolonial. It is anti-postcolonial in the sense that it represents "a reactive though emergent moment in global governance of forced dehybridization and homogenization," a moment that Mark Driscoll calls "reverse postcoloniality" (Driscoll 2004, 70).[21] Imperiality's uncanny and cunning (ab)use of the critical language of postcoloniality perhaps makes Edward Said's legacy of worldly, oppositional, contrapuntal criticism ever more urgent today.

The logic of imperiality is expressed in the ideology of permanent intervention and preemptive war (the war against terror is "a task that never ends"), in the systematic use of various forms of extreme violence and mass insecurity to prevent collective movements of emancipation. Imperiality universalizes material and moral insecurity to induce massive reproletarianization of labor, to minimize the possibilities of representation of the subaltern within the state apparatus, and to suppress the very possibilities of dissent. In this way imperiality makes the world "unbearable" (Amin 1992), unleashing worldwide terror and terrorism (Rodriquez, this volume). But the novelty of 911 imperiality lies in two particular developments: first, the ideology of imperiality is being felt within the borders of the United States itself, which is shifting from a social security to a national security state; second, the global power of the United States is showing some signs of morphing into dominance without hegemony (to draw on Ranajit Guha's famous Gramscian formulation).[22] The steady erosion of civil liberties, justified in terms of national security and patriotism, is a symptom of the first (Robin 2003). The simmering global dissatisfaction with American unilateralism (although geopolitically fractured), the massive militarization of the United States (which now includes the nuclear option), and the unabated insurgency in Iraq are symptoms of the second. That these developments have the potential to thwart imperiality may be the good news; the bad news, of course, is that before that happens, the cost in human lives could well be catastrophic.

## RESISTANCE

What, if any, are the subjects and sites of resistance in imperiality? Post-Fordist capitalism, it is widely claimed, opens up new possibilities for politics by promoting new forms of subjectivity. The demise of communism in Eastern Europe destroyed the imagery of a revolutionary alternative to capitalism, and the paralysis of social democracy in Western Europe undermined faith in the possibilities of class conflict. With capital successfully penetrating every corner of the globe, many theorists of globalization see little sense in thinking of anything outside or beyond capital. Postcolonial scholars, however, locate the limits of capital in its encounter with embodied alternative economic formations that remained partially unassimilated to its (universal/global) logic (Guha 1992; Chakrabarty 2001). From this perspective, although there is no exterior to capital, there is an exteriority to it (Mignolo 2001). But interestingly, this exteriority seems to enable mostly creative negotiation with(in) capitalism, rarely organized opposition to it. Indeed, in many postcolonial theorizations of globalization the resistant subject appears as a subversive consumer who uses things and ideas in unexpected, pragmatic, even playful, ways (Appadurai 1996; Zhen 2001). The representation of consumers as savvy pragmatic decision makers rather than as passive dupes is certainly both refreshing and empowering. But it does reduce agency to a reactive mode of manipulating something that is already established (Radhakrishnan 2001; Krishnaswamy 2002). Although vastly better than abjection or cynicism, can subversive consumption, like the practices of everyday life or the weapons of the weak, do more than dent the dominant structure?[23] As Audre Lourde has famously asked, can the master's tools ever dismantle the master's house? Can reform and regulation, which certainly make life more livable, bring about a revolution?

An influential manifestation of the trend toward reform and accommodation is the so-called Third Way, championed by Anthony Giddens (1999). The goal of Third Way politics is not to stop or control the forces of globalization but to harness the very energies of capitalism to foster social solidarity and civic values. Its main aim is to insulate vulnerable social groups, promote civil society (through public education, health care, etc.), and free individuals to pursue their own potential. Critics on the left have dismissed the Third Way as simply neoliberalism with a human face dressed up in an appealing language of "postideological politics." In particular, they have faulted Giddens' analysis for ignoring two crucial categories: inequality and conflict.[24] There is indeed some validity to this charge because Giddens' insistence that the primary public policy problem is exclusion rather than inequality minimizes growing disparities of income and wealth and ignores the active reproduction of inequality and conflict in globalization.

Post-Marxist theorists today generally believe that proletarian class analysis is exhausted, received notions of class agency and organization anachronistic, and the nation-state no longer an adequate framework for opposition to contemporary capitalism. These views have derived much inspiration from postcolonial deconstructions of classical Marxism's Eurocentric (as well as racist, sexist) bias and its mixed legacy in the third world. In particular, the category of the "subaltern," proposed by South Asianists, and the "damnes," proposed by Latin Americanists, have contributed much to the debate over class. Although some Marxist scholars have tried to engage with postcolonial studies and to reclaim the centrality of class as an analytical category (Bartolovich and Lazarus 2002), many theorists of postcolonialism and globalization today look not to the old socialist internationalism, which they believe is obsolescent, but to the internationalisms of the New Social Movements (women, ecology, peace, human rights) that operate transnationally and are not defined by class consciousness.[25] These movements seem to be the vanguard of a "globalization from below." Some see organized civil society (constituted by various voluntary associations, NGOs, World Social Forum, etc.) as the most promising agent of social transformation today (Hawley; Sassen, both this volume). Others equally disillusioned with class politics find hope in "disorganized" civil society (Hardt and Negri; Burgmann, both this volume). As Hardt and Negri declare, "the restructuring and global expansion of capitalist production," has, in "the absence of a recognition of a common enemy against which struggles are directed" (2000, 55), caused the death of class solidarity and given birth to a new proletariat that "is not a new industrial working class," but "the general concept that defines all those whose labor is exploited by capital, the entire cooperating multitude" (2000, 402). A mirror image of Friedman's "electronic herd," the "multitude" is a singular, disembodied, raceless, classless, sexless, odorless networked force that somehow comes into being without political mediation and remains united in spite of its diversity.[26] In the push to reconceive class as an analytical category, the very concept of class as a constituency seems to be vanishing into thin air. After postcolonialism, it is clear that class can no longer be deployed as an abstract homogenizing category that subsumes or occludes other oppressions; what is less clear is whether anticapitalist critiques can afford to discard the concept of class altogether. Different local struggles against exploitation, whether allied to ecological, feminist, workerist, or autonomous movements, can indeed bring about important and necessary transformations (Burgmann, this volume), but it remains to be seen if in the absence of class-consciousness, these movements can pose a real threat to the dominance of capital.

"Civil society," presented by many as the panacea for all ills, especially in postcolonial spaces, is not an unproblematic or uncontested category either. First of all, it may be useful to remember that neoliberal globalization itself has been a champion of "civil society," transferring to it responsibilities that were supposedly wrongly assigned to the state. As states everywhere pull out of public enterprises, social security, education, and healthcare, a notion of "civil society" closely compatible to the market and privatization is fast emerging even as increased collaboration with the state is rapidly diminishing the independence of this emerging civil society (Santos 2004). Then, there is the issue of participation. Although education can promote awareness and involvement, civil participation cannot be sustained unless the structure of everyday life is redefined. Therefore, without broader institutional reforms such as the establishment of a living wage and the reduction of the working day, the vast majority will simply not have the time necessary for daily engagement in civil society (DiFazio 2003). Finally, it is important to recognize that on closer inspection, "global civil society" frequently turns out to be a somewhat exclusive club composed largely of the self-selected, the networked, and the affect-based (Srivastava 2005; Buchanan and Pahuja, this volume).

The South Asian Subaltern historian Partha Chatterjee contends that the very concept of civil society (as developed in the Western tradition) is limiting because it applies only to democratic arenas of citizen action and hence excludes all those who, for whatever reason, do not have access to full citizenship or whose actions are not premised on the notion of rights-bearing individuals. Civil society, for Chatterjee, is thus a quintessentially bourgeois politics of private property, equality of law, and freedom of contract that operates powerfully, even pedagogically, only within a small elite zone in postcolonial societies. The vast majority of the people in these societies, however, are not bourgeois and do not operate within the traditionally defined arena of civil society when coping with lived localized forms of illegality, inequality, and violence. Chatterjee calls this arena "political society." The rumblings and churnings in this postcolonial political society, "not all of which is worthy of approval," should not, however, be dismissed (by the right and the left) as irrational forms of popular politics (ethnic violence, religious fundamentalism, or terrorism). Rather, they need to be grasped as awkward gropes and risky fumbles toward democratic forms of the modern state that were not thought out by the post-Enlightenment social consensus of the secularized Christian world (Chatterjee 2004, 176–77). It may be too early to tell if either "civil society" or "political society" has the potential to create a participatory (rather than representative) democracy. But in the meantime, it is not too early to admit that neither the violence and brutality of popular politics nor the craft and cunning of neoliberal imperiality should be underestimated (Callinicos 2003).

## CONCLUSION

To globalize or not—that is no longer the question. What kind of globalization—that is the question both postcolonial and globalization studies must grapple with. Part of that grappling clearly involves distinguishing between the different aspects as well as the differential impacts of globalization (Bhagwati 1977, 2004). Yet, as Amartya Sen (2002) points out, one cannot rebut the charge that the global system is unfair by showing that even the poor gain something from global contacts and are not necessarily made poorer, because the critical issue is not whether the poor are getting marginally poorer or richer or whether they are better off than they would be had they excluded themselves from globalized interactions (as if such "delinking" were indeed possible). The real issue, as Sen firmly asserts, is the distribution of globalization's benefits.[27] To which I would only add, the distribution of opportunities to shape the terms and conditions of globalization as well.

"A different kind of globalization is possible" is the hopeful cry of the World Social Forum. Postcolonial and globalization studies clearly have much to contribute to the debate on what that different kind of globalization or planetarity should look like and how it can be brought about. But this requires more open dialogue and productive contestation between the two fields. This volume attempts to create a space for such dialogue and contestation. In bringing together scholars from both fields, however, we have not simply sought to pit one camp against the other; rather we have tried to make it possible for all those who believe in the possibilities of a decolonized planetarity to clarify the connections, acknowledge the conflicts, and recognize the complicities between the postcolonial and the global. It is our hope that this exercise will help scholars as well as students chart new directions for producing knowledge about the fate of our fragile planet and its inhabitants.

## NOTES

1. Some attempts to rethink the postcolonial in relation to the global can be found in Ahmad (1992); Grewal and Kaplan (1994); Lowe and Lloyd (1997); Jameson and Miyoshi (1998); During (1998; 2000); Public Culture's "Millennial Quartet" (2001); O'Brien and Szeman (2001); Sarkar and De (2002).

2. Held and McGrew (2000) is a good example of the near absence of the postcolonial in social science theorizations. Few postcolonial contexts are analyzed at length in any of the contributions; practically no prominent postcolonial theorist is among the contributors. Muppidi (2004) offers an excellent critique of how reductively the postcolonial is treated in the social sciences and initiates a meaningful dialogue between theories of international relations and postcolonial studies; Applebaum and Robinson (2005) makes a more concerted effort to deal with postcolonial contexts; for a pioneering effort to revise world-system theory from the perspective of coloniality, see Grosfoguel in this volume.

3. For recent attempts to take stock of postcolonial studies and map out directions for a productive future, see Afzal-Khan and Seshadri-Crooks (2000) and Loomba et al. (2005).

4. For a polemical discussion of comparison in the context of literature, see Spivak (2003). The rapid inclusion and assimilation of diverse (non-Western/postcolonial) literatures in the Western/American academia, Spivak argues, makes the question of comparativity especially critical.

5. Homi Bhabha is of course the foremost theorist of hybridity (1994). The concept has now nearly become the unexamined center of contemporary cultural studies. See for instance how Naoki Sakai's theorizations of translation appeal to the notion of hybridity (1997).

6. An extended discussion of postcolonial critiques of modernity can be found in Kraniauskas (2005).

7. Ironically, it is this kind of culturalist thinking that also leads to Huntington's thesis about "the clash of civilizations," illustrating how globalization is producing ideological contradictions and blurring distinctions between left and right.

8. Pheng Cheah's essay in this volume outlines just such a project in relation to area studies.

9. For "the nation-state is dead/dying" position, see Keohane and Nye (1972, 1977); McGrew et al. (1992); Appadurai (1996); and Friedman (1999, 2005). For challenges to this position, see Jameson (1991); Ahmad (1992); Lazarus (1997); Aronowitz (2003); and Sassen (1996 and this volume).

10. For a critique of culturalist postcolonialism, see Krishnaswamy (2002); for a cautious infusion of postcolonial culturalism into theories of international relations, see Muppidi (2004).

11. Smith (2003) presents a succinct discussion of U.S imperial ambitions to get "beyond geography"; Fukuyama's (1992) heady endorsement of American triumphalism as the end of the history is well known; and "Flat World" is, of course, Friedman's latest phrase (Friedman 2005).

12. For some early critiques of postcolonial migrancy, see Ahmad (1992); Krishnaswamy (1995); and Cheah (1998).

13. For extended critiques of Hardt and Negri's *Empire*, see Balakrishnan (2003); Aronowitz and Gautney (2003); and *Interventions* 5, no. 2 (2003). For an analysis of how outsourcing is represented in the American media, see Hashmi (2006).

14. In their critiques of postcolonial studies, Lazarus (1997, 1999), San Juan (1998), Brennan (1977), and others have consistently argued for need to differentiate between different historical nationalisms.

15. See Sassen (1996); Jameson (2000); Panitch (2000); Gowan (2001); Radhakrishnan (2001); Cheah (2003); and Stiglitz (2003, 2004).

16. Laws of weaker states are made to comply with or merely replicate U.S./"international" law (Ahmad 2004; Buchanan and Pahuja, this volume); note for instance how Indian patent rights are being rewritten to accord with WTO specifications (see editorial in *Economic & Political Weekly* 2 [April, 2005]).

17. Russia used the war on terror to defeat Chechnya; Turkey to repress its impoverished Kurdish population; Israel to crush the Palestinians ever more brutally—all with tacit U.S. support. China and Pakistan had similar reasons and got similar rewards. Even more democratic countries in Europe (France, Denmark) have grown more authoritative and ethnophobic, legalizing persecution and sanctioning discrimination, all in the name of security and terror.

18. Tomlinson's culturalist deconstruction of "the West" interestingly intersects with Lazarus's Marxist criticism that postcolonial theory reductively deploys "the West" as an essentialist or homogenized category (much like "the East" in Orientalist discourse). Although I agree that we need to distinguish more carefully between different, particular manifestations of "the West," I think the term can still be put to the service of a Spivakian "strategic essentialism."

19. Although Hardt concedes that 9/11 and American unilateralism in the war on terror have downgraded Empire from an actuality to a potentiality, "a mere alternative within global politics," he fails to recognize that it is really not a radical departure from the so-called multilateralism of the Gulf War (Hardt 2002).

20. See the *New York Times* op ed, February 16, 2003.

21. Driscoll's notion of "reverse postcoloniality" interestingly questions the popular charge that postcolonial hybridity has been domesticated by the embrace of global capital. For Driscoll, globalization represents the "revocation of the post-World War II promise of the North to assist in the development of the former colonies of the South and the concomitant rollback of the global advances of postcolonial hybrid politicocultural forms" (2004, 70).

22. Guha explains that "hegemony stands for a condition of Dominance (D), such that, in the organic composition of the latter, Persuasion (P) outweighs Coercion (C)" (1992, 233). Dominance without hegemony therefore refers to a condition of state power in which Coercion outweighs Persuasion. Guha, of course, came up with the formula to characterize the British colonial state in India.

23. For an extended critique of subversive consumption, see Krishnaswamy (2002).

24. Some criticisms of Third Way politics include Callinicos (1999); King (1999); and Mouffe (2000).

25. See for instance Waterman (1993) and Lowe and Lloyd (1997). A nice overview/assessment of the New Social Movements is available in Sklair (1998).

26. Laclau (2001) contrasts Hardt and Negri's concept of "multitude" with Jacques Rancière's notion of "people." In many ways "multitude" belongs to the same set of "organismic" concepts Pheng Cheah discusses in *Spectral Nationality* (2003).

27. Sen (2002) draws an interesting comparison: "By analogy, to argue that a particularly unequal and sexist family arrangement is unfair, one does not have to show that women would have done comparatively better had there been no families at all, but only that the sharing of the benefits is seriously unequal in that particular arrangement. . . . But even when it is accepted that both men and women may typically gain from living in a family, the question of distributional fairness remains. Many different family arrangements—when compared with the absence of any family system—would satisfy the condition of being beneficial to both men and women. The real issue concerns how fairly benefits associated with these respective arrangements are distributed."

# Works Cited

Afzal-Khan, Fawzia, and Kalpana Seshadri-Crooks, eds. 2000. *The Pre-Occupation of Postcolonial Studies.* Durham, N.C.: Duke University Press.

Agamben, Giorgio. 2005. *State of Exception,* trans. Kevin Attell. Chicago: University of Chicago Press.

Ahmad, Aijaz. 1992. *In Theory.* London: Verso.

———. 2004. *Iraq, Afghanistan, & The Imperialism of Our Time.* New Delhi: LeftWord Books.

Ambedkar, B. R. 1987. "Buddha or Karl Marx" and "The Buddha and His Dharma." In *Dr. Babasaheb Ambedkar: Writing and Speeches,* ed. Vasant Moon, vol. 3 and vol. 11, respectively. Bombay: Education Department, Government of Maharashtra.

Amin, Samir. 1992. *Empire of Chaos.* New York: Monthly Review.

Anderson, Benedict. 1983. *Imagined Communities: Reflections on the Origins and Spread of Nationalism.* London: Verso.

Anderson, Perry. 1980. *Arguments within English Marxism.* London: Verso.

Appadurai, Arjun. 1996. *Modernity at Large.* Minneapolis: University of Minnesota Press.

Applebaum, Richard, and William Robinson. 2005. *Critical Globalization Studies.* NewYork: Routledge.

Aronowitz, Stanley. 2003. "Global Capital and its Opponents." In Aronowitz and Gautney: 179–95.

Aronowitz, Stanley, and Heather Gautney, eds. 2003. *Implicating Empire.* New York: Basic Books.

Balakrishnan, Gopal, ed. 2003. *Debating Empire.* London: Verso.

Balibar, Étienne. 2001. "Outlines of a Topography of Cruelty: Citizenship and Civility in the Era of Global Violence." *Constellations* 8, no. 1: 15–29.

Bartolovich, Crystal, and Neil Lazarus, eds. 2002. *Marxism, Modernity, and Postcolonial Studies.* Cambridge, UK: Cambridge University Press.

Bauman, Zygmunt. 1995. *Life in Fragments.* Oxford: Blackwell.

Bhabha, Homi. 1994. *The Location of Culture.* London: Routledge.

———. 2003. "Making Difference: The Legacy of the Culture Wars." *ArtForum* (April): 73.

Bhagwati, Jagdish. 1995. *Life in Fragments.* Oxford: Blackwell.

———. 1977. *The New International Economic Order.* Cambridge, Mass.: MIT Press.

———. 2004. *In Defense of Globalization.* New York: Oxford University Press.

Brennan, Timothy. 1997. *At Home in the World: Cosmopolitanism Now.* Cambridge, Mass.: Harvard University Press.

Bruce-Novoa, Juan. 2003. "Offshoring the American Dream." *CR: The New Centennial Review* 3, no. 1: 109–45.

Callinicos, Alex. 1999. "Social Theory Put to the Test of Practice: Pierre Bourdieu and Anthony Giddens." *New Left Review* I, no. 236 (July–August): 77–102.

———. 2003. "The Anti-Capitalist Movement after Genoa and New York." In Aronowitz and Gautney: 133–150.

Chakrabarty, Dipesh. 1993. "Provincializing Europe." In *The Nation and Its Fragments,* 117–236. Princeton, N.J.: Princeton University Press.

———. 1997. "Postcoloniality and the Artifice of History: Who Speaks for 'Indian' Pasts?" In *A Subaltern Studies Reader, 1986–1995,* ed. Ranajit Guha, 263–93. Minneapolis: University of Minnesota Press.

———. 2000. *Provincializing Europe: Postcolonial Thought and Historical Difference.* Princeton, N.J.: Princeton University Press.

———. 2001. "Universalism and Belonging in the Logic of Capital." In *Cosmopolitanism,* eds. Carol. A. Breckenridge, Sheldon Pollack, Homi K. Bhabha, and Dipesh Chakrabarty, 82–110. Durham, N.C.: Duke University Press.

Chakrabarty, Paula. 2005. "Weak Winners of Globalisation: Indian H1B Workers in the American Information Economy." *AAPI Nexus.*

Chatterjee, Partha. 1993. *The Nation and Its Fragments: Colonial and Postcolonial Histories.* Princeton, N.J.: Princeton University Press.

———. 2004. *The Politics of the Governed: Reflections on Popular Politics in Most of the World.* New York: Columbia University Press.

Cheah, Pheng. 1998. "The Cosmopolitical – Today." In *Cosmopolitics,* eds. Pheng Cheah and Bruce Robbins, 20–41. Minneapolis: University of Minnesota Press.

———. 2003. *Spectral Nationality*. New York: Columbia University Press.

Desai, Gaurav. 2006. "Capitalism, Sovereignty and the Dilemmas of Postcoloniality." *boundary 2* 33, no. 2: 177–201.

DiFazio, William. 2003. "Time, Poverty, and Global Democracy." In Aronowitz and Gautney: 159–78.

Driscoll, Mark. 2004. "Reverse Postcoloniality." *Social Text* 22, no. 1: 59–84.

During, Simon. 1998. "Postcolonialism and Globalisation: A Dialectical Relation after All?" *Postcolonial Studies* 1, no. 1: 31–47.

———. 2000. "Postcolonialism and Globalisation: Towards a Historicization of Their Inter-Relation," *Cultural Studies* 14, no. 3–4: 385–404.

Dussel, Enrique. 1998. "Beyond Eurocentrism: The World-System and the Limits of Modernity." In Jameson and Miyoshi: 3–31.

Eng, Ian, and Jon Stratton. 1996. "Asianing Australia: Notes toward a Critical Transnationalism in Cultural Studies." *Cultural Studies* 10, no. 1: 16–36.

Friedman, Thomas. 1999. *The Lexus and the Olive Tree*. New York: Farrar, Straus, & Giroux.

———. 2005. *The World Is Flat*. New York: Farrar, Straus, & Giroux.

Fukuyama, Francis. 1992. *The End of History and the Last Man*. New York: Free Press.

Gaonkar, Dilip Parameshwar, ed. 2001. *Alternative Modernities*. Durham, N.C.: Duke University Press.

García Canclini, Néstor. 1995. *Hybrid Cultures: Strategies for Entering and Leaving Modernity*, trans. Christopher L. Chiappari and Silvia L. Lopez. Minneapolis: University of Minnesota Press.

Giddens, Anthony. 1990. *The Consequences of Modernity*. Cambridge, UK: Polity Press.

———. 1991. *Modernity and Self-Identity: Self and Society in the Late Modern Age*. Cambridge, UK: Polity Press.

———. 1999. *The Third Way*. Cambridge, UK: Polity Press.

Gikandi, Simon. 2001. "Globalization and the Claims of Postcoloniality." *The South Atlantic Quarterly* 100, no. 3: 627–58.

Gilroy, Paul. 1993. *The Black Atlantic: Modernity and Double Consciousness*. Cambridge, Mass.: Harvard University Press.

———. 2005. *Postcolonial Melancholia*. New York: Columbia University Press.

Gowan, Peter. 2001. "Explaining the American Boom: The Roles of 'Globalization' and United States Global Power." *New Politica Economy* 6, no. 3: 359–73.

Grewal, Inderpal, and Caren Kaplan, eds. 1994. *Scattered Hegemonies*. Minneapolis: University of Minnesota Press.

Grossberg, Lawrence. 1999. "Speculations and Articulations of Globalization." *Polygraph* 11:11–48.

Guha, Ranajit. 1992. "Dominance without Hegemony and Its Historiography." In *Subaltern Studies VI*, ed. Ranajit Guha, 210–309. New Delhi: Oxford University Press.

———. 1997. "Introduction." In *A Subaltern Studies Reader, 1986–1995*, ed. Ranajit Guha, ix–xii. Minneapolis: University of Minnesota Press.

Hall, Stuart. 1996. "When Was the 'Post-Colonial'? Thinking at the Limit." In *The Post-Colonial Question: Common Skies, Divided Horizons*, eds. Iain Chambers and Lidia Curtis, 242–60. London: Routledge.

———. 2000. "Conclusion: The Multi-Cultural Question." In *Un/settled Multiculturalisms: Diasporas, Entanglements, Transruptions*, ed. Barnor Hesse, 209–41. London: Zed.

Hardt, Michael. 2002. "Folly of Our Masters of the Universe." *Guardian*, December 18.

Hardt, Michael, and Antonio Negri. 2000. *Empire*. Cambridge, Mass.: Harvard University Press.

Harootunian, Harry. 2005. "Some Thoughts on Comparability and the Space-Time Problem." *boundary 2* 32, no. 2: 23–52.

Harvey, David. 1982. *The Limits of Capital*. Chicago: University of Chicago Press.

———. 1989. *The Condition of Postmodernity: An Enquiry into the Origins of Cultural Change*. Oxford: Blackwell.

———. 2003. *The New Imperialism*. Oxford: Oxford University Press.

Hashimi, Mobina. 2006. "Outsourcing the American Dream? Representing the Stakes of IT Globalization." *Economic and Political Weekly*, January 21: 242–49.

Held, David, and Anthony McGrew. 2000. *The Global Transformations Reader*. Cambridge, UK: Polity Press.

Jameson, Fredric. 1991. *Postmodernism, or The Cultural Logic of Late Capitalism*. London: Verso.

———. 1998. "Notes on Globalization as a Philosophical Issue." In Jameson and Miyoshi: 54–77.

———. 2000. "Taking on Globalization." *New Left Review*: 49–68.

———. 2003. "The End of Temporality." *Critical Inquiry* 29, no. 4: 695–718.

Jameson, Fredric, and Masao Miyoshi, eds. 1998. *The Cultures of Globalization*. Durham, N.C.: Duke University Press.

Keohane, Robert, and J. S. Nye. 1972. *Transnational Relations and World Politics*. Cambridge, Mass.: Harvard University Press.

———. 1977. *Power and Interdependence*. Boston: Little, Brown.

King, Anthony. 1999. "Legitimating Post-Fordism: A Critique of Anthony Giddens's Later Works." *Telos* 115:61–78.

Kraniauskas, John. 2005. "Difference against Development: Spiritual Accumulation and the Politics of Freedom." *boundary 2* 32, no. 2: 53–80.

Krishnaswamy, Revathi. 1995. "Mythologies of Migrancy." *Ariel* 26, no. 1: 125–46.

———. 2002. "The Criticism of Culture and the Culture of Criticism." *Diacritics* 32, no. 2: 106–26.

———. 2003. "The Claims of Globalization Theory: Some Contexts and Contestations." *South Asian Review*, 24, no. 2: 18–32.

———. 2005. "Globalization and Its Postcolonial (Dis)contents:. Reading Dalit Writing." *Journal of Postcolonial Writing* 41, no. 1: 69–82.

Laclau, Ernesto. 2001. "Can Immanence Explain Social Struggles?" *Diacritics* 31, no. 4: 3–10.

Lazarus, Neil. 1997. "Transnationalism and the Alleged Death of the Nation State." In *Cultural Readings of Imperialism: Edward Said and the Gravity of History*, eds. Keith Ansell-Pearson, Benita Parry, and Judith Squires, 28–48. London: Lawrence & Wishart.

———. 1999. *Nationalism and Cultural Practice in the Postcolonial World*. Cambridge: Cambridge University Press.

Loomba, Ania. 1998. *Colonialism/Postcolonialism*. London: Routledge.

Loomba, Ania, Suvir Kaul, Matti Bunzl, and Antionette Burton, eds. 2005. *Postcolonial Studies and Beyond*. Durham, N.C.: Duke University Press.

Lowe, Lisa, and David Lloyd, eds. 1997. *The Politics of Culture in the Shadow of Capital*. Durham, N.C.: Duke University Press.

Marable, Manning. 2003. "9/11: Racism in a Time of Terror." In *Implicating Empire*, eds. Stanley Aronowitz and Heather Gautney, 3–14. New York: Basic Books.

McGrew, A. G., P. G. Lewis, et al. 1992. *Global Politics*. Cambridge, UK: Polity Press.

Mignolo, Walter. 2001. "The Geopolitics of Knowledge and the Colonial Difference." *Multitudes* 6:56–71.

Mouffe, Chantal. 2000. "A Politics without Adversary?" In *The Democratic Paradox*, 108–28. London: Verso.

Muppidi, Himadeep. 2004. *The Politics of the Global*. Minneapolis: University of Minnesota Press.

Nandy, Ashis, ed. 1988. *Science, Hegemony, and Violence*. Delhi: Oxford University Press.

O'Brien, Susie, and Imre Szemann. 2001. "Anglophone Literatures and Global Culture," special issue of *The South Atlantic Quarterly* 100, no. 3.

Panitch, Leo. 2000. "The New Imperial State." *New Left Review* II, no. 2: 5–20.

Quijano, Anibal. 1997. "The Colonial Nature of Power in Latin America." In *Sociology in Latin America*, eds. R. Briceno-Leon and H. R. Sonntag, 27–38. Madrid: International Sociological Association.

———. 2000. "Coloniality of Power, Ethnocentrism, and Latin America." *Nepantla* 1, no. 3: 533–80.

Radhakrishnan, R. 2001. "Globalization, Desire, and the Politics of Representation." *Comparative Literature* 53, no. 4: 315–32.

Robertson, Roland. 1992. *Globalization: Social Theory and Global Culture*. London: Sage.

Robin, Corey. 2003. "Fear, American Style: Civil Liberty After 9/11." In *Implicating Empire*, eds. Stanley Aronowitz and Heather Gautney, 47–64. New York: Basic Books.

Sakai, Naoki. 1997. *Translation and Subjectivity: On Japan and Cultural Nationalism*. Minneapolis: University of Minnesota Press.

San Juan, E. 1998. *Beyond Postcolonial Theory*. New York: St. Martin's Press.

Santos, Boaventura de Sousa. 1998. *De la mano de Alicia. Lo Social y lo Politico en la Postmodernidad*, trans. Consuelo Bernal and Mauricio G. Villegas. Bogota: Ediciones Uniades.

———. 2004. "In Search of a Global Citizenship." At: www.lolapress.org/artenglish/souza 18.htm.

Sarkar, Sonita, and Esha Niyogi De, eds. 2002. *Trans-Status Subjects: Gender in the Globalization of South and Southeast Asia*. Durham, N.C.: Duke University Press.

Sassen, Saskia. 1996. *Losing Control? Sovereignty in an Age of Globalization*. New York: Columbia University Press.

Sen, Amartya. 2002. "How to Judge Globalism." *The American Prospect* 13, no. 1: 1–14.

Sivakumar, Nadarajah. 2004. *Dude, Did I Steal Your Job? Debugging Indian Computer Programmers*. Bridgewater, N.J.: Divine Tree.

Sklair, Leslie. 1998. "Social Movements and Global Capitalism." In Jameson and Miyoshi: 291–311.

Smith, Neil. 2003. "After the American Lebenstraum." *Interventions* 5, no. 2: 249–70.

Spivak, Gayatri Chakravorty. 1999. *A Critique of Postcolonial Reason: Towards a History of the Vanishing Present*. Cambridge, Mass.: Harvard University Press.

———. 2003. *Death of a Discipline*. New York: Columbia University·Press.

Srivastava, Jayati. 2005. "NGOs at World Trade Organisation: The 'Democratic' Dimension." *Economic & Political Weekly,* May 7: 1952–57.

Stiglitz, Joseph. 2004. "Distant Voices." *Guardian* 12 (March)

———. 2003. "Do as the U.S. says, Not as It Does." *Guardian* 19 (October)

Taylor, Charles. 2001. "Two Theories of Modernity." In *Alternative Modernities*, ed. Dilip Parameshwar Gaonkar, 172–196. Durham, N.C.: Duke University Press.

Tomlinson, John. 1999. *Globalization and Culture*. Chicago: University of Chicago Press.

Tucker, Vincent. 1999. "The Myth of Development: A Critique of Eurocentric Discourse." In *Critical Development Theory: Contributions to a New Paradigm*, ed. Ronaldo Munck and Denis O'Hearn, 1–26. London: Zed.

Waterman, Peter. 1993. "Social Movement Unionism: A New Union Model for a New World Order?" *Review* 16(3): 245–78.

Willis, Ellen. 2003. "The Mass Psychology of Terrorism." In *Implicating Empire*, eds. Stanley Aronowitz and Heather Gautney, 95–105. New York: Basic Books.

Zhen, Zhang. 2001. "Mediating Time: The 'Rice Bowl of Youth' In Fin de Siecle Urban China." In *Globalization*, ed. Arjun Appadurai, 131–54. Durham, N.C.: Duke University Press.

# AGENCIES FOR RESISTANCE, PROSPECTS FOR EVOLUTION

## John C. Hawley

*When we got into Marx and Engels we were thoroughly spoilt by literature, its irony and humor.*

— Subcomandante Marcos, interview with Gabriel García Márquez and Roberto Pombo

Whether they are read as calls to arms or as occasions for more generous inclusion (Bauman 2004; Siddiqi 1974),[1] and whether their source is interpreted as ethical (Dussel 1996),[2] sociological (Bolaria 1997; Ong 1987; Scott 1985), political (Buck-Morss 2003; Chatterjee 2004), environmentalist (Shiva 2005), or economic (Smith and Guarnizo 1998; Elson 1997; Powelson and Stock 1990; Eder 1982), jeremiads against globalists are nothing new.[3] Some might wonder what difference these warnings have ever made, or could possibly make. Isn't globalization an implacable and impersonal force that works its inevitable course, willy-nilly, across national borders and roughshod over whatever well- or ill-natured opposition it faces? Is Thomas Friedman not correct in estimating the process to be "inexorable" (2000, 9)? Is being a "globalist" the "only way to systematically connect the dots, see the system of globalization and thereby order the chaos" (24)? Is he accurate when he tells a friend, "I wish we could slow this globalization train down . . . but there's no one at the controls" (343)?

Someone like Néstor García Canclini can accept globalization as an irreversible tendency, but nonetheless ask whether "the neoliberal mode of globalization is the only one, or the most desirable one, for carrying out a transnational restructuring of societies" (García Canclini 2001, 19; see also Condé 1998; Ahluwalia 2001; and in this volume, Krishnaswamy). The recent pope seems to offer an alternative mode, putting the moral case persuasively by seeking to awaken the consciences of the powerful. "No one, in fact, ever lives in isolation," he writes. And after 9/11, who can deny his point? "The challenge," in his view, "is to ensure a globalization *in solidarity*, a globalization *without marginalization*"— and this, he concludes, is "a clear duty in justice, with serious moral implications in the organization of the economic, social, cultural and political life of nations" (Karol Wojtyla 1998, section 3).

A clear duty? Even if one were to concede the point, how does one fight one's way to the controls? Friedman (2000), who writes most persuasively and with great dollops of statistics and fascinating personal anecdotes, clearly speaks for a great many of his readers who are anxious to see the system of globalization succeed, however that success may be variously defined, and who are happy at the notion that with the proper care it can be made to benefit many of those who are currently barely keeping their heads above the waves, or who have just now dropped from sight but may still be within reach. Friedman protests that he is "a journalist, not a salesman for globalization"; he is "keenly aware of globalization's downsides" and hopes that a clear analysis of the process and its intricacies can help its advocates figure out how the system can benefit the most people. But the collapse of the twin towers has made a great many such people wonder if they might not have been whistling in the dark; perhaps, some former neoliberals apparently believe, it's high time to cut out the "rising tide raises all boats" malarkey and start battening down the hatches.

Still, beyond the implied threats of terrorist anarchy that can elicit quite horrifying tactics of self-defense, there are the calmer (hopelessly naïve?) voices that continue to seek more generous ways to husband the world's resources—both material and spiritual. Some of these might part company with Friedman when he confidently proclaims that "globalization emerges from below, from street level, from people's very souls and from their very deepest aspirations" (2000, 348), and such doubters may wonder whether *these* are anyone's "deepest" aspirations? And when Friedman asserts that, "with all due respect to revolutionary theorists, the 'wretched of the earth' want to go to Disney World—not to the barricades" (364), the imagery is just too jarring.[4] For the sake of argument, let us grant that this desire for a bit of carefree fun is universal, and especially so in the lives of those beaten down by a miserable life—but it is even more obviously the case that millions upon millions are never going to get to Disney World or to any other fantasyland of capitalism.[5]

Much of the heat that quickly emerges in discussions of these topics draws its energy from the question of who is allowed to speak for these impoverished millions. As Partha Chatterjee (2004) puts it, "how can the particular claims of marginal population groups, often grounded in violations of the law, be made consistent with the pursuit of equal citizenship and civic virtue? To produce a viable and persuasive politics of the governed, there has to be a considerable act of mediation. Who can mediate?" (64). Who, in fact, is goading them on towards the "barricades" or, conversely, promising to introduce their children to Mickey Mouse? Ever the pragmatist, Friedman notes that, "with so many democracies around the world now, sometimes it only takes one environmentalist waving an E-mail message on the floor of his or her parliament to hold up a major power plant project or some other environmentally sensitive deal" (2000, 290)—and thus, he argues, some companies see a benefit in taking the environment seriously. Perhaps this is a significant concession to the forces of civil self-empowerment, offering a model to organizers with analogous concerns about globalization. After all, Friedman notes that the Davos Forum in 1996 elicited a backlash that has since become "more apparent and widespread." In fact, he writes that the emotions and anxieties "have come together to create a whirlwind that—for the moment—is only buffeting the globalization system but one day might become strong enough to destabilize it if we don't take the serious backlashers seriously" (2000, 329). So, let "us" do so by considering the World Social Forum.

"Another world is possible" is the slogan of the Forum, and it is also the name of the book edited by William F. Fisher and Thomas Ponniah (1996) that collects significant documents from the second such forum. The first was held in January of 2001; the second was in Porto Alegre, the largest city in southern Brazil, in January 2002; another has been held in 2004 in Mumbai, India. Porto Alegre was chosen as a fitting "response" to the choice of Davos, Switzerland, the site of the World Economic Forum. As Michael Hardt and Antonio Negri describe the contrast, "the heat of Brazil in January and the snows of Switzerland echoes the opposition between the two political strategies. . . . The meetings at Davos were restricted to a small elite and protected by armed guards whereas Porto Alegre is an overflowing event with innumerable participants" (Fisher and Ponniah 1996, xvi–xvii). In their view, Porto

Alegre is "the representation of a new democratic cosmopolitanism, a new anticapitalist transnationalism, a new intellectual nomadism, a great movement of the multitude" (xvi). Less generous critics have described the setting and its participants as sweaty, loud, and pointless.

Sweaty and loud it no doubt is—but hardly pointless. Ponniah and Fisher analyze the documents from Porto Alegre as falling into four categories:

- the production of wealth and social reproduction
- access to wealth and sustainability
- the affirmation of civil society and public space
- political power and ethics in the new society (see, in this volume, San Juan)

Under the first of these categories they consider such questions as: external debt, repercussions of the colonization of Africa/Brazil, the necessity of controls on financial capital, the comparative disadvantage of international trade, the need to limit the mobility of transnational corporations, the attack on the labor movement, and the relationship between "the solidarity economy" (91) and neoliberalism. Under the second category they consider the environment and sustainability, access to water, knowledge, and intellectual property rights, the availability of essential medicine, "food sovereignty" (161), the public's right to benefits associated with cities, and the sovereignty of indigenous peoples. Under the third heading they consider democratizing communications and the media (see, in this volume, Harlow), the commodification of education, the production of cultural homogeneity versus culture difference, the culture of violence and domestic violence, the combating of discrimination and intolerance, and perspectives on the global civil society movement. The final category discusses international organizations and the architecture of power; globalization and militarism; the universal nature of human rights (see, in this volume, Ahluwalia); sovereignty, nation, and empire; participatory democracy; and principles and values for a civilization of solidarity (see, in this volume, Grewal, Rodriguez, and Burgman). This ample list of topics demonstrates the strengths and weaknesses of calling together 55,000 activists! Ponniah and Fisher need hardly remind us that the Forum "is not an agent, but is instead a pedagogical and political space that enables learning, networking, and political organizing" (6).[6]

In his recent book, *The World is Flat: A Brief History of the Twenty-First Century*, Friedman (2005) again strives to find a fitting conceit to fix complex details in simple form (recall his earlier observation that "no two countries that both had McDonald's had fought a war against each other since each got its McDonald's" [2000, 248]), and in the new book he handily divides the world into 11/9, when the Berlin Wall was dismantled, and 9/11: "the two competing forms of imagination at work in the world today" (2005, 441). He complains that antiglobalization forces lost touch with the poor, and that this came about because they were driven by five disparate forces: (1) upper-middle-class American liberal guilt; (2) a rear-guard push from the Old Left who "wanted to spark a debate about *whether we globalize*" (2005, 385); (3) a passive reluctance from some who regretted the passing of the old way of doing things; (4) anti-Americanism; and, finally, (5):

> a coalition of very serious, well-meaning, and constructive groups—from environmentalists to trade activists to NGOs concerned with governance—who became part of the populist antiglobalization movement in the 1990s in the hopes that they could catalyze a global discussion about *how we globalize* . . . [but] in the end they got drowned out by the whether-we-globalize crowd. (386)

"What the world doesn't need now," he has decided, "is for the antiglobalization movement to go away. We just need it to grow up" (389). Looking back over the list of discussion topics at the World Social Forum, at its pedagogical emphasis, one suspects that a good many of the planners hardly need an admonition to grow up. In fact, Ponniah and Fisher directly confront the competing philosophies at Porto Alegre. Among them:

- revolution versus reform
- protecting the environment versus growing the economy and providing jobs
- human rights or protectionism
- the contest between Western values and universal values
- the competing emphases on localization of governance, or radical nationalism, or global organizations and standards (see, in this volume, Trivedi)

Admittedly, such deep-rooted disagreements threaten to paralyze activist groups (recall that Ponniah and Fisher emphasize that the Forum "is not an agent"), but these two editors note that all Porto Alegre's *targets* shared one characteristic: they "have eluded democratic accountability" (11). In fact, Chatterjee (2004) describes this as the principal contradiction of empire today: "The empire stands by democracy; yet so far it has not presented any framework of global democracy. Hence, although most people defer to the reality of empire's power, there is no moral legitimacy to its dominance" (104). The practical implications of this unfold on a daily basis, but the cumulative effect must be anticipated: "Like all empires, this one too will one day collapse. Its crisis will deepen precisely over the question of democracy—over the struggles, now being carried out in different parts of the world, to broaden and deepen the practices of democracy" (105).

Friedman (2005) congratulates the Forum on having had "a lot of energy and a lot of mobilizing capacity." But, he complains, "[w]hat it lacked was a coherent agenda for assisting the poor by collaborating with them in a way that could actually help them (389)."[7] Perhaps the operative word in Friedman's observation is "coherent," for the Forum surely had an agenda. As Ponniah and Fisher note, Porto Alegre proposes "the reinvention of society such that the mode of economic production, the structures of political governance, the dissemination of scientific innovation, the organization of media, social relations and the relationships between society and nature, are subjected to a radical, participatory and living democratic process" (13). This would entail, they write,

> democratic public control over external indebtedness, democratic regulation of corporations, the globalization of collective bargaining, decentralized local solidarity economies, a World Water Parliament, local food sovereignty, civil society monitoring of capital and the state, free education for all, enforceable social, economic and cultural rights, and new values for a civilization of solidarity. (15)[8]

This remarkably comprehensive and revolutionary agenda strikes many as ludicrous in its reach and impractical in its goals.

Nonetheless, a bit of leaven can have impressive results.[9] Another account of resistance (*We Are Everywhere*) focuses less on Porto Alegre and more on anticapitalist movements from 1994 to the present. "The powerful look at our diversity and see only miscellany," its editors write, "[and, it is true,] rather than one dominant political voice, one dogma, one party line, we present you with a collision of subjectivities" (Notes from Nowhere 2003, 14). Characteristically, what critics see as the movement's weakness—the hopeless fragmentation—is here described as the movement's greatest strength. "When we started to bring these stories together," they note, "we were excited to confirm what we'd always suspected—that separate movements converge, recognize each other as allies, and struggle together. . . . [T]he Zapatistas, from behind their masks, are saying not 'Do as we do,' but rather, 'We are you'" (15). Such purported solidarity may be romantic nonsense or cold comfort in the face of the juggernaut that Friedman describes. Still, it apparently offers a sense of agency, a sense that small corrections here and there can finally have a corrective, if not salutary, effect.

In fact, Immanuel Wallerstein (2001) would seem to imply that the World Social Forum's lack of a superstructure and its obviously unwieldy program of objectives are tactically necessary in a transitional era when a state-oriented strategy of opposition is less relevant. And at the same time, in his view, those in Davos who have a great deal invested in the present system also recognize that it is changing beyond recognition, and they will therefore try to ensure that the transition leads to "the construction of a new system that will replicate the worst features of the existing one—the hierarchy, privilege and inequalities" (271). In response to this counterreformation by the powerful, Wallerstein recommends that those represented by the World Social Forum need to adopt a strategy with four components: (1) there must first be "a process of constant, open debate about the transition and the outcome we hope for"; (2) there should, in the meantime, be "short-term defensive action, including electoral action"; (3) there should be "interim, middle-range goals that seem to move in the right direction"—for example, "selective, but ever-widening decommodification"; and finally, (4) there needs to be an ever-developing definition of what it means to have a world that is "relatively democratic and relatively egalitarian" (273). Participants in this amorphous resistance may well find themselves engaged now in one tactical component of such a strategy, and later in some other one.[10]

On the one hand, one must acknowledge that in a globalizing world there are few pockets of naïveté left. Thus, we learn that support for globalization is strongest in Nigeria (90 percent), South Korea (84 percent), Kenya (82 percent), Indonesia (79 percent), Vietnam (79 percent), and China (76 percent) [Pew Research Center]. But on the other hand, the citizens of developing countries sense their irrelevance in global decision making at the same time that they recognize a greater need of their labor in less-accessible markets. As Zygmunt Bauman (2004) recently argues, "The global spread of the modern form of life set loose and put in motion enormous and constantly rising quantities of human beings bereaved of their heretofore adequate ways and means of survival in both the biological and social/cultural sense of that notion" (7).[11] And Néstor García Canclini similarly notes that "the market's reorganization of production and consumption to maximize and concentrate profits transforms [intra-national] particularities into inequalities" (García Canclini 2001, 10). For good or for ill, and increasingly in all parts of the globe, consumption entails "doing something that sustains, nourishes, and to a certain extent constitutes a new mode of being citizens" (26).

The concluding documents of the World Social Forum take note of this developing definition of international responsibility, and García Canclini advises that this shapes the sort of protest that one can expect today: an odd meshing of confrontation, on the one hand, and on the other hand, participation in global commerce, in communications, and in both high and popular culture: "In order not to simplify what we mean by one or the other," he writes, "we need to rethink simultaneously policies and forms of participation. This means that we have to understand ourselves as citizens and consumers" (2001, 154).[12] This has practical consequences: rather than bemoan the growing universal desire for an interlocking global economy, reformers "need to imagine how to valorize the public interest in radio and television, in cutting-edge technologies, scientific experimentation, and aesthetic innovation that circulate through the mass media and information networks" (155; see, in this volume, Bowker).

If the process is, in fact, inexorable—except in the face of anarchy or massive international depression—we may turn with profit to Himadeep Muppidi's (2004) contention that "the systemic production of the global . . . is not outside of individual actors but is constantly reproduced or transformed through their identities, meanings, and practices" (28). Muppidi argues for the interpretive concept of social claims, "an analytical need to constantly reconstruct the social context" (23). He does not rely on metaphysics or some incontrovertible "global morality" to establish the legitimacy of such claims, but instead describes them as recognized to be "intersubjectively desirable and socially constituted."

In light of the dynamics described by the likes of Bauman, García Canclini, and Muppidi, such idealistic gatherings as the World Social Forum offer support to Peter Kropotkin's (1910) nineteenth-century notion that "mutual aid" could serve as the rhizomatic alternative to Darwin's gruff "*vae victis!*" Working toward the interpretive concept of social claims, writes Muppidi, "might mean an active engagement with those Others who have alternative conceptions of seemingly global morals (democracy, liberation, and freedom)." As sweaty and loud as this may be, it is hardly pointless.[13] It seems a far preferable alternative to "the unilateral and colonial assertion of one's preferences as the preferences of the world" (2004, 24; see also, in this volume, Mignolo and Tlostanova; Stam and Shohat).[14] In the first instance, the negotiation of social claims serves to temper cultural arrogance. Moreover, a case can be made for participation in a civil process such as the World Social Forum even if one were to concede that its outcome might be ephemeral. As Bauman notes, "Liquid modern culture no longer feels like a culture of learning and accumulation like the cultures recorded in the historians' and ethnographers' reports. It looks instead like a *culture of disengagement, discontinuity and forgetting*" (2004, 117). Relatively few bestir themselves to seek, in Wayne Gabardi's words, "a postmodern civic pluralism that exhibits both associational and agonistic features" (Gabardi 2000, 128, 138)—but more should.[15]

Recognizing the agonistic features returns us to Subcomandante Marcos's tongue-in-cheek reference to having been spoiled by literature, with which we began this chapter. Beyond the efficient machinery of economics and the cold equations of corporate profits, beneath the associational struggles of local resistance, such homage to the world of the imagination offers us all a refreshing reminder of our common humanity—and therein, perhaps a reminder of why "resistance" in its various forms may be worth the bother. Depending upon where you are seated while reading this essay, Chiapas will perhaps seem a remote site of rebellion—and that is both its romantic allure and its pitfall. As anthropologist James C. Scott writes, analogously, of a Malaysian village,

> One might well ask: Why are we here, in a village of no particular significance, examining the struggle of a handful of history's losers? For there is little doubt on this last score. . . .

> The justification for such an enterprise must lie precisely in its banality—in the fact that these circumstances are the *normal* context in which class conflict has historically occurred. By examining these circumstances closely, it may be possible to say something meaningful about normal class consciousness, about everyday resistance, about commonplace class relations where, as is most often the case, neither outright collective defiance nor rebellion is likely or possible. (Scott 1985, 27)

One must respect the sense of individual agency bolstered in the World Social Forum. Citizens of "the West" take a stand on global issues as an existential ethical challenge and generally do so in a safe environment; citizens of the global "South" generally do so because they must, and sometimes do so at personal risk (Chatterjee 2004; in this volume, Majid).[16] In a globalizing world, that risk can take on a life of its own and, indeed, even erase the comfort of borders.

A word on the rationale and organization of our volume: We suggest disciplinarity, planetarity, and imperiality as rhizomatic connections that imply an organic relationship between several of the essays. We might have included comparativity and translationality in another nodal system, but that strikes us as premature in this stage of the discussion. Susan Koshy (2005) notes that "geopolitical realignments, global capital movements, and population transfers are creating new local and transnational communities," and she is among those who contend that "it is crucial to understand and engage these structures and identities because the opposition to global capitalism will be articulated through these emergent formulations" (110). Such an engagement is what Revathi Krishnaswamy and I have attempted here in asking our contributors to comment on topics related to postcoloniality and globalism, fully expecting that they may speak at cross-purposes. Personal—sometimes disciplinary—alignments prompt authors to dramatize the limitations in alternative analyses of the issues here in question: in one essay, for example, there may seem to be a conflation of postmodernism and postcolonialism; in another, a reduction of postcolonialism to identity politics; perhaps, here and there, an avoidance of postcolonialism altogether and, in its place, a class/Marxian analysis without much explicit recognition of postcolonial engagements with Marx. Reading these essays side by side will demonstrate frictional areas of productive tension between the social sciences and the humanities where the two tectonic plates come into contact. Clearly, the writers in this volume are not all saying the same thing—nor, in the present state of the question, should they. But, as Naoki Sakai remarks on an analogous matter, "translation is believed to be necessary because incommensurability exists not between the addresser and the addressee but essentially between one linguistic community and another" (1997, 10).

The crises facing both study areas are suggested by the titles of two recent books: *Postcolonial Studies and Beyond*, edited by Ania Loomba et al. (Duke University Press, 2005) and *Critical Globalization Studies*, edited by Richard P. Appelbaum and William I. Robinson (Routledge, 2005). Loomba and company propose that it is the eclipse of postcolonial studies by globalization studies that has prompted their book's reassessment of what it is that postcolonial theorists are trying to do, and in the process they reassert the "vocation" of postcolonial studies to ask the following question: "what visions of a postcolonial world can we as humanists offer that will interrogate, perhaps even interrupt, the forms of globalization now dictated by politicians, military strategists, captains of finance and industry, fundamentalist preachers and theologians, terrorists of the body and the spirit, in short, by the masters of our contemporary universe?" (16). More specifically, they hope to "separate facile or tendentious visions of a neoliberal world-without-borders from genuine or progressive forms of transnationalism," and to "separate the abstract brand of freedom implied by market liberalization across the globe from the internationalist vision of freedom encapsulated in something like Fanon's rhetoric of liberation" (20). The call for an ethical response to a patently inequitable economic system seems at the heart of such a description of vocation.[17]

Perhaps it will come as a surprise to some that the intent of the contributors to the Appelbaum and Robinson (2005) book on globalization studies is remarkably similar. These editors first note that global studies emerged in the nineties in reaction to the emphasis on new nations that expressed itself in the field of international studies in the fifties. In contrast, global studies began addressing "emergent transnational realities" (xi). But critical globalization studies is now asking whether or not it was ever "enough to *study* globalization" (xii)—and is answering in the negative. More pointedly, such academics are now studying "the relevance of globalization studies to the global justice movement" (xii):

> We believe that it is our obligation as scholars to place an understanding of the multifaceted processes of globalization in the service of those individuals and organizations that are dedicated to fighting its harsh edges. We are not anti-globalists, but we are staunchly opposed to the highly predatory forms that globalization has assumed throughout history, and particularly during the past quarter century. (xiii)

These global theorists—mostly social scientists—are not naïve to the challenges they face.[18] But—sounding very much like postcolonial studies advocates—they contend that "within the field of global studies, there is a growing emphasis on the importance of understanding globalization from the situated viewpoint of oppression and resistance among peoples that are marginalized on the basis of race, class, and gender" (xxviii).

Thus we offer the present volume as an occasion for postcolonial studies and globalization theory to seek common cause. Pascale Casanova (2004) has recently noted that "the special perceptiveness of contestants on the periphery enables them to detect affinities among emerging literary (and political) spaces." In her view, "their shared literary destitution leads them to take each other as models and historical points of reference, to compare their literary situations, and to apply common strategies based on the logic of prior experience. This logic," she continues, "show[s] that small nations—or rather the international writers of small literatures—could act in concert to challenge their domination by the centers" (247–48). What Casanova describes in the literary realm is easily extended to the other arts, and then on to more directly political areas, as well: the spirit of Bandung continues to echo long after the philosophers of non-alignment have passed from the scene. In that spirit, we dedicate this volume to the memory of Edward Said, and to the cause of greater justice in the distribution of the world's freedoms and bounty.

## NOTES

1. On the one hand: "No shortcuts like Capitalism or Socialism can help Muslims bring out the best in them. In their present condition, the fate that awaits Muslims is visualized by Harold D. Lasswell in his article, "World Organization and Society," published in the *Yale Law Journal* (1946): . . . " 'unipolar world does not necessarily involve the sharing of an advanced civilization; on the contrary, many groups may be permanently relegated into castes and dependent peoples.' The writing on the wall is clear. Let Muslims take heed" (Siddiqi 1974, 78–79). And on the other hand: "The world that we inhabit is always a step, or a mile, or a stellar year ahead of the world we are experiencing. . . . The mission of ideals is to guide us into the territory as yet unexplored and unmapped" (Bauman 2004, 114).

2. "Is there a relationship between the wealth of the few and the poverty of the majority? Are these worlds that cannot communicate? Is there no commensurability that may be applied with the goal of establishing poverty as a *factum*, or point of departure, for an ethics, for a practical philosophy? This is exactly the origin of Liberation Philosophy, since it is necessary to co-relate 'worlds' apparently uncommunicable in order to obtain a world vision, universal, in relationship to humanity" (Dussel 1996, 217).

3. Similar, though less virulent, critiques of postcolonial theory (or at least its academic institutionalization) have also been offered. Consider Parry (2004), Shohat (1992), Dirlik (1994), Trivedi and Mukherjee (1996), Huggan (2001), and San Juan (2000), among others.

4. "Can we continue to presume that the West is essentially a cartographic category? Can we continue to overlook the fact that the distinction between the West and the Rest is increasingly independent of geography, race, ethnic culture, or nationality but is, in fact, a matter of cultural capital shaping the individual's socio-economic status? Can we continue to ignore the economic and social conditions that allow some people to *afford* to be 'Western' while others cannot?" (Sakai and Hanawa 2001, x).

5. A recent report from the Pew Research Center (2003) indicates the globalization is actually popular throughout the world in countries of all stripes and in all social classes. Where there is discontent, it is over the impact on one's personal life rather than its impact on one's country. Majorities think it is harder to find well-paying jobs, and working conditions have deteriorated. Great majorities think the disparity between the rich and the poor has greatly increased. Most think that diseases now spread more quickly, that health care has become less affordable, and that it is more difficult to tend to one's aging—but most do not blame globalization for these problems. Food is perceived to be more plentiful in stores; modern medicines appear to be more available generally. Growing interconnectedness, including swifter communications and increasing international commerce, is generally praised.

6. Chatterjee (2004) cautions against "the new liberal dogma: 'participation of civil society through NGOs.' Participation, however, has one meaning when it is seen from the standpoint of those who govern, i.e., as a category of governance. It will have a very different meaning when seen from the position of the governed, i.e., as a practice of democracy" (69).

7. "The activist groups that are helping alleviate poverty the most are those working at the local village level in places like rural India, Africa, and China to spotlight and fight corruption and to promote accountability, transparency, education, and property rights" (Friedman 2005, 389).

8. See the Forum's overarching principles, at: www.wsfindia.org/charter.php.

9. Vandana Shiva asserts as much: "Far away from the glare of global media," she writes, "ordinary people are making history, not by organizing arms to fight a brutal empire but by self-organizing their lives—their resources, their cultures, their economies to defeat the empire by turning their back to it, rejecting its tools and its logic, refusing its chains and its dictatorship" (Shiva 2005, 182).

10. Many commentators seem to concur on two points: that opposition comes in the form of a rebirth of the expression of one's citizenship, and that such expression is by definition in flux (Sandoval 2000, 179–80; Santos 1984, 50; Bello 2004, 69).

11. As Bruce Robbins (1999) notes, "It is hard to imagine that American readers would react so favorably to Jamaica Kincaid or Bharati Mukherjee . . . if they thought the entire Third World was being advised to emulate their upwardly mobile heroines and head for the nearest international airport" (121). See Georgio Agamben's (1998) suggestive work on related matters (e.g., *Homo Sacer*, 126–35).

12. "Unlike the epoch in which those who placed all their hopes in some magic transformation of the state were diametrically opposed to those who staked all change on the proletariat or the popular classes, now it is a matter of trying to remake the state and civil society in relation to each other" (García Canclini, 2001).

13. Note, too, as Partha Chatterjee (2004) writes: "I cannot claim to fully understand how criminality or violence are tied to the ways in which various deprived population groups must struggle to make their claims to governmental care. . . . [I]n the field of popular democratic practice, crime and violence are not fixed black-and-white legal categories" (75–76). And, Vandana Shiva: "We are fully aware that creating living economies based on self-organization and living democracies based on self-rule demands the commitment and courage to resist and disobey the unjust laws that render self-rule, self-provisioning, and self-sustenance illegal. Farmers are forced into corporate slavery by making seed saving illegal. The poor are forced into water markets by privatization contracts. We are all pushed into food fascism by laws that destroy local production and processing" (Shiva 2005, 183–84).

14. William E. Connolly (2002) similarly argues that "the possibilities of affirmative negotiation depend upon several parties relinquishing the provincial demand that all others subscribe to the transcendental, universal, imminent, or deliberative source of ethics they themselves confess. That ain't easy" (200).

15. Note, for example, André C. Drainville's (2002) comment that "there is more to cities than walls, and our analysis of the dynamics of order in the contemporary world economy ought not to stop at exclusionary processes, but should also look at the making of a compliant citizenry" (37).

16. Irish journalist Michael McCaughan asked Subcomandante Marcos what the roots of his personal rebellion were and received the following response: "It's a process. It's not a blow-up where you say it's now or never. You begin to take steps—first becoming interested in a situation, then understanding that there is injustice, then trying to understand the roots of this injustice. This invariably leads you to ask yourself: and you, what are you going to do about it? You begin by helping out in small ways, taking logical steps, without pressure, by your own initiative. The moment arrives when you realize that you are arriving at the point of no return as a human being. It doesn't mean that they are going to kill you or anything, but that to turn back would mean to surrender. It's there where you stop and say: okay, I'm either going to go ahead, or I'm going to turn back, or I'm going to look for another way forward. It's at that moment that you have to choose. In this case, turning back gives you a certain distance. You can keep a certain social prestige or status for sure, and still bet on good will and charity. You are a good man, then, in the social sense of the word, but you figure out that you'll have to make concessions, accommodations, compromises, small compromises that begin adding up. You know that it's a mirage, a deception. It's something that you know is not going to resolve the roots of the problem. More than anything, it's like an aspirin; when your head aches, it doesn't cure the illness, but only relieves the pain for a little while" (http://home.san.rr.com/revolution/marcos.htm).

17. So, too, the humanistic emphasis of Gayatri Spivak: "In this era of global capital triumphant, to keep responsibility alive in the reading and teaching of the textual is at first sight impractical. It is, however, the right of the textual to be so responsible, responsive, answerable" (2003, 101); also see

*Beyond Dichotomies: Histories, Identities, Cultures, and the Challenge of Globalization*, edited by Elisabeth Mudimbe-Boyi (2002).

18. "Scholars who carry their passions into the classroom may encounter strong resistance . . . by colleagues and administrators who regard the dominant scholarly discourse within a discipline as canonical 'truth,' and challenges to that discourse as 'biased'" (Appelbaum and Robinson 2005, xxviii).

## WORKS CITED

Agamben, Giorgio. 1998. *Homo Sacer: Sovereign Power and Bare Life*. Stanford: Stanford University Press.

Ahluwalia, Pal. 2001. *Politics and Post-Colonial Theory: African Inflections*. London: Routledge.

Appelbaum, Richard P., and William I. Robinson, eds. 2005. *Critical Globalization Studies*. New York: Routledge.

Bauman, Zygmunt. 2004. *Wasted Lives: Modernity and Its Outcasts*. Cambridge, UK: Polity.

Bello, Walden. 2004. "The Global South." In Mertes: 49–69.

Bolaria, B. S., and Rosemary Von Elling Bolaria, eds. 1997. *International Labour Migrations*. Delhi: Oxford University Press.

Buck-Morss, Susan. 2003. *Thinking Past Terror: Islamism and Critical Theory on the Left*. London: Verso.

Casanova, Pascale. 2004. *The World Republic of Letters*, trans. M. B. DeBevoise. Cambridge, Mass.: Harvard University Press.

Chatterjee, Partha. 2004. *The Politics of the Governed: Reflections on Popular Politics in Most of the World*. New York: Columbia University Press.

Condé, Maryse. 1998. "O Brave New World." *Research in African Literatures* 29, no. 3: 1–7.

Connolly, William E. 2002. *Neuropolitics: Thinking, Culture, Speed*. Minneapolis: University of Minnesota Press.

Dirlik, Arif. 1994. "The Postcolonial Aura: Third World Criticism in the Age of Global Capitalism." *Critical Inquiry* 20, no. 2: 328–56.

Drainville, André C. 2002. "The Fetishism of Global Civil Society: Global Governance, Transnational Urbanism, and Sustainable Capitalism in the World Economy." In Smith and Guarnizo: 35–63.

Dussel, Enrique. 1996. *The Underside of Modernity: Apel, Ricoeur, Rorty, Taylor, and the Philosophy of Liberation*, trans. and ed. Eduardo Mendieta. Atlantic Highlands, N.J.: Humanities Press.

Eder, James R. 1982. *Who Shall Succeed? Agricultural Development and Social Inequality on a Philippine Frontier*. Cambridge: Cambridge University Press.

Elson, R. E. 1997. *The End of the Peasantry in Southeast Asia: A Social and Economic History of Peasant Livelihood, 1800–1990s*. New York: St. Martin's Press.

Fisher, William F., and Ponniah, Thomas, ed. 1996. *Another World Is Possible: Popular Alternatives to Globalization at the World Social Forum*. London: Zed.

Friedman, Thomas L. 2000. *The Lexus and the Olive Tree: Understanding Globalization*. New York: Anchor/Random House.

———. 2005. *The World Is Flat: A Brief History of the Twenty-First Century*. New York: Farrar, Straus, and Giroux.

Gabardi, Wayne. 2000. *Negotiating Postmodernism*. Minneapolis: University of Minnesota Press.

García Canclini, Néstor. 2001. *Consumers and Citizens: Globalization and Multicultural Conflicts*, trans. and introduction by George Yúdice. Minneapolis: University of Minnesota Press.

Global Policy Forum. 2003. "Globalization with Few Discontents?" Pew Research Center. www.globalpolicy.org/globaliz/cultural/2003/0603globalopinion.htm.

Huggan, Graham. 2001. *The Postcolonial Exotic: Marketing the Margins*. London: Routledge.

Koshy, Susan. 2005. "The Postmodern Subaltern: Globalization Theory and the Subject of Ethnic, Area, and Postcolonial Studies." In *Minor Transnationalism*, eds. Françoise Lionnet and Shu-mei Shih, 109–31. Durham, N.C.: Duke University Press.

Kropotkin, Petr Alekseevich. 1910. *Mutual Aid: A Factor of Evolution*. London: Heinemann.

Lionnet, Françoise, and Shu-mei Shih, eds. 2005. *Minor Transnationalism*. Durham, N.C.: Duke University Press.

Loomba, Ania, Suvir Kaul, Matti Bunzl, and Antoinette Burton, eds. 2005. *Postcolonial Studies and Beyond*. Durham, N.C.: Duke University Press.

McCaughan, Michael. 2005. "Interview with Subcommandante Marcos." http://home.san.rr.com/revolution/marcos.htm.

Mertes, Tom, ed. 2004. *A Movement of Movements: Is Another World Really Possible?* London: Verso.

Mittelman, James H., and Mustapha Kamal Pasha. 1997. *Out from Underdevelopment Revisited: Changing Global Structures and the Remaking of the Third World*. New York: St. Martin's Press.

Mudimbe-Boyi, Elisabeth, ed. 2002. *Beyond Dichotomies: Histories, Identities, Cultures, and the Challenge of Globalization*. Albany: State University of New York Press.

Muppidi, Himadeep. 2004. *The Politics of the Global*. Minneapolis: University of Minnesota Press.

Notes from Nowhere, ed. 2003. *We Are Everywhere: The Irresistible Rise of Global Anti-Capitalism*. London: Verso.

Ong, Aihwa. 1987. *Spirits of Resistance and Capitalist Discipline: Factory Women in Malaysia*. Albany: State University of New York Press.

Parry, Benita. 2004. *Postcolonial Studies: A Materialist Critique*. London: Routledge.

Powelson, John P., and Richard Stock. 1990. *The Peasant Betrayed: Agriculture and Land Reform in the Third World*. Washington D.C.: Cato Institute.

Robbins, Bruce. 1999. *Feeling Global: Internationalism in Distress*. New York: New York University Press.

Sakai, Naoki. 1997. *Translation and Subjectivity: On "Japan" and Cultural Nationalism*. Minneapolis: University of Minnesota Press.

Sakai, Naoki, and Yukiko Hanawa, eds. 2001. "Specters of the West and the Politics of Translation." *Traces: A Multilingual Journal of Cultural Theory and Translation* 1, no. 1: v–xiii.

Sandoval, Chela. 2000. *Methodology of the Oppressed*. Minneapolis: University of Minnesota Press.

San Juan, Epifanio. *Beyond Postcolonial Theory*. London: Palgrave Macmillan.

Santos, Boaventura de Sousa. 1984. "On Modes of Production of Social Power and Law." Working Papers, University of Wisconsin–Madison Law School, Institute for Legal Studies.

Scott, James C. 1985. *Weapons of the Weak: Everyday Forms of Peasant Resistance*. New Haven, Conn.: Yale University Press.

———. 1990. *Domination and the Arts of Resistance: Hidden Transcripts*. New Haven, Conn.: Yale University Press.

Shiva, Vandana. 2005. *Earth Democracy: Justice, Sustainability, and Peace*. Cambridge, Mass.: South End.

Shohat, Ella. 1992. "Notes on the 'Post-Colonial'." *Social Text* 31/32:99–113.

Siddiqi, Aslam. 1974. *Modernization Menaces Muslims*. Lahore, Pakistan: Sh. Muhammad Ashraf/Kashmiri Bazar.

Smith, Michael Peter, and Luis Eduardo Guarnizo, eds. 2002 (1998). *Transnationalism from Below*. New Brunswick, N.J.: Transaction Publishers.

Spivak, Gayatri Chakravorty. 2003. *Death of a Discipline*. New York: Columbia University Press.

Subcomandante Marcos. "The Hourglass of the Zapatistas." Interviewed by Gabriel García Márquez and Roberto Pombo. In Mertes: 3–15.

Trivedi, Harish, and Meenakshi Mukherjee, eds. 1996. *Interrogating Post-Colonialism: Theory, Text, and Context*. Shimla: Indian Institute of Advance Study.

Wallerstein, Immanuel. 2004. "New Revolts against the System." In Mertes: 262–73.

World Social Forum. 2001. "Charter of Principles." www.wsfindia.org/charter.php.

Wojtyla, Karol. 1998. "From the Justice of Each Comes Peace for All," World Day of Peace. www.vatican.va/holy_father/john_paul_ii/messages/peace/documents/hf_jp-ii_mes_08121997_xxxi-world-day-for-peace_en.html.

# PART I

*Disciplinarity and Its Discontents*

# Disciplinarity and Its Discontents

Postcolonial studies and globalization theory appear to have developed in relative isolation and maintained relatively divergent disciplinary affiliations even though their historical or geopolitical points of reference converge on important issues such as modernity, imperialism, nationalism, and capitalism. To grasp the implications of these divergences and convergences more fully, it is necessary to understand the historical conditions and ideological factors that have contributed to the rise of postcolonialism and globalization theory, to have a sense of how these two fields have defined themselves as well as the objects they study, and to recognize how the disciplining and institutionalizing of these knowledges impact the project of decolonization worldwide. There are several important questions to consider: Is disciplinarity a necessary basis for knowledge production or does it contribute to radical functionalism? Has postcolonial studies been enabled or assimilated by globalization theory? To what extent has globalization theory engaged the concerns and contexts of the postcolonial? Can there be productive dialogue between postcolonialism and globalization theory, or are their goals and methods too incompatible for any meaningful exchange?

In "Postcolonial Studies and Globalization Theory," the first essay in this section, Tim Brennan traces the historical constitution of the two academic discourses or disciplines in order to explore the ideological convergences and complicities between them. By carefully tracking what each field disavows in the process of constituting itself, Brennan shows that not all studies of colonialism are recognized as "postcolonial studies," just as not all theories of globalization make up "globalization theory." But despite their shortcomings, Brennan acknowledges that both discursive formations have generated a highly complex, "internally riven" set of theories about the world we live in. He also credits them with promoting a "welcome intellectual generalism" that has the potential to transcend narrow disciplinary boundaries.

Pheng Cheah's essay, "Universal Areas: Asian Studies in a World in Motion," attempts to understand the "conceptual matrix of the formation of area studies," focusing particularly on its "division of labor" between the humanities and the social sciences. Recent criticisms of area studies, Cheah points out, have focused on the imbrication of "Asia" and "the West" in global modernity, but they have not questioned or deconstructed the foundational assumption underlying the discipline of area studies—the assumption that an area (the particular) is precisely that which is not a discipline (the universal). Showing how areas and area scholarship are placed in a subordinate relationship to the universal knowing subject of the disciplines, Cheah suggests a way to reinvent area studies in contemporary globalization that would define the area "neither as something particular that needs to be transcended to attain universality nor as concrete reality that needs to be affirmed over abstract universality, but instead, as the irreducible inscription of the universal in the singular."

History has, of course, been critical to the postcolonial project of dismantling Eurocentrism, but the discipline of history has itself been radically redefined in the process.

Radhakrishnan's essay, "Revisionism and the Subject of History," stages the encounter between a literary postcolonialism and a literalist history through a suggestive interpretation of Adrienne Rich. In the multivalent possibilities of Rich's poetry, Radhakrishnan locates an "agonized countermnemonic commitment" that eschews an imperialistic, "unerring or incorrigible remembering," to pursue a weaker but more ethical form of memory. Contending that the very notion of revisionist history is a tautology, because all historicizing is "taking a second look at what has already been otherwise," Radhakrishnan advocates reorienting history as "a compensatory discipline that has to both mourn over a loss that is beyond recuperation and at the same time name that loss multifariously and contingently."

In "The Many Scales of the Global: Implications for Theory and for Politics," Saskia Sassen seeks to redraw the "analytical terrain for studying and interpreting the global." She challenges the opposition between the national and the global in accepted narratives of globalization by arguing that the global is "endogenous to the national" and by suggesting an alternative way of "scaling" the global that inserts the national as well as the subnational into the transnational. Such an approach, Sassen contends, can reveal the "countergeographies of globalization" and develop a critical analyticity that is more than a critique of globalization.

The last essay in this section, "World-System Analysis and Postcolonial Studies: A Call for a Dialogue from the 'Coloniality of Power' Approach," calls for a critical dialogue between postcolonial theory and the world-system approach in order to rethink global capitalism. Clarifying the concepts and intellectual projects implied in the emerging exchange between the world-system approach and postcolonial critique, Ramón Grosfoguel provides an alternative reading of the "modern world-system" or the "modern/colonial world-system" by locating knowledge production geopolitically in terms of the "colonial difference" or the North-South divide. The main aim of Grosfoguel's essay is to show how a "world-system approach" provides an important conceptual framework to rethink the modern/colonial world, whereas an epistemic perspective from the subaltern side of the colonial difference contributes to certain counter limitations of the "world-system" approach.

# 1

# POSTCOLONIAL STUDIES
# AND GLOBALIZATION THEORY

*Timothy Brennan*

Neither "globalization theory" nor "postcolonial studies" are terms that easily reveal their meanings. The areas of knowledge to which they refer are not what they seem, and a great deal of confusion surrounds their uses. Readers would be forgiven for thinking that the first denoted an emergent body of writing called forth by inexorable recent developments in technology and communications, as well as radical shifts in the world economy and in geopolitics, all of them presaging the rise of a truly global culture—the obliteration of state sovereignty in a world marked by fluidity and border crossing. In turn, these readers might suppose that the second term referred to an inaugural critique of Eurocentrism prompted by a new diasporic wave of intellectuals from the former colonies resident in metropolitan centers who—informed by postwar theories of language and representation—began in the late 1970s to cast older versions of "Western Man" in doubt in an act of writing back to Empire.

Actually, neither is the case. One must begin by distinguishing between the study of global issues or colonial pasts per se and the fairly recent creation of schools of thought that retrospectively appropriate the more general cases fleetingly echoed in their names. When invoked in European or North American universities in the past decade, globalization theory and postcolonial studies turn out to be very specialized discursive formations passing for older and more varied types of inquiry. This slippage between connotation and code is one of the first things to understand about the conjunction of the two terms.

There have been many earlier traditions of investigating, on the one hand, globalizing features of world history and human societies and, on the other, colonial practices and anticolonial challenges in the cultural field. Indeed, these now-separate foci were in earlier periods conjoined. The ancestors of both, as unified phenomena, include systemic analyses of colonization dating from the early years of the European conquest in the sixteenth century (Las Casas 1552; Raleigh 1596; Montaigne 1595), Enlightenment novels and critiques protesting the ravages of imperial intervention in the eighteenth and early nineteenth centuries (Grafigny 1755; Voltaire 1759; Raynal 1774; Smith 1776; Bentham 1822), studies in the nineteenth and early twentieth centuries of the origins and dynamics of capitalism as a global phenomenon (Marx and Engels 1848; Marx 1894; Melville 1851; Hobson 1902; Pessoa 1925), economic and cultural critiques of the division of the globe at the apex of European colonization prior to World War I (Graham 1896; Morris 1901; Kautsky 1914; Lenin 1917), new forms of global or broadly regional histories associated with the Annales school and other historical schools after World War II (McNeill 1963; Braudel 1984 [1967], Hodgson 1974), Marxist world historiography based on the initiatives of the anticolonial movements (Kiernan 1969; Stavrianos 1981; Wolf 1982), dependency theory (Frank 1967; Rodney 1972; Santos 1978), and particularly—and very directly—world systems theory (Cox 1959, 1962, 1964; Wallerstein 1974; Amin 1976). We will look at some of these efforts in more detail.

In spite of reaching back several centuries, and despite being well developed, extensively documented, and self-conscious, these intellectual movements with their own canons of texts and scholarly pantheons are frequently discounted in contemporary globalization theory even as they are quietly accessed without acknowledgement. In a similar way, postcolonial studies—although in part resting on these foundations—draws on more immediate precursors, especially the anticolonial intellectuals of the 1950s and 1960s whose work was anticipated by, and directly inherits, interwar Marxist networks of anti-imperialism (Nehru 1946; Mao 1953; Ho Chi Minh 1968 [1960]; Guevara 1961; Fanon 1963; Lumumba 1972).[1] Motifs of cultural difference, epistemological othering, colonial subjectivity, and social contradiction—all common in later postcolonial studies—were inaugurated by that earlier generation of politically engaged intellectuals, who were often members of actual governments following formal independence. These "independence intellectuals," if one can call them that, were in turn the inheritors of a tradition forged by intellectuals from Africa, Asia, and Latin America, resident in Europe between the world wars, who in the communist milieu of those years had begun to forge a rhetorical and theoretical apparatus for studying colonialism as a comprehensive phenomenon, and even more importantly as a morally corrupt system of economic enrichment that could be defeated by organized counteractivity in which intellectuals from the colonies would play a prominent role.

The tendency of contemporary intellectual trends to supplant predecessors by erasing the history of their own making is not a chance occurrence, nor is it simply the work of uncharitable scholars. It is rather a characteristic feature of contemporary capitalist societies, which are at once *presentist*—that is, viewing each moment as the only reality while expunging the past in a gesture of calculated *anti*historicism—and *modernist* in the technical sense of needing to judge every current discovery as an utterly new departure, an absolute rupture with all that went before. This intellectual reflex is, in fact, a central feature both of what globalization theory argues the world has become, as well as what that theory unwittingly demonstrates about itself.

Contemporary modernism only celebrates what earlier modernists greeted with suspicion or disparagement (as in those writers of the early twentieth century, such as Franz Kafka, Marcel Proust, or William Butler Yeats, who despised mass culture and the decline of an aristocratic sensibility of the refined patron of the arts). Today, by contrast, mass culture is enshrined in terms of obscure and refined aesthetic pleasure with populist pretensions that form the bedrock ideology of the wealthiest and the most privileged. Both versions are "modernist" in that they cast the new as the never-before-seen: in the first case, as a heroically constructed, formal experimentalism that preserves the unsurpassed intelligence and insight of the chosen few of the past, serving as a bulwark against the vulgarity of the masses; in the second case (in what is typically called "postmodernism"), vulgarity and mass commercial appeal are sublimated, and the artist immerses him/herself in a kitsch that is archly mocked even as it is adopted, relieving the intellectual of the obligations of critique as well as the hope of any meaningful transition to a future *made* by an act of will. The future is rather perceived as a radical break with a history considered to be heading in an unpredictable direction which is, then, valorized precisely for that reason. Although one speaks of *post*modernism today, the "post" does not connote a time after, but rather a heightening. What is meant by the term is less the supersession of modernity than *ultra*modernity. The modernist does not merely express a neutral belief in the "year zero" of the now, as though dispassionately describing a fundamental historical fissure that evidence had forced him or her to accept. Instead, modernism (including its postmodern variant) is normative. The "now" is the new, and the new is rapturously and exuberantly embraced. Without ever questioning the fundamental self-contradiction of the move, the modernist then vigorously urges on a future that *should* unfold (because it is good) while simultaneously arguing that it *must* unfold (because it is inevitable). This style of thinking informs both globalization theory and postcolonial studies and is another of the major links between them. Let us now develop in more detail the arguments outlined previously.

The term *globalization* is marked by a fundamental ambiguity. On the one hand, it holds out hope for the creation of new communities and unforeseen solidarities; on the other hand, it appears merely to euphemize corporatization and imperial expansion. At its base, in other words, lies a tension between *process* and *policy*. Is globalization theory about describing a "process": that is, an amalgam of material shifts, spatial reorderings, anonymous developments and movements, the inexorable concatenation of changes in communication, transportation, demographics, and the environment? Or does it describe a "policy" (and is it a part of that policy): that is, a myth-making operation whose purpose is to project a world order that a small group of national and/or financial interests ardently desires to be the future for the rest of us—a future that has happily not yet arrived? There is, as well, a normative dimension to this tension. Does globalization presage a new openness to the previously foreign and the out of reach, or is it rather (and paradoxically) just the opposite: a veiled way of alluding to the Americanization of foreignness in a world dominated by U.S. power following the fall of the Soviet Union? (Bourdieu 2001; Foster 2002; Friedman 1999). As expected, given our observations, a similar ambiguity—structurally identical, in fact—marks postcolonial studies, where various critics have wondered aloud whether assaults on "imperial discourse" or the "epistemic violence" of colonial mentalities are the more sophisticated ways of battling Eurocentrism their authors claim, or merely a rendering of earlier radical positions of dissent in a form more accommodating to power by a professional diaspora to the imperial centers (Appiah 1991; Ahmad 1992; Dirlik 1997; Huggan 2001). Questions such as these interrogate globalization but are already outside "globalization theory," which does not typically open itself up to this kind of self-questioning. In particular, globalization theory would consider raising the issue of the *interestedness* of academic knowledge impertinent, for reasons we will describe.[2]

Current globalization theory, in its restricted sense, cannot logically doubt itself in the manner I have suggested because it does not merely claim that economic or cultural integration is occurring on a global scale. The import of what is being said goes significantly beyond that. The intended point is rather that the world is being reconstituted *as a single social space*. One might interpret this to mean that the world is becoming more homogenized, that we are seeing the creation of a single, albeit hybridized, world culture whose pace of life, tastes, and customs—conditioned by a similar regime of commodities consisting of cars, computers, and cellular phones—have increasingly fewer local variations. It could also be taken to mean that we are on the road to global political integration. But it is worth recognizing that it does not necessarily stipulate either of these positions. To say "a single social space" still allows for complex and dynamic internal variations across an interconnected system of localities and regions. The key component is a governing logic or social tendency that brings all these localities and regions into a unity unknown before.

The idea is further posited that globalization has become its own explanation: that is, not only has space/time been "distanciated" as a result of analyzable causal forces (that is, distances are less relevant to one's particular experience given the instant availability of images, objects, and information from afar); what is being claimed is rather that social theory itself has undergone a spatiotemporal reformulation in which the earlier modes of analysis are no longer tenable. Class antagonisms, geopolitical rivalries, the entrenched defense of privileges, imperial designs, and the blunt arguments of war and profit making—all of the earlier mechanisms of historical causation—are, in globalization theory, implicitly downgraded to second-order explanations.

As these are cast as vestiges of a vanishing social logic, globalization theory looks rather to a "new" dynamic forged by the happy chaos of an infinitely mobile citizenry, a constantly self-defined subjectivity, and a terrain of virtual space consisting of multifaceted niches of an always malleable and morphing freedom. As such (the argument goes) the mandate of reliable definitions crumbles away; the researcher, in order not to be left behind, sprints frantically after a reality vastly more innovative on its own than earlier utopias had been in the imagination. Social sense making is no longer determined by students of history or the organizers of thought known as philosophers; in the view of the globalization theorist, their structures of understanding only impede their ability to recognize the future unfolding before their eyes, which is being created by investors, technologists, managers, and organizers not—thankfully not, in their opinion—working according to plan, but swept along in a process that is anarchic and autopoietic (Bauman 1998; Giddens 1991; Agamben 1993).

The paradigmatic tone and style of globalization theory is perhaps provided best by sociologist Anthony Giddens, who gives a clear indication of the type of argument found in the field in our restrictive sense. For Giddens, people in ultramodernity live apocalyptically, experiencing levels of risk unknown before. As social institutions become more and more complex, they operate (and force us to operate) at increasing levels of abstraction, now built into the fabric of individual life. As a result, the subject is forced to *trust*, because abstract systems tend to "disembed" the subject from immediate experience, transforming intimacy from the previously anchored criteria of kinship and obligation to a "life politics" based on controlling one's own body. As deskilling renders most of us utterly dependent on expert systems whose functioning we simply have to trust, this biopolitical control becomes more important as a response to the "runaway world" of modernity, and the unitary framework of experience of which we are constantly reminded. Doubt as a pervasive feature of modern critical reason now permeates everyday life, becoming part of its existential dimension. Time and space are separable and controllable by way of the technologies of clock and map. Although aspects of this vision sound threatening at first, our initial impressions are deliberately confounded by Giddens' jubilant conclusions. For him, our ability in ultramodernity to outgrow providential reason produces an increasingly secular understanding of the nature of things, and so intrinsically leads to a safer and more rewarding existence (Giddens 1991).

Such an account is obviously at odds with a systematic account of financial forces or the impure motives of privileged agencies. By taking these conflicting approaches into consideration, one comes to recognize that globalization is not waiting to be found, discrete and safe, in the world of living social communities. There are no facts to be rehearsed in order to determine either whether the term *globalization* is merited, or whether (if so) this *thing* has not existed for many centuries without it being accompanied by the heraldic futuristic utterances that are now widely evident (utterances that often have the ring of a campaign). By themselves the facts, such as they are, are mute. One can freely concede the reality of those central features summoned by globalization theory without concluding that they collectively merit the term *globalization* or signify a radical break: for instance, the new ownership patterns of transnational corporations (TNCs), the explosive rise in Internet traffic, the radical breakdown of treaties governing international law, the increasing recourse to off-shore banking, the orchestrated planning imposed by the Bretton Woods institutions (International Monetary Fund, World Bank), or the flows of migrant labor in Southeast Asia.

To this extent, it is vital to grasp that debates over globalization are discursive. That is, they are debates over theory: over which explanatory mechanism makes the most sense given a body of (usually implicit) ethical and political objectives. The ensemble of theories of globalization invoked at the outset of this essay—centuries-old critiques of capitalism, Enlightenment protests against colonial excesses, conscious attempts over the past fifty years to write a fully world history, and the more recent exuberant "globalization theory" that characterises both poststructuralism and neoliberalism (often in similar terms)—have yielded five basic positions that again and again arise in various guises in the now-massive literature on globalization. Heuristically, it might be useful to spell them out at this point.

The first position argues that globalization—however much it is the unintended result of economic logics, technical discoveries, and population growth—finds its only real significance as a political promise. Here, finally, the great Enlightenment program of Immanuel Kant for a single world government under universal law is perhaps realizable (Kant 1795; Toulmin 1990; Kristeva 1993). Possibilities at last exist for either world citizenship under a single governmental entity (a new world state) or some flexible federalist structure allowing significant local autonomy. It is an exciting and welcome development, taking us beyond the petty factionalism, ethnic rivalries, and bloodletting of the past, associated with the ancient, premodern, and modern nationalist eras. Globalization, in this view, is welcome (Falk and Strauss 2000, 2001; Cronkite 1999).

By contrast, the second position argues that globalization is not so much a matter of formal political outcomes as the development of *trade* and of *finance*, in which the pure freedom of exchange revolutionizes human contact along with the potential for understanding, leisure, and cultural sampling. It is not political actors but the transnational corporations that are responsible for globalization, and therefore what is happening is happening deliberately *outside* political structures, and even in opposition to them (Sklair 1991). There is no clear local, or national, beneficiary of globalization, because the transnationals are indifferent to nations (they are, after all, technically owned by people from many countries) and hostile to them (they naturally desire the permeability of borders). They supersede nations, which have therefore become obsolete. In this variant, globalization can be considered either welcome or unwelcome. Theorist Jagdish Bhagwati—an economist at Columbia University who celebrates capitalism—considers these developments the fruit of the marvelous rationality of market forces, and Félix Guattari and Toni Negri (post-Marxist intellectuals who describe themselves as "communists") share much the same view, considering the runaway market as unleashing powerful utopian energies (Bhagwati 2001; Guattari and Negri 1990 [1985]). By contrast, billionaire financier George Soros deems the unrestricted mobility of finance to be a human catastrophe because it renders developing nations acutely vulnerable to collapse when shaky market conditions prompt capital flight (Soros 1998).

The third position combines the emphasis on politics and trade while shifting the criterion to geopolitical motive. In this variant, globalization is the result of developments in technology, transportation, and financial/corporate restructuring working in concert with an underlying *ideology* that is basically American (Valladao 1996; Bauman 1998). Thus globalization, although undoubtedly permeating the rest of the world and in some ways benefiting actors in several countries, is structurally American. It is the United States that primarily benefits, not only directly as a specific nation-state, but in the more ambitious sense that the United States is a mini-model of the future world—the world as it will appear when globalized. Were we to examine this recognizably American ideology as the dynamic contemporary expression of capitalism (the argument goes), we would see how important it has been in facilitating technological developments in media, travel, fashion, and entertainment in a wild and intrepid search for novelty without any thought to consequences. But in a more localized sense, it is the American twist on capitalism that has made globalization seem desirable, and it has done so by making the following concepts widely accepted, either because they are thought inexorable or because they are thought attractive (the fusing of the two qualities, again, is paradigmatic): pragmatism, pluralism, individualism, and suspicion towards the "state." Here globalization can, again, be thought either good or bad, with Thomas Friedman offering perhaps the most outspoken and extreme views on behalf of an irrepressible American genius and beneficence, and Paul Krugman, the economist and op-ed columnist for the *New York Times*, tirelessly exposing the emptiness of neoliberal ideology and the rampant corruption and cronyism at the heart of American profit making (Friedman 1999; Krugman 1997).

A fourth variant is less evolutionary than the third but retains its focus on the United States. It explicitly ties globalization to the problematics of the colonizing "West." Here, globalization is basically the form that imperialism takes in the late twentieth century (Amin 1990; Blaut 1993; Lapham 1998; Bourdieu 2001). It is a shibboleth whose emergence as a master term coincided exactly with the fall of the Soviet Union and the Eastern bloc—that period, in other words, in which the last credible adversaries to U.S. global hegemony were removed. Most of the features said to characterize globalization are American, and they are coercively imposed on others as a universal norm. Rather than the hybridity that is widely acclaimed as being on the rise, we are instead seeing the violent incorporation of global difference into a single national project that is importantly, even vitally, not perceived as such. Although the forms and styles of this imperialism are crucially different from those of the past, the intentions and effects are identical. Conquest, occupation, and the stealing of resources continue to enrich distinct national entities, but they are now performed not under the sign of "civilization" or "God" or "Britain" but in the name of "globalization" or simply the "new," which universalize the interests of that distinct national entity. This analysis presents globalization as a largely fictive enterprise, either cynical or guilty of wishful thinking. Here, globalization is seen as a threat.

The fifth position is the most distinctive. It avers that globalization does not exist. Although it concedes that travel and communication are much easier and more accessible than previously, and although it readily agrees that this increased human contact has had profound effects on the way people see the world, nothing qualitatively has changed. The nation-state structure is still the international norm; ethnic, linguistic, and religious divisions have only intensified; most of the world's people are entirely localized, provincial, traditional, and cut off from others, not only living outside this supposedly new globalized world, but outside modernity itself. Globalization is therefore not a description, but a projection; or more properly, it is a projection that passes itself off as a description. Once again, this is a mixed view, with globalization being thought either good or bad. As the self-styled Metternich of the late twentieth century, for instance, Henry Kissinger is not particularly happy to observe that globalization is an overweening fiction (Kissinger 1994). With grim pragmatism, therefore, he counsels his readers to be wary of obstacles still remaining to American supremacy, wishing in fact that globalization were more real than it is. In both Immanuel Wallerstein and Janet Abu-Lughod, by contrast, globalization collapses as a concept not because its champions are guilty of wishful thinking, but because they rush to unwarranted conclusions (Wallerstein 1984; Abu-Lughod 1989). An investigation of material relations makes it vain, in their opinion, to distinguish our own time from the high Renaissance (or even earlier); both eras are "global" in more or less the same ways, just as both equally fail to approximate the complete integration fancifully described in globalization theory.

These representative positions display more than different diagnoses or emphases; they are methodologically at odds as well. For instance, in his own primer on globalization, Anthony McGrew assumes that "global society" is uncontroversially real, seeking to introduce the topic only by discussing the conflicting explanations for this reality given by major voices in the field. He does not mention the fact, but his discussion reveals a paradox (McGrew 1992). His own argument is representative of only one of two major methodologies—which can be found throughout globalization discourse—that emerge as perfect dialectical opposites. A seesawing between the multiple and the unitary is highlighted in both, but the two elements play very different roles in each. On the one hand, the proponents of the view of an already achieved "global village" (McGrew's position combines the second and third positions mentioned previously) often tend to see a multiplicity, randomness, and disconnectedness at the heart of an overall, fortuitous unity portrayed as the result of a progressive telos. By contrast, some of the critics of globalization—both those skeptical of its desirability and those doubtful of its presence—see behind globalization an underlying, comprehensive set of motives and related processes working on behalf of limited and localized interests: a symmetrically inverted position. Theirs is a *total* explanation based on the repetition of patterns of power brokering from capitalism's past, whereas the proponents' explanation is, as a matter of taste and principle, individual, separable, and "federal," if you will, at the same time that it resists the suggestion of an organic or systemic familiarity.

The concept of totality employed by some critics of globalization theory is reminiscent of that theory, but again, inverts it. Totality does not merely stipulate a unity, but suggests that any contingent or local problem is only clearly seen as being conditioned by its place in a total relationship of objects and events, all governed by a dominant logic. So, for example, the idea presented by a globalization enthusiast such as McGrew that Immanuel Wallerstein, James Rosenau, and Robert Gilpin pose incompatible views on globalization because Wallerstein emphasized historical capitalism, Rosenau the shift from industrial to postindustrial order, and Gilpin the power and legitimacy of a hegemonic liberal state would, from the vantage point of totality, be a crude way of seeing the matter. A theory that conceives of society as a totality would tend not to separate the economic, the political, the social, and the aesthetic in this way. These modes of societal interaction all devolve from interests and material conditionings such that, say, the preferred goals of historical capitalism could be said to *demand* at a certain point precisely a "hegemonic liberal state" to oversee its concerns, managing the vast division of labor that involves moving basic industry to the third world while drawing on the highly trained citizens of the wealthier countries to set up information- and service-based businesses (the "postindustrial" ones). Capitalism is the logic in each phase of this operation, and there are not three explanations, but one.

In all of its variants, globalization theory presumes a knowledge of the following key terms:

- **Modernity**—apart from suggesting widely available technologies associated with "modern life" (televisions, cars, high-rises, computers), modernity more generally refers to a cast of mind, an attitude, and an approach to problems as much as to a period. Modernity begins with the Enlightenment and never ends (we are still in modernity). It centrally involves the idea of the "new", the break, the departure. Earlier, intellectuals (church clerics, for example) tended to base their arguments on Aristotle, Scripture, or the like. In modernity, legitimacy and authority are no longer based on principles derived from the past. Rather in modernity, the questioner (of law, of right, of religion, of truth) offers his or her own justification. Modernity means to create one's own normativeness out of oneself.
- **The West**—a historical rather than a geographical construct. It means developed, industrialized, urbanized, capitalist, secular, and modern. Any society that shares these features is usually thought of as existing in the orbit of the "West." Derived originally from the division of the Roman Empire, and later by the division of the Christian churches in the eleventh century, it took on a new, ideological coloring in the era of the Crusades, when the "Orient" (which referred at first only to Islam) was then allowed to stand in for everything East of it as well (China, India, Persia, and so on). In the Cold War, a new binary opposition arose using the terms "East" and "West" with

a slightly altered (but fundamentally similar) geopolitical significance (Lazarus 1991, 2002; Said 1993; Coronil 1997).

- **Space/Place**—The significance of the turn to space/place in globalization theory lies, first of all, in the overcoming of temporality. Time is supplanted by Space in a world-view that: (a) perceives the conflicts of history as being decisively decided in favor of one of the warring parties; or (for exactly opposite reasons) (b) recoils from the Hegelian notion of a progressive telos to history, to which it is allergic, and is therefore drawn methodologically to a synchronic analysis, expressed in metaphors of spatiality (we identified these opposed, but complementary, features of globalization theory in the terms *neoliberalism* and *poststructuralism*). In harmony with the assumption that globalization is an irrepressible unfolding, the logical issue is no longer what will happen, but when it will extend itself over a vast but finite territory. The optic logically shifts from pace to scale, and from the chronometric to the cartographic. As a matter of theory, the dual expression *space/place* means to suggest that a struggle over value is embedded in the way one thinks about spatiality (Dirlik 2001; Sassen 1998). "Space" is more abstract and ubiquitous: it connotes capital, history, and activity and gestures towards the meaninglessness of distance in a world of instantaneous communication and "virtuality." "Place" connotes, by contrast, the kernel or center of one's memory and experience—a dwelling, a familiar park or city street, one's family or community. An ambiguity of value is obviously contained in the pairing, because the former is both bloodless and forward looking, whereas the latter, although personally vital, is also static.

- **Cosmopolitanism**—colloquially associated with broad fellow feeling, world travel, openness to cultural otherness, and so on, cosmopolitanism discursively accompanies globalization as the political ethic of intellectuals as such, and specifically, of intellectuals as members of the mobile and enlightened middle classes. It both describes and endorses (endorses *as* it describes) the creation of a singularity out of newness, a blending and merging of differences becoming one entity. Furthermore, it stipulates a theory of world government and world citizenship in which the term's cultural meaning is carried over to its political one. In that sense, it is distinct from internationalism, which sets out to establish a global network of respect and co-operation based on differences of polity as well as culture (specifically, those polities known as nation-states). Cosmopolitanism sprouts from an already existing culture of intellectuals and middle-class travelers, researchers, and businessmen. Internationalism, on the other hand—although based no less than cosmopolitanism on the facts of global interpenetration, the homogenization brought about by capitalist mass culture, and the cultural consequences of mass migration – is an ideology of the domestically restricted, the recently relocated, the exiled, and the temporarily weak (Hannerz 1990; Nussbaum 1996; Brennan 1997).

- **Neoliberalism**—a position that became prominent in policy-making circles (and later in journalism and the academy) following the conservative electoral victories of Margaret Thatcher in Britain and Ronald Reagan in the United States. With the goal of dismantling the welfare state, neoliberalism argues that an unrestrained market logic, freed from governmental constraints, will cure social ills and lead to general prosperity. As Pierre Bourdieu explains, it "is not a discourse like others. Like psychiatric discourse in the asylum, as described by Erving Goffman, it is a 'strong discourse' which is so strong and so hard to fight because it has behind it all the powers of a world of power relations which it helps to make as it is, in particular by orienting the economic choices of those who dominate economic relations and so adding its own—specifically symbolic—force to those power relations" (Bourdieu 1998, 95). It is a faith rather than an analysis, which creates its own truth by imposing itself on the supposedly free agents of economic choice.

To turn now to postcolonial studies, one should begin by noticing that, like globalization theory, it ambiguously evokes an ethical program and presents itself as an iconoclastic departure from older modes of studying its field of interest. A teleology of shared mores links the two movements. On the one hand, postcolonial studies carries on the sensibilities formulated by anticolonial intellectuals who, given the conjunctures of foreign policy, caught the attention of metropolitan writers and thinkers at specific times (resistance intellectuals from Latin America throughout the nineteenth century, China of the 1920s, India of the 1940s, Algeria of the 1950s, Vietnam of the 1960s, Central America of the 1970s, and so on). Within the United States, many of the central motifs of postcolonial studies were formulated already in academia in the 1960s as a result of the anti-Vietnam War movement and the radicalizations that produced new Black Studies and Women's Studies departments. On the other hand, "postcolonial studies" is often taken to be something much more specific. It was less a discrete field than a collection of attitudes and styles of inquiry arising in a variety of disciplines more or less simultaneously in the early 1980s. Postcolonial studies in this sense alluded to its early parentage but thought of itself as being more directly influenced by poststructuralism; indeed, the growth of "theory" in the late 1970s and the rise of postcolonial studies in this more restricted sense were virtually contemporaneous.

In the broadest sense, postcolonial studies is an intellectual movement driven by a critique of Eurocentrism and patriarchy. In its general arc, the work involves collecting and disseminating information, formulating arguments, or explaining concepts with the end of achieving emancipation for minority, marginal, or formerly colonized peoples. However, it is also and at the same time involved in questioning value—that is, it seeks to reorient cultural values attendant upon learning to understand and aesthetically appreciate the cultural achievements of those outside the European sphere. It seeks to show how earlier scholars in the West have been narrowly obsessed, culturally limited, and tendentiously ignorant of many of the world's most consequential artistic and intellectual creations. Many trace the origins of the field to the publication of Edward Said's *Orientalism* in 1978 and the elaborations later provided (in a very different vein) by Gayatri Spivak, Homi Bhabha, and others. In practice, these later elaborations (unlike Said's) tended to merge colonial or non-Western themes with deconstruction, post-Marxism, discourse analysis, Lacanian psychoanalysis, and other expressions of poststructuralist literary theory, whereas Said was more consciously drawing on an earlier philological and social democratic tradition of historians and activists. Postcolonial studies, then, is far from a unified ideological field, and there are several important fissures within it.

There has been a good deal of argument about the term *postcolonial* because it suggests that colonies no longer exist (a suggestion that does not bear scrutiny). The term has, however, survived in part because it successfully euphemizes harsher terms such as *imperialism* or *racism* in professionally respectable academic environments, but also because many of its practitioners believe the fight over the independence of sovereign states (over which the colonial struggle had once been fought) was no longer the issue. In an age of globalization the issue was rather about Eurocentric assumptions rather than military occupations. Hence, the *post*.

As a matter of intellectual precedent, however, one clearly sees the ties of globalization to the problems of imperial practices, and so can appreciate a rather different kind of bond between them as well. "World systems theory" is often cited as the most obvious forerunner of globalization theory, and either Immanuel Wallerstein or Samir Amin is usually considered its most commanding presence if not its founder. Who came first is of less importance than that a left critique of development ideology arose in the 1950s and 1960s, creating the basis for much of what later became known as the theory of globalization. Amin was formulating its basic tenets in his dissertation in 1957 (published in 1970 as *Accumlation á l'échelle mondiale* [*Accumulation on a World Scale*]). For his part, Marshall Hodgson was publicly using the term *world system* already in 1965, and that was a year *after* Oliver Cromwell Cox had completed the third volume of his neglected trilogy on the foundations of capitalism as a world system (Hodgson 1974; Cox 1959). The central arguments of world systems theory are: (a) that intricately organized systems of trade, cultural contact, and borrowing are extraordinarily old, even ancient; (b) that capital accumulation is the motor force for such contact; (c) that history must be founded on a rejection of Eurocentric assumptions or by the artificial separation of cultural and economic questions; and, (d) that world systems have a center-periphery structure and alternate between a hegemony and rivalry marked by economic cycles of ascending and descending phases.

A related predecessor would be "dependency theory." If the high colonial era's naively ethnocentric evolutionary argument of European superiority and racial supremacy in the eighteenth and nineteenth centuries gave way after the Second World War to the more anodyne "modernization theory," the latter nevertheless adapted many of the former's assumptions. Both, for example, explain Europe's (and now the United States') dominant posture internationally by invoking a "European miracle"—the unique mastery of reason, freedom, and individualism in the West. These cultural traits are said to distinguish it among world civilizations (McNeill 1963; Landes 1998). Hence, the rest of the world is on the way to "modernizing" itself but cannot do so without the diffusion of European traits. The dependency theorists, primarily based in Latin America and the Caribbean, arose to contest this narrative. They argued by contrast that the dominant countries deliberately "underdeveloped" the third world, and that first-world wealth was derived not only from the theft of resources from the periphery, but from pressing home the artificial advantages won in an earlier period of conquest (Frank 1967, 1993; Rodney 1972; Santos 1978).

Theories of globalization, then—as Justin Rosenberg points out—are not necessarily "globalization theory," just as studies of colonialism, anticolonialism, and imperialism are not necessarily "postcolonial studies" (Rosenberg 2000).[3] In the university at least, both were driven by a set of *ethical* postulates popularized by poststructuralist theory: the striving for ambivalence as a matter of principle; the ardent belief that answering a question "forecloses" it; the elision of meaning in pursuit of epistemological doubt; and, most of all, the deployment of a variety of tropes such as "migrancy," "nomadism," "hybridity," and "decentering," which are marshaled in order to make the case that mobility and cultural mixing—not as contingent historical experiences but as modes of being—are states of virtue. What is implied is that these conditions are *ontologically* superior and that political life should be based today on approximating them. It is important not to confuse this ethical program with theories of globalization, because many critics believe such a program to be precisely an adjunct to the very corporate (and American) globalization being analyzed.

To its predecessors, as well as to its critics, globalization theory shares with postcolonial studies a dubious relationship to the power it purportedly questions. In these circles, one would want to emphasize not ethics but the large-scale structural determinants of both fields of inquiry: namely, *capitalism* and *the West*. What both are really attempting to do is expose the tyrannies of value lying behind the creation of the myth of "the West"—a myth continually reinvented in each subsequent era in order to outmaneuver the disrepute into which the older discrimination had fallen (Blaut 1993; Stokes 2001). But if globalization is a continuation of colonialism, what exactly is colonialism?

Both colonialism and imperialism entail the subjugation of one people by another. Traditionally, neither term refers to individuals within one society subjugating others within that same society. What is meant, rather, is that people who live in one region of the world—not just living together, but acting as organized members of a recognizable political territory such as a nation-state—subjugate those of another part of the world. So the concept suggests not only the largeness of the operation, or the ethnic, racial, or cultural differences of the parties, but the global scale upon which it is carried out. When we say "subjugation," we mean forcible, often violent, control over others: the rendering of people "subjects," which is to say placing them in a situation where their freedom is contingent upon the will of the dominant group.

Colonialism and imperialism, unlike other forms of subjugation, are not based on rank or privilege alone—as, for instance, in the inequalities experienced by people of different social classes in eighteenth-century France. That is, the dominant group is not composed only of the rich and powerful, or the generals who did the conquering, or the businessmen who profited from the conquest. On the contrary, the key idea that motivates colonialism and imperialism is that *everyone* from the conquering country is civilizationally superior to the conquered people. One can feel that one belongs to the dominant group simply by virtue of one's race (the racial identity that is preponderant in the home territory), one's nationality (whether one is a citizen of the conquering country), or one's cultural identity. In this way, the poor, the subservient, or the discriminated against within a given country often support imperialism because in *that* relationship they are considered members of the superior group.

What prompts this form of subjugation? Historically, several different factors exist at times in combination: to acquire new territory for expansion or settlement, to acquire raw materials needed in production (ones that cannot be found in the home territory); to acquire labor by enlisting laborers who can be forced to work for free or for less money than in the home country; to set up businesses that either could not exist in the home territory (because of the climate or the distances from essential commodities) or would not be tolerated at home (given the cruelty of the operation, the amount of pollution the business generates, or other legal or moral reasons). Other motives are less immediately linked to the extraction of wealth: to have a place for expelling unruly social elements (criminals, religious dissidents, unwanted racial populations, the diseased, or the insane); to have a place to flee persecution and so to become the persecutors in turn; or, simply, to create new markets. Here the point is not to *take* things from the colony, or make things in the colony less expensively, but to create a new culture that will be receptive to the things one makes in the home territory so they can be more readily sold there. This last point often entails the export of ideas and values: the setting up of new educational systems, the establishment of new local customs, the dissemination of books, dress, musical performances, and other artistic and broadly cultural practices, as well as religious indoctrination, in order to transform the local population into a "familiar" one.

There were many ancient and modern *empires*—that is, attempts by a people to conquer the known world and bring it under a single jurisdiction: the Persians, Macedonians, Romans, Mongols, Mughals, Ottomans (Turks), and Spanish all had extensive empires. But when one uses the word *imperialist* today, it does not refer to these empires. This is rather a modern, and more specific, term for a system that grew out of European colonial expansion between the fifteenth and nineteenth centuries and involves a comprehensive interconnected economic system, as well as an accompanying cultural penetration and unification rather than simply a conquest as in the ancient empires. Coined in the late nineteenth century by critics of empire who saw the global system as an organic outgrowth of capitalist expansion, the term *imperialism* in practice refers to the French, Dutch, Spanish, Portuguese, and especially British empires, but also to the U.S. empire, which after World War II inherited the system these European countries created (Brewer 1980; Chilcote 2000; Tabb 2000).

The basic difference between colonialism and imperialism (for they vary greatly from case to case) is that imperialism is a later and more systematic organization of the foreign exploitation pioneered by colonialism. Another way of expressing the idea is this: imperialism makes the process begun by colonialism more efficient and generalized, and it often (although not always) reduces the need for a bald, direct confrontation of peoples from two different cultures. In general, colonialism characterized the period before imperialism: roughly the fifteenth to the nineteenth centuries (it is, in this sense, a chronological term). Although widespread and even concerted, it tended to be pragmatic, occasional, and unsystematic. Colonies, especially in their origins, were often run by private ventures or holding companies rather than states. They were carried out either for purposes of settlement or for economic exploitation; they were largely conducted in terms of a confrontation between the white and the "dark" races; they often involved direct military occupation and the setting up of alternative cultural institutions for the purpose of creating a native caste that shared the same culture as those in the home country. Imperialism, by contrast, grows out of colonialism, both by extending its logic but also by responding more subtly to the demands for political independence launched by the freedom movements within the colonies during the twentieth century. It tends to be comprehensive and systematic, ruled by a central authority such as a state or decisive financial or political institutions effectively controlled by a state or an alliance of states. Imperialism can and does involve military invasion or occupation, but usually not for the purpose of settlement.

Under imperialism, conquest is often maintained from afar, by the *threat* of military invasion or by means of economic coercion. In its classical sense, imperialism is above all a structured system of economic disparity that places certain countries of the world in a position of dependence on those states whose economies are strongest, and whose strength is artificially (and coercively) maintained by unequal rates of exchange, punitive lending laws, and by other financial, commercial, and military means. One of imperialism's classic definitions, therefore, is simply "the export of capital." Under imperialism, the imperial center itself no longer runs (at least directly) the cultural institutions in the foreign country that serves the imperial center. A whole sector of "native" intellectuals and elites, inherited from the colonial era, identify with the imperial center and carry out its wishes either out of conviction or through payoffs, bribery, personal networks of affiliation, and so on. The ideology of civilizational superiority incipient under colonialism becomes under imperialism a given, and it is used by the imperial center as a natural justification for all its actions. There is no open enlistment, as under colonialism, of the rhetoric of a righteous cause or a confrontation of the enlightened versus the benighted. These categories are rather fully internationalized and bureaucratized and are no longer controversial. As the recent invasions of Iraq and the Balkans reminds us (although much the same could be said of the Reagan-era invasions of Nicaragua, El Salvador, and Grenada), the classic colonial relationship of military force and holy mission is often in practice fused with the more impervious imperial status quo, even in late modernity.

One can appreciate, then, why globalization theory so carefully dissociates the process of globalization from *national* identifications, ethnocentric attitudes, forcible inclusion, or the discourse of civilizational superiority, because unless it does so the continuities between its purportedly new and liberatory panorama and older exploitative arrangements would be obvious and uncomfortable. Taking globalization theory at its word, the classic features of colonialism seem not only alien to globalization, but its very opposite, because the latter is relentlessly cast as popularly willed, anonymous, permeating, and unplanned. But can this assumption be confidently maintained? One notices, for instance, that colonialism always worked by playing cultural differences off of one another in the name of acquiring material advantages. Differences, as such, were critical to a strategy of profit making that relied upon the dissemination of local values in the guise of global ones. If it is obvious that cultural differences were greeted negatively in earlier centuries, whereas they now stand at the very core of the universal ethic of global pluralism, the stark contrast is perhaps a little too easy to misinterpret. Rather than being opposites, these positions are complementary. In each case, a carefully nurtured segregation of locality, political knowledge, and cultural practice allows an educated caste with means to manipulate sectarian interests in order to benefit from the disparities that keep them in competition while calling forth a self-image as unifying force whose "inevitability" renders self-interest both invisible and benevolent.

What we are seeing today under the banner of globalization repeats a process, with some changes, that we saw over two centuries ago with the emergence of *national* markets (Polanyi 1944). The significant development today is only the larger scale on which the process occurs, and the smaller number of beneficiaries. Much has been made in recent years of the necessity of nations to create an artificial sense of belonging—a distinct national culture via print media and invented traditions (Anderson 1983; Hobsbawm and Ranger 1983; Hobsbawm 1987). In globalization—often portrayed as the transcendence of nationalism—the same dynamic pertains: homogenization takes place as a concentration of power on the road to monopoly. Samir Amin's account of the rise of finance capital demonstrates from another angle this parallelism between globalization and national state formation. Via immense deficit spending, the United States dictates terms of structural readjustment to other countries, just as the Bretton Woods institutions (under U.S. tutelage) form the nucleus of a new global megastate (Bourdieu 1998; Amin 1997). Many commentators, Amin argues, have falsely associated capitalism with "development" and "the market," whereas it is actually hostile to both. It thrives, rather, in the zero-sum contest of mobile finance drifting around the globe in search of investment, victimized by its own victorious monopolization, hungering for new worlds to conquer.

The underlying logic linking globalization theory and postcolonial studies has, in at least one respect, a perverse cast. The mutual hostility of both to the nation form (particularly as nation-*state*) is projected as an irrepressible ultramodernism. In turn, this ultramoderism in its contemporary variant is given an almost aesthetic accent in which mobility as an ontological condition is portrayed as the exciting play of an infinite self-fashioning. The cast is "perverse" because in accordance with such a logic one is forced contemptuously to revile, even while resonating with, a specific and conjunctural national-statist project (that of the United States) that in a vigorously broadcast system of images and slogans embraces the same hybridity, modernity, and mobility of globalization theory. Like that theory, it depicts the world as having moved *past* colonialism and imperialism.

It would be an enormous irony, of course, if this shared logic were purely and neatly self-contradictory. In fact, both discursive formations have helped generate, often in spite of themselves, a more complicated and internally riven set of theories. Even in their restrictive senses, both are institutional arenas where a welcome intellectual generalism has lately begun to flourish, pushing researchers into a rudimentary knowledge of sociology, economics, and social history. Particularly in the past few years, cultural theorists have moved past interrogations of methodology and epistemology (however important these gestures always were on their own terms, and however admirable when contrasted with the relative methodological complacency of the natural and social sciences). The globalization theorist has at last become part of the object of inquiry, placed in a field of interests and seen as functioning in a larger division of intellectual labor. In the shift in academic fashions, which has driven many postcolonial theorists to retool themselves as globalization theorists, this "economics" of the cultural intellectual may be the most consequential future field of action.

## Notes

1 For a closer look at the interwar sources of postcolonial studies, see Benita Parry (1997).

2 Interestedness—positions that are a matter of social convenience rather than the acknowledgment of inconvenient facts; for example, the bookish philosopher Derrida's prioritizing of writing over speaking in a culture of a televisual secondary orality, or New Criticism's unyielding principle of the self-enclosed, nonreferential artwork during an era when political contextualization was professionally dangerous. But this is not to say that one cannot transcend sectoral, class, or cultural interestedness. The logic of bringing "interest" as a category to the surface for discussion is precisely to bring this conclusion about.

3 A more detailed description of this process can be found in Ahmad (1992), Lazarus (1999), and San Juan (1998). See also Brennan (2000).

# WORKS CITED

Abu-Lughod, Janet. 1989. "On the Remaking of History: How to Reinvent the Past." In *Remaking History*, eds. Barbara Kruger and Phil Mariani, Seattle: Bay Press.

Agamben, Giorgio. 1993. *The Coming Community*. Minneapolis: University of Minnesota Press.

Ahmad, Aijaz. 1992. *In Theory: Classes, Nations, Literatures*. London: Verso.

Amin, Samir. 1976. *Unequal Development: An Essay on the Social Formations of Peripheral Capitalism*. New York: Monthly Review.

———. 1990. *Transforming the Revolution: Social Movements and the World-System*. New York: Monthly Review.

———. 1997. *Capitalism in the Age of Globalization: The Management of Contemporary Society*. London: Zed Books.

Anderson, Benedict. 1983. *Imagined Communities: Reflections on the Origins and Spread of Nationalism*. London: Verso.

Appadurai, Arjun. 1996. *Modernity at Large: Cultural Dimensions of Globalization*. Minneapolis: University of Minnesota Press.

Appiah, Kwame Anthony. 1991. "Is the Post- in Postmodernism the Post- in Postcolonial?" *Critical Inquiry* 17:336–57.

Bartolovich, Crystal, and Neil Lazarus, eds. 2002. *Marxism, Modernity, and Postcolonial Studies*. Cambridge: Cambridge University Press.

Bauman, Zygmunt. 1998. *Globalization: The Human Consequences*. New York: Columbia University Press.

Bentham, Jeremy. 1995 (1822). *Colonies, Commerce, and Constitutional Law: Rid Yourselves of Ultramaria and Other Writings on Spain and Spanish America*, ed. Philip Schofield. Oxford: Clarendon Press.

Bhagwati, Jagdish. 2001. "Why Globalization Is Good." *Items & Issues* 2:3–4, 7–8.

Blaut, J. M. 1993. *The Colonizer's Model of the World: Geographical Diffusionism and Eurocentric History*. New York: Guilford Press.

Bourdieu, Pierre. 1998. "Neoliberalism, the Utopia (Becoming a Reality) of Unlimited Exploitation." In *Acts of Resistance: Against the Tyranny of the Market,* trans. Richard Nice. New York: New Press.

———. 2001. "Uniting Better to Dominate." *Items & Issues* 2:3–4.

Braudel, Fernand. 1984. "Economies in Space: The World Economies" and "By Way of a Conclusion: Past and Present." In *The Perspective of the World* (vol. 3 of *Civilization and Capitalism, 15th–18th Century*). New York: Harper & Row.

Brennan, Timothy. 1997. *At Home in the World: Cosmopolitanism Now*. Cambridge, Mass.: Harvard University Press.

———. 2000. "The Illusion of a Future: Orientalism as Traveling Theory." *Critical Inquiry* 26, no. 3 (Spring): 558–83.

———. 2002a. "Cosmo-Theory." *South Atlantic Quarterly* 100, no. 3: 657–89.

———. 2002b. "Postcolonial Studies between the European Wars: An Intellectual History." In *Marxism, Modernity, and Postcolonial Studies*, eds. Crystal Bartolovich and Neil Lazarus, 185–203. Cambridge: Cambridge University Press.

Brewer, Anthony. 1980. *Marxist Theories of Imperialism*. London: Routledge and Kegan Paul.

Bukharin, Nikolai. 1917 (1973). *Imperialism and World Economy*. New York: Monthly Review.

Bukharin, Nikolai, (and Rosa Luxemburg). 1921 (1972). *Imperialism and the Accumulation of Capital: An Anti-Critique*. New York: Monthly Review.

Chilcote, Ronald H., ed. 2000. *Imperialism: Theoretical Directions*. Amherst, N.Y.: Humanity Books.

Coronil, Fernando. 1997. *The Magical State: Nature, Money, and Modernity in Venezuela*. Chicago: University of Chicago Press.

Cox, Oliver Cromwell. 1959. *The Foundations of Capitalism*. New York: Phil. Library.

———. 1962. *Capitalism and American Leadership*. New York: Phil. Library.

———. 1964. *Capitalism as a System*. New York: Monthly Review.

Cronkite, Walter. 1999. "Speech Given upon Receiving the Norman Cousins Global Governance Award" at the United Nations. San Francisco: World Federalist Organization.

Dirlik, Arif. 1997. *The Postcolonial Aura: Third World Criticism in the Age of Global Capitalism*. Boulder, Colo.: Westview Press.

———. 2001. "Place-Based Imagination: Globalism and the Politics of Place." In *Places and Politics in an Age of Globalization,* eds. Roxann Prazniak and Arif Dirlik. Lanham, Rowman and Littlefield.

Falk, Richard, and Andrew Strauss. 2000. "On the Creation of a Global Peoples Assembly: Legitimacy and Power of Popular Sovereignty." *Stanford Journal of International Law* 36, no. 2: 191–219.

———. 2001. "Toward a Global Parliament." *Foreign Affairs*, January–February: 212–20.

Fanon, Frantz. 1963. *The Wretched of the Earth.* Preface by Jean-Paul Sartre, trans. Constance Farrington. New York: Grove Press.

Featherstone, Mike. 1990. *Global Culture: Nationalism, Globalization, and Modernity.* London: Sage Publications.

Foster, John Bellamy. 2002. *The Rediscovery of Imperialism* 54, no. 6 (November): 1–16.

Frank, Andre Gunder. 1967. *Capitalism and Underdevelopment in Latin America.* New York: Monthly Review.

———. 1993. "The 5,000-Year World System: An Interdisciplinary Introduction." In *The World System: Five Hundred or Five Thousand?* eds. Andre Gunder Frank and Barry K. Gills, 3–57. London: Routledge.

Friedman, Thomas. 1999. *The Lexus and the Olive Tree.* New York: Farrar, Straus, and Giroux.

Giddens, Anthony. 1991. "The Contours of High Modernity." In *Modernity and Self-Identity: Self and Society in the Late Modern Age.* Stanford: Stanford University Press.

Grafigny, Mme de François d'Issembourg d'Happoncourt. 1993 (1755). *Letters from a Peruvian Woman,* trans. David Kornacker, introduction by Joan DeJean and Nancy K. Miller. New York: Modern Language Association of America.

Graham, R. B. Cunningham. 1896. *The Imperial Kailyard: Being a Biting Satire on English Colonisation.* London: Twentieth Century Press.

Guattari, Félix, and Toni Negri. 1990 (1985). *Communists Like Us: New Spaces of Liberty, New Lines of Alliance,* trans. Michael Ryan with a "Postscript, 1990" by Toni Negri. New York: Semiotext(e).

Guevara, Ernesto Che. 1969 (1961). *Guerrilla Warfare,* trans. J. P. Morray, prefatory note by I. F. Stone. New York: Vintage Books.

Hannerz, Ulf. 1990. "Cosmopolitans and Locals in World Culture." In *Global Culture: Nationalism, Globalization, and Modernity,* ed. Mike Featherstone, 237–551. London: Sage.

Harvey, David. 1989. *The Condition of Postmodernity: An Enquiry into the Origins of Cultural Change.* Cambridge, Mass.: Blackwell.

Hobsbawm, Eric. 1987. *The Age of Empire: 1875–1914.* London: Cardinal.

Hobsbawm, Eric, and Terence Ranger. 1983. *The Invention of Tradition.* Cambridge: Cambridge University Press.

Hobson, J. A. 1902. *Imperialism: A Study.* London: Allen & Unwin.

Ho Chi Minh. n.d. *Selected Works,* prologue by René Depestre. Havana, Cuba: Tricontinental.

———, trans. 1960. *Oeuvres choisies.* Hanoi: Foreign Languages Editorial.

Hodgson, Marshall. 1974. *The Venture of Islam: Conscience and History in a World Civilization.* Chicago: University of Chicago Press.

Huggan, Graham. 2001. *The Postcolonial Exotic: Marketing the Margins.* London: Routledge.

Kant, Immanuel. 1970 (1784). "Idea for a Universal History with a Cosmopolitan Purpose." In *Kant's Political Writings,* ed. and introduction by Hans Reiss, trans. H. B. Nisbet, 93–130. Cambridge: Cambridge University Press.

———. 1970 (1795). "Perpetual Peace: A Philosophical Sketch." In *Kant's Political Writings,* ed. and introduction by Hans Reiss, trans. H. B. Nisbet, 93–130. Cambridge: Cambridge University Press.

Kautsky, Karl. 1897. *Communism in Central Europe in the Time of the Reformation,* trans. J. L. Mulliken and E. G. Mulliken. London: T. Fisher Unwin.

———. 1914. "Ultra-imperialism." *New Left Review* 59 (January – February 1970).

Kiernan, V. G. 1969. *The Lords of Human Kind: European Attitudes to the Outside World in the Imperial Age.* London: Weidenfield and Nicolson.

Kissinger, Henry. 1994. *Diplomacy.* New York: Simon & Schuster.

Kristeva, Julia. 1993. *Nations without Nationalism.* New York: Columbia University Press.

Krugman, Paul R. 1997. *The Age of Diminished Expectations: U.S. Economic Policy in the 1990s.* Cambridge, Mass.: MIT Press.

Landes, David. 1998. *The Wealth and Poverty of Nations: Why Some Are so Rich and Some so Poor*. New York: W. W. Norton.

Lapham, Lewis H. 1998. *The Agony of Mammon: The Imperial World Economy Explains Itself to the Membership in Davos, Switerzland*. London: Verso.

Las Casas, Bartolomé de. 1552. *Breuissima relación de la destrucción de las Indias*. Seville: Sebastián Trujillo.

Lazarus, Neil. 1991. "Doubting the New World Order: Marxism and Postmodernist Social Theory." *differences* 3, no. 3: 94–138.

———. 1999. *Nationalism and Cultural Practice in the Postcolonial World*. Cambridge: Cambridge University Press.

———. 2002. "The Fetish of the 'West' in Postcolonial Theory." In *Marxism, Modernity, and Postcolonial Studies*, eds. Crystal Bartolovich and Neil Lazarus, 43–64. Cambridge: Cambridge University Press.

Lenin, Vladimir. 1917 (1925). *Imperialism: The Highest Stage of Capitalism*. London: New Left Books.

Lumumba, Patrice. 1972. *Lumumba Speaks: The Speeches and Writings of Patrice Lumumba* (in French), eds. Jean van Lierde and Helen R. Lane, introduction by Jean-Paul Sartre. Boston: Little, Brown.

Luxemburg, Rosa, and Nikolai Bukharin. 1921 (1972). *Imperialism and the Accumulation of Capital: An Anti-Critique*. New York: Monthly Review.

Mao, Zedong. 1953. *On Contradiction*. New York: International Publishers.

Marx, Karl. 1991 (1894). *Capital: A Critique of Political Economy* (vol. 3), trans. David Fernbach, introduction by Ernest Mandel. London: Penguin in association with New Left Review.

Marx, Karl, (with Friedrich Engels). 1848 (1998). *The Communist Manifesto*. New York: Monthly Review.

McGrew, Anthony. 1992. "A Global Society?" In *Modernity and Its Futures*, eds. Stuart Hall, David Held, and Tony McGrew, 466–503. Cambridge, UK: Polity Press and Blackwell.

McNeill, William. 1963. *The Rise of the West: A History of the Human Community*. Chicago: University of Chicago Press.

Melville, Herman. 1851 (1988). *Moby-Dick*. Oxford: Oxford University Press.

Montaigne, Michel de. 1595. "On Cannibals." In *Les Essais de Michel seignevr de Montaigne; Edition novvelle, trovvee apres le deceds de l'autheur, reueuë & augmantée par luy d'vn tiers plus qu'aux precedentes impressions*. Paris: Abel L'Angelier.

Morris, William. 1901. *News from Nowhere: Or, an Epoch of Rest, Being Some Chapters from a Utopian Romance*. New York: Longmans, Green.

Nehru, Jawaharlal. 1946. *The Discovery of India*. New York: John Day.

Nussbaum, Martha, et al. 1996. *For Love of Country: Debating the Limits of Patriotism*, ed. Josh Cohen. Boston: Beacon Press.

Parry, Benita. 1997. *Cultural Readings of Imperialism: Edward Said and the Gravity of History*, eds. Keith Ansell-Pearson and Judith Squires. New York: St. Martin's Press.

Pessoa, Fernando. 1925 (1988). *Always Astonished: Selected Prose*, trans., ed., and introduction by Edwin Honig. San Francisco: City Lights Books.

Polanyi, Karl. 1944. *The Great Transformation*. New York: Farrar, & Rinehart.

Raleigh, Sir Walter. 1596. *The discoverie of the large, rich and bevvtiful empire of Guiana, with a relation of the great and golden citie of Manoa (which the Spanyards call El Dorado) and the prouinces of Emeria, Arromaia, Amapaia, and other countries, with their riuers, adioyning*. London: Robert Robinson.

Raynal, abbé Guillaume-Thomas-François. 1991 (1774). *Histoire philosophique et politique des établissements & du commerce des Européens dans les deux Indes*. La Haye: Gosse.

Rodney, Walter. 1972. *How Europe Underdeveloped Africa*. London: Bogle L'Ouverture.

Rosenberg, Justin. 2000. *The Follies of Globalization Theory*. London: Verso.

Said, Edward. 1993. *Culture and Imperialism*. New York: Knopf.

San Juan, Epifanio. 1998. *Beyond Postcolonial Theory*. New York: St. Martins.

Santos, Theotonio dos. 1978. *Imperialismo y dependencia*. Mexico City: Ediciones Era.

Sassen, Saskia. 1991. *The Global City: New York, London, Tokyo*. Princeton, N.J.: Princeton University Press.

———. 1998. *Globalization and Its Discontents*. New York: New Press.

Sklair, Leslie. 1991. *Sociology of the Global System*. New York: Harvester Wheatsheaf.

Smith, Adam. 1776. *An Inquiry into the Nature and Causes of the Wealth of Nations*. Dublin: Whitestone.

Soros, George. 1998. *The Crisis of Global Capitalism: Open Society Endangered*. New York: PublicAffairs.

Stavrianos, Leften Stavros. 1981. *Global Rift: The Third World Comes of Age*. New York: Morrow.

Stokes, Gale. 2001. "Why the West?" *Lingua Franca* 11, no. 8 (November): 30–39.

Tabb, William K. 2000. "Capitalism and Globalization." In *Imperialism: Theoretical Directions*, ed. Ronald H. Chilcote, 315–21. Amherst, N.Y.: Humanity Books.

Toulmin, Stephen Edelston. 1990. *Cosmopolis: The Hidden Agenda of Modernity*. New York: Free Press.

Valladao, Alfredo G. A. 1996. *The Twenty-First Century Will Be American*. London: Verso.

Voltaire. 1759 (2001). *Candide: ou l'optimisme*. Paris: Maisonneuve et Larose.

Wallerstein, Immanuel. 1974. *The Modern World-System: Capitalist Agriculture and the Origins of the European World Economy in the Sixteenth Century*. New York: Academic Press.

———. 1984. *The Politics of the World Economy: The States, the Movements, and the Civilizations*. Cambridge: Cambridge University Press.

———. 1991. "Geopolitics: Post-America" and "Geoculture: The Underside of Geopolitics." In *Geopolitics and Geoculture: Essays on the Changing World System*. Cambridge: Cambridge University Press.

Wolf, Eric R. 1982. *Europe and the People without History*. Berkeley: University of California Press.

# 2

# UNIVERSAL AREAS: ASIAN STUDIES IN A WORLD IN MOTION

## *Pheng Cheah*

In recent years, the research enterprises called *area studies* have been increasingly challenged, especially by anthropologists influenced by Edward Said's critique of Orientalism, as well as by those interested in the impact of contemporary globalization on culture.[1] The primary thrust of these criticisms is directed at the organic and static understanding of the *area* as an object of scholarly inquiry. But although these criticisms have made indeterminate the surfaces of area studies by pointing to the mutual interpenetration of "Asia" and "the West" in global modernity, they have not questioned the implicit conceptual determination of area that places it in a negative relationship to that now-unfashionable but still-powerful ethico-philosophical epithet and hypostatization, "universal." For it seems such an obvious fact that it is scarcely worth pointing out that an area—the object of area studies—is that which is not universal. Or, to be more tendentious still, an area is precisely that which is not *capable* of universality.

This chapter is primarily an outsider's attempt to understand the conceptual matrix of the formation of area studies in the U. S. academy, particularly its division of labor in relation to the disciplines of the humanities and the social sciences, and the constraints placed upon the work of area studies by this conceptual matrix. I argue that the conceptual definition of *world area* in the programmatic literature of key funding bodies during area studies' high-growth years in the post–Second World War era places area scholarship and the areas themselves in a subordinate relationship to the universal knowing subject of the disciplines. I trace this definition of world area back to the Hegelian idea of *Volksgeist* in order to elaborate on the underlying relationship between universal and particular. This understanding of the universal and the particular still structures critiques of the Eurocentrism of disciplinary knowledge that reject Western universalism and denounce its parochialism. I suggest that another way to reinvent area studies in contemporary globalization is to see each and every area neither as something particular that needs to be transcended to attain universality nor as concrete reality that needs to be affirmed over abstract universality, but instead, as the irreducible inscription of the universal in the singular.

## THE "AREA" OF AREA STUDIES AND THE DENEGATION OF THE WEST

It is generally assumed that "area" in "area studies" refers to a cartographically delimited region that is isomorphic with a distinctive anthropological culture (Appadurai 1996, 16). An area is regarded as having the two fundamental characteristics of being non-Western and being bounded. These traits are necessary corollaries of each other. *Area* is shorthand for an expanse that is spatially distinct from the academic researcher or scholar—the knowing subject; and this distinctness implies the bounded nature of the area, the impossibility of the knowing subject's confusion of the area with the location from which he or she cognizes it. Moreover, because the knowing subject is almost always explicitly nationally marked as "American," the area that is studied is also qualitatively distinct in the sense of being "alien" or "foreign" in historical, social, or cultural terms. Thus, *non-Western* is inevitably a cognate, even a synonym of *area*. Such bounded units were aligned with areas of strategic interest or foreign affairs policy. Nevertheless, area studies were inscribed into institutional existence by referring to intellectual objectives that exceeded its practical objectives, namely its relation to the disciplines and its contributions to the production of universal knowledge.

Today, the general political criticism of area studies points to the coincidence of its rapid growth and the interdependence of its knowledge claims with U.S. national-governmental interests in the Cold War era. Such a criticism takes its cue from the instrumentalist view of knowledge that Edward Said articulated in *Orientalism*, where he argued that the Orientalist *mode of knowing* not only served to justify colonialism as civilizing mission, but was actually a way of stimulating interest in and exerting authority over the Orient (Said 1978, 12). Said had described U.S. area studies as a contemporary form of Orientalism but had gestured towards "'decolonializing' new departures" in area studies (325). Such a criticism, however, fails to explain how the intellectual objectives claimed by area studies in addition to its practical objectives are continuous with the latter without resorting to an instrumentalist account of the relationship between knowledge and power. Although Said implies, following Foucault, that power and knowledge are not in a relationship of exteriority, he fails to elaborate on the precise nature of the connection between Orientalist knowledge and British colonial power, but simply conflates two different meanings of the word *authority*, authority in the sense of intellectual mastery and in the sense of political domination (32). But in what sense does the vulnerability of an object to the Orientalist mode of knowing necessarily imply its vulnerability to political subjugation? How do the intellectual objectives of area studies articulate an intrinsic connection between the act of knowing and the well-being of the territorial site from which such knowing takes place (the national interest of the American knowing subject) that places this territorial site of knowledge-production in a position of strength vis-à-vis the world area that is studied, and hence, in a position capable of exerting power in the narrow sense over that world area?

The point that knowledge confers power to the knower has never been disputed, and indeed, has always been underscored as an important justification of area studies.[2] The question that Said never answers is *how* the style of knowing characterizing area studies confers power and, indeed, expresses the essential unity of (area) knowledge and (U.S. national) power. Pointing to the technical utility of area knowledge simply begs the question of how knowledge can be a technical force and, therefore, possess a real effectivity. These issues of how knowledge can confer power and why knowledge possesses real effectivity, I want to suggest, need to be related back to a certain philosophical definition of freedom as a self-determining consciousness that underpins the conceptual matrix of area studies and its institutional position vis-à-vis the disciplines. Simply put, the nation that can treat other places as areas to be studied in relation to itself, the nation that can position other places as the objects for area studies, achieves the optimal state of freedom and power vis-à-vis others insofar as it manages to attain the highest degree of self-consciousness and self-determination. Conversely, places that can only know or cognize themselves as areas can never attain genuine self-consciousness and self-determination.

Let us now look at how area studies was constrained from the moment of its institutionalization by this conceptual matrix that aligns areas with the particular and the disciplines with the universal. My purpose is not to dismiss area research as an intellectually weak enterprise, but to suggest that area studies should ask more of itself than it traditionally has. The two basic features of this conceptual matrix are as follows: an area is both non-Western and clearly delimitable. These two features are governed by a principle of consanguinity that allows the subject of knowledge to distinguish between what is part of its own historical-cultural makeup, its *Weltanschauung*, and what is not. Now, the distinction between West and non-West also corresponds to a distinction between the universal and the particular, and it is on this basis that area studies is separated from the disciplines in at least three related ways. First, area studies is supposed to be involved in the gathering of raw empirical data or concrete factual information. It is primarily descriptive, whereas the disciplines, which engage in theoretical generalization and abstraction, further the task of pure intellection. Second, it follows from the first distinction that area studies is intellectually subordinate to the disciplines in the same way that applied knowledges are subordinate to pure forms of knowledge. The latter provides the methodological and epistemological structures necessary for the conduct of research, which the former applies or puts into practice. Area research could not be conducted without the prior intellectual ground laying of the disciplines. The disciplines are therefore intellectually a priori to, have greater epistemological authority and are more powerful than, area studies. This is why an area studies scholar has often been described using the metaphor of dual occupations or dual citizenship: he or she must obtain a doctorate in a department of graduate study and "also have special competence relating to a particular area." But the two jobs or citizenships are not equal, for "in general the area training is *supplementary*" (Bennett 1951, 4; Pye 1975, 9).[3]

The third ground of division between area studies and the disciplines is the correlation of the former with the particular and the latter with the universal. The renowned Indonesianist and theorist of nationalism, Benedict Anderson, articulates this distinction succinctly and with justifiable pique when he voices the largely unaired but tacit general opinion of his discipline of political science that its

> search for universal/global, if you prefer transcendental models, its scientific attachment to parsimony, its ever more subtle and intricate vocabulary and its methodological sophistication, all make it fundamentally beyond Southeast Asian scholars. It is as though one heard people saying: 'They don't/can't think abstractly; they're uninterested in any country other than their own; they're not trained to use sophisticated mathematical or epistemological tools. They don't get the journals and if they did, they wouldn't read them'. (Anderson 1984, 42)

Hence, the oppositions between theory building and data collection, pure and applied knowledges, ultimately refer back to the opposition between universal and particular. The particular is that which is tied to the immediacy of experience—empirical evidence—whereas universality is the mark of discursive knowledge, knowledge that rises above immediacy through the mediation of abstract concepts that are universally communicable. Lucian Pye puts it this way:

> In part . . . the division has been one between those who crave knowledge in the form of universal propositions and discount the merit of "mere description," and those who revere the unending uniqueness of human experiences and see mainly empty words in abstract formulations. (Pye 1975, 5–6)

Insofar as the disciplines are seen as the guardians of standards for determining the universal validity of social phenomena (i.e., social scientific laws) and these standards are formulated from evidence that is indisputably confined to the North Atlantic fraternity, there is an unspoken but for that very reason all the more tenacious isomorphism between the universal structures of reason and the social structures of the West. This is not exactly the common-place criticism of the historical Eurocentrism of the social sciences.[4] I am not only saying that there has been a *historically contingent* conflation of the differentiated social structures of Western society with the divisions of the different social sciences. I am saying instead that the social sciences are inherently Eurocentric because the universality of their knowledge claims is predicated on the figure of self-consciousness, and this necessarily sets up an isomorphism between Western social structures and the universal phenomena that are the subject of the disciplines. For if universality is defined in terms of the ability of consciousness to reflect or turn back on itself in order to abstract from and transcend what is particular in it, thereby raising itself into something that possesses unconditional validity, then this injunction to know oneself is primarily governed by the principle of consanguinity. What belongs to the knowing subject's historical or cultural makeup—its Western-ness—will always be raised to the level of the universal. And what lies on the side of the unknown (the non-Western world area) can only ever be the mere object of factual knowledge rather than the subject of theory. This is the conceptual matrix that governs the parameters of area studies vis-à-vis the disciplines.

We would be mistaken to see the universalism of the disciplines as dogmatically abstract and Eurocentric in a simple manner. Within the constraints of this conceptual matrix, there can be much room for variation. The most important and commonly adduced intellectual objectives of area studies are (1) the fostering of interdisciplinary co-operation and teamwork that can bridge the humanities and the social sciences; and (2) the instilling of a healthy cultural relativism coupled with the accumulation of concrete material to be used as a data base for testing the abstract theoretical formulations and universal generalizations of the disciplines as a safeguard against excessive generalization. Co-operation between area research and the disciplines, between the particular and the universal, is allowed, indeed even deemed necessary to "the development of a universal and general science of society and of human behavior" (Wagley 1948, 5, 9, 48). We are also told that the separation of theory from area research is artificial and "unfortunate because there is no basic antagonism between the two—the full development of theory depends on the accumulation of comparable data from all available sources" (Taylor 1964, 9). Area research can combine "studies which illuminate the particularistic and unique elements in a society (language, literature, history, religion, etc.) with the sciences of society (the social sciences)," thereby enabling "the social sciences (and some fields in the humanities) to take into account the particular and unique as well as the universal elements in human experience" (ibid.).

Moreover, the same conceptual matrix can also accommodate an explicit anti-Eurocentric rhetoric (Wagley 1948, 6–7). Yet, instead of impinging upon and transforming the universal form of theoretical consciousness, what area research contributes is merely technical or applied know-how or even dogmatic knowledge as opposed to the critical knowledge that is articulated in the disciplines in the manner that Kant distinguished between dogmatic and transcendental philosophy, the former being occupied with objects, whereas the latter is concerned with our a priori mode of cognition of objects (Kant 1997, 11–12, 149). The attempt to reconcile theory and area research retains the epistemological priority accorded to theory, which is seen as something to be applied in order to give form to raw data from non-Western world areas. The vocabulary used to describe this reconciliation is always conservative in the most literal sense: it is a testing/checking of or tinkering with a pre-established or a priori eidetic structure using secondary material in order to reinforce it rather than a general rebuilding of that structure from the ground up using bits of newly acquired comparative knowledge. Thus, Hans Morgenthau suggests that area studies needs to be grounded in the underlying universalities of "man as such," the basic "contours of human nature." Its task is "to provide an empirical check upon . . . the correctness [of these contours] and that specific content and color."[5] Contemporary anti-Eurocentrism, for instance, recent arguments to "provincialize Europe," remains part of this discursive formation.

But what is "man" in his "as such"? Or, better yet, what are the universal structures of consciousness that enable, firstly, the cognition of "man as such" and, secondly, the setting up of institutional research fields in which non-Western areas can be apprehended and studied in order to check the correctness of and to specify the details of "man as such"? It is precisely here that the relationship between power and knowledge needs to be raised, not as a matter of the instrumentality of knowledge, but instead in terms of *how* area studies is positioned or set up by the conceptual matrix that governs its institutionalization. This matrix predetermines that non-Western areas are a priori distinct from a self-conscious subject of universal knowledge. This has two implications. First, these areas can gain access to universal self-consciousness only through an extended apprenticeship with the West, through training in the universal knowledge of the disciplines. But second, and more importantly, because they are, by definition, particular areas, they can know themselves only through area research as empirical data and as particular bounded objects. The only knowledge they can have of themselves comes from apprehending themselves through the eyes of the West, which amounts to saying that they can never fully know themselves. For these areas either give up the aim of self-knowledge, in which case they must remain mired in self-incurred tutelage because they have not achieved self-determination, or they attain self-determination only by being enthralled or possessed by the specter of the West, because they can know themselves only as its other.

Area knowledge thus empowers and disempowers in a very literal sense. Gabriel Almond captures only one side of the double bind when he observes

> the relative dominance of American investigators for developmental prospects in various parts of the world and for international affairs generally. This concentration of foreign area knowledge in the United States, and in the advanced countries generally, and the limited knowledge in Third World areas contributes to the weakness of these countries and to their inability to relate effectively to the forces of the outside world, to develop their own agendas, and to shape and implement their own goals effectively. From this point of view, the diffusion of social science competence and foreign area studies to the Third World must have a high priority. (Almond 1992, 200)

The dilemma is precisely that as U.S. area studies becomes disseminated throughout the globe, either through policy making or through the training of indigenous area experts by the U.S. academic industry, the inhabitants of these places are constitutively made to cathect the space of the world area, the space of the particularistic object of factual information, and are thus barred from genuine self-knowledge and self-determination. The problem is not necessarily solved by the fact that there are more and more Western-trained indigenous scholars based in their "home" areas who write in the vernacular for local audiences.[6] In itself, physical or geographical location is no guarantee that the conceptual matrix distinguishing areas from the universal knowing subject of the disciplines and subordinating them to it will be overturned, that these indigenous scholars will cognize the places they both inhabit and study as something other than mere areas, others of the West. One would need to ask: Who is this "they" (indigenous scholars) who have become much better at studying "themselves"? How is this "they" formed by the "we" of area studies' institutional origin and how is this "they" constitutively constrained by its conceptual matrix?

For this conceptual positioning, which is more powerful than the physical or geographical location of the area scholar, informs Asian studies in a very profound way. Regardless of how interdisciplinary or theoretically sophisticated Asian studies are or have become, it is always concerned with a bound object. Generally, its focus is information retrieval and not theoretical reflection and speculation that pertain to the whole of humanity. To take the most obvious example, whereas a certain strand of Christian monotheism has been sublated into universal secular ethics as such after the European enlightenment, the great religions of Asia have been museumized into mere markers of "cultural difference." Because these religions are considered as predating and deviating from the secular subject of universal reason, they have rarely been seriously studied as philosophies that can provide the bases for a universalizable secular ethics or practical action in contemporary life. At best, they are studied as "ethno-philosophy" or celebrated as mystical "nativist" exceptions to the excessive rationality of modernity that leads to Weber's iron cage.

But in order to overturn this conceptual matrix, we need to understand more fully the schema through which the subject of universal knowledge becomes isomorphic with the West and all other regions become consigned to particularity. To this end, I want to turn to an exemplary text in the history of Western philosophy: Hegel's *Lectures on the Philosophy of World History*, which, in my view, supplies the philosophical prototype for area studies' conceptual matrix. Unless one is a fan of Francis Fukuyama, this text is not widely read today. If it is read, it is mainly read in an accusatory manner: Hegel's remarks about "the Oriental World" are denounced as the Eurocentric expression of the West's will to power over Asia. But if we temper our will to diagnose, then we will begin to realize how much the discursive formation of Asian studies still inhabits the folds of Hegel's text.

Hegel's teleology of world history is designed to solve the problem of how to claim universal normativity for the actions of nation-states in view of the fact that international relations exist in a state of nature. In response to the ineluctable contingency of history, Hegel maps out a path of world-historical progress in which the spirit of a certain nation (*Volksgeist*) embodies the world spirit (*Weltgeist*) in a given epoch. This nation is the bearer of world-historical progress and will lead all other nations. "In contrast with this absolute right which it possesses as bearer of the present stage of the world spirit's development, the spirits of other nations are without rights, and they, like those whose epoch has passed, no longer count in world history" (Hegel 1991, §347, 374). For present purposes, two features of Hegel's argument are important: why he regards the German nation as the embodiment of the modern world spirit, and conversely, why the different nations of Asia no longer play a part in world-historical progress and the fate that befalls them in modernity.

For Hegel, "world history is the progress of the consciousness of freedom," where freedom is understood in an ontological sense as a self-determining consciousness, a form of conscious being (spirit or *Geist*) that knows itself as a universal being, and in this self-knowledge, is able to determine itself in accordance with universal ends, thereby actualizing its freedom through its own actions.[7] The bearer of freedom and the agent of world-historical progress is a *collective* form of self-consciousness. This is what Hegel calls objective spirit, which takes the shape of the nation (*Volk*) in world history.

Now, rational consciousness or spirit can be genuinely free only if it attains complete self-knowledge. Hence, to embody freedom concretely, spirit must be aware that it is, in its own essence, free. The realization of freedom thus involves spirit's gradual development to self-knowledge through various stages. What is important for us is that Hegel relates these different stages in the development of collective self-consciousness in world history to different types of national spirit, each with a finite life span. Thus, not only does he divide the development of world spirit into *distinct* temporal stages or epochs of the same historical process, he also correlates each of these epochs to a *bounded* and spatially localized configuration (*Gestaltung*) by arguing that in each epoch, there is one nation whose principle embodies the spirit of the age. These configurations are then designated as quasi-cartographical/seminatural realms or worlds (*Reich*). It is this underlying spiritual principle that determines the character of each nation. Each national spirit tries to understand and develop its underlying principle into actuality through its actions and the various spiritual and cultural products of each nation—its religion, arts, and knowledge—are the different intellectual means or media through which each nation seeks to understand itself.[8] The various aspects of national life— all its cultural products and political institutions—are thus related to each other and articulated into an organized/organic whole because they are elaborations of the same underlying spiritual principle. In turn, these various aspects enable a nation to know itself.

Now, for Hegel what distinguishes the Oriental *Volksgeist* or the various national self-consciousnesses of Asia from the Germanic *Volksgeist* that makes the latter the bearer of world spirit in modernity is that whereas the former does "not know that the spirit or man as such are free in themselves" (1980, 54), "the Germanic nations, with the rise of Christianity, were the first to realise that man is by nature free, and that freedom of the spirit is his very essence" (1980, 54).[9] Because freedom is the unity of universality and particularity, the consciousness of freedom involves, first and foremost, the transcendence (*Aufhebung*) of particularity.[10] Through this transcendence of one's particular limits, one attains a state of being that is universal. Thus, Hegel writes that "consciousness of freedom consists in the fact that the individual . . . sees himself in his distinct existence as inherently universal, as capable of abstraction from and renunciation of everything particular, and therefore as inherently finite" (1980, 144).

When this definition of freedom as the transcendence of particularity and finitude is applied to the self-consciousness of entire peoples within world history, what we see is the alignment of spatial boundaries with finitude or the limits of contingent existence. Those nations whose self-consciousness does not include the knowledge of human freedom are therefore mired in an existence that always remains limited, bounded, and particularistic. They cannot step beyond these limits into universality. Because they cannot step outside their own limits, they cannot fully apprehend themselves as objects for themselves. This means that they also cannot fully know and understand themselves. Thus, Hegel writes that "the Chinese are not yet conscious of their own nature as free subjectivity" (1980, 121–22), and that India and China "are lacking—indeed completely lacking—in the essential consciousness of the concept of freedom" (1980, 145).[11]

But more importantly, their particularistic nature also means that these nations can have only a very limited life in world history. In the contemporary era, Hegel suggests, they are no longer active bearers of progress. Because they cannot fully know themselves, they can only continue to exist as static or frozen objects to be known by others. They are the living dead.[12] "It may well be that nations whose concepts are less advanced survive, but they exist only on the periphery of world history" (1980, 60). Consigned to the sidelines, what these Asian nations have achieved in their moments of past glory—their contributions to world history—become raw materials that can be fully understood and retrieved only by those who are capable of universality. Thus, for Hegel, the Oriental world "can be likened to that of childhood in general," (1980, 202) and "Asia is the continent of sunrise and of origins in general" (1980, 190).

Much of Hegel's argument is indeed offensive to our more enlightened sensibilities. Yet, the taken-for-granted boundedness of the areas of area studies corresponds in a very startling way to the particularism and finitude that Hegel sees as a mark of the self-consciousness of Asian nations. I am, of course, not suggesting that the historical establishment of area studies took Hegel's charting of world history as its blueprint. My point is that there is a strong isomorphism between Hegel's arguments and the logic of area studies: First, in their implied opposition to disciplines with a universal subject matter, Asian studies are concerned with subject matters that are empirical rather than universal.[13] Second, Hegel's idea that all the cultural products and political institutions of a nation can be referred back to one basic principle is, of course, conceptually identical to the structural-functionalist idea of an interrelated whole that is so crucial to area studies.[14] Third, to say that these various empirical subject matters are attributes that are specific to the areas being studied implies that the collective self-consciousnesses inhabiting these areas are particularistic. Fourth, the reason why these self-consciousnesses cannot transcend their respective areas is because they do not know their own bounds. Because their limits have to be conferred upon them by a knowing subject, these areas and their self-consciousnesses are objects to be known by others.

The above presuppositions are most concretely illustrated by two common facts: (1) In Asian studies, Asia is regarded as the inexhaustible source of raw materials to be retrieved through field-work and processed for publication by scholars who are generally based in the West; (2) Even if the Asian studies scholar is of non-Western origin, he or she is usually a native informant who comes to the West to study his or her own area of origin because it is only through the structures and methods of Western knowledge (to which is added "native" experience that often makes for a shorter period of field research) that he or she can come to view this area of origin as an object of thematic knowledge.[15] In other words, Asian studies presupposes that Asia can fully know itself only through the more developed structures of self-consciousness of the West. The Indonesian novelist Pramoedya Ananta Toer captures this nicely by having his protagonist, a native youth educated in a Dutch school in the East Indies at the turn of the century, exclaim, "Only through Europe can I know my own people" (Toer, *ASB* 1982, 164, my translation).

The distinction between the particularistic self-consciousnesses of Asia and the universalistic self-consciousness of the West is also reproduced in the distinction between empirical and theoretical forms of knowledge that underwrites the division of intellectual labor separating Asian studies from disciplines concerned with universal truths and ideals. Whereas philosophy and other forms of theoretical inquiry in the Western academy continue to formulate "fundamental" concepts largely by abstracting from evidence confined to the socio-historical situation of the North Atlantic, Asian studies have generally remained atheoretical because they are by definition concerned with the specificity and particularity of Asian cultures. At the most, scholars in Asian studies try to find equivalents for concepts such as "civil society," "human rights," and "public sphere" (*Öffentlichkeit*) in Asian cultures. Following a well-known Freudian schema, this can be called civil society envy, human rights envy, and public sphere envy. Or else they suggest that these concepts are not applicable to Asian cultures. The alternatives represented here are either the dogmatic application of an untested universalism or a dubious cultural relativism.

But the cultural relativist's mesmerizing focus on the uniqueness of Asia is haunted by the specter of the West. Because their claims of local uniqueness are the inverted mirror image or phantom double of the universality claimed by the West, a relativistic Asian studies is a priori barred from access to universality. At the same time, Asian materials or data are ironically processed through the concepts and methodologies of (Western) theory, which remain dogmatically unquestioned. This means that Asian studies is in fact built upon the denegation (*Verneinung*) of the West *qua* universal. The situation is not remedied by a recent third alternative that is formed from the intersection of Asian studies and East Asian governmental cultural policy. I am referring to the East Asian chauvinism, loosely based on a repackaged Confucianism that reverses Max Weber, which sees the rapidly developing nation-states of East Asia as embodiments of a superior ideal of capitalist development capable of reconciling modernization with Asian ideals of community. This is not really an alternative form of modernity as some scholars claim but a displaced repetition of the chauvinism of Eurocentric modernity. It is, in fact, an Asianized version of Hegel's end of history. It has dangerous consequences in that some Asian governments have deployed it to circumvent humanitarian critique. Moreover, this alternative has been rendered implausible by the 1997 economic crises in East and Southeast Asia, which have shown us how much global economic hegemony is still centered in the North Atlantic.

## Universalizing Asia: The Example of Pramoedya Ananta Toer's Buru Quartet

I want to suggest that one way for Asian studies to escape the sterile polemics that pit cultural relativism against dogmatic universalism, or, which is not quite the same thing, empiricism against theory, is neither to denigrate the universal nor to claim an alternative and usually antagonistic Asian modularity, but for Asian studies to claim that their subject is a *part* of the universal, not just as a check to a preformulated universal, but as something that actively *shares in* and *partakes of* the universal in a specific way. In other words, instead of viewing the various phenomena and experiences that are specific to Asia as marginal to universal history, which is today sometimes explicitly discredited and coded as the history of the North Atlantic, one might consider these phenomena and experiences *as though* they were universalizable, shareable with the whole of humanity. But then, the idea of the universal will need to be transformed in such a way that it is no longer viewed as superior or antithetical to what is culturally specific or particular. Specialized research on cultural matters in area studies rarely pose problems at this level because it has only ever accepted or denigrated the concept of universality as such and never questioned it. What I want to suggest is that Hegel's philosophy of history has privative or exclusionary implications precisely because he understands the passage from particular to universal as a movement of sublation in which both terms become reconciled in an *individual* body.

Now, for Hegel, particularity refers to the moment when the absolute abstraction or universality of pure thought is given concrete content when the self understands that it is a determinate being: "Through this positing of itself as something *determinate*, 'I' steps into existence [*Dasein*] in general—the absolute moment of the finitude or particularization of the 'I'" (1991, §6, 39). The genuinely free will, however, is a will that pursues aims that are at one and the same time both determinate (and, hence, particular) and capable of self-reflection (and, hence, universal). Thus, Hegel writes that

> The will is the unity of both these moments—*particularity* reflected *into itself* and thereby restored to *universality*. It is *individuality* [*Einzelnheit*], the *self-determination* of the 'I', in that it posits itself as the negative of itself, that is, as *determinate* and *limited*, and at the same time remains with itself [*bei sich*], that is, in its *identity with itself* and universality; and in this determination, it joins together with itself alone. (1991, §7, 41)

The moment of individuality is, of course, central to Hegel's understanding of *Volksgeist*. Individuality is that which gives coherence and totality to each national spirit, allowing each to be distinguished from the others. The point that I want to make here is that Hegel sees universality and particularity as related through the moment of individuality because he regards the particular or the finite as something that needs to be transcended by thought in order to attain genuine universality.[16]

But then any *concrete* universality formed by sublating the finite inevitably involves a certain violence precisely because universality is *exclusively* identified with a specific body, an individuality. Because particularity is understood as a negation of abstract universality, which must in turn be negated and sublated to achieve genuine universality, this leads to the internment of universality within a specific body that is now raised to the higher level of infinity. As we have seen, in any particular world-historical epoch, the specific body that is raised to the higher level of infinity is set apart from all other specific bodies that have not been able to transcend their particularity. This elevation of one individuality, one national spirit over all others, has obvious colonialist and imperialist implications. Indeed, in the introduction of the

*Philosophy of Right*, as well as in his philosophy of history, Hegel automatically resorts to the metaphor of slavery as a counterexample when he attempts to illustrate what he means by a universal self-consciousness and a genuinely free will: "if the spirit knows that it is free, it is altogether different from what it would be without this knowledge. For if it does not know that it is free, it is in the position of a slave who is content with his slavery and does not know that his condition is an improper one" (1980, 48, cf. 1991, §21R, 52–53).

Consequently, in the Hegelian gallery of world history, nations, and indeed realms, are judged and ranked according to their capacity for genuine self-consciousness. At the endpoint of history, one nation or realm—the one that has attained the highest level of self-consciousness—Germanic or American, depending on whether one is Hegel or Fukuyama, it doesn't matter which, will stand as the ultimate judge. This is precisely the conceptual matrix governing the institutionalization of Asian studies. If Asia is universalized on this basis, we get something similar to the Confucian chauvinism I mentioned earlier. In contradistinction, the idea of universality that I think is able to accommodate a nonprivative universalizing of Asia is one that is marked not by the transcendence of finitude but, instead, by a radical openness to finitude, which is to say, also a radical openness to contamination by alterity.

To give an illustration of this other understanding of universality, let me look briefly at Pramoedya Ananta Toer's Buru quartet, a series of novels about the Indies national awakening published in the late 1970s and the early 1980s.[17] For present purposes, what is interesting about the quartet is its suggestion that the Indies national awakening, and not the Dutch colonial state, ought to be regarded as the heir to the European Enlightenment. What the quartet illustrates, I want to suggest, is a certain digestion of the universal in a specific territorial body. But, this digestion is not a sublation of that body's finitude. Consequently, at the same time that the universal is concrete and specific—it is *this* particular body—it also remains radically open to the possibility of being shared with other territorially located bodies.

The quartet contains repeated references to the French Revolution. However, in the second volume, entitled *Anak Semua Bangsa* (*Child of All Nations*), Minke, the protagonist and the founding father of the Indies, awakening is presented with other non-European models of modernity: imperialist Japan and also anti-imperialist China and the decolonizing Philippines.[18] The restless energy of this chain of events is now felt in the Indies, stimulating Minke's desire for modernity. The restlessness of modernity is infectious. Minke's desire to be modern is stimulated by a comparison between the Indies and other non-European models of modernity that results in feelings of shame and frustration at the backwardness of the Indies:

> I forced myself to think through on my own the connections between them all—Japan's advance, the anxieties/uneasiness of Young China, the native Filipino revolt against Spain and later the United States . . . And with my inward eye I cast my gaze around my own milieu. Not the slightest trace of movement! They were still sunk happily in dreams. And I myself was bewildered, angry, in my powerless awareness [*Dan aku sendiri pusing, geram, dengan kesedaran tanpa daya*]. (*ASB*, 86)

These repeated juxtapositions and comparisons cumulatively suggest that the newly-born nations of decolonizing Asia, and not the colonial state or the Dutch liberals, are the true heirs of the world-historical spirit of the French Revolution. In the fourth volume, *Rumah Kaca* (*Glass House*), Pangemanann, a Sorbonne-educated native official of the Dutch colonial state, who is Minke's destroyer, gradually comes to the same view. In his eyes, the spontaneous native awakening against European capital becomes even more powerful than the revolt in France against Louis XVI.[19] Meanwhile, beyond the Indies, the Russian Revolution indicates the actualization of a new form of power that is seen as analogous to the *pergerakan* in the Indies. This combination of political events within and beyond the Indies compels Pangemanann to admit that these native organizations rather than the colonial state are the true legatees of the ideal project of modernity (*RK*, 321–22). Indeed, Pangemanann suggests that Minke is no longer Javanese but European. Even if Minke has never studied European philosophy, as the first Javanese realist, he has inherited European philosophical ideals and methods through historical osmosis and activated them in his endeavors to foster an Indies nationalism (*RK*, 305–6).

But this passage of the world-historical spirit of freedom from Europe to Asia is emphatically not a sublation that interns the universal in a specific body or individuality evident in Hegel's philosophy of history. The quartet's narrative logic is not dialectical but aporetic. Nothing evokes the failure of dialectical sublation as suggestively as the role of Nyai Ontosoroh at the end of the narrative. Nyai Ontosoroh is Minke's spiritual mother (*ibu rohani*). The final volume of the quartet sees her reincarnated as Madame Sanikem Le Boucq, a legal resident in France, now married to Jean Marais, alias Le Boucq, the French painter who was a mercenary in the Dutch Indies and later a friend of Minke. A representative of the ideals of the French Revolution now embodied in a modern native person, Sanikem returns to the Indies to search for Minke and to judge Pangemanann for betraying his vocation as a person of education. Sanikem is the personification of the national spirit of modern Indonesia. As the recipient of Minke's manuscripts, she is also the trustee of its future. What her actions signify is that the future of the Indonesian nation can be secured only from outside the colonial world: in France, the nation where modern freedom was first born. But—another aporia—because the spirit of modern freedom was also betrayed by French colonialism in Indochina, Algeria, and elsewhere, it can live on only in the future of the Indonesian nation whose agent is—yet another aporia—the modern native expatriate.

The nation *qua* embodiment of universal freedom thus lives on abroad, so to speak, awaiting to be returned to itself, that is to say, repatriation. But meanwhile, it lives on uncannily (*unheimlich*), from outside its own home. At an even more mundane level this aporia is played out by the fact that Pramoedya's own writings are banned in Indonesia and are only accessible to Indonesian readers through Malaysian imprints and English translations and reviews and critical studies by commentators outside Indonesia.[20] This aporetic expatriation, I want to suggest, indicates a sharing/partaking of universality between the specific bodies of Europe (France) and Asia (the Indies/Indonesia). This means that universality is neither a static ideal of reason nor a self-conscious individuality. Instead, it is in this interminable movement of sharing between specific territorial bodies or areas that universality becomes articulated and redefined again and again.

Or better yet, universality *is* nothing other than this interminable movement of sharing. For is not this radical openness to finitude and to contamination by alterity the very "essence" of universality, the being universal of the universal? In the obvious instance, for a given issue to be worthy of the epithet, "universal," it ought to be able to accommodate every single particular example. More importantly, however, the universal must always show itself in a particular example. This is especially true of concrete or actual universality, because a concrete universal must have *exemplary* status. Yet, because to be exemplary is by definition to be both unique and also repeatable insofar as an example is an example of some 'X' that can have other examples, any concrete universal gives itself to be inscribed in an endless series of sensible particulars. In other words, a concrete universal is constitutively open to being affected by *other particulars* and, hence, by alterity and particularity in general. This radical openness to alterity and particularity is a type of finitude that cannot be transcended. The relationship between universality and particularity that is implied here is therefore not the internment of universality within the proper body of an individuality but one in which a given particular answers to the call of universality in its unique way and, in so doing, remains open to other equally singular responses to the universal. As Jacques Derrida puts it, "the value of universality . . . must be linked to the value of *exemplarity* that inscribes the universal in the proper body of a singularity, of an idiom or a culture, whether this singularity be individual, social, national, state . . . or not. Whether it takes a national form or not, a refined, hospitable or aggressively xenophobic form or not, the self-affirmation of an identity always claims to be responding to the call or assignation of the universal . . . Each time, it has to do with the discourse of *responsibility*: I have, the unique "I" has, the responsibility of testifying for universality. Each time, the exemplarity of the example is unique. That is why it can be put into a series and formalized into a law" (Derrida 1992, 72–73).

## ENVOI: THE UNIVERSALIZATION OF AREAS IN CONTEMPORARY GLOBALIZATION

The responsibility for testifying for universality of each unique territorial body, each culture and each area, is no longer a mere ethical ideal in the same way that, for Marx, the global spread of capital made cosmopolitanism a material reality in 1848. Responding to the call of the universal is now an urgent imperative because the division of intellectual labor between universal and particular knowledges, the theoretical disciplines and area studies, has become obsolete in contemporary globalization. The heightened interaction between nation-states and cultures in contemporary globalization has generated a discontinuous field of overlapping and contested universal areas.

To take Southeast Asia as a concrete example, the intensified integration of Southeast Asia by regional and global forces makes it imperative to study "Southeast Asia" as a regional entity and an important part of a shrinking world. Labor migration and foreign investment already link Southeast Asian nations. As these nations move towards the formation of an ASEAN Free Trade Area, official visions of an ASEAN consciousness, whether or not they reflect popular opinion, already abound. Moreover, as a site of foreign-investment-generated rapid economic growth, the region is attracting growing attention in the spheres of world political economy and international politics (Keyes 1992, 14). Not only is Southeast Asia the destination of foreign capital from the industrialized North; it is also the source of capital flows to Africa, Latin America, the Caribbean, and other parts of Asia. Before the financial crash of 1997, Malaysia and Singapore were increasingly regarded as alternative models of economic development through the attraction of foreign investment by many countries in the South (Lim 1995, 205–38; Edwards 1995, 239–56). But they and other Southeast Asian nations are also exemplary in the aftermath of the crash for the ways in which they have attempted to cope with the dangers of global financialization.

The challenge that lies ahead for Asian studies is to exorcize the specter of *Western* universality so that they can be spectralized by the call of the universal as such. It is the development of new conceptual perspectives that will enable us to understand the impact of these globalizing/regionalizing processes on local cultures and vice versa, without sacrificing the specialist expertise and loving attention to languages and local detail that is the enduring strength of area studies. This involves a double imperative: On the one hand, from the side of Asian studies, the imperative is to treat these experiences as universalizable, shareable with everyone else—in a word, as translatable. On the other hand, what is now commonly regarded as the universal as such—the ethical concepts and normative ideals of contemporary (Western) theory—ought to be opened up by "a strategy without finality, what might be called a blind tactics, or empirical wandering" into spaces with social and political histories that are different from the North Atlantic, "if the value of empiricism did not itself acquire its entire meaning in its opposition to philosophical responsibility" (Derrida 1982, 7). With this double imperative, the universal may at last become particularized into areas that possess historical effectivity at the same time as these particular areas become universalized.

## NOTES

1. For a lucid account by a Southeast Asianist to recent debates on the obsolescence of area studies among area research foundation donors, see O. W. Wolters, "'Regional Studies' in the 1990s" (Wolters 1999, 206–25).

2. "Sound research is valuable to the nation, whereas the national need cannot be served by inadequate scholarship. Only the soundest sort of area research can be in the genuine national interest and thereby also a factor for international well-being" (Wagley 1948, 9).

3. "The fact that American universities have universally agreed that after the master's degree all advanced work must be associated with a degree in a traditional discipline is generally translated in the minds of students to mean that disciplinary work is intellectually superior to area-oriented work. Therefore, some students fear that if they are overly tainted with an area specialization, it may suggest to others that they are academically inferior to the regular student" (Pye 1975, 9).

4. This is Pye's point: "The dilemma of the general and the particular in science became the source of increasing strain as the essentially Eurocentric social sciences sought to become truly global. Evidence of the inherent Western parochialism of much of contemporary social science can be found in the standard practice of giving universal, mankind-wide titles to studies based on European or American data while expecting a limiting designation for comparable studies focusing on some other part of the world" (Pye 1975, 6).

5. See H. J. Morgenthau, "International Relations as an Academic Discipline," in *The Decline of Democratic Politics* (Chicago, 1962), cited in Milton Singer, "The Social Sciences in Non-Western Studies," in Bigelow and Legters (1964, 42).

6. This is the optimistic solution proposed by many prominent Southeast Asian scholars, such as James C. Scott, Charles F. Keyes, Benedict Anderson, and Charles Hirschmann, in their contributions to Hirschmann et al. (1992). See especially Anderson's contribution, "The Changing Ecology": "[T]here exists today in Southeast Asia a group of people who did not exist in late colonial times: a substantial indigenous academic and non-academic intelligentsia. . . . Most are civil servants, and all, to different extents, understand their work as most relevant to a specific country (Burma, Indonesia, the Philippines), and to a lesser degree, its neighbors. They are area studies people ipso facto" (36).

7. See G. W. F. Hegel (1980, 54). This text is a translation of Johannes Hoffsmeister's 1955 edition.

8. The underlying principle is the content and the various spiritual powers are the various forms this content assumes. These various forms make up the culture of the nation. See Hegel (1980, 96–97, 102).

9. For a description of the Germanic people as the bearers of the spirit of modernity, see, for instance, Hegel (1991, §358).

10. "[S]pirit, in its consciousness of itself, is free; in this realisation, it has overcome the limits of temporal existence and enters into relationship with pure being, which is also its own being" (Hegel 1980, 53).

11. This lack of complete self-consciousness leads to partial and truncated development. Hence, the Chinese did not know how to use the gunpowder they invented, and the Indians had brilliant poetry but only a primitive legal system (Hegel 1980, 102).

12. These nations are literally zombies because even if they "live on, their existence is devoid of life and interest; their institutions have become superfluous, because the needs which created them have been satisfied, and nothing remains but political stagnation and boredom. . . . In a moribund state such as this, a nation . . . serves as material for a higher principle, and becomes the province of another nation in which a higher principle is active" (Hegel 1980, 59–60).

13. The *area* of area studies braids together three senses of "subject": first, as "topic," which is also a spatial term; second, as a topographical area; and third, as an intending collective consciousness.

14. Even in an area such as Southeast Asia, where it is difficult to point to any distinct organic totality because its cultures are historically derivative and hybrid and lack opulent classical traditions and a core civilization, some kind of organizational coherence is always found. Either the coherence of Southeast Asia is understood as coming artificially from the outside (i.e., through the encounter with colonialism in general) or "hybridity" is viewed as the underlying principle of the region's religious practices and its other cultural forms and spiritual powers.

15. It is probable that many Chinese, Indian, etc. graduate students who become China-, India-, etc. specialists in the West would not have done so if they had remained in their countries of origin.

16. "This universality is such that the immediacy of the natural and the particularity with which the natural is likewise invested when it is produced by reflection are superseded within it. But this process, whereby the particular is superseded and raised to the universal is what is called the activity of thought. The self-consciousness that purifies and raises its object, content, and end to this universality does so as thought asserting itself in the will" (Hegel 1991, §21R, 52–53).

17. The four volumes of the quartet in chronological order are: *Bumi Manusia* (Kuala Lumpur: Wira Karya, 1981); *Anak Semua Bangsa* (Kuala Lumpur: Wira Karya, 1982); *Jejak Langkah* (Kuala Lumpur: Wira Karya, 1986); *Rumah Kaca* (Kuala Lumpur: Wira Karya, 1988). I will be quoting from the Malay editions of the second and fourth volumes, hereafter *ASB* and *RK*. Translations of *ASB* are mine, and translations of *RK* are by Benedict Anderson, to whom I am indebted for correcting my translations.

18. Khouw Ah Soe, a revolutionary youth, is the personification of the nationalist youth movement in China and a model of emulation for Minke. He is the first to bring the Filipino revolt against the Spanish to Minke's attention as a world-historical example for all colonised peoples in Asia (ASB, 81). Minke also learns the importance of publishing to the life of a movement from him (ASB, 61).

19. "The State which represents Europe now faces a product of exactly that Europe: a nationalism which awakens and bursts forth. . . . *Educated, scientific Europe, teacher of a new civilization, is now confronted by its own student, the Native, who has more will than scientific knowledge—but a will to become a new bangsa.* . . . Riots are occurring wherever giant European capital is planted, perhaps even more violent than those in France against Louis XVI" (*RK*, 285, emphasis added).

20. The first extensive book-length study of Pramoedya is Teeuw 1993. Most of Pramoedya's works are published in Bahasa Malaysia (which is slightly different from Bahasa Indonesia) by the Kuala Lumpur-based publishing house, Wira Karya, run by Jomo Sundaram, a professor of political science at the University of Malaya who studied at Harvard. The English translation of the Buru quartet was first published by Penguin Australia. The Cornell University-based specialist journal, *Indonesia*, is the most important source for English translations of Pramoedya's shorter fiction and nonfictional prose and also a continuing forum for critical writing on Pramoedya.

## Works Cited

Almond, Gabriel. 1992. "The Political Culture of Foreign Area Research: Methodological Reflections." In *The Political Culture of Foreign Area and International Studies: Essays in Honor of Lucian W. Pye*, eds. Richard J. Samuels and Myron Weiner, 199–214. Washington D.C.: Brassey's.

Anderson, Benedict. 1984. "Politics and Their Study in Southeast Asia." In *Southeast Asian Studies: Options for the Future*, ed. Ronald A. Morse, 41–51. Washington D.C.: Lanham: University Press of America, Asia Center.

Appadurai, Arjun. 1996. *Modernity at Large: Cultural Dimensions of Globalization*. Minneapolis: University of Minnesota Press.

Bennett, Wendell C. 1951. *Area Studies in American Universities*. Social Science Research Council. June 4.

Bigelow, Donald, and Lyman Legters, eds. 1964. *The Non-Western World in Higher Education*. Philadelphia: American Academy of Political and Social Science.

Derrida, Jacques. 1982. *Margins of Philosophy*, trans. Alan Bass. Chicago: University of Chicago Press.

———. 1992. *The Other Heading: Reflections on Today's Europe*, trans. Pascale-Anee Brault and Michael B. Naas. Bloomington: Indiana University Press.

Edwards, Chris. 1995. "East Asia and Industrial Policy in Malaysia: Lessons for Africa?" In *Asian Industrialization and Africa: Studies in Policy Alternatives to Structural Adjustment*, ed. Howard Stein, 239–56. New York: St. Martin's Press.

Hegel, G. W. F. 1980. *Lectures on the Philosophy of World History: Introduction*, trans. H. B. Nisbet. Cambridge: Cambridge University Press.

———. 1991. *Elements of the Philosophy of Right*, trans. H. B. Nisbet, ed. Allen W. Wood. Cambridge: Cambridge University Press.

Hirschmann, Charles, et al., eds. 1992. *Southeast Asian Studies in the Balance: Reflections from America*. Ann Arbor, Mich.: Association of Asian Studies.

Kant, Immanuel. 1997. *Critique of Pure Reason*, trans. and ed. Paul Guyer and Allen W. Wood. Cambridge: Cambridge University Press.

Keyes, Charles F. 1992. "A Conference at Wingspread and Rethinking Southeast Asian Studies." In *Southeast Asian Studies in the Balance: Reflections from America*, eds. Charles Hirschmann, Charles Keyes, and Karl Hutterer, 9–24. Ann Arbor, Mich.: Association for Asian Studies.

Lim, Linda. 1995. "Foreign Investment, the State, and Industrial Policy in Singapore." In *Asian Industrialization and Africa: Studies in Policy Alternatives to Structural Adjustment*, ed. Howard Stein, 205–38. New York: St. Martin's Press.

Pye, Lucian. 1975. "The Confrontation between Discipline and Area Studies." In *Political Science and Area Studies: Rival or Partners?* ed. Lucian W. Pye, 9. Bloomington: Indiana University Press.

Said, Edward. 1978. *Orientalism*. Harmondsworth, England: Penguin.

Sakai, Naoki, and Yukiko Hanawa, eds. 2001. "Specters of the West and the Politics of Translation." *Traces: A Multilingual Journal of Cultural Theory and Translation* 1:37–70.

Taylor, George E. 1964. "The Leadership of the Universities." In *The Non-Western World in Higher Education*, eds. Donald Bigelow and Lyman Legters, 1–11. Philadelphia: American Academy of Political and Social Science.

Teeuw, A. 1993. Pramoedya Ananta Toer: *De verbeelding van Indonesië*. De Geus, Netherlands: Breda.

Toer, Pramoedya Ananta. 1981. *Bumi Manusia*. Kuala Lumpur: Wira Karya.

———. 1982. *Anak Semua Bangsa*. Kuala Lumpur: Wira Karya.

———. 1986. *Jejak Langkah*. Kuala Lumpur: Wira Karya.

———. 1988. *Rumah Kaca*. Kuala Lumpur: Wira Karya.

Wagley, Charles. 1948. *Area Research and Training: A Conference Report on the Study of World Areas*. Social Science Research Council, Pamphlet 6.

Wolters, O. W. 1999. "'Regional Studies' in the 1990s." In *History, Culture, and Region in Southeast Asian Perspectives*, 206–25. Ithaca, N.Y.: Cornell Southeast Asia Program.

# 3

# REVISIONISM AND THE SUBJECT OF HISTORY

## R. Radhakrishnan

First, the intransigent and raw immanence of Existence that is parsed into temporality that in turn is semanticized into history to be recovered and redeemed as anthropocentric meaning by the human subject: I begin with a series of cognitive neo-Hegelian displacements or slippages only to suggest that the emergence of historicity is in fact constituted by an inescapable asynchrony that bequeaths its lag as the affirmation of history. History neither nails time to an exact calendar, nor does it produce historicity as the exemplum of the temporal condition. History as a genre is rather like the legendary Ganesha in Indian mythology who transcribes into *ecriture* the orality of Vyasa's tale, and in doing so inaugurates the time of the between that articulates the time of the telling to that of the writing in a relationship of epistemological difference. Those of us who know that profound tale will remember that Vyasa insists as a precondition that his amanuensis, Ganesha, has to keep pace with the nonstop rapidity of the story telling. To bring Foucault to the Mahabharatha, what is being enacted here is the perennial drama of the "empirico-transcendental doublet" whose commitment to the reality of immanence can only be registered as the unreachability of meaning as transcendence.[1] Once it is made conscious of its ontological liminality, history as the representation of the Real can at best thematize its exquisitely timed belatedness even as it makes its generic truth claims about what happened, and indeed about the nature of "the about" as the precondition of all representation.[2]

If the foregoing paragraph is persuasive at all, then it follows that the very notion of revisionist history is a tautology; for, all historicizing is taking a second look at what has already been otherwise. It is in and through that glance towards the "what has been-ness" of a moment that seemed so one's own in the heat of the experience, that history emerges as a kind of a "diving into the wreck": for if moments do not die, then there is no history. But on the other hand, moments do not really die except by way of the historical imagination. My point is not just that (1) in the flow of time as a river one never touches the same drop again or (2) that the moment of the touching and the self-reflexive moment that recognizes the moment of touching as such are temporally nonidentical, but rather that the very constitution of historical reality is premised on an undecidable relationship between the immanent objectivity of what is "be-ing" and the representational truth claims of history with its transcendental will to meaning. Here is another way of saying it: of all the genres, history, with its representational claims about reality and facticity, and experience is best oriented as a compensatory discipline that must both mourn over a loss that is beyond recuperation and at the same time name that loss multifariously and contingently.[3] It is indeed possible, and that would be mute and inhuman, not to want to return to that loss presented to the human subject as a wreck of meaning and significance. But the opposite of that possibility is not an unerring or incorrigible remembering, but an agonized countermnemonic commitment that must learn to live in the tension between a rigorously historicized anthropocentrism and an ontological critique of anthropocentrism.[4] I will return to this theme in the heart of my essay where I will be interpreting the multivalent possibilities opened up by Adrienne Rich in her poem "Diving into the Wreck" (Rich 1973).

The issues that concern me here, in the context of "revisionism as return," are: why return, return to what, who returns, and what are the differences between the returns undertaken by different human subjects that occupy different locations and different positionalities. What is the structure of *the return as such* in all its generality, and a specific return such as the feminist return, the ethnic return, and so forth? I am assuming that there is indeed no universal or anthropological human subject that can speak in the voice of a fully achieved representation. For example, how would the look back at history as ventured by a subaltern location differ from that authorized by a dominant or hegemonic location?[5] Is the return to "what has been" necrophilic or biophilic in its orientation and motivation? To raise this question and a number of related issues in a textually concrete manner, I go now to that wonderfully nuanced poem by Adrienne Rich, "Diving into the Wreck": a poem that brings into tension the political and the aesthetic, the transitive with the intransitive, play with purpose, the instrumentally programmatic with the theoretically open-ended, the forever new with the look back, the humanly historical with the planetary and the oceanic.

The poem begins with the assumption that there indeed is a wreck: its ontology is pre-given as an a priori, even though the perceptual reality of the wreck must be verified a posteriori by the act of diving and finding. In other words, without the assumption of the wreck, the act of diving cannot be undertaken, leave alone justified. Why the return to the wreck in the first place: Why does the persona in the poem want to dive into the wreck? Is the motivation philosophical-academic and disinterested? Is it the spirit of discovery to be shored up in the name of nonpolemical knowledge? What is the nature of the call from the wreck that motivates the dive? Is it aesthetic, antiquarian, primordial, political, physical, metaphysical, or elemental? Is the call ontological or epistemological or both? Is the dive undertaken in the name of the wreck or in the name of the dive itself and its will to its own perspectival truth? How is the truthfulness of the dive mediated by the tacit truth of the wreck; and which of the two truths enjoys primacy over the other? The questions multiply endlessly; so I turn now to the body of the poem as it plunges into the deep in search of the wreck. The poem begins thus: "First having read the book of myths, / and loaded the camera, / and checked the edge of the knife-blade, / I put on / the body-armor of black rubber / the absurd flippers / the grave and awkward mask. / I am having to do this/not like Cousteau with his / assiduous team / aboard the sun-flooded schooner / but here alone."

The poem makes no bone about presenting the prolegomenon as such in a spirit of self-reflexive theoretical acumen. A number of themes and contradictions are set afloat in the opening section. First, there is the priority of the "first" and its relationship to the book of myths. But one can invoke the "first" here even without any content-oriented instantiation. In a purely formal manner, the "first" sets in motion the pattern of the "return" and the logic of endless serialization and of nonidentical repetition that is both the "same and not the same" at the "same" time.[6] Once this grammar of the return is acknowledged, the truth-value of any one determinate return can only be conegotiated with the structural temporality of the return as such. But this by no means eviscerates of its own ideological specificity any particular dive into the wreck. The dive is no spontaneous lark; it is indeed a premeditated project that acknowledges the different steps of preparation that lead up to the moment of the dive. There is indeed a Beginning, which is going to be problematized and called into question by an act of repetition that may or may not uphold the sovereignty of the "original."[7] Yet, the original is needed and invoked as a mere secular point of departure. The "first" takes the form of a "book of myths," a phrase that combines critically the belief structure of myths and the "written-ness of the book." This phrase highlights the reality that myths are not value-neutral fantasies float-ing in the void, but are indeed canonized structures that function in the form of normative publications and truth claims. The next few lines anticipate a dialectical tension that animates the entire poem: the tension between spontaneous naturalness and deliberate artificiality. In this poem, the sea is both the primordial sea that antedates humanity absolutely and over-whelmingly; but it is also the sea forever "anthropocentered" by the wreck and by human goings on in general. The camera and the knife blade and the armor and the flippers point up the constitutive disjunction between human nature and Nature; and it is not at all coincidental that the adjective used by the poet is *absurd*, the very word that Albert Camus turns into a concept as he positions rational human subjectivity in a relationship of chronic alienation with Nature.[8] Finally, the reason why the persona is undertaking the dive is articulated in the name of a categorical imperative ("having to do this" as a form of the "ought") that is contrasted immediately with the structure of gratuitous choice that informs Jacques Cousteau's scholarly investigations into the nature of the ocean. The contrasts are clear: Jacques Cousteau is a professional, well-funded, male explorer of the sea with no particular political or cultural "biases" or motivations. Moreover, he is part of a team whose only motivation is research for the sake of research: a kind of a superior "purposeless purposiveness." Finally, the ocean has not in any way interpellated him and his team. They are there by choice: they are not required to be there except as a matter of self-fulfillment or self-indulgence. They, unlike the Rich per-sona or the allegorically deluded man from the country in Kafka's *The Trial* who has been called to wait at the gate, will not have failed themselves and history in any way if they did not perform their scientific explorations.

The question I would like to pose here is the following: how exclusively is the urge for revisionism fueled by a quarrel with history? In other words, would a person, a collectivity, or a location even dream of a revisionist project, of rubbing history against the grain, if not for hurt and subjugated by history? But for that drive toward justice and redress and that sense of *ressentiment*, what would revisionism signify at all? Would a fat-cat millionaire, a tra-ditionally rich old boy, a well-fed, well-empowered subject who has been the beneficiary of generations of a munificent history ever want to look back and quarrel with history in a spirit of radical antagonism? Would such a person, unless he or she were unbelievably ethical and deconstructive, not want to perpetuate history as it is and claim its benefits as the results of putative hard work? Sure enough, Rich claims the revisionist project in the name of a pur-pose. She makes it abundantly clear, through her detailed physical descriptions of "equip-mentality,"[9] that her persona, as a gendered subaltern, is in no position to woo an aleatory politics of interpretation or prematurely launch herself into a critique of instrumental reason or of a politically motivated *plumpes denken* (i.e., vulgar thought or popularization). It is also at this point that the "I" in the poem turns into a "we," positing a collective identity as an act of will and as an act of self-recognition. It is interesting to note that throughout the poem, in all the movements between individual subjectivity and collective consciousness, between individual being and a species being, "purpose" is asserted in the context of a "we." Here, to know a thing is to use it: theory as knowledge is used up in the act and is not to be enjoyed as an excess. To put in Žižekian psychoanalytic terms here, there is no room here to shore up the symptom as excess and enjoy it as a form of intransitive jouissance. But this theme will reappear later in a different section of the poem.

No sooner does the poem make a commitment to historical revisionism than it pulls back in a dialectically opposite direction to focus on the phenomenology both of the self and of the circumambient ocean.[10] Stanza three ends with, "I crawl like an insect down the ladder / and there is no one / to tell me when the ocean / will begin." It is clear that Rich is creating a rich ambiguity between the phenomenological given-ness of the ocean, and its availability as a site for the human project. The ocean in a sense is always already there, with or without reference to human cognition and acknowledgment; but the ocean that the diver is descending into, layer after watery layer, is the ocean that already accommodates the wreck whose historicity is human and secular. Perhaps it is a bit too obvious, but it does serve to refer here to Jacques Derrida's celebrated "ambiguation" of the nature–culture nexus in the context of "incest."[11] For, in this poem too, there is a pervading double consciousness that shuttles between the oceanic and the "oceanic." What about the telling resonance of the verb "begin?" Perhaps, it already has ontologically, but not in quite an ontic manner: to refer to the famous ontico-ontological difference elaborated by Martin Heidegger (1977). There is a precious pattern of "not knowing" that coexists dialectically with a form of "knowing" that is tethered to a political will. The mystery of the ocean survives as an "authentic" interpellation without in any way nullifying the perspectival knowability of the historico-political project of revisionism. Also, in the context of this primordial encounter with the ocean, the "we" returns to the "I" in an attitude of what I would call mystified discipleship. To avail of Homi Bhabha's graceful vocabulary, the relapse into the "I" marks the transition from a transitive pedagogical certainty to an intransitive performative contingency. There is more to come.

The very next stanza houses these haunting lines: "the sea is another story / the sea is not a question of power / I have to learn alone / to turn my body without force / in the deep element." Before I attempt to do justice to these tantalizing lines, I would like to make a certain connection with Nietzsche in the context of the opening provided by these lines in the poem. So, what is not a question of power (the title of a powerful and poignant novel by Bessie Head [1986]), and what might it mean to swim without force in the deep element? How do the logic and the structure of the deep element both transcend and underwrite the anthropocentric-historical human will? Is historicity practicable without the burden of anthropocentrism? Can a meaningful "turning of the body" without force in the "deep element" be the beginning of a noninvasive relationship both with the nature of history and the history of nature? It is with these thoughts in my mind that I turn to the theme of the undecidability of nature in Nietzsche's philosophy. For to Nietzsche, too, the "human" represents the antagonism of nature with itself. I would like to broach this problem by way of "chance," and the technique of dice throwing. To Nietzsche, as we have already seen, chance is an affirmation of necessity. To get to this truth, Nietzsche doubles the logic of the game of dice. There are two ways of assigning human destiny to the play of throwing dice; and one of them is shortsighted and self-mystified, whereas the other really understands. To Nietzsche, the human being needs to learn to play and mock at the same time. It is the practice of mocking play that rearranges and re-understands what it means to win: not the determinate winning that is desired so desperately by the human subject under the spell of ressentiment, but a deeper winning that revolutionizes the deep structure of the game itself. Sure enough, "play" is an important motif in the Rich poem as well: play as an end in itself that makes one kind of investment in the game, and a directed and teleological play that associates winning exclusively with the production of a particular result that is incapable of a second-order understanding of what the game is all about. Yet, there is a poststructuralist linguistic turn that animates Rich's poem. At the linguistic level, the poem is not afraid to abandon itself "purposelessly" to play even as it is "intentional," political speaking. In the ongoing exchange between the illocutionary and the perlocutionary, between the constative and the performative aspects of language, Rich has no problem in understanding intentionality itself as being linguistically mediated.[12] In this poem, Rich does not attempt to shore up language in identitarian terms. In the middle of the poem the persona has the audacity to say that at a certain moment she almost forgets the purpose of the dive.

In Adrienne Rich's poem, there is an urge to speak for the wreck from a certain perspective as well as an urge to claim redress and representation as well as an abiding sensitivity to that something that is other than and deeper than the political: the ocean as such as it quite fortuitously houses the wreck in its heart and core. Rich's play with pronouns, her constant semantic shuffles between "what is being said" and "who is saying," between "speaking" and "speaking for," her ambivalence of purpose, and her "negative capability"[13] vis-à-vis nature that is not annulled by her political will to give truth a name and a perspectival bearing: all of these deliberative strategies are based on a different axiology than that of Nietzsche. Her concern not to reduce the ocean monomaniacally to "a question of power" and her willingness to go with the flow of the ocean do not result in her valorization of chance as an underlying universal principle that nullifies human signatures. If anything, in the poem the term "universal" resonates differently as it moves as a human imagining that is sometimes someone's, and at other times, no one's.[14] Besides, "the human universal," in the Rich poem, is not allowed to legitimate itself in an autotelic way. It is always staged in a setting that is eco-planetary and primordial with reference to human historicity. The two impulses, the humanly historical and the eco-planetary, are experienced in relational simultaneity by the persona in the poem. It is never one or the other. Rich is also careful not to inflate her solicitude for "nature" into an unmediated form of wisdom or communion with nature. The analytic separation between the human and "nature" is always acknowledged with respect even as that separation is not allowed to harden into hubris and insensitivity. The Self/Other theme swims all through the Rich poem on two levels: the allegorical level where the command of the Other is absolute and binding on every self/other configuration, and the historical-secular level where self-other effects are produced by a world that is structured in dominance.[15]

"I came to explore the wreck. / The words are purposes. / The words are maps. / I came to see the damage that was done / and the treasures that prevail. / I stroke the beam of my lamp / slowly along the flank / of something more permanent / than fish or weed." These lines are unequivocally didactic and revisionist. They have more in common with the Nietzsche of *The Use and Abuse of History* (1949) who proclaims that effective history has every right to bring any past to justice in the court of the present. It is difficult to see how such a strongly interventionary historicism can be reconciled with the strategy of the good dice player whose only certainty is "that the universe has no purpose, that it has no end to hope for any more than it has causes to be known." The heavy thematic emphasis both in Nietzsche and in the poem is on the category "purpose." Is "purpose" an ontological property that inheres in reality that the human subject intuits or represents? Or, is "purpose" a purely anthropocentric epistemological fiction to render life and the universe bearable? If indeed there is a "purpose," then how is natural purpose as instantiated in the tiger eating the lamb related to human cultural purpose? Does human purpose reiterate the organic purposiveness found in nature, or does it transcend it in the name of a "supplemental" humanity that creates its own culture and historicity as a "second nature?" Is it possible to act purposively and intentionally as human beings, and at the same time read human history as an instantiation of a deeper purposelessness that inheres in the universe? Does it make sense, for example, to maintain that projects of anticolonialism are purposive in and of themselves in an immanent sort of way but do not in any way get rid of or resolve the fundamental purposelessness of the universe? We can see in Nietzsche some of the early tendencies towards postmodernism, towards what we now call "the legitimation crisis." Nietzsche insists on an immanent plane that is forever de-linked from its binary companion (i.e., "transcendence"). Nietzsche realizes that "there is no truth" but cannot help shouting it out pseudo-ostensively. Nietzsche is convinced of the futility of transcendence, because there can be no transcendence that is not formally and modally based on anthropocentrism. The good player then becomes the "superhuman" who laughs and plays without teleological and causal guarantees, whereas the bad player is the "weakling" who tries to align the politics of ressentiment with universal meaning and purpose. It is precisely by virtue of his randomization of the human historical project in the name of an underlying purposelessness that Nietzsche becomes a dangerous philosopher. He leaves no room where differentiations can be made between the master's purposelessness and the slave's purposelessness.[16]

The Rich poem proposes a different politics as well as epistemology of purpose. I see the poem resorting to the representation of "traces," both in the Gramscian and the Derridean sense of the term.[17] On a strictly political register, a la Gramsci, the poem, in order to understand the meaning of the present, undertakes an inventory of past traces: traces that include "damage" as well as "treasures." There is indeed a double consciousness at work, but not a benign and given double consciousness that passively or reactively itemizes treasures and damages. On the contrary, what is at work is an actively transcribed double consciousness that transforms the given-ness of history into a project of agential intervention. Though in a sense the treasures and the damage are cohistorical, the lines in the poem make an active distinction between "subjugated knowledges" and the body of dominant historiography. "The treasures that remain" are a countermnemonic repudiation not of the reality of the damage, but of the influence of the damage on the history of the present. The "traces," in a Gramscian sense are evidentiary in the context of a revisionist project, but the same "traces," when given a Derridean inflection, take off in a slightly different direction: towards "the thing I came for:/ the wreck and not the story of the wreck / the thing itself and not the myth." These lines begin with an attempted complicity between ontology and epistemology, between the Real and representation. Let me explain. If, in the Gramscian context, the "traces" represent "what was" in the name of history, the Derridean "traces" insist that traces can be no more than representations of absence; and that not even the urgency of a political project, with its set of required beliefs and principles and purposes, can suture that grammatological distance between logocentric presence and *ecriture*.[18]

It is significant that the lines just quoted operate in a space of legitimation that lies between phonocentrism (i.e., interpretive biases in favor of speech) and grammatology. They partake of phonocentrism insofar as there is an "I" that claims it has come there with an intention. Even though the wreck, with its treasures and damage, would have been real anyway, in this poem the "I" authenticates both itself and the wreck by proving that "it" has been there. The words that speak emanate from a specific vocal box that belongs to a body that is located at the scene of the wreck. More illocutionary than perlocutionary, more constative than performative, the speech act here is wedded to a speaking agent who has a purpose. To go back then to the Nietzschean question, what is the phenomenology of "purpose," and where and how is it lodged? Is it intrinsic to personhood and extrinsic to language, or is it intrinsic to language under certain generic and historical conditions where the user of language can constrain language to bear the burden of a prelinguistic agency? Does the "purpose" belong to the realm of the a priori that is then appropriately embodied in and as language? In other words, does linguistic intentionality dangle between the pedagogical certitude of the a priori and the performative contingency of the historical articulation? According to the poem, the words are maps; the words are purposes.[19] That is not the same thing as the roads having maps and purposes. Here then is the Derridean slide. Though the ethico-political authority of the revisionist drive is pre-given in the form of an imperative, the search itself, the process of the search, is linguistic, and constitutively so. It is from within the immanence of language qua language that directions must be found and purposes recognized. The poem, to use Heidegger (1977) loosely, commits "the language of being" to "the being of language," and not the other way around. The poem establishes an identical connection between the ontology of language and its usability. It is therefore not a guarantee at all that the dive will not be purloined, that the dive will not reach the wreck. As a matter of fact, it is only when the wreck becomes "the wreck" that it becomes the destination of the revisionist dive.

Why then does Rich, given the perspectival nature of her revisionist dive, even talk about "the thing itself, and not the myth," "the wreck and not the story of the wreck"? Clearly the wreck cannot speak for itself; nor can any one story of the wreck naturalize itself as the wreck's intra-ontological self-predication. There would seem to be a natural sympathy between the revisionist dive and the Nietzschean dictum that "truth is nothing but a mobile army of anthropomorphisms." The truth of any revisionist vision is double-tongued. The vision knows what the truth is not, even though it cannot affirm what the truth actually is. I will assume then, given Rich and the range of her preoccupations as a poet-feminist activist-intellectual, that the wreck is nothing but the body of feminist/feminine subjugated knowledges.[20] These knowledges were "made a wreck of" by patriarchy and its many forces. There have been myths and stories about this wreck: stories and myths within the dominant historiography that saw the wreck as historically justifiable loss, as legitimate debris cast away by the historical process. What the revisionist project will claim, by speaking for the wreck, is that the wreck still lives and is reclaimable as a treasure and a legacy from a certain point of view. This task of reviving the wreck and making it speak to the present is a matter both of rubbing dominant historiography (its myths and its stories) against the grain and of telling another story, along its grain, as it were. The *topos* where "nature" and "history" come together, pretending to be versions of each other, is the site of dominance. For it is the dominant will-to-meaning that fabricates a story from its perspective, naturalizes that perspective as the Perspective of all perspectives, and naturalizes the object of its representation as the transcendent Real. The drive in the poem towards "the thing itself" is not so much an essentialist quest, but rather a destructive project that envisions the "thing itself" not as a presence, but as an active absence, or a series of absences in the body of the dominant historiography. "The thing itself" is then "the thing itself" of the dominant discourse under erasure, *sous rature*. On a political level, it is imperative for the revisionist perspective to seek the "thing itself" as an open possibility liberated from the sovereignty of the dominant discourse. But it is not that simple. The question remains: what should happen within the field of open possibility whose very purpose is to "let the thing itself be"?

It is under the aegis of this larger question that androgyny develops in the poem. "We circle silently/ about the wreck/ we dive into the hold. / I am she: I am he." It is important to note that the lines do not say, "She is him, and He is her." The he and she are mutually trans-gendered not on the basis of an I-Thou intersubjectivity, but with reference to a nameless third term in the form of an existential first person pronoun in all its irreducible specific generality. The finding of the wreck opens up a space of an empathic solidary and performative inclusiveness that enables the "her" and the "him" not to be fused into one, but to find an emergent space of solidarity in the name of the "I": the first person pronoun. The pronoun is here a performative device and not an ontological straitjacket.[21] Both the "he" and the "she" can simultaneously cohabit the "I": as a matter of fact, this "I" as topos does not exist except as a function of the transgendering performance. The overall movement of the poem is from a specific perspectival revisionism—for example, the feminist perspective that is itself internally heterogenized as heterosexual and lesbian—to an open revisionism that does not shore up its findings as its own private treasure but rather shares it in the name of all humanity. It is particularly appropriate that the poem ends not with a text, not with a body, and not with a state of being, but with the notion of "names." Rich uses all the connotative power of that word: representation, official legitimation, partaking with others in the task of creating a document and a point of reference. At the same time, she creates a contrapuntal relationship between the *imprimatur* of the name and the fluidity of a pronominal identification. She also takes care not to celebrate her state of arrival as the finding of a new name or a new affirmative positivity. The poem ends thus. "We are, I am, you are / by cowardice or courage / the one who find our way / back to this scene / carrying a knife, a camera / a book of myths / in which / our names do not appear." It is a mark of Rich's remarkable integrity as an artist-intellectual and revisionist-activist that she does not end the poem on a triumphalist note of arrival or with a gung-ho chest-thumping gesture of rectitude. After the we/you/I dance (with the "you" both addressing the reader and creating a different zone of address), Rich has the "courage or the cowardice" to include courage or cowardice as potential motivating resources for the revisionist project. Rather than launder revisionism in the name of an always already political correctness, she opens up the diving as a potential object of ambivalence. Her use of the progressive tense, "are carrying," emphasizes the reality that the highly motivated dive ends as process, which is another way of saying that it does not and cannot end. This is a revisionist politics of ongoing questions, as Michel Foucault (1980) would have it, and a "politics of the open end" in Gayatri Spivak's sense of the term (Spivak 1990). The ending makes the rich and undeniable suggestion that once the logic of repetition is inaugurated, repetitions will never end. Each repetition will invoke an "origin" or a "beginning" that will lose its inaugural status in the process of the dive. There is a symptomatic need to keep returning to the scene of the wreck: a return of the same, rendered nonidentical by the performance of the return. The ones who undertake the dives are identified, both ontologically and epistemologically, as the ones "who undertake the dive." The ending of the poem does not do away with the materiality of the search or all the baggage that constitutes the labor of the trip: the camera, the knife, and even the book "in which our names do not appear" continue their historical existence even after the arrival of the revisionist dive. The book in which our names will appear, as a result of the successful achievement of the dive, is never mentioned, and the only way names are invoked is in terms of a profound absence or a lack. The filling out or the rectification of the lack does not result in the production of a hegemonic name or a constituency as the sovereign filler of the lack. What is preserved perennially is revisionism as perspective, and not revisionism as guaranteed truth. What we have here is the rationale of "signifying" as an ongoing process that defers its own truth with extreme rigor and purposiveness.

The semantics of revisionism is necessarily double, and not just in the context of the antagonistic contact zone between subjugated and dominant knowledges, but in a broader theoretical sense as well. For example, how are the specific politics of feminist revisionism or postcolonial revisionism related to the general nature of revisionism as such? What are the differences between patriarchal dominant historiography as the object of a reading or a brushing against the grain and the historiography of colonialism or that of normative heterosexuality or that of racism subjected to a similar antagonistic reading? What are the specific assumptions about nature, human nature, gender, race and ethnicity, and sexuality that drive the semantics of each revisionist project under the broad syntactic umbrella called revisionism as such? With these questions in mind I turn to Frantz Fanon (1963); in particular, to his posthumously published *The Wretched of the Earth*. What makes Fanon relevant today, despite all the changes in world and postcolonial developments, is the fact that he is interested both in the psychic and the political dimensions of subject formation. His thought acknowledges that psychic duration and political temporality, however much they are interrelated within the organicity of a movement or revolution, cannot be synchronized. Of ongoing importance is the manner in which Fanon connects revisionism with a particular kind of historiography. Both solicitous and suspicious of history, both mnemonic and countermnemonic, Fanon produces, not represents, the native intellectual as national intellectual. Why is the look back towards the past necessary for the look forward into the future? Which look towards the past is legitimate and historical, and which apocryphal and self-deluded?

Of all the words in Fanon's vocabulary, the most troubling, the most problematic, and the least resolved is the term "native." If he were a contemporary political theorist, he would have helped us out with the simple device " " to help us understand where he means native, and where "native." The native, in places, stands for the given and is therefore to be suspected

deeply and rigorously, and at other places the "native" is an achieved and a historically produced native who is also a postcolonial "national." At times, the word native resounds with a
false autochthony, as a mere natal or place name whose ontology has not aspired to produce
its own epistemology. In other places, the word suggests a kind of knowledge, as in native
knowledge versus neocolonial knowledge. To put it in Cartesian terms, "The native thinks,
therefore, s/he is," but the haunting question in the aftermath of colonialist depredation is,
"what is thinking?" That is to say, what is right thinking, and what is wrong thinking? And
this is a question that cannot even begin to be answered without a correct and authoritative
understanding of the past, the precolonial past. Again, the question comes up: which is the
real past, and which is the past that is part of a stifling tradition invented by the colonizer to
stifle and paralyze the colonized?

A way to understand Fanon's revisionist program is to acknowledge that the teleological
drive behind it all is to rediscover the native as the postcolonial African national. Fanon
understands with remarkable clarity (1) that the way to history is itself historical and (2) that
the historiography of interventionism is neither fully representational nor entirely constitutive of history. As in the case of Rich's "dive into the wreck," here too an occult zone of instability opens up between the body of history and the meaning of history. Neither an absolute
given, nor entirely a polemical construct, the past as history dangles in that indeterminate
area of psycho-political disequilibrium. Can the truth of history be affirmed except at the level
of strategic usability? Is Africa's past true, real, and valuable only because it offers the African
subject a point of leverage against the white man's history? "The Negro is not. Any more than
the white man" (Fanon 1967, 231). Does this claim from *Black Skin, White Masks* concede too
much to the historicity of the binary form that is structured in colonial dominance? Is it not
conceivable to speak of the Negro without any reference to the white man at all? What is the
nature of that reality that will survive the nihilation of binarity? And from what perspective
will the value of that survival be registered? Through all these investigations, Fanon is raising
yet another fundamental problem: the relationship of belief as an a priori system to historical
knowledge as a secular a posteriori. One recalls Renan's ironic claim that the nation is the
function of a daily plebiscite. Or, in a frivolous vein, there is that exquisite skit in Monty
Python where an entire tenement building remains stable when its inhabitants believe in it;
but once, even if one of them begins to entertain doubts about its architectural integrity, fissures and fault lines begin to appear on the walls and on the ceiling. There is the need to
believe in a national culture even though such a culture can only be the result of a contingent
historical performance.

I would like to offer a few general theoretical speculations before I undertake a Fanon-
specific dissection of the heart of history. To Fanon, there is no *Ur* truth just as there is no *Ur*
history: no primordiality, no essentialism. Fanon would also agree with Nietzsche, with some
important provisos, that the truth of history is the truth of power and indeed that truth is a
mobile army of anthropomorphisms. But Fanon, like Amitav Ghosh (1988) in *The Shadow
Lines*, would ask insistently, "which anthropomorphism?" In other words, Fanon would not
acquiesce in the conflation of the epistemological questioning of truth with the political contestation, in a world structured in dominance, about the nature of historical truth. Yes, it is
important to Fanon that a new humanism is to be imagined ethically, philosophically, and
epistemologically; but such an imaginary will have to be predicated on the political dismantling of the vicious binary logic of colonialism. The dismantling of the very structure of binarity
at the metalevel has to go hand in hand with the project of addressing the unequal historical
realities brought into existence by binarity. To put it concretely, the very effect of the deconstruction of binarity as such will fall differentially on the master and the slave. The dialectical
model looks toward the perennial reproduction of the thesis-antithesis-synthesis in the hope
that this binary contestation will eventually find a resolution where all binarities will have

faded away and withered. The highly controversial discussion, within Marxist theory, about the nature of agency has had to do with readings of agency. Is agency immanent, or transcendent, or both? How does the dialectic carry, within its historical movement, the gesture towards a teleology? Is history, to use Althusser's formulation, "a process without subject or goals?" Is class a something in itself, or is it the expression of constantly shifting historical energies and trajectories? Is there a guarantee that the truth of the dialectic would produce the truth of Truth, particularly within an epistemological framework that does not allow for the existence of an a priori truth? To put it in less Hegelian and more Marxist terms, how does one know immanently that the proletarian perspective is *the* perspective most suited for the production of universal freedom? Fanon's revisionist drive takes shape within a temporality that acknowledges the relevance of binarity without at the same time surrendering the conflictual oppositionality that is required to read the binarity historically, and not just formally. "The Negro is not. Any more than the white man." But who is saying this, and from where? If the Negro or the white man within the binary structure is saying it, it will serve only to perpetuate the *longue duree* of colonialism for the simple reason that the articulation continues to represent the legitimacy of binarity. But the bind of course is that the statement cannot come from outside the structure of binarity, simply because the very fact that such an "outside" has been found renders the statement redundant. It is only by working from within the binary in a perspectival and antagonistic mode that the Negro can undertake the double task of decolonization from the white man, and decolonization from binarity as such. In other words, the metahistoricity of the binary structure cannot be deconstructed unless and until the historical unevenness brought about by binarity is eliminated in the first place. In Fanon's terms, the "human" has to be taken critically beyond the binary playing field that creates positions such as white and black, the haves and the have-nots.

So, which subject undertakes the project of historical revisionism: the master or the slave, the white man or the Negro, the colonizer or the colonized? How is the preoccupation of the colonized different from the colonizer's preoccupation, assuming in the first place that history even has a place in the colonizer's scheme of things? Fanon's unique insight is that the colonized need to be both solicitous and wary of history at the same time. There is a history that is to be legitimated but such a history does not exist as such until after the legitimation. There is a history to be avoided despite its seductiveness and easy availability. Also, like Gramsci, who insists that an inventory be made of the many critical traces of the past, Fanon too makes differentiations among different histories that have led up to the present. Some histories are unethical, politically incorrect, unjust, and unacceptable; and yet these histories have occurred successfully and hegemonically. One such example is that of colonialism. This history must be repudiated, and yet no radical repudiation can exorcize the fact that it is indeed a history. In the case of the colonized, colonialist history has become the most immediate sedimentation of history: an invasive history that has dispossessed the natives of their history and forced on them what is alien. What the native intellectual attempts is to repudiate the authority of colonial history, but not its given-ness. Consequently, a critical encounter with that history, which is not one's own, has become part of the revisionist postcolonial national project. As in the case of Rich's dive into the wreck, the wreck cannot be reached by way of one nonstop journey: pure origin to pure destination. The layered and the multimediated path towards the wreck must adopt the strategy of *Nethi* or *na ithi*: a process of negative or "not this" recognitions before it recognizes the wreck.

Says Fanon, "The colonized man who writes for his people ought to use the past with the intention of opening the future, as an invitation to action and a basis for hope" (Fanon 1963, 232). This triangulates an ethic as the basis for the look back into history: the usability of the past in the name of a future, historicizing as an invitation to action based on hope, and the bringing together of the "I" with the "we." "We must not therefore be content with delving into the past of a people in order to find coherent elements which will counteract colonialism's attempt to falsify and harm. We must work and fight with the same rhythm as the people to construct the future and to prepare the ground where vigorous shoots are already springing up" (Fanon 1963, 227).[22] The delving into the past, that certainly bears a resemblance to the dive into the wreck, has to go beyond a merely symmetrical refutation of colonialism towards a fellow-heartedness with the people and their rhythms. Revisionism has a theoretical or a meta- function in Fanon's imagination, and this function has to do with "preparing the ground"—that is, of articulating a temporality that will be organic with the shoots that are already in emergence. Fanon here is defining temporality along Foucauldian lines as a regime and as a kind of space or habitat that will be conducive for some growths and not for others. It is not enough for the people to have spoken and acted and for the shoots to have sprung. Those declarations and actions and emergences need to theorize into existence the right milieu where they can develop in their own way. Without such a careful theoretical production, the populist verities of a postcolonial nationalism might find itself growing in a soil that is still neocolonial; and this tragedy must be avoided at all cost. In much the same way that a sophisticated post-Gramscian Marxism would acknowledge the connectedness of the superstructure to the base without at the same time disallowing the capacity of the superstructure to translate the base to itself, Fanon's revolutionary thought locates intellectuality in a double relationship with the rhythms of the people. The origins of the intellectual are in the people, for intellectuals are "people" too; but again like Gramsci, Fanon would affirm that some of the people will need to function as organic intellectuals to prepare the ground toward the right kind of yield and harvest.

To conclude, the moment of "occult instability" in Fanon's theory need not be read merely as an ineffectual gesture towards the perennial revolution, or as an "always already" interruption of the political by the psychoanalytic, but as a blowing open of the blockage that disconnects the historicity of temporality from the temporality of historicity. If temporality pertains to the human condition and historicity has to do with the ideological instantiation of temporality in such regimes as colonialism, apartheid, racism, heterosexism, and so forth, then Fanon's theory may function both as an irreversible indictment of a specific historicity and as an invocation toward an other and nonbinary temporality.

## NOTES

1. The category of the "empirico-transcendental doublet" has been theorized brilliantly by Michel Foucault (1980).
2. My forthcoming essay "Why History, Why Now?" deals at length with the relationship between historical representation and what it is "about."
3. For more on the relationship between history and loss, see my forthcoming collection of essays.
4. Harvey (1998) offers a careful and diagnostic reading of the standoff between militant eco thinkers and Marxists-Socialists.
5. The theme of "looking back" to make sense of history has of course been made memorable by Walter Benjamin's brief but poignant reading of Paul Klee's "The Angel of Progress." An outstanding instance of a dominant subject position in the act of deconstruction and ethical autocritique is Nadine Gordimer's *Burger's Daughter*. For an analysis of this aspect of the Gordimer novel, see chapter 5 of Radhakrishnan (2003).
6. For a thorough philosophical reading of "repetition," see Deleuze (1994).
7. Said (1975) is a magisterial study of the phenomenology as well as the epistemology of "what it means to begin."
8. For more on Nature and the Absurd, see Camus (1965).
9. "Equipmentality" is a term that Martin Heidegger uses with telling hermeneutic effect in his analysis of the artwork in his essay "The Origins of a Work of Art."

10. There are some thematic overlaps between Rich's signification of the ocean and Julia Kristeva's notion of semiosis prior to oedipalization.

11. I refer here to Jacques Derrida's essay "Structure, Sign, and Play in the Human Sciences." See Derrida (1978).

12. For a searching analysis of the epistemological status of intentionality as a profoundly human mediation, see Maurice Merleau-Ponty (1962).

13. John Keats, the English Romantic poet, coined the term "negative capability" in opposition to the scientific rational way of knowing things.

14. Maxine Hong Kingston's *The Woman Warrior*, Ralph Ellison's *Invisible Man*, and Amitav Ghosh's *The Shadow Lines* politicize and psychologize the problem of "names and naming."

15. The small o/big O distinction is crucial to Lacanian psychoanalysis. Slavoj Žižek's ongoing work returns to this problematic in a variety of contexts. See Žižek (1993, 1999).

16. For more on the master-slave relationship, see Judith Butler (1987).

17. For a compelling reading of the Derridean notion of the "trace," see Gayatri Chakravorty Spivak's "Translator's Introduction" to Derrida's *Of Grammatology*.

18. Jacques Derrida's virtuosic essay "Ousia and Gramme" (1978) is an appreciative critique of the themes of presence and absence in Martin Heidegger's work.

19. Both Amitav Ghosh's *The Shadow Lines* and Nuruddin Farah's *Maps* are profound philosophical reflections on cartography and the politics of representation.

20. For more on "subjugated knowledges," see Foucault (1980).

21. The pronoun, as the representative speaking voice, represents both the attenuation and the vivid dramatization of human ontology.

22. For a comprehensive discussion of "occult instability," see a much longer version of this essay in my book forthcoming from Duke University Press.

## Works Cited

Benjamin, Walter. 1969. "Theses on the Philosophy of History." In *Illuminations*, trans. Harry Zohn, ed. Hannah Arendt, 253–64. New York: Schocken Books.

Butler, Judith. 1987. *Subjects of Desire: Hegelian Reflections in Twentieth-Century France*. New York: Columbia University Press.

Camus, Albert. 1965. *Notebooks 1942–1951*, trans. Justin O'Brien. New York: Knopf.

Deleuze, Gilles. 1994. *Difference and Repetition*, trans. Paul Patton. New York: Columbia University Press.

Derrida, Jacques. 1978. *Writing and Difference*, trans. Alan Bass. Chicago: University of Chicago Press.

———. 1982. *Margins of Philosophy*, trans. Alan Bass. Chicago: University of Chicago Press.

Ellison, Ralph. 1947. *Invisible Man*. New York: Vintage.

Eng, David, and David Kazanjian. 2003. *Loss: The Politics of Mourning*. Berkeley: University of California.

Fanon, Frantz. 1963. *The Wretched of the Earth*, trans. Constance Farrington. New York: Grove Press.

———. 1967. *Black Skins, White Masks*, trans. Charles Markmann. New York: Grove Press.

Farah, Nuruddin. 1986. *Maps*. London: Pan.

Foucault, Michel. 1970. *The Order of Things*. New York: Vintage.

———. 1980. *Power/Knowledge: Selected Interviews and Other Writings*, trans. Colin Gordon, Leo Marshall, John Mepham, and Kate Soper. New York: Pantheon Random House.

Ghosh, Amitav. 1988. *The Shadow Lines*. New York: Viking Penguin.

Gordimer, Nadine. 1979. *Burger's Daughter*. New York: Penguin Books.

Gramsci, Antonio. 1957. *The Modern Prince & Other Writings*, trans. Dr. Louis Marks. New York: International Publishers.

Harvey, David. 1998. "What's Green and Makes the Environment Go Round?" In *The Cultures of Globalization*, eds. Fredric Jameson and Masao Miyoshi, 327–55. Durham, N.C.: Duke University Press.

Head, Bessie. 1986. *A Question of Power*. London: Heinemann Educational.

Heidegger, Martin. 1977. "The Origin of the Work of Art." In *Martin Heidegger: Basic Writings*, trans. David Farrell Krell, New York: Harper & Row.

Kingston, Maxine Hong. 1989. *The Woman Warrior*. New York: Vintage.

Kristeva, Julia. 1986. *The Kristeva Reader*, ed. Toril Moi. New York: Columbia University Press.

Merleau-Ponty, Maurice. 1962. *The Phenomenology of Perception*, trans. Colin Smith. London: Routledge & Kegan Paul.

Nietzsche, Friedrich. 1949. *The Use and Abuse of History*, trans. Adrian Collins. New York: Bobbs-Merrill.

Radhakrishnan, R. 2003. *Theory in an Uneven World*. Oxford: Blackwell.

Rich, Adrienne. 1973. *Diving into the Wreck: Poems 1971–72*. New York: Norton.

Said, Edward. 1975. *Beginnings*. New York: Basic Books.

Spivak, Gayatri Chakravorty. 1974. "Introduction" to Jacque Derrida's *Of Grammatology*. Baltimore: Johns Hopkins University Press.

———. 1990. *The Postcolonial Critic: Interviews, Strategies, Dialogues*. New York: Routledge.

Žižek, Slavoj. 1993. *Tarrying with the Negative: Kant, Hegel, and the Critique of Ideology*. Durham, N.C.: Duke University Press.

———. 1999. *The Ticklish Subject*. London: Verso.

# 4

# THE MANY SCALES OF THE GLOBAL: IMPLICATIONS FOR THEORY AND FOR POLITICS

*Saskia Sassen*

In this short chapter I want to work on two key features of the many needed to critically remap the analytic terrain for studying and interpreting the global. One of these features is the need to destabilize the accepted narratives and explanations of globalization in order to generate new questions for research; whether critical or supportive of globalization, we now have dominant narratives that can easily close off the analytic terrain within which to study globalization. A second feature is the need to develop conceptual architectures that allow us to detect what we might think of as countergeographies of globalization—that is, structurations that might use the major corporate global infrastructures, but do so for purposes other than their original design or intent. There are multiple instances of these countergeographies. In this chapter I am particularly interested in types of spaces where we can find resistance to global power and as yet unrecognized forms of participation by actors typically represented as powerless, or victims, or uninvolved with global conditions. Such new narratives and conceptual architectures can help us in this effort to develop a critical analytics that is more than a critique of globalization.

These two necessary features for critical globalization studies stem in part from a basic assumption in my own fifteen years of research, to wit, that the global is partly endogenous to the national rather than a formation that stands outside and in opposition to the national. Endogeneity can be the result of an originally national condition that becomes reconstructed as global; for example, the fact that what we call global capital is an amalgamation of what often were national capitals. Global capital can then be seen as denationalized national capital. Or endogeneity can result from the partial insertion of global dynamics and entities into national institutional orders—for example, the fact that global electronic financial markets are partly embedded in, and dependent on, a network of national financial centers.

Such an approach has theoretical, empirical, and political implications for specifying the global. The global is not simply defined as that which is outside and in contestation to the national, nor is the global only that which is part of a space of flows that cuts across borders. There are components of globalization that we keep coding in national terms, and there are global actors whom we think of as local because they are immobile and do not move across borders, thus lacking the markers of what have become dominant representations of the global for both the supporters and the critics. If we understand the global as indeed partly endogenous to or endogenized into the national, we expand the range of actors who are conceivably global. We can then include even those who are immobile, resource poor, and not able to travel global circuits.

## The Subnational: A Site for Globalization

One starting point for me, then, has been to keep on asking the question: what is it we are trying to name with the term *globalization*? In my reading of the evidence, it is actually two distinct sets of dynamics. One of these involves the formation of explicitly global institutions and processes, such as the World Trade Organization, global electronic financial markets, the new cosmopolitanism, and the war crimes tribunals. The practices and organizational forms through which these dynamics operate are constitutive of what is typically thought of as global scales—by both critics and supporters of globalization.

But there is a second set of processes that does not necessarily scale at the global level as such, yet, I argue, is part of globalization. These processes take place deep inside territories and institutional domains that have largely been constructed in national terms in much, though by no means all, of the world. What makes these processes part of globalization even though localized in national, indeed subnational, settings is that they involve transboundary networks and formations connecting or articulating multiple local or "national" processes and actors. Among these processes I include cross-border networks of activists engaged in specific localized struggles with an explicit or implicit global agenda, as is the case with many human rights and environmental organizations; particular aspects of the work of states (e.g., certain monetary and fiscal policies critical to the constitution of global markets that are hence being implemented in a growing number of countries); the use of international human rights instruments in national courts; and noncosmopolitan forms of global politics and imaginaries that remain deeply attached or focused on localized issues and struggles, yet are part of global lateral networks containing multiple other such localized efforts.

A focus on such subnationally based processes and dynamics of globalization requires methodologies and theorizations that engage not only global scalings but also subnational scalings as components of global processes, thereby destabilizing older hierarchies of scale and conceptions of nested scalings. Studying global processes and conditions that are constituted subnationally has some advantages over studies of globally scaled dynamics—but it also poses specific challenges. It does make possible the use of long-standing research techniques, from quantitative to qualitative, in the study of globalization. It also gives us a bridge for using the wealth of national and subnational data sets as well as specialized scholarships such as area studies. Both types of studies, however, need to be situated in conceptual architectures that are not quite those held by the researchers who generated these research techniques and data sets, as their efforts mostly had little to do with globalization. One central task we face is to decode particular aspects of what is still represented or experienced as "national" that may in fact have shifted away from what had historically been considered or constituted as national. In many ways this effort at decoding the national is illustrated by the research and theorization logic developed in global-city studies. But there are many domains where this work has not yet been done.

Three instances serve to illustrate some of the conceptual, methodological, and empirical issues in this type of study. One of these instances concerns the role of place in many of the circuits constitutive of economic and political globalization. A focus on places allows us to unbundle globalization in terms of the multiple specialized cross-border circuits on which different types of places are located. I would include here the emergence of forms of globality centered on localized struggles and actors that are part of cross-border networks; this is a form of global politics that runs not through global institutions but through local ones and constitutes a horizontal, rather than hierarchical, space of globality. Global cities are subnational places where multiple global circuits intersect, and thereby these cities are positioned on various structured cross-border geographies, each typically with distinct scopes and constituted in terms of distinct practices, logics, and actors. For instance, at least some of the circuits connecting Sao Paulo to global dynamics are different from those of Frankfurt,

Johannesburg, or Bombay. Further, distinct sets of overlapping circuits contribute to the constitution of distinctly structured cross-border geographies. We are, for instance, seeing the intensifying of older hegemonic geographies, for example, the increase in transactions among New York, Miami, Mexico City, and Sao Paulo, as well as newly constituted geographies (e.g., the articulation of Shanghai with a rapidly growing number of cross-border circuits). This type of analysis produces a different picture about globalization from one centered on global markets, international trade, or the pertinent supranational institutions.

A second of these instances, partly connected to the first, is the role of the new interactive technologies in repositioning the local, thereby inviting us to a critical examination of how we conceptualize the local. Through these new technologies a financial services firm becomes a microenvironment with continuous global span. But so do resource-poor organizations or households; they can also become microenvironments with global span, as might be the case with activist organizations. These microenvironments can be oriented to other such microenvironments located far away, thereby destabilizing the notion of context that is often imbricated in that of the local and the notion that physical proximity is one of the attributes or markers of the local. A critical reconceptualization of the local along these lines entails an at least partial rejection of the notion that local scales are inevitably part of nested hierarchies of scale running from the local to the regional, the national, and the international.

A third instance concerns a specific set of interactions between global dynamics and particular components of national states. The crucial conditionality here is the partial embeddedness of the global in the national, of which the global city is perhaps emblematic. My main argument here is that insofar as specific structurations of the global inhabit what has historically been constructed and institutionalized as national territory, this engenders a variety of negotiations. One set of outcomes evident today is what I describe as an incipient, typically highly specialized, and partial denationalization of specific components of national states. Notable here are particular components of the work of ministries of finance, central banks, and regulatory agencies in key sectors such as finance and telecommunications.

In all three instances the question of scaling takes on very specific contents in that these are practices and dynamics that, I argue, pertain to the constituting of the global yet are taking place at what has been historically constructed as the scale of the national. With few exceptions, most prominent among which is a growing scholarship in geography, the social sciences have not critically distanced (i.e., historicized) the scale of the national. The consequence has been a tendency to take it as a fixed scale and to reify it and, more generally, to neutralize the question of scaling, or at best to reduce scaling to a hierarchy of size. Associated with this tendency is also the often-uncritical assumption that these scales are mutually exclusive, most pertinently for my argument here, that the scale of the national is mutually exclusive with that of the global. Finally, the three instances described go against those assumptions and propositions that are now often described as methodological nationalism. But they do so in a very distinct way. Crucial to the critique of methodological nationalism is the need for transnationalism, because the nation as container category is inadequate given the proliferation of transboundary dynamics and formations (e.g., Taylor 2000; Beck 2001; Chase-Dunn and Gills 2005; Datz 2007). What I am focusing on here is a different aspect, although it is yet another reason for supporting the critique of methodological nationalism: the fact of multiple and specific structurations of the global inside what has historically been constructed as national.

## THE DESTABILIZING OF OLDER HIERARCHIES OF SCALE

Various components of globalization bring with them a destabilizing of older hierarchies of scale—scales and hierarchies constituted through the practices and power projects of past eras, with the national scale eventually emerging as the preeminent one over the past few centuries. Most notable today is what is sometimes seen as a return to older imperial spatialities for the economic operations of the most powerful actors: the formation of a global market for capital, a global trade regime, and the internationalization of manufacturing production. It is, of course, not simply a return to older forms; it is crucial to recognize the specificity of today's practices and the capabilities enabling these practices. This specificity partly consists of the fact that today's transboundary spatialities had to be produced in a context where most territory is encased in a thick and highly formalized national framework marked by the exclusive authority of the national state. This is, in my reading, one of the key features of the current phase of globalization, and it entails the necessary participation of national states in the formation of global systems (Sassen 2006a, 2007).

The global project of powerful firms, the new technical capabilities associated with information and communication technologies, and some components of the work of states have together constituted strategic scales other than the national scale. Most especially among these are subnational scales such as the global city and supranational scales such as global electronic markets. These processes and practices also contain a destabilizing of the scale hierarchies that expressed the power relations and political economy of an earlier period. These were, and to a good extent continue to be, organized in terms of institutional size and territorial scope: from the international down to the national, the regional, the urban, and the local, with the national functioning as the articulator of this particular configuration. That is to say, the crucial practices and institutional arrangements that constituted the system occurred at the national level. Notwithstanding multiple different temporal frames, the history of the modern state can be read as the work of rendering national just about all crucial features of society: authority, identity, territory, security, law, and capital accumulation.

Today's rescaling dynamics cut across institutional size and across the institutional encasements of territory produced by the formation of national states. This does not mean that the old hierarchies disappear but rather that rescalings emerge alongside the old ones, and that the former can often trump the latter. Existing theory is not enough to map today's multiplication of practices and actors constitutive of these rescalings. Included are a variety of nonstate actors and forms of cross-border cooperation and conflict, such as global business networks, the new cosmopolitanism, NGOs, diasporic networks, and spaces such as global cities and transboundary public spheres. A second feature is the multiscalar character of various globalization processes that do not fit into either older conceptions of hierarchies of scale or conceptions of nested hierarchies. Perhaps most familiar here is, again, the bundle of conditions and dynamics that marks the model of the global city. In its most abstract formulation this is captured in what I see as one of the key organizing hypotheses of the global-city model, to wit, that the more globalized and digitized the operations of firms and markets, the more their central management and specialized servicing functions (and the requisite material structures) become strategic and complex, thereby benefiting from agglomeration economies. To variable extents these agglomeration economies are still delivered through territorial concentrations of multiple resources. This points to multiple scales that cannot be organized as a hierarchy or a nested hierarchy: for example, far-flung networks of affiliates of multinational firms along with the concentration of strategic functions in a single or in a very limited number of locations (e.g., GAWC). This is a multiscalar system, operating across scales and not merely scaling upward because of new communication capabilities.

## RECOVERING PLACE IN GLOBAL PROCESSES

Including cities in the analysis of economic globalization is not without its analytic consequences. Economic globalization has mostly been conceptualized in terms of the duality national – global where the latter gains at the expense of the former. This conceptualization has largely been in terms of the internationalization of capital, and then only the upper circuits of capital. Introducing cities into this analysis allows us to reconceptualize processes of economic globalization as concrete economic complexes partly situated in specific places (Knox and Taylor 1995; Orum and Chen 2002; Brenner and Keil 2005; Taylor 2006; Bryson and Daniels 2006). This contrasts with the mainstream account about globalization where place is typically seen as neutralized by the capacity for global communications and space-time compression. A focus on cities decomposes the nation-state into a variety of subnational components, some profoundly articulated with the global economy and others not (Parnreiter 2002; Yeung 2000; Sassen 2006b). It signals the declining significance of the national economy as a unitary category in the global economy.

Why does it matter to recover place in analyses of the global economy, particularly place as constituted in major cities? Because it allows us to see the multiplicity of economies and work cultures in which the global information economy is embedded (Low 1999; Eade 1996; Marcuse and van Kempen 2000; Samers 2002; Barlow 2003; Bada, Fox and Selee 2006; Buechler 2007). It also allows us to recover the concrete, localized processes through which much of globalization exists and to argue that much of the multiculturalism in large cities is as constitutive of globalization as is international finance, though in ways that differ sharply from the latter (Sassen 2006a, chapters 5 and 6; Iyotani, Sakai, and Bary 2005; Cordero-Guzmán, Grosfoguel, and Smith 2001; King 1996; Tardanico and Lungo 1995). It allows us to see an interesting correspondence between great concentrations of corporate power and large concentrations of "others" (e.g. Hagedorn 2006; Kirsch 2006; Lucas 2005). Large cities, perhaps especially in the global North, are the terrain where a multiplicity of globalization processes assume concrete, localized forms. A focus on cities makes legible not only the upper but also the lower circuits of globalization. Finally, focusing on cities allows us to specify a geography of strategic places bound to each other largely by the dynamics of economic globalization and cross-border migrations. I refer to this as a new geography of centrality, at the heart of which is the new worldwide grid of global cities. This is a geography that cuts across national borders and the old North—South divide. But it does so along bounded channels; it is a set of specific and partial rather than all-encompassing dynamics (e.g. Taylor 2006; Ribas-Matteos 2005; Hindman 2007).

It is against this context that I argue that one of the strategic working structures enabling the new imperial spatiality is the network of global cities, one that might eventually evolve into a grid of imperial and subimperial cities. This network is a strategic infrastructure enabling the production and specialized servicing of components crucial for the constituting of global corporate capital. Second, this network is a key structure for social reproduction, both in a narrow sense (its elites and cadres need to live) and a broader sense (the materializing of global corporate capital as a social force). The outcome is a new type of geography of centrality and space of power. It is different from earlier imperial structures in that it installs itself in multiple national territories and, in that regard, is not characterized by the types of interimperial rivalries of earlier periods. And, secondly, it constitutes itself institutionally—as distinct from geographically—partly outside the frame of national states and the interstate system. In this regard, my analysis signals the possibility of an empire not centered in a single dominant state. Here I would, then, diverge from much analysis that centers the new empire in the United States as the hegemonic power.

An emphasis on place and networks of places in a context of global processes makes possible a transnational economic and political opening for the formation of new claims and hence for the constitution of entitlements, notably rights to place. At the limit, this could be an opening for new forms of "citizenship." The city has indeed emerged as a site for new claims: by global capital, which uses the city as an "organizational commodity," but also by disadvantaged sectors of the urban population, frequently as much an internationalized presence in large cities as capital. The denationalizing of urban space and the formation of new claims by transnational actors raise the question: whose city is it? This is a type of political opening that contains unifying capacities across national boundaries for each of these transnational actors and sharpening conflicts within such boundaries among different transnational actors. Global capital and the new immigrant workforce are two major instances of transnationalized actors that each have unifying properties internally but find themselves in contestation with each other inside global cities. Global cities are the sites for the overvalorization of corporate capital and the devalorization of disadvantaged workers; but they are also the sites for new types of politics that allow the latter to emerge as political subjects.

## A New Geography of Centrality and Marginality

The new economic geography of centrality partly reproduces existing inequalities but also is the outcome of a dynamic specific to the current forms of economic growth. It assumes many forms and operates in many terrains, from the distribution of telecommunications facilities to the structure of the economy and of employment. The most powerful of these new geographies of centrality at the interurban level binds the major international financial and business centers: New York, London, Tokyo, Paris, Frankfurt, Zurich, Amsterdam, Los Angeles, Sydney, and Hong Kong, among others. But this geography now also includes cities such as Sao Paulo, Shanghai, Bombay, Bangkok, Taipei, and Mexico City. The intensity of transactions among these cities—particularly through the financial markets, transactions in services, and investment—has increased sharply, and so have the orders of magnitude involved. At the same time, there has been a sharpening inequality in the concentration of strategic resources and activities between each of these cities and others in the same country. The growth of global markets for finance and specialized services, the need for transnational servicing networks due to sharp increases in international investment, the reduced role of the government in the regulation of international economic activity, and the corresponding ascendance of other institutional arenas, notably global markets and corporate headquarters—all these point to the existence of transnational economic processes with multiple locations in more than one country. We can see here the formation, at least incipient, of a transnational urban system. These cities are not simply in a relation of competition to each other; they are part of emergent global divisions of labor (Sassen 2001, chapters 1, 5, and 7, 2006b; Taylor 2006; Yeung 2000).

Global cities are centers for the servicing and financing of international trade, investment, and headquarter operations. That is to say, the multiplicity of specialized activities present in global cities is crucial in the valorization—indeed, overvalorization—of leading sectors of capital today. And in this sense they are strategic production sites for today's leading economic sectors. This function is reflected in the ascendance of these activities in their economies. Whether at the global or regional level, urban centers—central cities, edge cities—are adequate and often the best production sites for such specialized services. When it comes to the production of services for the leading globalized sectors, the advantages of location in cities are particularly strong.

A focus on the work behind command functions, on the actual production process in the finance and services complex, and on global marketplaces has the effect of incorporating the material facilities underlying globalization and the whole infrastructure of jobs typically not marked as belonging to the corporate sector of the economy. An economic configuration very different from that suggested by the concept information economy emerges. We recover the material conditions, production sites, and place-boundedness that are also part of globalization and the information economy.

## The Less Visible Localizations of the Global

Cities make legible multiple localizations of a variety of globalization processes that are typically not coded as such in mainstream accounts. The global city is a strategic site for these instantiations of globalization in a double sense. Cities make some of these dynamics more legible than other types of spaces, such as suburbs and rural areas. Urban space enables the formation of many of these dynamics, and in this regard is productive space. Many of these less-legible localizations of globalization are embedded in the demographic transition evident in such cities, where a majority of resident workers are today immigrants and women, often women of color. For instance, Ehrenreich and Hochschild (2002) examine the formation of a global supply of maids and nannies in response to the new expanded demand for such workers in global cities (see also Parreñas 2001; Chang and Abramovitz 2000; Fernandez-Kelly, and Shefner 2005; Zlolniski 2006; Hagedorn 2006). These cities are seeing an expansion of low-wage jobs that do not the master images about globalization, yet are part of it. Their embeddedness in the demographic transition, evident in all these cities, and their consequent invisibility contribute to the devalorization of these types of workers and work cultures and to the "legitimacy" of that devalorization.

One of the localizations of the dynamics of globalization is the process of economic restructuring in global cities. The associated socioeconomic polarization has generated a large growth in the demand for low-wage workers and for jobs that offer few advancement possibilities. This is happening amid an explosion in the wealth and power concentrated in these cities—that is to say, in conditions where there is also a visible expansion in high-income jobs and high-priced urban space. Women and immigrants emerge as the labor supply that facilitates the imposition of low-wages and powerlessness under conditions of high demand for those workers and the location of those jobs in high-growth sectors. It breaks the historic nexus that would have led to empowering workers and legitimates this break culturally. Another localization that is rarely associated with globalization, informalization, reintroduces the community and the household as an important economic space in global cities. I see informalization in this setting as the low-cost (and often feminized) equivalent of deregulation at the top of the system. As with deregulation (e.g., as in financial deregulation), informalization introduces flexibility, reduces the "burdens" of regulation, and lowers costs, in this case especially the costs of labor.[1] Informalization in major cities of highly developed countries—whether New York, London, Paris, or Berlin—can be seen as a downgrading of a variety of activities for which there is an effective demand in these cities, but also as a devaluing and enormous competition, given low entry costs and few alternative forms of employment. Going informal is one way of producing and distributing goods and services at a lower cost and with greater flexibility. This further devalues these types of activities. Immigrants and women are important actors in the new informal economies of these cities. They absorb the costs of informalizing these activities. (See Sassen 1998, chapter 8, 2006b, chapters 6 and 7.) The restructuring of the labor market brings with it a shift of labor-market functions to the household or community. Women and households emerge as sites that should be part of the theorization of the particular forms that these elements in labor-market dynamics assume today.

## A Politics of Places on Global Circuits: The Local as Multiscalar

These localizations of the global can, in some cases, actually be constituted at multiple scales. This can be examined through the case of political practices among mostly resource-poor organizations and individuals who are shaping a specific type of global politics, one that runs through localities and is not predicated on the existence of global institutions. Because a network is global does not mean that it all happens at the global level. Yet there are two specific matters that signal the need for empirical and theoretical work on this dimension. One is that much of the conceptualization of the local in the social sciences has emphasized physical and geographic proximity and thereby a sharply defined territorial boundedness and, usually, closure. The other, partly a consequence of the first, is a strong tendency to conceive of the local as part of a hierarchy of nested scales. To a very large extent these conceptualizations probably express the actual practices and formations likely to constitute most of the local in most of the world. But there are also conditions today that contribute to destabilize these practices and formations and hence invite a reconceptualization of the local, even if it pertains to only a limited range of its features and of its instantiations.

Key among these current conditions are globalization and globality as constitutive not only of cross-border institutional spaces but also of powerful imaginaries enabling aspirations to transboundary political practice. Also important are new computer-centered interactive technologies that facilitate multiscalar transactions. All of this allows local actors to participate in a new type of cross-border politics, one centered in multiple localities yet intensely connected digitally. Adams (1996), among others, shows us how telecommunications create new linkages across space that underline the importance of networks of relations and partly bypass older hierarchies of scale. Activists can develop networks for circulating place-based information (about environmental, housing, political issues, etc.) that can become part of political work and strategies addressing a global condition—the environment, growing poverty and unemployment worldwide, lack of accountability among multinationals, and so on.

This is a particular phase in the development of these networks, one when powerful corporate actors and high-performance networks are strengthening the role of private digital space and altering the structure of public-access digital space (Sassen 2002). Digital space has emerged not simply as a means for communicating, but as a major new theater for capital accumulation and the operations of global capital. But civil society—in all its various incarnations—is also an increasingly energetic presence in cyberspace. (For a variety of angles, see, for example, Rimmer and Morris-Suzuki 1999; Poster 1997; Miller and Slater 2000; Aneesh 2006; Sassen 2006a, chapter 7.) The greater the diversity of cultures and groups, the better for this larger political and civic potential of the Internet, and the more effective the resistance to the risk that the corporate world might set the standards. The issue here is not so much the possibility of such political practices; they have long existed even though with other mediums and with other velocities. The issue is rather one of orders of magnitude, scope, and simultaneity. The technologies, the institutions, and the imaginaries that mark the current global digital context inscribe local political practice with new meanings and new potentialities.

Further, an important feature of this type of multiscalar politics of the local is that it is not confined to moving through a set of nested scales from the local to the national to the international, but can directly access other such local actors whether in the same country or across borders. This possibility does not preclude the fact that powerful actors can use the existence of different jurisdictional scales to their advantage (Morrill 1999) and the fact that local resistance is constrained by how the state deploys scaling through jurisdictional, administrative, and regulatory orders (Judd 1998). On the contrary, it might well be that the conditions analyzed, among others, by Morrill and Judd force the issue, so to speak. Why work through the power relations shaped into state-centered hierarchies of scale? Why not jump ship if this is an option? This combination of conditions and options is well illustrated by research showing how the power of the national government can subvert the legal claims of First Nation people (Howitt 1998), which has in turn led the latter increasingly to seek direct representation in international fora, bypassing the national state (Sassen 2006, part 3).[2]

In this sense, then, my effort here is to recover a particular type of multiscalar context, one characterized by direct local–global transactions or by a multiplication of local transactions as part of global networks. Neither type is marked by nested scalings.

There are many examples of such types of cross-border political work. We can distinguish two forms of it, each capturing a specific type of scalar interaction. In one, the scale of struggle remains the locality, and the object is to engage local actors—for example, a local housing or environmental agency—but with the knowledge and explicit or tacit invocation of multiple other localities around the world engaged in similar localized struggles with similar local actors. It is this combination of multiplication and self-reflexivity that contributes to constitute a global condition out of these localized practices and rhetorics. It means, in a sense, taking Cox's notion of scaled "spaces of engagement" constitutive of local politics and situating it in a specific type of context, not necessarily the one Cox himself might have had in mind. Beyond the fact of relations between scales as crucial to local politics, it is perhaps the social and political construction itself of scale as social action (Howitt 1993; Swyngedouw 1997; Brenner and Keil 2005) that needs emphasizing.

The second form of multiscalar interaction is one where localized struggles are aiming at engaging global actors (e.g., WTO or multinational firms), either at the global scale or in multiple localities. Local initiatives can become part of a global network of activism without losing the focus on specific local struggles (e.g., Cleaver 1998; Espinoza 1999; Ronfeldt et al. 1998; Mele 1999; Sassen 2006a, chapters 7 and 8).[3] This is one of the key forms of critical politics that the Internet can make possible—a politics of the local with a big difference: these are localities that are connected with each other across a region, a country, or the world. From struggles around human rights and the environment to workers' strikes and AIDS campaigns against the pharmaceuticals, the Internet has emerged as a powerful medium for nonelites to communicate, support each other's struggles, and create the equivalent of insider groups at scales going from the local to the global. The possibility of doing so transnationally at a time when a growing set of issues are seen as escaping the bounds of nation-states makes this even more significant.


## CONCLUSION

Let me conclude by emphasizing the political dimensions of this type of critical mapping of spaces and actors of globalization. An emphasis on cities and places on global networks makes visible the multiple scales of the global and the work of constructing the geographical scales at which social or political action can occur. Cyberspace can be a more concrete space for social struggles than that of the national formal political system. It can become a place where nonformal political actors become part of the political scene in a way that is much more difficult in national institutional channels. Nationally, politics needs to run through existing formal systems, whether the electoral political system or the judiciary (taking state agencies to court). Nonformal political actors are rendered invisible in the space of national politics. The city, especially the global city, also is a more concrete space for politics. In many ways, the claim-making politics evident today in cyberspace resonates with many of the activisms proliferating in large cities: struggles against police brutality and gentrification, struggles for the rights of the homeless and immigrants, struggles for the rights of gays and lesbians. Much of this becomes visible on the street. Much of urban politics is concrete, enacted by people rather than dependent on mass media technologies. Street-level politics makes possible the formation of new types of derogatory political subjects that do not have to go through the formal political system in order to practice their politics. Individuals and groups that have historically been excluded from formal political systems, and whose struggles can be partly enacted outside those systems, can find in cyberspace and in cities an enabling environment both for their emergence as nonformal political actors and for their struggles.

The types of political practice discussed here are not the cosmopolitan route to the global. They are global through the knowing multiplication of local practices. These are types of sociability and struggle deeply embedded in people's actions and activities. They are also forms of institution-building work with global scope that can come from localities and networks of localities with limited resources and from informal social actors. We see here the potential transformation of actors "confined" to domestic roles into actors in global networks, without having to leave their work and roles in their communities. From being experienced as purely domestic and local, these "domestic" settings are transformed into microenvironments located on global circuits. They do not need to become cosmopolitan in this process; they may well remain domestic and particularistic in their orientation and remain engaged with their households and local community struggles, and yet they are participating in emergent global politics. A community of practice can emerge that creates multiple lateral, horizontal communications, collaborations, solidarities, and supports.

## NOTES

1. For a broader treatment of the informal economy, including a focus on its reemergence with the end of the so-called *Pax Americana*, see Tabak and Crichlow (2000). For an in-depth examination of how globalization has reorganized the informal economy in the global South, see Beneria and Roldan (1987) and Buechler (2007).
2. Though with other objectives in mind, a similar mix of conditions can also partly explain the growth of transnational economic and political support networks among immigrants (e.g., Smith 2006; Cordero-Guzmán et al. 2001; Gzesh and Espinoza 2002).
3. One might distinguish a third type of political practice along these lines, one which turns a single event into a global media event, which then in turn serves to mobilize individuals and organizations around the world—either or both in support of that initial action—or around similar such occurrences elsewhere. Among the most powerful of these actions, and now emblematic of this type of politics, are the Zapatistas' initial, and several subsequent, actions. The possibility of a single human rights abuse case becoming a global media event has been a powerful tool for human rights activists.

## WORKS CITED

Adams, Paul C. 1996. "Protest and the Scale Politics of Telecommunications." *Political Geography* 15: 419–41.

Aneesh, A. 2006. *Virtual Migration: The Programming of Globalization*. Durham, N.C.: Duke University Press.

Bada, Xochitl, Jonathan Fox, and Andrew Selee. 2006. *Invisible No More: Mexican Migrant Civic Participation in the United States*. Washington D.C. The Woodrow Wilson International Center for Scholars.

Barlow, Andrew L. 2003. *Between Fear and Hope: Globalization and Race in the United States*. Lanham, Md.: Rowman & Littlefield.

Beck, Ulrich. 2001. "The Cosmopolitan Society and Its Enemies." In *New Horizons in Sociological Theory and Research: The Frontiers of Sociology at the Beginning of the 21st Century*, ed. Luigi Tomasi, 181–202. Aldershot, UK: Ashgate.

Beneria, Lourdes, and Marta Roldan. 1987. *Crossroads of Class and Gender: Homework, Subcontracting, and Household Dynamics in Mexico City*. Chicago: University of Chicago Press.

Brenner, Neil. 1998. "Global Cities, Glocal States: Global City Formation and State Territorial Restructuring in Contemporary Europe." *Review of International Political Economy* 5: 1–37.

Brenner, Neil, and Roger Keil. 2005. *The Global Cities Reader*. New York: Routledge.

Bryson, J. R., and P. W. Daniels, eds. 2006. *The Service Industries Handbook*. Cheltenham, UK: Edward Elgar.

Buechler, Simone. 2007. "Deciphering the Local in a Global Neoliberal Age: Three Favelas in Sao Paulo, Brazil." In *Deciphering the Global: Its Scales, Spaces, and Subjects*, ed. Saskia Sassen, 95–112. New York: Routledge.

Chang, Grace, and Mimi Abramovitz. 2000. *Disposable Domestics: Immigrant Women Workers in the Global Economy*. Boston: South End Press.

Chase-Dunn, Christopher, and Barry Gills. 2005. "Waves of Globalization and Resistance in the Capitalist World System: Social Movements and Critical Global Studies." In *Towards a Critical Globalization Studies*, eds. Richard Appelbaum and William Robinson, 45–54. New York: Routledge.

Cleaver, Harry. 1998. "The Zapatista Effect: The Internet and the Rise of an Alternative Political Fabric." *Journal of International Affairs* 51: 621–40.

Cordero-Guzmán, Héctor R., Ramón Grosfoguel, and Robert C. Smith, eds. 2001. *Migration, Transnationalism, and Race in a Changing New York*. Philadelphia, Pa.: Temple University Press.

Datz, Giselle. 2007. "Global-National Interactions and Sovereign Debt-Restructuring Outcomes." In *Deciphering the Global: Its Spaces, Scales, and Subjects*, ed. Saskia Sassen, 321–50. New York: Routledge.

Eade, John, ed. 1996. *Living the Global City: Globalization as a Local Process*. London: Routledge.

Ehrenreich, Barbara, and A. R. Hochschild. 2002. *Global Women: Nannies, Maids, and Sex Workers in the New Economy*. New York: Metropolitan Books.

Espinoza, V. 1999. "Social Networks among the Poor: Inequality and Integration in a Latin American City." In *Networks in the Global Village: Life in Contemporary Communities*, ed. Barry Wellman, 147–184. Boulder, Colo.: Westview Press.

Fernandez-Kelly M. P., and J. Shefner. 2005. *Out of the Shadows*. College Station: Penn State University Press.

GaWC. (ongoing). *Globalization and World Cities-Study Group and Network*. Available at: *www.lboro.ac.uk/gawc/*.

Gzesh, S., and R. Espinoza. 2002. "Immigrant Communities Building Cross-Border Civic Networks: The Federation of Michoacan Clubs in Illinois." In *Global Civil Society Yearbook 2002*, eds. Helmut K. Anheier, Marlies Glasius, and Mary Kaldor, 226–27. Oxford: Oxford University Press.

Hagedorn, John, ed. 2006. *Gangs in the Global City: Exploring Alternatives to Traditional Criminology*. Chicago: University of Illinois Press.

Hindman, Heather. 2007. "Outsourcing Difference: Expatriate Training and the Disciplining of Culture." In *Deciphering the Global: Its scales, Spaces, and Subjects*, ed. Saskia Sassen, 153–76. New York: Routledge.

Howitt, Richard. 1993. " 'A World in a Grain of Sand': Towards a Reconceptualisation of Geographical Scale." *The Australian Geographer* 24: 33–44.

———. 1998. "Recognition, Respect, and Reconciliation: Steps towards Decolonisation?" *Australian Aboriginal Studies*1: 28–34.

Iyotani, Toshio, Naoki Sakai, and Brett de Bary, eds. 2005. *Deconstructing Nationality*. Ithaca, N.Y.: Cornell University East Asia Program.

Judd, Denis R. 1998. "The Case of the Missing Scales: A Commentary on Cox." *Political Geography* 17, no. 1: 29–34.

King, A. D., ed. 1996. *Re-Presenting the City: Ethnicity, Capital, and Culture in the 21st Century*. London: Macmillan.

Kirsch, Max, ed. 2006. *Inclusion and Exclusion in the Global Arena*. New York: Routledge.

Knox, P. L., and P. J. Taylor, eds. 1995. *World Cities in a World-System*. Cambridge: Cambridge University Press.

Low, Setha M. 1999. "Theorizing the City." In *Theorizing the City*, ed. S. Low, 1–33. New Brunswick, N.J.: Rutgers University Press.

Lucas, Linda, ed. 2005. *Unpacking Globalisation: Markets, Gender, and Work*. Kampala, Uganda: Makerere University Press.

Marcuse, Peter, and Ronald van Kempen. 2000. *Globalizing Cities. A New Spatial Order*. Oxford: Blackwell.

Mele, Christopher. 1999. "Cyberspace and Disadvantaged Communities: The Internet as a Tool for Collective Action." In *Communities in Cyberspace*, eds. Marc A. Smith and Peter Kollock, 290–310. London: Routledge.

Miller, Daniel, and Don Slater. 2000. *The Internet: An Ethnographic Approach*. Oxford: Berg.

Morrill, Richard. 1999. "Inequalities of Power, Costs, and Benefits across Geographic Scales: The Future Uses of the Hanford Reservation." *Political Geography* 18: 1–23.

Orum, Anthony M., and Xiangming Chen. 2002. *Urban Places*. Malden, Mass.: Blackwell.

Parnreiter, Christof. 2002. "Mexico: The Making of a Global City." In *GlobalNetworks/Linked Cities*, ed. Saskia Sassen, 145–82. New York: Routledge.

Parreñas, Rhacel Salazar. 2001. *Servants of Globalization: Women, Migration, and Domestic Work*. Stanford, Calif.: Stanford University Press.

Poster, Mark. 1997. "Cyberdemocracy: Internet and the Public Sphere." In *Internet Culture*, ed. D. Porter, 201–18. London: Routledge.

Ribas-Matteos, Natalia. 2005. *The Mediterranean in the Age of Globalization: Migration, Welfare, and Borders*. Somerset, N.J.: Transaction.

Rimmer, P. J., and T. Morris-Suzuki. 1999. "The Japanese Internet: Visionaries and Virtual Democracy." *Environment and Planning* 31: 1189–1206.

Ronfeldt, David, John Arquilla, Graham Fuller, and Melissa Fuller. 1998. *The Zapatista "Social Netwar" in Mexico*. Santa Monica, Calif.: Rand.

Samers, Michael. 2002 "Immigration and the Global City Hypothesis: Towards an Alternative Research Agenda." *International Journal of Urban and Regional Research* 26, no. 2: 389–402.

Sassen, Saskia. 1998. *Globalization and Its Discontents: Essays on the Mobility of People and Money*. New York: New Press.

———. 2001. *The Global City*, 2nd ed. Princeton: Princeton University Press.

———. 2002. "Towards a Sociology of Information Technology." *Current Sociology, Special Issue: Sociology and Technology* 50, no. 3: 365–88.

———. 2006a. *Territory, Authority, Rights: From Medieval to Global Assemblages*. Princeton, N.J.: Princeton University Press.

———. 2006b. *Cities in a World Economy*, 3rd ed. Thousand Oaks, Calif.: Pine Forge Press.

———. 2007. *A Sociology of Globalization*. New York: W. W. Norton.

Smith, Robert C. 2006. *Mexican New York: Transnational Worlds of New Immigrants*. Berkeley, CA: University of California Press.

Swyngedouw, Erik. 1997. "Neither Global nor Local: 'Glocalization' and the Politics of Scale." In *Spaces of Globalization: Reasserting the Power of the Local*, ed. Kevin R. Cox, 137–66. New York: Guilford.

Tabak, Faruk, and Michaeline A. Crichlow. 2000. *Informalization: Process and Structure*. Baltimore: Johns Hopkins University Press.

Tardanico, Richard, and Mario Lungo. 1995. "Local Dimensions of Global Restructuring in Urban Costa Rica." *International Journal of Urban and Regional Research* 19, no. 2: 223–49.

———. "World Cities and Territorial States under Conditions of Contemporary Globalization." *Political Geography* 19, no. 1: 5–32.

Taylor, Peter J. 2006. *Cities in Globalization: Practices, Policies, and Theories*. London: Routledge.

Yeung, Yue-man. 2000. *Globalization and Networked Societies: Urban-Regional Change in Pacific Asia*. Honolulu: University of Hawaii Press.

Zlolniski, Christian. 2006. *Janitors, Street Vendors, and Activists: The Lives of Mexican Immigrants in Silicon Valley*. Berkeley: University of California Press.

# 5

# WORLD-SYSTEM ANALYSIS AND POSTCOLONIAL STUDIES: A CALL FOR A DIALOGUE FROM THE "COLONIALITY OF POWER" APPROACH

*Ramón Grosfoguel*

This chapter attempts to clarify some of the concepts and intellectual projects implied in the emerging critical dialogue between world-system approach and postcolonial critique. It provides an alternative reading of the "modern world-system" (Wallerstein 1974, 1979, 1991b) or, as Walter Mignolo has recently proposed, the "modern/colonial world-system" (Mignolo 2000). By "situating" or "geopolitically locating" knowledge production from the "colonial difference" of the North-South divide, I attempt to reinterpret important aspects of the capitalist world-system. I situate my knowledge production not in representation of, but from the subaltern experiences of, people in the South. Thus, I aim to show how a world-system approach provides an important conceptual framework to rethink the modern/colonial world, whereas an epistemic perspective from the subaltern side of the colonial difference contributes to counter certain limitations of the world-system approach. The first part of the paper is about "coloniality of power" and "symbolic capital," two crucial concepts that force us to rethink global capitalism. The second part discusses the geopolitcs of knowledge and the imaginary of the modern/colonial world-system. The third part is a call for a critical dialogue between two literatures: postcolonial critique and the world-system approach.

## "COLONIALITY OF POWER" AND "SYMBOLIC CAPITAL"

It might seem anachronistic to talk about colonies and colonialism today. However, a world-system approach from the perspective of the colonial difference offers a unique opportunity to reinterpret the modern world and to question the "common sense" assumption that the world has been "decolonized." I intend to rethink the modern/colonial world-system from the multiple locations and experiences of people from the South that reveal the limitations of the so-called decolonization of the modern world, both in terms of the global political-economy and the dominant geocultural imaginary. "Independent" republics in the periphery live the crude exploitation of the capitalist world-system. Moreover, migrants from the South experience the effects of racism in the metropoles as a hegemonic imaginary of the modern/colonial world-system. Colonial migrant experience illustrates how racial/colonial ideologies have not been eradicated from metropolitan centers, which remain in grave need of a sociocultural decolonization. In sum, thinking from the "colonial difference" highlights global processes that the world-system approach does not emphasize, such as "global symbolic/ideological strategies" (Grosfoguel 1994) and "global coloniality" (Quijano 1993).

It is impossible to understand today's global political-economy without taking into account the United States' global geopolitical symbolic/ideological strategies and its colonial/racist social imaginary. The manufacturing of Cold War "symbolic showcases" was crucial to sell the United States' developmentalist policies to the periphery of the world-economy in opposition to the Soviet model. The world-system approach's use of the notion of "geoculture" to address "global ideologies" is, however, insufficient to grasp such "showcase" strategies in the world-system. Pierre Bourdieu's concept of "symbolic capital" and Aníbal Quijano's notion of "coloniality of power" can, I believe, redress these limitations. Although Bourdieu developed the concept of symbolic capital for national and micro social analysis, it is a powerful tool to conceptualize the symbolic strategies involved in manufacturing "showcases" on a global scale. The United States developed different global symbolic/ideological strategies during the Cold War to showcase a peripheral region or an ethnic group as opposed to a challenging peripheral country in order to gain symbolic capital for its developmentalist model. These strategies are material and constitutive of global political-economic processes. They are economically expensive because they entail the investment of capital in nonprofitable forms such as credits, aid, and assistance programs. Nevertheless, the symbolic profits that accrue from such investments translate into economic profits in the long run.

The second concept I would like to discuss is the concept of coloniality developed by Peruvian Sociologist Aníbal Quijano to account for the entangled and mutually constitutive relations between the international division of labor, the global racial/ethnic hierarchy and the hegemonic Eurocentric epistemologies in the modern/colonial world-system. Although "colonial administrations" have been almost entirely eradicated and the majority of the periphery is politically organized into nation-states, non-European people are still living under crude Euro-American exploitation and domination. Coloniality on a world scale, with the United States having undisputed hegemony over non-European people, character-izes the globalization of the capitalist world economy today. The old colonial hierarchies of European/non-Europeans remain in place and are entangled with the "international division of labor". Herein lies the relevance of the distinction between colonialism and coloniality. Coloniality refers to the continuity of colonial forms of domination after the end of colo-nial administrations produced by colonial cultures and structures in the modern/colonial world-system. "Coloniality of power" refers to a crucial structuring process in the modern/colonial world-system that articulates peripheral locations into the international division of labor and inscribes third world migrants into the racial/ethnic hierarchy of met-ropolitan global cities.

Peripheral nation-states thus live today under the regime of global coloniality imposed by the United States through the International Monetary Fund (IMF), the World Bank (WB), the Pentagon, and NATO. This phenomenon cannot be understood from either a nationalist or a colonialist perspective that assumes automatic decolonization after the formation of a nation-state or from an approach that privileges the nation-state as the unit of analysis. Peripheral zones remain in a colonial situation even though they are no longer under a colonial administration. A colonial situation of exploitation and domina-tion, formed by centuries of European colonialism can and does persist in the present without the existence or the presence of a "colonial administration." I therefore use the word *colonialism* to refer to colonial situations enforced by the presence of a colonial administration such as the period of classical colonialism, and, following Quijano (1991, 1993, 1998), I use *coloniality* to address colonial situations in the present period in which colonial administrations have almost been eradicated from the capitalist world-system.

By *colonial situations* I mean the cultural, political, and economic oppression of subordinate racialized/ethnic groups by dominant racial/ethnic groups with or without the existence of colonial administrations.

It is crucial to point out that coloniality in the contemporary world-system stems from the long history of European colonialism that preceded it. Five hundred years of European colonial expansion and domination formed an international division of labor between Europeans and non-Europeans that is reproduced in the present so-called postcolonial phase of the capitalist world-system (Wallerstein 1979, 1995). Today the core zones of the capitalist world-economy overlap with predominantly white/European/Euro-American societies such as Western Europe, Canada, Australia, and the United States, whereas peripheral zones overlap with previously colonized non-European people. Japan is the only exception that confirms the rule. Japan was never colonized nor dominated by Europeans and, similar to the West, played an active role in building its own colonial empire. China, although never fully colonized, was peripheralized through the use of colonial entrepôts such as Hong Kong and Macao, and through direct military interventions.

My conceptualization here goes against the grain of commonly held assumptions. The social sciences and the humanities produce knowledge that is predominantly focused and oriented towards the nation-state as the unit of analysis (Wallerstein 1991b). The dominant assumption is that nation-states are independent units and the main explanation for global inequalities is accounted for by the internal dynamics of each nation-state. Although in the past decade, ongoing scholarship on globalization has challenged this assumption, none of this literature (Robertson 1992; Mittelman 1997; Sassen 1998) has adequately addressed the continued coloniality of formally independent states. The dominant representations of the world today assume that colonial situations ceased to exist after the demise of colonial administrations. This mythology about the so-called decolonization of the world obscures the continuities between the colonial past and current global colonial/racial hierarchies and contributes to the invisibility of coloniality today. For the past fifty years, states that had been colonies, following the dominant Eurocentric liberal discourses (Wallerstein 1991b, 1995), constructed ideologies of "national identity," "national development," and "national sovereignty" that produced an illusion of "independence," "development," and "progress." Yet their economic and political systems were shaped by their subordinate position in a capitalist world-system organized around a hierarchical international division of labor (Wallerstein 1979, 1984, 1995). The multiple and heterogeneous processes of the world-system, together with the predominance of Eurocentric cultures (Said 1979; Wallerstein 1991a, 1995; Lander 1998; Quijano 1998; Mignolo 2000), constitute a global coloniality between Europeans/ Euro-Americans and non-Europeans.

Thus, coloniality is entangled with, but is not reducible to, the international division of labor. The colonial axis between Europeans/Euro-Americans and non-Europeans is inscribed not only in relations of exploitation (between capital and labor) and relations of domination (between metropolitan and peripheral states) but also in the production of subjectivities and knowledges.

## GEOPOLITICS OF KNOWLEDGE AND THE IMAGINARY OF THE MODERN/COLONIAL WORLD

It is important as scholars to recognize that we always speak from a specific location in the gender, class, racial, and sexual hierarchies of a particular region in the modern/colonial world-system. Our knowledges, as the feminist thinker Donna Haraway (1988) contends, are always already "situated," but I will add, following Quijano (1993) and Mignolo (2000), that they are situated within the axis of the colonial difference produced by the coloniality of power in the modern/colonial world-system. The Western/masculinist idea that we can produce knowledges that are unpositioned, unlocated, neutral, and universalistic is one of the most pervasive mythologies in the modern/colonial world. Universal/global designs are always already situated in local histories (Mignolo 2000). Those in power positions in the European/Euro-American versus non-European hierarchy of the modern/colonial world often think in terms of global designs or universalistic knowledges to control and dominate colonized/racialized/subordinated peoples in the capitalist world-system. To speak from the subaltern side of the colonial difference is to look at the world from angles and points of view critical of hegemonic perspectives. This requires an effort on our part. "Border thinking" or "border epistemology" are the terms used by Walter Mignolo (2000), inspired by the work of Chicana and Chicano scholars such as Gloria Anzaldúa (1987), Norma Alarcón (1983), and José David Saldívar (1997), to refer to this in-between location of subaltern knowledges, critical of both imperial global designs (global coloniality) and anticolonial nationalist strategies (internal coloniality).

Mignolo's concept of colonial difference (Mignolo 2000) is epistemologically crucial here to overcome the paternalistic and elitist limits of both nationalist and colonialist discourses. The question to ask ourselves is: from which location in the colonial divide are knowledges produced? Nationalist and colonialist discourses are thinking from a power position in the colonial divide of the modern/colonial world, whereas subaltern subjects are thinking from the subordinate side of the colonial difference. Colonialist discourses reproduce the North-South global colonial divide, whereas nationalist discourses reproduce an "internal" colonial divide within national formations. The knowledge, critical insights, and political strategies produced from the subaltern side of the colonial difference serve as points of departure to move beyond both colonialist and nationalist discourses.

The point here is that we live in a world where the dominant imaginary is still colonial and founded on a very intricate and uneven set of narratives with long histories that are re-enacted in the present through complex mediations. Postcolonial literatures have contributed greatly to the critique of these narratives as they are produced and reproduced in the constitution of one group's superiority over an-Other. The process of "Othering" people has operated through a set of narrative oppositions such as the West and the Rest, civilized and savage, intelligent and stupid, hard worker and lazy, superior and inferior, masculine and feminine (sexual and racist narratives have been entangled to racist discourses), pure and impure, clean and dirty, and so on. There are world-systemic historical/structural processes that constituted these narratives that I can only simplify and schematically designate here, namely, the relationship between European modernity (e.g., citizenship, nation building, democracy, civil/social rights), European colonial expansion, colonial modernities, and white/masculinist supremacy.

The capitalist world-system was formed by the Spanish/Portuguese expansion to the Americas in the long sixteenth century (Wallerstein 1974; Quijano and Wallerstein 1992; Mignolo 1995, 2000). This first modernity (from 1492 to 1650) built the foundations of the racist/colonial culture and global capitalist system we are living today. Simultaneous to its expansion to the Americas in 1492, the Spanish Empire expelled Arabs and Jews from their land in the name of "blood purity" ("pureza de la sangre"). This "internal border" against Arabs and Jews was built simultaneously to the "external border" against people from peripheral geographical zones (Mignolo 2000). The Spanish and Portuguese expansion to the Americas constructed the racial categories that would be later generalized to the rest of the world. Nobody defined themselves as blacks in Africa, whites in Europe, or Indians in the Americas before the European expansion to the Americas. All of these categories were invented as part of the European colonization of the Americas (Quijano and Wallerstein 1992).

The formation of the international division of labor occurred simultaneously to the formation of a global racial/ethnic hierarchy. As Quijano states, there was neither "pre" nor "post" to their joint constitution. This is why Mignolo (2000) states that "Occidentalism" (the dominant discourse of the first modernity) is the sociohistorical condition of possibility for the emergence of Orientalism (the dominant discourse of the second modernity). Christianity was central to the constitution of the colonial imaginary of the world-system.

During the second modernity (1650 to 1945), the core of the world-system shifted from Spain and Portugal to Germany, The Netherlands, England, and France. The emergence of northwestern Europe as the core of the capitalist world-system continued, expanded, and deepened the "internal imaginary border" (against Jews, Arabs, and Gypsies) and the "external imaginary border" built during the first modernity (against the Americas and later expanded to include other geographical zones such as Africa, the Middle East, and Asia). The second modernity added a new border between northwestern Europeans and Iberian peoples to the old racial/colonial hierarchies. Hispanic/Latin southern European cultures were constructed as inferior to the northwestern Europeans. This hierarchical division within Europe would be extended to North America and be reenacted in the context of the U.S. imperial expansions of 1848 (Mexican-American War) and 1898 (Spanish-American War). The U.S. colonization of northern Mexico, Cuba, and Puerto Rico formed part of the white Anglo hegemony in the nineteenth-century colonial expansions of the second modernity. Hispanic cultures were subalternized and the notion of "whiteness" acquired different and new meanings. In the context of the U.S. colonial expansion, white Spaniards were expelled from the notion of "whiteness." "Hispanics" were constructed as part of the inferior others excluded from the superior "white, European" races. To make matters even more complicated, the U.S. notion of whiteness expanded to include groups that were internal colonial subjects of Europe under northwestern European hegemony (e.g., Irish, eastern Europeans, Italians, and Jews). At the time, European Orientalist discourses were also being articulated in relation to the colonized populations of Asia, Africa, and the Middle East. The history of the second modernity is crucial to understand both the present racialization of Puerto Ricans, Mexicans, and Latinos of all colors in the United States and the hegemony of Anglo-white-Americans. The Indian Wars in the late nineteenth century were part of this colonial expansion, although not recognized as such by mainstream historians and social scientists. The hegemonic white/black divide does not exhaust the multiple racisms deployed and developed in U.S. colonial expansion and colonial regimes. Given the social construction of race, whiteness is not merely about skin color. There are other markers that racialize people located on the "wrong side" of the colonial difference (e.g., accent, language, and demeanor).

The capitalist world-system expanded to cover the whole planet during the second modernity (Wallerstein 1979). European (understood here not merely in geographic terms, but in the broader cultural and political sense of white European supremacy) and Euro-American processes of nation building, struggles for citizenship rights, and development of parliamentary regimes were inscribed in a global colonial/racist imaginary that established internal and external borders (Quijano 1993; Mignolo 2000). The invisibility of global coloniality in the process of building modern nation-states in nineteenth-century Europe and the Americas shows how powerful and ingrained its colonial/racist culture was and still is. Although categories of modernity such as citizenship, democracy, and nation building were acknowledged for the dominant northwestern Europeans, the colonial "others" were submitted to coerced forms of labor and authoritarian political regimes in the periphery and semiperiphery. The Latin American periphery is no exception. White Creole elites continued to dominate the power relations of the newly independent republics of South and Central America in the nineteenth century. Latin American independence, achieved in struggles against Spain and Portugal, was hegemonized by Euro-American elites. It was not a process of social, political, cultural, or economic decolonization. Blacks, mulattos, Native Americans, and people of color remained in subordinated and disenfranchised positions in the coloniality of power constitutive of the emerging nation-states. Colonialism gave way to coloniality, that is, independence without decolonization. The myth that we live in a decolonized world needs to be challenged. This has crucial political implications in terms of how we conceive social change, struggles against inequality, scientific disciplines, knowledge production, utopian thinking, democracy, and decolonization.

## Postcoloniality and World-Systems: A Call for a Dialogue

Rethinking the modern/colonial world from the colonial difference modifies important assumptions of our paradigms. Here I would like to focus specifically on the implication of the coloniality of power perspective for the world-system and postcolonial paradigms. Most world-system analyses focus on how the international division of labor and the geopolitical military struggles are constitutive of capitalist accumulation processes on a world scale. Although this approach offers a useful point of departure, thinking from the colonial difference forces us to take more seriously ideological/symbolic strategies as well as the colonial/racist culture of the modern/colonial world. For instance, world-system analysis has recently developed the concept of geoculture to refer to global ideologies. However, the use of *geoculture* in the world-system approach is framed within the infrastructure-superstructure Marxist paradigm. Contrary to this conceptualization, I take global ideological/symbolic strategies and colonial/racist culture as constitutive, together with capitalist accumulation processes and the interstate system, of the core-periphery relationships on a world scale. These different structures and processes form a hierarchy (Kontopoulos 1993) of heterogeneous, complex, and entangled hierarchies that cannot be accounted for in the infrastructure/superstructure paradigm.

Postcolonialism shares with the world-system approach a critique of developmentalism, of Eurocentric forms of knowledge, of gender inequalities, of racial hierarchies, and of the cultural/ideological processes that foster the subordination of the periphery in the capitalist world-system. However, the critical insights of both approaches emphasize different determinants. Whereas postcolonial critiques emphasize colonial culture, the world-system approach emphasizes the endless accumulation of capital on a world-scale. Whereas postcolonial critiques emphasize agency, the world-system approach emphasizes structures. Some scholars of the postcolonial theory, such as Gayatri Spivak (1988), acknowledge the importance of the international division of labor as constitutive of the capitalist system, whereas some scholars of the world-system approach, such as Immanuel Wallerstein (1974, 1984, 1991a), acknowledge the importance of cultural processes such as racism and sexism as inherent to historical capitalism. However, the two camps in general are still divided over the culture versus economy and the agency versus structure binary oppositions. This is partly inherited from the two cultures that divide the sciences from the humanities, premised upon the Cartesian dualism of mind over matter.

With very few exceptions, most postcolonial theorists come from fields of the humanities such as literature, rhetoric, and cultural studies. Only a small number of scholars in the field of postcolonial studies come from the social sciences, in particular from anthropology. On the other hand, world-system scholars are mainly from disciplines in the social sciences such as sociology, anthropology, political sciences, and economics. Very few come from the humanities, with the exception of historians [seems curious to place historians in the humanities camp?] who tend to have more affinities with the world-system approach, and almost none come from literature. I have emphasized the disciplines that predominate in world-system approaches and postcolonial studies because I think that these disciplinary boundaries are constitutive of some of the theoretical differences between the two approaches.

Postcolonial critics characterize the capitalist system as a cultural system. They believe that culture is the constitutive element that determines economic and political relations in global capitalism (Said 1979). On the other hand, most world-system scholars emphasize economic relations as constitutive of the capitalist world-system. Cultural and political relations are conceptualized as instrumental to, or epiphenomenon of, the capitalist accumulation processes. The fact is that world-system theorists have difficulties theorizing culture and postcolonial theorists have difficulties conceptualizing political-economic processes. The paradox is that many world-system scholars acknowledge the importance of culture but do not know what to do with it or how to articulate it in a nonreductive way; whereas many postcolonial scholars acknowledge the importance of political economy but do not know how to integrate it to cultural analysis. Thus, both literatures fluctuate between the danger of economic reductionism and the danger of culturalism.

I propose that the culture versus economy dichotomy is a "chicken-egg" dilemma, or a false dilemma, that comes from what Immanuel Wallerstein has called the legacy of nineteenth-century liberalism (Wallerstein 1991b, 4). This legacy implies the division of the economic, political, cultural, and social as autonomous arenas. According to Wallerstein, the construction of these "autonomous" arenas and their materialization in separate knowledge domains such as political science, sociology, anthropology, and economics in the social sciences as well as the different disciplines in the humanities are a pernicious result of liberalism as a geoculture of the modern world-system. In a critical appraisal of world-system analysis, Wallerstein states that:

> World-system analysis intends to be a critique of nineteenth-century social science. But it is an incomplete, unfinished critique. It still has not been able to find a way to surmount the most enduring (and misleading) legacy of nineteenth-century social science—the division of social analysis into three arenas, three logics, three levels— the economic, the political and the socio-cultural. This trinity stands in the middle of the road, in granite, blocking our intellectual advance. Many find it unsatisfying, but in my view no one has yet found the way to dispense with the language and its implications, some of which are correct but most of which are probably not. (1991b, 4)

> [A]ll of us fall back on using the language of the three arenas in almost everything we write. It is time we seriously tackled the question . . . we are pursuing false models and undermining our argumentation by continuing to use such language. It is urgent that we begin to elaborate alternative models. (1991a, 271)

Of course, it could be argued that the separation of spheres has never been fully achieved in the peripheries (Lowe and Lloyd 1997), and this is yet another reason for taking the subaltern perspective I am advocating here. We need to find new concepts and a new language to account for the complex entanglement of gender, racial, sexual, and class hierarchies within global geopolitical, geocultural, and geoeconomic processes of the modern/colonial world-system where the ceaseless accumulation of capital is affected by, integrated to, constitutive of, and constituted by those hierarchies. In order to find a new language for this complexity, we need to go "outside" our paradigms, approaches, disciplines, and fields. I propose that we examine the metatheoretical notion of "heterarchies" developed by Greek social theorist, sociologist, and philosopher Kyriakos Kontopoulos (1993) as well as the notion of "coloniality of power" developed by Aníbal Quijano (1991, 1993, 1998).

Heterarchical thinking (Kontopoulos 1993) is an attempt to conceptualize social structures with a new language that breaks with the liberal paradigm of nineteenth-century social science. The old language of social structures is a language of closed systems, that is, of a single, overarching logic determining a single hierarchy. To define a historical system as a "nested hierarchy," as Wallerstein proposed in the Gulbenkian Commission report "Open the Social Sciences," undermines the world-system approach by relying on a metatheoretical model that corresponds to closed systems, precisely the opposite of what the world-system approach attempts to do. In contrast, heterarchies move us beyond closed hierarchies into a language of complexity, open systems, entanglement of multiple and heterogeneous hierarchies, structural levels, and structuring logics. The notion of "logics" here is redefined to refer to the heterogeneous entanglement of multiple agents' strategies. The idea is that there are neither autonomous logics nor a single logic, but multiple, heterogeneous, entangled, and complex processes within a single historical reality. The notion of entanglement is crucial here and is close to Wallerstein's (1974, 1984, 1991a) notion of historical systems understood as "integrated networks of economic, political and cultural processes." The moment we consider multiple hierarchical relationships to be entangled, according to Kontopoulos (1993), or integrated, according to Wallerstein, no autonomous logics or domains remain. Heterarchies keep the use of the notion of logics only for analytical purposes in order to make certain distinctions or to abstract certain processes that once integrated or entangled in a concrete historical process acquire a different structural effect and meaning. Heterarchical thinking provides a language for what Immanuel Wallerstein calls a new way of thinking that can break with the liberal nineteenth-century social sciences and focus on complex, historical systems.

The notion of coloniality of power is also helpful in terms of the culture versus economy dilemma. Quijano's (1991, 2000) work provides a new way of thinking about this dilemma that overcomes the limits of both postcolonial and world-system analysis. In Latin America, most dependentista theorists privileged the economic relations in social processes at the expense of cultural and ideological determinations. Culture was perceived by the dependentista school as instrumental to capitalist accumulation processes. Categories such as gender and race were frequently ignored and when used, they were reduced (instrumentalized) to either class or economic interests. Dependentistas reproduced the illusion that rational organization and development can be achieved from the control of the nation-state. This contradicted the position that development and underdevelopment are the result of structural relations within the capitalist world-system. Although dependentistas defined capitalism as a global system beyond the nation-state, they still believed it was possible to delink from or break with the world-system at the nation-state level (Frank 1970, 11, 104, 150; Frank 1969, chapter 25). This implied that a socialist revolutionary process at the national level could insulate the country from the global system. However, as we know today, it is impossible to transform a system that operates on a world scale by privileging the control/administration of the nation-state (Wallerstein 1992a). No "rational" control of the nation-state would alter the location of a country in the international division of labor. Rational planning and control of the nation-state contributes to the developmentalist illusion of eliminating the inequalities of the capitalist world-system from a nation-state level.

In the capitalist world-system, a peripheral nation-state may experience transformations in its form of incorporation to the capitalist world economy, a minority of which might even move to a semiperipheral position. However, to break with, or transform, the whole system from a nation-state level is completely beyond their range of possibilities (Wallerstein 1992a, 1992b). Therefore, a global problem cannot have a national solution. This is not to deny the importance of political interventions at the nation-state level. The point here is to not reify the nation-state and to understand the limits of political interventions at this level for the long-term transformation of a system that operates at a world scale. The nation-state, although still an important institution of historical capitalism, is a limited space for radical political and social transformations. Social struggles below and above the nation-state are strategic spaces of political intervention that are frequently ignored when the focus of the movements privileges the nation-state. The dependentistas overlooked this due, in part, to their tendency to privilege the nation-state as the unit of analysis and to the economistic emphasis of their approaches.

Quijano (1993) is one of the few exceptions to this critique. Coloniality of power is a concept that attempts to integrate as part of a heterogeneous structural process the multiple relations in which cultural, political, and economic processes are entangled in capitalism as a historical system. Quijano uses the notion of "structural heterogeneity," which is very close to the notion of heterarchy. Similar to world-system analysis, the notion of coloniality conceptualizes the process of colonization of the Americas and the constitution of a capitalist world economy as part of the same entangled process. However, different from the world-system approach, Quijano's structural heterogeneity implies the construction of a global racial/ethnic hierarchy that was simultaneous, coeval in time and space, to the constitution of an international division of labor with core-periphery relationships on a world scale. Since the initial formation of the capitalist world-system, the ceaseless accumulation of capital was entangled with racist, homophobic, and sexist global ideologies. European heterosexual males led the European colonial expansion. Everywhere they went, they exported their cultural prejudices and formed heterarchical structures of sexual, gender, class, and racial inequality. Thus, in "historical capitalism," understood as a "heterarchical system" or as a "heterogeneous structure," the process of peripheral incorporation to the ceaseless accumulation of capital was constituted by, and entangled with, homophobic, sexist, and racist hierarchies and discourses. As opposed to world-system analysis, what Quijano emphasizes with his notion of coloniality of power is that there is no overarching capitalist accumulation logic that can instrumentalize ethnic/racial divisions that precede the formation of a global colonial, Eurocentric culture. For Quijano, racism is constitutive and entangled with the international division of labor and capitalist accumulation at a world scale. The notion of structural heterogenerity implies that multiple forms of labor coexist within a single historical process. Contrary to orthodox Marxist approaches, there is no linear succession of modes of production (slavery, feudalism, capitalism, etc.). Capitalist accumulation on a world scale operates by simultaneously using diverse forms of labor divided, organized, and assigned according to the racist Eurocentric rationality of the coloniality of power. Moreover, for Quijano, there is no linear teleology between the different forms of capitalist accumulation (primitive, absolute, and relative, in this order according to Marxist Eurocentric analysis). Rather, the multiple forms of accumulation coexist simultaneously. As a long-term trend, the "violent" (called "primitive" accumulation in Eurocentric Marxism) and "absolute" forms of accumulation are predominant in the non-European periphery, whereas the "relative" forms of accumulation predominate in the "free" labor zones of the European core.

Another problem with the dependentista-type underestimation of cultural and ideological dynamics is that it impoverishes the political-economy approach. Ideological/symbolic strategies, as well as Eurocentric forms of knowledge, are constitutive of the political economy of the capitalist world-system. Global symbolic/ideological strategies are an important structuring process of the core-periphery relationships in the capitalist world-system. For instance, core states develop ideological/symbolic strategies by fostering Occidentalist (Mignolo 1995) forms of knowledge that privilege the West over the Rest. This is clearly seen in developmentalist discourses, which became a so-called scientific form of knowledge in the past fifty years. This knowledge privileges the West as the model of development and offers a colonial recipe on how to become like the West.

Although the dependentistas struggled against these universalist/Occidentalist forms of knowledge, they perceived this knowledge as a "superstructure" or an epiphenomenon of some "economic infrastructure." Dependentistas never perceived this knowledge as constitutive of Latin America's political economy. Constructing peripheral zones such as Africa and Latin America as "regions with a problem" or with a "backward stage of development" concealed European and Euro-American responsibility in the exploitation of these continents. The construction of "pathological" regions in the periphery, as opposed to the so-called normal development patterns of the West, justified an even more intense political and economic intervention from imperial powers. By treating the Other as underdeveloped and backward, metropolitan exploitation and domination were justified in the name of the "civilizing mission."

The ascribed superiority of European knowledge in many areas of life was an important aspect of the coloniality of power in the modern/colonial world-system. Subaltern knowledges were excluded, omitted, silenced, and/or ignored. This is not a call for a fundamentalist or an essentialist rescue mission in the name of authenticity. The point here is to put the colonial difference (Mignolo 2000) at the center of the process of knowledge production. Subaltern knowledges are those knowledges that emerge at the intersection of the traditional and the modern. They are hybrid, transcultural forms, not merely in the traditional sense of syncretism or "mestizaje," but in Aimé Cesaire's (1946/1970) sense of the "miraculous arms" or what I have called "subversive complicity" (Grosfoguel 1996) against the system. These are forms of resistance that resignify and transform dominant forms of knowledge from the point of view of the non-Eurocentric rationality of subaltern subjectivities thinking from border epistemologies. They constitute what Walter Mignolo (2000) calls a critique of modernity from the geopolitical experiences and memories of coloniality. According to Mignolo (2000), this is a new space that deserves further explorations both as a new critical dimension to modernity/coloniality and, at the same time, as a space from where new utopias can be devised. This has important implications for knowledge production. I believe that world-system analysis from the subaltern side of the colonial difference takes the side of the periphery, the workers, women, racialized/colonial subjects, homosexuals/lesbians, and antisystemic movements in the process of knowledge production. This means that although world-system takes the world as a unit of analysis, it is taking a particular perspective of the world. Still, world-system analysis has not found a way to incorporate subaltern knowledges in processes of knowledge production. Without this, there can be no decolonization of knowledge and no utopistics beyond Eurocentrism. The complicity of the social sciences with the coloniality of power in knowledge production and imperial global designs makes a call for new institutional and noninstitutional locations from which the subaltern can speak and be heard.

One crucial implication of the notion of coloniality of power is that the first decolonization was incomplete. It was limited to the juridical-political independence from the European imperial states. This led to the formation of colonial independences. As a result, the world needs a second decolonization, different and more radical than the first one. A future decolonization would need to address heterarchies of entangled racial, ethnic, sexual, gender, and economic relations that the first decolonization left untouched. This second decolonization would necessarily imply the demise of the existing modern/colonial capitalist world-system. If Immanuel Wallerstein's (1974, 1984, 1991a) assessment is correct, that is, that we are living a bifurcation, a moment of transformational time-space towards a new historical system that could be better or worse than the capitalist world-system, depending on the imagining of new alternatives and the effectivity of the agencies involved, then we need to listen to the subaltern speak from non-Eurocentric, nonmetropolitan locations.

## Works Cited

Alarcón, Norma. 1983. "Chicana Feminist Literature: A Re-Vision through Malintzín/or Malintzín: Putting Flesh Back on the Object." In *This Bridge Called My Back: Writing by Radical Women of Color*, eds. Cherríe Moraga and Gloria Anzaldúa, 182–90. New York: Kitchen Table/Women of Color.

Anzaldúa, Gloria. 1987. *Borderlands/La Frontera: The New Mestiza*. San Francisco: Spinsters/Aunt Lute.

Cesaire, Aimé. 1946 (1970). Les armes miraculeuses. Paris: Gallimard.

Frank, André Gunder. 1969. *Latin America: Underdevelopment or Revolution*. New York: Monthly Review.

———. 1970. *Capitalismo y Subdesarrollo en América Latina*. Buenos Aires, Argentina: Siglo XXI.

Grosfoguel, Ramón. 1994. "World Cities in the Caribbean: The Rise of Miami and San Juan." *Review* 17, no. 3: 351–81.

———. 1996. "From Cepalismo to Neoliberalism: A World-System Approach to Conceptual Shifts in Latin America." *Review* 19, no. 2: 131–54.

Haraway, Donna. 1988. "Situated Knowledges: The Science Question in Feminism and the Privilege of Partial Perspective." *Feminist Studies* 14:575–99.

Kontopoulos, Kyriakos. 1993. *The Logics of Social Structures*. Cambridge: Cambridge University Press.

Lander, Edgardo. 1998. "Eurocentrismo y colonialismo en el pensamiento social latinoamericano." In *Pueblo, época y desarrollo: la sociología de América Latina*, eds. Roberto Briceño-León and Heinz R. Sonntag, 87–96. Caracas, Venezuela: Nueva Sociedad.

Lowe, Lisa, and David Lloyd. 1997. *The Politics of Culture in the Shadow of Capital: Worlds Aligned*. Durham, N.C.: Duke University Press.

Mignolo, Walter. 1995. *The Darker Side of the Renaissance: Literacy Territoriality and Colonization*. Ann Arbor: University of Michigan Press.

———. 2000. *Local Histories/Global Designs: Essays on the Coloniality of Power, Subaltern Knowledges, and Border Thinking*. Princeton, N.J.: Princeton University Press.

Mittelman, James H. 1997. *Globalization: Critical Reflections*. Boulder, Colo.: Lynne Rienner.

Quijano, Aníbal. 1991. "Colonialidad y Modernidad/Racionalidad." *Perú Indígena* 29:11–21.

———. 1993. "'Raza', 'Etnia,' y 'Nación' en Mariátegui: Cuestiones Abiertas." In *El Otro Aspecto del Descubrimiento*, ed. Roland Forgues, 167–87. Lima, Perú: Empresa Editora Amauta S.A.

———. 1998. "La colonialidad del poder y la experiencia cultural latinoamericana." In *Pueblo, época y desarrollo: la sociología de América Latina*, eds. Roberto Briceño-León and Heinz R. Sonntag, 139–55. Caracas, Venezuela: Nueva Sociedad.

———. 2000. "Coloniality of Power, Ethnocentrism, and Latin America." *Nepantla* 1, no. 3: 533–80.

Quijano, Aníbal, and Immanuel Wallerstein. 1992. "Americanity as a Concept, or the Americas in the Modern World-System." *International Journal of Social Sciences* 134:583–91.

Robertson, Roland. 1992. *Globalization*. London: Sage Publications.

Said, Edward. 1979. *Orientalism*. New York: Vintage Books.

Saldívar, José David. 1997. *Border Matters*. Berkeley: University of California Press.

Sassen, Saskia. 1998. *Globalization and Its Discontents*. New York: New Press.

Spivak, Gayatri. 1988. *In Other Worlds: Essays in Cultural Politics*. New York: Routledge, Kegan, and Paul.

Vila, Carlos M. 1992. *La Costa Atlántica de Nicaragua*. Mexico: Fondo de Cultura Económica.

Wallerstein, Immanuel. 1974. *The Modern World-System*. New York: Academic Press.

———. 1979. *The Capitalist World-Economy*. Cambridge: Cambridge University Press.

———. 1984. *The Politics of the World-Economy*. Cambridge: Cambridge University Press.

———. 1991a. *Geopolitics and Geoculture*. Cambridge: Cambridge University Press.

———. 1991b. *Unthinking Social Science*. Cambridge, UK: Polity Press.

———. 1992a. "The Collapse of Liberalism." In *The Socialist Register*, eds. Ralph Miliband and Leo Panitch, 96–110. London: Merlin Press.

———. 1992b. "The Concept of National Development, 1917–1989: Elegy and Requiem." *American Behavioral Scientist* 35, no. 4/5 (March–June): 517–29.

———. 1995. *After Liberalism*. New York: New Press.

# PART II

## Planetarity and the Postcolonial

# Planetarity and the Postcolonial

In his Economic Philosophic Manuscripts of 1844, Karl Marx lists four types of alienation: from our product, from our productive activity, from our species being, and from other human beings. Building on the third of Marx's four types of alienation, that of alienation from our species being, Gayatri Spivak in *Death of a Discipline* (2003) offers a suggestive contrast that may open up this division of our book: "if we imagine ourselves as planetary subjects rather than global agents, planetary creatures rather than global entities, alterity remains underived from us; it is not our dialectical negation, it contains us as much as it flings us away" (73). Thus, the notion of how those in rich nations might engage in a conversation with the rest of the world by allowing themselves to be imagined afresh in a collectivity of equals may circumvent the appropriation of the poor nations by the dominant. This section, therefore, asks what "level playing field" might be available to imagine a collectivity in which the colonized are seen and see themselves as a source of knowledge and power. Is the choice of planetarity anything more powerful than a comforting semantic trick in the face of realpolitik and the New World Order? Is this redux humanism that shrivels in the face of genuine aggression from the indeterminable other? Some discourses on globalization claim that the subversive consumption of modernity in the margins is an active process through which postcolonial subaltern subjects construct their own "alternative" or "vernacular" modernities. If they do, would the rest of the world see this as a threat, an opportunity, or simply as a quaint and romantic oddity?

Walter D. Mignolo and Madina Tlostanova, in "The Logic of Coloniality and the Limits of Postcoloniality," follow on the paradigm shift implied in Spivak's book to suggest that the panorama that scholars concerned with the persistence of the colonial matrix of power are facing is the need to decolonize their own knowledge. This, they argue, must be pursued outside Western categories of thought. In an imaginative presentation of a pre-Marxist Russia, combined with the decolonizing projects of writers such as Waman Puma de Ayala, Mahatma Gandhi, Frantz Fanon, and Gloria Anzaldùa, they propose that we seek a cosmology larger than those embraced by Western theology and secular philosophy.

Proponents of multiculturalism in its various manifestations are no longer surprised to confront criticism from the right, but in "Culture Debates in Translation," Ella Shohat and Robert Stam also provocatively engage the criticism that comes from the left. They do so to contextualize the concept of culture itself and to relate it to globalization, which they conclude can be "oppressive or resistant, conservative or emancipatory." They then go on to argue that all national cultures, so vigorously defended by the critics of multiculturalism, exist in (and always have) "internations," in which there are "competing constellations of models" of what the national culture may or should be. Thus, these two writers also seek a shift in our knowledge paradigm.

Perhaps the most obvious such shift, the most pressing example of a "counter-" weltanschauung to that of the West, is that of the Islamic world—a far-from-univocal manifestation of alterity that makes no apologies about its resistance. Anouar Majid's "The Postcolonial

Bubble" explains why the "clash of civilizations" thesis is a move to relocate the source of global discord in ancient antagonisms (based on culturalist/essentialist assumptions) and prevents people from seeing how both West and East, the United States and Islamic countries, are losing under the iron laws of capitalism. Majid argues that capitalism is endangering cultural sovereignties and reducing all humans to passive spectators without agency. In his view postcolonial studies may well have been a tangent that has delayed a better reading of an accelerating erosion of human freedoms.

E. San Juan Jr.'s "Globalized Terror and the Postcolonial Sublime: Questions for Subaltern Militants" argues that postcolonial theory has heretofore rejected the universalist claims of national-liberation struggles as forms of Eurocentric mimicry and has celebrated ideals of hybridity, in-between or borderland experience, and other fantasmatic performances of agency parasitic on the liberal market and the circulation of heterogeneous commodities. In the process, he argues, it found itself endorsing the war against Islamic fundamentalism (the "internal enemies" of the pluralist order), and it unwittingly became complicit with the decentering program of the World Bank, International Monetary Fund, and the World Trade Organization. His essay underscores the reality of reciprocal accountability—perhaps the very foundation of an "internation."

In "Empire and the 'New' Politics of Resistance," Pal Ahluwalia moves the question of definition back to the individual, positing the personal experience of belonging to a diaspora as a self-reflexive moment underscoring the role of borders of all sorts in the political fabric of daily life. His essay offers a further interrogation of the intellectual données that still shape the discussion of postcolonial resistance to globalization.

Inderpal Grewal's "Amitav Ghosh: Cosmopolitanisms, Literature, Transnationalisms" may somewhat temper E. San Juan Jr.'s criticism of the celebration of hybridity by focusing on its impact on the works of a writer who uses his own cosmopolitanism to imagine a convincing alternative to the Western stranglehold on transnational commerce and cultural exchange, and the Eurocentric hegemonic view of progress. At the same time, the work in question also underscores the fact that globalization has roots that stretch back many centuries.

Moving yet more insistently to the particular, Barbara Harlow relates a specific moment in the history of the antiapartheid movement in South Africa. Describing two pivotal texts from the sanctions movement, one edited by Ronald Segal and the other coauthored by Ruth First with Jonathan Steele and Christabel Gurney, she nonetheless uses the intricacies of these individuals and their commitment to their cause to raise the broader question of the possibility of any new international solidarity movement. Is this an example of the internation, or does it more immediately suggest the folly of such optimism?

We conclude this section with Harish Trivedi's "From Bollywood to Hollywood: The Globalization of Hindi Cinema" as a paradigmatic example of an internation, par excellence, and a model for the celebratory, sometimes-resistant, often-complicit, frequently escapist, commodity that may have defined the Western concept of itself and, no less, the South Asian concept of itself in the twentieth century. When does the vernacular find a finely tuned voice, and when is its audience truly planetary?

# 6

# THE LOGIC OF COLONIALITY AND THE LIMITS OF POSTCOLONIALITY

## Walter D. Mignolo and Madina Tlostanova

*I am talking about societies drained of their essence, cultures trampled underfoot, institutions undermined, lands confiscated, religions smashed, magnificent artistic creations destroyed, extraordinary possibilities wiped out . . . I am talking about millions of [wo]men torn from their gods, their land, their habits, their life—from life, from the dance, from wisdom.*

—Aimé Cesaire, Discourse on Colonialism

## THE COLONIAL MATRIX OF POWER: RACISM, IMPERIAL AND COLONIAL DIFFERENCES

In July of 2001 the authors of this article were teaching a summer seminar, supported by Open Society Institute at the European Humanities University, in Minsk, Belarus. During a lunch conversation, in which we were talking about "postcoloniality," one of the participants in the seminar asked: "What exactly is coloniality? When you talk about postmodernity, I know what modernity is (at least I am familiar with the idea and the term), but when you talk about postcoloniality, I haven't the slightest idea what coloniality is or may be."[1] This article is a belated response to that question.[2] By addressing the limits of postcoloniality, we are not placing ourselves "against" it but, on the contrary, attempting to move postcolonial critique out of the celebratory mood in which it has been cajoled by the book market in the English language and for an English-speaking market audience.[3]

The student's perplexity is understandable for several reasons. First of all, "coloniality" is a disturbing concept that has been introduced by Peruvian sociologist Anibal Quijano in the late eighties to unveil the hidden side of "modernity." Secondly, coloniality invokes colonialism, which is indeed the complement of imperialism. Thus, whereas imperialism/ colonialism refers to specific sociohistorical configurations (i.e., the Spanish and British Empires' colonies in the Americas and Asia), modernity/coloniality refers to the conceptual and ideological matrix of the Atlantic world that, since 1500, has expanded all over the globe. Third, coloniality or what is the same, the colonial matrix of power, describes a specific kind of imperial/colonial relations that emerged in the Atlantic world in the sixteenth century and brought imperialism and capitalism together. The Roman Empire, for example, was not a capitalist empire. Neither was the Ottoman Empire that coexisted in the sixteenth century side by side with the Spanish Empire. The colonial matrix of power explains the specificity of the modern/colonial world and the imperial/colonial expansion of Christian, Western, and Capitalist empires: Spain, England, and the United States. Coloniality is disturbing because it forces you to move back the clock of modern history, as the focus of modernity has been placed in the working class conceived after the industrial revolution. Coloniality underlines the massive land appropriation and massive exploitation of labor at the foundation of colonialism/ capitalism where the focus is in the "wretched damnes," the racialized Indian and black workers of silver and gold mines and agricultural plantations. It is disturbing also because from the damnes you cannot derive a post-Fordist concept of multitude (those who produce surplus value) but that they are cleansed from any racial (and of course, gender and sexual) characterization. It is disturbing, finally, because it forces you to a new beginning of modern/colonial history, to see the foundation of capitalism in the very "primary originary accumulation" that Karl Marx, with his progressive view of history, saw as a precondition of *real* capitalism in the Northern European industrial revolution. Globalization, as it is understood today, goes hand in hand with coloniality, with the foundation of the colonial matrix of power.[4] Postcolonial studies and theories, as currently understood in the United States and certain European countries, start from a different historical version that places the British Empire and sometimes French colonial expansion at the center of modern/colonial history. This is one of the limits of postcolonial studies seen from the perspective of global coloniality.

If modern/colonial empires are one and the same with the foundation and history of capitalism and the idea of Europe, then the question that follows is: how does the colonial matrix of power, thus defined, relate and explain the Russian and the Ottoman Empires, to take the examples of empires coexisting with the capitalist and Western Christian ones?[5] To answer this question, we need to introduce the concepts of the "colonial and imperial differences," both implied in the very structure of the colonial matrix of power. Imperial discourses are built on the bases of the differences with people, languages, religions, economies, and political organizations of the colonies. In order to exploit, it is necessary to dominate, and in order to dominate, it is necessary to build discourses and belief systems that produce the imperial image as the locus of the right and unavoidable march of history and the colonies as the locus of the erroneous, the inferior, the weak, the barbarians, the primitives, and so on. To conflate differences with values in human beings' hierarchical order is not just to *identify* "cultural" differences but to *build* "colonial" differences justified in a "racial" configuration of human being in the planet, their languages and religions, their economies, and their social organizations. That is, modern imperial discourses have been founded on the basis of "colonial differences" at all levels of the social. On the other hand, in order to maintain the upper hand vis-à-vis competing empires, it is also necessary to assert the superiority of imperial hegemony and to found the "imperial difference" with coexisting and competing empires. Thus, the Russian Empire that took off with Ivan the Terrible toward 1555 (but that indeed can be traced back to the designation of Moscow as the Third Rome) and the Ottoman Empire, whose moment of splendor with Suleiman the Magnificent coincided with Charles V of the Holy Roman Empire (Charles I of Castile), were soon located in the margins of the Western Christian imperial discourses. The Russians were Christian but Orthodox, their alphabet was Cyrillic, and their language was Slavic not Latin, whereas the Ottoman Empire was Muslim and its language Turkish and Arabic. Russian and the Ottoman may have been empires, like the Spanish one, but certainly only second class. That is, the imperial difference recognizes the similar but immediately reduces it to a second-class empire by extending to it the features of the colonial difference. That is to say, both the Russian and Ottoman Empires were inferior in terms of religion and language. Consequently, the imperial difference was constructed on the same principle of the colonial difference, except that it was applied to sociohistorical configurations that were not reduced to colonies.[6]

The colonial matrix of power emerged and was founded as the consequence of the Christian and Castilian colonization of the Americas. Radical changes took place during that period in the history of humankind. The changes in scale and orientation could be described in four interrelated spheres of social organization. Firstly, at the economic level, and for the first time in the history of humankind, massive appropriation of land and massive exploitation of labor (e.g., African slaves) were oriented to produce commodities for a global market. As Anibal Quijano and Immanuel Wallerstein (1992) have suggested, the Americas were not incorporated into an already existing capitalist economy, but, on the contrary, a capitalist economy as we know it today could not have existed without the discovery of America. The complementary movement of land appropriation and labor exploitation meant, simultaneously, the dismantling and overruling of other existing relations between human beings, society, land, and labor, such as the one already in place in the so-called Inca and Aztec Empires. Secondly, simultaneous to the appropriation of land and exploitation of labor, Spanish and Christian institutions were established in order to control authority. This meant the dismantling and overruling of existing forms of control of authority between Incas and Aztecs. Thirdly, the control of gender and sexuality followed suit to the control of economy and authority. Christian morality, the idea of the family, and patriarchal superiority were imposed at the same time that homosexuality was condemned and placed on the side of the Devil. The control of gender and sexuality also overruled gender relations and sexual practices existing among Aztecs, Incas, and other communities reached by the spread of Christian itinerant missionaries.[7] Last but not least, control of knowledge and subjectivity was part of the package of the colonial matrix of power upon which the imperial control of the colonies was organized. Christian colleges were created all over the Spanish dominions. The Renaissance University, already at work in places such as Salamanca and Coimbra, were installed (like McDonalds today) in Santo Domingo, Mexico, Peru, and Argentina during the sixteenth century; and in the seventeenth century, Harvard (1636) was founded as the first university in the British colonies. With the control of knowledge goes the control of subjectivity, from the Christian subject modeled according to Theo-logical principles of knowledge to the secular subject modeled according to the Ego-logical, emancipating, and sovereign principles. Obviously, together with the control of knowledge and subjectivities went the dismantling and overruling of Aztec and Inca systems of knowledge and formations of subjectivity, which were framed neither on Christian Theo-logical principles nor on secular Ego-logical principles. From the late eighteenth century on, the colonial matrix of power that was put in place during the sixteenth century under Christian and Iberian forms of governments and economy was translated and adapted to the needs of the new emerging imperial powers, mainly France and England. We do not have time here to go into details, but the reader can do his or her own homework and find the transformations of the colonial matrix of power at the level of economy, authority, gender and sexuality, and subjectivity and knowledge.

The four levels of the colonial matrix of power are interrelated and interdependent. Each of them impinges on the other. But what glues them together? The answer is: racism. By *racism* we do not mean a classification of human beings according to the color of their skin, but more basically, the classification of human beings according to a certain standard of "humanity." Skin color was the secular device used since the eighteenth century when the religious racism based on blood purity was no longer sufficient to accommodate, in the classification, peoples around the world that were not Muslims or Jews. In the sixteenth century then, while Christians in Europe were building a discourse that disqualified, in religious terms, Moors and Jews, the same Christians were building in the Americas a discourse that disqualified not only Indians and blacks, but also mestizos and mulattos, that is, the mix between Spanish and Indians and

Spanish and black. Although this classification was necessary for Spanish and Creoles of Spanish descent in the Americas, Spaniards from Spain introduced a new distinction to cast Creoles of Spanish descent in America inferior to those Spanish born and raised in Spain. Thus, *racism* is an instrumental term in which the colonial difference is built and the colonial wound infringed: racism is a device to deprive human beings of their dignity.

The control of knowledge in the colonies implied, simultaneously, the denial of knowledges and subjectivities in Nahuatl, Aymara, or Quechua languages. In the sixteenth century Arabic had been already cast out and, in the nineteenth century, Hindi, Urdu, and Bengali would follow the same path. The denial of knowledge and subjectivity created a *spatial epistemic break* than cannot be captured by Tomas Kuhn's (1962) paradigmatic changes or Michel Foucault's (1968) epistemic breaks. Today, the spatial epistemic break is turning into the geo- and body-political epistemic shift: those managed by the body-politics of the State (unveiled by Foucault) are turning miseries into celebration and claiming the geo- and corpopolitical epistemic rights of enunciation. Both "breaks" are chronological and within the regional history of Europe. The spatial break emerged in the decolonial attitude that can be traced back to the sixteenth and seventeenth centuries (Waman Puma de Ayala in the Viceroyalty of Peru), but that became more visible in the nineteenth and twentieth centuries (Gandhi, Mariátegui, Césaire, Cabral, Fanon, Menchú, Anzaldúa). The very concept of coloniality emerged in that context, in the context of the decolonial attitude, of decolonization of knowledge and subjectivity. Making visible the logic of coloniality implies a shift in the geography and the biography (i.e., a version of body-politics of knowledge), shift toward a geopolitical and corpopolitical perspective that places at the center of knowledge production the "colonial wound" rather than the "achievements of modernity." Needless to say, and according to our thesis, there are no modern achievements without engendering colonial wounds. This logic of coloniality is implied in the racialization of people, languages, knowledges, religions, political regimes, systems of law, and economies. Racialization of the sociohistorical spheres on a world scale means to degrade whatever does not correspond with the imperial ideals of modernity, and to persecute and shoot whoever disagrees with the racial classification of the world. That hidden logic, the logic justifying shooting and killing in the name of modernity, is precisely the constitutive logic of coloniality.

Thus, a shift in the geo- and corpopolitics of knowledge is of the essence and the decolonization of knowledge an imperative that postcolonial studies have not yet clearly articulated. As long as postcolonial remains in the sphere of "studies," it remains also within the subject/object distinction of modern social sciences and the humanities. The shift in the geo- and corpopolitics of knowledge must take place precisely at this level. The future of the world may not continue to be decided from Western Europe and the United States, be those decisions made by neo-Liberals, neo-Marxists or postcolonials. That is why Mariátegui, Césaire, Fanon, or Anzaldúa become the equivalents of Descartes for the decolonial epistemology that is already well underway and, although not visible in the publications of university presses, more and more attentive to the market. The concept of coloniality is not only a concept that describes a reality but also a concept that affirms its own locus of enunciation; a concept that anchors the shift in the geo- and corpopolitics of knowledge. This argument is not only describing a phenomenon but also mainly arguing from the new perspective that the phenomenon described allows us to create.

## COLONIALITY: THE CONSTITUTIVE AND HIDDEN SIDE OF MODERNITY

Following up on the previous observations, our thesis is that the analysis and understanding of the logic of coloniality presupposes a reframing of the current view of history and of modernity.

Consequently, the very concept of postcoloniality (and its corollaries, postcolonial studies and theory) shall also be reframed once the logic of coloniality is brought out of its invisibility and placed side by side with the rhetoric of modernity. The idea of modernity, first of all, has been conceived from the perspective of European history and has been framed based on the historical process and subjective experience of Western European countries and people—more specifically, on the complicity between Western Christendom and the emergence of capitalism as we know it today. Europe and modernity have become synonymous and essential components of modern European identity. Coloniality, instead, has been wiped out and made invisible in the Eurocentered narratives as an encumbrance for the glorious march of modernity. Where coloniality is visible every day is in the colonies, semicolonies and ex-colonies of Western empires since the sixteenth century. For that reason, it is not surprising that the concept of "coloniality" has been brought out in Latin America, whereas the concept of "modernity" is a European invention. These are not, however, concepts that stand at the same level in power relations. We can talk about modernity ignoring coloniality, as it has been obvious and still is. But you cannot talk about coloniality without invoking modernity. That imbalance in power relations brings about the splendors and misery of coloniality. The misery is its dependency on modernity. The splendor, its power to reveal the colonial matrix of power, to illuminate the colonial difference, to make understandable the colonial wound, and to provide epistemic energy for a radical shift in the geo- and corpopolitics of knowledge: the history and interpretation of the world can no longer be achieved from the universal perspective of the modern social sciences and humanities. Perspectives from modernity (from the left and from the right, neo-Liberals or neo-Marxists) provide only half the story.

Whether the historical foundation of modernity is located in the sixteenth century, the "discovery" of America and the European Renaissance, or in the European Enlightenment and the French Revolution, modernity has been explicitly and implicitly linked with Western Christendom, secularization, Western types of imperialism (i.e., Spain, England, the United States), and capitalist economy. In that Eurocentered version of modernity, fashioned from the very imperial history of Europe, coloniality had to remain silenced. But in our thesis there cannot be modernity without coloniality. Coloniality is constitutive of modernity; thus, the triumphal march of modernity cannot be celebrated from the imperial perspective without bringing to the foreground that religious salvation implied the extirpation of idolatry; civilization the eradication of non-European modes of life, economy, and political organization; development within capitalist economy and market democracy within Western political theory. In that version of history there are two major issues that are left in the background (a background that helps in enhancing the idea of modernity and hiding the logic of coloniality).

The first issue is the uneven conceptualization of modernity and its hidden complicity with the spatial and temporal "differences" and with colonization. Modernity, in order to be conceived as such, needed (and still needs) a break with the past within internal European history, and so the idea of the Middle Ages had to be invented. Thus, the historical foundation of modern time took place. Almost simultaneously, the very concept of "discovery of America" (i.e., the discovery of a continent that did not exist yet—there was not such a thing as America when Columbus landed in the Caribbean islands; furthermore, the Christian conceptualization of the "discovery" of a continent that has been inhabited for about thirty thousands years according to current estimates and the efforts of Christian intellectuals in the sixteenth century to make the "new" continent and people fit Biblical history) contributed to the historical foundation of modern space. By the eighteenth century, when the "barbarians" in space where transformed (e.g., Lafittau) into the "primitives" in time, the colonization of the world by the European Empire brought together and distinguished the time/space of modernity from the time/space of premodern Europe and premodern America, Asia, and Africa. "Modern" imperialism and, therefore, colonialism (as distinct from Roman, Islamic,

Ottoman, Russian) rests on two basic and interrelated pillars: the internal colonization of time in the internal history of Europe (e.g., the Middle Age) and the external colonization of space in the external history of Europe (of the Americas first by Spain and Portugal, of Africa and Asia since the nineteenth century by England and France, and of strategic places of the globe mainly since the second half of the twentieth century by the United States).

Thus, we are making here a distinction between imperialism/colonialism as singular, historical processes on the one hand, and the rhetoric of modernity/the logic of coloniality on the other. From the Biblical macronarrative, we inherited the idea that there is a linear history from the creation of the first woman and the first man by God, until the final judgment. From George W. F. Hegel we inherited the secular version of the sacred narrative: the idea that history is a linear process that began in the East many centuries ago, moved West and, at the time Hegel was writing, History was dwelling in Germany, although its future was already destined to move further West to the United States of America. From Francis Fukuyama (1992) we have inherited the idea that History has arrived at its end. Although these macronarratives are Christian and Western, the expansion of the West all over the globe has made these narratives points of reference (not necessarily of conviction) for the entire world—similar to the way Hollywood and Wall Street are also global reference points. The concepts of colonial and imperial differences alter significantly the calm waters of a linear history that has arrived at its end with the collapse of the Soviet Union, as Fukuyama has it. The rhetoric of modernity (i.e., the Renaissance idea of "les ancients et les modernes") was founded and expanded, in the internal history of Europe and the United States, on the language of progress and newness. To be modern, people or countries had to be at the tip and the top of history, at the tip and top of "human" evolution. With regard to the Muslims in the North of Africa, the Indians in America, the Africans in Africa and in the Americas, and the Ottomans, to be "modern" meant to be civilized and distinct from the barbarians (and after the Enlightenment, distinct from the primitives). Thus, the foundation of the rhetoric of modernity consisted of affirming the point of arrival of the societies in which the men who were telling the story and conceiving modernity were living in; it provided and still provides the justification for the continuing colonization of time and space: "bringing" modernity to the world (in terms of conversion to Christianity, to civilization, to development and market democracy) became a "mission" that, in the name of progress and development, justified colonization from the conquest of Mexico to the conquest of Iraq.

## BEYOND HEGEL: COEXISTING EMPIRES AND COLONIES

We have thus far argued around the constitutive complex modernity/coloniality and described the colonial difference and the production and reproduction of the colonial wound in the name of the achievements of modernity. It is necessary now to displace Hegel's version of world history anchored in modernity and to shift the geo- and body-politics and to anchor new world histories from the perspective of coloniality.[8] We have suggested how the implementation of the colonial matrix of power created the conditions for the emergence of spatial epistemic breaks that emerged around the world as decolonial projects and orientations, silenced in the map of world history by the rhetoric of modernity. We will move now to the complex imperialism/colonialism as far as the imperial and colonial differences have been defined by the rhetoric of modernity and implemented within Western, capitalist, Christian, and secular empires. The imperial and colonial differences are not of course "matters of fact," ontological realities, but imperial construction upon which the entire racial matrix of the modern world has been built and continues to be so. Think, for instance, of the characterization of Islam in sixteenth-century Christian Spain and its counterpart, the characterization of Islam in twenty-first century United States.

A genealogy of the word *imperium* is thus of the essence. Imperium has sovereignty and management of the colonies as one of the basic meanings. These legacies were handed down to Spain, particularly through Charles V, Holy Roman Emperor (1519–1558), and were later on appropriated by the kings and queens of England and France. In a nutshell, the genealogy goes from the foundation of the idea of Empire in Rome to its continuation in Spain, England, and France. That is, in the foundation of Western capitalist empires (Rome was not capitalist in the sense of the Western capitalist and Atlantic empires), there are legacies of the Roman Empire. This narrative is quite well known in the West, but it is particularly interesting that the Russian Empire has been left out as a silent and absent historical agent. The imperial difference begins, from the perspective of modernity, with this silence, which implies the inferiority of those who are, if not altogether out of history, on its very margin, even if they are also imperial people. At the beginning of the sixteenth century, when Spain was not yet an empire but just a kingdom that had the luck of bumping into what is today America, Russian imperial vision declared itself an heir of Rome, self-defining and christening Moscow as "The Third Rome." A British scholar of Russian descent, Dominic Lieven (2000), published a book titled *Empire: The Russian Empire and its Rivals*.[7] Lieven begins with the coetaneous existence, toward the first century of the Christian era, of the Roman and the Chinese Empires, of Latin and Sanskrit as the two imperial languages and the carriers of a complex system of knowledge. Secondly, Lieven moves to the three heirs of the Roman Empire: the Islamic Empire that arose toward the eighth century AD; the Russian Empire, rising at the end of the fifteenth century; and the Western Christian (as Lieven puts it), which carried the torch for the rise and growth of Western empires (capitalist, Catholic, and Protestant).

The connections between these two genealogies of empire were forged in the eighteenth century. At this point, the working of the imperial difference is crucial to understand not only historical changes but also to reread Hegel's imperial version of world history. The Russian Empire began a process of affirmation of sovereignty and establishment of colonies that transformed "frontiers" into "borderlands" (i.e., the political divisions with adjacent empires, such as the Ottoman and Persian Empires in the South, Qing China in the East, and Europe in the Southwest). Caucasus developed into a borderland between Islam and Orthodox Christianity as well as into a colony of the Russian Empire. Thus, imperial and colonial differences were established in the very act of setting up physical and geographical borderlands at once—the colonial difference with Caucasus was simultaneously the locale of the imperial difference with the Ottoman Empire. The Russian Empire that from the eighteenth century on imitated and followed the imperial, capitalist, and liberal patterns emerging in England, France, and Germany—at least on the surface—had a local history that prevented its governors, intellectuals, scholars, and civil society from feeling that they also inhabited the house of the "Absolute Spirit." Thus, the imperial difference was established and Russia became a lesser empire in the ascending history of "European modernity." Russia and the Soviet Union as empires had their own colonies subordinated through their own adaptation of the colonial difference (e.g., Chechnya). The colonial difference in Russia and the Soviet Union had been subordinated, however, to the imperial difference and subjected to the superiority of Western imperial rhetoric. Hegel was clear in laying out the imperial rhetoric. Fyodor Dostoyevsky (1977 [1881]) and Victor Yerofejev (2000), to name just two Russian thinkers) were clear in expressing the imperial wound to which they were subjected.

All the Atlantic empires that came into power through the exploitation of labor and extraction of natural resources from America were Catholic or Protestant, whereas the Ottoman Empire was Muslim and the Russian was Orthodox. Historically, then, it so happened that capitalism was complicit in the materialization of the Atlantic economy, with Catholicism and Protestantism. The very idea of "modernity" thus became part of the vocabulary and the rhetoric that went together with the coming into sight of the Western empires of the Atlantic and their colonies in the Americas. The colonial control of labor in the Atlantic was based on two systems of exploitation of labor to produce commodities for the world market that the Americas generated. It was based upon two brutal systems, encomienda[9] and slavery, of which the Spanish, Portuguese, French, and British took ample advantage. The implantation of labor systems that founded colonial capitalism displaced and destroyed the labor system in the Aztec and Inca Empire, which, whatever it was, was not capitalist. In contrast, Russia was not involved in the type of exploitation of labor that the encomienda and the transformation of the slave system implanted in the Atlantic (i.e., the triangular trade) during the sixteenth and seventeenth centuries.

Russia's road to the status of empire in the late fifteenth century was similar to Spain's. In both cases, it was an assertion of sovereignty—in the case of Spain by expelling the Moors, and in Russia's case by ceasing to pay tribute to the Golden Horde. The creation of the new Muscovite principality (the future Russian Empire) soon started to eliminate all alternative economic and political forms that existed in other Russian states at the time. This is what happened with the Novgorod tradition with its protodemocratic forms of government that allowed merchants to play a central part in the social, political, and economic structure of the cities. Novgorod had rich merchant traditions and, from the fourteenth to the sixteenth centuries, functioned according to the so-called Magdeburg law and was a member of the Hanseatic unity. But any possible continuity with alternative political and economic systems such as the Novgorod one was displaced when Moscow built its own authoritarian system, which, ironically, was similar in some respects to the political yoke it had just cast off. The Muscovite tradition brought with it the undivided authority of the Prince, later Tzar, and his feeble boyars. In contrast with the Spanish colonization of America, Russian colonization did not take the shape of massive exploitation of labor to produce commodities for the global market. Geopolitical, military, and religious goals prevailed, as Russia did not find itself in the situation of having to deal with a "new" continent and its natural resources, and the only massive labor force it could exploit was that of its own peasants. Thus, if Spain and Russia had a similar beginning in their road to empire (e.g., "liberating" themselves from the Moors and the Golden Horde), soon the differences became apparent: Russia was not part of the Atlantic monopolistic capitalism and, therefore, it found itself on the margins of European modernity and the emerging logic of coloniality.

In recently published works (Hardt and Negri 2000; Ferguson 2004a, 2004b; Smith 2003; Spivak 1999) touching upon the typology of empire(s), Russia/Soviet Union remains nonexistent or at the border, which, however, does not mean that its experience is not relevant for other locales. In fact, because of their uniqueness, the discourses and practices of the Russian and Soviet Empires, the "dark other" of Western Europe, can be used to illustrate and partly reformulate the problematic of modern colonial and imperial differences throughout the world. To understand from a border epistemic perspective how the European colonial model was replicated and transformed in subaltern empires such as Russia is one of the goals of this argument. In order to do so, it may be interesting to briefly trace the main aspects of modernity/modernization in Russia/Soviet Union interpreted both internally and externally. By *internally* and *externally* we mean both the frame of its complicated relations with the capitalist empires of the West and the frame of its no-less-complicated and varied imperial discourses with respect to its own quite different colonies. Khazhismel Tkhagapsoev (2006), intellectual and activist from Caucasus, has mapped the making of the imperial difference in the relationship between Russia and the West, starting from the "beginning," that is the adoption of Christianity, to the present of Vladimir Putin's presidency:

> In general the Russian reality appears as an existence of "transmuted forms" on all
> crucial and turning points in its history. For example, in the ninth century, Russia

adopted Christianity, but it got so transformed within the Russian social-cultural context that it became very much imbued with the spirit and forms of pagan culture and it acquired a "transmuted nature (form)" in relation to Western European Christianity, based on the systemic-rational philosophy of Aristotle and Aquinas. In the eighteenth century, Russia began to assimilate European economic, political, and cultural ideas and forms of modernity—the ideas and forms of capitalism, market economy, and technological culture. However for another two hundred years (up to the beginning of the twentieth century), Russia preserved the dominance of the political class of landowners (latifundium), while the capitalist (bourgeois) class was denied access to the political decision making. So capitalism also acquired in Russia a transmuted nature (form) as it was driven not so much by the rules of the market as by the subjective will of the main landowner of the country, the "tsar-autocrat." In 1917 a new turn took place in the history of Russia—the Bolsheviks pushed it into the new historical trajectory, that of socialism. But, as is well known, Stalin's model of socialism, which had never undergone any principal changes under other Communist party general secretaries from Khruschev to Gorbachev, had little to do with the Swedish social political system." (Tkhagapsoev 2006, 519–20)

The exemplary case of Russia shows how the canonical concept of "universal history," a Christian invention and a fundamental tool of modernity/coloniality later secularized by Kant and Hegel, could be reframed in terms of borders and differences—imperial and colonial. Universal history in this sense is none other than the history of the world from the epistemic perspective of European modernity (Christian and secular), fashioning itself as such and building on the imperial difference with other rival empires and on the colonial difference with subjugated people.

## RACISM RECONSIDERED: THE COLONIAL/IMPERIAL DIFFERENCES AND THE COLONIAL WOUND

The logic of coloniality has been hidden under the rhetoric of modernity that accompanied the sprouting and growth of Atlantic mercantile or colonial capitalism. The rhetoric of modernity was built around the "Christian mission" and the compromises between the Roman Papacy and the Crown of Spain (from 1480 to 1555, from Ferdinand and Isabelle to Charles I of Spain and Charles V of the Holy Roman Empire). In the eighteenth century, with the shift in the leadership of the Atlantic economy from Spain and Portugal to England and France, the rhetoric of modernity changed the name of the "mission" from Christianizing to civilizing the world. When imperial leadership changed hands again after WWII, U.S. development and modernization displaced the British Empire's mission. When development and modernization failed because it was not possible for capitalist economy to develop underdeveloped countries, the mission changed again to market democracy as the supreme point of arrival of neoliberal philosophy. Through five hundred years of Western capitalist empires (Spain, England, the United States, and their supporters), the rhetoric of modernity (i.e., the different type of "salvations" that the elites in power articulate in their discourses) at once justified and hid the logic of coloniality implanted during the sixteenth and the seventeenth centuries.

In the unfolding of this linear history of Western empires that coincided with the history of capitalism (Arrighi 1995), the making and remaking of the imperial and the colonial difference became the empire's companion, as Spanish philologist and grammarian Elio Antonio de Nebrija said when Queen Isabella asked him what would be the use of the grammar of the Spanish language. The foundation of imperial and colonial differences was articulated in the sixteenth century from the privileged perspective of Western Christendom and with the imperial foundation of Castile, with the "discovery of America" in 1492, and with the kingdom of Charles V of the Holy Roman Empire that occupied almost the entire half of the sixteenth century. It was in Christian Castile and the historical role it attributed to itself in the simultaneous events of expelling Moors and Jews from the Iberian Peninsula, of conquering two empires in what became the New World, and of initiating a massive appropriation of land and exploitation of labor (followed by Holland, France, and England) that created the conditions for a theological discourse in which the imperial differences with the Ottoman and the Russian Empires were established. Simultaneously, the colonial difference was articulated in the process of colonization of the Indians and the massive trade of African slaves.

Racism, in the final analysis, rests on the control of knowledge/understanding and subjectivity. The modern imperial missions were as much about the control of economy and authority as of producing new subjects, modeled according to Christian, Liberal, and Marxist concepts of society and the individual. Knowledge has been, together with language, the companion of empires and, in the case of Western empires founded in capitalist economy (from mercantilism to free trade, from monarchy to nation-states), knowledge has been under the control of Theo-logy and Ego-logy. By *Ego-logy*, we refer to the new principles of knowledge ("I think") and subjectivity ("I am"), which were both twisted by René Descartes (1596–1650) in his well-known "I think, therefore I am." One cannot exist without the other, although Knowledge was placed before and above Being. And both contributed to a new direction in European thought and subjectivities that was already in place, for instance, in Miguel de Cervantes Saavedra's *Don Quixote* (1605, explicitly stated in the Preface). The Cartesian thinking subject and constitutive being was not supposed to be a black African or a brown Indian from the Americas, a brown Indian from Asia, or a brown Arab from North Africa and what is today the Middle East. The Cartesian subject was immaterial and disembodied, without color and odor—an empty signifier of a sort (controlled by the principles of the Theo and Ego politics of knowledge) that embraced all, every skin color and religious belief under the control of the experience of white European man and Christian religion. Immanuel Kant was clear, following Descartes' route, that "these" people were not yet ready to reach the highs of the Beautiful and the Sublime and, even less, of Reason.[10]

The logic of coloniality (the colonial matrix of power) is the "missing" half in current definitions of "modernity." Take, for example, Anthony Giddens' short description of modernity: "'modernity' refers to modes of social life or organization which emerged in Europe from about the seventeenth century onwards and which subsequently became more or less worldwide in their influence" (Giddens 1992, 1). Giddens' concept of modernity is very shortsighted, for he sees only one side of it—the European imperial side. From the perspective of coloniality, however, world history since the sixteenth century has had different colors and shades, different geohistorical locations for accumulations (of money as well as of meaning), enjoyments, and sufferings. We can therefore paraphrase Giddens' description of modernity to render visible the logic of coloniality, as follows:

> "Coloniality" refers to the modes of control of social life and economic and political organizations that emerged in the European management of the colonies in the Americas and the Caribbean from about the beginning of the sixteenth century onwards and that subsequently became more or less worldwide in their influence. This associates coloniality with a time period and with an initial geographical location but for the moment leaves its major characteristics safely stowed away in a black box. Yet, they are being applied today in Iraq and the Middle East and North Korea, in Georgia (Transcaucasia) and Chechnya; in redefining the internal imperial difference between the United States and the European Union, and the external imperial

differences between the United States and the European Union on one side and Russia, China, and Japan on the other. Coloniality, indeed, has become since the sixteenth century more or less worldwide in its "influence." (Mignolo and Tlostanova's paraphrase of Giddens' [1992] definition of modernity)

The logic of coloniality (or the colonial matrix of power) is constitutive of modern Western and capitalist empires, as well as its communist counterpart. The imperial difference, however, establishes a distinction between them, because the Soviet Union was an empire based on the same logic but with different content: a communist rather than a liberal empire that was already solidly grounded in the industrial revolution and in the second stage of Western imperial expansion. In this respect, one can speak of postsocialism in Russia to account for the neoliberal turn that followed the demise of the Soviet Empire. Conversely, a more revealing conceptualization of the history of Western capitalist empires would be postliberalism rather than postcolonialism. What Russia, the European Union, and the United States have in common today is that the rhetoric of modernity and the logic of coloniality are articulated through a neoliberal philosophy of democracy and civilization: the market rules and brings democracy (and when this is not possible, the army makes it work). At the same time, what Russia does not have in common with the United States and the European Union is that, in the history of the modern/colonial world, Russia and the Soviet Union have always been second-class empires (i.e., the articulation of the imperial difference).

Among the great number of interpretations of Russia's extremely belated modernization, the most widely spread ones are largely Eurocentric. Shaped under the influence of Russian emigrants of all waves (Vishnevsky 1998; Yanov 1988), these interpretations were uncritically accepted by both Western historians of Russia and today by the "remaining" Russian historians themselves. Indeed, scholarly and intellectual life in Russia in the past two hundred years has been a constant effort to successfully adapt Euro-American models of the social sciences and the humanities. Such efforts also resulted in a "nationalistic" critique of "foreign" ideas. Neither position offers a way out. What is necessary is an attempt to understand Russia through a double differential of power: the imperial differential with the West and with the East (China and Japan) and the colonial differential between Russia and its colonies. Eurocentric theories of modernization and globalization are largely built on the linear historical projection from the Roman Empire to the United States, dismissing other imperial/colonial histories and, above all, dismissing colonial sites as locus of epistemic enunciation. Knowledge in its dominating and oppositional versions is imperial knowledge that, through the imperial and colonial epistemic differences, rules out and disregards knowledges in second-class empires and in the colonies. Because of both Western imperial enforcements and non-Western imperial self-subordination, there is a tendency to look at the world through the eyes of the West (Christians, Liberals, and Marxists). Similar tendencies can be located in the colonies, although a breakthrough emerged from the awareness of the consequences of the colonial epistemic difference (Yevtukhov, Gasparov, and Ospovat 1997). It is at this point that the geopolitical (nodes configured by the imperial and colonial differences) and biopolitical (subjectivities—the damnes—configured by the imperial and colonial differences) epistemic displacement are of the essence.

## SHIFTING THE ETHICS AND POLITICS OF KNOWLEDGE: THE DECOLONIAL ATTITUDE AND THE LIMITS OF POSTCOLONIAL STUDIES/THEORY

Postcolonial "studies" and "theories," as institutionalized through the U.S. academy and in ex-Western European empires, fell back into the epistemic frame of Eurocentered modernity: the distinction between the knowing subject/known object is implied in both the notion of "study" and in the notion of "theory." Gandhi, Fanon, or Anzaldúa did not "study" or "theorize" British imperialism in India, black experience in the Caribbean, Berber and Arabic experiences in North Africa, or chicana experiences in the United States. Their political stance went together with a decolonial shift in knowledge production—the shift we are conceptualizing in terms of geo- and body-politics of knowledge. What kind of knowledge, for what, and for whom? These are the questions that their writings elicit. What they all have in common, beyond their differences, is that they inhabit, dwell in, the colonial wound. The three of them "thought" and wrote from that "experience," the experience of the colonial wound. And the knowledge produced from the colonial wound is not a knowledge that aims to change the "disciplines" but rather to "decolonize" knowledge, to undo the imperial and colonial differences. Thus, one of the vexing questions that emerged in the late eighties about the relations between identities and epistemologies becomes a mute point: Fanon is not "studying the blacks" but instead "thinking" ethically and politically from the colonial wound and shifting the ethics and politics of knowledge articulated in the distinction between the knowing subject and the known object.

What about postsocialist Russia? Who are the equivalents to Gandhi, Fanon, or Anzaldúa? The complication in Russian history is that the Soviet revolution turned Marxism into a model of imperial domination and Marxism became as oppressive as Christianity and Liberalism. Postsocialist Russia is facing the dilemma of having burned out one of the "hopes" still alive among Western Marxists and of not having the other way out of joining the new philosophy of Western empires—neoliberalism. Consequently, whereas decolonial projects and practices emerged in the colonies of Western empires as early as the sixteenth century, Russian modern/colonial history was characterized by the imperial difference with the West and the particular nature of the Russian and Soviet empires' colonies. So within the history of today's Russian Federation, the decolonial attitude starts, paradoxically, with the imperial wound. Intellectuals and writers such as Dostoyevsky and Yerofejev described this as follows: "In Europe we were hangers-on and slaves, whereas in Asia we shall go as masters" (Dostoyevsky 1977 [1881]); "From Moscow I can go to Asia, if I want, or to Europe. That is, it is clear where I am going to. It is not clear—where I am coming from . . ." (Yerofejev 2000). It is not clear yet what will come from the ex-colonies of the Russian and Soviet empires, as well as from some of the colonies that remain under the Russian Federation (such as Chechnya). What is clear, however, is that a shifting in the ethics and politics of knowledge that would cast Russian history beyond the Hegelian dictum and beyond its double dependency with the West—Liberal and Marxist—will emerge at some point at some place, because neither Christian Orthodoxy (very much like Christian Catholicism and Protestantism in the West) nor second-class liberalism offers a promising future. Marxism as a model for the organization of society has also run its course in Russia as well as in Western industrialized countries (Europe and the United States) and their dependent countries (Latin America and the Caribbean).

The panorama we—scholars and intellectuals concerned and critical of the formation, transformations, and current persistence of the colonial matrix of power—are facing is not so much the "study of colonialism" or "postcolonial studies" around the world, but the need to "decolonize knowledge." And decolonization of knowledge can be hardly attained from within Western categories of thought—neither Spinoza nor Nietzsche will do. We need to move in different directions. To move in those direction means to follow the decolonial projects and the visions of Waman Puma de Ayala, Mahatma Gandhi, Frantz Fanon, and Gloria Anzaldúa, among others. Who produces knowledge and what for? Shifting to geo- and body-politics of knowledge brings decoloniality to the foreground instead of the critique of bio-politics within Western history itself (and more specifically France). Decoloniality (as synonymous with decolonization of knowledge and of being) cannot be knowledge at the service of the monarch, the church, the state, or the corporations, but knowledge that comes from the perspective of and empowering of the "colonial subalterns"—that is, those whose languages, religions, social organization, and economic production have been denied and suppressed by structures based on the Theo- and the Ego-politics of knowledge. Decoloniality emerges from the legacies in colonial histories instead of from the legacies of European imperial histories. The first took away the geo- and biographical location of knowledge and the knower in the name of God; the second—in the name of Transcendental Reason. The epistemic imperial and colonial differences were the instruments through which Theo- and Ego-politics of knowledge were established. The decolonial shift relocates the geo- and biopolitics of knowledge and reveals that both the Theo-logy and Ego-logy implemented a philosophy of knowledge that denied its own geo- and biographical location while projecting, as universal, what was indeed anchored and located at the geographical and biographical location of imperial agencies. Decolonial projects and actions cannot be subsumed under paradigmatic or epistemic *breaks* within the universal times of Western modernity, but should be considered as a *geo- and body-politics epistemic shift* fracturing a cosmology without alternatives, other than Christian, Liberal, and Marxist.

The spatial epistemic shift generated by the repressive logic of coloniality engendered, as we suggested, decolonial projects and practices, including knowledge and subjectivity, and prompted the question of the ethics and politics of knowledge: where do intellectuals stand in this enterprise? How do their subjectivities formed by ethnic belonging and discrimination based on race, gender, languages, regional histories, and so forth impinge on how they think, how they are seen, and how they want to imagine and create a future beyond discrimination? To answer these questions, it is necessary to start from the fact that the Soviet variants of modernization successfully assimilated cultures in order to create a new Soviet identity. This process continues to define post-Soviet subjectivity for which Western modernization and Eurocentrism remain the only possible points of reference, whereas the ethnic-cultural elements still remain strictly exotic. This is what makes the post-Soviet thinkers reflecting on the colonial/imperial difference so crucially different from Anzaldúa and other border thinkers (Tlostanova 2004).

Imperial and colonial differences inflicted wounds and created borders—physical and mental lines that can be policed between one country and the other; between one neighbor and another; between an employer and an employee; between the population of ex-imperial countries (such as Russia) and the immigrants in imperial ones (such as the core countries of the European Union and the United States); between the police and the civil society. Borders are lines that divide people in the street and allow the police and the embassies of dominant countries to control entire populations in other parts of the world. And borders are also conceptual and mental lines that divide different types of knowledge. What we need is the *epistemic geopolitical and body-political potential emerging from the borders (in the ex- and neocolonies as well as in the ex- and neoempires) to displace the epistemic privilege of modern epistemology* (Theo- and Ego-logical; Eurocentrically oriented). The line of the colonial difference is common through time and space to all those who have been wounded by the coloniality of knowledge and of being, one domain of the colonial matrix of power. Silenced through the history of modernity told from the perspective of modernity, those who have been wounded are taking the lead, not in the academicism of postcolonial studies but in the ethical and political arena of the epistemic decoloniality. Decoloniality (the undoing of coloniality, that is, of the colonial matrix of power) implies two simultaneous moves: to unveil the hidden logic of modernity (e.g., coloniality) and to work toward another globalization, as the World Social Forum has it.

# NOTES

1. The bibliography on the concept of coloniality is extensive by now, including: a summary in Anibal Quijano (2000); on coloniality of knowledge, Edgardo Lander (2000); on coloniality of being, Enrique Dussel (1977); and on being and geopolitics of knowledge, Nelson Maldonado-Torres (2004). "Coloniality" contributed to the move from Eurocentered works on the sociology of knowledge toward the geopolitics of knowledge as decolonization. On this, see Walter Mignolo at www.incommunicado.info/node/view/18.

2. As far as we (Madina Tlostanova and Walter Mignolo) carried within us the memories of being born and raised in Moscow (with ties to Uzbekistan and Caucasus) and Argentina (with ties to Northern Italy), respectively, the postcolonial academic talk in the United States remained somewhat—and for different reasons—outside the realms of our imperial/colonial experiences and our sociohistorical formation of subjectivity. Interestingly enough, we found in Gloria Anzaldúa (1987) and Frantz Fanon (1952; who are neither Russian nor from European descent) a guide for our thoughts and reflection of our subjectivities.

3. The idea that "globalization" as understood today is a process that starts with the "discovery" of America is shared by European political theorists such as Carl Schmidt who, in his *The Nomos of the Earth* (1952) makes a clear distinction between the "preglobal" and the "global" age. "Globalization" in this view is not a human phenomenon from time immemorial but a historical qualitative turn in appropriation of land, massive exploitation of labor, and international law that is concentrated both in the hands of European and capitalist imperial countries.

4. What we mean by "second-class" empire can be seen today in the case of Georgia and Ukraine. President Mikhail Saakashvili is denouncing Putin's imperial ambitions, but he himself has no quarrel with joining Western imperial ambitions. A similar case is Ukraine. In South America and Caribbean countries the situation is radically different because from their independence in the nineteenth century, they all wanted to join France and England, and now the United States, which form the history of Christian and Liberal capitalist empires of the West.

5. The idea that globalization is a historical process that originated with the "discovery" of America was proposed by conservative thinker Carl Schmidt (1952). Schmidt linked massive land possessions, since then, and international law as a clear Eurocentered expansionist phenomenon.

6. Notice that until the beginning of the nineteenth century, "Latin America" doesn't exist and there is no such a thing as "Latin America" countries. We are referring here mainly to the Spanish (and indirectly to the Portuguese) colonies in the New World. In the case of Spanish colonies, they extended to today's California and Colorado, including Texas, New Mexico, and to a certain point Louisiana and of course Florida. It is common, however, to repeat the mistake of labeling the period between 1500 and 1800 "colonial Latin America." What we have are "Spanish colonies in the Indias Occidentales," sometimes also called New World and America.

7. See Dominic Lieven (2000). A useful counterpart for the Atlantic Empires is Anthony Pagden (1995).

8. The concept of body-politics of knowledge is radically different from Michel Foucault's bio-politics. Whereas in Foucault bio-politics is conceived in terms of management of power (and is still anchored in the modern) and an imperial conception of knowledge, body-politics of knowledge displaces epistemology from its Eurocentric location to the places (geo-politics) and racialized bodies of the colonies (men and women of color, gays and lesbians of color, indigenous and Muslims, Arabic and Aymara languages instead of Greek and Latin, etc.). Body-politics of knowledges refers to epistemic and philosophical creativities in places, bodies, languages, and memories that have been disqualified as thinkers and philosophers. Border thinking refers precisely to the articulation of the displaced appropriating the global expansion of Western categories of thinking and principles of knowledge (e.g., epistemology). From all of this, decolonial thinking emerges, which does not mean that all blacks and Indians, Muslims and Aymaras, and women and men of color will endorse it. Assimilation is the alternative to decolonial thinking and the decolonial option.

9. A system of charges in the Spanish colonies, by means of which a group of individuals owed retributions to other groups (the colonizer) in terms of labor or other means.

10. See Eze (1997, part 4).

# WORKS CITED

Anzaldúa, Gloria. 1987. *Borderlands/La Frontera. The New Mestiza*. San Francisco: Spinster's Ink/Aunt Lute Books.

Arrighi, Giovanni. 1995. *The Long Twentieth Century*. London: Verso.

Dostoyevsky, Fyodor. 1977. "Geok-Tepe. Chto takoye Azia dlya nas?" *Dnevnik Pisatelja*, 1881, Sobranije Sochineniy, tom 27 ["Geok-Tepe. What Is Asia for Us?" *Writer's Diary*, 1881, complete works, Vol. 27]. Leningrad: Nauka.

Dussel, Enrique. 1977. *Philosophy of Liberation*. Maryknoll, N.Y.: Orbis Books.

Eze, Emmanuel Chukwudi. 1997. "The Color of Reason: The Idea of 'Race'." In *Postcolonial African Philosophy: A Critical Reader*, 103–40. London: Blackwell.

Fanon, Frantz. 1952. *Peau noire, maskes blanches*. Paris: Gallimard.

Ferguson, Niall. 2004a. *Empire: The Rise and Demise of the British World Order and the Lessons for Global Power*. New York: Basic Books.

———. 2004b. *Colossus: The Price of America's Empire*. New York: Penguin Press.

Foucault, Michel. 1968. *Les mots et les choses*. Paris: Gallimard.

Fukuyama, Francis. 1992. *The End of History and the Last Man*. New York: Avon Books.

Giddens, Anthony. 1992. *The Consequences of Modernity*. Stanford, Calif: Stanford University Press.

Hardt, M., and A. Negri. 2000. *Empire*. Cambridge, Mass.: Harvard University Press.

Kuhn, Thomas. 1962. *The Structure of Scientific Revolutions*. Cambridge, Mass.: Harvard University Press.

Lander, Edgardo. 2000 (1985). *La colonialidad del saber: Eurocentrismo y Ciencias Sociales*, trans. Aquilina Martinez and Christine Morkovosky. Eugene, Ore.: Wipf and Stock.

Lieven, Dominic. 2000. *Empire: The Russian Empire and Its Rivals*. New Haven, Conn.: Yale University Press.

Maldonado-Torres, Nelson. 2004. "A Topology of Being and Geopolitics of Knowledge." *London*, Vol. 8, no. 1: 29–56.

Mignolo, Walter, ed. Forthcoming. "Double Critique: Knowledges and Scholars at Risk in the Post-Socialist World." *South Atlantic Quarterly*.

Padgen, Anthony. 1995. *Lord of All the World: Ideologies of Empires in Spain, Britain, and France c. 1500–c. 1800*. New Haven, Conn.: Yale University Press.

Quijano, Anibal. 2000. "Coloniality of Power, Eurocentrism, and Latin America." *Nepantla: Views from South* 1/3:533–80.

Quijano, Anibal, and Immanuel Wallerstein. 1992. "Americanity as a Concept, or the Americas in the Imaginary of the Modern World-System." *International Journal of Social Science* Vol. 1, 134,549–556.

Schmidtt, Carl. 2003 (1952). *The Nomos of the Earth*. New York: Telos Press.

Smith, Neil. 2003. *American Empire: Roosevelt's Geographer and the Prelude to Globalization*. Berkeley: University of California Press.

Spivak, G. Ch. 1999. *A Critique of Postcolonial Reason: Toward a History of the Vanishing Present*. Cambridge, Mass.: Harvard University Press.

Tkhagapsoev, Khazhismel. 2006. "On the Way to Mirage: Russian Metamorphoses of Liberalism and the Problem of Their Interpretation." *The South Atlantic Quarterly* 105, no. 3: 501–26.

Tlostanova, Madina. 2004. *Postsovetskaja literatura i estetika transkulturatsii: Zhit nigde, Pisat niotkuda* [Living never, writing from nowhere: post-Soviet fiction and the trans-cultural aesthetics]. Moscow: Editorial URSS.

Ulmen, G. L. 2003. *The Nomos of the Earth in the International Law of the Jus Publicum Europaeum*. New York: Telos Press.

Vishnevsky, A. 1998. *Serp I Rubl'*. Moscow: OGI.

Yanov, A. 1988. *Russkaia ideia i 2000–i god*. New York: Liberty Publishers.

Yerofejev, Victor. 2000. *Pjat Rek Zhizni*. Moscow: Podkova.

Yevtukhov, K., B. Gasparov, and A. Ospovat, eds. 1997. *Kazan, Moscow, St. Petersburg: Multiple Faces of the Russian Empire*. Moscow: OGI.

# 7

# CULTURE DEBATES IN TRANSLATION

## Ella Shohat and Robert Stam

*American "multiculturalism" is not a concept, nor a theory, nor a social or politi-
cal movement, while pretending to be all those things at the same time . . . a screen-
discourse . . . which deludes those who are part of it as it deludes those who are not
part of it.*

—Pierre Bourdieu and Loic Wacquant, *Le Monde Diplomatique*

## MULTICULTURALISM: THE CRITIQUE FROM THE RIGHT

The U.S. right wing has fostered a number of myths about multiculturalism. Some of these
myths, unfortunately, have been circulated abroad by the media, even by the supposedly left
media (in France, *Liberation;* in Brazil, *Isto E*). Some of the right-wing myths include the following: (1) the idea, usually felt rather than stated, that multiculturalism is something that
"they" (African Americans, native Americans) do and something that is only in "their" interest, not in the general interest; (2) that multiculturalism is a recent phenomenon; (3) that
multiculturalism is anti-Western, anti-European, and anti-American; (4) that multiculturalism is separatist and "disuniting America"; (5) that multiculturalism is "therapy for minorities" or "underdog history"; (6) that multiculturalism anachronistically imposes contemporary
"p.c." values on the teaching and conceptualization of social issues and history; and (7) that
multiculturalists are puritanical party poopers, as unpleasant people anxious to spoil the
good times of fun-loving Americans. At the same time, paradoxically, the neoconservatives
portray multiculturalists as irresponsible hedonists, the heirs of the permissive 1960s with
its credo of "sex, drugs, and rock 'n' roll," leading one to ask: which is it? Are multiculturalists heirs of the self-indulgent do-your-own-thing 1960s or uptight puritans? It is difficult to
be both.

An important anticipatory figure in this sense was Pascal Bruckner and his 1983 book
*Le Sanglot de L'Homme Blanc* (The White Man's Sobs). A veteran of May 1968, Bruckner used the
language of third-worldism (i.e., of third world victimization) in an upside-down manner to make
the West the real victim. In a kind of inverted camera obscura Fanonianism, Bruckner offers the
white man's version of Fanon's (1952) *Black Skin, White Mask.* Whereas Fanon spoke of the colonialist and racist mechanisms that generated self-hatred on the part of blacks, Bruckner speaks of
the ways that third-worldism itself has supposedly oppressed white Europeans by imbuing them
with irrational guilt. Bruckner rejects what he calls Fanon's "ridiculous" plea to "go beyond" Europe,
arguing that "it is impossible to go beyond" democracy. "If the peoples of the third world are

to become themselves," Bruckner warns, "they must become more Western" (Bruckner 1983, 156). This equation of Europe and democracy is, of course, a staple of Eurocentric discourses. Yet Bruckner makes this equation just four decades after the advent, in the very heart of Europe, of the dictatorships of Mussolini, Franco, Hitler, and Petain. He makes it just three decades after Algerians under French colonialism had either no vote at all or one that represented a fraction of the vote of a European in Algeria. Yet Bruckner equates Europe with "democracy": Fanon had called for going "beyond Europe" precisely because Europe had not been democratic. Bruckner also resurrects the old narcissistic cliché—going at least as far back as Hegel—that only the West is self-critical and "capable of seeing itself through others' eyes" (156). Interestingly, Bruckner makes this claim shortly after demonstrating that he himself is incapable of seeing Europe through third-worldist eyes. But in any case, these claims of a unique capacity for self-criticism—coming just after Bruckner has displayed his own hypersensitivity to criticisms of the West—seem very strange. How did Bruckner acquire such transhistorical God-like powers? Or is he just a latter-day avatar of the West's "Prospero complex"? Has he, like Ines in Sartre's *No Exit*, looked into others' eyes only to see himself?

Bruckner (1983) does, admittedly, make a few points with which we entirely agree, although he is not the first to make them. He calls attention to a certain religious (largely Christian) substratum in some left-wing thought (but then that is equally true, if not more so, of right-wing thought). He criticizes the tendency of some Western leftists to project themselves into proxy struggles abroad and to idealize third-world revolutionaries. We too have criticized the upside-down narcissism that sees Europe as the source of all evil, and the naïveté of those who imagine that third-worldist movements are exempt from contradiction or oppression. Bruckner also rightly criticizes the uninformed enthusiasm of Western third-worldists who praised revolutions that they knew nothing about. First-world Maoists, for example, were convinced that the cultural revolution in China had produced a new mutation in human sexuality, thus misrecognizing a repressive form of one-party and cult of personality rule (and the sexual manias of Mao himself). Bruckner also scores the hypocrisies of third-worldists who failed to see the continuities between French imperialism and American imperialism, which he compares to a case of "the old prostitute, now impoverished and needy, denouncing the perversity of the young whore as a way of whitening her earlier misdeeds." These are all valid points, even if we might have expressed them differently and within a different purpose. But what strikes us, looking at his text in the light of the later "culture wars," is the extent to which Bruckner anticipated the hysterically lachrymose tone of victimization—the real "culture of complaint"—of the antimulticulturalists in the United States (and in France) a decade later.[1] Poor Europeans! Poor whites! Powerless and persecuted and penniless all over the globe, confined everywhere by an oppressive color line, subject everywhere to racist taunts, disproportionately imprisoned, harassed by police, misrepresented by the media, stereotyped as lazy and criminal, the last hired and the first fired, their culture repressed, living in poverty because of their race, guilty of nothing more than the color of their skin! It turns out that Bruckner really does not mind "the white man's sobs," as long as those "sobs" are for the white man himself, the product of the white man's own self pity. Here we have the new "white man's burden" of not being appreciated as the beautiful and generous creatures that they are. Here Bruckner anticipates the besieged tone of the antimulticulturalists in the United States, presumably defending the ramparts of a threatened Western civilization. Like them, Bruckner conveniently forgets that the West is overwhelmingly empowered in military, economic, cultural, political, and media terms.

At times, and especially in the footnotes, one senses that for Bruckner, in the period of the "Zionism is racism" proposition in the UN, Israel and Jews are at the very kernel of the West; for him, a threat to one is a threat to the other (1983, 219). In a transfer of affect, Bruckner attributes to the imperial and often anti-Semitic West the historic legacy of Jewish suffering. Apart from the fact that few of the West's critics call the West a "cosmic catastrophe" or a "monstrosity to be wiped off the map," Bruckner here transfers the language of exterminationist anti-Semitism to movements that are critical of certain oppressive features of the "West." Here Bruckner displays an astonishingly short historical memory. After centuries of Western anti-Semitism, going all the way back to the Inquisition and even earlier to medieval blood libels and pogroms, writing only forty years after the Jewish Holocaust taking place in Europe, a Holocaust practiced only by Europeans, and just four decades after the Vichy government sent over 50,000 Jews to the death camps, Bruckner portrays the "Jewish state" as consubstantial with the West. One would have thought that Israel was founded, at least in part, because the experiment with Jewish equality and safety in Europe had failed, not because it had succeeded. And in what sense is Israel "Western," and why would this "Westerness" necessarily be such a good thing? Is Judaism an exclusively Western religion? Israel is physically situated next to Egypt, Jordan, and Lebanon—are they "Western" countries? Are Hebrew and Arabic (the language of Palestinian Israelis and of Arab Jews who were displaced to Israel) Western languages? In demographic terms, the majority population of Palestinian Arabs and Oriental Jews (Mizrahim, coming from Islamic countries dominated by French and British colonialism) is Eastern, not Western, and even Israel's Ashkenazi Jews (the "Ostjuden") came largely from the "East" of Europe. What leads Bruckner to pronounce all those Iraqi and Iranian and Moroccan Jews honorary "Westerners"? And more important, how did Israel, and presumably Jews, become part and parcel of a West seen as synonymous with democracy and tolerance, given the West's shameful and endlessly documented history of diabolization of its perennial inernal other—the Jews? Here contemporary geopolitical polemics get superimposed on a simplistic reading of a complex history.

The subtitle of Bruckner's (1983) book was "The Third-World, Culpability, and Self-Hatred," and the book's special feature is its psychologistic stress on the "imbecilic masochism" and needless feelings of guilt forced on white Westerners. For us, in contrast, the issue is not so much guilt over the West's past and present actions—although guilt is on one level a perfectly normal reaction to slavery, anti-Semitism, and colonialism—but rather lucidity and responsibility to make sure that such ills do not occur again, and that their memory—as in the slogan "never again"—is preserved. But as Kristin Ross points out, the dominant emotion among third-worldists, whether in Paris or Rio or Berkeley, was not guilt but anger. Third-worldist discourse, as Ross puts it:

> far from being masochistic or self-hating in its attention to the unevenness and disequilibrium between rich and poor nations, was an aggressive new way of accusing the capitalist system—multinational firms, aid programs from the United States or western Europe—the whole neo-imperialist apparatus, culminating in Vietnam. Third-worldists did not feel "personally" responsible for third-world misery, as Bruckner asserts; rather, they were actively pointing a finger at those—the military, state leaders, big business—who they thought indeed were responsible. (Ross 2004, 163)

Is Bruckner suggesting, Ross asks, that the United States did well to drop three thousand tons of bombs per minute on Vietnam, or that the French empire in Vietnam and Algeria should have been maintained? Bruckner would presumably not answer "yes" to such questions, thus he is virtually obliged to develop a hysterical discourse of victimization in defense of a West presumably on the verge of extermination, yet in fact as dominant as ever.


## LEFT CRITIQUES

Although we can easily mock or ignore the hysterically uninformed attacks on multiculturalism from the Right, it would still be useful to address some of the more "friendly" critiques sometimes made from the Left. In France, both the Left and the Right were united in rejecting multiculturalism. Within the multicultural debate, French intellectuals have generally taken the antimulticultural side. Some of the milestones in the debate include the "affaire du foulard" (or the Islamic headscarf affair) in the late 1980s, various journalistic articles about "le politiquement correct" in the 1991s, the attacks on the "sexuellement correct" in 1993, and the publication of the Bourdieu/Wacquant "cunning of imperial reason" essay in 1997 in *Actes de la Recherche en Sciences Sociales*, and the recent banning of religious insignia in French schools. The American right-wing spoof on p.c., *The Official Politically Correct Dictionary and Handbook*, was translated into French in 1992, mistakenly understood not as a parody but as a work of Zolaesque naturalism by many French intellectuals. For a time in the early 1990s, a large swath of the political spectrum in France seemed to delight in denouncing multiculturalism as a symptom of American decadence and hysteria. Journalists spoke of a "frightening" America. Rather than a critical antiracist and anti-imperial project, "multiculturalism" was mobilized in the usual comparative manner, coming to evoke everything about American "race relations" that France did not want.

This apparent French united front against multiculturalism has led to bizarre alignments. The Left, incarnated by *Les Temps Modernes* and *Esprit* and *Liberation,* seemed not to notice that it was siding with George Bush, Pat Buchanan, and the extreme Right in the United States. To our multiculturalist ears, French leftists end up sounding like U.S. right-wingers. French leftists and centrists, not unlike American neoconservatives (and some liberals), see the multiculturalist movement as antidemocratic and divisive. They too appeal to the same tropes of "Balkanization," "Lebanonization," and "the cult of difference" deployed by American right-wingers such as Samuel Huntington. Some French antimulticulturalists even link the multiculturalist "cult of difference" to fascism, much as right-wing American talk-show hosts speak of "thought control" and "feminazis." The same left French intellectuals, who would have normally denounced George Bush père in terms of his neoliberal and neoimperial policies, adopt a Bushite rhetoric on the issue of multiculturalism and "political correctness." It was George H. W. Bush, after all, who used the p.c. phrase, even if he did not invent it, to condemn radical Left movements on campus. His purpose was to put all alternative thinking on campus on the defensive. We see the paroxysm of this transatlantic malentendu when the formerly "leftist" (now centrist) newspaper *Liberation* turns for an account of American multiculturalism to none other than Dinesh d'Souza, the American neoconservative whose book *The End of Racism* argues, to put it crudely, that slavery wasn't so bad (and anyway Africans did it too), that segregation was well intended, that racial discrimination can be "rational," and that African Americans have reintroduced "barbarism into the midst of Western civilization."

One "left" critique claims that the very concept of multiculturalism is itself Eurocentric, designed to account for cultural diversity only within the nation-states of the North, which ethnocentrically imposes its inappropriate concepts on the South.[2] According to this critique, "Northern" multicultural ideas end up becoming a means of Eurocentric intellectual domination. In the South itself, meanwhile, the concept of multiculturalism is seen as encouraging dangerous forms of separatist communitarianism. This critique is doubtless valid for some "shallow" and epidermic forms of official multiculturalism. But it all depends, in the end, on precisely which multiculturalism one is talking about. Multiculturalism is a constellation of discourses, a master code in which competing discourses do ideological battle. Like any term that crystallizes very complex debates, it does not have a single valence, whence the need to characterize the specific drift of the multicultural project one is defending. In any case, we would question the idea that the relevance of multiculturalism is limited to the nation-states of the North. Can it plausibly be argued that a critical discussion of the patterns of racial hegemony in the settler states of the Americas is relevant only to the United States, but not to Mexico or Brazil? Most of the countries of the Americas configure the same racialized stratifications created by colonial history, involving indigenous genocide (true of most of the Americas), slavery (true of most of the Americas), immigration, syncretism, and so forth. It is absurd to say that issues of reparations, affirmative action, and multicultural education are relevant to only one settler state in the Americas.

It is our assumption that structural oppressions with racial undertones are common to the black Atlantic and even to the former colonizing countries themselves. Racism, in this sense, is a pan-European disease. The 2002 Durban Conference on Racism and Xenophobia called attention to these unacknowledged continuities by bringing representatives from the entire world—indigenous Americans, black Brazilians and Americans, and Dalits from India—to accuse countries such as the United States, France, and Brazil of being complicit with racism and colonialism, making them the objects of demands for reparations and other compensatory measures of redress. The South and the North have much more in common, then, than some would like to recognize; they are coimplicated, interdependent, linked in multifarious ways. Finally, the critique assumes that the South (aka the third world) exercises no intellectual agency within the multicultural project. But in fact the various worlds are intellectually commingled. Many of the source ideas of multiculturalism—anticolonialism, dependency theory, the critique of European humanism—are associated as much with the South as with the North. The North/South divide, although heuristically useful, is premised on overly stark lines of separation; the lines in fact are much more porous.

A second "left" critique of multiculturalism, one associated with the journalist David Rieff and the theorist Slavoj Žižek, suggests that multiculturalism is the perfect expression of the cultural logic of multinational or global capitalism (one without a homeland) and a new form of racism. In a 1993 essay in *Harper's*, Rieff argued that multiculturalism was the bedfellow of consumer capitalism: the collapse of borders, far from being the liberating event that the academic multiculturalists have envisaged, has brought about the multiculturalism of the market, not the multiculturalism of justice. For Rieff, corporate executives are no longer committed "to notions of European superiority."[3] On the one hand, Rieff makes a good point—people of all races can staff market economies and multinational corporations, but they do not bring about justice. But what Rieff's critique misses is that corporate executives are the last people who need to consciously argue for European superiority; it is enough that the corporations themselves inherit the unequal structures and tendentious perspectives bequeathed by centuries of European economic domination. And even "insiders" such as Niall Ferguson argue that globalization is merely a new name for (what he sees as a benevolent) imperialism.[4]

Žižek, meanwhile, argues that multiculturalism is "the ideal ideological form of global capitalism" that posits a kind of global viewing position that treats "local cultures in the way that the colonizer treated colonized people" as "natives whose customs should be studied and respected." Multiculturalism, for Žižek, is indirectly racist, in that it operates from an invisible vantage point presumed to be universal from which it can appreciate or depreciate other cultures, ultimately "affirming its own superiority" (Žižek 1997, 44).

Like most critics of multiculturalism, Žižek never mentions any actual multicultural work or thinkers who exemplify the trends he is denouncing, making it difficult to even evaluate his accusations. For us, Žižek's hasty slippage from multiculturalism to global capitalism ignores the fact that radical versions of multiculturalism are deeply aware of the pernicious role of multinational corporations and global capitalism. But more importantly, the Žižek critique involves a number of "low blows" and boomerang arguments. Žižek borrows multiculturalist arguments, as if they were his own, to discredit multiculturalism. Indeed, his critique seems persuasive only to the extent that radical multiculturalism has prepared the ground for the acceptance of his criticisms, in that his essay encodes concepts, such as the critique of false universalism and of narcissistic monoperspectivalism, which are already axiomatic and hyperfamiliar from *within* radical multiculturalist discourse. In this example of (presumably unconscious) appropriation masquerading as critique, Žižek draws virtually every term and argument, here supposedly marshaled against multiculturalism, from the multiculturalist corpus itself. In other words, the very field that Žižek is demonizing prepared the ground that makes his argument sound persuasive. It is as if someone were to borrow Marxist concepts to accuse Marx himself of "alienation" or "commodity fetishism," without acknowledging that the concepts themselves were developed by Marx. The critique of the arrogant yet unmarked Western vantage point, that of the "monarch-of-all-I-survey" within colonialist travel literature, for example, is examined in Mary Pratt in *Imperial Eyes*.[5]

The Žižek critique, then, reproduces what is by now the standard repertoire of multicultural ideas. The critique of normative whiteness as "unmarked," for example, can be found in the work of Toni Morrison, Caren Kaplan, Richard Dyer, and George Lipzitz. Nor is radical multicultural work a cute endorsement of folkloric customs, as Žižek suggests; rather, it denounces the ethnocentric binarism that produces the very concept of "folklore" as an allochronic residue of the past rather than a vital cultural production in the present. In sum, Žižek stereotypes the debate itself, borrowing from multicultural concepts and topoi even while discrediting multiculturalism, attributing to a totalized movement the very terms and procedures that radical versions of that movement have denounced. Indeed, there is a double problem with Žižek's generalizations: he attributes multicultural ideas to those who do not claim them (e.g., transnational corporations) while hiding the fact that multiculturalists do claim the very ideas that he is advancing.

Furthermore, Žižek's spatialized imagery—which positions multiculturalism as having a superior vantage point from above—assumes that multiculturalism always comes from the top and has a diffusionist idea of its own knowledges. Žižek forgets that multiculturalism, which initially emerged from minoritized communities and racialized groups as well as from privileged (or unprivileged) academics, has won for the marginalized perspective a "looking space" from which to view the dominant society. In our view, the right wing is wrong to demonize the multiculturalist movement, but it is not wrong in seeing the movement as an updated version of 1960s antiracist radicalism. The energies that fed into multiculturalism do indeed trace back to the minoritian and revolutionary movements of the 1960s, whether decolonization in the third world or civil rights and black and Latino power movements in the first world, just as the right-wing attack on multiculturalism traces back to the counterinsurgency government operations and the racist backlash against these very same movements. By obscuring these historical origins and movements, Žižek has muddied that historical narrative by denying all cultural agency and political productivity to those groups whose work flows into the larger stream of the movement. The fact that the multicultural movement has tended to be strong on campuses does not mean that the movement is "only academic." That native Americans, blacks, and Latinos now have even a limited voice in the academe was the result of struggles that went far beyond the academe. And in any case, can one defame a movement simply because some academics—people not unlike Žižek himself—participate in it? Cannot people on the "top" side with people at the "bottom," and work to undo the effects of social/racial hierarchies, and cannot the people at the "bottom" also produce knowledge? And are left multicultural academics, in a world increasingly dominated by conservatives and the Far Right, in any real sense on "top"? Does not such an argument risk aligning itself with the right-wing populism that focuses not on the corporate-military-political elite but only on liberal intellectuals? The actual connections and articulations between progressives in the universities and resistant members of the communities are much more complexly articulated than Žižek implies. Despite Žižek's outrageous charge that the multiculturalist project—a project where antiracism has been the norm—is implicitly racist, it seems to us that Žižek has practiced his own form of intellectual racism by denying agency to the people of color who form part of the multicultural coalition. It is as if Žižek cannot imagine that people of color actually came up with these ideas. Like the Eurocentrics who tried to explain away the majestic ruins of Zimbabwe as somehow European in origin, Žižek seems to think that only white people could have thought them up.

A third "left" critique argues that multiculturalism is apolitical, eliding relations of power, exploitation, and inequalities. The silently paternalist notion of "tolerance" does not oblige any real interaction with the "other." Here again, we would suggest, it all depends on which multiculturalism one is actually talking about. The innocuous and by now taken-for-granted concept of "tolerance," which goes back to John Locke in the Protestant world, or even to the Ahel-al-Kitab ("peoples of the book") in the Islamic world, cannot be seen as a central point in the multiculturalist project. Again, radical multiculturalists have criticized "tolerance" in similar terms, just as they have criticized psychologistic and moralistic approaches to issues of racism. This critique presumes, again, that multiculturalism always comes from a top that paternalistically tolerates cultural difference. But the critique resonates only if one is speaking of the most superficial aspects of multiculturalism—what a Peter Sellers sketch once mocked as the "take-an-Indian-to-lunch-this-week" syndrome—rather than of its fundamental formulations.

George Yúdice—who certainly does know the multicultural literature—develops a much more sophisticated but in some ways cognate critique of multiculturalism as apolitical when he argues that "cultural expression" and "artistic trends such as multiculturalism that emphasize social justice" are "not enough." To which we say: of course; nothing is enough, yet everything is important. Although we agree with Yúdice that cultural expression alone cannot solve racial strife and end imperialism, that does not mean that culture is not an important sphere of political action. Art does have real effects; it does not merely reverberate in the valley of its expression. Popular art and culture, for example, shape collective fantasy, move the body politic. They can offer, to use Yúdice's own words, "a knowledge of social reality otherwise unavailable" (Yúdice 2003, 130). Indeed, the examples of bottom-up cultural agency that Yúdice brilliantly explores in *The Expediency of Culture* inspire a certain amount of optimism, even if they are "not enough." Nor do we think the multicultural project is only artistic; the multicultural corpus is multidimensional, and at its most radical it does address deep structural inequalities, even if it offers no easy remedy. What Renato Rosaldo (1989) in the late 1980s called "cultural citizenship"—the idea that groups of people bound by shared social cultural and physical features should not be excluded from the public sphere—is in our perspective one answer to the deformations of master race rule. It is too easy to conflate "multiculturalism" with the simulacral and merely epidermic diversity promoted by George Bush, for example, as Yúdice does when he says that "the Bush administration acutely sought to parlay its tutti-frutti (albeit homogeneously conservative) multicultural composition into political capital" (Yúdice 2003, 339). The word *multicultural* here becomes a synonym for multiracial; it has nothing to do with a multicultural project that the right wing has consistently opposed. Bush, to our knowledge, never endorsed the multicultural project; indeed, his father and his ideological alliances (such as William Bennett and Lynne Cheney) consistently demonized it and concretely undermined projects—such as affirmative action or multicultural pedagogy or revisionist history—that formed a standard part of the multicultural project. The multicultural movement in the United States cannot be limited to Karen Finley-style provocations; it also includes concrete educational projects concerning how history is taught, projects that the right wing has fought tooth and nail.

A fourth "left" critique suggests that the multicultural project is tethered to a nation-state frame, giving special status to those peoples whose collective existence is subordinated to the hegemony of the constitutional orders of the nation-state. This critique, as we have suggested in our own work, is perhaps valid in terms of some aspects of the top-down multiculturalism in places such as Australia or Canada, or in terms of some forms of "diversity" multiculturalism in the United States, but it is hardly true of the more radical versions of multiculturalism as a transnational and diasporic project. Indeed, the drift of our work here, and of the work of the other figures that we cite, is precisely to think outside of "the box" of the nation-state.

A fifth "left" critique, finally, suggests that multicultural studies, specifically those areas conventionally called cultural studies and postcolonial studies, privileges themes of mobility and migration and diaspora with a special emphasis on postcolonial diasporic intellectuals, while downplaying other situations characterized by forced or subordinate mobility (refugees, migrant workers, etc.). This emphasis is seen in the hybridity theory too often attributed exclusively to Homi Bhabha (despite the long-term theoretical antecedents of hybridity theory in Latin America and the Caribbean) or in the exclusive emphasis on literary and expressive forms of culture, which universalizes the category of displacement, as if the voluntary movements across borders of elite diasporic upper-class postcolonial intellectuals could in any way be equated with the painful and humiliating itineraries of desperate refugees. In our view, this is a valid critique of some of the work in question, but we would add that the multicultural field in the broadest sense is full of critiques of exactly this type (Kaplan 1996).

As for the undue privileging of culture, it must be remembered that culture is no longer "just" culture; in the era of global capitalism especially, culture has become the privileged space of the articulation (and sometimes the disarticulation) of the reproduction of capitalist social relations. For David Lloyd and Lisa Lowe, culture gains political efficacy when it enters into contradiction with political or economic logics of exploitation and domination (Lowe and Lloyd 1997). The point is not to look for a pure space of resistance outside of capitalism, but rather to discern what elements emerge historically in difference with and in relation to capitalism. Here many have questioned the Eurocentric forms of Marxism that tend to subordinate all struggles to class struggle, minimizing the importance of struggles revolving around race, ethnicity, gender, ecology, and so forth. Feminist theory, postcolonial theory, subaltern studies, poststructuralism, queer theory, all offer conceptual instruments relevant to these other struggles. The multidimensional character of the forms of oppression engender equally multidimensional and variegated forms of resistance and struggle, shaping new social actors, new vocabularies and strategies.

An alternative, counterhegemonic globalization, to return to our initial discussion, strives to diminish social inequalities both between and within countries. It seeks a more equal exchange between countries, not free trade but fair trade. (The propaganda coup of the globalizers was to portray the "antiglobalizers"—as for example in the euphoric pronouncements of journalist Thomas Friedman—as hostile to trade and progress.) With an alert eye to the possibilities of dialectical jujitsu, Portuguese critic Boaventura de Sousa points to five "fields" in which counterhegemonic globalization creates viable opportunities: (1) participatory democracy; (2) alternative systems of production; (3) multicultural justice and citizenship; (4) biodiversity and communitarian knowledge versus corporatized intellectual property rights; and (5) new working-class transnationalism. While provoking new forms of racism, globalization can also create new conditions for the emergence of transnational and multicultural resistance. Globalization can therefore be oppressive or resistant, conservative or emancipatory. And to our mind, all these issues are imbricated with multicultural issues; "participatory democracy" is an answer to "master race democracy"; biodiversity is linked to the indigenous peoples of the Americas; a new working-class transnational solidarity depends on transcending racism, and so forth.

## TRANSNATIONAL RELATIONALITIES

The various discursive positions for and against conquest, slavery, racism, and imperialism have been "available" for a long time; contemporary versions of multiculturalism are merely "revised" editions of those earlier debates. The various multicultural positions are not static or transhistorical, they are "situated utterances" molded by evolving events and conditions. Yet there are discernible patterns within all the mutations; there are lines that lead, in a kind of historical morphing, from Columbus to George Bush, for example, or from the Spanish priest Bartolome de las Casas to present-day liberation theology, or from the sixteenth-century Brazilian Tupinamba rebel Cunhambebe to the present-day Kayapo activist Raoni.

We have argued for, and tried to demonstrate, the cognitive power of transnational comparison and the "mutual illumination" it affords. The topos of the unitary nation camouflages the possible contradictions within the nation. The unity, furthermore, tends to be imagined in terms of those who are dominant in the nation. The nation-states of the Americas, for example, "hide" the existence of indigenous nations within the larger nation. All nations are, in Bakhtinian terms, "polyglossic"—featuring the speaking of many "natural" languages—and "heteroglossic," characterized by a multiplicity of social dialects, jargons, discourses, and ideologies. In all countries there are competing constellations of models. All nations, furthermore, are really internations; they are indelibly marked by the presence of the other nations with which they have come into hostile or friendly contact, for and against which they have defined themselves diacritically, with and against other nations. The paradox of identity, as Amin Malouf (2003) puts it, is that "everyone of [one's] allegiances links [one] to a larger number of people. But the more ties [one has] the rarer and more particular [one's] identity becomes."[6]

Although we have often critiqued the narcissism operative in some forms of U. S. multiculturalism, other narcissisms can also be at the root of some international opposition to multiculturalism. Despite their different geopolitical positioning, U. S., Brazilian, and French societies all bear the traces of various forms of Eurocentric educational systems and inferentially racist cultural institutions, of racist economic structures and political organizations, just as they all feature forces actively engaged in challenging such discourses and systems. Virtually all European countries, like the United States, have their racist and anti-Semitic movements: skinheads in Germany, Jean-Marie Le Pen in France, the Spanish expelling (again) the "Moros," the Czechs segregating the gypsies. The French newspapers, including Le Monde, are full of news items about discrimination in France based on appearance, name, and national origin. Polls, meanwhile, show that a fairly high proportion of citizens think there are "too many immigrants" or "too many Arabs" in France. This situation calls not only for a reflexivity about national narcissism but also for a transnational examination of the linked modes of institutional racism within diversely globalized spaces, all seen as rooted in a long international history. They all form part of historically linked and contrapuntally imaginable histories.

In the background of this search for new international and multicultural alliances is the perceived demise of "common dreams," a mourning for lost utopias, the lack of a strong response to what seems like the overwhelming forces of globalization, not only in the United States but also in Europe and in the third world. Concepts such as "cultural citizenship," "the progressive public sphere," "civil society," and "multiculturalism," as we suggested earlier, rush into the gap left by the defeat of third-world revolution and first-world socialism in the era of globalization. In such a situation, where the loss of utopian projects grounded in the universal is rudely felt, it becomes a temptation to scapegoat one nation, or one kind of scholarship. But one does not strengthen the Left by denouncing difference, and one does not strengthen a new internationalist alliance against globalization by insulting potential allies.

## NOTES

1. See Pascal Bruckner (1983, 12, my translation).
2. When we give talks on Eurocentrism, we often hear this critique, usually worded as follows: "By denouncing Eurocentrism, aren't you still being Eurocentric?" That, we usually respond, is like saying that by writing against fascism we are being fascist.

3. See David Rieff (1993).
4. George Yúdice (2003), although ultimately agreeing with Rieff about a putative multiculturalist rejection of Marxism, points out that Rieff's (ultimately insincere) invocation of Marxism has an element of social resentment, that of the "public intellectuals" against presumably privileged academics.
5. We ourselves have examined the "imperial gaze" and the normative regard toward the third world as it operates in TV network news, in Hollywood westerns, and in first-world films set in the third world. See Shohat and Stam (1994).
6. See Amin Malouf (2003, 18).

## WORKS CITED

Bruckner, Pascal. 1983. *Le Sanglot de L'Homme Blanc: Tiers-Monde, Culpabilite, Haine de Soi*. Paris: Seuil.

Kaplan, Caren. 1996. *Questions of Travel*. Durham, N.C.: Duke University Press.

Lowe, Lisa, and David Lloyd, eds. 1997. *The Politics of Culture in the Shadow of Capital*. Durham, N.C.: Duke University Press.

Malouf, Amin. 2003. *In the Name of Identity*, trans. Barbara Bray. New York: Penguin.

Rieff, David. 1993. "Multiculturalism's Silent Partner." *Harper's 70* (August): 67–72.

Rosaldo, Renato. 1989. *Culture and Truth: The Remaking of Social Analysis*. Boston: Beacon Press.

Ross, Kristin. 2004. "The French Declaration of Independence." *Contemporary French and Francophone Studies 8*, no. 3: 273–84.

Santos, Boaventura de Sousa. 2004. The World Social Forum: A User's Manual. At: www.ces.uc.pt/bss/documentos/fsm_eng.pdf (accessed April 13, 2006).

Shohat, Ella, and Robert Stam. 1994. *Unthinking Eurocentrism*. London: Routledge.

Yúdice, George. 2003. *The Expediency of Culture*. Durham, N.C.: Duke University Press.

Žižek, Slavoj. 1997. *Plague of Fantasies*. London: Verso.

# 8

# THE POSTCOLONIAL BUBBLE

## Anouar Majid

The ambiguity inherent in the term *postcolonial* has accounted for both the inconclusive path to true liberation among the formerly colonized and the not insignificant cultural and literary contributions postcolonial subjects have added to the world culture as a whole. This ambiguity has allowed the late Edward Said to defend "subaltern" rights *and* preach the West's secular humanistic traditions as the only way out of the impasse confronting the world today. It also allowed Homi Bhabha, among others, to show how Euro-American hegemony is never a finished process, fraught as it is with ambivalences and the constant undermining of the West's or colonizer's claim to superiority through the mimicry of elites in colonies, or perhaps, even in the diaspora. The harder the West tries to disseminate its superior ways, the more anxious it is about its Others adopting them so thoroughly and successfully; thus, the West's racial and cultural claim to exclusivism will be undermined by the West's own universalist—and universalizing—ideologies. Because the colonized can potentially be domesticated, familiarized, and incorporated, the "colonial discourse produces the colonised as a social reality which is at once 'other' and yet entirely knowable and visible" (Bhabha 1994, 66–92). Otherness becomes troublingly slippery. (This anxiety is felt at the imperial centers, too, where high-tech and computer industries are disproportionately filled with the West's Others who are treated just as ambivalently by the "white" culture. When nuclear secrets in the United States are passed on to China, suspicion falls on the ethnically Chinese, because cultural essentialisms are working just as effectively at "home" as they do in the "Orient." Racial and ethnic profiling merely confirm that suspicion must first fall on the racially and ethnically Other.)

Such theoretical approaches to the question of the Other are no doubt illuminating and help us tease out the contradictory and inconsistent strains that often run in what seems to be a unified theory of culture or power; yet, in the final analysis, postcolonial theory has also been somewhat disabling because what it reveals is not too much of a revelation. We all know that life is more complex than it appears in any age or circumstance (absolutes are more often fiction than not), that some sort of exchange happens whenever and wherever paths cross, that power is always contextual and negotiable; yet knowing this does not preclude one from asserting that global power relations and national class divisions can be quantified with a better degree of certainty, and it is this assessment that leads me to conclude that postcolonialism, both semantically and theoretically, has, in the aggregate, made it more difficult for people to take stock of the colonial project and its aftermath. "When compared with neocolonialism, the term post-colonial," Ella Shohat wrote in 1992, "comes equipped with little evocation of contemporary power relations" (Shohat 1992, 105).

Arif Dirlik was equally unambiguous in his objections to the whole array of assumptions evoked by the term *postcolonial*. He saw it as the false consciousness of globalization, particularly because "postcolonial critics have been silent on the relationship of the idea of the postcolonial to its context in contemporary capitalism; indeed, they have suppressed the necessity of considering such a possible relationship by repudiating a foundational role to capitalism in history" (Dirlik 1994, 328–56). Again and again, and in a remarkably lucid argument, Dirlik shows how postcolonialism is in effect the cultural expression of capitalism in its current phase and that postcolonial theory disguises this relationship by being equally vague about its agenda. Dirlik's trenchant critique was joined by Aijaz Ahmad, who demonstrated how a concept that initially arose to describe a certain political condition confused things considerably when it was adopted by literary theory and criticism in the 1980s (Ahmad 1995, 1–20). The concept is so vast and slippery that it almost means nothing. What accounts for the properly postcolonial in the first place? And, to paraphrase Nathan Glazer's reference to multiculturalism (Glazer 1997), aren't we all postcolonials now because, regardless of our subject positions, the colonial experience, which is assumed to be superseded, no longer structures social relations?[1] Is postmodernity the cultural expression of postcolonialism? Even if that were the case, the epistemological dilemma would remain intact: aren't we all postmodern—Peruvian peasant and urban German, Islamist and latte-sipping computer whiz—regardless of our degree of awareness of this new global identity? To describe cultural diversities in privileged cosmopolitan spaces as sure signs of postcoloniality or postmodernity doesn't mean that those without the power to describe are not part of this new reality. We are all postcolonials and postmoderns—colonized and colonizers, Berber nomads and globe-trotting celebrities, starving children in Africa and suburban bike riders in North America—or we are not.

One can see how it's much better (at least theoretically) to stick to the basic Marxist formula and agree with Ahmad that "we should speak not so much of colonialism or postcolonialism but of capitalist modernity which takes the colonial form in particular places and at particular times" (Ahmad 1995). It is capitalism that defines social relations, driving the world into the dual but opposite raptures of faith and dissolution, the quest for authenticity and the drive for constant renewal and self-fashioning, a world of fortress builders and daring trespassers. A world of gross inequalities, fixations on imagined glorious pasts, radical capitalists with no vision of a collective human future, and self-appointed expansionists who are convinced of their mission to rescue Others. A world, in short, that fosters the conditions for terror.

Almost half a century after decolonization, the struggle for sovereignty continues in earnest, as the category of Otherness has been expanded through delocalization and, in many instances, deracialization. Colonial subjects are not only in India, Morocco, Ghana, and Nicaragua, but they are also in white towns and cities across the Euro-American map. The process of (neo)colonialism (managed by a global alliance of imperial elites and their comprador partners, a fact noted and derided by Frantz Fanon) is intensifying even as we look for cracks in its fabric. And as Shohat, Dirlik, and Ahmad have suggested a long time ago, this colonialism cannot be explained without reference to capitalism (whether one prefers to qualify it as "late," "advanced," or "global").

Once we accept the notion that colonialism (defined here as the dispossession of a people of their sovereign or "natural" rights, in the early Marxist sense) shows no signs of abating under the influence of diasporic contestations, slowed down by the rich legacies of a (Western) humanist tradition, or sabotaged by the subversive powers of mimicry and ambivalence, we can then account for two major theoretical lacunae in the corpus of postcolonial studies: the absence of religious revivalism, particularly Islam, from any serious discussion (except for Edward Said who was alone in trying to cover huge cultural expanses at once) and the insignificant attention given to the titanic "clash of civilizations" spectacle being thrust on the world community in the present. More than any other subaltern or national culture, it is Islam that has been fixed as the universal Other, and it is the Muslim who is now embodying the whole array of negative stereotypes typically assigned to all non-whites with equal measure. The clash between Islam and the West has coalesced whole histories of religious rivalries, racism, Eurocentrism, imperialism, and anticolonial struggles into one gigantic duel. But much like the ongoing hand wringing and nail biting over the issue of race in the United States, this fight merely delays the inevitable reckoning with the apocalyptic environment in which both the West and its Others are hopelessly entangled. The "clash" is a *danse macabre*, a death ritual among many others occurring across the globe, a sign that unless a new global order sees the day, we will not see our way out of a thickening darkness.

In more ways than one, the world has entered a phase of terror that seems to have no end under the prevailing economic conditions. The proliferating cult of the suicide bomber in the Middle East is part of a continuum of global violence that is affecting every sphere of life and cannot be read except as the cultural expression of a failed global system and civilizational model. And it is merely one form of suicide. According to the World Health Organization, the global death toll of suicide in 2001 exceeded those of homicide and war combined, and now accounts for about a million fatalities a year, costing billions of dollars. In 2003, more than 50 percent of violent deaths in Virginia were caused by suicide, including by men older than sixty-five and by veterans of the armed forces, while across the United States, "50,000 suicides and homicides are committed" each year. Among the causes listed for such grim statistics, the World Health Organization cites poverty, unemployment, personal loss, breakdown in human relations, and work problems—all features of capitalism, commonly known as globalization.[2] "Terror," Arjun Appadurai wrote in a recent book dealing with the "fear of small numbers" and the "geography of anger," is "the nightmarish side of globalization" and "the rightful name for any effort to replace peace with violence as the guaranteed anchor of everyday life" (Appadurai 2006, 32–33). In fact, the past few decades are marked by the growing attention of jurists, economists, and health professionals to violence. As if it needed proof, the authors of a study funded by the World Bank found a strong correlation between income inequality and crime (Fajnzylber, Lederman, and Loayza 2002), and another study by Paul Collier, director of the Development Research Group in the World Bank, showed that economists such as H. I. Grossman tend to see insurgents as "indistinguishable from bandits or pirates" and concludes that "dependence on primary exports, low average incomes, slow growth and large diasporas" are a toxic mix when it comes to the stability of country or region (Collier 2000). And in a first report of its kind ever, the World Health Organization reported in 2002 that violence is one of the leading causes of death and injury in the world (World Health Organization 2002). It is in this context that one can make sense of the mounting despair of the non-Western poor and the death toll it generates, a picture too grim to be explained away by the failure of Islam or other monotheistic religions.

No other event brought this reality more forcefully to the world's attention than the suicide of a humble South Korean farmer in the Mexican resort of Cancún. On September 16, 2003, the *New York Times* displayed a moving image that, at first sight, could have fooled even the best culturally trained eye. Twelve men or so, shoulder to shoulder, were photographed kneeling down on a small carpet, their shoes taken off and placed behind them, and bowing down in Muslim-like fashion. A second closer look quickly shows that these men were not facing toward Mecca (although the room in which the picture was taken could have easily passed for any of the makeshift mosques that dot the Western landscape) but toward the white-and-yellow photograph of Lee Kyung Hae, a gentle-looking man with a blue jacket and tie, surrounded by two elegantly knotted green ribbons, the picture sitting in an altar filled with white and green bouquets, the whole surrounded by elegant Korean script. The photograph produced an eerie impression, briefly collapsing two different cultural and religious traditions (Korean and Islamic) into a common ritual. For what makes this Korean ceremony of mourning similar to the ones being held for other Muslim "martyrs" is that Kyung Hae was a fifty-six-year-old farmer and president of the Korean Advanced Farmers Federation who had gone to Cancún to attend the Fifth World Trade Organization (WTO) Ministerial Conference held between September 10 and 14, 2003, with the determined purpose to commit suicide. On the day the WTO conference opened (coinciding with the Korean Thanksgiving holiday of Chusok and around the second anniversary of 9/11), Kyung Hae climbed the steel barricades separating protesters from officials and stabbed himself to death, thus concluding a long attempt (including a self-stabbing in Geneva a decade earlier) to bring the world's attention to the destructive impact of globalization on South Korean and, by extension, all the world's farmers. Before he killed himself, he distributed a handout denouncing the devastating impact of globalization on South Korea's rural communities: "I am crying out the words to you that have boiled so long time inside my body," he wrote (Becker and Thompson 2003).

Kyung Hae was now a hero in his rural community of Jangsu, much like many terrorists and suicide bombers become heroes in their native slums or barren suburbs (Brooke 2003). Indeed, Kyung Hae immediately acquired the status of a global martyr because his suicide was in fact quite common among the world's poor farmers struggling against agribusiness monopolies. That bloody moment in the sunny Mexican resort brought the world's attention to the plight of farmers around the world. Christine Ahn of the Food First/Institute for Food and Development Policy reported that in one year alone in India (1998–99), more than a thousand farmers committed suicide. One Indian activist told marchers in Cancún that "650 farmers committed suicide [in India] in just one month," a tragic statistic foreshadowing the catacombs of 2003, when 17,107 farmers, reeling from the combined effects of debt and shame at not being able to make ends meet, ended their lives, some by drinking pesticide. So desperate is the situation of Indian farmers that the celebrated writer Arundhati Roy declined "the prestigious Sahitya Akademi Award" in early 2006 to highlight their plight. And such tragic conditions are not the lot of India alone: even in prosperous Britain and Canada, suicide rates are much higher among farmers than in the rest of the population (Ahn 2003a, 2003b; Sengupta 2006).

Farmers are not alone. Miners and indigenous people, still brutally exploited in Latin America and Australia, are also blowing themselves up in protest against the antisocial policies of globalization. In March 2004, a miner blew himself up in Bolivia's congress, killing two people and injuring many others, capping a list of grievances ranging from the privatization of Bolivia's "vast reserves of gold and other mineral deposits" to the vanishing benefits for the working class (*Taipei Times* 2004; Perlez 2004). Bolivia, like the rest of Latin America, suffers from some of the highest forms of inequality in the world, and its people had just forced out Gonzalo Sánchez de Lozada, a president who had planned a $5 billion pipeline scheme to transport gas through Chile to the United States and Mexico. To Bolivia's indigenous people, globalization is a mere smokescreen for the same policy of dispossession that they have been subjected to since the Spaniards came looking for silver and gold about five hundred years ago. A foreign aid official in Bolivia reported in 2005 that Indians were still subjected to a "pigmentocracy of power," a system of apartheid that still bars them—the majority of the country's population—from some swimming pools and keeps most of them in abject poverty (Peter 2003; Slack 2003; Rohter 2003a; Powers 2005). In Chile, Latin America's poster country for prosperity and stability, the one-million strong Mapuche Indians, whose medicinal powers are being increasingly recognized, are being persecuted under terrorism laws and charged with "generating fear among sectors of the population" for standing up for their historic rights and reclaiming their lands that are being exploited and polluted by the timber industry. One Mapuche leader, exhausted by the government's stalling maneuvers, bluntly said, "We have the right to recover what was stolen from us, even if that means incorporating violence within our struggle" (Rohter 2004a; Devalpo 2006; Ariaga 2007).

Globalization didn't spare once-prosperous and rather egalitarian Argentina, either. By 2003, that country had spiraled down into shocking levels of poverty. According to statistics issued in January of that year, "at least 60 percent of the country's 37 million people [were living] in poverty, defined as an income of less than $220 a month for a family of four. That [was] nearly double the number toward the end of 2001. Even more alarming, more than a quarter the population [was] classified as 'indigent,' or living on less than $100 a month for a family of four." So bad had the situation become that Argentine doctors were "treating patients with kwashiorkor, a disease caused by lack of protein and characterized by its victims' distended bellies and reddish hair." It was only after Argentina's government chose to default on its more than $100 billion debt and defy the economic orthodoxy of the U.S.-controlled International Monetary Fund that the country regained its momentum and renewed the confidence of its citizens, who now poured more of their money into their economy, giving it the impetus to grow at the rather exceptional rate of 9 percent per annum. The economist Mark Weisbrot, commenting on the spectacular outcome of breaking away from global economic common sense, deemed Argentina's comeback "a remarkable historical event, one that challenges 25 years of failed policies." (Argentina's economic recovery did not, however, narrow the gap between the rich and the working classes) (Rohter 2003b, 2004a, 2006b, 2006c). Brazil, of course, has always been a study in gross class divisions. Income inequalities in this joy-exuding, samba-happy country have given rise to a mainstream culture of kidnapping, one in which average middle-class people could be ransomed for as little as $500. Trying to explain this routine form of business, one professor said that the socially excluded are refusing to be docile, and that "daily, well-structured acts of violence are no longer just the tools of the rich." The situation is so dire that a news magazine published a kidnapping "survival guide" in one of its issues. And whether fueled by poverty or not, drug gangs in Mexico are beheading people and dumping severed heads in bars to instill terror in rival gangs and government officials alike (Romero 2002; McKinley Jr. 2006).

Class disparities and poverty levels have become so bad in Latin America that leaders are being ousted in violent protests, politicians are being lynched by angry mobs, and people would rather have an honest tyranny than a democracy that serves as cover for plundering the people's resources (Forero 2004). (The drift toward authoritarianism is noticeable in Russia, too.)[3] No wonder the "Negro e Indio" (black and Indian) Bolivarian president of Venezuela, Hugo Chávez, keeps overcoming its well-organized and financed middle-class opposition to his attempt to improve the lot of the overwhelming Negro e Indio landless and hopelessly poor majority of that country. At the Sixth World Social Forum held in Caracas in January 2006, Chávez, who called President Bush "Mister Danger" and the United States a "perverse, murderous, genocidal, immoral empire," heralded the rise of indigenous peoples across America and proclaimed the rebirth of a new socialism and the defeat of U.S. imperialism. "There will be nothing beyond the 21st century if we don't change," he announced to an international crowd. The choice, he said, is between socialism and the extinction of the human species (*Chicago Tribune* 2006a; Navarro 2006).

And he is not alone to espouse such views. In 2004, Dr. Tabaré Vázquez, a socialist oncologist from a working-class background opposed to U.S.-backed free-market policies, won the presidency of Uruguay, supported by a coalition of progressives that included former Tupamaro guerilla fighters (Rohter 2004c). By the end of 2005, when Evo Morales—a forty-six-year-old Aymara Indian, a former herder of llamas who lost four siblings in childhood, a promoter of coca farming, a foe of globalization, a leader of the Movement Toward Socialism, and a champion of "communal socialism" —was given the mandate to run Bolivia, he immediately declared war on imperialism and the "neoliberal" economic model (also known as the Washington consensus). On the day before he was sworn in as president in the Bolivian Congress, Morales, barefoot and dressed in the costume of an ancient indigenous civilization, underwent a purification ceremony at the sacred site of Tiwanaku, about fourteen thousand feet above sea level in the presence of tens of thousands of Aymara and Quechua Indians, and vowed to end five hundred years of exploitation. "Today begins a new era for the indigenous peoples of the world, a new life of justice and equality," he announced. The following day, he told supporters that his "democratic, cultural fight is part of the fight of our ancestors. It is the continuity of the fight of Che Guevara." Soon after, Morales appointed a cabinet of Indians, Marxist intellectuals, and union members, then slashed his and their salaries by more than 50 percent, so that the president of Bolivia now makes less than $2,000 a month (the minimum wage in Bolivia is slightly more than $56 a month). On May 1, 2006, Bolivia became the first country in the twenty-first century to nationalize its hydrocarbon resources, until then scandalously exploited by foreign companies, and secured a majority of the revenues of all exploited gas fields. And by late November of that same year, Morales managed to confiscate unproductive private land to redistribute among the country's indigenous population. As a result of such measures, Bolivia quickly posted hundreds of millions of dollars in additional revenue and Morales presided over the best economy in forty-five years.

To his credit, David Brooks, the *New York Times* columnist, had seen this coming. When the United States was engrossed in the National Security Agency's spying on American citizens in late 2005, Brooks offered a Christmas gift to his readers by noting that the election of Morales "illustrated many of the combustible phenomena we'll be dealing with for the rest of our lives. It demonstrated that economic modernization can inflame ethnic animosity, that democracy can be the enemy of capitalism and that globalization, far from bringing groups closer together, can send them off in wild and hostile directions." Brooks wrote about how Bolivia's white elites, enriched through globalization schemes, had dispossessed most of the native Indians, and why the toxic mixture of race, ethnicity, and inequality in emerging democracies is likely to cause "ever-growing resentments and flare-ups" (Forero 2005a, 2005b, 2005c, 2006; Forero and Rohter 2006; Henningan 2006; Smith 2006a, 2006b; Crespo 2006; Lemoine 2006; Keane 2006; Romero 2006; Brooks 2005).

Not long after this dramatic victory of indigenous rights in a continent long bathed in the blood of the natives, Michelle Bachelet, a fifty-four-year-old single mother, pediatrician, agnostic, and socialist, won the presidency of Chile, defeating her billionaire opponent, owner of Chile LAN airlines, vowing to seek "change with continuity" and to work for women and the poor people's rights. And she didn't wait to declare her intention to work with Chávez and Morales, whom she considers legitimate "presidents elected by their peoples." By the time Bachelet was sworn in as president of her conservative country on March 11, 2006, she had appointed a cabinet equally divided between men and women (McDonnell 2006a, 2006b; Rohter 2006a; Reel 2006). Around the same time in Mexico, the fifty-two-year-old Andrés Manuel López Obrador (known as AMLO) of the Party of Democratic Revolution, the "plain-spoken and direct" son of a shopkeeper from the state of Tabasco, a former social worker and uncompromising leftist inspired by the legacy of the nineteenth-century Zapotec president Benito Juárez, running on a popular campaign to root out corruption, to cut down the privileges of elites, including slashing the salaries of government officials, to redistribute wealth and resources, and to stand up to Mexico's northern neighbor, was ahead of his two rivals in the presidential campaign. (He lost the election amid highly contested ballot counts.) Yet even this fiery politician was not convincing to significant segments of the downtrodden in Mexican society. On January 1, 2006, the enigmatic rebel/poet of Mexico, the ski-masked, pipe-smoking Subcomandante Marcos emerged from his Zapatista stronghold in the Lacandonian jungle of Chiapas to launch his own educational anticapitalist campaign, one powered not by big money and PR ads but by the *viento de abajo* (wind from below), and challenge the Mexican Left, including Obrador, to live up to its principles. Naming himself Delegate Zero, his message in the words of the *Los Angeles Times* was simply, "Capitalism is bad. Globalism is bad. Racism is bad. All politicians, all parties are the same—bad. The rich get all the breaks; the young and poor are ignored." Meanwhile, Mexicans who live in slums and make a living outside of the law are giving up on the country's traditional saints and creating their own, ones that sympathize with their plight. Thus, Santa Muerte, or Saint Death, "a scythe-wielding skeleton with a blood-curdling grin," a *cabrona*, or bitch, who prefers mariachi music, has appeared to lend succor to growing numbers of people living "on the fringes of a society besieged as much by renegade cops and corrupt politicians as by crime" (McKinley Jr. 2006a; Ponce 2006; Enriquez 2006; Thompson 2004).

In Peru, the forty-three-year-old nationalist caudillo Ollanta Humala, campaigning on a platform against globalization and elitism, and aligning himself with Latin America's leftist leaders, was the front-runner in that country's 2006 presidential race (Forero, 2006b). Haiti's endemic poverty and violent political culture may not inspire much hope in the future, but there, too, sixty-three-year-old René Préval, once a bakery owner, the "twin brother" of Jean-Bertrand Aristide, the exiled "fiery slum priest who could command this country's poor masses as firmly as Moses did the Red Sea," won an election despite avowed opposition from that country's elite (Armengaud 2006; Thompson 2006). In November 2006, when American voters were in the process of giving majorities in both houses of the U.S. Congress to Democrats, the Sandinista Daniel Ortega, long the leftist nemesis of U.S. administrations, won the presidential election in his country Nicaragua and wasted no time denouncing the U.S. military intervention in Iraq and vowing to work with Fidel Castro and Hugo Chávez. A few days later, Rafael Correa, a leftist forty-three-year-old mestizo who speaks Quechua, the main indigenous language of the country's Indians, and who counted Chávez as a friend, won the presidency of Ecuador, easily defeating a banana tycoon and promising radical changes in favor of the dispossessed. Like Michelle Bachelet of Chile, Correa immediately transformed the face of Ecuadorian politics, appointing seven women to his cabinet, including to the ministry of defense. Hugo Chávez, too, won a landslide reelection in early December 2006, giving further impetus to the Bolivarian revolution he had started. At his inauguration ceremony for another six-year term on January 10, 2007, he consolidated his pantheon of socialist leaders by adding Jesus Christ to the list. Jesus, he said, perhaps in reply to the Catholic Church's opposition to his socialist agenda, is "the greatest socialist in history."

And so, as the year 2006 was coming to a close, the rise of champions of the poor and dispossessed all over Latin American continued unabated, giving the Southern Hemisphere a political life and dynamism rarely witnessed in the world's major capitalist centers. "Five centuries after the European conquests," writes Noam Chomsky, "Latin America is [finally] reasserting its independence." Chomsky's enthusiasm is well justified, for when do full-blooded indigenous people or single, agnostic mothers ever have the chance to win the presidency in the more advanced North (Chomsky 2006)? Or, as Hugo Chávez had commented on the outcome of earlier elections in Brazil, Bolivia, Chile, and his own, "In Latin America, you have a laborer becoming president, that's Lula; an Indian, Evo, has arrived; a socialist woman; and a soldier—that's me, a revolutionary soldier—building a new South American project that is vital for the salvation of our people." Chávez may be dismissed in the U.S. media as a ranting ideologue, but many Latin Americans, as the Argentine novelist Luisa Valenzuela has noted, feel empowered by his politics (Ramirez 2006; *Chicago Tribune* 2006b; Hedgecoe 2006; Valdivieso 2006; Buncombe 2006; Romero 2006; Valenzuela 2007). Is it, then, surprising that when Chávez's fortune was ascending and Morales was elected in Latin America on populist platforms promising better lives for the poor and the indigenous, and vowing to face down the United States, the forty-nine-year-old Mahmoud Ahmadinejad, the son of a blacksmith, was elected president of Iran on a similar platform, defeating the much savvier, millionaire Ayatollah Ali Akbar Hashemi Rafsanjani? Although many Iranians are chafing under clerical cultural edicts, and businessmen tried to keep the socialist candidate out of the president's office, most Iranian people in 2005 were, in the end, more interested in securing a living and providing for their families. The economic policies of the outgoing President Mohammed Khatami, often praised in the West as a moderate, had benefited the upper classes while the condition of the poor and middle classes kept deteriorating. Ahmadinejad was elected because he denounced the "mafia of the rich" and promised a better life to the working poor. "People have been talking about head scarves and TV shows and music. Wonderful," opined a thirty-year-old Iranian, "but what about talking about having enough to eat or raise a family?" An exit poll, the *Washington Post* reported, "found many voters were motivated by anger over the gap between rich and poor. Even after the ultraconservative man who calls the United States "world oppressor" had become the object of satire in his own country and earned the fear and loathing of the West for his pernicious remarks on the Holocaust and his dogged pursuit of a nuclear agenda, he was still being appreciated throughout Iran, particularly in the long-neglected provinces, as the spokesman for the masses. He looked familiar to an eighteen-year-old bakery worker who said, "TV showed us his house. It was very simple. He is making these efforts for the people and all he wants is Iran's dignity." President Ahmadinejad's strong sense of social justice was revealed in his famous eighteen-page letter to President George W. Bush on May 8, 2006. After defending the rights of all the oppressed people in the world, the Iranian president said, "the people are protesting the increasing gap between the haves and the have-nots and the rich and poor countries." Even the Iranian activist and 2003 Nobel laureate, Shirin Ebadi, once the target of assassination by the clerical regime's henchmen, declared that, in the case of U.S. military intervention, "we will defend our country till the last drop of blood."[4]

The Korean Kyung Hae's death signaled yet another reversal. Twenty-one of the world's developing nations (known as G-21), such as India, Malaysia, Brazil, and South Africa, joined hands with even poorer nations in what was reported as an "attack" on the West by refusing to compromise on what a Senegalese delegate called their survival (*Times* (London) 2003; *Le Monde* 2003). The collapse of WTO talks in Cancún was considered an epoch-making event, the first major triumph of the colonized at the negotiations table. John Cavanagh and Robin Hood later wrote that the failure of the summit was "a turning point in the increasingly contentious globalization debate" because "for the first time in decades of globalization negotiations, democracy trumped narrow elite interests" (Cavanagh and Hood 2003).

Of course, this fiasco could have been avoided. Almost two months earlier, the *New York Times* had warned about such an outcome. In an exceptionally long editorial (covering its entire editorial space) warning against the consequences of the onslaught on the world farmers (96 percent of whom reside in developing and poor countries) through rich state subsidies to agribusinesses, it condemned such practices as "morally depraved." Such subsidies (at the rate of $2 per cow a day, double the income of about one billion people) allow the rich to dump their products at below cost in poor countries' markets, thereby undermining the world's struggling small farmers. "In the aftermath of 9/11," the *Times* continued, "Americans have desperately been trying to win the hearts and minds of poor residents of the Muslim world," but in countries like the Philippines, where farmers have suffered grievously since joining the WTO in 1995, Al-Qaeda is making inroads among the groups that are suffering the most (such as in the corn-producing region of the Mindanao island). "The United States and its wealthy allies will not eradicate poverty—or defeat terrorism, for that matter—by conspiring to deprive the world's poor farmers of even the most modest opportunities. And the threat of a devastating antiglobalization backlash set off by widespread resentment of 'northern' trade practices is enormous."[5]

In one brilliant editorial move, the *New York Times* managed to insert terrorism and Islamic extremism into the larger culture of despair produced by capitalism (termed euphemistically in all public discourse as "globalization"). It had put its finger on one of the primary causes of terror through acts of suicide. By charging the current economic regime with the rise of terror, it, in effect, mutatis mutandis, suggested that religion is less important than it appears in the rise of what one could only call the politics of suicide. The influential *New York Times* columnist and champion of globalization, Thomas Friedman, writing after the collapse of trade talks in Cancún, began his column, "The U.S. war on terrorism suffered a huge blow last week—not in Baghdad or Kabul, but on the beaches of Cancún" and blamed U.S. trade policies and double standards (Friedman 2003). In fact, Joseph Stiglitz, the Nobel prize laureate in economics, has shown that although the United States puts pressure on the poor to privatize, the United States supports new technologies and subsidizes farming, for it knows from experience that the role of government in developing the country is crucial. The International Labor Organization (ILO), then chaired by the presidents of Finland and Tanzania and whose board members included the head of Toshiba, saw globalization as not only having failed but, according to Stiglitz, as contributing to "social distress." "Premature capital market liberalization" and "unbalanced intellectual property provisions" are dangerous to so-called developing countries. Even a Pentagon report on countering terrorism, part of which was released in February 2006, recommended encouraging "economic prosperity abroad" as one of the strategies to overcome the insidious trend of terrorism (Stiglitz 2003, 2004; Shanker 2006).

Two months after the exceptional *New York Times* editorial was published, Robert A. Pape wrote for the same paper confirming, through research he had conducted between 1980 and 2001 and the data he had collected, that "religion is rarely the root cause" of suicide bombings, because the movement that is the leading instigator (75 out 188 incidents in the period covered by Pape) is Marxist-Leninist and opposed to religion—the Tamil Tigers in Sri Lanka. As if to confirm Pape's thesis, in the course of two days in October 2006, two Tamil suicide bombers were responsible for killing more than 110 people and wounding at least another 150 for the sake of their nationalist cause.

Religion is used as a strategy of recruitment, but the main (and secular) goal of Muslims and non-Muslims alike is the liberation of their territory from what they perceive as foreign occupation. Pape's findings helped explain, too, the futile attempt to destroy the Lebanese organization and militia Hezbollah in the summer of 2006, as Israel had hoped to do through military intervention in Lebanon. Examining the records of Hezbollah's suicide bombers in the 1980s, Pape's researchers were shocked to find out that out of thirty-eight identified suicide attackers, "only eight were Islamic fundamentalists. Twenty-seven were from leftist political groups like the Lebanese Communist Party and the Arab Socialist Union. Three were Christians, including a high-school teacher with a college degree. All were born in Lebanon." Hezbollah, despite its religious rhetoric, was, in other words, an umbrella organization akin to the "multidimensional American civil-rights movement" of the 1960s. (On the same day that Pape's article on Hezbollah appeared in the *New York Times*, the *Chicago Tribune* wrote on the raging popularity among all social classes, faiths, and denominations of Hezbollah's leader, Sheikh Hassan Nasrallah, in the Arab and Muslim worlds, confirming Pape's thesis that religious rhetoric often masks what are essentially political disputes. By the time the cease-fire was mandated in August, the *Times* reported that Hezbollah and its leader, with their unambiguous Islamic ideology, were widely celebrated as heroic resistance fighters restoring Arab dignity. Following the publication of the Iraq Study Group in December 2006, Pape strongly recommended that "American combat forces" leave Iraq because "more than 95 percent of all suicide terrorist attacks around the world have been caused by the presence of foreign combat forces on territory the terrorists value."

In a recent work, Mike Davis, the renowned scholar of cities and urban life, traced the history of suicide bombings to the earlier decades of the twentieth century, when all sorts of political movements used car bombs—a device inadvertently perfected by the Provisional Irish Liberation Army in 1972—to fight back against stronger states. It's hard to believe, but Wall Street was the target of terrorists in September 1920, when Italian anarchist Mario Buda, intent on avenging his comrades Nicola Sacco and Bartolomeo Vanzetti, packed his horse-drawn carriage with explosives, parked it near J. P. Morgan's offices, and walked away. His target, J. P. Morgan, was in Scotland, but the blast killed forty people and wounded more than two hundred.[6]

"Suicide bombing as a tool of stateless terrorists," legal scholar Noah Feldman writes, "was dreamed up . . . by European anarchists immortalized in Joseph Conrad's *Secret Agent*" and "became a tool of modern terrorist warfare only in 1983, when Shiite militants blew up the U.S. Marine barracks in Lebanon." According to Alan B. Krueger and Jitka Malecková, writing in the *Chronicle of Higher Education*, the rise of terrorism is "a violent, inappropriate form of political engagement," a "response to political conditions and longstanding feelings of indignity and frustration that have little to do with economic circumstances" (Feldman 2006; Krueger and Malecková 2003). Michael Shermer, reviewing a crop of books on suicide and suicide bombing, found out that religion and poverty play a minor role (if at all) in this troubling phenomenon, ranking behind political tyranny, a sense of hopelessness, and loyalty to preexisting bonds. Shermer coined the word *murdercide* to describe suicide bombers who seek death by maliciously plotting the death of others (in the United States some choose what's called "suicide by cop," putting themselves in a situation to be shot at by police officers). As the psychologist Thomas Joiner phrased it in his 2006 book *Why People Die by Suicide*, "people desire death when two fundamental needs are frustrated to the point of extinction; namely, the need to belong with or connect to others, and the need to feel effective with or to influence others." Nichole Argo, a graduate student and former freelance journalist for the *Jerusalem Post* in the Palestinian territories (from 2003 to 2004), found no convincing correlation between an irrational faith and suicide bombing, after both experiencing the situation on the ground and reviewing current scholarly works. (Argo thinks a more apt description of suicide bombers is "human bombs," because humans turn themselves into bombs to fight back.) The preliminary findings of a two-year Gallup poll in eight Muslim countries (published in May 2006) revealed that "fear of U.S. domination, not religious fanaticism" is what explains the rise of extremism, even in historically West-oriented nations such as Morocco and Turkey. Soon after the fifth anniversary of 9/11, U.S. intelligence agencies found that the U.S. invasion of Iraq had made terrorism worse. Most important, though, "according to neuroscientific studies, ritual effects do not require religion" because "any social ritual, where people are brought together in repetitive acts imbued with meaning, will do."[7]

In Cuban culture, suicide is so deeply embedded in the national psyche and ideology that it has practically become a fact of life, an idiosyncrasy that also explains Cuba's remarkable resistance to its mighty northern neighbor for almost five decades. "For more than 150 years," writes Louis A. Pérez Jr., "the rate of suicide has ranked consistently among the highest in the world." Cuba's national anthem, "La Baymesa" (1868), straightforwardly states that "To die for the patria is to live" (*Morir por la Patria es vivir*), a notion that survived in the twentieth-century revolutionary slogan "*Patria o muerte*" (Pérez Jr. 2005, 5–6). The motif of Cuban resistance fighters sounds eerily similar to the language of Muslim suicide bombers. In a poem titled "De la madre al hijo," a mother enjoins her son to choose death over indignity:

> Although I am your mother and love you
> > as son of the blood of my heart,
> I prefer to see you dead in campaign
> > than to see you slave.
> Act like a warrior,
> > for whom death does not frighten:
> The dangers of war
> > have been made for who is a man.
> And if you want to make a name for yourself
> > go fight for your land (Pérez 2005, 118–19).

It is this same sense of indignity among ghettoized and socially dispossessed African Americans that is the cause of the perplexing rise in murders over petty disputes in the United

States, young people killing each other over "mean mugging," code for dirty looks, or simply a perceived slight. For the downtrodden and hopeless, dignity is the last line of defense. The same thing is happening in class-divided France. A recent report found that gratuitous violence against individuals, triggered by nothing more than an argument over cigarettes or using the wrong word, is on the rise, even as general crime rates are declining.[8]

Ian Buruma, the coauthor of *Occidentalism: The West in the Eyes of Its Enemies* (2004), pointed out in an op-ed article that "history shows that the forceful imposition of even decent ideas in the claim of universalism tends to backfire—creating not converts but enemies who will do anything to defend their blood and soil." After explaining to a seemingly mystified audience of readers that "the main fault line crossing most Muslim societies isn't even between secularists and religionists, but between Muslims with different ideas about the proper role of religion," Buruma warned that Western military intervention (in Muslim societies) only strengthens the hand of extremists (Buruma 2004; Buruma and Margalit 2004). (Ironically, on the day Buruma's op-ed piece appeared in the *New York Times*, the same newspaper reported on the newest poll by the Pew Research Center for the People and the Press, conducted before the terrorist attacks on Madrid in March 11, 2004, showing the continued decline of the U.S. image abroad) (Sachs 2004).

The rise of political Islam in Iraq, Palestine, and across much of the Islamic world only proves that religion is the refuge of the oppressed. "History shows," explains Dilip Hiro, "that when an ethnic, racial, or social group is persecuted or overly oppressed, it tends to turn to religion to find solace. In the Americas, this was true, for instance, of the Africans brought in as slaves. It is not accidental that today African Americans are still more religious than white Americans." When the Palestinian political party Hamas—designated as a terrorist organization by the United States—shocked the world with its landslide victory in the legislative council elections of January 25, 2006, a taxi driver from Ramallah was quoted in the *New York Times* as saying that he favored Hamas because "it has clean hands, puts the poor before the rich and will resist the occupier." Meanwhile, the recourse to terrorism in Iraq had become so common after the U.S. invasion in 2003 that the Iraqi insurance industry, a surprisingly successful business even in the chaos of war and insurgency, was the first in the world to cover that risk.[9]

An injurious form of globalization, underwritten by the increasing militarization of diplomacy and international affairs, is, I am arguing, the main producer of extremism and violence in the world today. One need only recall that even an ideology as odious as Hitlerism was justified by Germany's rejection of globalization. As Doug Henwood noted in *Wall Street: How It Works and for Whom*, Hitler sounded deceptively progressive in *Mein Kampf* (1943) when he wrote that

> the task of the state toward capital was comparatively simple and clear; it only had to make certain that capital remain the handmaiden of the state and not fancy itself the mistress of the nation. This point of view could then be defined between two restrictive limits: preservation of a solvent, national, and independent economy on the one hand, assistance of the social rights of the workers on the other. . . . The sharp separation of stock exchange capital from the national economy offered the possibility of opposing the internationalization of the German economy without at the same time menacing the foundations of an independent national self-maintenance by a struggle against all capital. The development of Germany was much too clear in my eyes for me not to know the hardest battle would have to be fought, not against hostile nations, but against international capital (Henwood 1998, 303).

That globalization is running roughshod on the world's traditions and cultures, dehumanizing rich and poor, making life untenable for the latter, and fueling violent reactions and the politics of terror, is a condition that has not changed much in the past hundred years or so, regardless of the political status of newly developed nations, or the class membership of citizens in rich societies.

The despair generated by the classic capitalist syndrome of dire poverty in the midst of excess and waste is the reigning condition today. By the end of 2004, a report by the United Nations Children's Fund (UNICEF) drew the world's attention to the ravages of poverty among a billion children across the world, including in the advanced economies of the West. Noting that global military spending was $956 billion, while the cost of effectively combating poverty could range from $40 to $70 billion, one would think that the UNICEF report was a clear challenge to the global community to set its priorities straight. Even while the United States and Britain were fighting for more freedoms in the Middle East, child mortality in both nations was the worst recorded in twenty-four developed nations, according to a British study published in 2007. Children just seem to be another unfortunate casualty of capitalism (Dugger 2004; Dobson 2007).

Take a look at the figures provided by the Worldwatch Institute in its 2004 report to gauge the severity of the global condition. Not only is the misery of the poor intensifying, but the world's 1.7 billion members of the "consumer class" are literally consuming themselves—and our planet—out of existence (*State of the World 2004* 2004, 4). (Before it was recycled by spin doctors in the last part of the twentieth century, the word *consumption* itself had long been associated with violence, illness, and death) (Rifkin 2004, 379). Although family sizes are shrinking, houses are getting bigger. By 2006, a whole industry had emerged to organize the ever-expanding garages of befuddled homeowners, while an increasing number of full-time American workers, priced out of one-bedroom apartments, were turning their cars into residences (Brown 2006; Kocieniewski 2006; Urbina 2006). More than one billion people worldwide, according to the latest report from the Earth Policy Institute, do not have access to safe water supplies, yet bottled water, often no better than tap water, is now a $100-billion industry, one that adds to the world's pollution substantially and takes away from the resources needed to provide clean water for all (Arnold and Larsen 2006). Soda, meanwhile, is the world's third-favorite beverage, after tea and milk. "Luxury foods" with "marginal nutritional value" are doing a brisk business: "The $57-billion trade in coffee, cocoa, wine, and tobacco is worth more than international trade in grain," and depending on how it is defined, the "chocolate business is worth $42–60 billion annually," according to the same Earth Policy Institute report (Arnold and Larsen 2006, 4–5, 71, 94, 97). (In 2004, during a recovering economy with persistent unemployment and low-paying jobs, luxury products such as Porsche cars sold very well, as did merchandise at the elite stores Neiman Marcus, Nordstrom, and Saks Fifth Avenue, outpacing sales even at Wal-Mart, Sears, and Payless Shoes) (Strope 2004).

Despite the promise of computer technology, the consumption of paper has never been as high as it is today. Semiconductors are "more materials-intensive than most 'traditional' goods. A single 32-megabyte microchip requires at least 72 grams of chemicals, 700 grams of elemental gasses, 32,000 grams of water, and 1,200 grams of fossil fuels. Another 440 grams of fossil fuels are used to operate the chip in its typical life span." Welcome to the era of e-waste. Not that we are doing better with old-fashioned solid refuse. People in rich countries are producing so much of it (basically, 560 kilos of municipal waste per person per year) that the cost of America's contribution alone was calculated in the mid-1990s to be "at least $2 trillion (*State of the World 2004*, 2004, 44, 15)." Waste and pollution work in tandem. The plastic bag, scourge of the world's landscape, has been christened the "national flag" in Ireland and the "national flower" in South Africa, and although it doesn't make it out of the recycling bin or trash can in the United States, "Americans throw away 100 billion plastic grocery bags each year" (Strope 2004, 17, 22–23,44). And now that poorer countries are racing to catch up with the United States and the West, the situation will only get worse.

Who will fuel China (whose pollution levels are frightening) and India's meteoric growth when oil production is on course to shrink in the coming decades? In fact, nothing less than the fate of the world rests on what developmental model these emerging giants choose to pursue. According to the 2006 edition of *State of the World*, "if China and India were to consume resources and produce pollution at the current U.S. per-capita level, it would require two planet Earths just to sustain their two economies." These two countries' need for fresh water, oil fuel, grain, soybeans, and wood products far outstrips available resources, while their reliance on "coal-dominated energy systems" is directly affecting global climate change through the emission of high quantities of carbon dioxide. The Worldwatch Institute may see a glimmer of hope in these two nations' pursuit of sustainable models of development (Worldwatch Institute 2006), but their feeble attempt may well be too little too late.

James Lovelock, the British scientist who coined the term *Gaia* in the 1970s to describe how the Earth keeps itself fit for life and "conceived the first wholly new way of looking at life on Earth since Charles Darwin," shocked public opinion in early 2006 by asserting that we have passed the point of no return in damaging our habitat, and the best we can hope for now is a soft landing and a concerted effort to live with fewer resources in an ailing planet. The eighty-six-year-old environmental scientist was not a man given to alarmist statements, since in the 1970s he thought the Earth could take care of itself forever. But now he was warning that unless we do our best to make amends with our environment immediately, we will most likely end up in a dystopian world "led by brutal war lords." Soon after Lovelock's views were made public, no less than Britain's prime minister, Tony Blair himself, contributed the foreword to a new study titled *Avoiding Dangerous Climate Change*, accepting and warning of the impending prospect of disruptive climate change in this century. "It is now plain," Blair wrote, "that the emission of greenhouse gases, associated with industrialization and economic growth from a world population that has increased six-fold in 200 years, is causing global warming at a rate that is unsustainable" (Lovelock 2006; McCarthy 2006a, 2006b, 2006c; Weaver 2006).

The development of more efficient technologies—another mantra of progress—is only accelerating the current human catastrophe. "Modern industrial workers [can] now produce in a week what took their eighteenth-century counterparts four years," reports the *State of the World 2004*. A Toyota plant in Japan "rolls out 300 completed Lexuses per day, using only 66 workers and 310 robots." Supertrawler fishing vessels "can process hundreds of tons of fish per day. They are part of the reason that communities of many oceanic fish have suffered declines on the order of 80 percent within 15 years of the start of commercial exploitation." In fact, if present patterns of fishing continue unmodified, scholars in late 2006 predicted a "global collapse" of all marine species by the middle of this century. And yet corporations continue to spend heavily on advertising. In 2002, global spending on advertising reached $446 billion, more than half of which was spent in the United States. Even when the state restricts access to harmful products, advertisers find creative ways to reach consumers. For instance, according to the *State of the World*, "smoking is three times more prevalent in the movies than in the actual U.S. population" (*State of the World 2004* 2004, 17, 29; Dean 2006).

Ever since the salesman King Camp Gillette came up with the idea of disposable razor blades, a culture of "planned obsolescence" has taken root and is now financed primarily through debt. By 2002, the average outstanding balance on an American's credit card was $12,000, which at an average interest rate of 16 percent would cost the cardholder "about $1,900 a year in finance charges—more than the average per capita income (in purchasing power parity) in at least 35 countries" (*State of the World 2004* 2004, 12–15, 97). By the end of 2005, annual U.S. household savings were at their lowest since the Great Depression, with Americans spending $42 billion more than they earned and owing "$800 billion in credit card debt," while more than two million people applied for bankruptcy that same year. Much the same is happening in Britain, which by the end of 2005 accounted for two-thirds of the

European Union's credit card debt, while France's consumer credit is getting worse. And the number of insolvent Britons was expected to grow from "around 20,000 in 2005 to more than 100,000 by the end of the decade" (Thornton 2006; Egan 2005; Hickman 2006; Osborne 2006; Lentschner and Visot 2005; *Guardian* 2006a).

Needless to say, the political economy of globalization is directly responsible for the amount of violence that terrorizes the world today. (So accustomed have Americans become to violence that New York City at the end of 2005 celebrated the low murder toll of 537, a figure that compared quite favorably with 649 deaths in 2001 and 2,245 in 1990!) (Baker 2005). According to the director of the department of injuries and violence prevention at the World Health Organization, more than a million people, mostly in poor or middle-income countries, "die in road accidents, and 20 to 50 million are injured and survive, often with disabilities for the rest of their lives." Despite the decline in smoking, "tobacco-related medical expenditures and production losses cost the United States more than $150 billion" in 1999 (*State of the World 2004* 2004, 17, 29; Mohn 2007). While a recent report in the UK-based *Food Magazine* shows that intensive farming is depleting our vegetables, fruits, meat, and dairy products of minerals (*Food Magazine* 2006, 10; Lawrence 2006), obesity is now a global epidemic, with *National Geographic* giving it front-cover attention in its August 2004 issue, as if confirming that human evolution had entered a new phase with the ballooning sizes of our malnourished bodies. So many children are becoming obese that health officials are expecting this generation of children to die before their parents. Yet if people ate less ice cream, used less makeup, and spent less on pet food, the world's poor could be provided adequate food, clean water, and basic education (*International Herald Tribune* 2006; *State of the World 2004* 2004, 10).

A casual reading of any newspaper would reveal the depths to which our civilization is descending in the name of antiquated economic and political philosophies, yet the silence on such horrors is as deafening as the loud condemnations of religion as the main culprit of violence in the world today. When people are literally leasing or even permanently selling their foreheads as spaces for advertising and buying life insurance policies to resell to investors to collect profits upon their death, glaciers are melting and lakes are evaporating at a rapid pace (Striker 2005; Duhigg 2006; Chang 2005; Harvey 2005), and entire nations are struggling to keep up with a destructive way of life, isn't it time to widen our perspective and raise questions about the future of the planet itself? Just as many Muslims are unable to be self-critical or to think beyond their zone of comfort, so are the champions of capitalism, whether it be the Anglo-Saxon model, supply-side economics, or the Keynesian approach, unwilling to open the pages of their newspapers and periodicals to a robust, nonpartisan discussion of the reigning economic system. Those who are inclined to oppose adventurous wars in faraway lands somehow remain indifferent to the violence generated by the precarious social conditions of billions of people worldwide. Just as with the environment, such an approach is ruinous to winners and losers alike in the long run. The sooner we adopt that broader perspective, the better our chances for surviving and, perhaps, developing a more harmonious form of globalization.

It is in this context that the conflict between the world of Islam (which consists mostly of poor countries) and the West must be read, if we are looking for serious solutions to this global crisis. Many Muslims use religion as an ideology as much as other nations use patriotism and the defense of liberty to change their citizens' tendency toward disengagement and indifference and rally them to an old-style nationalism. It is true that the much-discussed Huntingtonian notion of the "clash of civilizations" seems to be justified by current events, that Islam seems to be on an ongoing course of collision with a Judeo-Christian West; but as I described, that is clearly not the case, and the divisions are not that neat. Even the notion that the West is roughly the domain of Christianity not only is a profoundly erroneous and misleading belief, but it also occludes the new schisms within Christianity itself, and how such schisms are further polarizing the world in unpredictable ways.

Philip Jenkins's thorough study of the New Christendom irrefutably proves that Christianity, not Islam, is the fastest-growing religion in the world. Basing his numbers on current estimates, Jenkins predicts that there will be around 2.6 billion Christians by 2025, and three Christians to every two Muslims in the world by 2050 (Jenkins 2002). The faithful of all major churches (mainstream and alternative) will be overwhelmingly Southern and poor. In Africa, where Christians outnumbered Muslims for the first time in the 1960s, and now form roughly one-half of the continent's population, Christian growth was phenomenal in the twentieth century. At least in Africa, the twentieth century was indeed a Christian Century.

Though often introduced by Europeans or Americans, Christianity in the South—not just Africa—quickly assumed messianic, millenarian, utopian, charismatic, prophetic, anticolonial, activist overtones, a trend that fit well with the expansion of Pentecostalism (the most successful movement in the twentieth century). As Laurie Goodstein explains,

> The world's fastest growing religion is not any type of fundamentalism, but the Pentecostal wing of Christianity. While Christian fundamentalists are focused on doctrine and the inerrancy of Scripture, what is most important for Pentecostals is what they call "spirit-filled" worship, including speaking in tongues and miracle healing. Brazil, where American missionaries planted Pentecostalism in the early 20th century, now has a congregation with its own TV station, soccer team and political party.[10]

Much like medieval Europe, the separation of state and church, or the Western notion of secularism, doesn't make any sense to this rising Christianity. The spheres of the temporal and the spiritual are one and the same. Sermons focusing on prayers for worldly success fill giant churches and stadia. In the Philippines, "El Shaddai followers raise their passports to be blessed at services, to ensure that they will get visas they need to work overseas. Many open umbrellas and turn them upside-down as a symbolic way of catching rich material blessings they expect to receive from on high," notes Philip Jenkins (Jenkins 2002, 67). Much as Christianity developed in its infancy (Jenkins 2002, 76), the next Christendom is fired not simply by biblical truths but also by a response to poverty and alienation in the world system:

> One common factor is that various Southern churches are growing in response to similar economic circumstances. Their success can be seen as a by-product of modernization and urbanization. As predominantly rural societies have become more urban over the past thirty or forty years, millions of migrants are attracted to ever larger urban complexes, which utterly lack the resources or infrastructure to meet the needs of these "post-industrial wanderers." Sometimes people travel to cities within the same nation, but often they find themselves in different countries and cultures, suffering a still greater sense of estrangement. In such settings, the most devoted and fundamentalist-oriented religious communities emerge to provide functional alternative arrangements for health, welfare, and education. This sort of alternative social system has been a potent factor in winning mass support for the most committed religious groups, and is likely to become more important as the gap between popular needs and the official capacities to fill them becomes ever wider (Jenkins 2002, 72–73).

This surge in Christian fundamentalism is spelling trouble for coexistence among faiths and between the South and the secular West. "Evangelical Christians [now] speak of the great missionary territory of the future as 'the 10–40 window,' a vast and densely populated rectangle stretching across Africa and Asia, from 10 degrees north to 40 degrees north of the equator." This is the "Resistant Belt" of Islam. Given this missionary zeal, the West should be as worried about a new "crusade" as it is about jihad. And Muslims won't be the only targets: in due time, the secular, capitalist, underpopulated North will be facing "the flags not of red revolution, but of ascendant Christianity and Islam." As it turns in disgust against this new Christianity, what some Westerners see as a "jungle religion," the West will come to be seen as "the final Babylon," the real "Heart of Darkness," ripe for conversion and overtaking (Jenkins 2002, 191–201). Already, African missionaries are preaching in New York and other parts of the United States, while entire segments of the Episcopal Church USA are seceding from their liberal dioceses in the United States to join more conservative affiliates in Africa and Latin America. By the end of 2006, Archbishop Peter J. Akinola, leader of the Anglican Church in Nigeria, famous for his condemnation of homosexuality, was "the spiritual head of 21 conservative churches in the United States" (Watkin 2004a, 2004b; Banerjee 2004a, 2004b; Goodstein 2006; Turque and Boorstein 2006; Polgreen and Goodstein 2006).The Nigeria-based Redeemed Christian Church of God is ministering in what has until recently been the whitest areas in Texas, such as Hunt County, and the Church's proclaimed goal is nothing less than "to establish parishes within five minutes' driving distance of every family in every city and town in the United States" (Romero 2005).

The clash between secularism and religion may be escalating, a clash in which poor literalist Christians from the Southern Hemisphere are rushing to the rescue of their wealthier brethren in the North, but the prognosis for relations between this Southern Christianity and Islam is getting worse (even though both are fighting the same demons of poverty and tyranny). Potential hot spots include Indonesia (where people asserted their Islamic identity during the Cold War to avoid the charge of communism), the Philippines (mostly Catholic but with a Muslim separatist group), Nigeria, Sudan, and even Kenya and the Ivory Coast (Jenkins 2002, 166, 169, 171, 177).

There is also no avoiding a proper accounting of the material conditions that undergird the proliferation of violence, extremism, and the clash of civilizations if we are to think our way out of this deadly impasse. Recent economic analyses have shown clearly that the global capitalist system has entered a phase of decline and crisis that is being reflected in global social and cultural breakdowns, including the rise of nativism across cultures. Not only is it abundantly clear that the rich are getting richer since the "financialization" of capital in the 1970s, but according to Giovanni Arrighi, the capitalist system that emerged in Renaissance Italy in an attempt to overcome the chaos that preceded it is itself breaking down, partly because the United States is unwilling to cede the torch to the next major capitalist player, East Asia (Arrighi 1994, 356). Even as the power of the nebulous middle class in high-capitalist societies is getting more precarious than ever (without a social or class consciousness to awaken it to its plight), the state's recourse to debt places it even more firmly in the grip of capitalist interests, thereby ensuring the longevity of the global dysfunctional system. It is, in fact, the booming trade in credit that is perpetuating class and global divisions, reflecting at once the usurious exploitation of the poor (through loans to the masses who are made to believe that they can borrow their way out of poverty) and the benefits of a "legal form of graft" (bailing out the state through the purchase of government and tax-exempt municipal bonds in exchange for tax subsidies and reductions that also punish the poor through austerity measures that always reduce benefits to the poor) (Henwood 1998, 23, 26–27, 314). Indeed, as Robert Brenner notes, the rise of private credit (household and corporate) is a counter-Keynesian move because it shifts the onus of the burden from the public to the private sector: "Crudely put, rising equity prices [by the second half of the 1990s] were now enabling U.S. economic growth to depend for its expansion to an ever-increasing extent on the growth of U.S. private indebtedness" (Brenner 2002, 178).

Hence the contradictions of capitalism are, once again, becoming glaringly apparent: although, as Marx once put it, "the ultimate reason for all real crises always remains the poverty and restricted consumption of the masses, in the face of the drive of capitalist forces as if only the absolute consumption capacity of society set the limit to them" (Henwood 1998, 234), capitalist ideology is growing more socially ruinous. Instead of addressing the global problem of "over-capacity and over-production in manufacturing, in which competition had over-ridden complementarity and redundant production had prevailed over mutually beneficial specialization" (Brenner 2002, 129), the stress is falling on individuals to address the fundamental flaw in capitalism—that is, how to spread the wealth generated by production, while, at the same time, insisting on extracting maximum profit from a declining base of consumers. The United States, once a net exporter of durable and nondurable goods, has lost significant share value in both to foreigners, increasingly relying on specialized, nonexportable services (such as recreation and health care) and some high-tech manufacturing. "We are becoming a nation of advisers, fixers, entertainers, and high-tech engineers," wrote Daniel Altman in early 2006, "with a lucrative sideline in treating our own illnesses." It is not only the United States that is losing its manufacturing base. The lack of complementarity in international manufacturing (resulting in a sort of rich man's race to the bottom, or an unstoppable decline in the rate of profit) is having such a deleterious effect on societies and businesses that the *Economist* suggested in early 1999 that the world may well be entering a phase similar to the one of the 1930s (Brenner 2002, 271; *Economist* 1999, 19–22; Altman 2006).

In fact, scholars have long been predicting the resurgence of premodern conflict within the dual processes of globalization and waning state power—a period of "turbulence," in James Rosenau's expression (quoted in Arrighi 1994, 79). Because the United States is unwilling to let go of its hegemony to new capitalist centers (in East Asia, for instance) by appropriating "through force, cunning, or persuasion the surplus capital that accumulates in the new centers and thereby terminate capitalist history through the formation of a truly global empire," escalating violence in the post–Cold War period may very well be a sign of the collapse of the system that regulated capitalism since its inception in Renaissance Italy and the return to the chaos that it tried to overcome. In other words, we may be talking about the end of capitalism, if not, more ominously, the end of humanity itself in the furnace of an overarmed world (Arrighi 1994, 78–79, 355–56). The sleep of reason produces monsters indeed!

Again, it is this troubling global picture that has been papered over by the discursive strategies of a postcolonial theory that has not met Fanon's basic test that native intellectuals (here expanded beyond its "third-world" category, because we all know that the subaltern is more the norm than not) be allowed to speak clearly about issues of concern to the survival of world cultures. The global condition needs to be defined as it is if we are to move beyond literary conceits and language games. Because naming is supremely important, we must at once state that the world we live in is in no way postcolonial, for the conditions that made colonialism inevitable are the prevailing forces in the global economy today. Postcolonial states are not sovereign states, but "quasi-states," juridical entities without much control over their destiny (Jackson 1990, 21). They have not achieved the degree of self-sufficiency that was available, let's say, to America's thirteen colonies before and after independence. John Plamenatz put it this way in 1960:

> The colonies now claiming independence are not societies of the same kind as the thirteen colonies which signed the Declaration of Independence in 1776. The freedom of the individual was about as well respected in those colonies as in the mother country, and they were already much closer to democracy. If capacity for freedom is our test, the thirteen revolted colonies, in spite of Negro slavery, were fit for self-government; or at least not less fit than the country they rebelled against. It is by no means clear that the colonies now clamouring for independence are all fit for self-government in the same way (Plamenatz 1960, 21–23).

Might one then ask whether the same principle applies to subjects?

The time has come to do away with postcolonial theory and replace it with a bird's-eye view of the entire human condition, one in which the geography of conflict is remapped to get rid of disabling binaries. In the world briefly described here, the colonial and the postcolonial, wealth and wretchedness, peace and terror can coexist in the same location or across geographical divides. We are not witnessing the clash of cultures as much as their implosion. Nativism takes on a multitude of guises—religious or secular—all prompted by the same sense of dispossession and fear. If a rigorous Marxist interpretation no longer appeals to fashionistas, then an equivalent theory that doesn't take away from Marx's sure-footed analyses will do. Theories, like all things in life, must evolve and take on local color; the tragedy, however, is that our civilization seems only to be regressing into a more uniform darkness. To pin this global reality into a workable formula might help us overcome our academic complacencies and open up new spaces of hope.

## Notes

1. See Dirlik (1994, 337). This argument is also the basis of Edward Said's call for a contrapuntal reading (Said 1993).

2. See World Health Organization (2004); Jamie Stockwell (2005); Robert Roy Britt (2005). In the United States, for instance, there is a well-established pattern, going back to the 1980s, of disgruntled postal workers shooting their colleagues before turning their guns on themselves. The annual number of murder-suicides (killing others before turning the gun on oneself) in the United States may reach, according to the Violence Policy Center, two thousand fatalities a year, and people continue to die for the most trivial reasons. To cite but one random example from 2006 of the precariousness of life in the United States, a sixty-six-year-old man in Ohio shot his neighbor's fifteen-year-old teenager dead simply because he walked across his lawn on his way home. "I shot him with a goddamn 410 shotgun twice," the killer told the emergency services operator. Indeed, one might consider the United States, with its 30,136 deaths by firearms in 2003, a war zone comparable to the worst areas in the globe. See Steve Chawkins and Michael Muskal (2006); Julian Borger Washington (2006).

3. Historically, and as polls continue to show, Russians have tended to be more comfortable with authoritarian systems. See Seth Mydans (2004). For democracy and electoral politics in Russia, see Michael McFaul and Nikolai Petrov (2004).

4. See Brian Murphy (2005); Michael Slackman (2005, 2006); Karl Vick (2005); Alexandre Leroi-Ponant (2006); Shirin Ebadi (with Azadeh Moaveni 2006); *Guardian* (2006b); also, see Shirin Ebadi (2006). In this article, Ebadi warned that if the United States attacked Iran, "Iranians will unite, forgetting their differences with their government, and they will fiercely and tenaciously defend their country." The awkward English translation of President Ahmadinejad's letter was published on *Le Monde's* Web site at www.lemonde.fr/web/article/0,1-0@2-727571,36-769886@51-677013,0.html.

5. See *New York Times* (2003). The editorial is part of an occasional series dealing with the West's unfair trade practices with the poor. They are collected under the title of "Harvesting Poverty."

6. See Robert A. Pape (2003); Shimali Senanayake (2006a, 2006b). The escalation of suicide bombings in U.S.-occupied Iraq in 2005 only confirmed Pape's contention. See Robert A. Pape (2005); on the futility of trying to wipe out Hezbollah, see Robert A. Pape (2006); on the popularity of Hezbollah's Sheikh Hassan Nasrallah, see Liz Sly (2006) and Michael Slackman (2006b); on the response to the Iraq Study Group's recommendations, see Robert Pape (2006); Mike Davis (2007, 1–3).

7. See Michael Shermer (2006); Nichole Argo (2006). Argo writes that most jihadi forms of suicide bombing occurred after 9/11: "According to a recent study by Bruce Hoffman of the RAND Corporation, 81 percent of human bombs since 1968 occurred in the four years *after* September 11. And, while secular organizations perpetrated approximately half of the human bombs up to 2001, Hoffman says, 31 out of 35 groups perpetrating terror today are jihadi." For the Gallup poll results, see *Wall Street Journal* (2006); Mark Mazzetti (2006).

8. See Kare Zernike (2006); Chistophe Cornevin (2006); Piotr Smolar (2006). The rate of such homicides in cities such as Hartford, Connecticut, are so high that civic leaders are calling for

cease-fires, and frightened citizens are willing to give up their civil rights and expand police powers to stem the tide of violence. See Susan Haigh (2006).

9. See Dilip Hiro (2006); Steven Erlanger (2006). For more on initial reactions to the victory of Hamas, see Simon Freeman (2006); Robert F. Worth (2006).

10. See Laurie Goodstein (2005, 2006). For a thorough report on Pentecostalism, see http://pewforum. org/surveys/pentecostal.

## WORKS CITED

Ahmad, Aijaz. 1995. "The Politics of Literary Postcoloniality." *Race & Class* 36, no. 3: 1–20.

Ahn, Christine. 2003a. "Death at the WTO." *CommonDreams.org*, September 12.

———. 2003b. "Suicide at WTO Meeting Highlights Farmers' Plight." *CommonDreams.org*, September 12.

Altman, Daniel. 2006. "Exporting Expertise, If Not Much Else." *New York Times*, January 22.

Appadurai, Arjun. 2006. *Fear of Small Numbers: An Essay on the Geography of Anger*. Durham, N.C.: Duke University Press.

Argo, Nichole. 2006. "The Role of Social Context in Terrorist Attacks." *Chronicle of Higher Education*, February 3.

Ariaga, Carolina. 2007. "Chile Rediscovers Native Mapuche Remedies." www.Yahoo!News.com, March 25.

Arnold, Emily and Janet Larsen. 2006. "Bottled Water: Pouring Resources down the Drain." Earth Policy Institute, http://www.earth-policy.org, February 2.

Armengaud, Jean Hébert. 2006. "'Le frère jumeau' d' Aristide." *Libération* (France), February 16.

Arnold, Emily. 2006. "Bottled Water: Pouring Resources down the Drain." Earth Policy Institute, February 2. At: www.earth-policy.org/Updates/2006/Update51.html.

Arrighi, Giovanni. 1994. *The Long Twentieth Century: Money, Power, and the Origins of Our Times*. New York: Verso.

Baker, Al. 2005. "Crime Numbers Keep Dropping across City." *New York Times*, December 31.

Banerjee, Neela. 2004a. "American Ruptures Shaking the Episcopal Church." *New York Times*, October 3.

———. 2004b. "Two Washington Churches Leave the Episcopal Church USA." *Seattle Post-Intelligencer*, October 19.

Bardach, A. L. 2006. "Cuba at the Crossroads." *Washington Post*, February 12.

Becker, Elizabeth, and Ginger Thompson. 2003. "Poorer Nations Plead Farmers' Case at Trade Talks." *New York Times*, September 11.

Bhabha, Homi K. 1994. *The Location of Culture*. London: Routledge.

Brenner, Robert. 2002. *The Boom and the Bubble: The US in the World Economy*. New York: Verso.

Britt, Robert Roy. 2005. "The Odds of Dying." *LiveScience.com*, January 6.

Brooke, James. 2003. "Farming Is Korean's Life and He Ends It in Despair." *New York Times*, September 16.

Brooks, David. 2005. "Trade, Oppression, Revenge." *New York Times*, December 25.

Brown, Paul. 2006. "There Is No Place Like Home." *New York Times*, January 21.

Buncombe, Andrew. 2006. "Chavez Hails Landslide Election Victory as Defeat for 'Devil' Bush." *Independent*, December 5.

Buruma, Ian. 2004. "Killing Iraq with Kindness." *New York Times*, March 17.

Buruma, Ian and Avishai Margalit. 2004. *Occidentalism: The West in the Eyes of Its Enemies*. New York: Penguin.

Cavanagh, John, and Robin Hood. 2003. "A Turning Point for World Trade?" *Baltimore Sun*, September 18.

Chang, Alicia. 2005. "Scientists: Greenland Glaciers Retreating." *Associated Press*, December 8.

Chawkins, Steve, and Michael Muskal. 2006. "Ex-Postal Worker Kills 6, Commits Suicide in Goleta." *Los Angeles Times*, January 31.

Collier, Paul. 2000. "Economic Causes of Civil War and Their Implications for Policy." *World Bank*. Accessed at http://econ.worldbank.org/files/13198_EcCausesPolicy.pdf.

*Chicago Tribune*. 2006a. "Chavez Calls U.S. 'Immoral'." *Chicago Tribune*, January 29.

———. 2006b. "Ortega Vows to Work with Castro, Chavez." *Chicago Tribune*, November 9.

Chomsky, Noam. 2006. "Latin America Declares Independence." *International Herald Tribune*, October 3.

Cornevin, Chistophe. 2006. "500 agressions gratuites chaque jour en France." *Le Figaro*, February 14.

Crespo, Luis. 2006. "Morales: abajo los sueldos." *BBC Mundo.com*, January 26.

Davis, Mike. 2007. *Buda's Wag on: A Brief History of the Car Bomb.* London: Verso.

Dean, Cornelia. 2006. "Study Sees 'Global Collapse' of Fish Species." *New York Times*, November 3.

Devalpo, Alain. 2006. "Opposition pacifique des Mapuches chiliens." *Le Monde diplomatique*, February: 18–19

Dirlik, Arif. 1994. "The Postcolonial Aura: Third-World Criticism in the Age of Global Capitalism." *Critical Inquiry* 20, no. 2: 328–56.

Dobson, Roger. 2007. "Rise in UK's Child Mortality Rate Is Linked to Inequality." *Independent*, April 1.

Dugger, Celia W. 2004. "Unicef Says Children in Deprivation Reach a Billion." *New York Times*, December 10.

Duhigg, Charles. 2006. "Late in Life, Finding a Bonanza in Life Insurance." *New York Times*, December 17.

Ebadi, Shirin (with Azadeh Moaveni). 2006. "Reading a Death Warrant in Tehran." *New York Times Magazine*, April 9.

*Economist.* 1999. "Could It Happen Again?" *Economist*, February 20.

Egan, Timothy. 2005. "Newly Bankrupt Raking in Piles of Credit Offers." *New York Times*, December 11.

Enriquez, Sam. 2006. "Masked Marxists with Marimbas." *Los Angeles Times*, January 23.

Erlanger, Steven. 2006. "Hamas Routs Ruling Faction, Casting Pall on Peace Process." *New York Times*, January 27.

Fajnzylber, Pablo, Daniel Lederman, and Norman Loayza. 2002. "Inequality and Violent Crime." *Journal of Law and Economics* 45, no. 1: 1–40.

Feldman, Noah. 2006. "Islam, Terror and the Second Nuclear Age." *New York Times Magazine*, October 29.

*Food Magazine.* 2006. "Meat and Dairy: Where Have the Minerals Gone?" *Food Magazine.* January/March, 10.

Forero, Juan. 2004. "Latin America Graft and Poverty Trying Patience with Democracy." *New York Times*, June 24.

———. 2005a. "Advocate for Coca Legalization Leads in Bolivian Race." *New York Times*, November 26.

———. 2005b. "Bolivia's Newly Elected Leader Maps His Socialist Agenda." *New York Times*, December 20.

———. 2005c. "Coca Advocate Wins Election for President in Bolivia." *New York Times*, December 19.

———. 2006a. "Indians in Bolivia Celebrate Swearing In of One of Their Own." *New York Times*, January 23.

———. 2006b. "Nationalism and Populism Propel Front-Runner in Peru" *New York Times*, April 2.

Forero, Juan, and Larry Rohter. 2006. "Bolivia Leader Tilting Region Further to the Left." *New York Times*, January 22.

Freeman, Simon. 2006. "World Reaction to the Hamas Victory: 'Fasten Your Seatbelt'." *Times* (London), January 26.

Friedman, Thomas L. 2003. "Connect the Dots." *New York Times*, September 29.

Glazer, Nathan. 1997. *We Are All Multiculturalists Now.* Cambridge, Mass.: Harvard University Press.

Goodstein, Laurie. 2005. "More Religion, But Not the Old-Time Kind." *New York Times*, January 9.

———. 2006. "Episcopalians Are Reaching Point of Revolt." *New York Times*, December 17.

*Guardian.* 2006a. "Insolvent Britons Set to Rise by 400%." *Guardian*, October 24.

———. 2006b "Nobel Laureate Says Iran Would Defend Self." *Guardian*, April 21.

Haigh, Susan. 2006. "Cities Struggling with Increased Violence." Yahoo!News, June 8.

Harvey, Fiona. 2005. "UN Warns of Poverty as World's Lakes Evaporate." *Financial Times*, October 31.

Hedgecoe, Guy. 2006. "Ecuador: Protest and Power." www.OpenDemocracy.net, November 28.

Henningan, Tom. 2006. "Leader Takes Power from Earth God on Ancient Site." *Times* (London), January 23.

Henwood, Doug. 1998. *Wall Street: How It Works and for Whom*, updated ed. New York: Verso.

Hickman, Martin. 2006. "Britons in Debt to the Tune of 1. 13 Trillion." *Independent*, January 3.

Hiro, Dilip. 2006. "The Rise of Political Islam: The Palestinian Election and Democracy in the Middle East." *TomDispatch.com*, January 25.

*International Herald Tribune.* 2006. "Obesity Called 'Scourge' Afflicting Entire World." *International Herald Tribune*, September 3.

Jackson, Robert. 1990. *Quasi-States: Sovereignty, International Relations, and the Third World.* Cambridge: Cambridge University Press.

Jenkins, Philip. 2002. *The Next Christendom: The Coming of Global Christianity*. New York: Oxford University Press.

Keane, Dan. 2006. "Bolivian Senate Oks Sweeping Land Reform." *Washington Post*, November 29.

Kocieniewski, David. 2006. "After $12,000, There's Even Room to Park the Car." *New York Times*, February 20.

Krueger, Alan B., and Jitka Malecková. 2003. "Seeking the Roots of Terrorism." *Chronicle of Higher Education*, June 6: B10–11.

Lawrence, Felicity. 2006. "Mineral Levels in Meat and Milk Plummet over 60 Years." *Guardian*, February 2.

*Le Monde*. 2003. "L'ampleur des désaccords Nord-Sud met l'OMC en échec." *Le Monde*, September 15.

Lemoine, Maurice. 2006. "Nationalisations en Amérique Latine." *Le Monde diplomatique*, May 18.

Lentschner, Keren, and Arie Visot. 2005. "Consommation: la belle surprise de fin d'année." *Le Figaro*, December 22.

Leroi-Ponant, Alexandre. 2006. "L'Iran du président Mahmoud Ahmadinejad." *Le Monde diplomatique*, December, 8–9.

Lovelock, James. 2006. "The Earth Is About to Catch a Morbid Fever That May Last as Long as 100,000 Years." *Independent*, January 16.

McCarthy, Michael. 2006a. "Climate Poses Increased Threat, Admits Blair." *Independent*, January 30.

———. 2006b. "Environment in Crisis: 'We Are Past the Point of No Return." *Independent*, January 16.

———. 2006c. "Why Gaia Is Wreaking Revenge on Our Abuse of the Environment." *Independent*, January 16.

Mazzetti, Mark. 2006. "Spy Agencies Say Iraq War Worsens Terrorism Threat." *New York Times*, September 24.

McDonnell, Patrick. 2006a. "Former Political Prisoner Is Chile's New President." *Los Angeles Times*, January 16.

———. 2006b. "Socialist Bachelet Wins Chilean Presidency." *New York Times*, January 16.

McFaul, Michael, and Nikolai Petrov. 2004. "Russian Democracy in Eclipse: What the Elections Tell Us." *Journal of Democracy* 15, no. 3: 5–19.

McKinley Jr., James C. 2006. "With Beheadings and Attacks, Drug Gangs Terrorize Mexico." *New York Times*, October 26.

Mohn, Tonya. 2007. "The Biggest Little Noticed Hazard." *New York Times*, April 17.

Murphy, Brian. 2005. "Newsview: Economy Key to Iranian Election." *Yahoo!News*, June 25.

Mydans, Seth. 2004. "Give Me Liberty, but Not Too Much: This Is Russia." *New York Times*, April 21.

*New York Times*. 2003. "The Rigged Trade Game." *New York Times*, July 20.

Navarro, Luis Hernandez. 2006. "Socialismo o muerte de la especie humana, la disyuntiva: Huga Chavez." *La Jornada* (Mexico), January 28.

Osborne, Hilary. 2006. "Bankruptcies and Repossessions Rise." *Guardian*, February 3.

Palast, Greg. 2004. "Dick Cheney, Hugo Chavez, and Bill Clinton's Band." *CommonDreams.org*, August 16.

Pape, Robert A. 2003. "Dying to Kill Us." *New York Times*, September 22.

———. 2005. " Blowing Up an Assumption." *New York Times*, May 18.

———. 2006a. "Ground to a Halt." *New York Times*, August 3.

———. 2006b. "We Can Watch Iraq from the Sea." *New York Times*, December 10.

Pérez Jr., Louis A. 2005. *To Die in Cuba: Suicide and Society*. Chapel Hill: University of North Carolina Press.

Perlez, Jane. 2004. "Aborigines Say Australia Pushes Their Plight to Sideline." *New York Times*, April 18.

Peter, Jon. 2003. "Protests Force Bolivian Leader to Resign." *Washington Post*, October 18.

Plamenatz, John. 1960. *On Alien Rule and Self-Government*. London: Longmans, Green, & Company.

Ponce, Fernando Matamoros. 2006. "L' 'au tre campaigne' des zapatistes." *Le Monde diplomatique*, February 20.

Powers, William. 2005. "Bolivia, the Poor Little Rich Country." *International Herald Tribune*, June 13.

Ramirez, Silene. 2006. "Leftist Fiesta in Chile for Bachelet Inauguration." *Reuters*, March 11.

Reel, Monte. 2006. "Bachelet Sworn In as Chile's President." *Washington Post*, March 12.

Rifkin, Jeremy. 2004. *The European Dream: How Europe's Vision of the Future Is Quietly Eclipsing the American Dream*. New York: Tarcher/Penguin.

Rohter, Larry. 2003a. "Bolivia's Poor Proclaim Abiding Distrust of Globalization." *New York Times*, October 17.

———. 2003b. "Once Secure, Argentines Now Lack Food and Hope." *New York Times*, March 2.

———. 2004a. "Mapuche Indians in Chile Struggle to Take Back Forests." *New York Times*, August 11.

———. 2004b. "Uruguay's Left Makes History by Winning Presidential Vote." *New York Times*, November 1.

———. 2004c. "Argentina's Economic Rally Defies Forecasts." *New York Times*, December 26.

———. 2006a. "A Leader Making Peace with Chile's Past." *New York Times*, January 16.

———. 2006b. "For Argentina's Sizzling Economy, a Cap on Steak Prices." *New York Times*, April 3.

———. 2006c. "A Widening Gap Erodes Argentina's Egalitarian Image." *New York Times*, December 25.

Romero, Simon. 2002. "São Paulo Becomes the Kidnapping Capital of Brazil." *New York Times*, February 13.

———. 2005. "A Texas Town Nervously Awaits a New Neighbor." *New York Times*, August 21.

———. 2006. "In Bolivia's Affluent East, Anger at Morales Is Growing." *New York Times*, December 26.

Sachs, Susan. 2004. "Poll Finds Hostility Hardening toward U.S. Policies." *New York Times*, March 17.

Said, Edward. 1993. *Culture and Imperialism*. New York: Knopf.

Senanayake, Shimali. 2006a."Suicide Bomber Kills 94 in Northern Sri Lanka." *New York Times*, October 17.

———. 2006b. "Suicide Boats Explode in Sri Lanka Port, Killing 16." *New York Times*, October 19.

Sengupta, Somini. 2006. "On India's Despairing Farms, a Plague of Suicide." *New York Times*, September 19.

Shanker, Thom. 2006. "Pentagon Hones Its Strategy on Terrorism." *New York Times*, February 5.

Shermer, Michael. 2006. "Murdercide." *Scientific American* 26 (January): 34.

Shohat, Ella. 1992. "Notes on the 'Post-Colonial.'" *Social Text* 31/32:105.

Slack, Keith. 2003. "Poor vs. Profit in Bolivian Revolt." *Los Angeles Times*, October 19.

Slackman, Michael. 2005. "Iran Vote: Dark Horse Rises. " *New York Times*, June 24.

———. 2006a. "A New Face in Iran Resurrects an Old Defiance." *New York Times*, January 30.

———. 2006b. "And Now, Islamism Trumps Arabism." *New York Times*, August 20.

Sly, Liz. 2006. "Hezbollah Chief Wins Admirers." *Chicago Tribune*, August 3.

Smith, Fiona. 2006a. "Bolivia's Morales Announces Cabinet, Including Marxist Energy Minister." *San Diego Union-Tribune*, January 23.

———. 2006b. "Morales da inicio a la rebaja salarial en cargos jeráqui cos." *La Rázon* (Bolivia), January 23.

Smolar, Piotr. 2006. "Hause de 6.6% des atteintes volontaires à l' intégrité physique." *Le Monde*, February 14.

*State of the World 2004: A Worldwatch Institute Report on Progress toward a Sustainable Society.* New York: W. W. Norton.

*State of the World 2006: A Worldwatch Institute Report on Progress toward a Sustainable Society.* New York: W. W. Norton.

Stiglitz, Joseph. 2003. "Do as the US Says, Not as It Does." *Guardian*, October 29.

———. 2004. "Distant Voices." *Guardian*, March 12.

Striker, Jeff. 2005. "Forehead Billboards." *New York Times Magazine*, December 11.

Stockwell, Jaime. 2005. "Va. Violent Deaths Are Mostly Suicide." *Washington Post*, October 12.

Strope, Leigh. 2004. (Associated Press). "Gap between Rich and Poor Widening in Troubled Economy." At: www. Commondreams.org, August 17.

*Taipei Times*. 2004. "Suicide Bomber Strikes in Bolivia." April 1.

Thompson, Ginger. 2004. "On Mexico's Mean Streets, the Sinners Have a Saint." *New York Times*, March 26.

———. 2006. "Préval's Silence Obscures Quiet Bid to Reunite Haiti." *New York Times*, February 20.

Thornton, Philip. 2006. "U.S. Savings Rate Sinks to Lowest since Great Depression." London: *Independent*, January 30.

*Times* (London). 2003. "West Attacked over Cancún Collapse." September 15.

Turque, Bill, and Michelle Boorstein. 2006. "7 Va. Episcopal Parishes Vote to Sever Ties." *Washington Post*. December 18.

Urbina, Ian. 2006. "Keeping It Secret as the Family Car Becomes a Home." *New York Times*, April 2.

Valdivieso, Jeanneth. 2006. "Ecuador Names 1st Female Defense Chief." London and Manchester: *Guardian*, December 27.

Valenzuela, Luisa. 2007. "What We See in Hugo Chávez." *New York Times*, March 17.

Vick, Karl. 2005. "Class Is Pivotal in Iran Runoff." *Washington Post*, June 24.

*Wall Street Journal*. 2006. "U.S. Domination Fear Fuels Muslim Anger," May 4.

Washington, Julian Borger. 2006. "Gunned Down: The Teenager Who Dared Walk across His Neighbour's Prized Lawn." London and Manchester: *Guardian*, March 22.

Watkin, Daniel J. 2004a. "In New York, Gospel Resounds in African Tongues." *New York Times*, April 18.

———. 2004b. "Nowadays, New York City Is Prime Conversion Ground." *New York Times*, July 11.

Weaver, Matt. 2006. "PM Issues Blunt Warning on Climate Change." London and Manchester: *Guardian*, January 30.

World Health Organization. 2002. "First Ever Global Report on Violence and Health Released." At: www.who.int/mediacentre/releases/pr73/en/, October 3.

———. 2004. "Suicide Huge but Preventable Public Health Problem." At: www.who.int/mediacenter/news/releases/2004/pt61/en.

Worldwatch Institute. 2006. Press release for *State of the World 2006: China and India Hold World in Balance*. At: www.worldwatch.org/press/news/2006/01/11.

Worth, Robert F. 2006. "New Business Blooms in Iraq: Terror Insurance." *New York* Times, March 21.

Zernike, Kare. 2006. "Violent Crime Rising Sharply in Some Cities." *New York Times*, February 12.

# 9

# GLOBALIZED TERROR AND THE POSTCOLONIAL SUBLIME: QUESTIONS FOR SUBALTERN MILITANTS

## E. San Juan Jr.

A few months before his death, Edward Said, arguably the founding "patriarch" of postcolonial studies, reassessed his critique of "Orientalism" by affirming the value of "humanistic critique to open up the fields of struggle" so as to enable the speaking of "issues of injustice and suffering" within the amply situated contexts of history and socioeconomic reality. He invoked sentiments of generosity and hospitality so that the interpreter's mind can actively make a place for "a foreign other," the "active practice of worldly secular rational discourse." He strongly denounced the current U.S. government policy of celebrating "American or Western exceptionalism" and demonstrating contempt for other cultures, all in the service of "terror, pre-emptive war, and unilateral regime change" (Said 2003, 1–6). In an earlier interview, Said asserted that his main interest was in neocolonialism, not postcolonialism (which, to him, was a "misnomer"), in "the structures of dependency and impoverishment" in the global South due to the operations of the International Monetary Fund and the World Bank (1999, 82). Overall, a modernist humanism, not postcolonial hybridity, deconstruction, or genealogy of speechless subalterns, was for Said the paradigmatic framework of inquiry for a comparative analysis of cultures and societies in an epoch of decolonization.

After more than two decades of intellectual specialization and investment, postcolonial inquiry has now enjoyed sufficient legitimacy and prestige in the Euro-American academy to make it serviceable for reinforcing the Establishment consensus. Decolonization is over. The natives now run the government. Long live the free market around the planet! Works by Homi Bhabha, Gayatri Spivak, and others are institutionally consecrated "touchstones," to use the Arnoldian rubric, that, though somewhat vitiated as products of a "comprador intelligentsia," nevertheless serve to authorize a validation of colonialism and its legacies as a useful if ambivalent resource. Informed by theoretical protocols and procedures hostile to nationalist movements, not to speak of anti-imperialist revolutionary struggles and other "meta-narratives" (Edgar and Sedgwick 2002, 253) inspired by Fanon, Mao, Ho Chi Minh, Che Guevara, and others, postcolonial studies today function as supplements not to the critical theories of Derrida, Foucault, or Deleuze, but to the official apologetics of the "new world order" called "globalization." This was ushered in with the demise of the Soviet Union and the end of the Cold War, that is to say, the end of history and the eternal triumph of capitalism and its attendant ideology, neoliberal globalism. As Arif Dirlik summed it up, postcolonial discourse has become an academic orthodoxy in its "self-identification with hybridity, in-betweeness, marginality, borderlands"—a fatal move from the "language of revolution infused with the vocabulary of political economy to a culturalist language of identity politics" (Dirlik 2000, 5).

What happened to revolution and the decolonizing emblem prefigured by Caliban and personified by Rizal, Sandino, Nelson Mandela, and others? In his master work *Culture and Imperialism*, Said (1994) paid homage to the revolutionary militants, Amilcar Cabral, Frantz Fanon, C. L. R. James, and others, as the locus classicus of emancipatory "third world" discourse who engaged the recovery of lost integrity in the context of regaining the territorial habitat of memory—places instead of spaces—and popular sovereignty. But today, nationalism and national liberation struggles are anathema to postcolonialists. And with the neoconservative counterrevolution after the defeat of U.S. aggression in Indochina, a "cultural turn" effectively replaced the revolutionary process in history with an endless process of "abrogation and appropriation" of colonial texts and practices in quest of an identity that is ultimately and forever decentered, shifting, borderless, fluid, aleatory, ambivalent, and so on. What encapsulates all these qualities is the term *transnational*, the prefix *trans* functioning as the magic word that would bridge the immense gap between the terrible misery of peoples in the underdeveloped South and the affluent suburban megamalls of the North. One might ask: Would transnationals and transculturals resolve questions of suffering and injustice that confront us daily in Iraq, Palestine, Afghanistan, Colombia, the Philippines, and of course in the "internal colonies" of North America and Europe?

## POSTCOLONIAL SINGULARITIES

In the canonical handbook *Key Concepts in Post-Colonial Studies* (1998) by the same Australian authors (Bill Ashcroft, Gareth Griffiths, and Helen Tiffin) of *The Empire Writes Back*, we do not find any entry for "Liberation" but one for "Liminality." And, more telling, there is no entry for "Revolution" either. Aside from the valorization of the liminal as the in-between hybrid notion, "rhizome" is privileged by our postcolonial experts as the concept (attributed to Deleuze and Guattari, but defined in Foucauldian terminology) that best describes colonial power: "it operates dynamically, laterally, and intermittently." Ashcroft, Griffiths, and Tiffin assert that "There is no 'master plan' of imperialism, and its advance is not necessarily secured through violence and oppression"; and therefore we should focus on the way "cultural hegemony" operates through "an invisible network of filiative connections, psychological internalizations, and unconsciously complicit associations" (1998, 207). Surely these generalizations will strike anyone as quite dubious, departing radically from Gramsci's use of "hegemony" as a historically variable combination of force and consent.

One sign of the terminal exhaustion of this antitotalizing stance is the reduction of the issue of globalization to "the nature and survival of social and cultural identity," thus evacuating the arena of political and socioeconomic struggle that Said and his models (Fanon, C. L. R. James) considered salient and inescapable. Disturbed by this trend, students and teachers at McMaster University in Ontario, Canada, recently organized a conference on "the politics of postcoloniality." Anticipating an "Empire Resurrected," they posed the following questions in a futuristic or subjunctive mode (reproduced from a widely circulated flyer): "What are the chances of establishing direct colonialism again in the twenty-first century? Why did the old empires give up their old colonies in favor of indirect colonialism? What are the conditions that would make them revert back to direct colonialism? What are the circumstances (economical/political/cultural/social) that would facilitate the resurrection of direct colonialism/empire? How can colonial schemes be countered? What should be the new mode of resistance? What is the role of civil disobedience in this case? Is terrorism/radical resistance the new mode for countering the new empire? What are the viable modes of resistance?

How can postcolonial theory respond/react to such a possibility? What would be its role?" These are fresh winds blowing from the dusty ivory towers and archives of academe, betokening grassroots unrest that might stir us up from dogmatic slumber induced by the seductive pleasures of postcolonial contingency and disjuncture.

We are at a pivotal juncture in critical self-reflective inventory. Instead of elaborating fully the historical circumstances that might explain this shift, a transition I have sketched in *Beyond Postcolonial Theory* (San Juan 1998), what I would like to attempt here is to explore briefly the most suggestive ways in which we can restore the critical edge in postcolonial critique by engaging the problem of terrorism and its polar antithesis, the "New American Century" and the project of globalization designed to re-establish an imperial hegemony not dreamed of by either Cecil Rhodes or the architects of Pax Americana erected on the ruins of Hiroshima, Berlin, and Stalingrad. What I have in mind is the interrogation of the discourse of imperial neoliberalism as the wily, duplicitous mimicry of postcolonial agency. What is urgently needed is a new analytic approach to twenty-first-century imperial hegemony and a corollary strategy of demystification that would advance the antiglobalization actions to take into account crucial developments since the disaster of September 11, 2001, and its aftermath, the ongoing devastation of Afghanistan and Iraq. This is both a pedagogical and mobilizing task aimed at sectors of the petit bourgeois intelligentsia and middle strata open to an evolving neo-postcolonial critique.

## Approaching Imperial Neoliberalism

Imperial neoliberalism, the rationale of actual political and economic globalization, reveals itself most lucidly in the "Project for the New American Century," the manifesto of advisors closest to President George W. Bush (Source Watch, 2007). The designers of this new aggressive U.S. foreign policy premised on an unprecedented military buildup were participants in the invasions of Panama and Grenada, counterinsurgency wars in Central and South America (particularly Colombia and Peru), the Cold War showdown with the Soviet Union in Afghanistan, and the arming of Iraq to counter radical Islamists in Iran and elsewhere. Basically, the project centers on a doctrine of unilateral pre-emptive war against any nation or power seeking to rival the United States rather than containment and multilateral internationalism of terrorist groups. The goal is total war, endless war, premised on accelerated militarization of society and "moral clarity." What the last phrase means may be grasped by quoting portions of the manifesto: "American foreign and defense policy is adrift. . . . As the twentieth century draws to a close, the United States stands as the world's pre-eminent power. . . . Does the United States have the resolve to shape a new century favorable to American principles and interests?" This domination of the planet is based on "unquestioned U.S. military preeminence" beefed up with a new generation of nuclear weapons and sufficient combat forces deployed to a wider network of forward-operating bases to fight and win multiple wars, including forces for "constabulary duties" with American rather than UN leadership. Are we facing here an aberrant act committed in a moment of absent-mindedness?[1]

In a blueprint entitled "Rebuilding America's Defenses: Strategy, Forces and Resources for a New Century" released in September 2000, this neoconservative group outlined its grand plan for world hegemony: "The United States is the world's only superpower, combining preeminent military power, global technological leadership, and the world's largest economy. America's grand strategy should aim to preserve and extend this advantageous position as far into the future as possible. Yet no moment in international politics can be frozen in time; even a global Pax Americana will not preserve itself. . . . The presence of American forces in critical regions around the world is the visible expression of the extent of America's status as a superpower." The report urges the control of the Persian Gulf region by the United States, proceeding through the conquest of Iraq, followed by Syria, and eventually Iran. For this plan to be "saleable" to the public, a catastrophic and catalyzing event "like a new Pearl Harbor" was needed; this was promptly supplied by September 11, 2001. Although the ostensible excuse for the invasion of Iraq included Hussein's tyranny, putative weapons of mass destruction, and terrorism, it was in effect the desire of the U.S. ruling elite for a permanent role and base in this strategically important region of the world, rich in resources but also geographically situated in a way that would provide springboards for intervention into Europe, Russia, China, and the Indian subcontinent.

In President Bush's 2002 State of the Union address, the doctrine of "preemptive war" as the lynchpin in the endless war against terrorism, against rogue states that form the axis of evil (Iraq, Iran, and North Korea), was announced. The right to act preemptively, using nuclear strikes and other "operational capabilities," was no longer being exercised to punish the perpetrators of the crime of September 11 by the savage onslaught on Afghanistan where Al-Qaeda and Osama bin Laden had strongholds, but it was a measure necessary "to defend our liberty and to defend our lives." The phantasmagoric danger of terrorism scattered around the world now justifies this militarization of foreign policy and the willingness to intervene and engage even in "lots of small, dirty fights in remote and dangerous places" in the process of "draining the swamp" of civil society (to quote Defense Secretary Rumsfeld; Mahajan 2002, 97; Shank 2003). In addition to the "shock and awe" war against Iraq, endless and borderless war against anyone perceived or declared as "terrorist," that is, anti-American, seems overreaching and out of proportion to the catastrophe of September 11 (Ullman and Wade 1996). The aim of fighting and winning multiple, simultaneous, major theater wars seems a postmodernist avant-garde invention. But the reality of events appear to confirm the intent: Afghanistan was subjugated at the expense of some 20,000 lives, Iraq at more than triple the number and still counting.

What strikes most people as sinister is the plan of a secret army or "superintelligence support activity" labeled as the "Proactive Pre-emptive Operations Group," or P2OG. It will combine the CIA and military covert action, information warfare, and deception to provoke terrorist attacks that would then require U.S. "counterattacks" against countries harboring the terrorists. But this is humdrum routine for the "civilizing mission" since the conquistadors landed in the "New World" and the European traders-missionaries began the merchandising of the bodies of African slaves (Isenberg, 2002).

In retrospect, one can discern an uncanny similarity with the events before the war against Iraq in 1991, which inaugurated the era of "total war." The depressed economic situation and the scandals of corporate criminality cannot be remedied by further dismantling of the welfare state, so the public must be diverted. Noam Chomsky's analysis of that situation sounds prescient and historically grounded in a well-defined pattern of political sequences that condense half a century of postcolonial interventions:

> Two classic devices are to inspire fear of terrible enemies and worship of our grand leaders, who rescue us just in the nick of time. The enemies may be domestic (criminal Blacks, uppity women, subversives undermining the tradition, etc.), but foreign demons have natural advantages. . . . As the standard pretext [i.e., Communists] vanished, the domestic population has been frightened—with some success—by images of Qaddafi's hordes of international terrorists, Sandinistas marching on Texas, Grenada interdicting sea lanes and threatening the homeland itself, Hispanic narco-traffickers directed by the arch-maniac Noriega, after he underwent the usual conversion from favored friend to Attila the Hun after committing the one unforgivable crime, the crime of disobedience. . . . The scenario requires Awe as well as Fear. . . . (Chomsky 1992, 408)

Awe as well as fear—this "structure of feeling," which postcolonial critics have so far ignored, frames the situation of the war against terrorism carried to the imperial margins, this time in the Philippines. I would now like to call the attention of the reader to the Philippines, a former colony of the United States (now arguably a genuine U.S. neocolony) and the continuing *l'aff aire* Abu Sayyaf and its use as a pretext for the invasion by over a thousand U.S. troops of this second front of the war against terrorism, after Afghanistan.

Since the seventies at the time of the Marcos dictatorship, the severely impoverished Muslims in the southern Philippines, called "Moros" (who were never actually subjugated by the Spaniards, Americans, or Japanese throughout their history), have mounted a fierce struggle for autonomy and dignity, and for some measure of self-determination. While the Moro National Liberation Front (MLNF) has compromised with the government, another more formidable group, the Moro Islamic Liberation Front (MILF), has continued its struggle. But its fighters are now branded "terrorists" and their legitimate cause criminalized. It is expected that the MILF will be classified as a "foreign terrorist organization"—foreign, of course, to Americans, but not to Filipinos. When President Arroyo allowed the U.S. Special Forces to participate in the pursuit of the Abu Sayyaf, a bandit group that is really a creation of both the CIA and the Philippine Armed Forces, did she not violate the Philippine Constitution? Indifference to this question is a symptom of the larger problem of either ignorance of the plight of the Moro people, or complicity with the ruling class in the oppression and exploitation of at least 7.5 million citizens who happen to subscribe to another faith.

Thousands, perhaps over a hundred thousand now, have died since the flare-up of Christian-Muslim hostilities in the sixties. The U.S.-backed Marcos dictatorship declared martial law in 1972, summarily torturing and killing thousands of civilians and destroying entire communities; Marcos' barbaric rule, which ended in 1986, was inaugurated with the battle of Jolo, Sulu, in 1972. The city was actually burned by government forces, producing 2,000 corpses and 60,000 refugees in one night. A ceasefire was reached after the Tripoli Agreement of 1976, but it was often honored in the breach. The split of the MILF-led Hashim Salamat from Misuari's more secular MNLF introduced a sectarian but also conciliatory element in the scene, precipitating in 1976 the formation of the Abu Sayyaf along the lines of the government-sponsored and CIA-funded Bangsa Moro Liberation Organization (BMLO). Such is the complexity of the original situation that the current media portrayals obscure or simplify for State propaganda purposes.

The Abu Sayyaf has been represented in the U.S. mass media as an awesome and fearful force, mysterious yet intelligible. It is now public knowledge that the Abu Sayyaf, like the MILF, was set up by the Philippine government to split the Moro struggle for self-determination and pressure the MNLF into capitulation. But since 1995 the Abu Sayyaf has turned into a Frankenstein's monster devoted to hostage-taking for ransom and terrorizing civilian communities. In the midst of U.S. intervention, an International Peace Commission went to Basilan on March 23–27, 2002, and produced what I think is the most comprehensive and detailed report on conditions in the region. The conclusion of their report, entitled *Basilan: The Next Afghanistan?*, is unequivocal: the Abu Sayyaf is a symptom of the disastrous failure of the state in ensuring not only peace and security but an honest and efficient government— both provincial governance and military-police agencies—in a milieu where the proverbial forces of civil society (business, church, media) have been complicit. Enmeshed in corruption that involves local officials, military officers, and central government, the region where the Abu Sayyaf thrives has witnessed the reign of complicitous government and vigilante terror over civilians. Nowhere in the entire Philippines are the violation of human rights and the brutalization of civilian suspects so flagrant and ubiquitous as in Basilan where this group operates. In this context, the deployment of U.S. troops in Mindanao, compliments of the Arroyo administration, has only worsened the situation, demonized and mystified the Abu Sayyaf as an Al-Qaeda accomplice, and promoted hostility and mayhem among various ethnic groups.

## ENGAGING THE NEOCOLONIAL RETURN

Given this context, let us examine how metropolitan wisdom has employed "postcolonial" resources to represent this whole conjuncture to the academic public. One example is Charles O. Frake's article, "Abu Sayyaf: Displays of Violence and the Proliferation of Contested Identities among Philippine Muslims," in a 1998 issue of *American Anthropologist*. Although Frake is quite erudite in referencing the history of the Muslims from the Spanish times to the present, he never examines seriously, except in a tokenizing gestural mode, the political and economic context of land dispossession and economic marginalization of the Muslim majority. Instead, typical of postcolonial discourse, he focuses on the Abu Sayyaf as an attempt to solve "the logical gap in the identity matrix of Philippine Muslim insurgency." Because the Moro movement has been fragmented by ethnic antagonisms among Tausugs, Maguindanaos, Maranaos, Yakans, and so on, the Abu Sayyaf, according to Frake, is "militantly Islamicist." And because its leadership draws from the displaced and unaffiliated youth, as well as the traditional outlaw areas, the group represents "a new layer in the strata of kinds of identity laid down in the long history of conflict in the Muslim Philippines" (Frake 1998, 48). In short, the Abu Sayyaf (according to Frake's postmodernist optic) is a symptom of the problem of "identity proliferation," because the fault lines of identity construction are often revealed in explosions of political violence. Empire, class, and nation have all been expunged from the functionalist, co-optative frame of analysis.

Frake is an example of a knowledge producer intent on unwitting mystification. The result of applying Geertz's "thick description," that is, the focus on how participants interpret everyday happenings, instead of clarifying the nexus of causality and accountability, muddles it. Frake wants to answer the question: "How can such nice people [meaning the anonymous members of the Abu Sayyaf], at times, do such horrible things?" But his premise—that the central motivation of individuals in society is to be recognized as somebody, to establish an identity—is completely detached from historical specificities, even from the basic determinants of any cultural complex or location. Despite the empirical citations and putative data, Frake's attempt to deploy postmodern ethnography on the Abu Sayyaf phenomenon results only in a simplistic reduction: that in situations of struggle, people fail to unite because they continually interpret what's going on around them, thus multiplying "contested identities." I am afraid such "thick descriptions" are really opaque ruses obscuring instead of illuminating the plight of the Moro people. Vincent Crapanzano's critique of Geertz may be quoted here: the method of "thick description" offers no understanding of the native from the native's point of view, . . . no specifiable evidence for his attributions of intention, his assertion of subjectivity, his declarations of experience" (quoted in San Juan 2002, 234).[2]

Recalling Said's critique of Orientalist scholarship cited earlier, I cannot imagine any intellectual who, endeavoring to grasp the roots of a long-enduring, complex "Moro problem," will preemptively assert or claim a detached or disinterested stance. A few postmodernist scholars openly announce their point of view, their subject positions—if only to wash their hands, of course, of any complicity with U.S. imperialism. Professions of neutrality have been replaced with gestures of liberal guilt manifest in philanthropic compassion. Unfortunately, these gestures only prolong the Orientalizing supremacy of Western knowledge production and its hegemonic influence. Of course it is now commonplace to note that all disciplinary research performed in state institutions, all pedagogical agencies (in Karl Mannheim's phrase, the "everyday constituent assembly of the mind"), are sites of ideological class struggle, and none can be hermetically insulated from the pressures of material local and global interests. There is no vacuum or neutral space in the planetary conflict of classes and groups for hegemony.

## Perseverance in Commitment

In my recent work (San Juan 2002, 2004), I called attention to recent developments in Cultural Studies as a disciplinary practice in North America and Europe that have subverted the early promise of the field as a radical transformative force. In every attempt to do any inquiry into cultural practices and discourses, one is always carrying out a political and ethical project, whether one is conscious of it or not. There are many reasons for this, the main one being the inescapable political-economic constitution of any discursive field of inquiry, as Pierre Bourdieu has convincingly demonstrated. Also, in the famous theoretical couplet that Foucault has popularized—knowledge/power—the production of knowledge is always already implicated in the ongoing struggles across class, nation, gender, locality, ethnicity, and so on, which envelops and surrounds the intellectual, the would-be knower, learner, investigator, scholar, and so on.

This is the moment when I would like to close with some reflections, and questions, on why problems of culture and knowledge are of decisive political importance for the postcolonial critic.[3] Although we always conceive of ourselves as citizen-subjects with rights, it is also the case that we are all caught up in a network of obligations whose entirety is not within our conscious grasp. What is our relation to Others—the excluded, marginalized, and prostituted who affirm our existence and identity—in our society? In a sense we (Filipinos, Americans) are responsible for the plight of the Moros—yes, including the existence of the Abu Sayyaf— insofar as we claim to live in a community of singular persons who alternatively occupy the positions of speakers and listeners, I's and you's, and who have obligations to one another, and reciprocal accountabilities. We should also keep in mind the new historical milieu characterized by what Alain Badiou calls "the disjunctive synthesis of two nihilisms," capitalist nihilism and the anonymous fascist nihilism manifested in the 9/11 attack (Badiou 2003, 160). To overcome this cynical milieu, we need to aspire to practice the "critical universality" that Michael Lowy invokes in his instructive treatise, *Fatherland or Mother Earth? Essays on the National Question* (1998). This ethical challenge sums up, to my mind, the riposte that postcolonial agency must pose to neoliberal imperialism (instanced by Frake's discourse, among others) if it is to sustain its tradition of critique, that uncompromising questioning of absolutisms and sacralizing mystifications that Edward Said initiated at the beginning of his exemplary intellectual adventure.[4]

## Notes

1. We can cite here the principle of global leadership embodied by the realist statesmanship of George Kennan, former head of the U.S. State Department Policy Planning Staff in the early days of the Cold War. Kennan may be the presiding genius behind the neoconservative "conspiracy" to rehabilitate imperial dreams when he wrote (in Document PPS23, February 24, 1948): "We have about 60% of the world's wealth but only 6.3% of its population. In this situation we cannot fail to be the object of envy and resentment. Our real task in the coming period is to devise a pattern of relationships that will permit us to maintain this position of disparity. We need not deceive ourselves that we can afford today the luxury of altruism and world benefaction. We should cease to talk about such vague and unreal objectives as human rights, the raising of living standards and democratization. The day is not far off when we are going to have to deal in straight power concepts. The less we are then hampered by idealistic slogans, the better" (U.S. Government 1950).

2. The same caveats apply to two indefatigable American anthropologists intending to explain Filipinos to themselves: Thomas McKenna's *Muslim Rulers and Rebels* (1998) and Nicole Constable's *Maid to Order in Hong Kong: Stories of Filipina Workers* (1997). I am not indicting all of American or Western anthropology, let alone the hermeneutic methodology of the social sciences. But I would like to mention here two other sources of historical and political inquiries, aside from the writings of Cesar Adib Majul: one is the work of the Indian scholar Aijaz Ahmad (1982), and the other the essay of political scientist Robert Stauffer (1981). In both these thinkers, the differentiated totality of Filipino society and its historical imbrication in the world-system of global capitalism are the two necessary requisites for grasping the concrete linkages and contradictions in the Moro struggle for autonomy and dignity. For these intellectuals are not only practitioners of a mode of scientific analysis of history but also protagonists in the search for solutions to the most urgent social and political problems of our time.

3. I am following an argument elaborated by the late Canadian scholar Bill Readings in his provocative book, *The University in Ruins*. Speculating on the impossibility of subjective self-identity, of being free from obligation to others, Readings comments on an attitude prevalent in the United States—an attitude that, I think, became more articulate when, after September 11, most Americans, newly self-anointed as victims, refused to see any responsibility for what happened to them and disclaimed any share in causing such horrendous disaster, what is indeed a terrible tragedy because it is uncomprehended and disconnected from the flaws of the "egotistical sublime," hence the hunger for revenge. Readings of course includes his fellow Canadians in the following remark—which we can immediately apply to our own relations with the Moros, Igorots, and other ostracized neighbors: "It is the desire for subjective autonomy that has led North Americans, for example, to want to forget their obligations to the acts of genocide on which their society is founded, to ignore debts to Native American and other peoples that contemporary individuals did not personally contract, but for which I would nonetheless argue they are responsible (and not only insofar as they benefit indirectly from the historical legacy of those acts). In short, the social bond is not the property of an autonomous subject, since it exceeds subjective consciousness and even individual histories of action. The nature of my obligations to the history of the place in which I live, and my exact positioning in relation to that history, are not things I can decide upon or things that can be calculated exhaustively. No tax of 'x percent' on the incomes of white Americans could ever, for example, make full reparation for the history of racism in the United States (how much is a lynching 'worth'?). Nor would it put an end to the guilt of racism by 'whiteness' " (Readings 1996, 186).

4. Noam Chomsky and other public intellectuals have called the United States itself "a leading terrorist state" (Chomsky 2001, 16). Just to give an example of how this has registered in the lives of Filipinos in the United States: In 2003, 62 Filipinos (among them, doctors, and engineers) were apprehended by the U.S. Immigration and Naturalization Services for overstaying their visa or for lack of appropriate documentation. They were arrested as "absconders," handcuffed, and manacled in chains while aboard a plane on the way to the former Clark Air Base in Pampanga. About 140 Filipinos are now being treated as hardened criminals, according to Migrante International, thanks to the U.S. Patriot Act. Together with the Military Commissions Act of 2006, this act cancels the constitutional right of habeas corpus and allows torture of political prisoners by U.S. military and state personnel wherever Bush's "global war on terrorism" prevails (as in the territory of the Republic of the Philippines). Over a thousand persons, most of them people of color, are now detained in the United States as suspects, already being punished. I am not referring to the prisoners captured in Afghanistan and confined to cells in Guantánamo, Cuba; I am referring to American citizens who have been jailed on suspicion that they have links with Osama bin Laden or other terrorist groups listed by the U.S. State Department (which now includes the Communist Party of the Philippines and its armed wing, the New People's Army; see San Juan [2007]). Just last November, there was a report of eight Filipino aircraft mechanics who were detained since last June without bail due to "suspected terrorist links"; they are now being deported because of alleged inaccuracies in their immigration papers. I conclude with this question: how many more Filipinos will suffer globalized state terrorism spearheaded by the U.S. Government, a fate that may befall any one of us who as citizens (here or in the United States) may be branded as unpatriotic or traitors because we dare to criticize, dare to think and resist?

# Works Cited

Ahmad, Aijaz. 1982. "Who Is the Moro?" and "Class and Colony in Mindanao." *Southeast Asia Chronicle* (February): 2–10.

Asad, Talal. 2002. "Some Thoughts on the WTC Disaster." *ISIM Newsletter* 9 (January): 5–6.

Ashcroft, Bill, Gareth Griffiths, and Helen Tiffin. 1998. *Key Concepts in Post-Colonial Studies.* London: Routledge.

Badiou, Alain. 2003. *Infinite Thought: Truth and the Return of Philosophy.* London: Continuum.

Chomsky, Noam. 1992. *Deterring Democracy.* New York: Hill and Wang.

———. 2001. "The United States Is a Leading Terrorist State." Interview by David Barsamian. *Monthly Review* 53, no. 6 (November): 10–19.

Constable, Nicole. 1997. *Maid to Order in Hong Kong: Stories of Filipina Workers.* Ithaca, N.Y.: Cornell University Press.

Dirlik, Arif. 2000. *Postmodernity's Histories.* Lanham, Md.: Rowman and Littlefield.

Edgar, Andrew, and Peter Sedgwick, eds. 2002. *Cultural Theory: The Key Concepts.* London: Routledge.

Frake, Charles. 1998. "Abu Sayyaf: Displays of Violence and the Proliferation of Contested Identities among Philippine Muslims." *American Anthropologist* 100, no. 1: 41–54.

Isenberg, David. 2002. "P2OG Allows Pentagon to Fight Dirty. Asian Times, November 8.

Lowy, Michael. 1998. *Fatherland or Mother Earth? Essays on the National Question.* London: Pluto Press.

Mahajan, Rahul. 2002. *The New Crusade: America's War on Terrorism.* New York: Monthly Review.

McKenna, Thomas M. 1998. *Muslim Rulers and Rebels.* Berkeley: University of California Press.

Readings, Bill. 1996. *The University in Ruins.* Cambridge, Mass.: Harvard University Press.

Said, Edward. 1994. *Culture and Imperialism.* New York: Alfred Knopf.

———. 1999. "Edward Said, in Conversation with Neeladri Bhattacharya, Suvir Kaul, and Ania Loomba, New Delhi, 16 December 1997." *Interventions* 1, no. 1: 81–96.

———. 2003. "A Window on the World." *The Guardian* 2 (August): 1–6.

San Juan, E. 1998. *Beyond Postcolonial Theory.* New York: Palgrave Macmillan.

———. 2002. *Racism and Cultural Studies.* Durham, N.C.: Duke University Press.

———. 2004. *Working through the Contradictions: From Cultural Theory to Critical Practice.* Bucknell, Pa.: Bucknell University Press.

———. 2007. *U.S. Imperialism and Revolution in the Philippines.* New York: Palgrave Macmillan.

Shank, Duane. 2003. "The Project for a New American Empire: Who Are These Guys? And Why Do They Think They Can Rule the World?" *Sojourner* (August 22).

Source Watch. 2007. "A Project of the Center for Media and Democracy." Source Watch. July 31. At: *http://www.Sourcewatch.org/.*

Stauffer, Robert. 1981. "The Politics of Becoming: The Mindanao Conflict in a World-System Perspective." In *Dependency Series No. 31.* Quezon City: University of the Philippines, Third World Studies Center.

Ullman, Harlan, and James Wade. 1996. *Shock and Awe: Achieving Rapid Dominance.* Washington D.C. NDU Press.

U.S. Government. 1950. *Foreign Relations of the United States*, vol. 1, 1948, made public in 1975.

# 10

## DEATH AND POLITICS: EMPIRE AND THE "NEW" POLITICS OF RESISTANCE

### *Pal Ahluwalia*

It is now commonplace to speak of a global culture, the global village as well as the speed and spread of globalization processes that are gripping the world. Globalization is not an entirely new phenomenon. Nevertheless, new information, communication, transport, and manufacturing technologies, as well as trade regimes, effected through such multilateral organizations as the GATT and tariff reductions, have allowed production, commerce, and finance to be organized and operated on a global scale. The rise and spread of multinational corporations operating across nation-state boundaries raises questions about the capacity of the state to function within the national interest. In addition, the mass migrations of peoples from different parts of the world have intensified. Although there are considerable arguments for and against the extent and impact of globalization, there is no denying that the phenomenon currently is ongoing (Giddens 1990; Waters 1995; Hoogvelt 1997; Appadurai 1990, 1996; Jameson and Miyoshi 1998). Still, there is little agreement across disciplines on how to theorize globalization. Malcolm Waters claimed that just as "post-modernism was the concept of the 1980s, globalization may be the concept of the 1990s, a key idea by which we understand the transition of human society into the third millennium" (1995, 1).

I want to begin by reflecting on two personal issues precisely because of the broader implications that they raise about globalization and sovereignty. These are my citizenship and my Sikh identity, both of which intersect in an obvious manifestation of empire, globalization, and diasporic identity. These two issues raise also the more fundamental questions about where sovereignty ultimately resides—that is, in the nation-state or in the body. In many ways, I might well be described as the consummate global citizen who has circulated among the nations of the Commonwealth. I was born a third-generation Kenyan to parents of "Indian" origin, hence my prominent Sikh identity. I went to Canada as a child, moved to Australia to study, and ended up living there for the longest period of my life in any single country before moving to the metropolitan center when I took up the Chair of Politics at Goldsmiths College, University of London.

As I reflect on my own movements around the Commonwealth, I am struck by how my identity has been continuously constructed and reconstructed in contrast to the identity that I may choose to imagine. What I find remarkable about this rootlessness, and to a certain extent uncomfortableness about belonging, is the manner in which I have been entrapped by those most obvious symbols of modernity—the passport and citizenship.

It is these two markers of identity that have followed me wherever I have gone. In Kenya, as an Asian Indian subject (note that in East Africa the term Indian was conflated with Asian), my Africanness was questioned. I was perceived as part of a settler class, albeit a settler class that was inferior to the Europeans who lived there. The sense of vulnerability, despite my parents having been born there and being Kenyan citizens both by virtue of birth and the taking of formal citizenship at the time of independence, was only revealed in 1972 when Idi Amin in the neighboring Commonwealth nation of Uganda expelled Asians regardless of their citizenship. This singular event no doubt marked the Asians of East Africa, and my parents migrated to Canada.

Canada and Saskatchewan of the 1970s brings back memories of my world turning upside down. I was no longer a *Singha Singha* (as I was referred to in common parlance in Kenya) but was now part of a new community to which I never even knew I belonged—I 'became' East Indian. Remarkably, I was transformed from an Asian into an East Indian. I was immediately made an outsider. My African identity was all but erased as this new East Indian identity was thrust upon me.

I remember traveling to the UK and France with my parents a couple of years later and realizing that as a Kenyan citizen my passport was a barrier to the places to which I could travel without a plethora of visas and questions about my intent.[1] It seemed that everyone was worried that I was a threat, that I would overstay my welcome. My Kenyan identity, which had been transformed into East Indian, was I discovered, a further barrier to being a Commonwealth citizen. There was a certain cachet in 'belonging' to the white settler colonies of the Commonwealth. This situation lay behind my parents' decision that I should become a Canadian citizen once I fulfilled the necessary residency requirements. I now had a new citizenship and was formally a Canadian. Having a Canadian passport meant that I was no longer forced to obtain visas in most of the Western world, but at every border I was constantly reminded that I was not a 'normal' Canadian. Wherever I traveled, immigration officials were, and are, particularly keen to examine closely my passport—fearing, I suspect, that it may be forged.

In 1984, I went to Adelaide, Australia, to pursue my PhD in African Studies. In Australia, no one ever doubted that I was an Indian. It was always a shock when I said that I was born in Kenya and had lived for many years in Canada. Just as in Canada, I was ascribed a new identity, this time Indian as opposed to East Indian. I had never lived in India and had only visited there as a very young child and yet, everywhere in the white settler colonies, I was an Indian. At best, I existed with a hyphenated identity—East Indian, Indo-Australian, British-Asian, and so on.[2]

A few months after I arrived in Australia, I remember waking up one morning to the news that the Indian army under orders from the Prime Minister, Indira Gandhi, had attacked the Golden Temple. I remember having a sense of nausea and baulking at the very idea that I was an Indian. Alone, amongst a very small Sikh community in Adelaide, I began to come to terms with the indignity that every Sikh felt at having their holiest shrine brutally invaded. Operation Bluestar, the Indian Army's code word for the attack, and the subsequent mass killings of Sikhs after the assassination of Indira Gandhi by her Sikh bodyguards, left an indelible mark not only on me but also on Sikhs everywhere. It was not until the next year when I went to India with my Australian wife that I was to discover that, as a Canadian East Indian, I was perceived as a terrorist threat and was denied a visa to visit Punjab and the Golden Temple in Amritsar. I realized that my ascribed 'Indianness' in both Canada and Australia was meaningless. It was at this moment that my Sikh identity, which was always a part of me, came to the fore—indeed I was not an Indian, I was a Sikh regardless of the passport I carried. It was as Edward Said wrote, "my uniquely punishing destiny" (Said 1978). It mattered little that I always viewed myself as an African who practiced the Sikh religion, who had a commitment to the continent, and who had dedicated my intellectual life to that project and continue to do so.

# EMPIRE

In this context let us consider the question of Michael Hardt and Antonio Negri's *Empire* (2000) and the notion of sovereignty. The Commonwealth, and moving amongst its various countries, clearly evokes a deep sense of the cosmopolitan nature of diasporic identity, a sense of rootlessness, mobility, and indeed globalization that has become characteristic of this postmodern, postcolonial world—one in which, some argue, nation-state boundaries and national sovereignty are being eroded. Yet, as I travel around the globe, I am constantly reminded of the demarcations that so clearly divide us, the borders that have been erected to keep us separate, and the power of citizenship and the passport—those formal markers of identity that can mean everything to an immigration officer at various border posts around the world.

Hardt and Negri assert that a new epoch has emerged that can be captured best by borrowing a term from classical antiquity—*empire*. The term invokes the idea of the power (imperium), as opposed to the idea of territorial acquisition, that became integral to the way the term was thought of in relation to recent European empires such as the British and French Empires. The idea of "place," Hardt and Negri insist, belongs to the past, to modernity, whereas the transition to Empire signals a new "space of imperial sovereignty" which "in contrast, is smooth" (2000, 190). In this new smooth space of Empire, "there is no *place* of power—it is both everywhere and nowhere. Empire is an *ou-topia*, or really a *non-place*" (190). Hardt and Negri argue:

> Empire is materializing before our very eyes. Over the past several decades, as colonial regimes were overthrown and then precipitously after the Soviet barriers to the capitalist world market finally collapsed, we have witnessed an irresistible and irreversible globalization of economic and cultural exchanges. Along with the global market and the global circuits of production has emerged a global order, a new logic and structure of rule—in short, a new form of sovereignty. Empire is the political subject that effectively regulates these global exchanges, the sovereign power that governs the world. (2000, xi)

Their project involves tracing the genealogy of sovereignty and its most obvious linkages to modernity. Modern sovereignty is linked inextricably with Europe, where it emerged in conjunction with modernity itself. It was through the project of colonialism that modern sovereignty spread beyond the borders of Europe, rendering it as "two coextensive and complementary faces of one development: rule within Europe and European rule over the world" (70). Empire is not some form of reconstituted imperialism from a previous epoch; it is essentially a new form of rule. It is here that the multitude, supposedly mobile and innovative, can be free of the very constraints of modernity.

Whereas modernity was from its very beginning seen as being in a state of crisis when the multitude came into conflict with forms of ordering authority, under the new form of sovereignty, "Empire is a mere apparatus of capture that lives only off the vitality of the multitude" (Hardt and Negri 2000, 62). The passage to Empire is the informatization /modernization of the economy that leads to the dominance of the world market over the nation-state as the latter has little ability to contain the amorphous capacity of the dynamics of capital. This passage of sovereignty is best seen as a move towards immanence.

As Tony Schirato and Jen Webb (2003) have noted so perceptively, for Hardt and Negri, globalization *is* Empire. Thus, the significance of Empire is the very emergence of a global system of power. Hardt and Negri are adamant that the establishment of Empire is a progressive move and reject any political strategy that seeks to return power to the nation-state so that it can challenge global capital (Hardt 2000, 43). The very formation of Empire is a "*response* to proletarian internationalism" (51) so that, central to their characterization of Empire is the assertion that "globalization . . . is really a condition of liberation of the multitude" (52). Hardt and Negri argue that Empire—a new supranational and deterritorializing form of sovereignty—is the terrain in which a new mode of critical and revolutionary action is carried out by the multitude. Their claim that there is no outside to Empire underscores the point that there is no capacity to organize resistance from the outside. Rather, a politics of resistance has to come from within it.

In fact, the spread of globalization is desirable precisely because it creates the conditions conducive to an intensified resistance by the multitude. A new form of solidarity and militancy can be seen in varied struggles, such as Tiananmen Square, the Intifada, Chiapas, the race riots in Los Angeles, as well as the French and South Korean mass strikes. Although there seems to be little communication between these largely localized struggles, "in fact they all directly attack the global order of Empire and seek a real alternative" (Hardt and Negri 2000, 56–57). Hardt and Negri further argue that "postcolonialist theory [while] a very productive tool for rereading history . . . is entirely insufficient for theorizing contemporary global power" (146).[3] The end of colonialism and the diminishing powers of the nation "are indicative of a general passage of the paradigm of imperial sovereignty" (136).

Nonetheless, Anthony Burke (2002) notes that it is the perverse perseverance of sovereignty that marks the end of formal colonial rule; Susan Marks similarly challenges the notion of the irrelevance of postcolonial theory as a theoretical tool for understanding the contemporary postcolonial world. She reminds us that it is important to remember that, "with deterritorialization comes reterritorilization, in the sense that old dichotomies shape the operations of the new more complex systems of domination" (2000, 464). Furthermore, she argues that Hardt and Negri themselves point out that the geographical and racial modes of oppression that were established during colonialism not only have not decreased but rather have increased exponentially (Hardt and Negri 2000, 43). This suggests that rather than the nation-state disappearing, it has most likely been restructured.

Partha Chatterjee interrogates closely the thesis that the nation-state's demise is inevitable and imminent, and he argues that the so-called crisis of the nation-state can be attributed to two sets of arguments. The first concerns the inability of the state to govern effectively: that is, its inability to meet the "welfare" needs of its population. The second outlines the "decay or lack of appropriate civil-social institutions that could provide a secure foundation for a proper relationship between autonomous individual lives in society and the collective political domain of the state" (Chatterjee 1998, 65), and it is this that explains the dictatorial and authoritarian role of the nation-state. Chatterjee argues to the contrary that it is the collapse of these two arguments that in turn sets up a dichotomy between globality and modernity that nation-states are unable to mediate. In their place he posits two kinds of mediation: "one between globality and modernity, and the other between globality and democracy. The two, at least apparently, cannot be performed by the same set of institutions" (65–66). For him, this is the current crisis of the nation-state. The way in which global modernity is being advanced is "profoundly colonial," whereas the articulation of democracy "will pronounce modernity itself as inappropriate and deeply flawed" (68). An awareness of these twin pressures will permit movement beyond the nation-state, and it is precisely this dilemma that is most acutely highlighted by postcolonial theory—but this is a point that Hardt and Negri fail to understand. It is in this context that Sanjay Seth (2002) asks how they can be sure that the forward march of globalization is superior to what it is replacing.

Globalization illustrates most vividly the insatiable desire for Western consumer goods that pervades the postcolonial world, and it was the failure of the Left to account for this desire in the former communist world that rendered its theoretical elaborations most problematic. Adam Smith argued that it was the role of commodities that distinguished between "civilized" and "barbarous" nations. An abundance of "objects of comfort" was the litmus test that distinguished "civilized and thriving nations" from "savage" ones, "so miserably poor" they were reduced to "mere want" (1776, lx). The purpose of destroying barbarism was to create consumption through what Smith called desire—which is central to capitalism and becomes its most important export.

Paradoxically, it is the maintenance of different levels of consumption that remain the real markers of difference between nations. The greatest weakness of Empire, as Crystal Bartolovich points out, is its avoidance of the desire for commodities, set against the patterns of consumption between and within nations:

> For consumerism indicates why there is still an investment in the 'people' of certain nation-states, or groups of nation-states (EU), seen as interest blocs—in a continued 'boundedness', not predicated merely on Freud's 'narcissism of minor differences' manipulated to the benefit of elites, but on the protection of real generalized privilege. There might not be any 'outside' of capital, but there is definitely an outside to those who benefit from it, relatively and absolutely. (2003, 182)

It is this logic of contemporary patterns of consumption that ensures the maintenance of boundaries between people and groups of people who reside in the postcolonial world. Global inequality, Bartolovich argues, "is *directly* a function not only of 350 or so billionaires, the captains of industry, the heads of wealthy states, but of considerable swathes of the *settled* population in the 'developed' countries who benefit from the status quo at great cost to others" (195). Hence, it is not surprising that Benita Parry has argued that, "where inequalities persist, so do borders remain in place and so are flows of population, cultures and socialities distorted" (2003, 302).

It is this maintenance of borders and boundaries between the Western and the postcolonial world, coupled to the deep investment in and persistence of identity politics with which I began this chapter, that together raise problems simply not adequately dealt with by Negri and Hardt. The question then arises, where does sovereignty reside if it is no longer existent within the nation-state? It is here that postcolonial theory may well provide insights because postcolonial subjects have had to confront these issues.

## HOMO SACER AND THE PARADOX OF SOVEREIGNTY

In order to reflect on these questions, it is important to turn to Giorgio Agamben and his discussion of *homo sacer*. The term *homo sacer* refers to the juridical category of ancient Roman law where someone who has committed a crime cannot be sacrificed for that crime. It was from the Roman writer Pompeius Festus that we learn what is critical about *homo sacer* is that although "it is not permitted to sacrifice this man, yet he who kills him will not be condemned for homicide" (as cited in Agamben 1998, 71). Giorgio Agamben traces this idea throughout Western political thought and argues that it represents a key element of sovereign power. The paradox of sovereignty is that:

> The life caught in the sovereign ban is the life that is originally sacred—that is, that may be killed but not sacrificed—and, in this sense, the production of bare life is the originary activity of sovereignty. The sacredness of life, which is invoked today as an absolutely fundamental right in opposition to sovereign power, in fact originally expresses precisely both life's subjection to a power over death and life's irreparable exposure in the relation of abandonment. (83)

The paradox of sovereignty "consists in the fact the sovereign is, at the same time, outside and inside the juridical order" (15). That is, the sovereign who has the legal power to proclaim a state of exception, in the Schmittian sense, is legally also placed outside the law. Agamben explains that the exception is a type of exclusion where, "the exclusion from the general rule is an individual case" (17). However, what is excluded is not without relation to the rule. The state of exception, he argues, "is thus not the chaos that precedes order but rather the situation that results from its suspension" (18).

A link then is established between sacredness, sovereignty, and life, where sovereignty functions to delimit a zone of indistinction that constitutes life as sacred. This sacredness, however, is not linked to any divine notions of sacrifice. Davide Panagia notes, "sovereign power and bare life are linked precisely because it is sovereignty that constitutes a life as bare through the foundation of a zone of indistinction" (1999, 1). Bare life for Agamben is before the law and as such can be taken only without being sanctioned by the law. Such a bare life is manifested, he argues, in the Foucauldian notion of biopower.[4] Bare life is, in short, the object of that power, and it is the inability to differentiate between our biological body and our political body that raises questions about where sovereignty ultimately resides: If one has no confidence in the sovereign or rather if the sovereign power is seen to be illegitimate as it was for colonial subjects, where does sovereignty lie?[5] What is the relationship between the biological and political body within such a context? Furthermore, what are the implications of this for a politics of resistance?

## "NECROPOLITICS" AND THE POLITICS OF RESISTANCE

It is with this in mind that we need to engage with Achille Mbembe's recent intervention, "Necropolitics." Working in response to Foucault, Mbembe's central problematic is to ascertain the relationship between politics and death in those systems that can function only in a state of emergency or a state of exception. He shows how the trope of death operates in the formulation of one being rendered a subject through an exploration of the very "work of death."[6] Foucault's formulation of biopower appears to function through dividing people into those who must live and those who must die. For Foucault, it was the Nazi state that constituted the most comprehensive example of a state exercising its right to kill. The manner in which the imaginary of sovereignty operates under modernity is along the lines that my life is threatened by the existence of the other, which means that in order to secure the potential of my life and security it is necessary to kill the other. This means that "the ultimate expression of sovereignty resides to a large degree, in the power and the capacity to dictate who may live and who may die. Hence, to kill or to allow to live constitutes the limits of sovereignty, its fundamental attributes" (Mbembe 2003, 11–12).

For Mbembe, politics in the age of late capitalism is underpinned by the concept of reason that is critical to both the "project of modernity and the topos of sovereignty." Politics in such a configuration is "a project of autonomy and the achieving of agreement among a collectivity through communication and recognition" (13). It is precisely such a politics of reason that demarcates the civilized from the barbarian and what differentiates politics from a state of war.[7] However, as Agamben has illustrated, in a state of exception or in a zone of indistinction the very lines between the sacredness of life and the proliferation of death are extremely blurred. Mbembe therefore seeks to understand how "contemporary forms of subjugation of life to the power of death (necropolitics) profoundly reconfigure the relations among resistance, sacrifice, and terror" (39). He sums up his project arguing that the notion of necropolitics and necropower are aimed at understanding how "weapons are deployed in the interest of maximum destruction of peoples and the creation of *death-worlds*, new and unique forms of social existence in which vast populations are subjected to conditions of life conferring upon them the status of *living dead*." Furthermore, under these conditions, "the lines between resistance and suicide, sacrifice and redemption, martyrdom and freedom are blurred" (40).

Mbembe explores different sites of exception that have a bearing on our discussion of sovereignty. One of the first instances of biopolitical experimentation was slavery. The plantation system was itself a paradoxical figure of the state of exception. Slave life was in many ways a form of death-in-life. For the system to operate, it was essential that the slave not have agency.[8] The very existence of the slave was a condition of loss, a "loss of a 'home,' loss of right over his or her body, and loss of political status. This triple loss is identical with absolute domination, natal alienation, and social death (expulsion from humanity altogether)" (Mbembe 2003, 21).

Another obvious site of exception is the colony, which in modern European thought and practice "represents the site where sovereignty consists fundamentally in the exercise of a power outside the law" (Mbembe 2003, 23). The designation of the colony as a site of exception demonstrates in Schmittian terms the definition of sovereignty. Colonies are:

> . . . zones in which war and disorder, internal and external figures of the political stand side by side or alternate with each other. As such, the colonies are the location par excellence where the controls and guarantees of judicial order can be suspended— the zone where the violence of the state of exception is deemed to operate in the service of civilization. (24)

Perhaps the most extreme example of contemporary necropower, Mbembe argues, is the colonial occupation of Palestine where "sovereignty means the capacity to define who matters and who does not, who is *disposable* and who is not" (27). The Palestinian case "is a concatenation of multiple powers: disciplinary, biopolitical, and necropolitical"—a lethal combination providing the "colonial power an absolute domination over the inhabitants of the occupied territory" (29).

It is this absolute domination, whether in the case of slavery, the colony, or Palestinian occupation, that renders the subject powerless. Sovereignty in these death worlds resides in what the subject considers an illegitimate power—the master, the colonizer—who has the ultimate power to decide between who can live and who can die. The only agency that is possible is to be found in the very act of actual death. Actual death as opposed to social death is the very instance where agency itself can be exercised.[9] This capacity for agency has been acknowledged by Paul Gilroy who argues that, in those slaves who committed either individual or mass suicide when confronted by slave catchers, death can be seen as being representative of agency—precisely because it is over death that one has power (1993, 63).

Globalization, Étienne Balibar points out, has brought in its wake "*the new visibility of extreme violence,*" largely due to modern techniques of media coverage and broadcasting (2001, 23). What is important about Balibar's observation is that the globalization of this extreme violence has resulted in a world that can be characterized by life-zones and death-zones. It is between these zones that there has been an appearance of "a decisive and fragile superborder, which raises fears and concerns about the unity and division of mankind— something like a global and local 'enmity line,' like the 'amity line' which existed in the beginning of the modern European seizure of the world" (24). Although we may well be in the midst of certain developments that are challenging the sovereignty of the nation-state, including forms of international terrorism, it is important to remember that it is the existence of these life- and death-zones that produce and reproduce conditions that are akin to the very zones of exception such as slavery and colonial occupation that gave rise to certain forms of agency of which death is both the most gruesome and the most powerful.

## POLITICAL VIOLENCE AND RESISTANCE

In the wake of September 11 and the globalization of violence, Susan Buck-Morss's (2003) intervention is particularly helpful. She argues that what Hardt and Negri fail to deal with is the problem of the legitimate use of violence—which is absolutely central to the very question of sovereignty. She argues that, "the hope that a felicitously reconstituted 'postmodern' sovereignty will come about as a new paradigm of power . . . now seems clearly overly optimistic" (36).

She sets out to examine how the Left can think past terror. In reflecting on the attacks on the twin towers, she notes that Timothy McVeigh, the Oklahoma City bomber who was executed in 2000, and the events of September 11 were not allowed to be connected because "to relate them is to acknowledge the global, rather than domestic, context of political acts" (2003, 27). Rather than dealing with the complexity of the message of September 11, that very complexity was reduced simply by George Bush to the proclamation that "you are with us or against us."[10] For Buck-Morss, there are two Americas—a democratically elected republic under threat since the Bush election and the security state that always requires an enemy.[11] For the U.S. security state, the biggest threat is that the enemy might disappear. It has to constantly reinvent enemies, which paradoxically means "that the undemocratic state claims absolute power over the citizens of a free and democratic nation" (29).

If we were to remove ourselves from the context of the 9/11 attacks, it is not difficult to see that terrorism is not the worst kind of violence nor does it necessarily result in the greatest loss of life, as in the case of a war. Indeed, if one looks at the current intifada, there are far more Palestinians who have lost their lives at the hands of the Israeli military than Israelis themselves. What is remarkable in the post-9/11 world is that to talk of suicide bombing has itself become a taboo subject. If one broaches the subject, she or he is treated with suspicion and outrage. For example, when a British M.P. spoke out recently, pointing out vehemently that although she condemned the practice, she could nevertheless understand why Palestinian youth took this route—given their deplorable conditions—she was immediately challenged and shunned by her parliamentary colleagues and vilified by the media. She, of course, was not alone in feeling the effects of this new policing and the political risk of speaking out against the injustices being endured by Palestinians.[12]

Colonialism has always entailed resistance, often violent resistance. The anticolonial resistance of Fanon and Gandhi entailed certain violence regardless of their methodologies— the very reversal of the colonial order that they sought was violent (Ahluwalia 2003). As Edward Said noted, to "ignore or otherwise discount the overlapping experience of Westerners and Orientals, the interdependence of cultural terrains in which colonizer and colonized coexisted and battled each other through projections as well as rival geographies, narratives, and histories, is to miss what is essential about the world in the past century" (1993, xxii–xiii). The ANC in South Africa, for example, under Nelson Mandela, engaged in such a campaign of violence as a means to end apartheid. It is ironic that Nelson Mandela, a recipient of the Nobel Peace Prize, advocated violent resistance to attain liberation. Moreover, it is important to recognize that this global icon of reconciliation never renounced what he considered the legitimate right to political violence. What is particularly interesting is the politics of how one can go from being a convicted terrorist leader to a universally revered global leader or indeed, as in the case of Yassir Arafat despite his Nobel Peace Prize, be reclassified a "terrorist." What is significant about Nelson Mandela, Mahatma Gandhi, and Yassir Arafat, leaders who sought justice and freedom for their people, is that their place in history is in part the result of the configurations and machinations of global power politics and the legitimacy or illegitimacy of sovereign power against which they exercised their different modes of resistance.

The phenomenon of suicide bombings is by no means new or unique to Islam, as is often portrayed in the media. It is a practice that has been widely deployed as an effective weapon in war. An obvious example is that of the Japanese kamikaze pilots of the Second World War who chose to die in honor of their country. John Seery notes that: "Most of us Westerners view non-Western cases of political suicide as culturally pathological, and we generally lump together 'terrorists,' guerrilla fighters, *sati* and *satyagrahaas*-crazed fanatics. Joyous Day of the Dead celebrations we discuss as dark-skinned exotica" (as cited in Euben 2002, 8). Hilal Khashan's empirical study of Palestinian suicide bombing (PSB) unsurprisingly reveals that political Islam was indeed a factor in one being prone to suicide bombing, "especially among refugee camp inhabitants, where dismal poverty coalesces with radical Islam. Disposition to partaking in suicide attacks cannot take place without provocation that produces intolerable frustration" (2003, 1064). We might well ask then what makes the PSB particularly repugnant? Is it merely the fact that their targets are often civilians? Ghassan Hage explains:

> The PSBs disrupt the ability of the colonizers to consolidate a 'normal peaceful life' inside the colonial settler state of Israel. As such they do not respect the Israeli colonizer's division of labor between the military who engage in protecting and facilitating the process of colonization and the civilian population who can peacefully enjoy the fruits of this process. Furthermore, the practice is condemned and considered socially pathological because it involves what anthropologists call *self-sacrifice* on the part of the perpetrators. (2003, 68–69)

The manner in which we approach PSBs and anticolonial violence differently is indicative of the "symbolic violence that shapes our understanding of what constitutes ethically and politically illegitimate violence. Indeed, the fact that the terrorist groups never classify themselves as terrorists, instead calling themselves revolutionaries, martyrs, nationalists or freedom fighters, is an indication of the depth of this symbolic violence" (Hage 2003, 72).

We have pointed out that in the death world of the contemporary colonial occupation of Palestine, the Palestinian subject must accept the reality of living as socially dead with little or no agency and the inability to challenge what they consider an illegitimate sovereign power. It is in this context that we need to think about why it is that Palestinian youth (across the gender divide) embrace a culture of suicide bombing. The ability to face one of the most formidable military machines with rocks and to risk death is to accumulate the highest cultural capital—whose ultimate expression lies in death as a mode through which life itself is given meaning. Hage explains that the PSBs, "become a sign that Palestinians have not been broken. They are a sign of life. For what better sign of life is there, in such violent conditions, than the capacity to hurt despite the greater capacity of the other to hurt you" (74). The point is that Palestinian suicide bombings are a terrible curse and social evil with profound and horrific consequences for both the victims and the Palestinians, who in turn face further violence as the Israeli state engages in a politics of retribution and recrimination. But they should also be a reminder that evil "resides more in certain social conditions of life where the possibilities of a meaningful life are shrinking, rather than in the individuals trying to survive in such conditions" (Hage 2003, 88–89).

Thus, global capitalism needs to be evaluated much like the U.S. security state—it is paradoxical because "on the one hand, it is the very foundation of the whole possibility of a global public sphere. On the other hand, because it thrives on uneven development and the lack of universal rights within that sphere, it continues to be an indefensible system of brutal exploitation of human labor and nature's labor" (Buck-Morss 2003, 36). A globalization that increasingly divides the world between what Balibar calls life-zones and death-zones, a globalization that operates through furthering the interests of a hegemonic power, and that operates with duplicity and double standards, is unlikely to lead to the new forms of sovereignty envisaged by Hardt and Negri. As Buck-Morss points out:

> Democracy means treating people democratically. If we in the West find that under present economic, political and cultural arrangements of power we cannot do this without danger to our own existence, then the defense of democracy demands not military force, but a radical questioning of these power arrangements. (2003, 52)

The task of creating a global sphere where the multitude can indeed operate in a new mode of critical and revolutionary action is to recognize that the system of consumption in which the West has a parasitical relationship with the postcolonial world must change. As long as postcolonial subjects are not allowed true freedom from the very death worlds in which they have been entrapped, they will increasingly encroach on the West's freedom. As Walter Benjamin noted: "Whoever has emerged victorious participates to this day in the triumphal procession in which the present rulers step over those who are lying prostrate. . . . There is no document of civilization which is not at the same time a document of barbarism" (as cited in Buck-Morss 2003, 104).

## CONCLUSION

For Carl Schmitt, all political actions and intentions could be summed up in the distinction between friend and enemy. Politics itself was underpinned by the notion that it was possible to kill without hate. The politics of commitment, whether motivated by religion or indeed by a secular cause, meant that one could and did transcend oneself to kill the *public enemy*. The politics of consumption that has created such a wide gulf between the West and the majority of postcolonial subjects is producing a different configuration of power and a different sort of politics—a politics that increasingly looks like that of Agamben's *Homo Sacer*—where a war machinery kills without fear of being held responsible. Whilst most in the West are unwilling to transcend themselves, to die in a war for the nation or indeed their convictions, those trapped in death worlds, largely the making of the West, seem all the more prepared to embrace a Schmittian mode of politics. In such a configuration, the very question of sovereignty and resistance cannot be reduced to that of an all-encompassing multitude. As Bashir Abu-Manneh points out, the irony of Hardt and Negri's position is that, "after presenting Empire as a realm 'beyond politics' they end up advocating a reformist sort of politics—like the right to global citizenship, a social wage, and the right of reappropriation" (2003, 171). Whilst such a reformist agenda is welcome, the present reality is one that entraps postcolonial and diasporic subjects within a web of citizenships, passports, and ascribed identities.

## NOTES

1. It is important to note that the policing of the borders has been heightened with the perceived influx of refugees. In Australia, refugees have not been allowed to enter the mainland with extraterritorial zones of exception established to deal with the issue. The idea of hospitality and the responsibility to refugees seems to have been all but eroded.
2. The question of this hyphenated identity and the fact that people of color do not have the choice to lose the hyphen are explored in "When Does the Settler Become a Native." See Ahluwalia 2001b.
3. I do not have the space here to engage fully with Hardt and Negri's reading of postcolonial theory that they seem to equate essentially with Homi Bhabha. For a fuller discussion, see Ahluwalia (2001a) and Ashcroft and Ahluwalia (2001).
4. Tony Schirato and Jen Webb define *biopower* as: the technologies, knowledges, discourses, politics, and practices used to bring about the production and management of a state's human resources. Biopower analyzes, regulates, controls, explains, and defines the human subject, its body, and its behavior. For Michel Foucault it is associated most particularly with official institutions that construct spaces and ways of regulating (and so producing) people — schools, hospitals, and prisons (2003, 214).
5. As Peter Fitzpatrick points out, Agamben offers two ways of thinking about what constitutes modern bare life and its relationship to sovereign power: "One mode is that of the totality, a mode in which the pall of bare life/sovereignty is about to encompass all in a 'catastrophe.' Even now, 'homo sacer is virtually confused with the citizen' and politics has been 'totally transformed into biopolitics,'

so much so that it is no longer possible to differentiate 'between our biological body and our political body'. . . . The other mode of conceiving of bare life/sovereignty comes with its varied instantiation—in 'the camp', refugees, *zones d'attentes*, and others—added to the rendering of one of them, 'the camp' as paradigm" (2001, 11–12).

6. It should be noted that although Mbembe's notion of "becoming subject" is arrived at very differently, it does bear some resemblance to Mahmood Mamdani's differentiation between citizen and subject. See Mamdani 1996; Ahluwalia 2001a.

7. It is this demarcation that underpins the very idea of Huntington's "Clash of Civilizations" and the triumphalism of Fukuyama's end of history. See Huntington 1996; Fukuyama 1992.

8. Susan Buck-Morss explores the importance of slavery in Western thought and particularly in Hegel. See Buck-Morss 2000.

9. I am deeply indebted to Abdul JanMohamed for this insight. This problematic is thoroughly worked out by him in his *The Death-Bound-Subject: Richard Wright's Archaeology of Death* (2005).

10. John Kelly has made some interesting observations about the flag and American patriotism. Like the tattered flags flying on cars, he suggests "patriots face the guilty problem of deciding when enough is enough, and how to dispose of their own decayed fetish of love, hate, and unfocussed will" (2003, 368).

11. On the invention of an enemy, see Ahluwalia and Sullivan (2000).

12. In recent times, other prominent figures, including both Ted Turner and Cherie Blair, were similarly also silenced and forced to apologize for their views.

## Works Cited

Abu-Manneh, Bashir. 2003. "The Illusions of Empire." *Interventions* 5, no. 2: 159–76.

Agamben, Giorgio. 1998. *Homo Sacer: Sovereign Power and Bare Life*, trans. Daniel Heller-Roazen. Stanford, Calif.: Stanford University Press.

Ahluwalia, Pal. 2001a. *Politics and Post-Colonial Theory: African Inflections* . London: Routledge.

———. 2001b. "When Does a Settler Become a Native? Citizenship and Identity in a Settler Society." *Pretexts* 10, no. 1: 63–73.

———. 2003. "Fanon's Nausea: The Hegemony of the White Nation." *Social Identities* 9, no. 3: 341–56.

Ahluwalia, Pal, and Michael Sullivan. 2000. "Edward Said and the World." In *International Relations Still an American Social Science?* eds. Daryl Jarvis and Robert Crawford. New York: State University of New York Press.

Appadurai, Arjun. 1990. "Disjuncture and Difference in the Global Cultural Economy." *Public Culture* 2, no. 2: 1–24.

———. 1996. *Modernity at Large* . Minneapolis: University of Minnesota Press.

Ashcroft, Bill, and Pal Ahluwalia. 2001. *Edward Said*. London: Routledge.

Balibar, Étienne. 2001. "Outlines of a Topography of Cruelty: Citizenship and Civility in the Era of Global Violence." *Constellations* 8, no. 1: 15–29.

Bartolovich, Crystal. 2003. "The Eleventh September of George Bush: Fortress U.S. and the Global Politics of Consumption." *Interventions* 5, no. 2: 177–99.

Brennan, Timothy. 2003. "The Subtlety of Caesar." *Interventions* 5, no. 2: 200–206.

Buck-Morss, Susan. 2000. "Hegel and Haiti." *Critical Inquiry* 26:821–65.

———. 2003. *Thinking Past Terror: Islamism and Critical Theory of the Left*. London: Verso.

Burke, Anthony. 2002. "The Perverse Perseverance of Sovereignty." *borderlands e-journal* 1, no. 2: 1–14.

Chatterjee, Partha. 1998. "Beyond the Nation? Or Within?" *Social Text* 16, no. 3: 57–69.

Euben, Roxanne. 2002. "Killing (for) Politics: Jihad, Martyrdom, and Political Action." *Political Theory* 30, no. 1: 4–35.

Fitzpatrick, Peter. 2001. "Bare Sovereignty: Homo Sacer and the Insistence of Law." *Theory and Event* 5, no. 2. At: http://muse.jhu.edu/journals/theory_and_event/v005/5.2fitzpatrick.html.

Foucault, Michel. 2003. *"Society Must Be Defended" Lectures at the Collège De France 1975–1976*, trans. David Macey. New York: Picador.

Fukuyama, Francis. 1992. *The End of History and the Last Man*. London: Hamish Hamilton.

Giddens, Anthony. 1990. *The Consequences of Modernity*. Cambridge, UK: Polity Press.

Gilroy, Paul. 1993. *The Black Atlantic: Modernity and Double Consciousness*. Cambridge, Mass.: Harvard University Press.

Hage, Ghassan. 2003. " 'Comes a Time We Are All Enthusiasm': Understanding Palestinian Suicide Bombers in Times of Exighophobia." *Public Culture* 15, no. 1: 65–89.

Hardt, Michael, and Antonio Negri. 2000. *Empire*. Cambridge, Mass.: Harvard University Press.

Hoogvelt, Ankie. 1997. *Globalisation and Postcolonialism*. London: Macmillian.

Huntington, Samuel. 1996. *The Clash of Civilizations and the Remaking of World Order*. New York: Simon and Schuster.

Jameson, Fredric, and Masao Miyoshi, eds. 1998. *The Cultures of Globalization*. Durham, N.C.: Duke University Press.

JanMohamed, Abdul. 2005. *The Death-Bound-Subject: Richard Wright's Archaeology of Death*. Durham, N.C.: Duke University Press.

Kelly, John. 2003. "U.S. Power, after 9/11 and before It: If Not Empire, Then What?" *Public Culture* 15, no. 2: 347–69.

Khashan, Hilal. 2003. "Collective Palestinian Frustration and Suicide Bombings." *Third World Quarterly* 24, no. 6: 1049–67.

Mamdani, Mahmood. 1996. *Citizen and Subject: Contemporary Africa and the Legacy of Late Colonialism*. Princeton, N.J.: Princeton University Press.

Marks, Susan. 2002. "Empires Law." *Indiana Journal of Global Legal Studies* 10:449–66.

Mbembe, Achille. 2003. "Necropolitics." *Public Culture* 15, no. 1: 11–40.

Olma, Sebastian. 2001. "Globalization, the Pudding, and the Question of Power." *Theory, Culture, and Society* 18, no. 4: 111–22.

Panagia, Davide. 1999. "The Sacredness of Life and Death: Giorgio Agamben's Homo Sacer and the Tasks of Political Thinking." *Theory and Event* 3, no. 1. At: http://muse.jhu.edu.sculib.scu.edu/journals/theory_and_event/v003/3.1r_panagia.html.

Parry, Benita. 2003. "Internationalism Revisited or in Praise of Internationalism." *Interventions* 5, no. 2: 299–314.

Said, Edward. 1978. *Orientalism*. New York: Pantheon Books.

———. 1993. *Culture and Imperialism*. London: Chatto and Windus.

Schirato, Tony, and Jen Webb. 2003. *Understanding Globalization*. London: Sage.

Schmitt, Carl. 1996. *The Concept of the Political*, trans. George Schwab. Chicago: University of Chicago Press.

Seth, Sanjay. 2002. "Back to the Future?" *Third World Quarterly* 23, no. 3: 565–75.

Smith, Adam. 1776 (1994). *An Inquiry into the Nature and Causes of the Wealth of Nations*, ed. Edwin Cannan. New York: Modern Library.

Waters, Malcolm. 1995. *Globalization*. London: Routledge.

Watson, Tim. 2001. "An American Empire?" *Postcolonial Studies* 4, no. 3: 351–59.

# 11

# AMITAV GHOSH: COSMOPOLITANISMS, LITERATURE, TRANSNATIONALISMS

## Inderpal Grewal

The cosmopolitanism of the last decade of the twentieth century was a product of two subjects: the liberal subject as a possessor of rights and the subject of international trade. Whereas the former emerged from the nineteenth-century idea of "the world citizen" as a form of belonging to the world and a subject of rights on a global scale, the other was the subject of global economic exchange and trade that began many centuries ago (Stevenson 1997) and gained renewed force and dissemination through its late capitalist incarnation of consumer culture. These two ideas emerged as key aspects of cosmopolitanism so that one could not exist without the other. Quite often, however, the interlinked nature of these processes has been mystified so that the connectivities between the two become invisible. This mystification has been as important in producing cosmopolitan subjects at the end of the twentieth century as it was in earlier centuries. Whereas in earlier formations it was mostly Europeans who could be cosmopolitan, by the end of the twentieth century, forms of globalized consumption and trade produced postcolonial cosmopolitans among formerly colonized and non-European Others through relations of power with the West and histories of colonialism (Brennan 1997).

If the fundamental cosmopolitan position in the West has been that political participation is a human right of the first order, then the fullest extension of this argument leads to a claim of a transnational political participation and to the eclipse of national citizenship. As one scholar, William Barbieri, describes the dominant meaning of the term, cosmopolitanism "militates against the intrinsically territorial idea of sovereignty and thus is ultimately impractical . . . its individualistic logic leads ultimately to the reduction of national differences, to a sort of overall human homogeneity and conceivably to the destruction of the cultural diversity that many take to be an essential human good" (Barbieri 1998, 105–9). Barbieri's claim, that cosmopolitanism was at odds with national sovereignty, was common in nineteenth- and twentieth-century European thought. However, this very claim of disaffiliation to a nation became a mode of nomadic power that used colonial power and racial privilege to cross national boundaries. As Caren Kaplan has argued, nomadism cannot be seen as a loss of privilege but as an assertion of power. This nomadism, Kaplan explains, has allowed cosmopolitanism to be associated with the representations of Europeans as "world citizens," that is, as those who are able to wander and travel at will to become "native" in "foreign" lands while retaining their identity and power as Europeans (Kaplan 1996).

As a consequence of such a mode of power, for the cosmopolitan "world citizen," the project of European civilization and the goal of cosmopolitanism has been to produce a notion of the "universal" that could erase differences. However, the strategies and epistemes of imperialism also relied heavily on ideas of cultural, racial, and gender differences, so that the work of hegemonic knowledges was to identify differences through the "comparative" mode of knowledge production. This project emerged as a powerful idea through the nineteenth century and into the twentieth as an important mode of organizing knowledge about the world. In this form of cosmopolitanism as an ability to produce comparative knowledge, the universal and the global become collapsed so that both sameness and difference are produced as temporal and spatial categories. Johannes Fabian has theorized the production of temporal difference through the concept of "coevalness" and the time lag produced within colonial hierarchies (Fabian 1983).

The debate on cosmopolitanism regarding the relationship between nomadism, nationalism, and cosmopolitanism has led to some new theorizations of the concept. For example, Bruce Robbins argues that rather than operating as an "ideal of detachment, actually existing cosmopolitanism is a reality of (re)attachment, multiple attachment, or attachment at a distance" (Robbins 1998). Robbins and Pheng Cheah follow James Clifford's important theorization of "discrepant cosmopolitanisms" (Clifford 1992, 96–112), leading Cheah to articulate cosmopolitanism as "a variety of actually existing practical stances" (Cheah 1998, 20–41). In his consideration of cosmopolitanism, Cheah observes that the opposition between cosmopolitanism and nationalism has always been "unstable" (20–41). As Caren Kaplan has argued, cosmopolitanism demarcates center from periphery and erases possibilities of imagining distance in less binary and more complicated ways within transnational cultural production (Kaplan 1996).

Despite this clear link to nationalism, late twentieth-century cosmopolitanism presumed the insufficiency of the nation-state and its necessary transcendence in favor of international regimes or of nomadic and global subjects and universal knowledges. Although nineteenth-century European cosmopolitanism, articulated as the condition of being a "citizen of the world," presumed that national affiliations were easily ignored, its power lay in the ability of its subjects to believe that nationalism could easily be forgotten even while it was the standpoint, via imperialism, from which cosmopolitanism could be articulated. Furthermore, even the form of internationalism that became hegemonic assumed its conflation with cosmopolitanism.

By the end of the twentieth century, the cosmopolitan position, allied to neoliberal logics of efficiency and privatization, not only saw the nation as insufficient but also often, for some nationalisms, as dangerous and a "global" or "world" citizenship as an opposition to the work of a mobile capitalism (Hardt and Negri 2000). Thus, for instance, international human rights instruments came to be understood as the only protection for displaced or resisting subjects within some nations. Yet, both internationalism and cosmopolitanism often mystified national belonging and the nation-state even while nationalisms produced gendered, raced, or classed standpoints that could operate within and through discourses of cosmopolitanism. For instance, Tim Brennan argues that cosmopolitanism gives space to the nationalism that it disavows. Yet cosmopolitanism cannot simply be decried, as Brennan does, as a mode of postcolonial globalization that leaves out the socialists, the nationalists, and those who are, as he calls them, "incommensurable" to the global. Neither nationalists nor socialists can be understood without the global networks in which they are produced; thus, it is important to see nationalism or socialism as being supported by many transnational processes within the "global." Furthermore, Brennan's search for the authentic subaltern underlies his view of cosmopolitanism both as "selling out" and as a form of homogenization into an imperial American popular culture. In Brennan's account, writers who write in English and who participate in the global publishing industry are the postcolonial cosmopolitans with a false consciousness that allies them with colonial power structures. Although Brennan's charge about postcolonial cosmopolitans as elites is not without some merit, his account relies on an idea of subjects as homogeneous and whole, unchanging and static, as well as without histories. Why some postcolonial subjects could more easily participate in cosmopolitan circuits of knowledge is a question that needs to be answered with some attention to specific historical formations. Elites also need to be analyzed and examined historically, especially if class is understood as a dynamic formation. Furthermore, elite positions include many varied classes, genders, races, and sexualities that participate in the transnational productions of knowledge about cultures and nations. Thus, it seems important to trace the genealogy of various cosmopolitan knowledges that produce such subjects and their changing relation to colonial and postcolonial formations.

Postcolonial cosmopolitanisms with specific genealogies of class, race, and gender produced an explicit and articulated relationship to nationalism from the perspective of a colonized subjectivity that was both privileged yet subordinate to the West. For Amitav Ghosh, for instance, a valorization of mobility was central to the production of a liberal, colonized subject produced not in relation to one state but to a broadly conceived global or international arena of anticolonial struggle and solidarity. In his text, *In an Antique Land* (Ghosh 1992), Ghosh recuperated this cosmopolitan subject that could be understood to be postcolonial and transnational in that it positioned itself within a world connected through its resistance to European colonization and the construction of new histories of a world without Europe.

Ghosh's texts write against diasporic consciousness, preferring to articulate instead a cosmopolitanism that is understood to the authentically non-Western and emerging from a historical narrative suppressed by many Western histories. Because historical accounts privilege relations between West and non-West, the accounts of connections between two non-Western regions have been erased from history. Despite this important intervention, however, Ghosh's text remains tied to a romanticized notion of the precolonial, which suppressed conflict and contention in favor of narratives of cosmopolitan tolerance and peaceful coexistence engendered by trade.

The production of this text has a genealogy that connects it to an earlier phase of globalization engendered by British colonial policies in India in the nineteenth century, and this history provided the precondition for the author's participation in the cosmopolitanism of the late twentieth century. Ghosh comes from a particular social formation, the Bengali English-educated middle class created by British colonization in India during the nineteenth century (Visweswaran 1997). The British policy of providing an "English" education to Indians, as articulated in Thomas Macaulay's 1835 "Minute on Education," was initiated to produce a middle class that might function in the British government as an intermediary between the colonial state and the Indian population (Macaulay 2000). Well versed in British literature and in the English language, this group emerged in Bengal in particular as a vocal group, which became active in nationalist and anticolonial politics and produced famous writers and poets. It came to constitute an elite through knowledge of and contact with the West (Chatterjee 1993). Although many other groups of Indians came to be influenced by an English education, each group had a particular history and genealogy; the Bengali middle classes were important targets of English education. However, it can be argued that the entire class of English-educated Indians came to have a colonial cosmopolitanism that inserted them into circuits of knowledge about Britain and about India that were not previously open to them. This cosmopolitanism, although quite different from the postcolonial cosmopolitanism of the 1990s, was nevertheless a condition of possibility for that later articulation. Ghosh also belongs to what Salman Rushdie called "midnight's children," in his 1981 novel of that title, that is, born just before or after Indian independence, a generation wrestling with the legacy of colonialism and the problems of decolonization (Rushdie 1995). As such, he was brought up with a British colonial education and the Indian state's attempts to decolonize such education. There is a considerable literature on this particular group that tells us about its relation to British colonialism, its postcoloniality, its public culture, its educational systems, and in the case of Bengal, its relation to Bengali nationalism (Chakrabarty 2000; Chatterjee 1993).

Within such postcolonial cosmopolitanisms, the publication and circulation of literary works, especially those written in English, was made possible by an earlier phase of globalization of the publishing industry and of something called "literature" and the ability of such texts to circulate across national boundaries (Dharwadkar 1997). Which texts circulated depended not only on the language of these texts but also on histories of literacy, of publishing, and of trade as well as on the kinds of representations that enabled readers to consume texts in different ways in various locations (Dharwadkar 1997, 108–33). These connectivities of representational practices and of knowledge production participated in transnational networks of knowledge production that encompassed India, Europe, and the United States, anticolonial nationalisms and American nationalisms, and literary connections and postcolonial networks. Nineteenth-century English education in India created a class that was able to move into the West with a facility that was not possible for others in India not well versed in this education (Helwig 1990).

Within transnational connectivities created by contemporary diasporic formations and postcolonial histories, literary and aesthetic productions by such subjects as Ghosh participated in the circulation of knowledges about India. Although novels were a small part of these circulating knowledges, given the presence of music, movies, academic texts, and informal networks, they were, nevertheless, key to the production of aesthetic and political value among dominant classes. These texts were both products and producers of such knowledges, and their transnational publication and readership as well as their use of English enable the circulation of a range of knowledges about India and its diasporas. Though the anticolonial nationalism and cosmopolitanism of Amitav Ghosh was in marked contrast to the American and Bengali nationalism of an author such as Bharati Mukherjee, their works expressed a cosmopolitanism that circulated in different connectivities—the former within networks of anticolonial histories and the latter in neoliberal nationalist identity formations. However, their work participated in the production of a "literature" that by means of its aesthetic qualities disseminated representations of India and the West. Within such work, late twentieth-century cosmopolitanism can be seen not merely as a "discrepant" version (Clifford 1992) or a liberal goal for a transnationalized civil society but also as a class-, gender-, and racially specific network of discursive practices circulating within transnational connectivities.

To a certain extent, the question of class needs to be understood in relation to historical changes in ideas of place and nation. How ideas and discourses circulated and were articulated in particular places through cosmopolitan or nationalist or international subjects requires a historical analysis. As Amitav Ghosh argued in his essay "The March of the Novel through History: The Testimony of my Grandfather's Bookcase," on the emergence of "world" and "international" literature and its institutions, cosmopolitanism was as much about placement as about displacement (Ghosh 2002). The circulation of texts, particularly novels, canonized by institutions such as the Nobel Prize across what came to be understood, within an emerging cosmopolitan discourse, as an "international" arena, enabled the production, in the second half of the twentieth century, of a new discourse of cosmopolitanism as a form of belonging that placed through the articulation of displacement; it understood its place in comparison with others. The international novel, Ghosh argues, produced cosmopolitans in all kinds of sites, distinguished by their access to the texts, mainly novels that institutions of "world literature" such as the Nobel Prize identified as "literature." Not only did this cosmopolitanism produce the sense of place nurtured by the novel form, as Ghosh has noted, but it also inserted persons across the world into the consumption of literary texts as a source of aesthetic and artistic value, which in turn gave readers and buyers a new cultural capital. For instance, that

Rabindranath Tagore, the Bengali writer, won the Nobel Prize for literature in 1913 meant that subsequent generation of Bengalis (and Indians) were inserted into the world of "international" literature in new ways. Ghosh's understanding of the subjects of a literature that is international begins from this position. One can speculate that Ghosh's grandfather's collection of Nobel prize–winning literature received its inspiration from Tagore's Nobel Prize, and Ghosh's participation in the production and consumption of these novels within the international literary world becomes possible through this familial and colonial history.

In his essay, Ghosh describes a postcolonial cosmopolitanism as a condition made possible by the circulation and articulation in India of a genre such as the novel.[1] The novel, according to Ghosh, has been "international" for over a century, and within which forms of intertextuality between the novels in Russian, Spanish, English, and French emerged as a result. Ghosh points out that institutions such as the Nobel Prize for literature brought together many different writers from different nations within one bookshelf and created cosmopolitan readers as well as writers. However, rather than argue that such a cosmopolitanism transcended location or place to become a version of the "international" that is understood to be nomadic and placeless, Ghosh suggests that the genre of the novel, as it circulated within India through the institution of the Nobel award, was about producing a particular sense of place and laying claim to it. Thus for Ghosh, the emergence of the Bengali middle class, educated in English, with access to a set of books sanctioned as "great literature" by the institution of the Nobel Prize, produced a cosmopolitanism that was nationalist in its allegiance to place of belonging to Calcutta and Bengal, and India in the case of Tagore, but was also produced in relation to a somewhat different idea of internationalism from that of the "world citizen" articulated by Barbieri.

To extend Ghosh's analysis, it can be argued that this notion of internationalism was created by the ability to participate, from a colonized position that was subservient to the West but privileged among those colonized, in the idea of an "international" aesthetic that could cross national boundaries as national literatures. The literary cognate to the "world citizen" of nineteenth-century cosmopolitanism was Goethe's concept of "world literature," which he defined as the creation of a "common world literature transcending national limits" and which was to be produced because, according to Goethe writing in the nineteenth century, "nowadays, national literature doesn't mean much: the age of world literature is beginning."[2] No doubt Goethe's idea was produced by the circulation of a body of writing deemed "literature" within European culture in which it was possible to compare, judge, and combine rather than see cultural productions as incommensurable, and which led to what Vinay Dharwadkar calls "the internationalization of literature" (Dharwadkar 1996). This idea was later institutionalized through institutions such as the Nobel Prize for literature, created by Alfred Nobel through the funding from his invention, patenting, and manufacturing of dynamite. The Nobel prize was (and is, to this day) a sign of "international literature," of the Western idea of the "literary" as "universal," that is, of a common aesthetic that could be found by means of comparison across the world through its ability to be national as well as "international." Whereas Nobel's will stipulated that the prize for literature be given to works with an "idealistic tendency," during the first half of the twentieth century these awards, for the most part, were mainly given to European writers of many different genres and philosophies. Tagore's prize in 1913 was the first to a writer from Asia, facilitated by his ability to translate his own work into English. Although the emergence of the idea that one winner could be judged out of the many different aesthetics and ideas of the "literary," which is itself a European aesthetic as Christopher Prendergast points out, Tagore's prize was a choice that resonated in political ways (Prendergast 2001). It made Tagore into an "Indian" and a "Bengali" writer as it gave value, within an international arena, to the voice of an emerging English-educated Indian elite as well as to the notion of a literature with a national identity.

Yet it is noticeable that in Ghosh's account, this cosmopolitan internationalism is gendered as a masculine articulation, because Ghosh's grandfather's bookcase found its reader in Ghosh himself rather than any of his female relatives. The cosmopolitan world of connections remained one of connections between males, maintained and produced patriarchally by the "grandfather's bookcase" as a legacy to the grandson, Ghosh. The legacy was, in Ghosh's account, crucial to his sense of himself as an author who could be read in many parts of the world and to his insertion into a world that could both move him away from the site of reading and the bookcase to other national cultures represented in the books that he read as a child to an international discourse of literature and literariness. However, there were soon women writers from India creating a female version of this literature in English that could cross borders; Sarojini Naidu comes to mind, as does Toru Dutt.

With new technologies of connection between South Asia and the United States, and greater interest in reading multicultural and postcolonial writers in the West, late twentieth-century writers such as Mukherjee and Ghosh gained audiences in both India and the United States. Technologies that enabled transnational connectivities circulated knowledge with greater facility and intensity than in the past. Indian and U.S. publishers, for instance, copublish Amitav Ghosh's works, so that they reach multiple markets and audiences almost at the same time. His writings about the histories of precolonial, postcolonial, and colonial South Asia produced a cosmopolitanism that moved across time and place, creating knowledges that could circulate across South Asia and its diasporas as well as to other audiences. Written in English, historical and erudite, his work gained appeal across scholarly and literate audiences. Ghosh's writings identify him as a writer about British colonization and Indian nationalism rather than as a writer about the immigrant experience, although it is clear that living in the West has not only informed his politics through an interest in borders and crossings but also expanded the audience for his writings. However, his work on border crossings and migration does not directly address the immigrant experiences in the United States as a movement from repression to freedom, but rather as a problem created by colonial powers that drew and redrew boundaries to alter national affiliation, thus creating migrant communities cut off from earlier homes.[3] His research and emphasis on histories of South Asia and his postcolonial cosmopolitanism leads Ghosh to write against the West, though from the cosmopolitan subjectivity of the writer of literature, instead of probing the complexity of living within it. Within his writings, travel and migration do not constitute movements from East to West, but rather from one part of the East to another part of it. Thus these are not diasporas in the way that these have been understood in recent years through examinations of communities of migration in the West, but rather as forced migrations within Asia and Africa or as intrinsic to movements of trade. For Ghosh, diasporas can be understood through a history of colonialism that produced such hybrid communities in Africa and Asia. Cosmopolitanism provided a means to forge connections with regions with similar colonial histories and to imagine a "world without Europe" and without invidious nationalisms; cosmopolitanism existed in trading communities that lived without violence before the coming of the Europeans. Yet this version was not so far from the European conceptualization of cosmopolitanism in which it did not create "world citizens" but produced traders who worked together despite national boundaries and nationalisms.

Analyses of diasporas and colonialism in the 1980s and 1990s came to be connected through the work of theorists such as Edward Said, Homi Bhabha, and Stuart Hall (Bhabha 2004; Hall 1997a; Said 2000). However, Ghosh's text *In an Antique Land* took this connection into another direction—that of examining the redrawing of national borders by colonial regimes that created diasporas. Furthermore, rather than examining diasporas created by such movements in the West, and thus about the movements of migrants from East to West, which were the primary focus of such theoretical formulations, he writes about a much more pervasive form of displacement from one part of the non-West to another. Although Ghosh's text suggested the concept of "imaginative recovery," which Stuart Hall claimed was one way in which an "imaginary coherence" could be created out of the "experience of dispersal and fragmentation which is the history of all enforced diasporas" (Hall 1997b, 51–58), it is possible to understand Ghosh's important work not as a strategy of diasporic identification but rather as an anticolonial political project. For Hall, the Caribbean was a site where displacement and European and American regimes of colonial representation led to new hybrid and syncretic formations. Caribbean diaspora was produced as a specific formation created from within itself, as well as from resistance to Europe and America. However, Africa appeared in this diaspora theory only as a place of aporia rather than as a site of anticolonial resistances and social movements that spread across the world and across the Caribbean itself. "Africa," for many diasporic subjects living in Europe or North America, remained in the past once again, whereas diasporas and the West were seen as modern with syncretic identities, creating a division between "home" and "host" that emerged as foundational to diaspora studies.

Whereas theories of migration focused on movements from a "home" country to a "host" country as a process of assimilation and acculturation from one essential identity to another, diaspora studies emerged to account for the heterogeneity of many national and cultural formations (Lowe 1996, 60–83). Yet some theorizations of diaspora suggested that diasporas were resistant to a nation-state or to a nation (Gilroy 1997, 301–46), leading to groups becoming "alienated or insulated" from their "host society" (Safran 1991). For the most part, although the nationalism of a diaspora was seen as disentangled from a "host" nation, or the homogeneity of the diasporic group is disaggregated by gender, sexuality, or class, the creation of a binary of diaspora and of the "host" culture within which a diaspora was produced, created a unproblematized "host" nation whose homogeneity was unquestioned (Lowe 1996, 60–83). In addition, the consequence of this binary led to yet another binary of diaspora and "home" or origin through which, quite often, the site that was represented as the "origin" became temporally noncoeval. However one could argue that if Africa or Asia were not to remain within the logic of noncoevalness or of "origin" narratives that could never be recovered, then their syncretism also needed to be acknowledged along with the ways in which anticolonial nationalisms emerged as transnational movements through the twentieth century. Ghosh's articulation of a long non-Western history of cosmopolitanism brought to crisis the ways in which diaspora theories produced new continental divides between the "old world" and the "new."

Instead of the break with the past that diaspora theories suggested, Ghosh's text produced continuities of many kinds, especially of the precolonial past with the transnational present. In fact, the text argued for a cosmopolitanism that he suggested was not Western in its origin but rather a product of Indian Ocean trading practices of the tenth and eleventh centuries. His work created a golden past not of the nation, but of cosmopolitan connections between groups divided by religion but unified through trade. By formulating the *histories* of itineraries and routes as a way to understand cultural connections, *In an Antique Land* mapped the Indian Ocean and the spice trade in the way that Paul Gilroy's work, *The Black Atlantic*, mapped the slave trade (Gilroy 1993). Ghosh's work can also be seen as a powerful corrective to the ways in which Gilroy's work delinked the Atlantic from the Indian Ocean. Yet unlike Gilroy's *Atlantic*, within which Africa was subsumed in favor of the cultural productions of those created in the New World, Ghosh's project was to produce a new map of the Old World as the world without Europe. Moving away from the contest between a "West" and the "non-West," the text created a world in which the West was either nonexistent or irrelevant and where the focus was the relationship between two "non-Western" regions. The book proposed a new field whose history and geography could be examined from medieval times to the present in the service of an idealized non-Eurocentric postcolonial cosmopolitanism. More importantly, its difference from the theorizations of Western cosmopolitanism lay in its refusal to produce universal claims and knowledges, content to keep its project to the historical specificity of tenth- and eleventh-century Indian Ocean trading practices. Yet, as we shall see, Europe and the New World could not be erased and Ghosh's text, in its romanticizing of the Old World, cannot escape its condition of production in postcolonial and national knowledges produced within contexts of cosmopolitanism that were linked to those histories of cosmopolitanism that the text hoped to disavow. Like the European cosmopolitanism that Ghosh hopes to discredit, this text too argues that nationalism and cosmopolitanism are opposed to each other. In particular, "the premodern" as the past without Europe becomes the focus of this postcolonial cosmopolitan imaginary that can capture the seductive power of postcolonial history for a past purified of colonialism's taint. It is perhaps this imaginary that has enabled the literature of postcoloniality to have a transnational appeal.

In proposing a new cartography, Ghosh presented a postcolonial reversal of European cosmopolitanism, arguing that the nationalisms and internationalisms of the nineteenth and twentieth centuries could not be seen as positive versions of cosmopolitanism. Rather, the text represented the so-called cosmopolitanism of modern Europe as an inferior version compared to that produced by the tenth- and eleventh-century spice trade of the Indian Ocean. Jonathan Ree pointed out this aspect of Ghosh's project, stating that in this work, readers could get a glimpse of premodern experience of cultural and geographic difference as an experience "innocent" of any ideas of national character or identity from the "beautiful" reconstruction of the life of a twelfth-century Jewish merchant (Ree 1992, 3–11). Ree's terms "innocent" and "beautiful" captured the nostalgia for a nonnational perspective cosmopolitanism that pervades Ghosh's text. Interspersing his self-reflexive ethnography of contemporary rural Egypt, where he traveled for fieldwork, with the story of Bomma, the Indian slave of Jewish traders in the twelfth-century Indian Ocean spice trade, Ghosh contrasted past and present, the noncosmopolitans and nationalists in the present with the cosmopolitan traders of the past. The narrative cuts back and forth in time and space between Egypt, Mangalore, and Princeton, in the transnational pursuit of knowledges to help bring the eleventh-century Indian Ocean trading culture to life.

In contrast to modern capitalism's roots in the "Black Atlantic" and the horrors of the Atlantic slave trade, the text suggested, somewhat problematically and romantically, that the spice-trade circuit was much more benign; the book produced an alternative history of slavery in order to contrast it to the Atlantic slave trade. It presented the medieval spice route as a corrective to the idea that the first explorers were Europeans, the first global economy the European one, and the first cosmopolitanism was that produced by Western Europe. The Eurocentric history of travel was thus shown to have erased the world that existed before, in which there existed the global economy that linked the Mediterranean and the Indian Ocean. Accounts that had been erased include those of the cosmopolitan cities of the Indian Ocean. In Cairo's section of Fustat, the text states, the merchandise came from as far afield as East Africa, southern Europe, the western Sahara, India, China, and Indonesia; and Fustat itself was the conjuncture of some of the most important trade routes in the known world and the nucleus of one of the richest and most cosmopolitan cities of the world (Ghosh 1992, 38). The Jewish traders of Fustat, according to the text, "traveled regularly between three continents and their travels and breadth of experience and education seem astonishing even today, on a planet thought to be newly shrunken" (55). There were scholars, doctors, and philosophers among these traders. The counterparts to Cairo on the Indian coast were the towns of Mangalore and Calicut, places that attracted visitors because of their wealth and as gateways to the largest spice-producing areas of the world.

In Ghosh's text, the medieval cosmopolitan community of spice trade was contrasted to the religious and cultural nationalisms of contemporary Egypt and the imperial power of colonial Europe that nurtured these nationalisms. European colonialism, for instance, was described as "that unquenchable demonic thirst that has raged ever since, for almost five hundred years, over the Indian Ocean, the Arabian Sea and the Persian Gulf" (288). According to the text, such was this demonic thirst that it swallowed even the Jews who became European, forgetting their Arab past, and who helped denude the Geniza of its documents by thievery and trickery. This same thirst destroyed the spice trade of the Indian Ocean, not only changing the relation of Egypt to India but also subordinating these cosmopolitan places within another hierarchy. The Portuguese, who demanded that the Hindu ruler expel all Muslims, destroyed Calicut's cosmopolitanism. *In an Antique Land* attributed the tolerance of all religions in the spice trade as emerging not only from the demands of trade but also from the pacifism of some of the Indian communities participating in the trade. All this was destroyed by the European entry into the spice trade, and by the violence and aggression of the Europeans.

Not only was European colonial aggression antithetical to cosmopolitanism, but other nationalisms emerging in the context of European colonization were also represented as destroying the cosmopolitanism of the Egyptian and Indian past. The gulf between Egypt and India in the past and the present was visible, according to the text, in the ignorance among the villages of Nashawy and Lataifa about Indian and Hindu customs. This ignorance, in the narrative, was attributed to the destruction of the spice trade and its routes by the European colonizers, as well as to the nationalisms that taught ethnocentrism. Histories were erased, according to this account, that needed to be remembered, and this work, like all his other works, relied on historiography as a political project. Despite the presence of words, customs, and beliefs found in Egypt and which enabled the narrator to connect Egypt to India, the villagers were ignorant of India and looked toward the West rather than to India for constructing their identity. For instance, one policeman who questioned Ghosh's presence in Egypt could not imagine there was any religious identity beyond Muslim, Christian, or Jew.

The village men and boys who questioned Ghosh about customs in India were astonished that men and women there were not circumcised and that most people did not believe in Islam. This religious nationalism as it articulated with state nationalism frightened Ghosh because it recalled other nationalisms in India that were not so benign. In particular, questions about whether Ghosh himself was circumcised reminded him of religious nationalisms in South Asia, in particular the history of the Partition. In both Punjab and Bengal, Muslim and Hindu males were differentiated and identified by whether they were circumcised or not and thus either killed or let go. Death or deliverance on different sides of the religious divide depended on just this bodily practice. In Nashawy, therefore, innocent questions about India and astonishment that men and women are not circumcised became intolerable and a source of terror. Even if Ghosh saw these questions as innocent, the book suggests that such innocence was frightening and painful because it signaled an ignorance that translated into a loss of cosmopolitanism that could be contrasted with the religious pluralism and tolerance practiced in medieval times in the context of the spice trade. The presence of water-pump technology from India, one modern example of the ancient link between India and Egypt, could not shake his sorrow at the loss of connection. Thus, in this account, the West had destroyed cosmopolitanism instead of nurturing it. Implicit here is a claim that the origins of cosmopolitanism could be located outside Europe.

Moreover, according to Ghosh's text, there were those who were not so innocent of difference but downright intolerant of it. These were subjects of colonialism and its product, modern nationalisms, which were based on forgetting the connections of the past. The Imam in Nashawy, for instance, berates Ghosh for not working to change Hindu traditions that he called "savage" (235), "primitive and backward." He asks Ghosh, "You've been to Europe; you've seen how advanced they are. Now tell me: have you ever seen them burning their dead?" (235). In response, Ghosh used the narratives of Indian nationalism to respond to the Imam's Egyptian nationalism. Ghosh's own response reinforced his belief that nationalisms had divided people who were earlier connected. Thus, the text stated that instead of being cosmopolitans, both he and the Imam had become travelers in the West and thus living within the West's representational histories. He understood the Imam's citation of the West as a form of participating in Western knowledges that produced conflicts instead of cooperation: "We were both traveling, he and I: we were traveling in West. The only difference was that I had actually been there, in person" (236). The argument displayed their difference from their ancestors who participated in the Indian Ocean trade, and Ghosh bemoaned the loss of "the centuries of dialogue that had linked us" (236). Ghosh blamed the loss on the impact of Western colonization and its civilizational hierarchies that placed India and Egypt on the "ladder of Development." The incident suggested to the narrator that he was a "witness to the extermination of a world of accommodations that I had believed to be still alive and in some tiny measure still retrievable" (237). It is this "dialogue," the "world of accommodations" defined cosmopolitanism, as a different form of mobility than modern travel within which coevality was not possible. In colonial contexts, both Ghosh and the Imam had become travelers in a hierarchy within which they were equally subordinate to Europe.

The subtitle of this work says that it is "History in the Guise of a Traveler's Tale." It would be more accurate to call it a postcolonial history that attempted to move travel away from its Western origins to another time and place, and in fact, a utopian time and place. Vinay Lal has suggested that such a recuperation is a daring act of historiography.[4] However, though it was certainly a wonderfully daring history that built on transnational and anticolonial affiliations between Egypt and India, this history itself was guided by colonial narratives of migration and trade and the forms of travel, which, as Ghosh implicitly acknowledged, became the only way to reach histories of connection between Egypt and India. For instance, the definition of cosmopolitanism as a "world of accommodations" in which nationalism could be erased was itself the ideal of cosmopolitanism that had been articulated in the West for many centuries, and which, as many scholars have pointed out, resulted from the link between trade and cosmopolitanism in the West. Ghosh's narrative of a lost cosmopolitanism created the same connection between trade and cosmopolitanism that had been central to Western constructions of cosmopolitanism since the trading communities of Jews in Europe were considered cosmopolitans who could not belong to any nation.

Yet, it cannot be said that Ghosh's cosmopolitanism was the same articulation as the "world citizen" of nineteenth-century cosmopolitan Western travelers or even of the new formulations of this position in recent works such as *Empire* (Hardt and Negri 2000). The postcolonial aporia of this history lies in the problem that Ghosh's historical connection was possible only through Europe and, of course, "America" as repository of the documents that made this history possible. The Eurocentric perspective of the production of the "premodern" and the "precolonial" has been critiqued by Kathleen Biddick, for instance, who also takes to task the "neo-Orientalism" of those who search for the "real" precolonial in European archives (Biddick 2002). Yet even when an archive's source is not Europe, the archive is often housed in Europe and North America and these locations produce their own erasures. For example, although Ghosh cited the work of Professor Goitein for bringing the history of medieval trade to life, Goitein's opus was entitled *A Mediterranean Society* rather than the society of the Indian Ocean (Goitein 1967). To a scholar such as Goitein, it was Egypt's relation to the Mediterranean that was of interest rather than its relation to India.

It is not only the problem of the archive as it was interpreted or dispersed that revealed the difficulty of reclaiming medieval history as postcolonial cosmopolitanism, but also the construction of gender and class in Ghosh's text. How do we understand the increasingly mobile lives of the poor late twentieth-century villagers who leave Egypt to work in Iraq or the Gulf, or those like Ghosh himself who travel, or the Imam who Ghosh calls a traveler in the ideas produced by Europe? Were all these subjects cosmopolitan? Or even if these subjects revealed the "discrepant" cosmopolitanisms that, as Jim Clifford suggests, were characteristic of the end of the twentieth century, surely we need to see how these cosmopolitanisms combine with other subject positions for the scholar, the traveler, and the migrant worker. If the scholar and anthropologist rearticulated cosmopolitanisms, the migrant workers, like Ghosh's friends from Nashawy, were able to return, if they were lucky, to their villages after being expelled from Iraq—their cosmopolitanism was somewhat unstable and uneven. Furthermore, how do we differentiate these cosmopolitanisms from those of the Europeans in the nineteenth and twentieth centuries? If Ghosh's text suggested that the Europeans did not practice the cosmopolitanism of the medieval traders in the Indian Ocean, then how are we to understand the cosmopolitanism of colonial trade or the "world traveling" of nineteenth-century English travelers such as Isabelle Eberhardt, both of which were Western articulations?

Certainly, one way to resolve this issue is to argue that what Ghosh's medieval history and colonial nomadism had in common, unlike the villagers from Nashawy, was the ease of travel, the power to cross oceans and borders without impediment. Colonial cosmopolitanism may not have had the "dialogue" between Egyptians and Indians, or care to have a dialogue with any but other imperial powers, but Ghosh's medieval traders were also powerful and wealthy, though they were not Europeans. Yet the text also very importantly brings attention to this problem of relying on mobility as a standpoint for cosmopolitanism. In the story of Bomma, the Indian slave, Ghosh summoned the fissures in the cosmopolitan narrative, as we learn that the slave was paid very little, spoke against his master, and resisted the power of the wealthy traders. The "Slave of Ms H.6," though the impetus of the book, remained somewhat shadowy throughout the book, so that the historical narrative recreates much more of the life of the masters than of the slave. The text was at pains to show that subalterns were not easily visible in archives.

If the slave remained in shadow and gestured to the power relations that marred the utopian narrative, the fate of Ben Yiju's daughter, as related in the text, suggested other contradictions. According to Ghosh, Ben Yiju, the trader, moved to Mangalore in India from North Africa and married Ashu, a slave whose freedom he granted. When Ben Yiju decided to return to Cairo to see his family, he took his children from the union with Ashu but not Ashu. Ghosh explained this event by stating that Ashu's membership in the matrilineal Nair community would have prevented her from accompanying Ben Yiju to Egypt. Yet if Ashu's family is matrilineal, it was not clear how her daughter was able to leave with the father. Perhaps Ghosh did not delve too far into this contradiction because such contradictions would have unraveled the cosmopolitan story valorized in the text. Moreover, the daughter's future provided Ghosh with an even more interesting example of the reach of the spice trade. The daughter married her cousin from Sicily in Fustat, Cairo, bringing together a Nair woman with a Jewish man from across the Mediterranean. Ghosh resolved this failed cosmopolitanism through the narrative of the hybrid spread of cultures in which postcolonial hybridity became a response to Eurocentric histories.

Although these contradictions in the text complicated the utopian narrative of precolonial trade, they bring to our attention the kinds of histories that connected subalterns in the past to those of the late twentieth century. In the process of acquiring the facility to cross boundaries, immigrants and refugees became cosmopolitan subjects, but such subjectivities were unstable and often short lived. Migrants such as Nabeel, one of the villagers from Lataifa, led dangerous and precarious lives in Iraq, as they were unable to transcend or to mystify the continuing and emerging nationalisms that destroyed them. Their cosmopolitanism did not have the long history that Ghosh's own cosmopolitanism did. Ghosh's account mentioned that Nabeel had "vanished into the anonymity of History" (Ghosh 1992, 253), and as Vinay Lal suggests, by so doing he became the subaltern whose identity would be researched by some historian in the future.[5] Shuttling between nationalisms, their cosmopolitanism could not enable their passages out of poverty and their class positions dictated by long histories and national and global conditions.

Although Ghosh's text well described the divisions and inequities of the end of the twentieth century, it created a golden past of transnational trade. In Ghosh's text, nationalists could not be cosmopolitans, though this was the case for colonial cosmopolitan travelers. Certainly, Ghosh's own investments in his Indian identity are visible in the book and in its project to create a history without a European presence. Yet we cannot see this postcolonial cosmopolitanism as emerging out of the same nationalist project as that of the right-wing intolerance of many nationalists that have emerged by century's end in both India and Egypt, which was about creating borders rather than seeking the international and regional solidarities and connections of the past.

Trade created the first cosmopolitans, in Ghosh's account, and to a certain extent, Ghosh's cosmopolitan hopes for the future were made possible by the trade in knowledges and books. Both nineteenth- and twentieth-century cosmopolitans in Europe were produced through a narrative of trade, whether colonial or precolonial, and the relation between trade and national boundaries was both shifting and powerful. Ghosh's narrative inserted the histories of trade into questions of nationalism and belonging that enabled the emergence of cosmopolitan subjects. Many versions of cosmopolitanism ignored this narrative of trade and consumption to produce the subject of rights, whether national or international, as either delinked from economic histories or in opposition to them. Nationalisms as well as internationalisms relied on the transnational movements of finance capital that created the power relations that I have identified as cosmopolitanisms as well as their unstable relation to discrepant modern, national, and postcolonial subjects. Thus movements of goods and finance were integral to transnational connectivities, though it is difficult, in this current phase of the power of capital flows across many transnationalisms, to think of trade as either benign or as emptied of colonial power relations.

## Notes

1. See Amitav Ghosh (1989) at www.amitavghosh.com/bookcase.html.
2. Quote cited in Moretti (2004).
3. See Ghosh (1989).
4. See Lal (1997).
5. See Lal (1997).

## Works Cited

Bhabha, Homi. 2004. *The Location of Culture*. NY: Routledge.

Barbieri, William. 1998. *Ethics of Citizenship: Immigration and Group Rights in Germany*. Durham, N.C.: Duke University Press.

Biddick, Kathleen. 2002. "Translating the Foreskin." In *Queering the Middle Ages*, eds. Glenn Burger and Steven Kruger, 193–212. Minneapolis: University of Minnesota Press.

Brennan, Timothy. 1997. *At Home in the World: Cosmpolitanism Now*. Cambridge, Mass.: Harvard University Press.

Chakrabarty, Dipesh. 2000. *Provincializing Europe: Postcolonial Thought and Historical Difference*. Princeton, N.J.: Princeton University Press.

Chatterjee, Partha. 1993. *The Nation and Its Fragments*. Princeton, N.J.: Princeton University Press.

Cheah, Pheng. 1998. "Introduction II." In *Cosmopolitics: Thinking and Feeling beyond the Nation,* eds. Pheng Cheah and Bruce Robbins, 20–41. Minneapolis: University of Minnesota Press.

Clifford, James. 1992. "Traveling Cultures." In *Cultural Studies*, eds. Lawrence Grossberg, Cary Nelson, and Paula Triechler, 96–112. New York: Routledge.

Dharwadkar, Vinay. 1996. "The Internationalization of Literature." In *New National and Postcolonial Literatures*, ed. Bruce King, 59–77. Oxford: Clarendon Press.

———. 1997. "Print Culture and Literary Markets in Colonial India." In *Language Machines: Technologies of Literary and Cultural Production*, eds. Jeffrey Masten, Peter Stallybrass, and Nancy Vickers, 108–33. New York: Routledge.

Fabian, Johannes. 1983. *Time and the Other: How Anthropology Makes Its Object*. New York: Columbia University Press.

Ghosh, Amitav. 1989. *The Shadow Lines*. New York: Viking.

———. 1992. *In an Antique Land: History in the Guise of a Traveler's Tale*. New York: Vintage Departures.

———. 2000. *The Glass Palace*. Delhi: R. Dayal.

———. 2002. "The March of the Novel through History: The Testimony of my Grandfather's Bookcase." In *The Imam and the Indian*, 287–304. Delhi: Ravi Dayal.

Gilroy, Paul. 1993. *The Black Atlantic: Double Consciousness and Modernity*. Cambridge, Mass.: Harvard University Press.

———. 1997. "Diaspora and the Detours of Identity." In *Identity and Difference*, ed. Kathryn Woodward, 301–46. London: Sage.

Goitein, S. D. 1967. *A Mediterranean Society: The Jewish Society of the Arab World as Portrayed in the Documents of the Cairo Geniza*. Berkeley: University of California Press.

Hall, Stuart. 1997a. "The Local and the Global: Globalization and Ethnicity." In *Dangerous Liaisons: Gender, Nation, and Postcolonial Perspectives*, eds. Anne McClintock, Aamir Mufti, and Ella Shohat, 173–87. Minneapolis: University of Minnesota Press.

———. 1997b. "Cultural Identity and Diaspora." *Identity and Difference*, ed. Kathryn Woodward, 51–58. London: Sage.

Hardt, Michael, and Antonio Negri. 2000. *Empire*. Cambridge, Mass.: Harvard University Press.

Helwig, Arthur. 1990. *An Immigrant Success Story: East Indians in America*. Philadelphia: University of Pennsylvania Press.

Kaplan, Caren. 1996. *Questions of Travel*. Durham, N.C.: Duke University Press.

Lal, Vinay. 1997. "Review-Article on Amitav Ghosh. *In an Antique Land*." At: http://www.sscnet. ucla.edu/southasia/History/British/Amitav_Ghosh.html.

Lowe, Lisa. 1996. *Immigrant Acts: On Asian American Cultural Politics*. Durham, N.C.: Duke University Press.

Macaulay, Thomas Babington. 2000. "Minute on Education of India." In *Literature and Nation: Britain and India 1800–1990*, eds. Harish Trivedi and Richard Allen, 204–5. London: Routledge.

Moretti, Franco. 2004. "Conjectures on World Literature." *New Left Review* (Jan–Feb 2000). At: www.newleftreview.net/NLR23503.Shtml (accessed May 12, 2004).

Prendergast, Christopher. 2001. "Negotiating World Literature." *New Left Review* 8:100–121.

Ree, Jonathan. 1992. "Internationality." *Radical Philosophy* 60:3–11.

Robbins, Bruce. 1998. "Introduction." In *Cosmopolitics: Thinking and Feeling Beyond the Nation*, eds. Pheng Cheah and Bruce Robbins, 3. Minneapolis: University of Minnesota Press.

Rushdie, Salman. 1995. *Midnight's Children*. New York: Penguin.

Safran, William. 1991. "Diasporas in Modern Societies: Myths of Homeland and Return." *Diaspora* 1, no. 1: 83–99.

Said, Edward. 2000. "Reflections." In *Reflections on Exile and Other Essays*, 159–72. Cambridge, Mass.: Harvard University Press.

Stevenson, Nick. 1997. "Globalization, National Cultures, and Cultural Citizenship." *Sociological Quarterly* 38, no. 1: 41.

Visweswaran, Kamala. 1997. "Diaspora by Design: Flexible Citizenship and South Asians in U.S. Racial Formations." *Diaspora* 6, no. 1: 5–29, 66.

# 12

# Sanctions against South Africa: Historical Example or Historic Exception?

## Barbara Harlow

*Let me also make a fresh appeal: those who boycotted South African goods should now buy them. To create jobs, the houses, the schools, and the hospitals that our people cry out for, we must have the support of a new international solidarity movement.*

—Walter Sisulu, Foreword to Peter Hain's, *Sing the Beloved Country*

When South Africa's apartheid regime released its political prisoners and unbanned "illegal" organizations in early 1990, there were many students of that country's history who credited the sanctions movement for having enabled the ensuing negotiations that had brought about an end to official apartheid and the much-heralded "transition to democracy." International sanctions, it seemed, could work. In the decade since South Africa's liberation and its first-ever democratic, nonracial elections in April 1994, however, a decade that has overseen the beginnings of a "post-bi-polar world order," the issue of sanctions has been differently invoked, from Cuba to Iraq, and just as differentially endorsed. What then has become of that earlier South African example—the precedents it set, the pitfalls it sidestepped, and the provisos that it warrants now? What can its erstwhile narrative tell now?

Two pivotal texts from the South African sanctions movement, *Sanctions against South Africa* (1964), edited by Ronald Segal, and *The South African Connection: Western Investment in Apartheid* (1972), coauthored by Ruth First with Jonathan Steele (reporter for the London *Guardian*) and Christabel Gurney (then-editor of the *Anti-Apartheid News*), remain telling as to the tale of South African sanctions. Segal and First, both distinguished antiapartheid activists, were South Africans living in exile in London in the crucial decades of the 1960s and 1970s. Segal had left South Africa in 1960 when he escorted Oliver Tambo—the future leader of the ANC-in-exile—out of the country. Ruth First arrived in London with her three daughters in 1964, following her release from prison under the 90 Days Detention Act, where she joined her husband Joe Slovo. Slovo had been working with the ANC (African National Congress) and its armed wing of Umkhonto we Sizwe (MK) in addition to being involved with the South African Communist Party (SACP). *Sanctions against South Africa* is a collection of the papers presented by expert witnesses invited to a conference organized by Ronald Segal in London in April 1964, which First attended shortly after her arrival in the

United Kingdom. *The South African Connection* examines, in turn, the investment practices of "Western" companies—from Polaroid to Shell/BP—and their contribution to the furtherance of apartheid policies. Apartheid forces in Mozambique assassinated Ruth First in 1982; Ronald Segal continues to live and write in London. Questioning the role of these authors/activists in the sanctions movement against apartheid over several decades raises important concerns not only about the consequences of the South African example in the contemporary postapartheid, postcolonial world order but also about the controversial significance of sanctions as a political strategy, whether of persuasion or punishment or prurient predation, within a globalized political economy. Already in the early twentieth century, Woodrow Wilson had argued for the effectiveness of sanctions: "Apply this economic, peaceful, silent, deadly remedy and there will be no need for force. It is a terrible remedy. It does not cost a life outside the nation that is boycotted" (cited in Addis 2003, 621–22). Madeleine Albright was similarly cavalier later in the same century, as Mahmood Mamdani shows in citing (and commenting on) an interview that the former U.S. ambassador to the United Nations gave on prime-time television:

> The moral indefensibility of the [Iraq] sanctions regime was clear as early as 1996, when Madeleine Albright, U.S. ambassador to the UN, was asked by Lesley Stahl on the TV program *60 Minutes* about the price of "containing" Saddam: "We have heard that a half million children have died. I mean, that's more than died in Hiroshima. And, and you know, is the price worth it?"
>
> Madeleine Albright responded: "I think this is a very hard choice, but the price, we think the price is worth it."
>
> How and by whom was such a death toll justified for so long? (Mamdani 2004, 190)

After nearly a decade of manipulating UN sanctions against Iraq to suit United States interests (the result of which was a devastated Iraqi infrastructure and a decimated population), U.S. policymakers have, during the last decade of the twentieth century, "effectively turned a program of international governance into a legitimized act of mass slaughter" (Gordon 2002). Writing in late 2002, as the United States prepared its case for an all-out war on that country, Joy Gordon concludes her critique of the Iraq sanctions regime with the admonition that "destroying Iraq, whether with sanctions or with bombs, is unlikely to bring the security we [sic] have gone to such lengths to preserve" (Gordon 2002).

At least 116 cases of sanctions were imposed between World War I (1914–18) and the first Gulf War (1990–91), but the sanctions stratagem has a long history. It was used in the ancient and medieval worlds, the American Civil War, and the Paris Commune (Simons 1999). Identifying a targeted group, sanctions, as a coordinated and/or systematic, uni- or multilateral policy, seek to deprive a society or country of the "means to an effective economic life" (11). Or, as James A. Paul (1998) has described it in his analysis for the Global Policy forum, "Typically, sanctions cut off trade and investments, preventing a country from buying and selling goods in the global marketplace." Paul goes on to remark that "[s]anctions enjoy a good reputation that many now question. Increasingly, critics charge that sanctions are cruel, unfair and even violent." Indeed, sanctions have been seen, according to Paul, to cause "suffering of the innocent," especially women, children, ordinary citizens, and to wreak havoc, "collateral damage," on neighboring countries and trading partners. Furthermore, Paul points out, "[f]or all the pain they impose, sanctions usually do not succeed." That earlier history notwithstanding, the "UN Security Council imposed only two sanctions regimes in its first forty-five years. Surprisingly enough, both are generally considered effective. They targeted Southern Rhodesia (now Zimbabwe) and South Africa, both white-only settler regimes" (Paul 1998).

The issue of international sanctions against South Africa was first raised in the early years of the newly established United Nations, when, in 1946 (the same year as the African miners' strike and two years prior to the Nationalist takeover of the South African government), the Indian government asked that the treatment of Indians residing in the Union of South Africa be considered by the UN's General Assembly in its first session of that year. The South African Indian community's passive resistance campaign that began that same year was eventually followed by the nationwide 1952 Defiance Campaign launched by the ANC and the South African Indian Congress together with the Congress of Democrats. A series of UN resolutions followed during the 1950s, condemning various aspects of apartheid and the government's refusal to recognize the right of all racial groups to enjoy the same fundamental freedoms. In his 1987 retrospective "United Nations and Apartheid: Forty Years," E. S. (Enuga Sreenivasulu) Reddy, who for two decades (1965–1985) headed the UN Centre against Apartheid, observes: "A turning point was General Assembly Resolution 1761 of November 6, 1962, sponsored by the African states which urged member states to impose economic and other sanctions against South Africa and established a Special Committee (now the Special Committee against Apartheid) to keep the situation under constant review" (Reddy 1987). But, Reddy comments as well, there were "many types of boycotts": "The non-economic measures," he writes, " especially the sports and cultural boycotts—have been effective in demonstrating the abhorrence of apartheid. They have involved millions of people in many countries and have helped to educate public opinion" (Reddy 1987).

The British Anti-Apartheid Movement (AAM) began in 1959, when, according to Christabel Gurney—coauthor with Ruth First and Jonathan Steele of *The South African Connection* and editor of the *Anti-Apartheid News*—on June 26 of that year, "a group of South African exiles and their British supporters met in London's Holborn Hall to call for a boycott of fruit, cigarettes and other goods imported from South Africa" (Gurney 1999). Several months later, Julius Nyerere, leader of Tanzania, wrote to *Africa South*, edited by Ronald Segal: "Can we honestly condemn a system and at the same time employ it to produce goods which we buy, and then enjoy with a clear conscience? Surely the customers of a business do more to keep it going than its shareholders. We who buy South African goods do more to support the system than the Nationalist Government or Nationalist industrialists" (Nyerere 1959). Albert Lutuli, President-General of the ANC and Nobel Peace Prize winner, joined the appeal in a statement issued together with G. M. Naicker of the South African Indian Congress and Peter Brown of South Africa's Liberal Party in December 1959 on the eve of the fiftieth anniversary of the Union of South Africa: "Next year it is proposed to conduct a limited boycott of South African produce in Britain for a period of one month. The boycott is a protest against apartheid, the removal of political rights, the colour bar in industry, the extension of passes to African women and the low wages paid to Non-White workers." Economic boycott, it was argued, was "one way in which the world at large can bring home to the South African authorities that they must either mend their ways or suffer for them" (Lutuli 1959). Reinforcing the exceptionalism of the South African sanctions movement and perhaps controverting subsequent critiques based on the "suffering of the innocents", Oliver Tambo, speaking in 1958, maintained, albeit with important caveats, that "we do not conceive of sanctions as a substitute for our struggle; it is additional. So we will continue, we will certainly embark on massive strike actions, we will do all the things that we can and must do for our own freedom, but sanctions are additional and sanctions alone would not bring about any results" (cited in Maloka 1999, 178). Invoking the slogan, "Sanctions Hurt but Apartheid Kills!" labor advocate Tshidiso Maloka asserted that although "[o]ne of the strongest arguments against the use of sanctions is that often ordinary people in the target state—rather than the political elite—are most hurt, . . . it is important to keep in mind . . . that in the South African case, the call for isolation was part of the over-all political strategy of the internal black opposition" (178).

The International Conference on Economic Sanctions against South Africa was convened by Ronald Segal in April (14–17) 1964. Segal had arrived in London in 1960, in the company of Oliver Tambo, whose escape from South Africa's apartheid forces he had egregiously aided and abetted. His departure was not, as he remembers it in his memoir, *Into Exile* (1963), written shortly after his arrival in England, an easy decision. There were occupations—and preoccupations—to be tended to in South Africa. Ruth First's husband, Joe Slovo, for example, had just been detained. And then too, there was the journal, *Africa South*, which Segal had founded in 1956. According to Segal, "I felt that to leave now was a desertion, and that I would find my exile sour and shameful as no imprisonment would be. And I wondered too, whether flight would not put an end, beyond return, to any real chance I might have of helping to shape a new South Africa" (Segal 1963, 283). Ronald Segal, that is, furtively, righteously, clandestinely left South Africa together with Oliver Tambo, and both men took up residence in Britain, where, Segal would recall that "[i]n a crowded London street, I will see a coloured handkerchief wrapped round a head, or smell a pile of oranges on a barrow, and my blood will bound" (319). No less importantly, however, Segal will remind himself—and his readers then and now—that "South Africa remains our country, whatever passports we carry, and wherever we live, we remain—grudgingly or gladly, always helplessly—with its people. Yet it is also everyone's country and people. *Can anyone, anywhere, any more separate himself?*" (319, emphasis added).

Thus perhaps, with this question—"Can anyone, anywhere, any more separate himself?"—as beacon, Ronald Segal, in the year following the publication of his account of his foray "into exile," convened the Sanctions against South Africa conference. It was a "principle of universality," he argued, that determined both the venue and the participants: "I refused," writes Segal in the introduction to the conference proceedings, "to involve the Conference and so, by implication, the international struggle against *apartheid* in the overwhelming distractions of the cold war" (Segal 1964, 10). What was implicated in that "principle of universality"? And what is yet to be made of the "distractions of the cold war"?

The International Conference on Economic Sanctions against South Africa had as its aim to "root the whole issue in reality" (Segal 1964, 7). Oliver Tambo was there, at the Friends House in London's Euston Road to remind the audience that, though the "boast persists: 'South Africa has never had it so good.' . . . [I]ndeed it has not. On the weary and laden shoulders of African labourers stand the great finance houses of the Western world" (26). The interventions would eventually become capitalized. Per Haekkerup, the Danish Minister of Foreign Affairs, invoked the "feelings of international solidarity and responsibility that have emerged since the Second World War, due not least to the United Nations" (43). Taking up the internationalist appeal, Peter Calvocoressi insisted that the "development of sanctions as a regular part of international politics, accompanied as it must be by an evolution and elaboration of international law in practice, appeals to the internationalist on general grounds just as it scares the nationalist" (60). Other speakers, such as D. H. N. Johnson, from the University of London, and Rosalyn Higgins, of the Royal Institute of International Affairs, addressed concerns about the legal aspects of sanctions and domestic jurisdiction. Colin and Margaret Legum, scholars, critics, and political activists, themselves South African exiles living in London, wondered: "Has the United Nations the right to condemn a member for its domestic policies? Do South Africa's domestic policies constitute a threat to world peace? Is there any effective action which could be taken with the hope of redistributing power in South Africa without racial violence?" (Legum and Legum 1964, 235). As the Conference Steering Committee stated, "Whatever the claims of the South African Government with respect to its sovereign rights and jurisdiction, its policies of apartheid and race discrimination have become major issues of international dispute and tension, imperiling good relations between states and peoples everywhere" (Segal 1964, 94).

The Conference had asked its participants to provide committee reports at its conclusion. These reports suggest important critiques of both historical precedents and contemporary procedures, as well as for political processes with regard to the South African example of a "sanctions regime." Commissions I and II, asked to look at matters of world trade and payments systems, reported that "although economic sanctions would have a very serious effect on the South African economy, they should not have serious effects on world trade and payments as a whole. Such disturbance as did occur could easily be taken care of by the same kind of international agreement that resulted in a programme of collective sanctions" (Segal 1964, 249). According to Commission III, "The effects of sanctions would fall on all the people of South Africa." But, the report continued, again anticipating the concern for the "suffering of the innocent, . . . Africans are used to privation and prepared for more. It is they who have repeatedly asked for sanctions because they believe that if the Government is deprived of outside assistance it would be easier for them to achieve their objectives" (254). Finally, Commissions IV and V, whose remits were "legal and political" and "policing," respectively, submitted the opinion that the "apartheid system is especially inflammatory because it is a racial form and this race rule—unique in the world in its brutality and rigidity and official character—is a threat to peace by its very existence" (257)—and an "ever-present incitement to the rest of Africa" (258).

"Sovereign rights and jurisdiction" have once again become critical to the debate over the legitimacy and effectiveness of sanctions as political strategy and in the contested politics of global policing in the name of "humanitarian intervention." As Justin Conlon has pointed out, the apparent contradiction between human rights on the one hand and state sovereignty on the other continues to riddle the rationales for the continued prosecution of an imperial agenda. Reviewing the recent instances of just such an agenda, from Iraq, immediately prior to and following the first Gulf War (1990–91), Somalia (1993), Haiti (1994), Bosnia (1992), and eventually, again, Iraq (2003–) (and now there is the humanitarian crisis in Darfur and threatened sanctions against the Sudan [2004]), Conlon concludes—all too controversially, to be sure—that there is "no easy answer to the question of human rights, but it seems clear that imperialism, as its bloody history has shown, is not the answer" (Conlon 2004, 96).

And indeed, the distorted versions of a late twentieth–early twenty-first-century "humanitarian interventionism" have their antecedents, precedents, and prototypes in the paradigms of a nineteenth-century imperialism's "civilizing mission"—expressed and counterexpressed by "Little Englanders" and their opposing jingoists and the representatives, such as economist J. A. Hobson, of a "new Imperialism," or journalist W. T. Stead, of an "Imperialism of responsibility." According to Hobson's "psychology of jingoism," jingoism is that "inverted patriotism whereby the love of one's own nation is transformed into the hatred of another nation, and the fierce craving to destroy the individual members of that other nation" (Hobson 1901, 1), a sentiment that found its expression and new etymologies from the newspapers to the music hall in such ditties as:

> We don't want to fight
>     But, by Jingo, if we do,
> We've got the men,
>     We've got the ships,
> We've got the money too— (cited in Hobson 1901, 2)

Jingoism, wrote Hobson, involved the full "modus operandi of the various forces of public opinion" (Hobson 1901, 2). Stead, however, one of those "forces" and a close, if sometimes disapproving, friend of Cecil Rhodes, preferred to advocate on behalf of an "Imperialism of responsibility," an imperial posture that would be grounded in a "closer union with the Colonies" (Stead 1902). The issue of South African sanctions too had derived significantly from an earlier, nineteenth-century imperial project—as subsequent contributions to the Sanctions against South Africa conference indicate. William Gutteridge, for example, takes that imperial history into the Bandung era, in which the "views of Afro-Asia are now so important an element" (Segal 1964, 107). There are also the primary resources to be considered (once plundered, now prized): oil (Brian Lapping) and gold (Roger Opie), as well as the dreadful, all-too-lethal residues, such as asbestos (Elliot Zupnick).

Indeed, throughout the previous decade, since the establishment of the AAM at least, there had been important and effective emphases on consumer boycotts, sports boycotts, and cultural boycotts against South African products, teams, artists, and venues. Peter Hain, for example, who has since gone on to become a prominent member of Britain's Labour government, was an enthusiastic organizer of the sports boycott, most notoriously perhaps in the Stop the Seventy Tour (STST) in 1969–70 (which, incidentally, got Hain arrested and a letter bomb sent to his family's home). In his memoir of that extended episode, *Radical Regeneration: Protest, Direct Action and Community Politics* (1975), the erstwhile boycotter reflects: "to take the two examples of the Suffragettes and sports apartheid: it is clear direct action actually persuaded more people than would otherwise have been the case, because the novelty and impact of the strategy created an unrivalled platform for discussion and debate" (Hain 1975, 113). Two decades later, in a new memoir that called on Alan Paton's 1950s novel *Cry the Beloved Country* for its own title of renewal, *Sing the Beloved Country* (1996), Hain recalled those heady days of South African sports, their boycott, and their complicated and contested connection to British race relations: "The West Indian Campaign against Apartheid Cricket," Hain remembers, were "launched after the leading black activist, Jeff Crawford, contacted me; this introduced an important extra dimension which fused the battle against racism in Britain with our campaign" (Hain 1996, 58). But as Hain also recollects, there continued the debate over the relative efficacy of sports boycotts and economic sanctions—a debate with which *The South African Connection* directly engages.

Milton Temple Smith, the United Kingdom publisher of *The South African Connection: Western Investment in Apartheid* (1972), had advertised the book in an appeal that began with questions to its British readership: "Does our investment in South Africa accelerate 'modernisation,' raise African living standards, and help to liberalise the system from within? Or on the contrary does it shore up a regime which might otherwise have to give ground?" Taking the discussion from the pitches to the portfolios and boardrooms of those multinational corporations doing business in and with apartheid South Africa, First, Steele, and Gurney, the coauthors of *The South African Connection*, argue that "Demonstrators have nearly always taken political institutions as the objects of their opposition, with foreign embassies the favourite targets. It is surely time to question this approach as a preoccupation with the outward symbols of political power and a lopsided scale of tactical priorities." They go on to claim that "This question is probably more important in the discussion of apartheid than of any other world issue. For, controversial though the British government's policy towards South Africa is, its influence *is* small compared with the effect of trade and industry" (First, Steele, and Gurney 1972, 9, emphasis in original).

By the time that First, Steele, and Gurney came to research *The South African Connection*, it seemed apparent that, as the title to chapter 11 suggests, "western trade follows the South African Flag." The analysts follow that pursuit in nine case studies (chapter 8: "The Companies: Image and Reality") of corporations who were "prepared to provide information on their wages" paid to black workers (First, Steele, and Gurney 1972, 160). These business interests included the mining outfit Rio Tinto-Zinc; British Leyland, a motor vehicle manufacturer; Imperial Chemical Industries; the British Steel Corporation; Dunlop Holdings, which opened its first tire depot in South Africa in 1896; Guest Keen & Nettlefords, a manufacturer of steel products; General Electric Company; General Motors; and Caltex Petroleum Corporation. According to the researchers, while "[f]ew firms will admit that hiring more Africans at lower wages is good business," it turned out to be the case that '[a]ll firms argue that their involvement in South Africa does not imply approval of apartheid" (148). After all, as First and her coauthors point out, "[n]othing is more embarrassing to a large company than to find itself confronted with overwhelming evidence that it is, in fact, illiberal" (12). But there were also "experiments and failures" in corporate attempts to counteract this evidence, experiments such as Polaroid's project (as compensation for its contribution to the pass system perhaps) to provide improved working conditions and benefits for its African laborers, and Barclays Bank's similar, if less apologetic, attempt at avoiding withdrawal of its interests from the country altogether. Most egregious perhaps was the "Oppenheimer phenomenon." Harry Oppenheimer, head of the largest employer in South Africa after the government itself, still took as his role model Cecil Rhodes and espoused the Rhodes-ian "great vision" of a "great modern industrialized state in South Africa in which all civilized men could enjoy equal rights" (cited in First, Steele, and Gurney 1972, 206). But as First, Steele, and Gurney are quick to assert, these might seem to be "[i]nspiring words, except for that one phrase—'all civilized men'" (207).

When First, Steele, and Gurney published in London in 1972 *The South African Connection* (their close reading of "Western investment in apartheid"), the issues of economic, even cultural and sporting, boycotts, embargos, and political sanctions as instruments of international policy—and policy setting—were once again being refashioned. And within the tensions being fomented even then were those still-vexed collaborations between what would later be referred to by Rob Nixon as "exiles in league with foreign solidarity movements" and the "democratic movement inside South Africa" (Nixon 1994, 157). Among the conclusions that the coauthors of *The South African Connection* reached at the time, however, was that of the decisive and overdetermined "interpenetration of Western and South African business interests" (279). The designation "metropolitan," used by the authors of *The South African Connection* to speculate on the country's future, has often—in the lexicons of dependency and "postcolonialism"—been juxtaposed to that of "periphery," and the resulting geographical localizations and hierarchies have been organized accordingly. Not only are the colonial orders of space challenged, however, by this concluding, if hardly conclusive, question that would reidentify South Africa as "metropolitan," but the very political order that already identifies axial placements and axiomatic relationships is reconfigured. The allegedly postmodern semantics of "world order" have been more recently still, in their postbipolar/postapartheid versions and visions, subjected by the pressures of current global and local events to further redefinition: from first/second/third worlds to a "first world" and a "two-thirds—or two-thirds of the—world," from West/East to North/South, from nationalism to globalization, from developing countries to emerging markets, from area studies to regional trading blocs, from national liberation movements to nongovernmental organizations. The narrative of the turn of the nineteenth century into the late twentieth century might be read as large as it was written as the more-than-semantic replacement of the rhetorical pieties of a "civilizing mission" with the perorations of calls to "humanitarian intervention." The pundits and panderers of the twentieth-first century are now invested in the all-too-terrifying "war on terror."

Back in 1966, however, two years after Ronald Segal's Sanctions against South Africa conference, and some six years before the publication of *The South African Connection*, Ruth First, together with Ronald Segal, had called together in London still another international conference, this time on South West Africa, the former German colony still (since the post–World War I Versailles Conference) administered at the time by South Africa. The purpose of the meeting was to discuss precisely the local contradictions and internal conflicts of South Africa's mandated oversight of that neighboring territory and the imperative of international involvement in their resolution.

As First had put it in the introduction to her 1963 study, *South West Africa*, published shortly before she herself went into exile, "If the South West Africa issue expresses the essential dilemma of the apartheid state, it also touches the exposed nerves of the UN" (First 1963, 20). The London conference found in 1966, however, that the "South West African question ha[d] become a crucial test of—and challenge to—the principle of international commitment and responsibility. The role of the United Nations system in preserving peace and security depends on an adequate international response" (Segal and First 1967, 323). But the findings were subsequently contravened by the decision of the International Court, which announced that Ethiopia and Libya, who had brought South West Africa's case once again before the judicial body, "had no legal right or interest in the subject matter of their complaints." The Court, Ruth First would argue two months afterwards, in an article in the journal *Labour Monthly*, had been "used as an essentially Western Big Power instrument to forestall decision and action, specially where the liberation of subject peoples is at stake" (First 1966, 420).

Over two decades later and after a protracted struggle, South West Africa did successfully gain its independence and Namibia became part of the international community of nations—although in 2004, the centenary of the Herero genocide, the country was still looking to Germany for reparations. But sanctions meanwhile had become part of the arsenal of international crisis management, rather than a weapon in the struggle for self-determination and national liberation. The fulfillment of promises of the "rights of small nations" that had characterized the disparate if complementary work of both Woodrow Wilson and Vladimir Lenin following the First World War and which were written into the charter of the United Nations following the Second World War had given place to another way with words. At the turn of the twentieth into the twenty-first century, medicine and foodstuffs were in short supply in Cuba and children were dying of malnutrition in Iraq as the United States wielded sway over another "world order," even as China remained one of its "most favored" trading partners.

In his study of "un-sanctioned suffering in Iraq," Roger Norman pointed out that the "United Nations Charter gives the Security Council broad powers to maintain international peace and security. However, East-West divisions throughout the Cold War prevented the Security Council from fulfilling this mandate. As a result, between 1945–90 the Security Council imposed multilateral sanctions only twice—a trade embargo against Rhodesia in 1966 and an arms embargo against South Africa in 1977." Norman goes on: the "end of the Cold War brought calls for a 'New World Order' based on universal respect for international law. It also breathed new life into the moribund Security Council. Since 1990, the Council has imposed multilateral sanctions against eight different states, and occasionally authorized military force, most notably against Iraq in 1991" (Norman 1996). But in that latest guise, sanctions looked more like "collective punishment" than support against political peril, an assault on civilians, women, and children, and in flagrant disregard of either a peacetime regime of human rights or a wartime agenda of humanitarian intervention. There was still to come the United States's even more cataclysmic "war on terror."

## Conclusion

Ruth First was assassinated in August 1982 by a letter bomb sent to her from Pretoria—well before sanctions gave way to negotiations and democratic elections. Christabel Gurney, who for more than a decade edited the *Anti-Apartheid News*, wrote in 1999: "In 1959 the Boycott Movement was formed from an initiative of South Africans who were suffering under apartheid, which was taken up by people in Britain. If it holds a lesson, it is that change comes through partnership and that people in the industrialised North who want to improve living standards in the South should listen to, and work together with, those they are trying to help" (Gurney 1999). Jonathan Steele continues to write for the *Guardian* as senior foreign correspondent, from Central Asia, from the Horn of Africa, and from the Gaza Strip, as he did in May 2004 under the headline "More Carnage in Gaza as the US mutters Its Disapproval" (May 21, 2004). And he argued with regard to Darfur, "Diplomacy Is Forgotten in the Mania for Intervention" (August 6, 2004). Where is the support that Walter Sisulu asked for, for a "new international solidarity movement"?

South Africa and sanctions: example or exception?

## Works Cited

Addis, Adeno. 2003. "Economic Sanctions and the Problem of Evil." *Human Rights Quarterly* 25, no. 3: 573–623.

Bond, Patrick. 2004. "Pretoria Chooses Subimperialism." *Foreign Policy in Focus*. At: www.fpif.org.

Conlon, Justin. 2004. "Sovereignty vs. Human Rights or Sovereignty and Human Rights?" *Race and Class* 46:75–100.

de Waal, Alex, ed. 2000. *Who Fights? Who Cares? War and Humanitarian Action in Africa*. Trenton, N.J.: Africa World Press.

First, Ruth. 1963. *South West Africa*. Harmondsworth, UK: Penguin.

———. 1966. "South-West Africa." *Labour Monthly* (September).

First, Ruth, Jonathan Steele, and Christabel Gurney. 1972. *The South African Connection: Western Investment in Apartheid*. London: Temple Smith.

Gordon, Joy. 2002. "Cool War: Economic Sanctions as a Weapon of Mass Destruction." *Harper's Magazine* 305, no. 1830 (November): 43–50.

Gurney, Christabel. 1999. "When the Boycott Began to Bite." At: www.anc.org.za/ancdocs/history/aam/aamhist.html.

Hain, Peter. 1975. *Radical Regeneration: Protest, Direction, and Community*. London: Quartet Books.

———. 1996. *Sing the Beloved Country: The Struggle of the New South Africa*. London: Pluto Press.

Hobson, J. A. 1901. *The Psychology of Jingoism*. London: G. Hobson.

Legum, Colin, and Margaret Legum. 1964. *South Africa: Crisis for the West*. London: Pall Mall Press.

Lutuli, Albert. 1959. "Statement Appealing to the British People to Boycott South Africa." At: www.anc.org.za/ancdocs/history/lutuli/lutuli59.html.

Maloka, Tshidiso. 1999. "Sanctions Hurt but Apartheid Kills!: The Sanctions Campaign and Black Workers." In *How Sanctions Work: Lessons from South Africa*, eds. Neta C. Crawford and Audie Klotz. London: Macmillan.

Mamdani, Mahmood. 2004. *Good Muslim, Bad Muslim: America, The Cold War, and the Roots of Terror*. New York: Pantheon.

Nixon, Rob. 1994. *Homelands, Harlem, and Hollywood: South African Culture and the World Beyond*. New York and London: Routledge.

Normand, Roger. 1996. "Iraq Sanctions, Human Rights, and Humanitarian Law." *Middle East Report* 200:40–43, 46.

Nyerere, Julius. 1959. "On the Boycott of South Africa." At: www.anc.org.za/ancdocs/history/people/nyerere/boycotsa.html.

Oppenheimer, Harry. 1970. "A Reassessment of Rhodes." *Optima* (September):

Paul, James A. 1998. "Sanctions: An Analysis." *Global Policy Forum*. At: www.globalpolicy.org/security/sanction/analysis.htm.

Reddy, E. S. 1987. "United Nations and Apartheid: Forty Years." At: www.anc.org.za/un/reddy.

Sampson, Anthony. 1987. *Black and Gold: Tycoons, Revolutionaries, and Apartheid*. London: Hodder and Stoughton.

Segal, Ronald. 1963. *Into Exile*. London: Jonathan Cape.

———. ed. 1964. *Sanctions against South Africa*. Harmondsworth, UK: Penguin.

Segal, Ronald, and Ruth First. 1967. *South West Africa: A Travesty of Trust*. London: Andre Deutsch.

Simons, Geoff. 1999. *Imposing Economic Sanctions: Legal Remedy or Genocidal Tool?* London: Pluto Press.

Stead, W. T., ed. 1902. *The Last Will and Testament of Cecil Rhodes*. London: Review of Reviews Office.

Steele, Jonathan. 2004a. "More Camage in Gaza as the US mutters its Disapproval." *Guardian*. May 21.

———. 2004b. "Diplomacy is Forgotten in the Mania for Intervention." *Guardian*. August 6.

# 13

# FROM BOLLYWOOD TO HOLLYWOOD: THE GLOBALIZATION OF HINDI CINEMA

*Harish Trivedi*

Though postcolonialism and globalization are both phenomena that have arisen more or less together over the past couple of decades, at least in terms of academic discourse, and are currently very much with us, the intersection between them is far more than chronological or coincidental. In fact, the similarity and overlap between the two processes is so wide in terms of their political orientation and economic thrust that it is possible to see one as an extension of the other. The history of Western colonialism shows not only that the adventurist exploration of other countries and continents was very often driven by the motive of commercial gain but that it was to protect and propagate commercial interests that the Western powers conquered and colonized other nations. The Rev. Dr. David Livingstone himself allied his determined quest for the source of the Nile to the broader motivation of wanting to open up Africa to "commerce and Christianity" (in that order); and in India, it was of course the East India Company, a consortium of London merchants founded in 1600, that ruled large parts of the country until the "Mutiny" of 1857. But this near-terminal threat to free private enterprise promptly led the British government, in the name of Queen Victoria, to intervene and take over, in a manner reminiscent of some recent U.S. government interventions in which the ulterior motive seems to have been no less commercial. There is thus irony in the fact that both (post)colonialism and globalization are in current discourse sometimes traced back, in order to give them a long lineage, to the common nascent moment of 1492.

Nevertheless, the distinction is often made that whereas postcolonialism represents the aftermath or even afterglow of colonialism, which came to an end in the middle of the twentieth century in most parts of the world, and is by and large cultural and hegemonic, globalization in its present manifestation is a far more recent phenomenon, which came into existence after territorial occupation and direct foreign rule had become obsolete, and is to be understood in predominantly economic terms. But to subscribe to this view would be to be beguiled by a framework in which culture is not quite as materialist a formation as economics; it would be to elide the fact that what is now called globalization is a project that was routinely called by the name of neocolonialism in the 1960s and the 1970s, especially in Africa by political leaders such as Kwame Nkrumah and writers such as Ngugi wa Thiong'o. It is easier to draw a line between former colonization and current globalization in terms of their respective modes of operation than in terms of their ultimate effect, which in both cases is an inextricable blend of the cultural and the economic.

Few cultural phenomena could illustrate this nexus between the cultural and the economic, the postcolonial and the global, better than some recent developments in Hindi cinema (also called "Bombay cinema" after its main center of production and more recently

200

"Bollywood"). By far the most popular form of mass entertainment in India and thus both a mirror and matrix of popular Indian culture, Hindi cinema has lately been undergoing a major makeover such as bodes to redefine or even obliterate its very identity. In this essay, I seek to explore some of these developments in terms of rubrics that are of significance equally to postcolonial and global discourses—the nation, language, and crossover modes of both production and consumption—and I conclude with examining a parallel between global cinema and postcolonial literature.

## HINDI CINEMA AND THE NATION

More films are produced every year in India than in any other country, and though this vast output of about eight hundred films annually (Chakravarty 1998, 9) is spread over half a dozen Indian languages including Bengali, Kannada, Malayalam, Marathi, Tamil, and Telugu, it is films in Hindi, far the most widely spoken language in the country and the official language of the state, that have an unmatched circulation and pre-eminence and therefore "an undeniable national character" (Prasad 1998, 4). Right from the beginning, Indian films have had an unmistakable indigenous content and narrative idiom, with the first silent film *Raja Harishchandra* (1913) by Dadasaheb Phalke taking its story from the foundational Sanskrit epic the *Mahabharata* and deriving its style from the Parsi theater companies whose stage productions were the direct predecessors of the cinema in India and that had performed a play of the same title over 4,000 times at venues across India in the preceding decades. Thus, filmmaking in India was from the start "conceived of . . . as a nationalist, specifically 'swadeshi,' enterprise" (Prasad 1998, 2), "swadeshi" signifying not only homegrown and indigenous, which is what the word means, but also a nationwide anti-British movement against the partition of Bengal that began in 1905 and culminated successfully in the partition being annulled in 1911. Indian films remained throughout British rule a national and sometimes covertly nationalist form of expression and entertainment.

Although films from Britain and Hollywood were imported into India from an early date, they drew as audience only an infinitely small fraction of the urban elite because of the gap in culture as well as language. As late as in the 1970s, even highly educated Indians, who had been taught Shakespeare and Milton and used English routinely in colleges and offices, still could not follow English as spoken realistically and in unfamiliar accents by foreign characters, though some of them may have snobbishly pretended to understand it better than they did. If such persons still went to see an English or American movie, often put on for just the one show on Sunday mornings even in towns big enough to be state capitals, it was with the expectation to see some kissing (forbidden in Indian films) or other forms of exotic conduct, as depicted, for example, in a satirical Hindi short story "Who Isn't Afraid of Virginia Woolf?":

> [The audience] were sitting around hoping that Burton would kiss Taylor again and again. But he wasn't kissing her at all. He wasn't divorcing her and he wasn't shooting at her. Nothing at all was happening which they had hoped might happen. (S. Joshi 2000, 382)

Not only because foreign films were so alien but even more because India had quickly developed its own flourishing film industry rooted in its own distinctive culture, Hollywood was not able to become the main or even a significant subsidiary stream of cinema in India. Indian cinema represents and speaks for the nation and remains India's national cinema in a way few cinemas do anywhere else in the world, including Europe.

"But what is a 'nation'?" asks Sumita S. Chakravarty at the outset of her study titled *National Identity in Indian Popular Cinema: 1947–1987* (Chakravarty 1998, 10) while explaining that her own metropolitan critical project involves "wrenching . . . the Bombay cinema out of its native moorings . . . and giving it a somewhat globalized profile" (Chakravarty 1998, 8). Such radical interrogation of the very idea of the nation, especially in the Third World, has become de rigueur, of course, in both postcolonial studies and the discourse on globalization, in which the nation is seen as an altogether oppressive, regressive, and reactionary category. Thus, Ravi Vasudevan, after acknowledging that the Bombay cinema "constitutes something like a 'nation space' against the dominant norms of Hollywood", proceeds to argue that this cinema "generates an enlarged and standardized identity" that is located in its "construction of masculine authority and its privileging of a symbolic Hindu identity" (Vasudevan 2000, 381, 395). Although he concedes that such privileging of Hindu identity "is comparable to the way in which the white hero became the norm for the U.S. commercial cinema" and is thus part of a wider universal phenomenon, he fails to balance out the construction of Hindu identity against the construction, for example, of Muslim identity in Hindi films (for the casual reason that he has "not seen enough of these highly popular 'Muslim social' films)." But that does not prevent him from concluding that the "construction of the Indian nation" in Hindi films was "dominated by the Hindu" (Vasudevan 2000, 398, 399)—as if this were by itself a matter of surprise or opprobrium in terms of representation in a popular medium in a country in which over 80 percent of the population is Hindu.

The national function of Hindi cinema is formulated and problematized somewhat more complexly by Gayatri Chakravorty Spivak in her discussion of the Indian English novel *The Guide* by R. K. Narayan, with reference to the enormously popular Hindi film of the book made under the same title (1965).

> *The Guide* in the Hindi film version is the condition and the effect of the vox populi. As such the film brings into bold relief the multiculturalism of (the now-precarious) official Indian self-representation, [and] the religious tolerance of the Hindu majority that was still ideologically operative in the Nehruvian atmosphere of the 1960s . . . the film translates the novel from the elite colonial to popular national, from English to Hindi. (Spivak 1994, 142)

This seems to give more of due credit to both Hindi and the national in terms of their popular basis and strength, though the "national" must, of course, ultimately be debunked in postcolonial discourse and shown to be merely a stage in an ever-progressive trajectory, in "the itinerary from colonial through national to postcolonial and/or migrant subjects" (Spivak 1994, 147). Some ways in which Hindi cinema itself (as distinct from the critical and theoretical discourse on it) has in recent decades become less national and more postcolonial and global are indicated here.

## THE LANGUAGE OF HINDI CINEMA

Because it is not the cinema of a region, unlike all other cinema in India, Hindi cinema has always attracted actors, writers, directors, producers, and other personnel from diverse linguistic regions of India; it is as if Hindi cinema were too big and important to be left only to Hindi speakers. For this and other reasons, the language used in Hindi cinema has been all kinds of Hindi, inflected by numerous other Indian languages and dialects: from Urdu earlier spoken by a section of the old north Indian aristocracy including its accomplished courtesans to rural Bhojpuri spoken by the poor peasants in eastern Uttar Pradesh and Bihar to the macho and inventively ungrammatical street language spoken by characters walking the borderline between what they often see as socially just crime and the law in the Bombay underworld.[1] Beyond these earlier developments, however, Hindi cinema has in recent years taken another linguistic turn, which is both postcolonial and global, to use more and more English words or, through frequent code mixing, a mixture of Hindi and English sometimes called "Hinglish."

An early justification for this trend was that over the past decade or so, beginning spectacularly with *Dilwale Dulhaniya Le Jayenge* (Brave Hearts Will Win the Brides, 1995), which has just completed an uninterrupted ten-year run in a Bombay cinema house, any number of successful Hindi films have been made that have foreign locales not only as inert and exotic backdrops as in earlier films but as places where characters from Hindi films actually visit or live, even outside the magic-realist world of Hindi film songs. This reflects an upper-class cosmopolitan Indian mobility that has now become a staple subject matter of Hindi films, much as the villages were half a century ago—but the villages have now vanished from the Indian imaginary, as Ashis Nandy has recently pointed out in his *An Ambiguous Journey: The Village and Other Odd Ruins of the Self in the Indian Imagination* (2001). If the "real" India was not so long ago believed to live in its villages, as Gandhi repeatedly asserted, a significant proportion of it, at least on the evidence of these Hindi films, now lives abroad. The Indian diaspora numbers about 10 million persons worldwide, compared with the 1.2 billion Indians who still live in India, but it has begun to register its presence and its allure in Hindi films in a way that may be disproportionate in numbers but is in keeping with the foreign-currency wealth and glamour of the diaspora.

Another ruse through which to admit Hinglish- or even English-speaking characters in Hindi films had been through the spate of anticolonial films beginning with *1942: A Love Story* (1994) and running right through five film versions of the life story of Bhagat Singh (a bomb-exploding "terrorist"/patriot who was hanged by the British government), all released within 2001–02, right up to *Lagaan* (2002), in which the British were the villains whom a ragtag team of Indian villagers defeated at their own game of cricket. But these British characters speaking English were of course a special, aberrant category, including the young English woman in *Lagaan* who defected to the Indian side and became in the process probably the first white character in Hindi films actually shown to be learning Hindi. However, it is the phenomenally increasing presence of upper-class Hinglish-speaking Indians who are shown to shuttle between the East and the West and who, for all their Westernization, still mouth feel-good sentiments in praise of India (as in the song "Yeh mera India / Mathe ki bindiya" [This India of mine / The crown of the world]), which forebodes to change the very character of Hindi cinema and its potential viewership.

The use of English words and sentences in earlier Hindi films was often something of an exhibitionist bravura performance, as when Amitabh Bachchan, in the middle of a Hindi song in *Amar Akbar Anthony* (1977) delivered in one breathtaking breath the crazy sentence, "Wait, Wait, Wait! You see, the whole country of the system is juxtapositioned by the hemoglobin of the atmosphere because you are a sophisticated rhetorician intoxicated by the exuberance of your own verbosity!," though this particular outburst was perhaps partly in character (a Goan Christian: "My name is Anthony Gonsalves"). Even longer back, the use of English was a confident parody and critique of the West, as when Mehmood sang:

> Angrezi mulk men, kitna romance hai!
> Baahar ka chhokri, kitna advance hai!
> (Oh! the foreign countries are full of romance / And the girls there so advanced!)

But now, Hinglish is used in Hindi films in all earnestness as reflecting realistically the language in which the Westernized upper- and upper-middle-class characters normally speak. The extent and the nature of code mixing that goes on in metropolitan India between the local Indian language and English is accurately caught in some recent Hindi films. In *Taal* (Musical Beat, 1999), for example, Akshaye Khanna plays the scion of a stinking-rich Bombay family who go for a holiday in the North Indian hills where Khanna falls in love with a village belle, and back in Bombay, when it comes to the crunch, he coolly tells his family: "No tantrum, no fuss, *lekin shadi yehi hogi* (but I'll marry as I like)." Significantly, such resort to English often goes hand in hand in Hindi films with a protest against the traditional norm of arranged marriages and an assertion of romantic love, leading to what until a couple of decades ago used to be called "love marriage." In a recent film that has acquired something of a cult status among younger metropolitan viewers (sometimes disapprovingly called the bubble-gum generation), *Dil Chahta Hai* (What the Heart Desires, 2001), the relatively high proportion of Hinglish/English dialogue includes Saif Khan saying straight out, "Mom, *yeh* arranged marriage *vagairah mujhse nahin hoga"* (Mom, this arranged marriage stuff is not for me), and when Pooja Bhatt, with whom he is thrown together by his parents anyhow, finds out that these are his views in the matter, she says, in English: "I'm so happy. . . . Oh, that's such a relief!"

But there are other contexts too in which Hinglish is frequently used, and here too the insertion of the occasional English sentence, or of English words in a Hindi sentence, is symptomatic of a broader cultural pattern. Such mixed usage often serves as the small change of polite social intercourse among members of a Westernized upper class, or as formulaic emotional responses. In *Biwi No One* (The First and Foremost Wife, 1999), for example, a film in which the plot revolves around two couples (one married and the other apparently adulterous) going on holiday in Switzerland at the same time, sentences such as the following, spoken by various characters, are strewn all over the film: "May I help you." "You've come to the right place, sweetheart." "I hate you, I hate you, I hate you!" "I love you." "I love you too." "I am very, very, very upset." "I am sorry." More interesting perhaps are some examples of code switching, such as Salman Khan's "Tu kya mujhe *henpecked* samajhta hai?" (Do you think I am henpecked?) or Sushmita Sen's "Yeh kutta jagah jagah *shit* karta rahta hai"(This dog keeps shitting all over the place). In both of these sentences, it is just the operative, unpleasant word that is in English, for it may compromise the class-related sophistication of such characters to say it in Hindi.

## Hinglish and Body Language

Such insertion of Hinglish in Hindi cinema is not only a reflection of (a narrow but possibly glamorous fraction of) contemporary social reality but probably also a proleptic glimpse of a greater transformation yet to come. Over the past decade or so, a few Indian directors have made some films largely or entirely in English, including *Hyderabad Blues*, *Rockford*, and *Bollywood Calling*, all by Nagesh Kukunoor; *Bandit Queen* by Shekhar Kapoor; *English, August* (based on the novel in English of the same title by Upamanyu Chatterji) by Dev Benegal; and *Monsoon Wedding* by Mira Nair. Some Indians have also directed a very few mainstream Hollywood films in English, such as *Elizabeth* by Shekhar Kapur; *The Sixth Sense*, starring Bruce ("Diehard") Willis, one of the biggest grossers of the year in the United States, and an Oscar nominee for best director, by M. "Night" Shyamalan; and *Vanity Fair* by Mira Nair. From the other side of the fence, so to say, Baz Luhrmann's *Moulin Rouge* came as close in mode and idiom to Hindi cinema as perhaps any Hollywood film has ever done and showed unmistakable signs of Luhrmann having put himself through a crash course in watching mainstream Hindi films beforehand, as he said he had done.

All these are signs writ large of what can only be called globalization and of a kind of hybridity that might have been difficult to imagine even a decade ago. It seems fairly clear that more and more films will be made in India that will have not merely a greater Western visual content but also more and more of Hinglish or straight English dialogue. A remarkable example of a Hindi film with a Western visual content is *Kaante* (Thorns, 2002), which has an Indian cast but was shot entirely on location in Los Angeles with an all-American production crew and followed the bank robbery plot of the Hollywood movie *Reservoir Dogs*; this marked an advance on the innumerable unacknowledged adaptations of the plots of successful Hollywood films to an Indian situation, such as *Black* (in Hindi, 2004), which a film journalist has described as being "a frame-by-frame copy" of the Hollywood film *The Miracle Worker* (Faleiro 2005, 27).[2]

The proportion of English dialogue in *Monsoon Wedding*, a film set entirely in Delhi, was 60 percent by the director Mira Nair's own reckoning (Lahr 2002, 109). A large proportion of the younger Hindi film actors and actresses as well as directors seem rather more comfortable speaking English and living their lives in it than in Hindi or any other Indian language; indeed, they give the impression that they would speak Hindi only when paid handsomely to do so. In interviews and chat shows with them on Hindi TV channels, the interviewer may typically begin by asking a short and simple question in Hindi or a somewhat longer and less simple question in Hinglish, but the actor, after beginning with a token phrase or halting half-sentence in Hindi, would quickly switch almost completely to English, such a procedure perhaps demonstrating that although Hindi may have all the questions, it is English apparently that has all the answers.

A particularly significant case in this regard is that of Abhishek Bachchan, son of the greatest Hindi actor ever, Amitabh Bachchan, who has himself been launched as an actor (for the world of Hindi films is even more unabashedly dynastic than that of Indian politics). With all his other assets and advantages, Bachchan Jr. apparently cannot speak much Hindi, and the father, with his own authentic Hindi-heartland lineage and upbringing, has recently offered some poignant reflections on this situation.

> The most important quality or qualification [of an actor] is his knowledge of the language. Only through knowing the language can you produce the right expression on the screen. You can never do that merely by mugging up the dialogue. That's just what's the problem with Abhishek. He and people like him were born in Mumbai [i.e., outside the Hindi-speaking region], this is where they grew up, and then they went abroad for their education. So they are still rather more of foreigners than Indians. He knows only a little Hindi. I keep asking him to speak with me in Hindi but he is scared of doing so. (Bachchan 2002, 16, my translation)

There was a time not too long ago when most Hindi actors and (especially) actresses could not have spoken even a single sentence in English to save their lives, and it is a fair bet that a substantial proportion of the viewers of mainstream Hindi films cannot do so even now. There was always, of course, a great gap between the lives that the viewers themselves led and the lives of the characters they saw depicted on the cinema screen, especially as Hindi films always had an element of glamour and fantasy unlike the realism of many Hollywood films. But the gap now is not simply that between poverty and wealth; it is now increasingly that between Hindi and English.

Related to this partial shift in language is a corresponding transformation also in the body language of Hindi films. It is perhaps a constant and universal complaint that, as time passes, more and more nudity and sex are shown in films and on television, but in a conventional and "backward" society such as India, the change in this regard seems more notable and is, significantly, highlighted, castigated, and lamented rather more in the Hindi press than in the English-language press. For example, the annual "Bollywood Visheshanka" (Bollywood special number) for 2003 of the Hindi magazine *Indiya Tude* had for its focus "Heroine ka Badalta Chehra" (The Changing Faces of the Heroine), in which the lead article, titled "Sita se Soniya tak" (From Sita to Soniya), contrasted Sita, the resolutely and ideally chaste heroine of the epic *The Ramayana*, with the heroine named Soniya of the film *Jism* (Body, 2003), "probably the 'dirtiest' Bollywood heroine of the past decade." The writer of the film, Mahesh Bhatt, was inspired by the Hollywood film *Body Heat*, and the director,

Amit Saxena, explained: "We were trying to fashion a new Indian woman, someone like Sharon Stone (made famous by *Basic Instinct*) who, rather than hide her sexuality, exploits it" (Chopra 2003b, 10). In some recent Hindi films, kisses have been permitted by the censor board, thus reversing a taboo in the Indian performative tradition that dates back to the earliest Indian treatise on poetics, *The Natyashastra* (c. the first century BCE).[3]

## GOING GLOBAL: FROM BOLLYWOOD TO HOLLYWOOD

It is often pointed out, especially by the champions of the process, that globalization benefits everyone,that is, both the globalizer and the globalized. That some of the globalized may at least attempt to benefit from it is borne out by the moves made by a few players of the Hindi film industry, though they have sought to do so not by remaining globalized but by wishing to go out and globalize in turn. The Hindi film has had a significant circulation beyond India but not in the First World, finding a market as an alternative to local cinema in its older sub-altern diaspora (i.e., in countries ranging from Fiji and Mauritius through East Africa to Trinidad and Guyana), where migrant laborers from India had been exported under colonial coercion in the nineteenth century (as distinct from the middle-class diaspora that came into existence in the 1960s with the willing migration of Indian professionals to the First World), and in the U.S.S.R. and the Middle East. Now, Hindi films are being made depicting move-ment between persons living in India and Indians living in the First World (bureaucratically called NRIs or Non-Resident Indians), and often hinging on love and marriage between (usually) an NRI boy and an Indian girl. As some of these films have a built-in market among the NRIs, they circulate in the West in cinema halls and as DVDs, and a few white Westerners probably watch the more successful of these as well. Some films made by Indians born and brought up in America (sometimes called ABCDs, meaning American-Born Confused Desis, *desi* being the Hindi term for an unreconstructed Indian, here used ironically) also fall into this category though their language is English (two emblematic titles being *ABCD* and *American Desi*) and their representation infused with nostalgia for a home away from home. Although it may be true, as Jigna Desai claims in her book-length study of such offshore Indian cinema, that "its politics of the 'beyond' is central to the narration of postcolonial migration in globalization," it is less clear how this cinema "traffics with . . . local and global processes, back and forth, departing and arriving" (Desai 2004, 229), for it is hardly visible in India and does not reflect or impinge on the Indian cultural landscape.

The spate of the so-called NRI films in the past decade, however, is generated not only by nostalgia but even more by hard financial calculations. Given the wide disparity in exchange rates between the Indian rupee and the British pound or the U.S. dollar, even a small audience abroad is as lucrative as a large one at home; a ticket for *Monsoon Wedding* at a theatre in Leicester Square in London sold for 12 pounds sterling, which converted to approximately 1,000 rupees, whereas the most expensive seat in the poshest Delhi cinema hall sells for 150 rupees. The current calculation is that the rights for foreign distribution of such Hindi films are sold for an amount that equals that for two out of the five "territories" into which all of India is divided for the purpose of film distribution.

If Indian cinema is to have any valid claims to winning global recognition and circulation, directors who make Indian films on Indian terms, or actors who work mainly in India, must succeed abroad. Two Indians who have distinguished themselves with the keenness of their efforts to succeed in Hollywood are director Mira Nair and actress Aishwarya Rai. Nair was born and brought up in India and was a student at Delhi University when she left to go to Harvard; she has since lived abroad. She received international recognition with her film *Monsoon Wedding* (2001), which won the top award at the Venice Film Festival and went on to become "the eighth-highest-grossing foreign film of all time in the United States" (Lahr 2002, 100). Her previous films included *Salaam Bombay* (1988), about the "street" or slum children of Bombay; *Mississippi Masala* (1991), about black-Asian relations in the United States; and *Kama Sutra* (1996), an exotic erotic period piece. After the success of *Monsoon Wedding* (but there are, traditionally, no weddings in India during the monsoon, a fact that goes unmentioned in the film), she made *Vanity Fair*, based on W. M. Thackeray's novel, with Reese Witherspoon in the lead, presumably because, among other things, it afforded her an opportunity to blow up and concretize with caparisoned elephants and such the hazy off-stage allusions to India in the novel. Nair seems to look at India exotically enough; as she told the *New Yorker*, "What I love about shooting in India is to choreograph the chaos" (Lahr 2002, 108).

Aishwarya Rai won the Miss World title in 1994 and turned to film acting in 1997; she is regarded as exceptionally beautiful, although somewhat stiff and limited as an actress. Since May 2002, when she went to the Cannes Film Festival as the heroine of the Hindi blockbuster *Devdas* and attracted attention, she has developed some kind of an international profile summed up in a (highly skeptical) journalistic piece as follows:

> Featured on CBS *60 Minutes*. Broadcast on *Good Morning America*. Interviewed on the *David Letterman Show*. A jury member at Cannes. A statue at Madame Tussaud's. Brand ambassador for Longines. Coke. L'Oreal. De Beers. Splashed on the *Time* magazine cover. Blown up on the *Beijing Review* . . . [Appeared on the] *Oprah Winfrey* [show]. Declared the most beautiful woman in the world. By *GQ*. Julia Roberts. Roger Ebert. Richard Branson. Hello! Everybody. (Faleiro and Chaudhury 2005, 24)

The one international or "crossover" film she has appeared in so far is *Bride and Prejudice* (2004), an adaptation of the Jane Austen novel by the British director of Indian descent, Gurinder Chadha. The foremost Indian newsmagazine *India Today* ran a cover story on her titled "Aishwarya Rai: Global Goddess," which said: "She is a genetic masterpiece and her beauty transcends cultures and languages. . . . She can convincingly be Spanish, South American, or Italian" and quoted the London-based Indian film critic Nasreen Munni Kabeer as saying: "Her English is impeccable and her beauty is global. She could be a big star here" (Chopra 2003a, 30, 35). When she made it to Madame Tussaud's, the film magazine *Filmfare* put her on the cover under the caption "Global Gal" with an interview inside titled "Global Glitter" (Choudhary 2004); and when *Bride and Prejudice* did badly in the English version and even worse in the Hindi version, the newsmagazine *Outlook* had a cover caption "Ash Takes a Tumble" and ran a story inside titled "How Hot Is Ash, Really?" (N. Joshi 2004, 44).

There are rumors and reports from time to time of Rai signing other international roles, and she is accused of "chicanery" when they do not materialize (Faleiro and Choudhury 2005, 26). The Indian media, it may appear, has higher expectations of her turning into a global star than she herself may; it seems to be a national aspiration, or rather a postcolonial aspiration, for the patriotic nationalist urge behind it (which rose to a chauvinist crescendo, for example, when Rai was crowned Miss World and another Indian, Sushmita Sen, was crowned Miss Universe the same year) still seeks compensatory recognition for all the oppression, derision, devaluation, and misrepresentation that India was subjected to under Western colonial rule. Having written back with spectacular success, the Empire apparently wishes to act and direct back, too.

## POSTCOLONIAL LITERATURE: GLOBAL CINEMA

"I'm often asked," Mira Nair has stated, "why there is no movement comparable to Indo-Anglian writing in Indian film-making" (Nair 2003, 48). Presumably, this question is asked by anglophone diasporic Indians such as Nair herself is and as many of the eminent Indian writers in English are: Salman Rushdie, Amitav Ghosh, Rohinton Mistry, Bharati Mukherjee, Jhumpa Lahiri, to name a few. It may be relevant to recall here that by his own account, Rushdie was roused to "write back" to the metropolis through provocation caused by the misrepresentation of India not in literary works but in the visual media in the West, notably the British TV series *The Far Pavilions* and *The Jewel in the Crown* and Richard Attenborough's film *Gandhi*, which, Rushdie complained, "were only the latest in a long line of fake portraits inflicted by the West on the East" and propagated "a number of notions about history which must be quarreled with, as loudly and as embarrassingly as possible" (Rushdie 1991, 88, 101).

But the enviable example of the successful globalization of Indian writing in English also holds out some dire concomitants. The increased visibility of Indian writing in English over the past couple of decades has meant at the same time a corresponding occlusion, in Western as well as elite Indian regard, of the writing in all the other Indian languages. Indeed, Indian writing in English has come to stand for all of Indian literature, as in the *Vintage Anthology of Indian Writing*, coedited by Salman Rushdie, in which only two of the forty-two selected pieces are from Indian languages other than English, for the reason, as Rushdie ignorantly put it (in an article later reprinted as the introduction to his anthology), that Indian writing in English over the past half century "is proving to be a stronger and more important body of work than most of what has been produced in the eighteen 'recognized' languages of India, the so-called vernacular languages, during the same time" (Rushdie 1997, 50).

If a similar globalization of Indian cinema were to come about, would not that lead to a similarly distorted perception, to the effect that the few Hinglish or Indian English films shown in the new swank multiplexes in the half a dozen metropolitan cities of India and in the United Kingdom and the United States become more "significant" than all the hundreds of Hindi or other Indian-language films shown in all the rest of the vast country every year, and would not the latter then in one stroke be rendered B grade? This would be even more egregious an error than in the case of Indian literature, for whereas literature in the Indian languages is produced and consumed to a considerable extent by the educated urban middle class, the strength of Hindi cinema has lain in its ability to reach far more widely to the semiliterate and even illiterate masses, to the *rickshaw-wallahs* (rickshaw pullers), as was commonly alleged in derisive put-downs before the discourse on Hindi cinema became anglophone and respectable.

In fact, ever since the birth of Hindi cinema, some sporadic attempts have been made to win for it an international visibility and circulation. The first Indian feature film to have been made in both Hindi and English appears to have been *Karma/Nagan ki Ragini* (1933; in English, Fate/Song of the Serpent); it was produced by Himansu Rai who with Devika Rani also acted in it, and directed by J. L. Freer-Hunt at the Stoll Studios in London. Himansu Rai had earlier, in the silent era, produced or acted in four other international films, with largely German collaboration, and it was only the fact of all these films turning out to be flops that led Rai (who had been trained in London where he had met and married Devika Rani, who had herself been trained at the Royal Academy of Dramatic Arts) to set up Bombay Talkies in 1934 and begin to make films in Hindi, including the memorable *Achhut Kanya* (The Untouchable Girl, 1936; Rajadhyaksha and Willemen 1999, 183–84, 192). There is a parallel here with the early Indian novelists in English, Raja Rao and Mulk Raj Anand, who too had lived and studied abroad for some years before publishing their first novels in 1935 and 1938, respectively, from London—with the difference that neither of them subsequently turned to writing in their own languages. There was similarly a later attempt in 1965 to make a big bilingual Hindi/English film, *Guide/The Guide*, which was based on a novel by another early Indian novelist in English, R. K. Narayan; this provided a rare moment at which Hindi cinema and Indian writing in English actually met. Although a huge hit in Hindi, the film in its substantially different American version (written by Pearl S. Buck and produced and directed by Tad Danielewski) sank without a trace.

But has the breakthrough moment of Hindi/Hinglish/Indian English cinema now finally arrived, which in popular journalistic writing in India is already called by the wannabe name of "Bollywood" to make its cloning ambitions plain? More than any other single factor, it may be recalled, it was the award in 1981 of the Booker prize to Salman Rushdie that served to turn the international limelight on Indian writing in English and to gain it a global readership. Will the award of an Oscar or two in the coming years to Mira Nair, Gurinder Chandha, or Shekhar Kapoor open the floodgates of Hinglish/English cinema both in the world and within India, thus drowning out Hindi cinema, in terms of commercial reward and visibility if not in terms of wide subaltern popularity? And will the imminent trickle of Indian cinema in Hinglish and English also be promptly and peremptorily proclaimed as representing "a stronger and more important body of work" than the "vernacular" cinema in Hindi, in consonance with the new financial and cultural global order?

## NOTES

1. For a detailed discussion, see Trivedi (2006).
2. It is characteristic of the attitude to such plagiarism or appropriation on the part of the Bombay filmmakers that when Faleiro said this during an interview with Vidhu Vinod Chopra, a front-ranking director himself, Chopra responded: "Is it? I didn't know that. I haven't seen *The Miracle Worker*. I'm shocked! I'll see it and decide who did a better job. Maybe Bhonsali [the director of Black] did!" (Faleiro 2005, 27).
3. For a comparative discussion, among other things, of the lack of kisses in Sanskrit drama and their profusion in a Western play such as Shakespeare's *Romeo and Juliet*, see Trivedi (2005).

## WORKS CITED

Bachchan, Amitabh. 2002. "Amitabh Bachachan se Batcheet" [A Conversation with Amitabh Bachchan], an interview with Sumant Mishra. *Kathachitra: Cinema ka Hindi Traimasik* [Kathachitra: A Cinema Quarterly in Hindi] 1, no. 4:

Chakravarty, Sumita S. 1998. *National Identity in Indian Popular Cinema 1917–1987*. Delhi: Oxford University Press.

Chopra, Anupama. 2003a. "Ashwarya Rai: Global Goddess." *India Today*, May 12: 30–38.

———. 2003b. "Sita se Soniya tak." *Indiya Tude Bollywood Visheshanka*: 8–14.

Choudhary, Anuradha. 2004. "Aishwarya Rai: Global Glitter" (interview). *Filmfare* (October): 46–54.

Desai, Jigna. 2004. *Beyond Bollywood: The Cultural Politics of South Asian Diasporic Film*. New York: Routledge.

Faleiro, Sonia. 2005. "I Hate Indian Critics" [interview with Vidhu Vinod Chopra]. *Tehelka: The People's Paper,* June 11: 27.

Faleiro, Sonia, and Shoma Chaudhury. 2005. "Indian Cinema's Greatest PR Trick?" *Tehelka: The People's Paper,* April 32: 24–26.

Joshi, Namrata. 2004. "How Hot Is Ash, Really?" *Outlook,* October 25: 44–47.

Joshi, Sharad. 2000. "Who Isn't Afraid of Virginia Woolf?" trans. Harish Trivedi. In *Literature and Nation: Britain and India 1800–1990,* eds. Richard Allen and Harish Trivedi, 378–84. London: Routledge.

Lahr, John. 2002. "Whirlwind: How the Filmmaker Mira Nair Makes People See the World Her Way." *New Yorker,* December 9: 100–109.

Mishra, Vijay. 2002. *Bollywood Cinema: Temples of Desire*. New York: Routledge.

Nair, Mira. 2003. "Bring into Focus." *India Today*, "The Global Indian" special issue, January 13: 48.

Nandy, Ashis. 2001. *An Ambiguous Journey: The Village and Other Odd Ruins of the Self in the Indian Imagination*. Delhi: Oxford University Press.

Prasad, M. Madhava. 1998. *Ideology of the Hindi Film: A Historical Construction*. Delhi: Oxford University Press.

Rajadhyaksha, Ashish, and Paul Willemen. 1999. *Encyclopedia of Indian Cinema*. Delhi: Oxford University Press.

Rushdie, Salman. 1991. *Imaginary Homelands: Essays and Criticism 1981–1991*. London: Granta Books.

———. 1997. "Damme, This Is the Oriental Scene for You!" *New Yorker*, June 23: 50–61.

Spivak, Gayatri Chakravorty. 1994. "How to Read a 'Culturally Different' Book." In *Colonial Discourse/ Postcolonial Theory*, eds. Francis Baker, Peter Hulme, and Margaret Iversen, 126–50. Manchester: Manchester University Press.

Trivedi, Harish. 2005. "Colonizing Love: *Romeo and Juliet* in Modern Indian Disseminations." In *India's Shakespeare: Translation, Interpretation, and Performance*, eds. Poonam Trivedi and Dennis Bartholomeusz, 74–91. Newark: University of Delaware Press.

———. 2006. "All Kinds of Hindi: The Evolving Language of Hindi Cinema." In *Fingerprinting Popular Culture: The Mythic and the Iconic in Indian Cinema*, eds. Vinay Lal and Ashis Nandy, 51–86. Delhi: Oxford University Press.

Vasudevan, Ravi. 2000. "Addressing the Spectator of the 'Third World' National Cinema: The Bombay 'Social' Film of the 1940s and 1950s." In *Film and Theory: An Anthology*, eds. Robert Stam and Toby Miller. Malden, Mass.: Blackwell.

# Part III

## Imperiality and the Global

# Imperiality and the Global

Is globalization simply a continuation of Western/American imperialism in a new guise, or does it inaugurate the end of imperialism and open up possibilities for the emergence of a radically different democratic world? This question, which has been at the heart of many heated debates in both postcolonial and globalization studies, has become even more pressing in the wake of 9/11. Although postcolonial scholarship has generally tended to view globalization as a form of imperialism, there has been a marked trend, in recent years, to rethink that position and to find new forms of subaltern subjectivity and novel avenues for postcolonial agency. Globalization theory produced in the social sciences is also deeply divided over the role of the West and the rest in the emerging world (dis)order, although those divisions are not always along predictable ideological fault lines. Representing a critical intervention in this debate, the essays in this section offer a range of perspectives on how imperiality, sovereignty, law, ethics, technoscience, capital, and resistance operate in contemporary globality.

In "Discourses of Globalization: A Transnational Capitalist Class Analysis," Leslie Sklair examines how capitalist discourses of globalization, competitiveness, and sustainable development are promoted everywhere to conceal the severity of the two central crisis of capitalist globalization: the class polarization crisis and the ecological crises. Sklair argues that because the transnational capitalist class and its fractions have colonized societies all over the globe by extending the scale and scope of the commodification process in ways undreamt of by classical Marxists, other noncapitalist ways of resolving these crises are urgently required.

John McMurtry's essay, "The Postmodern Voice of Empire: The Metalogic of Unaccountability," elaborates on the "unspeakable secret" that joins postmodernism, postcolonialism, and free-market capitalism across their apparent oppositions. Behind their proclamations of "free markets and democracy," "the liberation of differences," and the "cosmopolitan perspectival," McMurtry finds a terrifying ethical unaccountability casting a shadow of totalitarianism, prescribing to all peoples alike how they must live and assuming the right to make war on whatever does not comply. The ultimate irony, McMurtry suggests, is that although postmodern thinkers and schools challenge all other closed systems, they "silently acquiesce in the totalizing globalization of a monocultural given by the iron laws of capitalism."

"Striking Back against Empire: Working-Class Responses to Globalization," shifts the emphasis from the power of capital to the creativity of labor. Drawing on the autonomist Marxist tradition, Verity Burgmann identifies some experimental models or ways in which labor is acting as a "dynamic subject" in the context of corporate globalization, presenting itself in ways distinctively novel as a problematic other for capital's globalization project and thereby recomposing itself. These new forms of resistance, Burgmann believes, point to an alternative way of understanding globalization and its working-class oppositions.

In "Localizing Global Technoscience," Geoffrey C. Bowker turns the spotlight on the role of science and technology in globalization. For all its universal aspirations, global technoscience, Bowker points out, is ineluctably the outcome of a very particular (Western) historical tradition. How then can we prevent the global information infrastructure from being just a covert "proselytizer for the very local knowledge of 'our' globalizing ethnos," and open it to other ways of knowing? The key to developing democratic technoscientific policy in the context of the new knowledge economy, Bowker suggests, requires deep understanding of the nature of information infrastructures, strict monitoring of standards and classification systems being layered into models and simulations, as well as radical redesigning of institutions so they can take advantage of new collaborative and information-sharing possibilities.

"Law, Nation, and (Imagined) International Communities" examines the role of law in mediating and legitimating the relationship between community and nation/nation-state. Focusing on three specific cases—U.S. unilateral action in relation to the war in Iraq; responses to the crisis of legitimacy of the World Trade Organization; and changes in the discourse of development emanating from the World Bank—Ruth Buchanan and Sundhya Pahuja unpack the way in which the "international community" has increasingly become the rhetorical vehicle by which legitimacy is sought for the decisions of international institutions. Their discussion reveals how the concept of "international community" functions to reinforce the modern, unequal system of nation-states—a situation that stands in sharp contrast to the promise of inclusion that the idea of international community would seem to invoke.

"How do we speak about globalization after 9/11?" asks Ileana Rodríguez in "Globalization as Neo-, Postcolonialism: Politics of Resentment and Governance of the World's Res Publica," the final essay of the section. Rodríguez identifies two complementary approaches to globalization that she sees as constitutive of the res publica of the world at large: the approach of intellectuals hired by "development" agencies and NGOs who address globalization in terms of politicoeconomic policies such as fiscal responsibility and its effects on administration, governability, and democracy; the approach of academics in metropolitan nations who analyze globalization in terms of commodity circuits and their effects on human consciousness, giving rise to theories of postmodernism and postcolonialism with their emphasis on multiculturalism, neo- and post- ethnicity, racism, and feminism. Against the backdrop of these approaches, Rodríguez examines chronic poverty and criminality, by-products of globalization that give rise to a global politics of resentment expressed in terror, terrorizing, and terrorism.

We conclude with an interview with Arjun Appadurai and a discussion of the globalizing of the imagination and its relationship to democracy.

# 14

# DISCOURSES OF GLOBALIZATION: A TRANSNATIONAL CAPITALIST CLASS ANALYSIS

*Leslie Sklair*

Remarkably for a subdiscipline in the social sciences, theory and research on globalization appears to have reached a mature phase, in terms of volume of publications if not their quality, in a relatively short period of time. Most attempts to survey the field, despite their differences, agree that globalization represents a serious challenge to the state-centrist assumptions of most previous social science.[1] The apparently "natural" quality of societies bounded by their nation-states, plus the difficulty of generating and working with data that cross national boundaries, plus the lack of specificity in most theories of the global, all conspire to shore up the crumbling defenses of state-centrist social theory against the onslaught of globalization in its several versions. Thus, just as the idea of globalization is becoming firmly established, the skeptics are announcing the limits and, in some extreme cases, the myth of globalization. Globalization, in the words of these scholars and populists alike, is nothing but "globaloney."

I have a good deal of sympathy with the skeptics. What I label global system theory, paradoxically, is an attempt to limit drastically the theoretical scope of the concept of globalization and its concrete application in the sphere of empirical research. Globalization is, nevertheless, in my view, a world-historic phenomenon and one that must be confronted in theory and research if we are to have any grasp of the contemporary world. This chapter aims to outline global system theory and to illustrate its central themes through an examination of how the transnational capitalist class has colonized societies all over the world.

Although many critics argue that globalization is simply imperialism in another form,[2] this is to deny that there is anything significantly new about capitalist globalization. The argument of this chapter is that there are, indeed, at least three respects in which capitalist globalization differs significantly from previous phases of capitalism. First, technological and organizational changes in transnational corporations (TNCs) have facilitated the globalization of capital and the production of goods and services on a historically unprecedented scale. Whereas capitalism has always been an international system of production and exchange to some extent, quantitative changes that took place in the second half of the twentieth century have created qualitative transformations in capitalism as a global system.[3] Second, the rise of new transnational forms of organization of the capitalist class has transformed the ways in which capitalism organizes itself politically in the global arena. Third, the electronic revolution and accompanying technological and regulatory transformations in the global scope of TNCs that own and control the mass media, notably the television industry, the transnational advertising agencies, and increasingly the internet, have made possible the emergence of a global culture-ideology of consumerism, based on the promotion of global-brand consumer goods and services.

It is important at the outset to distinguish between three distinct but often confused conceptions of globalization. The first is the *international* or *state-centrist* conception of globalization, where internationalization and globalization are used interchangeably. This usage signals the fact that the basic units of analysis are still nation-states and the pre-existing, even if changing, system of nation-states. This is the position of most of those who are in globalization denial. The second is the *transnational* conception of globalization, where the basic units of analysis are transnational practices, forces, and institutions. In this conception, states (or, more accurately, state agents and agencies) are just one among several factors to be taken into account and, in some theories of globalization, no longer the most important. The third is the *globalist* conception of globalization, in which the state is actually said to be in the process of disappearing.[4] It is obviously important that all those who write about globalization are clear about the sense in which they use the term, but not all are, with resultant confusions. In order to make my own position clear, I should note that I use the terms *transnational* and *globalizing* interchangeably, in order to signal that the state, or rather some state actors and agencies, do have a part to play in the globalization process, however diminished relative to their previous roles. This distinction between globalizing state agencies and actors on the one hand and localizing state agencies and actors on the other hand highlights the distinction between my own "globalizing" approach that takes account of struggles over globalization and the "globalist" approach that assumes that the triumph of capitalist globalization is complete and irreversible.

The concept of globalization propounded here rejects both state-centrism (realism) and globalism (the end of the state). The transnational conception of globalization postulates the existence of a global system. Its basic units of analysis are transnational practices (TNP), practices that cross state boundaries but do not originate with state agencies or actors. Analytically, TNPs operate in three spheres, the economic, the political, and the cultural-ideological. The whole is the global system. Although the global system is not synonymous with global capitalism, what the theory sets out to demonstrate is that the dominant forces of global capitalism are the dominant forces in the contemporary global system. The building blocks of the theory are the transnational corporation, the characteristic institutional form of economic transnational practices; the transnational capitalist class in the political sphere; and in the culture-ideology sphere, the culture-ideology of consumerism. The literatures on TNCs and consumerism are enormous.[5] Here, the focus is on the transnational capitalist class and how it has constructed a discourse of globalization to capture the idea of globalization to further its own interests.

The question, "Is globalization a 'good thing' or a 'bad thing'?" confuses the issue. The relative success of what I have termed the transnational capitalist class in monopolizing the discourse of globalization needs to be analyzed in order to bring clarity to the debate. Clearly, where capitalist globalization is identified with globalization as such (and this is, more often than not, exactly what happens most of the time), it is easy to portray the critics of globalization as narrow-minded, parochial, and even as Luddites. As I attempt to demonstrate in the following sections on competitiveness and sustainable development, by redefining the central terms of the discourse (globalization, competitiveness, sustainable development), the transnational capitalist class has made it much more difficult for noncapitalist discourses of globalization, for example discourses focused on the globalization of human rights of various kinds, to thrive.

## Transnational Capitalist Class (TCC)

The transnational capitalist class can be analytically divided into four main fractions (whose members can and do overlap).

1. Owners and controllers of TNCs and their local affiliates (corporate fraction)
2. Globalizing bureaucrats and politicians (state fraction)
3. Globalizing professionals (technical fraction)
4. Merchants, media, and marketers (consumerist fraction)[6]

To some extent the exact disposition of these four fractions and the people and institutions from which they derive their power in the system can differ over time and locality. To study globalization and the state, for example, it makes most sense to couple globalizing bureaucrats and politicians, whereas for other issues other alliances may be more appropriate. It is also important to note, of course, that the TCC and each of its fractions are not always entirely united on every issue. Nevertheless, together, leading personnel in these groups constitute a global power elite, dominant class, or inner circle in the sense that these terms have been used to characterize the dominant class structures of specific countries (Domhoff 1967; Useem 1984; Scott 1996). The transnational capitalist class is opposed not only by anticapitalists who reject capitalism as a way of life and/or an economic system but also by capitalists who reject globalization. However, those who entirely reject globalization and espouse extreme nationalist ideologies are comparatively rare, and although there are anticonsumerist elements in most societies, there are few cases of a serious anticonsumerist party winning political power anywhere in the world.

The TCC is transnational (or globalizing) in the following respects:

(a) The economic interests of its members are increasingly globally linked rather than exclusively local and national in origin. As rentiers, their property and shares are becoming more globalized through the unprecedented mobility of capital that new technologies and new global political economy have created.[7] As executives, their corporations are globalizing in terms of four criteria: foreign investment, world best practice and benchmarking, corporate citizenship, and global vision. As ideologues, their intellectual products serve the interests of globalizing rather than localizing capital, expressed in free market neoliberal ideologies and the culture-ideology of consumerism. This follows directly from the shareholder-driven growth imperative that lies behind the globalization of the world economy and the increasing difficulty of enhancing shareholder value in purely domestic firms. Although for many practical purposes the world is still organized in terms of discrete national economies, the TCC increasingly conceptualizes its interests in terms of markets, which may or may not coincide with a specific nation-state, and the global market, which clearly does not.

(b) The TCC seeks to exert economic control in the workplace, political control in domestic, international, and global politics, and culture-ideology control in everyday life through specific forms of global competitive and consumerist rhetoric and practice. The focus of workplace control is the threat that jobs will be lost and, in the extreme, the economy will collapse unless workers are prepared to work longer and for less in order to meet foreign competition. A term first introduced around 1900 to describe how the capitalist class controls labor—the race to the bottom—has been rehabilitated by radical critics to characterize the effects of economic globalization.[8] This is reflected in local electoral politics in most countries, where the major parties have few substantial strategic (even if many tactical) differences, and in the sphere of culture-ideology, where consumerism is rarely challenged within realistic politics.

(c) Members of the TCC have outward-oriented global rather than inward-oriented local perspectives on most economic, political, and culture-ideology issues. The growing TNC and international institutional emphasis on free trade and the shift from import substitution to export promotion strategies in most developing countries since the 1980s have been driven by members of the TCC working through government agencies, political parties, elite opinion organizations, and the media. Some credit for this apparent transformation in the way in which big business works around the world is attached to the tremendous growth in business education with a global focus, notably international MBAs, since the 1960s, particularly in the United States and Europe, but increasingly all over the world.

(d) Members of the TCC tend to share similar lifestyles, particularly patterns of higher education, and consumption of luxury goods and services. Integral to this process are exclusive clubs and restaurants, ultraexpensive resorts in all continents, private as opposed to mass forms of travel and entertainment and, ominously, increasing residential segregation of the very rich secured in gated communities by armed guards and electronic surveillance, from Los Angeles to Moscow, from Mexico City to Beijing, from Istanbul to Mumbai.

(e) Finally, members of the TCC seek to project images of themselves as citizens of the world as well as of their places and/or countries of birth. Leading exemplars of this phenomenon include the legendary Akio Morita, born in Japan, the founder of Sony and widely credited with having introduced global vision into Japan; and Rupert Murdoch, born in Australia, who took U.S. nationality to pursue his global media interests.

## NATIONAL COMPETITIVENESS AS A DISCOURSE OF CAPITALIST GLOBALIZATION

One need not indulge in the fantasy of conspiracy theory to understand why politicians and professionals have been so engrossed with contentious ideas of the national interest and national competitiveness. Krugman's devastating critique, "Competitiveness: A Dangerous Obsession" (Paul Krugman 1996), explains the latter (though not necessarily the former) with admirable clarity. The argument, briefly, is that only corporations and similar institutions can compete with one another and that the idea that nations can compete with one another is a "dangerous obsession" that interferes with the economic efficiency of business. Although Krugman's assumptions about the impossibility of industrial strategies can be challenged, the logic of his case on the incoherence of the idea of national competitiveness appears more convincing. This is central to the way in which globalizing politicians, bureaucrats, and professionals in the service of the transnational capitalist class relate to the state.

A good illustration of these processes at work is provided by the political trajectories of five individuals who fit well into my category of globalizing politicians, what Jorge Dominguez terms "technopols." These five technopols are F. H. Cardoso (president of Brazil), A. Foxley in Chile, D. Cavallo in Argentina (relative successes), P. Aspe in Mexico, and Evelyn Matthei in Chile. They all take seriously ideas that are cosmopolitan and meet normal international professional standards, and they succeed by selling sound economic policy in their own countries. Technopols are technocrats with added characteristics: they are political leaders, they go beyond narrow specialisms, and they are active in the politics of remaking damaged social and political systems. Democratic technopols choose freer markets over state intervention because it is what their professional training has taught them to do. Technopol support for free markets also makes them more liable to favor democracy, but this is the democracy of pluralist polyarchy and not any wider conception of representative democracy. In a statement redolent with meaning for those who would dare to oppose global capitalism, Dominguez argues: "Only democratic political systems embody the compromises and commitments that may freely bind government and opposition to the same framework of a market economy" (Dominguez 1997, 3).

The careers of these five notables illustrate how technopols in Latin America and, I would argue, globalizing politicians all around the world, are made in five settings: elite schools, religious and secular faiths, policy-oriented teams, the world stage, and specific national contexts. The Latin American five all studied either directly in the United States or were inspired by those who had (notably in the economics and political science departments at Chicago, MIT, and Harvard). They made their moves when statist democrats (Alfonsin in Argentina, Sarney in Brazil, Allende in Chile, for example) failed and when economic crisis facilitated acceptance of some version of the neoliberal consensus. Technopols, thus, incorporate two transnational pools of ideas—one favoring free markets, the other democracy. It is also important to note that technopols are not extreme neoliberals out to kill off the state, but politicians who want to recraft the state from "fat to fit," to encourage growth with a measure of equity. Above all, technopols understand that corporations and those who own and control them expect policy continuity to safeguard their investments. Thus, technopols need to develop a political and, increasingly, a globalizing agenda to establish a cosmopolitan vision to lock in their countries to free markets, international trade agreements, and globalization and to create political openings to bring all important social groups on side for "national development in a competitive international marketplace."

The significance of these examples, and they could be reinforced by many others from all over the world (Sklair 2002), is that they challenge the popular misconception that globalization is a Western imperialist plot. Although there is no doubt that corporations domiciled in Western countries still largely dominate the global economy, capitalist globalization has transformed the meaning of this fact. Crude dependency ideas of American corporations exploiting Latin America as instruments of the U.S. state or British corporations exploiting Africa as instruments of the British state have given way to more nuanced theories of globalizing alliance capitalism and global shift to accommodate new technologies of production, financing, and marketing (Dunning 1998; Dicken 1998; Sklair 2002, chapter 4).

Major corporations indulge these views for obvious reasons. Many major corporations interpret globalization in terms of being global locally. Corporations cope with the responsibilities of being local citizens globally by mobilizing national competitiveness on behalf of their mythical national interest in whatever part of the world the corporation happens to be doing business. The role of the globalizing politician is to ensure that all businesses, particularly the "foreign" corporations who have traditionally felt themselves discriminated against (sometimes true, often the opposite of the truth), receive at least equal treatment and, where possible, privileges. These privileges, in the form of development grants, fiscal holidays, training subsidies, and other "sweeteners," are routinely justified by the argument that attracting foreign investment will enhance the national interest. This can happen directly, with the addition of world-class manufacturing facilities, and/or indirectly, with the introduction of new ideas, methods, and incentives for local supplier industries. The ability of corporations seeking such investment opportunities to show that they are world class and thus could enhance the industrial environment they seek to enter is a political requirement for these privileges. Without this promise of increases in national prosperity, a corollary of global competitiveness, subsidies for "foreign" firms would be much more difficult to sell to local populations who might see better uses for their taxes.

Through the discourse of national competitiveness, the transnational capitalist class facilitates the insertion of the nation-state into the global capitalist system. The TCC achieves this through creating alliances of globalizing politicians, globalizing professionals, and the corporate sector. Globalizing politicians create the political conditions for diverting state support of various types (financial, fiscal, resources, infrastructure, ideological) towards the major corporations operating within state borders under the slogan of "national competitiveness." Parliamentary democracies based on geographical constituencies encourage this, resulting in "pork-barrel politics" in the United States and its equivalents elsewhere. Globalizing politicians, therefore, need global benchmarks in a generic sense to demonstrate that they are internationally competitive. Their "national" corporations and, by extension, their "nation," must seek out world best practice in all aspects of business. Global capitalism succeeds by turning most spheres of social life into businesses, by making social institutions—such as schools, universities, prisons, hospitals, welfare systems—more businesslike. Various forms of benchmarking are used in most large institutions to measure performance against actual competitors or an ultimate target, zero defects, for example.

Although globalizing politicians are responsible for creating the conditions under which "world best practice" (WBP) becomes the norm for evaluating the effectiveness of any social institution, they rarely become involved in its techniques. This is the responsibility of the globalizing professionals. The role of globalizing professionals is both technical and ideological. Their technical role is to create and operate benchmarking systems of various types; their ideological role is to sell these systems as the best way to measure competitiveness at all levels and, by implication, to sell competitiveness as the key to business (and national) success. It is, paradoxically, the way that national economic competitiveness has been raised to the pinnacle of public life that explains the empirical link between WBP, benchmarking, and globalization.

WBP is bound to be a globalizing practice in the global capitalist system and, thus, part of the discourse of capitalist globalization. It is quite conceivable that benchmarking could be restricted to small, localized communities of actors and institutions interested solely in providing a local service in terms of agreed criteria of efficiency. In a global economy, however, there are relentless pressures on small local businesses to become more global, either through predatory growth or, more typically, by allying themselves with major globalizing corporations. Therefore, to become world class it is not necessary to be big, but it is necessary to compare yourself with what the big players in your business sector do and to do what you do always better (Kanter 1996). Benchmarking is the measure through which all social institutions, including the state, can discover whether they are world class.

Benchmarking is normally defined as a system of continuous improvements derived from systematic comparisons with world best practice. New York University professor and soon-to-be management guru William Edwards Deming introduced the idea of continuous improvement shortly after the end of the Second World War. This became the driving force behind the total quality management (TQM) movement, which has had profound though uneven effects on big business all over the world. Japanese corporations working with state agencies first adopted these ideas, seeing in them the best way to rebuild their war-shattered economy. The Deming Prize for the best quality circles was established in Japan in 1951. By the 1990s the number of quality circles exceeded 100,000 with about 10 million members throughout Japan.

The Malcolm Baldrige National Quality Award was established in the United States in 1987, then the European Quality Award was introduced in 1991, followed by a veritable flood of quality initiatives covering almost all sectors of industry all over the world. These gave public recognition throughout business and beyond to the TQM movement that had swept through boardrooms, office complexes, and shop floors whenever an enterprise was faced with competition, particularly from "foreign" companies, from the mid-1980s. An important aspect of these awards and quality standards and the movements they were part of was the centrality of the role of leadership, particularly the leadership of the most senior executives, in the quest for continuous improvement. And what the leaders of the major corporations were saying, almost unanimously, was that business success lay in putting the customer first and that customer satisfaction depended on quality.

TQM, WBP, and benchmarking were given added impetus by the increase in global competition as protectionist walls have been breached all over the world and as rapidly growing new companies, particularly in the high-tech sector, have threatened the market dominance of their older and, perhaps, less-innovative rivals. WBP and benchmarking are logical strategies for globalizing corporations because when competition can, in principle, come from anywhere in the world, it is necessary for companies who wish to hold on to their market share, let alone increase it, to measure their performances against the very best in the world. "The very best," of course, is a highly contentious idea. It can mean "best returns on capital invested" or "best stock market price increase" or "best environmental performance" or "best employer" or any number of other things. An additional and crucial factor is that most major corporations are in industries in which most of their products are quite similar to (sometimes virtually identical with) those of their competitors. Thus, it is vital to ensure that any competitive advantage that a product has, however small, is matched by competitive advantages in bringing it to market. The TQM movement ensured that all aspects of company performance, from manufacturing widgets to answering telephones, from delivering and servicing the product to monitoring energy use in factories and offices, were liable to be benchmarked. The numerous criteria included for both the Deming Prize in Japan and the Baldrige National Quality Award in the United States were significant motivators in operationalizing the idea of total quality for customer-driven business.

The pioneers in global benchmarking were technology-intensive companies whose very survival depended on continuous innovation, such as Motorola and Xerox. Also influential in the theory and practice of benchmarking were global management consultants, notably Anderson Consulting and McKinsey. There are literally hundreds of different quality measures, some firm specific, others product or industry specific, some specifically aspiring to zero defects. Some cover environmental standards, others citizenship standards. Some are regional in scope (the United States, United Kingdom, European Union, and Japan, for example, all have various types of quality standards) and some are virtually global (for example, the International Standards Organization ISO series).

The links between state agencies and corporations in the creation of benchmarking and best practice systems can be briefly illustrated with the cases of Australia, Brazil, and the United States. In Australia and Brazil, the globalizing fractions of the state and business were united in their belief that the protectionism of the past could no longer be maintained if they were to enter the global economy. The two governments embarked on two different paths to implement world best practice but with the same end in view, to make their companies internationally competitive. In Australia, best practice was seen largely as a problem of changing labor practices, and a Best Practice Demonstration Program was introduced in 1991 by the Department of Industrial Relations, working with the Australian Manufacturing Council. DuPont, ICI, and BHP in Australia are cited as enthusiastic supporters of the program. The official magazine of the best practice program was entitled *Benchmark*, and its pages in the 1990s exemplified the alliance between globalizing politicians, bureaucrats, professionals, and big and small business, all striving for the quality improvements that would enhance national competitiveness.

In Brazil, the government agency responsible for quality standards was the National Institute for Standardization, Metrology, and Industrial Quality (Inmetro). The president of Inmetro declared to an international meeting in Holland in 1998 that: "The efforts made by Brazilian firms to improve the quality of their goods is linked to the beginning of competition in Brazil's economy. Up to 1990, when the economy was closed to imports, our companies did not bother about quality. After the opening of the economy in 1992, the need grew to show international standards of quality."[9] Inmetro worked closely with the Brazilian Program for Quality and Productivity and the Brazilian Foreign Trade Association, for enhanced quality in Brazil was necessary not only to compete against imports but, more importantly, to increase the potential for companies in Brazil to export.

In the United States, although quality standards and benchmarking have come largely from private industry initiatives, the Baldrige National Quality Award, perhaps the most prestigious mark of quality in the United States, was established in 1987 as a joint venture between government and industry. Although modeled on the Japanese Deming Prize, the Baldrige process is transparent and provides an audit framework, which companies could use for self-assessment. Robert Cole has gone so far as to predict the death of the quality movement as quality improvement becomes part of normal management activity (Cole 1999).

This is not the case outside the United States and a few major economies, however. Although over 70 countries were reported as having agencies for accreditation and inspection of technical standards laboratories, it is commonly accepted that standards vary from place to place. An International Accreditation Forum (IAF) was established precisely to ensure comparability of standards and by 1998 had eighteen member countries, with more applications, including Inmetro, in the pipeline. Accreditation by IAF meant recognition for technical standards in U.S., Canadian, Chinese, Japanese, and EU markets and a reasonable guarantee that the WTO technical rules, often seen as a form of disguised protectionism, were less likely to be used to block imports. What the three cases of Australia, Brazil, and the United States suggest is that globalizing state agents and professionals have joined forces with corporations to promote best practice in the service of national competitiveness. In this way the transnational capitalist class uses the discourse of national and international competitiveness to impose more intensive discipline on the workforce and in some cases to impose unnecessarily high standards that drive smaller competitors out of the market. In addition, the imposition of world best practice and benchmarking beyond the narrow confines of manufacturing industries is another important step in the commodification of everything that is closely connected with the culture-ideology of consumerism.

## THE CORPORATE CAPTURE OF SUSTAINABLE DEVELOPMENT

Similar processes can be observed in the corporate response to the environmental challenge. For decades, theorists of a singular ecological crisis have argued over the future prospects for life on the planet with those who conceive of the issue in terms of multiple, but manageable, environmental problems. Major corporations always tried to keep these ideas apart, but disasters such as the Torrey Canyon (1967) and Santa Barbara (1969) oil spills, toxic contamination that provoked hundreds of antipollution suits in Japan in the 1970s, Bhopal in 1984, and Exxon Valdez in 1989 exacerbated the problems. The argument climaxed in the late 1980s and early 1990s under the pressures of capitalist globalization just as the discourse of sustainable development was emerging as the common language for those who were thinking about almost any environmental issue (McManus 1996, 48–73; Sklair 2002, chapter 7). Sustainable development was seen as a prize that everyone involved in these arguments wanted to win. The winner, of course, gets to redefine the concept.

We can trace the first indication that some members of the corporate elite were beginning to take the ecological crisis seriously to the publication of *The Limits to Growth* (1972), sponsored by the Club of Rome.[10] This gave a modicum of business respectability to the profoundly anticapitalist thesis that growth had limits; but, in general, those who spoke for global capitalism were able to shrug off the deeper lessons of the "limits to growth" school as alarmist and naive. However, the problem would not go away and the more-forward-thinking members of the global business community knew that they were going to have to deal with it, eventually. By the late 1980s it became clear that the rhetoric of sustainable development provided a convenient solution, and it was eagerly taken up by globalizing corporations as they tried to cope with the emerging force of the arguments around the singular ecological crisis.

The corporate response in the United States and Europe to a spate of environmental catastrophes, notably Bhopal, evolved gradually throughout the 1980s. The chemical industry was clearly under pressure to be seen to be taking decisive action. An initiative of the Chemical Manufacturers Association (CMA) in 1988 in the United States resulted in the Responsible Care Program. This was adopted by more than 170 members of the CMA, including Union Carbide, and announced to the investing public and concerned citizens in full-page advertisements in the *New York Times* and the *Wall Street Journal* on April 11, 1990. The British Chemical Industries Association had adopted its Responsible Care Programme in 1989.

Not only industries but international organizations of various types took it upon themselves to "do something" about the environment. The European community introduced a community-wide environmental auditing scheme in 1993. The World Bank began to discuss the environmental aspects of lending in the 1970s, with controversial results. Similarly, the Environmental Committee of the OECD has been discussing the issue since the early 1980s. Why has it proved so difficult to enact effective legislation to protect the environment? One factor was clearly the phenomenon of poacher-turned-gamekeeper in the leadership of some bodies charged with environmental protection. It is clear from the evidence of the 1980s that even antiregulatory right-wing governments, such as those of Reagan and Thatcher, could no longer entirely ignore environmental violations. For example, while the Reagan administration was pulling the teeth of the Environmental Protection Agency, at the same time it permitted the establishment of a powerful Environmental Crimes Unit in the Department of Justice.

The major corporations were not, of course, standing idly by while the struggle over the environment was accelerating. Globally, big business response was orchestrated by the International Chamber of Commerce (ICC), which had been promoting an environmental agenda since the first UN environment conference in Stockholm in 1972. The ICC had members in more than one hundred countries, though it was most active in Europe. It founded its own Commission on Environment in the 1970s, and its first World Conference of Environmental Management in 1984 attracted five hundred leaders of industry, government, and environmental groups from seventy-two countries. The ICC was chosen to give the official business community input to the Bergen Ministerial Conference that led to the report of the UN World Commission on Environment and Development where the concept of sustainable development was firmly established. In the frank words of an ICC analyst of this process: "the Brundtland Report called on the co-operation of industry . . . the business community is willing to play a leading role, and to take charge" (Willums 1990, 3). And take charge of sustainable development it did.

An immediate consequence of the work of ICC was the Global Environmental Management Initiative (GEMI) of 1990, formed to implement the Business Charter for Sustainable Development. Nineteen leading U.S. transnational corporations announced their support for GEMI, including Union Carbide, desperate to rebuild its reputation after Bhopal. GEMI soon took on an institutional form in Washington D.C. The organization that eventually resulted from these efforts, the World Business Council for Sustainable Development (WBCSD), was probably the most influential of the many green business networks that were established in the 1990s. For all their differences—local, national, or global, general or industry specific, well or less well resourced—they all had one thing in common, their emphasis on self-assessment and voluntary codes where possible, but a decisive input into regulation where necessary. In this respect, the globalizing neoliberal revolution associated with the Thatcher-Reagan attempt to mold state legislation to promote rather than to restrict the corporate interest, or "free enterprise" as it was ideologically constructed, was very successful.

The roots of the distinctive global capitalist theory of sustainable development can be traced to the discussions around the Brundtland Report, *Our Common Future*, presented to the General Assembly of the United Nations in 1987. The uneasy compromise between conceptualizing the problem as a set of environmental challenges and as a much more serious singular—indeed, planetary life threatening—ecological crisis suited big business very well.

Stephan Schmidheiny, a Swiss billionaire who was to play a crucial role for big business at the Rio Earth Summit in 1992, gave an insight into corporate thinking on the issue. In a series of high-profile articles, public pronouncements, and consultations,[11] Schmidheiny argued that environmental protection had been a defensive, negative, antiprogress concept, but environmentalists and industrialists were beginning see each other's points of view and to compromise. Thus, the idea of "sustainable growth" had replaced the idea of "conservation" and industry could get on with its job. Limits to growth were not, as originally thought, limits on supplies but rather limits on the disposal of resources used and transformed in the productive process. Accepting that industry must operate within existing frameworks, it can, nevertheless, act to use these frameworks for its own advantage by taking the offensive and shaping ecological legislation.

The negative environmentalism that had forced industries to respond to specific challenges on pollution and toxic hazards gave way to more general conceptions of "sustainable growth" and "sustainable development," entirely compatible concepts in the corporate analysis. Corporate environmentalism, therefore, both as a social movement and as a discourse, co-existed easily with this moderate conception of sustainability. From this powerful conceptual base big business successfully recruited much of the global environmental movement in the 1990s to the cause of sustainable global consumerist capitalism. This achievement is an object lesson in how dominant classes incorporate potential enemies into what Gramsci called new historical blocs.

Historical blocs are fluid amalgamations of forces that coagulate into social movements to deal with specific historical conjunctures, reflecting concrete problems that have to be confronted by different social groups. In the struggle for hegemony, historical blocs form and dissolve and re-form. Big business mobilized a sustainable development historical bloc against what it saw as a threatening counterculture organized around the powerful idea of the singular ecological crisis by the deep green or ecological movement.

The sustainable development historical bloc began in earnest in the period leading up to the Earth Summit in Rio in 1992. The close relationship between Maurice Strong, the virtual CEO of the Earth Summit, and Stephan Schmidheiny is a matter of public record. The environmental arm of the ICC, the Business Council for Sustainable Development, represented big business in Rio and was successful in keeping any potential criticism of the TNCs off the official agenda (Panjabi 1997). There was, as a consequence, formidable corporate input into the formation of the UN Commission on Sustainable Development (CSD), the major institutional result of UNCED. The CSD has become a major transnational environmental organization in its own right. It evolved into the Division for Sustainable Development at the UN, and its major task was to monitor how member governments tested, developed, and used over one hundred indicators of sustainable development. The extent to which it redirects attention away from the discourse of singular ecological crisis, a discourse that challenges the very existence of global capitalism, and onto the discourse of multiple environmental challenges that corporations can cope with and global capitalism can live with will be a critical test for the success of the sustainable development historical bloc. The signs are not promising for deep ecologists. The basis on which the CSD approached its task of measuring consumption and production was as follows:

> Sustainable consumption and production are essentially two sides of the same coin. Sustainable consumption addresses the demand side, examining how the goods and services required to meet peoples' needs and improve the quality of life can be delivered in a way that reduces the burden on the Earth's carrying capacity. The emphasis of sustainable production is on the supply side, focusing on improving environmental performance in key economic sectors such as agriculture, energy, industry, tourism, and transport. (United Nations 1998)[12]

Despite some inspiring small-scale UN-CSD projects, from the ecological point of view this approach is based on two fallacies. The first is the anthropocentric approach itself, where sustainability for people and societies takes precedence over sustainability for the planet. The second fallacy is the idea that "sustainable consumption" and "sustainable production" are essentially two sides of the same coin. Radical ecologists argue that it is fallacious to assume that "meeting needs," "improving quality of life," and "improving environmental performance" are parts of the solution to the ecological crisis. They are not. They are parts of the problem, particularly in terms of distinguishing real from artificial needs and establishing universal norms for an ecologically sound quality of life. It need hardly be said that those who hold these views—radical ecologists—are a small minority, even in the environmental movement, but the capture of the discourse of sustainable development from the environmental movement by the transnational capitalist class has made it even more difficult to mount a radical critique of capitalist globalization in general, and the culture-ideology of consumerism in particular, than would otherwise have been the case.

## CONCLUSION

The combination of the discourse of sustainable development with that of national and international competitiveness provides a powerful weapon for the transnational capitalist class. Although capitalism increasingly organizes globally, resistance to global capitalism can be effective only where it can disrupt its smooth running (accumulation of private profits and claims of hegemony) locally and can find ways of globalizing these disruptions. No social movement appears even remotely likely to overthrow the three fundamental institutional supports of global capitalism that have been identified, namely the TNCs, the transnational capitalist class, and the culture-ideology of consumerism. Nevertheless, in each of these spheres social movements are active, as are transnational networks that have the potential to grow into social movements that could challenge the hegemony of global capitalism as a whole or of one or more of its essential supports. The TNCs, if we are to believe their own propaganda, are continuously beset by opposition, boycott, legal challenge, and moral outrage from disappointed or injured consumers of their products, by disruptions from their workers, and by protests from communities adversely affected by their actions. The transnational capitalist class often finds itself opposed by vocal coalitions when it tries to impose its will in the old and new ways. And what is widely referred to as the spiritual crisis of our era, from both theological and secular perspectives, has a root-and-branch critique of the culture-ideology of consumerism at its core. The problem for global capitalism is that each of its economic, political, and culture-ideology victories throws up mass movements on the local, national, and global scales to challenge its hegemony.

Opposing capitalism, from households, communities, and cities, all the way up to and beyond the level of the nation-state, has always been practically difficult in terms of resources, organization, and ideology. In most capitalist societies movements for social democracy have led to many uneasy alliances between those who are hostile to capitalism, those who struggle to alleviate its worst consequences, and those who simply want to ensure that capitalism works with more social efficiency than the so-called free market allows. This has inevitably meant that anticapitalists (principally socialists) of many kinds have seen no alternative to using capitalist practices to undermine the foundations of capitalist hegemony.

TNCs can be and have been successfully challenged. Where TNCs have been disrupted and have been forced to change their ways and to compensate those who have grievances against them, it has usually been due to local campaigns that have attracted worldwide publicity. The knowledge that worker, citizen, feminist, religious, and other concerned groups in communities all around the world are monitoring their activities clearly encourages some TNCs to act more responsibly than they otherwise might be doing. New technologies of communication also help transform local disruptions of TNC activities into global challenges to capitalist hegemony. As these challenges have become more effective, the response of the TNCs has become more systematically directed toward defusing and marginalizing the growing crises of class polarization and ecology that capitalist globalization appears to be making worse rather than resolving.

Resolving these crises requires opposition to capitalist globalization but not to globalization as such and, similarly, opposition to the capitalist version of sustainable development but not to sustainable development as such. The issue of genuine democracy is central to the practice and the prospects of social movements against capitalism, local and global. The rule of law, freedom of association and expression, freely contested elections, and transparency in public affairs, as minimum conditions and however imperfectly sustained, are as necessary in the long run for mass-market-based global consumerist capitalism as they are for any viable socialist alternatives. This applies in two ways. First, social movements against capitalism must be democratic in their own practices, even when this appears to be disadvantageous in the short term. Large majorities of people will take alternatives seriously only if they are persuaded that they are serious alternatives. Second, holding those in power and authority over the whole range of capitalist institutions (including some agencies of government) to democratic account on every issue on every single occasion does force changes that can shift the balance of social advantage from more-privileged capitalist interests to less-privileged popular interests. However small these shifts might be (for example, the establishment of a ridiculously low minimum wage, or marginally progressive antiracist or antisexist legislation, or making taxation systems slightly more fair to the poor) and however often they may be reversed and need to be won again, they are worth fighting for. Finally, the struggle over discourse is an important complement to the struggle over material resources in the quest for a peaceful transition out of global capitalism and into other forms of local and global organization that could reverse the tendencies of the capitalist global system to class polarization and ecological crisis. The capacity to reconceptualize globalization, therefore, must be reclaimed from the transnational capitalist class.

## NOTES

1. See, for example, Lechner and Boli (2003) and Sklair (2002), from which this chapter borrows.
2. This view is well represented in the contributions to Mander and Goldsmith (1996).
3. See Dunning (1998) and Dicken (1998) for critical accounts of the evidence for these claims.
4. Few writers take this extreme position, and of these, Ohmae (1995) has been the most influential. If Ohmae did not exist, then antiglobalization theorists would have had to invent him!
5. Surveyed in Sklair (2002), where global system theory is elaborated.
6. See Sklair (2000), from which the following paragraphs are adapted.
7. Despite the arguments that national governments still exert regulatory powers over capital flows and that most financial corporations are still focused mainly on their home economies (see Kapstein 1994), it is nevertheless true to say that there has been a globalization of capital in recent decades. Certainly, in my own interviews with executives in *Fortune* Global 500 financial corporations (banks and insurance companies), the constant theme was "we have to globalize because our clients are going global" (Sklair 2002, chapter 3). Harmes (1998, 92–121) gives this argument significant support.
8. See Brecher and Costello (1994). In Sklair (2000) the race to the bottom is connected with the class polarization crisis of global capitalism; that is, the simultaneous enrichment of some rapidly increasing minorities and impoverishment of other rapidly increasing and more numerous minorities all over the world.
9. "Brazilian Companies Invest in Quality," *Financial Times*, August 26, 1998.

10. See Meadows et al. (1972). A second edition published in 1992 received relatively little attention.
11. The most accessible source is Schmidheiny (1992).
12. See United Nations (1998).

## WORKS CITED

Brecher, Jeremy, and Tom Costello. 1994. *Global Village or Global Pillage*. Boston: South End Press.

Cole, Robert. 1999. *Managing Quality Fads: How American Business Learned to Play the Quality Game*. New York: Oxford University Press.

Dicken, Peter. 1998. *Global Shift: Transforming the World Economy*, 3rd ed., ed. Paul Chapman. New York: Guilford Press.

Domhoff, G. William. 1967. *Who Rules America?* Englewood Cliffs, N.J.: Prentice Hall.

Dominguez, Jorge, ed. 1997. *Technopols: Freeing Politics and Markets in Latin America in the 1990s*. University Park: University of Pennsylvania Press.

Dunning, John. 1998. *Alliance Capitalism and Global Business*. New York: Routledge.

Harmes, Andrew. 1998. "Institutional Investors and the Reproduction of Neoliberalism." *Review of International Political Economy* 5 (Spring): 92–121.

Kanter, Rosabeth Moss. 1996. *World Class: Thriving Locally in the Global Economy*. New York: Simon and Schuster.

Kapstein, Ethan. 1994. *Governing the Global Economy: International Finance and the State*. Cambridge, Mass.: Harvard University Press.

Krugman, Paul. 1996. *Pop Internationalism*. Boston: MIT Press.

Lechner, Frank J., and John Boli, eds. 2003. *Globalization: A Reader*. Oxford: Blackwell.

Mander, Jerry, and Edward Goldsmith, eds. 1996. *The Case against the Global Economy*. San Francisco: Sierra Club Books.

McManus, Phil. 1996. "Contested Terrains: Politics, Stories, and Discourses of Sustainability." *Environmental Politics* 5, no. 1: 48–73.

Meadows, D. D., et al. 1972. *The Limits to Growth*. New York: New American Library.

Ohmae, Kenichi. 1995. *The End of the Nation-State*. New York: Free Press.

Panjabi, R. K. L. 1997. *The Earth Summit at Rio: Politics, Economics, and the Environment*. Boston: Northeastern University Press.

Schmidheiny, Stephan. 1992. *Changing Course: A Global Business Perspective on Development and the Environment*. Cambridge, Mass.: MIT Press.

Scott, John. 1996. *Stratification and Power: Structures of Class, Status, and Command*. Cambridge, Mass.: Polity Press.

Sklair, Leslie. 2000. *The Transnational Capitalist Class*. Oxford: Blackwell.

———. 2002. *Globalization: Capitalism and Its Alternatives*. Oxford: Oxford University Press.

United Nations. 1998. "Workshop on Indicators for Changing Consumption and Production Patterns." New York: Division for Sustainable Development. (March 2–3).

Useem, Michael. 1984. *The Inner Circle: Large Corporations and the Rise of Business Political Activity in the U.S. and UK*. New York: Oxford University Press.

Willums, J. O. 1990. *The Greening of Enterprise: Business Leaders Speak Out*. Bergen: International Chamber of Commerce.

# 15

# The Postmodern Voice of Empire: The Metalogic of Unaccountability

## John McMurtry

### Image and Reality in the Postmodern Global Market

There is a general consensus among postmodern thinkers that our problems of oppression and silencing have followed from terrorist universals, the nation-state, and grand narratives of progress and necessity. Our release, postmodern voices imply, is to be found in an open cosmopolitan perspectivalism of particularity and indeterminate subjectivity that will not be imposed on by any foundational principle.

The true, the universal, and the obligatory are thus dead. A thousand shards and prisms of light open in the clearing of the forest where the dread monoliths of the rational universal, the patriarchal, and the Marxist are unravelling or fallen. There is a liberated lightness of being, a bursting free of all essences and grounds as traps and delusions, a liberation of euphorically elaborating voices from the snares of ultimate structure and reductive system. The Promethean imagination of the postmodern is no longer pinned to any unifying meaning.

It follows from this consensual given of the postmodern that there can be no accountability to logical structure, universal value, or truth in the realm of openness to differences and free subjectivities. No common thread or general conclusion is acceptable. Instead, a fury of subaltern voices and flourishings beyond inherited orders are set free from the trammels of history and all past prescriptions. The categories of substance, the transcendental subject, and the economic base alike are dissolved into postmodern air. In the new freedom from all identities and colonial structures of the mind, a transcontinental outburst of destructured thoughts erupts in ironic, iconoclastic, and neologistic cascades of linguistic circuitries, elaborations, and visionary escapades.

In the postmodern, as Yeats anticipated in The Second Coming, "things fall apart, the centre cannot hold." But the falling apart for Yeats was within the widening turns of the gyre of historical becoming to another epoch. This too is a grand narrative and a metaphysic of illusion for the postmodern. In its place, a "mere anarchy is loosed upon the world." More exactly for the postmodern, *meaning itself is liberated from any unifying form to confine it*. What is left in this kingdom of indeterminate plurality of voices with no ground or accountability across their differences is, at the highest reach of postmodern "responsibility," an undeconstructable "openness to the other"—so long as no nation-state law, universal program, or course of cooperative action imposes the threat of the "totalitarian" on this indeterminate individual subjectivity.[1]

The "postcolonial" and the "global" have become so intertwined in the postmodern release into dematerializing wordplays, novelties, tropes, strings of reverie, reversals, hybridic theories, insubordinate affirmations, perpetual pessimisms, and systemic indecisions that an unsuspected and unspeakable secret joins them across their apparent world divide of opposition. The postmodern market of freely circulating subjectivities and perspectives and the corporate market of freely circulating money and things are as a cultural hall of mirrors to a totalizing real that is always deferred out of sight. In each's preoccupation with self-referential circuitries of expansion, however, neither can see beyond its own decoupled codes of elaboration. It can only behold ever more expressions of itself. Yet a vast arc of *complicity of the unaccountable* spans unseen across the chasm—between, on the one hand, the multiplicitously appearing and intersubjectively unaccountable global corporate market of "a new reality" beyond the state or any public authority regulating and prescribing to it any universal of law or responsibility to the common life-ground and, on the other hand, a multiplicitously appearing and unaccountable postmodern unreality of no foundation or center or any ground whatever. Each always conforms to an underlying absolute of responsibility—an infantile repudiation of any accountability to any reference body or requirement beyond its own assertions. The global market is restless in perpetual motion of self-regulating money codes and multiplying priced objects. The postmodern is restless in perpetual motion of self-regulating cultural codes of multiplying signifiers without objects. Each acts out a strange identity of theme—*an omnivorous shared abyss posited for every agent of no responsibility to anything beyond ungrounded sequences of affirmation, negation, and denial in endless expression of its code's permissions of open-endedness. Each is united beneath words in abhorrence of any center, history, unifying principle, or ground, including the conditions of human existence, life itself.*

In the telling words of one of the editors of this volume, "the two have now become one and the same—to be global is first and foremost to be postcolonial and to be postcolonial is always already to be global." To this I add an explanans: *where* the global is no more than corporate-market public relations with no truth but that it sells to desire, and thus no limit to its falsehoods because it is free; and *where* the postcolonial is the postmodern that is one with the corporate global in denouncing as tyranny all ideas of the universal or public good, or any grand system except the actual global corporate system that rules. Through all differences of appearance and claim, each rejoices in a euphoric celebration of manufactured images and differences, and each repudiates the distinction between true and false as an authoritarian oppression. Above all, each anathematizes as impossible and overbearing any shared activatable ground of social purpose. Any unifying idea of an *alternative* system is impossible, futile, and deplored as the dead monument of the totalitarian.

The shared metalevel of meaning here cannot compute to the postmodern or corporate confinement of self-representation to the particular, the fleeting, and the self-elaborating, and so its exposure of sameness across differences cannot ever be found in anything either *says*. For each is in a priori denial of any integrating structure of problem or solution—the unravelling Thanatos of both. The way of differences only and undecidability always repels understanding of the social and the political necessarily—because both postmodern and market subjectivities presuppose obligatory ties of *the together* across private selves. But "the together" or the civil commons—all that enables universal access to life goods—can no more be seen through the lenses of the postmodern or the market metaphysic than market images and voices at any moment can find unity of truth or ground across their plurality of expressions. Yet all alike remain variations on one metatheme—the omnivorously consuming and privileged unaccountable.

In fact, beneath the paeans to the liberations of heterogeneity in globalization or "the postcolonial global," the reality is universally homogenizing and mechanistic. A single uniform pattern that postmodernism is preconsciously structured to evade, *the global corporate market as total obligatory system*, increasingly rules across all lines of nature and culture, demanding a devastation of human and environmental life organization so planetary and systematic that the question—what is *not* subjugated by its demands?—has become a challenge to answer in the living world. But because postmodern method denies us any access to any reality beyond signifiers, it rules out seeing what is in fact there. In both kingdoms of the unaccountable, signification can have no signified that is not endlessly reconstructed in ungovernable monetary or linguistic circuitries of proliferation. At the same time, the denied reality that remains there despite its dissolution into market and postmodern deferrals and signs with no referents has been so saturated with slogans of the new, the different, the plurally democratic, and the emancipated that we have come to live in an opiated dwelling place of only images, creative ads, and proclamations with no life-ground connection at all. Yet circuitously concealed in its own multiplying representations is always the unspeakable global corporate system that rules without ever being admitted or permitted opposition.[2]

We may recognize the debauchery of a global market carnival of endlessly diverse commodities that are ubiquitously hawked for sale across all the media and signs of global discourses, while people on the ground starve by the thousands every hour and the global ecosystem itself unfastens from its cycles. Yet how can a debauchery of the self-fascinated well-off, with no bound to their new desires and perspectives, be made accountable to the world that is stripped to serve the indeterminate freedom of their consumer subjectivities? How is this postmodern diversity of voices any more than the theoretical shadow world of the image and commodity carnival of the global market bazaar in ceaselessly stylized pluralities delinked from any common life base or social purpose? How can we tell the postmodern and the corporate market apart as both dissolve into ever more expressions and indulgences of the uselessly novel and superfluous? How, to be more direct, do the postmodern cascades of self-referential signs and sequences differ from the decoupled order of multiple varieties of money sequences, each expressing their different consumer-and-investor paths of free choice answerable only to their own contingent desires and code elaborations? Let them eat, if not cake, more proclamations of freedom and difference.

In both styles of disconnection from the necessities and interconnections of the life-ground—which is all the conditions required to take our next breath—there is a shadow of narcissist hysteria. The liberties of the diverse and the contested are pervasively asserted by both in torrents of words but with no foundation or possibility of united course of action. Meantime, in the life reality that is avoided by prior methodological commitment to existing representations only, an actually uniform global empire homogenizes all in its path, but is compulsively blocked out of view by escapist routes of proliferating signs with no real signified. As the global corporate market deconstructs all foundations on the level of the real by free flows of capital and commodities washing over all boundaries released from former state universals of life-protections and common grounds of existence, the transnational postmodern performs these same operations of life-base decoupling on the level of theory—with self-determining linguistic circuits, like money sequences on the ground, propelled only by self-referential codes and expressions of limitless reproduction and growth.

The global postcolonial is in these ways a growing chaos set free from any life commitment or comprehension, and with no center of responsibility of the market or the postmodern to anything beyond its own liberties and codes of articulation—rather like a carcinogenic sequencing metastasizing with no committed function to the life-host in its autonomous proliferations. The revel of deregulation, privatization, and multiplying signifiers and signs in place of life-regulating responses and interconnections is the postmodern and market bacchanalia all at once—the system and its illusory representations at once in disconnection from any life-serving function. As one culture and ecosystem after another is deconstructed of its actual foundations, each order of delinked perspective and open borders with no regulating ground are, in an ultimate irony of the real, transfigured by their own self-representations into heroic salvations of the poor and the life oppressed—both the postmodern and the market global proclaiming through their differences ever-new liberties of voice. In the reality that is off-limits to discuss, bread for the hungry, public voice, and life security beyond individual handouts or hospitalities are denounced as "totalitarian."

In the free global, money alone talks, but the meaning is unspeakable to its tongues. Market and postmodern thought systems so exactly presume the same emancipation of the individual subject from the state, the universal, and the socially obligatory that one might argue that the liberal and postmodern are merely diverse elaborations of one supreme but unnameable ruling code. In both, the self is a greedy emptiness of desire and subjectivity—the one in ceaseless tracking of commodity and profit pluralities in the open market, and the other in ceaseless tracking of its manifolds of signs and open subjectivities. For each, the facts of life despoliation and their regulating causal structure are decoupled as "freedom from any foundation." A question thus arises that may be too poignant to ask of ourselves in this time. Where in the postcolonial-cum-global literature of celebrating difference and freedom and the contingent particular over the foundational and the essential? Has any postmodern voice noticed what is actually happening to the *lives of peoples* in the world, or the world itself, and exposed in theoretical rather than ideological voice any actually regulating thought system that might explain their coming apart at the seams? Who dares, above all, to speak that the "global free market" itself expresses a closed and totalitarian Logos of itself? It seems that only *its* regulating system of silencing and oppression is a priori off limits to interrogate. Rather than any discourse on its universal command assumptions and prescriptions, postmodern insurgency against the universal, necessary and the obligatory talks only about its fallen enemies instead—patriarchy, dialectical materialism, the nation-state, and the rest of received pantheon of the acceptably oppressive. The postmodern defers, on the other hand, to the supreme rule of the global corporate system that is at the same time *legitimated by postmodern excoriations of all conceptions of alternative orders to it*. The free global, like Yahweh, is the unspeakable before which no Other may stand or be represented. Only its signs and signifiers, and traces of its fallen enemies, are the given to decode—revealing the evidences, counterpunctilia, and coded manifestations as the unspeakable One's infinite pluralities of possibility.

Postmodernism does not, thus, confront the actual terrorism of the universal, the necessary, and the unconditionally prescribed but, rather, imitates its prestidigitations of image, diversions from the base, and emancipatory slogans of a thousand faces of desires and releases. Subliminal methods, catchphrases, repetitive incantations, cynicism of all truth, mind-boggling tropes, sound-bite captures of attention, and submergence in the transient join postmodern and market voices in a silent ideological partnership across cultural realms. Together their disconnection from ground and substance produces a licentious field of popular and intellectual entertainment by a method of rootless spectacles and diversions. The ravenous global machine—everywhere transforming the real world into commodities, wastes, and distracting images—cannot be conceived by either as a shared problem or condition because no common ground exists beneath proliferations of self-referential expressions.

At bottom, the postmodern principle of difference is the theoretical correlative of divide-and-rule. An ever-deferring blind eye to global ecogenocide and an up-market mordant pessimism about all social alternatives keep the doors of postmodern and market perception firmly shut against any movement of the soul towards responsive connection to the threatened life conditions of all. In corresponding hothouses of ideation without ground, both market and postmodern ideologies remain silent about any sociopolitical conception beyond the subjectivities of atomic selves and desires. There can be no imaginative bonding or embodied solidarity in such a world because the pluralizing privatization of perspective allows no common reality or shared way out.

The planetary life-ground itself—the capabilities of ecosystems and societies to reproduce to enable the *actual* diversity of life's free expressions—is thus dissolved into word plays of the privileged imaginary disconnected from the mutual foundations upon which all that is expressed depends. Disjunction from the real, the true, and the ground is boasted with no determinate trace left—unaccountable, like money-capital sequencing, to anything but decoupled circuitries of self-propelling elaborations, nightmares, and messianism with no social meaning.

## INTERROGATING THE POSTMODERN INTERROGATION

Postmodern thought is first and foremost the denial of all *essences*—which former philosophy from Plato through Thomism to the rationalist idealists of modernity asserted over three millennia as the binding frame of truth and substance. Now "antiessentialism" is the certitude of the postmodern. No essence can be uttered without mockery. But in the spirit of exposing the denial as silent affirmation, let us lay bare to view what the denial of essence entails.

Is not breath and respiration the essence of all life—*that without which it cannot be what it is*? Is not this life-breath of the animate and this respiration of the rooted not that which distinguishes each from all that is inanimate and dead in all cases? Why, then, assume that essence is delusion, and proclaim antiessentialism as thought's liberation from it? In denying any such essence, does it not follow that we deny breath as the essence of life? But do not even postmodern words depend on breath to say and write what they do? Is not postmodernity's own ground of possibility therefore denied? When we deconstruct the postmodern, does not its proclaimed freedom from all essences and foundation reveal a systematic disconnection from the conditions of existence itself?

The postmodern denies even the ground of a human subject. For only subjectivity and codes of meaning exist. Yet how can we make sense of a philosophy that repudiates the primary assumption of its own affirmations—here, the very subject that must be *presupposed* for the freedom to express itself as different to exist. Postmodernism's vocation of contesting and exposing all closed systems of prescription that deny liberty of difference and voice must itself always presuppose this human subject, or there is no one there to be silenced or oppressed. Freedom and diversity of voice can be coherently affirmed against oppression and sameness only if there *is* a life subject who has its own voice.[3]

What are we to make of these incoherences of assertion? But it is not only internal confusion that is at work. For postmodernity's denial of the human subject is at the same time *enforced on the ground* by the global corporate system. Peoples everywhere are released from any human universals of life-security standards and nation-state protection as working and citizen subjects. Does not, then, the denial of and freedom from "the economic," "the state," and "foundations" become an ideological complicity with the actually ruling structure of oppression of peoples and their environments, who are left with no public order to protect their lives from privatized and deregulated corporate exploitation? Bosses too see no human subjects nor life-ground there, nor any moral obligation to a mere factor of production or a modern phantom. Do the cosmopolitan postmodern and the transnational corporate covertly agree in their erasure of the human subject as an illusion?

The questions multiply once we find our life-ground. Why would the most recognizable essential foundations of being alive or human—the obligatory necessities of means of existence of clean water, nourishing food, element-protective shelter, sentient variety of surroundings, and a form of life-expression of worth to others—be so perfectly *blinkered out* on both levels in corresponding life-blindness? If the deplored grand narrative of Marxism lost the life-ground to a monstrous modern technostructure driven by iron economic laws, do not post-modern thinkers lose it in silent ideological complicity with the more universal capitalist empire? There is a hidden logic of irresponsibility and denial at work. The self-referential academic circuitries whose systems speak their subjects in theory reflect the money capitalist circuitries that speak their subjects on the ground.

Why would the very idea of universal life goods that are everywhere under threat be repudiated in principle on both planes in such perfect coincidence? Is this correlating repudiation of all common ground, all universal bonds, and all social obligation merely accidental? Or does this eradication of all binding truth and deeper life-grounds as "our freedom" imply a compulsory universal acquiescence in whatever *dehumanizing and rootless* condition the global market system demands next? Does not the antifoundational demand the *overriding* of any shared ground of meaning and value as the new "liberty" that allows market empire to reorder the life-world as private and deregulated money and commodity sequences with nothing left to which it can be held accountable?

The postmodern unaccountable, however, always defers meaning to new routes of diversionary avoidance. How can we know that what is clean air and water for one is clean air and water for another? All who are postmodern and antifoundational already know that correspondence of signifier to signified does not exist. So to say that there even *is* clean water and air across cultural differences, linguistic traditions, and plurality of perspectives is already ruled out. That there could be a *universal value* to enable all life capabilities to continue and grow, as opposed to disease and die, is an affront in principle to "free subjectivity," the theoretical correlative of "consumer sovereignty." All binary oppositions are inadmissible to their infinitely plural meaning. How, then, can the universal value of means of life for human life and ecosystems, or the value of life versus death, oblige anyone's recognition or defense? Why not, then, ecogenocide or suicide as the new diversity of dissipation into limitless plurality? But because reason and logic are also perceived as tyrants of logocentric reductionism, another escape hatch from accountability to reality and human value-ground opens to indeterminate free subjectivity.

The lines of force on the ground play out this nightmare imaginary as real. Beneath the disconnected elaborations of texts and consumables in Dionysian free subjectivity, life fabrics and means of life everywhere are being polluted, drawn down, enclosed, and disaggregated to turn them into ever-more-fleeting private commodities for infinite desires that propel global money sequences across all borders—just as postmodern perspectives everywhere declare simultaneously that there are no life-grounds, no necessitating obligations, no common yard-sticks of value, no Archimedean point of grounding position, no universal truths or values, and no correspondences of claims to fact whereby any of these problems can be recognized or responded to. Least of all can any truth or moral obligation be claimed across the plurality of perspectives that could conceive of any necessary joint action? In the real global corporate system for which every one of these life goods and reference bodies of meaning are "externalities," the postmodern fits the invisible hand like a glove.

## THE ABSOLUTIST UNIVERSALS OF THE GLOBAL FREE-MARKET ORDER

Subjugation by "the global" has a unifying form underneath all the postmodern talk of free and indeterminate subjectivity, contingent particularity, and plurality of voices. Beneath the illusion of emancipation from the state and the universally prescriptive by massive *capitalist deregulation* across the world, there has been a simultaneous *binding reregulation* of every society on earth by more total and absolute global rights of transnational corporations with no limiting conditions on their totality of rule—from the reengineered genes of the world's food to the contents of classroom curricula to the enclosure of the natural and civil commons across all borders. This is the real meaning of "the global postcolonial" that is taboo to notice within the new deregulated ontologies and discourses.[4]

Behind the pervasive proclamations of "free markets and democracy," "the liberation of differences," and the "cosmopolitan perspectival," a shadow totalitarianism prescribes to all peoples alike how they must live, with the assumed right to make war on whatever does not comply. It is not led by any past oppressor or reign of terror that postmodern thought posits as our unfreedom—foundations, essence, truth, universal concepts, patriarchy, reason, the canon, representation epistemology, the nation-state, the metaphysics of presence, logocentricity, transcendental arguments, Marxian grand narrative, or—in general—*any non-or-anti-market system*. The subject that ultimately rules within and across elites and peoples is a metaprogram that no one questions, including, in particular, postmodern interrogations. The metaprogram is a metaphysical, epistemological, and moral totality, more absolutist in social prescription than dialectical materialism or rationalist essentialism. Although postmodern thinkers and schools challenge all other closed systems, they all the while silently acquiesce in the totalizing globalization of a monocultural given by the iron laws of capitalism.

We can unpack the layers of this universal and obligatory system by a fifteen-step algorithm of its organizing Logos within which the postmodern itself operates with no overt transgression. The global corporate market's inner logic of command, which need not be expressed so long as no word contradicts or proposes alternatives to it, operates as a syntax of perception, understanding, and judgment. Yet unlike Kant's a priori forms and categories, it is entirely constructed while being universally assumed by its creatures. Postmoderns obey it just so far as they never call into question the following command assumptions. So presupposed are they as a regime of universal necessity, order, and obligation that they operate together as a metacode *within subjectivity itself*—organizing perception, understanding, and judgment by erasure, selection, and denial as what we may call "*the regulating market group-mind*" of the total world system. Its algorithm of grand narrative can be deconstructed as follows:

1. Pursuit of maximal monetary assets and commodities for oneself is natural for humans, however this natural fact may be denied, and rationalized in all places and times.
2. There is no rightful limit on capital and commodity accumulation or inequality, which are always entitled to their unfettered freedom of private-property right and global market expression.
3. Freedom to buy and sell in self-maximizing transactions of money and priced commodities is the proven basis of all economic efficiency, and there is no outer limit to this system's universalization.
4. The market's money-price system always optimally allocates resources and distributes goods and services in every society to ensure the best of all possible worlds across all cultures.
5. Competitive money-profit maximization by investors is the engine of all freedom and progress and must be everywhere liberated from state regulation or "monopoly" public ownership.
6. Government intervention in self-regulating market competition is always and everywhere "dictatorial" by any transgression or obstruction of "free market flows of commodities and capital."

7. Individual consumer desires are permanently increasing and unlimited, and what all people everywhere want are more commodities to satisfy their elaborating desires for ever more satisfactions.

8. Every consumer need or want must be produced and distributed by the open market in proportion to the effective demand for it, that is, the possession of sufficient money to pay as the economy's selector of fitness to continue expressing or living.

9. The public interest and human welfare can be achieved and developed only by market competition of producers and sellers because it alone provides incentives for labor, cost efficiencies, and technological innovations that are the bases of all wealth of human well being.

10. Market growth is therefore always beneficial with no limit to its conversion of planetary and human life-organization into more market activities, more commodities for consumers, and more investment profits for successful firms in the limitless expansion of "development," "diversity," and "civilization."

11. Protection of domestic production is the disastrous limit of "protectionism," which is modernity's greatest threat to the global free market and the liberation of desires to market growth and demand.

12. Whatever facts of life-disaster, such as mass loss of livelihood and environmental despoliation, may seem to contradict the necessity and validity of market principles 1 through 11, they are always correctable by free-market initiatives and enterprises.

13. If the "creative destruction" by global capitalism destroys ancient settings and ways of life, these are unavoidable costs of its global freedom from "dictatorial state prohibitions."

14. Individuals, groups, or governments that doubt or criticize: (i) the supremacy of the market system, (ii) the inherent efficiency of its production and distribution of goods, or (iii) the freedom of its individual agents thereby attack the grounds of individual liberty, self-expression, and plurality.

15. Any and all societies, parties, or governments that choose or seek any alternative of economic organization are "despotic" and must be overcome to défend the free world with isolation, embargo, and the armed force of private freedom from the terror of the state and the socially universal.

These system commands masquerading as the freedom of the individual constitute the ruling order of the free global that strips the world's ecosystems as "growth and progress" while perpetually invading and expropriating others' common resources for their "market liberation." The universal corporate market thus comes to rule across the globe, but any conception *of* it or any program of alternative is anathema to postmodern perspectivalism and particularity. September 11 occurs as strategic occasion of the totalizing corporate system to expand its globe-girding rule by armed-force proxies or invasions at the control nodes of the publicly owned oil fields and resources of Latin America, the Middle East, and Central Asia, but no postmodern deconstruction stands to speak the repression of difference or the terrorist totalitarian at work. Only particular spectacles and signifiers of culture in sanitized disconnection from the invasive regime of transnational corporate money sequences and militarism are selected for indeterminate subjectivity to interpret in liberty from any shared responsibility to decide or to defend.

A final question thus arises out of this silent complicity with the actually totalizing intolerant global system that tolerates no alternative to itself. Is it the unspoken servo-function of postmodern thought to pillory every *other* "grand narrative" as silencing and oppressive, but to submit to the one actually ruling the world as "postcolonial freedom"? From Jacques Derrida, Michel Foucault, and Jean-François Lyotard to Richard Rorty, from their antifoundationalist market industries and the mad Gilles Deleuze to the social arch-reactionary Nietzsche, can we think of one exception to the great avoidance of the actual world regime of monocultural prescription? Do we find the actually ruling terrorist universals once named, the monolithic closed rationality of market capitalism once interrogated as a system, its universal corporate mechanisms once decoded or called into question, its overbearing and provocative essentialism of "necessity," "growth," "optimum," and "no alternative" ever mocked as world-suffocating metanarrative? Where in the postmodern, postcolonial, and cultural-studies canons do we find anyone to unravel the ruling code of globalization itself?

## CONCLUSION

Postmodern thought links the principle of indeterminacy to the principle of difference as the inner logic and generating core of all its expressions. Its polyverse present of particularities without history is perceived as an emancipatory opening of cultural space, the exposing of all value grounds, universalist claims, and unifying essences as delusions. The irony of this antimetaphysic of the postmodern flight is that it defers everywhere to the totalizing global system of money power and commoditization by default, while propagating a complicit ideology of unaccountable freedom of assertion with no limits, while speaking in tongues an American military-market empire that repudiates all limits of universally binding principle on its freedoms of expression.

Stripped of any recourse to the common life-ground of resistance, postmodernism becomes a theoretical alibi of self-determining linguistic plays, unmoored textual elaborations, and utopian dream worlds unfolding while ravenous money circuits and military clearing operations expand the one total system that is never called into question. The postmodernism of endless displacement and diversion operates by an algorithm of silencing, legitimation, and mockery that plays Nero to a burning world by: (1) a methodological evasion of taking any stand on anything in principle because no obliging principle can be decidable nor applicable across differences; (2) an abdication a priori of any principled or nonarbitrary basis for any politics of unifying struggle against any actual structure of oppression; (3) a complicit retreat to a euphoric and self-referential narcissism of particular subjectivities as the only horizons of the open, while (4) the dominant structure of subjugation and consumption of the living Other is deferred to with no question.

Who hears the call of this Other to interrogate and deconstruct the one universal structure of necessity and oppression whose world regime silences all alternatives to its rule? There is where the opening awaits the voices of the living to contest the repressed empire of mind.

## NOTES

1. Thus Jacques Derrida (1999) says (italics added), "This *nonresponse* conditions my responsibility, there where I *alone must respond*—[otherwise] we could simply unfold knowledge into a *program or course of action*. Nothing could make us more irresponsible; nothing could be more *totalitarian*. One wonders how, say, a universal health program can qualify as nontotalitarian to this standpoint. It cannot, which, as we will see ahead, does not prevent, but silently corresponds to the new totalitarian position."
2. Even Fredric Jameson seems confined within the circle of representations and representations of representations ad infinitum, the production of *representations* as found in literature rather than philosophy, as the only tangible and concrete fullness to engage—a preference for the concrete of literature shared by philosopher Richard Rorty (Jameson 1991, 209). The social and ecological life-ground *beneath* representations is, as always, within our era of the linguistic disconnect and dissolved from view within words about words as the limit of what we can critically talk about.

3. The only argument that exposes this contradiction between postmodern assertion and the necessary presupposition of it is Jeffery Noonan (2002). Noonan focuses on Lyotard, Derrida, and Foucault but reveals the same underlying performative contradiction at work in the radical feminist postmodernism of Iris Young.

4. A systematic explanation and documentation of the totalitarian logic of the global corporate market system can be found in John McMurtry (2002).

## WORKS CITED

Derrida, Jacques. 1999. *Adieu to Emmanuel Levinas*. Stanford, Calif.: Stanford University Press.

Jameson, Fredric. 1991. *Postmodernism, or The Cultural Logic of Late Capitalism*. Durham, N.C.: Duke University Press.

McMurtry, John. 2002. *Value Wars: The Global Market versus the Life Economy*. London: Pluto Press.

Noonan, Jeffery. 2002. *Critical Humanism and the Politics of Difference*. Montreal: McGill-Queen's University Press.

# 16

# STRIKING BACK AGAINST EMPIRE: WORKING-CLASS RESPONSES TO GLOBALIZATION

*Verity Burgmann*

Marxist theory has generally emphasized the dominance of capital and its accumulative logic as the unilateral force shaping the world (Tronti 1979, 1; Dyer-Witheford 1999, 65). The phenomenon of globalization fits with such analysis, if one accepts the common depiction of globalization as an inexorable and inevitable process happening *to* the world because of the internal momentum or dynamism of capital. However, the autonomist Marxist tradition— articulated, for example, in the work of Antonio Negri, Michael Hardt, Mario Tronti, Mariarosa Dalla Costa, Harry Cleaver, and Nick Dyer-Witheford—offers an alternative way of understanding both globalization and its working-class oppositions.

In contrast to the traditional Marxist emphasis on the power of capital, autonomist Marxism argues that Marx's analysis affirms the power not of capital but of the creative human energy Marx called "labor":

> Far from being a passive object of capitalist designs, the worker is in fact the active subject of production, the wellspring of the skills, innovation, and cooperation on which capital depends. . . . Labor is for capital always a problematic "other" that must constantly be controlled and subdued, and that, as persistently, circumvents or challenges this command. (Dyer-Witheford 1999, 65)

For Cleaver, who coined the term, autonomist Marxism unites those threads of the Marxist tradition that have emphasized the "self-activity of the working class" and stressed the autonomy of the working class vis-à-vis capital (Viller 2003, 10). The working class to Negri (1988, 209) is a "dynamic subject, an antagonistic force tending toward its own independent identity." In *Marx beyond Marx: Lessons from the Grundrisse*, Negri anticipates "autovalorization" or "self-valorization" in which the dialectical spiral speeds the circulation of struggles until labor tears itself away from incorporation within capital; for the working class can do away with capitalism but capital will always require a working class (Viller 2003, 29).

Furthermore, as Mario Tronti suggests in a crucial autonomist formulation, it is working-class struggles that determine capitalist development and "set the pace to which the political mechanisms of capital's own reproduction must be tuned." Berating Marxists for working with "a concept that puts capitalist development first, and workers second," he called for a reversal of this polarity, for "the beginning is the class struggle of the working class" (Tronti 1979, 1). Building on Marx's observation in *Capital* that the impetus for capital's intensifying use of industrial machinery came from proletarian movements demanding a shorter working day, the autonomists argue that capital does not unfold according to a self-contained logic but is driven by the need to forestall, co-opt, and defeat "the other" that is simultaneously indispensable and inimical to its existence (Dyer-Witheford 1999, 66–67; Viller 2003, 13).

The history of capitalist forms, according to Hardt and Negri (2000, 268), is always necessarily a *reactive* history: "Capitalism undergoes systemic transformation only when it is forced to. . . . The power of the proletariat imposes limits on capital and not only determines the crisis but also dictates the terms and nature of the transformation." Where traditional Marxism emphasizes the logical development of capital and relegates class struggle to a "but also" role, autonomist theory liberates class struggle from this role by insisting that capital depends upon the working class for its reproduction and therefore labor insubordination is the driving force of capital. In the beginning is the scream (Holloway 2002, 1, 163–66). For example, Keynesianism was a response to the revolution of 1917, which made clear that capital could survive only by recognizing and integrating the working-class movement (Negri 1988, 5–42; Holloway 2002, 166).

The autonomist notion of "cycles of struggle," developed by Negri (1988, 1989), is helpful for understanding labor-capital relations historically and therefore for interpreting the present and predicting the future. The process of composition, then decomposition, then recomposition of the working class constitutes a cycle of struggle. Forms of struggle at any particular time are expressions of the composition of the working class; when capitalism introduces changes to restore order, it aims to bring about a decomposition of the working class; this decomposition gives rise in turn to the development of new forms of struggle or a recomposition of the class (Holloway 2002, 162).

In this paradigm, globalization can be understood not as a natural phenomenon somewhat like the weather, but as a strategy and rhetoric actively pursued by capital to control, subdue, and subordinate labor to enhance profit. During the immediate postwar period relatively strong labor movements had restrained capital's ability to maximize profit. The strength of that new composition was expressed in the struggles of the 1960s and 1970s, which went far beyond the factory to contest all aspects of capital's management of society (Holloway 2002, 162–63). By the late 1970s, the problematic otherness of labor had become very apparent to corporate and right-wing political elites, especially in Britain and the United States. At this point capital abandoned the Keynesian-Fordist form of management to develop new forms of attack: neoliberalism or "Empire" in Hardt and Negri's terminology (Holloway 2002, 163).

In the past quarter century, the neoliberal globalization project of capital has been motivated by the urge to "decompose" labor to enhance profitability, an intention expressed clearly in the discourse of globalization that disdains to conceal its views and aims: "World-best practice" is increased dividends for shareholders and multimillion-dollar packages for corporate executives; but for employees it is downsizing, lower real wages, and reduced social wages, with job security and decent wages deemed "market imperfections" (Leisink 1999, 1). Decomposition has undoubtedly occurred; but recomposition, according to autonomist theory, will eventuate. "Empire" is a mere apparatus of capture that lives off the vitality of the "multitude"; and the creative movement of the multitude "acts as an absolutely positive force that . . . appears as the distinct alternative" (Hardt and Negri 2000, 62).

Autonomist Marxism is thus better able than mainstream Marxism to countenance the capacity of labor to contest corporate globalization. Indeed, the ennui of social democracy and Labo(u)r Party politics expressed in "third way" acceptance of the inevitability of corporate globalization is inspired in part by traditional Marxist assumptions about the all-conquering command of capital. This pessimistic viewpoint seems well founded. A powerful weapon for capital in its globalization project has been its actual or threatened locational freedom, used to good corporate effect against both governments and workforces. Other policies associated with globalization—such as privatization, decreased public-sector spending, and antiunion industrial relations legislation—weaken workers' power and rights in myriad ways. These developments are part of the explanation for declining levels of union membership (Frege and Kelly 2003, 16; Heery, Kelly, and Waddington 2003, 79; Myconas 2003, 266). Academic writers have reflected upon the "crisis of trade unionism" (Hyman 1999, 98). Economy and society have been deliberately restructured in ways detrimental to employee interests. At the same time, conservative ideology has gained an alarming and perplexing dominance in many sections of society formerly the domain of progressive and labor-orientated politics (Frank 2004).

However, workplace organization is also starting to adapt creatively to the challenges of globalization: more imaginatively than allowed in traditional industrial relations theory, perhaps also bearing the mark of mainstream Marxist pessimism, in which the trade union is a less powerful labor-market actor that responds merely defensively and in ad hoc ways to employer initiatives. Labor movements around the world are in the midst of major debates and efforts to create alternative union forms—variously termed "social unionism," "class struggle unionism," "transformative unionism," or "social justice unionism"—precisely because existing models of trade unionism have been called into question by the rampage of capital and its flagrant unwillingness to come to any sort of accommodation with the working class and the trade-union movement (Hassan 2000, 73–74). In a special issue of the *European Journal of Industrial Relations*, the conclusion notes that intensified international capital mobility, trade competition, and new work organization are driving unions into *expanded political participation*: "Unions everywhere respond to the pressures of global capitalism by recasting themselves and deepening their efforts as political actors, beyond more limited traditional roles as labor-market intermediaries" (Baccaro, Hamman, and Lowell 2003, 128).

The industrial relations literature has started to ponder "labor movement revitalization" (Frege and Kelly 2003; Baccaro, Hamman, and Lowell 2003). In an article on this seemingly curious phenomenon, Lucio Baccaro and others note:

> Unions are everywhere relaunching themselves as "political subjects," as actors engaged not just in collective bargaining and work-place regulation, but also in the broader aggregation of political and social interests. . . . The exact forms taken . . . are shaped differently in each country . . . But in all cases, the shift toward a fuller political subject orientation lies at the centre of contemporary strategic adaptation and revitalization. (Baccaro, Hamman, and Lowell 2003, 119–20)

Revitalization research is characterized by incredulity—and inability to explain this surprising phenomenon.

Again, autonomist Marxism is as helpful in understanding working-class opposition to globalization as it is in interpreting globalization in the first place. If capital has pursued corporate globalization to subdue and control the problematic other of labor, to "decompose" the working class, recent developments on the labor side of the class divide can be understood as resourceful responses in which labor "recomposes" and presents itself in ways newly problematic to capital. The paradigm that brought us the notion of Empire enables us also to conceptualize Counter-Empire. Yet, in proffering omens such as "The organization of the multitude as political subject, as posse, thus begins to appear on the world scene" and in awaiting "the maturation of the political development of the posse," Hardt and Negri (2000, 411) insist they do not have any models to offer for this event. "Only the multitude through its experimentation will offer the models and determine when and how the possible becomes real."

This chapter aims to identify some of the multitude's experimental models or ways in which labor is acting as a "dynamic subject" in the context of globalization, presenting itself in ways distinctively novel as a problematic other for capital's globalization project and thereby recomposing itself. What are specific characteristics of corporate globalization that challenge labor and to which labor has responded as an antagonistic force tending toward its own independent identity? Four recent developments bear out the insights of autonomist Marxism.

## LABOR TRANSNATIONALISM V. CAPITAL MOBILITY

The threat of capital flight as much as its actuality enables corporations to extract financial incentives, reduced company taxation, and antilabor legislation from governments and intimidate workforces with prospects of relocation if wage demands are pressed. It matters not whether such threats are idle. A climate of labor-force vulnerability encourages self-policing of wage demands (Leisink 1999, 16). Nonetheless, footloose corporations are starting to be confronted by new forms of labor organization that chase capitalism to the farthest corners of the globe. Beverly Silver argues that, as the labor movement is weakened in sites of disinvestment, it is strengthened in the new sites of expansion; automobile corporations have been chasing cheap and disciplined labor around the world, "only to find themselves continuously re-creating militant labor movements in the new locations" (Silver 2003, 41, 64). Growth of organized labor in the new investment sites—and transnational corporate employment patterns in which an injury to a distant worker becomes an injury to all and can be resisted by all—fosters newfound collaborations.

In direct response to expanded capital mobility, there is an increasing practice of labor transnationalism, which involves unions and union federations acting across borders utilizing transnational networks and international solidarity efforts organizing global resistance campaigns (Hurd, Milkman, and Turner 2003, 114; Baccaro, Hamman, and Lowell 2003, 120–29; Waterman and Wills 2001). Much of this transnational labor movement activity is "rank-and-file internationalism"—international exchanges, networks, and cross-border solidarity campaigns taking place outside the official union hierarchy (Moody 1997, 249–75). However, there are also new and important solidarity campaigns involving international union federations (Greenfield 1998, 181; Bandy and Mendez 2003, 180).

George Myconas reveals how the transnational network of labor organizations has evolved in ways that enable it now to assert a more unified presence across state boundaries, suggesting organized labor is entering a transitional phase of some significance, a process marked for the moment by "an integration of a kind; an autonomy of a kind; and, ultimately, a globalization of a kind." This more integrated network of transnational labor organizations "has grown more coherent and unified as still more interests converge"; and the converging interests that motivate and sustain labor transnationalism are efforts to ameliorate "the deleterious effects of neoliberalism," which is "creating a greater sense of urgency throughout the network" (Myconas 2003, 242, 252, 257–58, 262, 295).

Integration has been aided by the demise of the Soviet-backed World Federation of Trade Unions, enabling the International Confederation of Free Trade Unions (ICFTU) to emerge as an unrivaled peak confederation with an increasing number of affiliates. In 1996 the ICFTU declared it "aims to be at the centre of a worldwide social movement." Although there has been no surrender of autonomy by affiliates, the ICFTU is the organizational hub of the network, with the ten industry-specific trade secretariats important actors; in 2000 these adopted the name Global Union Federations. There are also significant regional labor organizations, such as the South Pacific and Oceanic Council of Trade Unions or the Asia Pacific Labor Network (Myconas 2003, 244, 245, 249, 281).

One of the Global Union Federations is Union Network International (UNI), "a global union for skills and services workers" (www.union-network.org/), which represents 15 million members in over 140 countries with more than 900 unions worldwide. UNI points out that workers in UNI sectors throughout the world "are being exposed to the harsh realities of globalization" and describes the deteriorating "new work realities" faced by workers in both the North and the South. (UNI 2004, 1–2) Its response to off-shoring and outsourcing is internationalist: "UNI would like to state that it would be dangerous to respond to employer initiatives to relocate work to other countries with arguments that could be misconstrued as xenophobic or protectionist" (UNI 2004, 2). Explaining that its aim is "to ensure job security and compliance with decent labor standards," (UNI 2004, 2–3) it concludes that off-shoring and outsourcing affect the whole range of jobs from the lowest to the highest skilled ones, and, as companies act globally, so trade unions must act together across the world to limit the costs globalization imposes on societies in both the source and destination countries (UNI 2004, 4).

Since 1995 global union federations have established formal mechanisms of engagement with multinational corporations by way of a quasi-legal device known as a framework agreement: an agreed set of principles relating to working conditions and to how industrial relations within a specific corporation should be conducted. By 2002 there were twenty such agreements with multinational corporations that submitted to this engagement with the transnational labor movement, representing a new phase in efforts to establish regimes of transnational collective bargaining (Myconas 2003, 287–89).

Along with the Trade Union Advisory Committee to the OECD, the ICFTU and the Global Union Federations have formed a joint Web site called Global Unions at www.global-unions.org/default.asp. The Internet, enhanced by advances in language-translation software, is a crucially significant tool enabling unions to connect with each other across national borders (Lee 1996; Myconas 2003, 248, 263). Stuart Hodkinson (2001, 7) argues the labor movement's "net-internationalism" is used in three overlapping ways: the informational, the organizational, and the solidaristic. Myconas (2003, 251, 286) suggests that the remarkable increase in instantaneous, computer-mediated interaction and cooperation across the network of transnational labor organizations constitutes a pattern of interaction that may in the future form the basis of more profound integration. Indeed, Peter Waterman (1998, 214) claims that global informational capitalism provides more favorable terrains for emancipatory movements than those of industrial capitalism. Perhaps the potential of the labor movement for truly international organizing capacity is closer to realization now than when Marx overoptimistically called upon the workers of the world to unite.

Regional collaborations are an important component of labor transnationalism. Within Europe since the mid-1990s there has been concerted cross-border trade union collaboration to exchange information and coordinate bargaining policy on the issue of wage levels in particular, and to create supranational bodies with resources and some authority (Leisink 1999, 27; Behrens, Fichter, and Frege 2003, 35–36). After many years of European Trade Union Confederation lobbying, between 1993 and 1998 about 500 European Works Councils covering at least 15 million employees across 1,500 multinational corporations established on-site representation for workers of the same corporation operating across the European Union; and another 2,000 such Councils are awaiting certification. Impressed with European successes, UNI is now calling for "global works councils" (Myconas 2003, 289–90). U.S. unions, too, have developed transnational capabilities in support of organizing drives and collective bargaining, forming alliances with unions and political actors in other countries to access crucial pressure points, especially in industries with transnational capital structures where employers are aggressively antiunion (Hurd, Milkman, and Turner 2003, 113; Brown and Chang 2004, 21).

More unions in the developed world are making practical efforts to bring the standards of all workers up in order to make all workers safe (Starr 2000, 88–89). For example, Victoria Carty's study of transnational labor mobilization in two Mexican maquiladoras reveals that NAFTA has enhanced the connection between workers in the North and South as they came to realize they share a common enemy in their respective struggles: "globalization is creating common interests . . . that transcend both national and interest-group boundaries." AFL-CIO-sponsored speaking tours about "the race to the bottom" encouraged workers in the North to recognize that workers in the South were also victims of NAFTA and that solidarity across borders was necessary in forging resistance (Carty 2004, 304–6). Australian unions, faced with growing competition of low-wage Asian competitors, decided during the 1990s to sponsor union organizations in these countries to demand fair wages and employment conditions, from which Australian workers would also benefit. Writing about recent disputes in the Asia-Pacific region, Rob Lambert (1999, 244) observes a "renewal" that reveals a trade unionism far from being the spent force that conservatives predicted: "Deep international linkages now exist between these union movements. A new internationalism is being forged as each comes to the aid of the other in the midst of . . . ferocious battles."

This new internationalism is a response quite distinct from earlier (protectionist) posturing about developing countries' labor standards; more genuine efforts to enforce core labor standards are producing alliances between unions in the developed and the developing world (Leisink 1999, 23; Panitch 2001, 379; Sutherland 2000). This more class-conscious internationalist unionism, and labor transnationalism in general, reveals labor's capacity to confound capital's attempt to divide and rule workers on a truly world stage for the first time in history.

## SOCIAL-MOVEMENT UNIONISM V. WORKFORCE FRAGMENTATION

Unions have become more aware of the need to integrate the most vulnerable sections of the workforce. In part this has occurred under the influence of new social movements, but it has developed dramatically in astute response to heightened levels of workforce fragmentation in the period of globalization (Kelley 1997; Moody 1997, 290; Leisink 1999, 11; Bandy and Mendez 2003, 174). The autonomist Marxist understanding of the connection between class exploitation and racial and gender-based forms of domination is that, although capital's overarching structure of domination compels key issues of sexuality, race, and nature to revolve around a hub of profit, the capitalist international division of labor often incorporates, and largely depends on, discrimination by gender or ethnicity to establish its hierarchies of control; Negri thus anticipates increasing intersection between labor and new social movement struggles (Dyer-Witheford 1999, 9–10, 160).

As a dynamic subject, the working class is challenging the fragmentation imposed upon it by globalizing capital. In its more militant manifestations the new inclusiveness is expressed in the phenomenon of "social-movement unionism," a term coined in 1988 by Waterman (1993), which emerged in the mid-1990s in North and South America, South Africa, South Korea, and the more industrialized parts of the third world. Social-movement unionism is characterized by militancy, ultrademocratic forms of organization, and a determination to embrace the diversity of the working class in order to overcome its fragmentation; it grew out of the new material circumstances imposed by corporate globalization (Moody 1997, 290, 309).

Significantly, mainstream unionism has also responded to the challenge of fragmentation. Leo Panitch (2001, 369) observes: "Labor is changing in ways that make it a more inclusive social agent." At the ICFTU World Congress in 1996, the general secretary reported on "a world of widening divisions" and stressed the importance of "building solidarity, attacking poverty . . . and strengthening the voice of working men and women." At the World Congress in 2000, affiliates committed to a global social justice agenda in a raft of resolutions on relations with NGOs, equality for women, third-world debt, and poverty (Myconas 2003, 258–59). Global union federations are also campaigning against child labor and slavery and for women's rights. Myconas argues there has been a discernible shift in priorities across the entire ensemble of labor organizations away from the instrumental, parochial, and functional; and to a set of interests that reflect concern for human rights, equity, and justice. We have seen through the 1990s a renewed and concerted focus on the amelioration of the most pernicious aspects of the prevailing neoliberal order. These bread-and-butter issues relate to child labor, discrimination, safety and environment, the power of multinational corporations, and labor rights. Linked to all this is the re-doubling of efforts to have social clauses—in their various guises—inserted into trade agreements, and into various compacts with governments. (Myconas 2003, 261)

Though this tendency is still inclined towards the ameliorative and reformist, "it nevertheless represents a more contrary and oppositional ideological disposition than has been the case in recent decades" (Myconas 2003, 262).

American unions have recently indicated much greater commitment to marginalized workers and have built radical coalitions with organizations representing racial and ethnic minorities, women, and homosexuals (Bystydzienski and Schacht 2001). In 1995 the AFL-CIO began prioritizing the organizing of workers in poorly paid and insecure jobs, many of them held by women, minorities, and immigrants (Delp and Quan 2002, 1; Baccaro, Hamman, and Lowell 2003, 122). American unionism's improved propensity to represent the most vulnerable is evident, too, in the Justice for Janitors campaign, which organizes the predominantly nonwhite cleaners of commercial buildings for better wages and conditions (www.seiu.org/building/janitors/about_justice_for_janitors; Kelley 1997; Hurd, Milkman, and Turner 2003, 109). Another example is the campaign to unionize Californian homecare workers, who look after elderly and disabled people in these people's homes. These workers are overwhelmingly nonwhite and female, dispersed in different homes throughout 4,083 square miles, speaking more than one hundred languages, and have a high turnover rate; but the campaign has improved unionization levels by more than 100,000 in the past decade (Delp and Quan 2002, 4). This reshaping of U.S. trade unionism is all the more significant for the fact that it is taking place when conservative forces have ratcheted up their attacks on affirmative action, basic democratic rights, and political power for oppressed nationalities (Hassan 2000, 73).

In Europe there are significant actions against social exclusion on the part of unions, such as campaigns against deportation of migrants. The radical European Marches network has campaigned around policies relating to migrants and women (Taylor and Mathers 2002, 101–2). In the UK in recent years the Trade Union Congress has campaigned against race discrimination and developed joint initiatives with ethnic minority organizations; developed policy on equality for gays and lesbians at work and launched an annual Pride march in conjunction with homosexual organizations; and linked trade-union concerns with those of campaigners on family and sex equality issues in joint action around the agenda of family-friendly working practices. Many British unions in the past few years have introduced representative mechanisms specifically for women, young workers, and ethnic minorities, which have increased the number of people from these groups assuming senior positions within unions (Heery, Kelly, and Waddington 2003, 84, 87). In the 1990s, UNISON embraced a new organizational principle of permitting four self-organized groups (SOGs) to operate within the union, so that members marginalized on account of race, gender, sexuality, or disability could participate in union structures that formally acknowledged their other identities; these SOGs have become a well-established and accepted part of the union structure (Humphrey 2002).

In Australia, the Textile, Clothing, and Footwear Union launched the Fairwear campaign in 1996 to unionize and improve the situation of outworkers—mainly non-English-speaking immigrant women—who work from home for very low pay. After constant pressure and embarrassing publicity resulted in legislative victories, most retailers now co-operate with the union in providing the records necessary for the union to police compliance with stipulated wages and conditions (www.awatw.org.au/fairwear.html). In Mexico, women workers have mobilized to improve working conditions in maquiladora factories; and unions have become more inclusive, attending to issues such as maternity leave, second shifts, homework, discrimination, wage inequalities, reproductive health, and sexual harassment. Bandy and Mendez conclude that, as dialogue regarding gender and economics expands, resistance to neoliberal globalization becomes translocal and "coalitional" with greater potential to transcend binaries of global/local, North/South, worker/woman (Bandy and Mendez 2003, 174–83). Labor recomposes itself against fragmentation by capital.

## Community Unionism v. Marketization

A prominent feature of corporate globalization is marketization or "neoliberal austerity": privatization and declining government spending on both service provision and welfare, and emphasis on cutting labor costs in the private sector. This policy orientation is expressed spectacularly in the Structural Adjustment Programs imposed upon poorer countries, to which labor has responded with riots, demonstrations, and strikes from the 1980s onwards. For instance, thousands of workers at India's state power company went on strike in 2000 to prevent privatization of electricity generation (Bacon 2000, 84). The frequency of riots against austerity measures in Argentina has established the term *estallido* (explosion or outburst) as a category of practice by those who study the "new and unconventional forms of protest that abound in contemporary Argentina" (Auyero 2003, 140).

However, the first world is also undergoing "structural adjustment" in the interests of corporations, equivalent to processes experienced in the third world: cutting social expenditure, privatization, deregulation undermining wage rates, and other labor gains (Bello, Cunningham, and Rau 1994). As elsewhere, unions have responded. For example, in late 1995, France was rocked by strikes by around five million workers in protest against reductions to the minimum wage and cuts to welfare, health, education, and the public service (Starr 2000, 48). The movement received overwhelming support, according to Pierre Bourdieu, because it was seen as a necessary defense of the social advances of the whole society, concerning everything public: "In a rough and confused form it outlined a genuine project for a society, collectively affirmed and capable of being put forward against what is being imposed by the dominant politics" (Bourdieu 1998, 52–53).

The autonomist concept of the "social factory" refers to the way in which the principles of domination and production evident in the workplace are imposed increasingly upon the wider society; and as the processes engaged to valorize capital in production spill over into society, struggle extends beyond the workplace and communities become a significant terrain for confronting capital (Viller 2003, 14–15). For Negri, the result of capital insinuating itself everywhere is that class struggle is refracted into a multiplicity of points of conflict. The front of struggle snakes through homes, schools, universities, hospitals, and media and takes the form not only of workplace strikes and confrontations but also of resistance to the dismantling of the welfare state, demands over pay equity, child care, parenting and health benefits, and opposition to ecological despoliation (Dyer-Witheford 1999, 159–60).

The wider society has indeed become a terrain for struggle against capital. Incessant marketization—a hallmark of capitalist globalization—has spawned new forms of community-based resistance. An early academic study of this phenomenon was entitled "The Community as a Source of Union Power" (Craft 1990). Labor geographers have analyzed the way unions have exercised "spatial power" by organizing power from local communities, achieved most readily from locally based union-community relationships (Herod 1998; Tattersall 2004, 5). Carla Lipsig-Mummé (2003, 48, 52), in her research on alliances between unions and the community on issues of job defense and job creation in North America and Australia, observes that alliances usually begin with the union and reach out to the community; and that the coining of the term *community unionism* in Canada attests to the habitual nature of these alliances.

The term *union-community coalition* is also used to describe the trend of unions "reaching out." Amanda Tattersall (2004) has developed a typography that distinguishes these terms, but such detail need not concern us. Whatever the relationship brokered, this trend towards union links with the wider community is born of the common interest of employees, local residents, and consumers in opposing processes associated with corporate globalization, such as downsizing and closure of services, both public and private. It is significant that unions often initiate or emerge as natural leaders within these newly minted alliances between people adversely affected by marketization.

A growing body of academic literature describes and analyzes community unionism. In the United States, an important early book is Jeremy Brecher and Tim Costello's 1990 edited collection, *Building Bridges: The Emerging Grassroots Coalition of Labor and Community*; and in 2004 David Reynolds' edited *Partnering for Change: Unions and Community Groups Build Coalitions for Economic Justice*. Case studies have also proliferated. The focus of this literature echoes trends in the real world. Early work on labor-community coalitions centered on struggles to prevent plant closures (Nissen 2004, 68). By the 1990s there was a new emphasis on struggles to save public-sector service provisioning (Lipsig-Mummé 2003, 48).

When the Canadian Union of Postal Workers campaigned in the 1990s against the privatization of up to 5,000 postal outlets, it reached far beyond its normal constituency, drawing strength from community groups reliant upon a high standard of mail delivery, such as farmers, pensioner groups, students, the disabled, and retirees (Myconas 2003, 279). In Australia, union-community collaborations have emerged in the banking industry, prompted by drastic job losses and branch closures. In 1996 the Finance Sector Union, stressing the connection between consumer protection and employees' interests, initiated a nationwide coalition of community groups with grievances against the banks, especially in the normally conservative rural communities disproportionately affected by branch closures (Burgmann 2004, 118–21).

One specific example of a union-led campaign to save an important community service is the defense of the Los Angeles public hospital system. In 2002 the Department of Health Services presented plans to dismantle the public health care system. With over 20,000 union members in public health and at least 5,000 union jobs on the line, SEIU Local 660 mobilized patients, patient advocacy groups, doctors, political leaders, community groups, and other unions in the Coalition for Healthy Communities. Its most remarkable success was the November 2002 ballot-initiative victory—Measure B—the first property-tax increase in California in over twenty years, which will generate an extra $168 million a year for L.A. County trauma and emergency services (Hall and Schaefer 2004, 52, 63, 64). Nationwide, Jobs with Justice (JwJ), created in 1987 under AFL-CIO auspices, brings together over 1,500 organizations in 25 states and has been spectacularly successful in recent years, with its campaigns supported by mass community mobilizations (Beaudet 2004, 142–43).

Policies associated with globalization have provoked people adversely affected to coalesce in opposition; community unionism expresses this new pattern that aligns workers and most people in any community on the same side of an increasingly sharp divide. That unions are frequently foremost in mobilizing the discontents of these new coalitions suggests the capacity of labor to develop novel anticapitalist strategies and alliances, revealing its ingenuity as antagonistic other for capital.

## The Cybertariat v. Corporate Control of New Technology

An intriguing development is the nascent trend for technologically skilled labor to resist capital's attempt to exploit its skills and monopolize the benefits of the new technology. The autonomist concept of "cycles of struggle" is especially pertinent here, because it reminds us that from one cycle to another the leading role of certain sectors of labor may decline, become archaic, and be surpassed, without equating such changes with the disappearance of class conflict; for each capitalist restructuring must recruit new and different types of labor and thus yield the possibility of working-class recomposition, involving different strata of workers with fresh capacities of resistance and counterinitiative (Dyer-Witheford 1999, 66, 71). The skilled engineers of the nineteenth century were often at the forefront of labor struggles because of industrial capitalism's dependence upon their skills. Informational capitalism has also created a new layer of workers upon whom it relies; indeed, the ultimate dependence of capital upon labor is glaringly evident in the case of information technology (IT) workers.

Especially interesting, then, are the first signs of collective consciousness amongst IT workers, as they realize their power at the point of production and the increasing extent of their exploitation. The first Australian IT workers' strike occurred in 1999 when the software engineers at Sydney's Software Systems Centre, part of a large Japanese multinational corporation, "downed mouses" in response to management's refusal to negotiate a collective agreement to replace the individual contracts under which they were experiencing deteriorating conditions, especially increased working hours. They succeeded in securing a collective agreement (Barnes 2001, 34–42). In October 2001, the IT Workers Alliance Web site, an international "virtual union" was launched at www.itworkers-alliance.org. Within forty-eight hours this site had received 1,895 visitors and twenty-two applications to join a real union via the site's electronic Join-a-Union form (*Workers OnLine* 115, October 12, 2001).

If this technologically capable workforce organized collectively in concerted ways, it would have significant industrial power. Capital's interest in subduing this particularly skilled workforce upon which it is so dependent is apparent in the trends towards off-shoring and outsourcing of IT work to India and the flying-in of Indian software engineers to sites where their skills are needed. In the mid-1990s, a global convergence began in IT workers' wages, resulting in reining in of real wage increases (if not actual decline) in developed countries (Huws 2001, 17–19). After the dot-com crash and the passing of the Y2K bug fear, IT workers are experiencing rising stress levels and deteriorating pay and conditions, enduring coercion and chronic unpaid overtime due to fears of the "reserve army" of unemployed IT workers now available to replace them (Viller 2003, 42, 51–52). Chris Benner (2002) shows how Silicon Valley, a global center for innovation and production in information technologies, is no longer a workers' paradise of high incomes and respect, but a world starting to feel the need of strengthened bargaining for wages and conditions (McFarlane 2003, 98). Ursula Huws (2001, 20) argues that "a new cybertariat is in the making", but "whether it will perceive itself as such is another matter."

Autonomist Marxist theory suggests that when capital attacks the remuneration and conditions of workers that once enjoyed higher status and greater autonomy, collective resistance is more rather than less likely to ensue. In *Working Class Sabotage and Capitalist Domination* (1977), Negri observed: "the more the form of domination perfects itself, the more empty it becomes; the more the working class refusal grows, the more it is full of rationality and value" (quoted in Wright 1996, 20). Capital's efforts to control, even if successful in the short term, ultimately multiply its difficulties (Wright 1996, 15). A member of the executive of UNIFI, a British IT workers' union, quotes workers at a union meeting stating that off-shoring "made us realize we are just a commodity" (Milner 2004). A Seattle-based union activist claimed in

2002 that computer workers in the Pacific Northwest were becoming more amenable to unionization, because "they have discovered they no longer have an infinite capacity to eat shit" (Rieder 2005).

Respondents in Andrew Viller's research on IT workers emphasized the growing significance of solidarity between IT workers *across* competing enterprises, which counteract the difficulties in securing feelings of collective power in typically small IT work teams: "You have a stronger workforce with external IT guys than you have with people in the company you're working for" and "the IT community is probably the largest in the work community. . . . IT people don't give a shit about interbusiness rivalry" (Viller 2003, 59). A study of European Works Councils found that IT union activists subverted information flows within companies to develop transnational networks that undermined the operation of management benchmarking and performance indicators (Taylor and Mathers 2002, 99). Another example of "external solidarity" is "brain dumping": the Web sites where IT workers help each other pass the tedious exams set by Microsoft as a requirement for an IT worker to become Microsoft-certified (Viller 2003, 66). Other Web sites, such as www.corporatemofo.com, feature articles on IT organizing, corporate worker discontent, hacking news, software piracy, and the political contests with Microsoft. It is at these sites that IT workers share information and strategize: "where they connect and become composing class subjects" (Viller 2003, 69). Though Ken Wark's *A Hacker Manifesto* pertains to knowledge workers more generally, "the abstracters of new worlds," his observations are especially relevant to the cybertariat: "a class still becoming, bit by bit, aware of itself as such" (Wark 2004, 2, 6).

Resistance on the part of IT workers is less likely to express itself in traditional organization than in the writing of viruses or other forms of sabotage (Huws 2001, 20). The potential power of IT workers is strikingly borne out in their capacity to cause chaos through viruses. The media rarely addresses the issue of motivation behind viruses. For instance, there was little coverage of the fact that the Blaster virus that caused so much disruption late in 2003 also included a message for its principal target: "Billy gates, why do you make this possible? Stop making money and fix your software!!" (*Age*, August 14, 2003: 7). Viruses remind us that capital at each and every stage creates new forms of labor upon which it is particularly dependent, and that its capacity to control this labor is only ever partial. The new forms of knowledge and communication are instruments of capitalist domination, but also potential resources for struggle against capital (Hardt and Negri 2000, xv).

Deeply significant in this respect is hacking. Paul, one of Viller's respondents, estimated that about 90 percent of hackers were IT workers and that they rarely got caught. Santiago, another interviewee, insisted most IT people were hackers. Another, Dave, observed how his IT worker friends become politicized through hacking: "It started for them as fun, but as they found out more about the companies they worked for (through hacking), they now use it to act against their current or former workplaces" (Viller 2003, 63). Viller's respondents expressed their feelings of potential power as they assessed management fear of this power. Paul reckoned:

> They are very scared of IT workers; they're scared of the damage it can cause. Like, if you think about it, there's so much damage you can cause in a business . . . and it's not traceable and you don't even have to be there. (Viller 2003, 64)

Santiago revealed:

> There's a thing called 'mean time to belly up,' MTBU. And what that means is the average time it takes a company to go bankrupt without computer systems . . . (So) you can properly budget your back-up systems and things like that . . . you can also use that for other areas like . . . sabotage. (Viller 2003, 64)

Such statements suggest the vulnerability of capitalist domination and express IT workers' "antipower" (Holloway 2002, 40). It is hardly surprising that hackers are pathologized as delinquent and disturbed, a media representation rejected in an early sociological study that investigated hackers' motivations and discerned rational community amongst them (Jordan and Taylor 1998).

Although hackers are not usually associated with the formal expressions of the labor movement, their activities can be understood as an emergent form of resistance by labor to globalizing capital, akin to the instances of industrial sabotage that signaled the early stages of development of the nineteenth-century labor movement. "It is from the leading edge of the working class," according to Wark, "that hackers may yet learn to conceive of themselves as a class" (Wark 2004, 86). Hacking and virus writing are the Luddism of the twenty-first century but, unlike Luddism, these activities utilize directly the technology of the time in opposition to its uses by capital. To paraphrase Negri, IT workers' organic relationship to technoscience enables them to express sabotage's dialectical partner of "invention power" (Dyer-Witheford 1999, 163). The technology that facilitates exploitation also enables the globalization of anticorporate resistance: In virus writing and hacking it is clearly being deployed by those most proficient in its uses against the corporations for whom the new technology is primarily a means to increase exploitation.

Technologically skilled labor, a recomposing class subject, offers great possibilities for confronting and circumventing the power of capital. Capitalist social relations are acting as fetters upon computer technology, preventing the realization of its true usefulness to society. Owned and controlled by capital, its capacity to increase each worker's productivity is used simply to return higher profits to the few and increase unemployment (so as further to increase the power of capital), rather than to reduce working hours and increase the remuneration of the many. It would be possible for IT workers to use the creative capacity on which capital depends for its incessant innovation in order to reappropriate technology; only labor has an interest in unleashing the full potential of the new technology for the benefit of all rather than the enrichment of the few. Not capital but labor, the dynamic subject, will shape the future course of events.

There is one problem that will always remain with capital. That is corporations' ultimate dependence upon, and therefore the power inherent in, the commodity upon which globalizing capital is dependent for profit making: labor. Class composition is in a state of constant flux, but because capital is a system that depends on labor, it cannot completely destroy its antagonist (Dyer-Witheford 1999, 66). Labor transnationalism, social-movement unionism, community unionism, and the rise of the cybertariat are tentative and often faltering new directions for labor, but straws that indicate the way the wind is blowing. Despite labor's disarray at the commencement of corporate capital's globalization project (Munck 2000), labor has begun to respond resourcefully, revealing its capacity to be always a problematic other for capital—and suggesting the efficacy of autonomist Marxism for comprehending the past and present and predicting the future.

## NOTES

I wish to acknowledge the help of Robin Cohen, Jan Aart Scholte, and others in the Centre for the Study of Globalization and Regionalization at the University of Warwick during my visit to the Centre in 2004.

## WORKS CITED

Auyero, Javier. 2003. "Relational Riot: Austerity and Corruption Protest in the Neoliberal Era." *Social Movement Studies* 2, no. 2: 117–45.

Baccaro, L., K. Hamman, and T. Lowell. 2003. "The Politics of Labour Movement Revitalization." *European Journal of Industrial Relations* 9, no. 1: 119–33.

Bacon, David. 2000. "World Labor Needs Independence and Solidarity." *Monthly Review* 52, no. 3: 84–102.

Bandy, J., and J. B. Mendez. 2003. "A Place of Their Own? Women Organizers in the Maquilas of Nicaragua and Mexico." *Mobilization* 8, no. 2: 173–88.

Barnes, T. 2001. "The Geeks Fight Back: Class Struggle in the Information Technology Industry." In *Work, Organisation, Struggle*, eds. P. Griffiths and R. Webb, 34–42. Canberra: ASSLH.

Beaudet, Pierre. 2004. "Proletarian Resistance and Capitalist Restructuring in the United States." In *Globalizing Resistance: The State of Struggle*, eds. F. Polet and DETRI, 136–44. London: Pluto.

Behrens, M., M. Fichter, and C. M. Frege. 2003. "Unions in Germany: Regaining the Initiative?" *European Journal of Industrial Relations* 9, no. 1: 25–42.

Bello, W., with S. Cunningham and B. Rau. 1994. *Dark Victory: The United States, Structural Adjustment, and Global Poverty*. London: Pluto Press.

Benner, Chris. 2002. *Work in the New Economy: Flexible Labor Markets in Silicon Valley*. Malden, Mass.: Blackwell.

Bourdieu, P. 1998. *Acts of Resistance: Against the New Myths of Our Time*. Cambridge, Mass.: Polity Press.

Brown, E. L., and T. F. H. Chang. 2004. "PACE International Union vs. Imerys Groupe: An Organizing Campaign Case Study." *Labor Studies Journal* 2 no. 1: 21–41.

Burgmann, Verity. 2004. "Active Citizenship against Marketization: Community Resistance to Neo-Liberalism." In *The Vocal Citizen*, ed. G. Patmore, 116–31. Melbourne: Arena.

Bystydzienski, Jill M., and Steven P. Schacht, eds. 2001. *Forging Radical Alliances across Difference: Coalition Politics for the New Millennium*. New York: Rowman and Littlefield.

Carty, V. 2004. "Transnational Labor Mobilizing in Two Mexican Maquiladoras." *Mobilization* 9, no. 3: 295–310.

Craft, J. 1990. "The Community as a Source of Union Power." *Journal of Labour Research* 11, no. 2: 145–60.

Delp, L., and Katie Quan. 2002. "Homecare Worker Organizing in California." *Labor Studies Journal* 27, no. 1: 1–23.

Dyer-Witheford, N. 1999. *Cyber-Marx: Cycles and Circuits of Struggle in High-Technology Capitalism*. Urbana: University of Illinois Press.

Frank, T. 2004. *What's the Matter with Kansas? How Conservatives Won the Heart of America*. New York: Metropolitan Books.

Frege, C. M., and J. Kelly. 2003. "Union Revitalization Strategies in Comparative Perspective." *European Journal of Industrial Relations* 9, no. 1: 7–24.

Greenfield, G. 1998. "The ICFTU and the Politics of Compromise." In *Rising from the Ashes? Labor in the Age of "Global" Capitalism*, eds. E. M. Wood, P. Meiksins, and M. Yates, 180–89. New York: Monthly Review.

Hall, A., and D. Schaefer. 2004. "The Coalition for Healthy Communities." *Labor Studies Journal* 2, no. 1: 43–66.

Hardt, M., and A. Negri. 2000. *Empire*. Cambridge, Mass.: Harvard University Press.

Hassan, Khalil. 2000. "The Future of the Labor Left." *Monthly Review* 52, no. 3: 60–83.

Heery, E., J. Kelly, and J. Waddington. 2003. "Union Revitalization in Britain." *European Journal of Industrial Relations* 9, no. 1: 79–98.

Herod, A. 1998. *Organising the Landscape: Geographical Perspectives on Labor Unionism*. London: University of Minnesota Press.

Hodkinson, Stuart. 2001. "Problems @ Labour: Towards a Net-Internationalism?" Paper presented to the GSA Conference, Manchester, July 3–5.

Holloway, John. 2002. *Change the World without Taking Power*. London: Pluto Press.

Humphrey, Jill C. 2002. *Towards a Politics of the Rainbow: Self-Organization in the Trade Union Movement*. Aldershot, England: Ashgate.

Hurd, R., R. Milkman, and L. Turner. 2003. "Reviving the American Labour Movement." *European Journal of Industrial Relations* 9, no. 1: 99–118.

Huws, U. 2001. "The Making of a Cybertariat?" In *Socialist Register 2001*, eds. L. Panitch and C. Leys, 1–23. London: Merlin Press.

Hyman, R. 1999. "Imagined Solidarities: Can Trade Unions Resist Globalization?" In *Globalization and Labour Relations*, ed. P. Leisink, 94–115. Cheltenham, UK: Edward Elgar.

Jordan, T., and P. Taylor. 1998. "A Sociology of Hackers." *The Sociological Review* 46, no. 4: 757–80.

Kelley, R. D. G. 1997. "The New Urban Working Class." *New Labor Forum* 1, no. 1: 6–18.

Lambert, R. 1999. "Australia's Historic Industrial Relations Transition." In *Globalization and Labour Relations*, ed. P. Leisink, 212–48. Northampton, Mass.: Edward Elgar.

Lee, E. 1996. *The Labour Movement and the Internet: The New Internationalism*. London: Pluto.

Leisink, P. 1999. "Introduction." In *Globalization and Labour Relations*, ed. P. Leisink, 1–35. Cheltenham, UK: Edward Elgar.

Lipsig-Mummé, Carla. 2003. "Forms of Solidarity: Unions, the Community, and Job-Creation Strategies." *Just Policy* 30 (July): 47–53.

McFarlane, A. 2003. "Review." *Melbourne Journal of Politics* 28: 97–98.

Milner, Richard. 2004. Conversation with author. June 5.

Moody, K. 1997. *Workers in a Lean World: Unions in the International Economy*. London: Verso.

Munck, R. 2000. "Labour in the Global: Challenges and Prospects." In *Global Social Movements*, eds. R. Cohen and S. M. Rai, 83–100. London: Athlone Press.

Myconas, George. 2003. "The Globalizations(s) of Organized Labour 1860–2003." PhD thesis, Monash University, Australia.

Negri, A. 1988. *Revolution Retrieved: Selected Writings on Marx, Keynes, Capitalist Crisis, and New Social Subjects*. London: Red Notes.

———. 1989. *The Politics of Subversion: A Manifesto for the Twenty-First Century*. Cambridge, Mass.: Polity Press.

Nissen, B. 2004. "The Effectiveness and Limits of Labor-Community Coalitions." *Labor Studies Journal* 2, no. 1: 67–89.

Panitch, L. 2001. "Reflections on Strategy for Labour." In *Socialist Register 2001*, eds. L. Panitch and C. Leys, 367–92. London: Merlin Press.

Rieder, Ross. 2005. Conversation with author. June 11.

Silver, B. 2003. *Forces of Labor: Workers' Movements and Globalization since 1870*. Cambridge: Cambridge University Press.

Starr, A. 2000. *Naming the Enemy: Anti-Corporate Movements Confront Globalization*. Sydney: Pluto Press.

Sutherland, P. 2000. "The WTO and Global Governance." *Overseas Development Council*. Washington D.C. At: www.ilo.org.

Tattersall, Amanda. 2004. "Towards a Definition of Community Unionism." Paper presented to the Australasian Political Studies Association Conference, University of Adelaide, September 29–October 1.

Taylor, G., and A. Mathers. 2002. "Social Partner or Social Movement? European Integration and Trade Union Renewal in Europe." *Labor Studies Journal* 27, no. 1: 93–108.

Tronti, Mario. 1979. "Lenin in England." In *Working Class Autonomy and the Crisis*, 1–6. London: Red Notes.

UNI. 2004. "European Parliament Public Hearing on Effect of Off-Shoring and Outsourcing on Employment of Europe." Presented by Oliver Roethig, Head of UNI Finance, April 5.

Viller, Andrew. 2003. "Cyber-Marx, Class Relations, and Worker Resistance in the IT Industry." BA thesis, University of Western Sydney.

Wark, McKenzie. 2004. *A Hacker Manifesto*. Cambridge, Mass.: Harvard University Press.

Waterman, P. 1993. "Social Movement Unionism: A New Model for a New World Order." *Review* 16, no. 3: 245–78.

———. 1998. *Globalization, Social Movements, and the New Internationalisms*. London: Mansell.

Waterman, P., and Jane Wills. 2001. *Place, Space, and the New Labour Internationalisms*. Oxford: Blackwell.

Wright, S. 1996. "Negri's Class Analysis: Italian Autonomist Theory in the Seventies." *Reconstruction* 8 (Winter–Spring): 10–22.

# 17

## LOCALIZING GLOBAL TECHNOSCIENCE

### *Geoffrey C. Bowker*

*In subjects of pure Science an Individual can speak as if he were all Mankind: for tho' it is he who speaks, yet that which is spoken is the Reason, which is one in all men. From whatever point of the periphery, or of its Area, the Word proceeds, in the moment of its utterance it becomes the same everywhere within the sphere of its audibility.*

—S. T. Coleridge, Notebooks

Just who we universals are is not an obvious question. The Athenians grounded their equality in their autochthony (Loraux 1996): It was a foundation of their equality—a foundation that excluded women (not born of the earth) and outsiders. The phrase is resonant today—the French with their terroirs at home and universalizing French empire abroad still refer to themselves as "autochthones" (Braudel 1986; Détienne 2003). The tension between universality and rooted locality runs deep. Possibly closest to our globalizing ethnicity (I speak for my fellow universals) is that of the Goths: They have an unfortunate reputation vested on them by their victors as ravaging hordes, but they are arguably the first political group for which *ethnicity* was not an issue. One became a Goth through ascribing to the Gothic political organization (Wolfram 1988), just as one becomes a member of Axis of Good through ascribing to a given form of political organization that goes under the universalizing name of democracy. We universals are the only group to have a nonlocal history—the truths we discover were always already there; they are not rooted in a creation myth tied to this spring or that species: Stefan Tanaka has a brilliant analysis of the work of *synchronizing* the local with the global as Japan "entered the world stage" (Tanaka 2004). We are the group that has a maximal break with the past—as Michelet taught us, we are not determined by our climate (others are); as Comte taught us, our knowledge is not tied to its roots in metaphysics and religion but is increasingly liberated from same (unlike the knowledge of others). We are the group that maximally rejects its past except as pure flow into an ideal eternal present—the real present that lurks beneath the appearance of disorder.

Key to our universality is our particular knowledge/power nexus: scientific knowledge and technological prowess marching hand in hand today as did the missionaries and the merchants in the nineteenth century. Learning to use the Internet is integrally about learning to accept the categories of Western knowledge, there is no separation of science and infrastructure. Indeed, the global sweep of the imperial move to impose our ways of knowing on the world is potentiated by its association with a very specific, locally grown infrastructure. In this chapter, I lay out some ways in which this association is produced and maintained. I argue that global technoscience, for all its universal aspirations, is ineluctably the outcome of a very particular historical tradition.

## Global Technoscience/Global Infrastructure

For the past few hundred years, many books and articles have begun with the phrase: "We are entering a period of rapid change unimagined by our ancestors."

The statement is both as true and as false now as it has been over the previous two centuries. It is true because we are as a society adjusting to a whole new communication medium (the Internet) and new ways of storing, manipulating, and presenting information. We are, as Manuel Castells and others remind us, now in many ways an information economy, with many people tied to computers one way or another during our working day and in our leisure hours (Castells 1996). It is false because we are faced with the same old problems—getting food, shelter, and water to our human population; living in some kind of equilibrium with nature—as ever we were.

## What Is Infrastructure?

Central to the new knowledge economy has been the development of a new information infrastructure. When we think of infrastructure in a commonsense way, we picture that which runs "underneath" actual structures—railroad tracks, city plumbing and sewage, electricity, roads and highways, cable wires that connect to the broadcast grid and bring pictures to our TVs. It is that upon which something else rides, or works, a platform of sorts. This commonsense definition begins to unravel when we populate the picture and begin to look at multiple, overlapping, and perhaps contradictory infrastructural arrangements. For the railroad engineer, the rails are only infrastructure when she or he is a passenger. Almost anyone can flip an electric switch, for a variety of purposes. When the switch fails, we are forced to look more deeply into the cause—first check the light-bulb, then the other appliances on the same circuit, then look at the circuit-breaker box, then look down the block to see if it is a power outage in the neighborhood or city, and finally, depending on one's home repair skills, consider calling an electrician. Increasingly, many of us are faced with infrastructures, designed by one group, that may not work for us. For instance, someone in a wheelchair appreciates the tiny (and not so tiny) barriers that are considered "wheelchair accessible" by the able-bodied. Four stairs can be a mountain if the specific conditions of usability are overlooked. So we have three separate themes here:

1. The moving target of infrastructure, from easy-to-use black box to active topic of work and research
2. The breakdown of infrastructure that opens the taken for granted
3. The relative usefulness of infrastructure for different populations

One thing that unites each of these strands is the notion that infrastructure is not absolute, but relative to working conditions. It never stands apart from the people who design, maintain, and use it. Its designers try to make it as invisible as possible, while leaving pointers to make it visible when it needs to be repaired or remapped. It is tricky to study for this reason.

I will work from Star and Ruhleder's definition of the salient features of infrastructure in order to bound and clarify the term:

- *Embeddedness.* Infrastructure is sunk into, inside of, other structures, social arrangements, and technologies.

- *Transparency*. Infrastructure is transparent to use, in the sense that it does not have to be reinvented each time or assembled for each task, but invisibly supports those tasks.
- *Reach or scope*. This may be either spatial or temporal—infrastructure has reach beyond a single event or one-site practice.
- *Learned as part of membership*. Being able to take for granted artifacts and organizational arrangements is a sine qua non of membership in a community of practice. Strangers and outsiders encounter infrastructure as a target object to be learned about. New participants acquire a naturalized familiarity with its objects as they become members.
- *Links with conventions of practice*. Infrastructure both shapes and is shaped by the conventions of a community of practice, for example, the ways that cycles of day-night work are affected by and affect electrical power rates and needs. Generations of typists have learned the QWERTY keyboard; its limitations are inherited by the computer keyboard and thence by the design of today's computer furniture.
- *Embodiment of standards*. Modified by scope and often by conflicting conventions, infrastructure takes on transparency by plugging into other infrastructures and tools in a standardized fashion.
- *Built on an installed base*. Infrastructure does not grow de novo; it wrestles with the inertia of the installed base and inherits strengths and limitations from that base. Optical fibers run along old railroad lines; new systems are designed for backward compatibility; and failing to account for these constraints may be fatal or distorting to new development processes.
- *Becomes visible upon breakdown*. The normally invisible quality of working infrastructure becomes visible when it breaks: the server is down, the bridge washes out, there is a power blackout. Even when there are back up mechanisms or procedures, their existence further highlights the now-visible infrastructure.

Something that was once an object of development and design becomes sunk into infrastructure over time. Therefore a historical, archeological approach to the development of infrastructure needs to complement sociological, regulatory, and technical studies.

## International Technoscience: The Promise

There has been much hope expressed that in the developing world, the new information infrastructure will provide the potential for a narrowing of the knowledge gaps between countries. Thus an effective global digital library would allow third-world researchers access to the latest journals. Distributed computing environments (such as the GRID, being developed in the United States) would permit supercomputer-grade access to computing to scientists throughout the world. The example of the use of cell-phone technology to provide a jump in technology in countries without landlines has opened the possibility of great leaps being made into the information future. As powerful as these visions are, they need to be tempered with some real concerns. The first is that an information infrastructure such as the Internet functions like a Greek democracy of old—everyone who has access may be an equal citizen, but those without access are left further and further out of the picture. Secondly, access is never really equal—the fastest connections and computers (needed for running the latest software) tend to be concentrated in the first world. This point is frequently forgotten by those who hail the end of the "digital divide"—they forget that this divide is in itself a moving target. Thirdly, governments in the developing world have indicated real doubts about the usefulness of opening their data resources out onto the Internet. Just as in the nineteenth century, the laissez-faire economics of free trade was advocated by developed countries with the most to gain (because they had organizations in place ready to take advantage of emerging possibilities), so in our age, the greatest advocates of the free and open exchange of information are developed countries with robust computing infrastructures. Some in developing countries see this as a second wave of colonialism—the first pillaged material resources and the second will pillage information: there are many calls for "data repatriation"—our twenty-first-century version of the Greeks' continual call for the UK to cede the Elgin Marbles. All of these concerns can be met through the development of careful information policies. There is a continuing urgent need to develop such policies.

International electronic communication holds out the apparent promise of breaking down a first-world/third-world divide in science. Developments such as the remote manipulation of scientific equipment (see the University of Michigan's UARC—upper atmospheric research collaboratory—project), where scientists on the Internet can manipulate devices in the Arctic Circle without having to go there, are trumpeted. The possibility of attending international conferences virtually is also being held out. And if universities succeed in wresting control over scientific publications from the huge publishing houses (a very open question), then easy, cheap access to the latest scientific articles becomes possible for a researcher in outback Australia. At the same time, there are a number of forces working to reinforce the traditional center/periphery divide in science internationally. Even with the move to open up access to scientific publications and equipment, there is no guarantee that the "invisible colleges" (that operate informally and determine who gets invited to which conference and so forth) will change: indeed the evidence seems to be to the contrary. Further, at the current state of technological development, there is a significant gap between information access in different regions of any given country, or different parts of the world. Consider the analogy of the telephone. In principle, anyone can phone anywhere in the world; in practice, some regions have more or less reliable phone services, which may or may not include access to digital resources over phone lines.

We can go beyond the continuing digital divide, however, to consider the possibility of mounting very large-scale scientific data collection efforts. Such efforts are central to the social sciences, and to the sciences of ecology and biodiversity. With the development of handheld computing devices, it is becoming possible for a semiskilled scientific worker with a minimum of training to go into the field and bring back significant results. Thus in Costa Rica, the ongoing attempt to catalog botanical species richness is being carried out largely by "parataxonomists" who are provided with enough skills in using interactive keys (which help in plant recognition) to carry out their work almost as effectively as a fully trained systematist. Computer-assisted workers, together with the deployment of remote sensing devices whose inputs can be treated automatically, hold out the possibility of scaling up the processes of scientific research so that they are truly global in scale and scope.

## THE OWNERSHIP OF KNOWLEDGE: CUI BONO?

It has often been asserted that science is a public good: meaning that scientific work does not fit into the globally dominant market economy. In the new knowledge economy, however, we are increasingly seeing the penetration of the market right down to the molecular level, right down to the stuff of scientific enquiry. Thus it is possible to patent genes, genetically modified plants, animals, and so forth. Taking a fairly wide definition of ownership, we can see three main sets of issues arising from the implementation of this knowledge/information market: control of knowledge, privacy, and patterns of ownership.

By control of knowledge, I refer to the question of who has the right to speak in the name of the science. Since the mid-nineteenth century this has been a fairly simple question to answer: Only professionally trained scientists and doctors can speak for science and medicine in turn. Only they had access to the resources that were needed in order to speak authoritatively about a given subject—they had the journals, the libraries, and the professional experience. Within the new information economy this is not the case. For example, many patient groups now are being formed on the Internet. These groups often know more about a rare condition (for example, renal cell carcinoma) than a local doctor does—they can share information twenty four hours a day, and they can bring together patients from all over the world. This flattening out of knowledge hierarchies can be a very powerful social force. It carries along with it, though, the need to educate the enfranchised public about critical readership of the Web. There are many Web sites that look official and authoritative but in fact only push the hobbyhorse of a particular individual. We have through our schools and universities good training in reading and criticizing print media; but we have little expertise as a culture in dealing with highly distributed information sources.

Privacy concerns are a significant dimension of science and technology policy in the new economy. It is now technically possible to generate and search very large databases, and to use these to integrate data from a whole series of domains. As this happens, the potentialities for data abuse are increasing exponentially. Much has been written, for example, about data mining of the Icelandic population. After much public debate, citizens of Iceland agreed to sell medical and genealogy records of its 275,000 citizens to a private medical research company. There were two central reasons for choosing Iceland: it has a population that has a relatively restricted gene pool; and it has excellent medical records dating back some thousand years. Although the science may prove useful (the question is open), it certainly opens the specter of genetic screening of prospective employees by any given company. It is extremely difficult to keep records private over the new information infrastructure—many third-party companies, for example, compile data from a variety of different agencies in order to generate a new, marketable form of knowledge. There is no point in trying to adhere to the old canons of privacy; however, open public debate and education about the possibilities of the new infrastructure are essential.

Science has frequently been analyzed as a "public good." According to this line of argument, it is in the interests of the state to fund technoscientific research because there will be a payoff for society as a whole in terms of infrastructural development. With the increasing privatization of knowledge (as we turn into a knowledge-based economy), it is unclear to what extent the vaunted openness of the scientific community will last. Many refer back to a "golden age" when universities were separate from industry in a way that they are not today. Although a lot of this talk is highly exaggerated (science has always been an eminently practical pursuit), it remains the case that we are in the process of building new understandings of scientific knowledge.

A key question internationally has been that of who owns what knowledge. This is coming out in fields such as biodiversity prospecting, where international agreements are in place to reimburse "locals" for bringing in biologically active plants, and so forth. However, the ownership patterns of knowledge of this sort are very difficult to adjudicate in Western terms. For example, consider a Mexican herbalist selling a biologically active plant in a market in Tijuana. He owns the plant, but is not the source of knowledge about biologically active plants. This knowledge does not go back to a single discoverer (as is needed in many Western courts of law adjudicating matters of ownership of intellectual property) but to a tradition held, often, by the women of a collectivity. The herbalist may well not be able to trace the chain of ownership that goes back to the original harvesting of the specific plant he or she is selling. Similarly, Australian aborigines or the Native Americans had very different concepts of land ownership from the white settlers, leading to complex negotiations that continue today about the protection of natural resources. We need anthropological/sociological studies of local knowledge (to the extent to which this is being mined by scientists) again in order to help design just frameworks and studies of issues of data ownership in different countries. There is a danger when we talk of the explosion of information in the new knowledge economy that we forget the role of traditional knowledge in the development of sustainable policies for a region. Thus, research has shown that management of some parks in the Himalayas has relied on models brought in from the outside and taught to villagers through the distribution of television programs—while at the same time ignoring centuries of local ecological knowledge because it is practice based and has its own intricate weaving of knowledge about the environment, religious belief, and mythological expression and cannot be easily conjured into a form that can be held on a computer (Padel 1998).

## KEEPING KNOWLEDGE LOCAL

We are currently, as a globalizing presence, seeking to preserve many kinds of diversity—linguistic, cultural, ethnic, genetic, to name but a few. And yet that preservation has its price: Ethnic and linguistic diversity can best be maintained by sequestration, which is good for the connoisseur of the diverse but not necessarily for the diverse themselves. Databases are often seen as a good site for preservation without politics, from the Mayan cultural atlas (Toledo Maya Cultural Council and Toledo Alcaldes Association 1997) through the efflorescence of museums of indigenous knowledge. Really listening to other ways of knowing entails more than databasing—after all, indigenous knowledge tends to end up in text fields in scientific databases, collocated with the real data but nonmanipulable and hence unusable. How should we record and remember other ways of knowing?

I attended in May 2001 a three-day workshop on "indigenous knowledge." Our workshop was a follow-up from the Innovative Wisdom conference in Florida the previous year, responding to Article 26 of a World Conference of Science report (which led to controversy in the journal *Nature*). The offending article read as follows:

> 26. That traditional and local knowledge systems as dynamic expressions of perceiving and understanding the world, can make and historically have made, a valuable contribution to science and technology, and there is a need to preserve, protect, research and promote this cultural heritage and empirical knowledge (p. 4, *Science International*, September 1999).

The International Council of Scientific Unions (ICSU) took collective umbrage at this statement, arguing that there was no such thing as traditional knowledge, and if there were, it certainly had not contributed to science and technology. Additionally if it had in the past contributed, then there was certainly no need to promote it in the future because the light of modern science could shine brighter and cheaper into local territory. I was part of a group of historians, philosophers, and sociologists of science charged with defending Article 26 to ICSU.

"Innovative wisdom" is a nice phrase. There is a great dearth of words for what it is that locals have and universals do not. If we call it "indigenous knowledge," then we are denying the role of the urban dweller who has moved in from another area, or the mestizo, the half caste. Many anthropologists and others also oppose the term *traditional*, which implies knowledge that is lodged in an eternal past (where our knowledge uncovers the eternal present). At a recent conference in Nairobi of signatories to the Convention on Biological Diversity, African delegates said that they felt insulted if their knowledge was referred to as traditional; "indigenous" refers for them to community and is the correct unit of analysis. In Latin America, "indigenous" is also considered a reasonable epithet. However, delegates from Morocco don't consider themselves indigenes and reject "traditional," which has connotations of being backwater. ILO Convention 169 refers to the rights of indigenous and tribal peoples; the Nairobi conference ended up adopting "indigenous and local." In the (highly ironic) Museum of Jurassic Technology in Los Angeles, an exhibit on local knowledge refers to a society established in Edwardian England for the Restitution of Decayed Intelligence (Weschler 1996)! Of course there's always *"pensée sauvage,"* but that wildflower is untranslatable.

One is giving the game away at the outset if one says that some knowledge is local, because by extension, there exists some other knowledge that is universal. We produce knowledge that is true in all places at all times; they produce knowledge that is particular to their region. Bruno Latour and Harry Collins have in different ways shown us that our "universal" knowledge is restricted to highly localized space and time—the space and time of the laboratory (Collins 1985; Latour 1987). When a science test starts with the phrase "All things being equal . . . ," asking then how fast a falling body will take to light, it points in the direction of all the work that is done in making other things equal—excluding vibrations, foreign products invisible to the naked eye, and weather conditions—so that in this very small, highly localized place called the laboratory, universal knowledge can be produced. Mark Meadow and Bruce Robertson's Microcosms project (www.microcosms.ihc.ucsb.edu/) shows just what a strange array of objects university knowledge is conjured out of: They inventoried and then exhibited collections of objects in libraries and in departments across the University of California system, showing how like they are to Cabinets of Curiosities. Further, as Latour points out, this highly localized knowledge can only travel along very sparsely populated networks (from one laboratory to another) before it begins to make the necessary set of alliances and affect (or effect, depending on your point of view) the world (Latour 1987). So I don't want to say that at universities we produce universal knowledge and then in the outback others produce local knowledge. Knowledge is always firmly tied to a locality, and to a temporality. ICSU took particular offense at the phrase "traditional and local knowledge" because the state of Kansas in the United States had recently voted evolutionary theory to be nonscientific and thus not teachable as science in the classroom. How, they asked, could we maintain lines distance between church and state—a long-cherished divide, constructed over several centuries in Western science—without being able to challenge hocus pocus like the oxymoronic "creationist science" or the knowledge of the shaman or astrologer? Local knowledge became *at this time* something that true science had to challenge—at other times the issue would not have arisen, or fear of political fallout would have suppressed the assertion. The historical junctures at which universalism asserts itself are invariably those where other knowledge systems threaten the monotheistic trick borrowed from that other great universalizing tradition.

Careening through our universal space, we risk being dashed against the Scylla and Charybdis of local knowledge—the Scylla being that its space cannot be recognized as socially performed and it cannot be historically constructed if it is to be knowledge, and the Charybdis being that if it does not conform to (or overly complicates) traditional rules of intellectual property, then it will be ignored or worked around. So it can only be knowledge at the price of denying its very nature.

## SO WHY KEEP KNOWLEDGE LOCAL AND LOCAL KNOWLEDGE?

The first answer is that it is anyway. All knowledge, as pointed out previously, is irredeemably local. Howard Becker (personal communication) has a nice mantra for the state of scientific knowledge: "They used to believe, but now we know." The astonishing thing, at any level of temporal granularity, is that so many think that our most cherished notions are established for all time. Now we know. It is a terrible hubris to say that one has access to the only way of knowing. We ourselves—whoever that may be—have several, contradictory, very powerful ways of knowing. Attention beyond reason to a single way of knowing is attaching to a fetish demanding obsession, not treading the one, true, right, and only path. Michel Serres long ago stated that his role as a philosopher of science was to keep the spaces between the disciplines open (Serres 1980). Disciplines did what they did very well, but they also had an imperial tendency to deny any knowledge that did not conform to their way of knowing.

More substantively, I could perhaps call to mind the beautiful lines in Leibniz's *Writings on China* about the difference between Chinese and European knowing (Leibniz et al. 1994). He argues that where the West has mathematical and logical knowledge down, the East understands the Art of Society. This resonates with much current Vulgate about the Other— they know how to live, how to laugh, how to subsist in harmony with nature. The power and the glory are on our side, but they get the rest. However, Leibniz also hails as one of the greatest discoveries of all time the invention of binary notation, which he discovered through the I Ching and its hexagrams. The powers of binary arithmetic are not to be denied in the computer age. Crucially, however, the argument can be made that the binary has become a tool for thinking with in our culture, as it was in China. One has only to look at the binary oppositions of the structuralists to see its penetration into anthropological and philosophical discourse in the 1980s. If we can say that we have learned a tool for thinking with, rather than wrested a nugget from a blank slate, then we can say that we are listening forth to all knowledge.

## CONCLUSION

We are globally faced with problems that cannot be solved by the generation of knowledge alone. Producing massive lists of flora and fauna will not of itself lead to a way to preserve biodiversity. However, I have tried to argue that the information economy does promise some major new tools. The real key to developing technoscientific policy in the context of the new knowledge economy is operating a deep understanding of the nature of information infrastructures. For many, the development of science policy evokes ethical and political questions, such as genetic screening, cloning, and so forth. This is important work; but much more important is the work of monitoring the standards and classification systems that are getting layered into our models and simulations, and of changing our institutions so that they can take maximum advantage of the new collaborative and information-sharing possibilities. Equally crucial is learning to make our rampant information infrastructure a genuinely flexible playground for all ways of knowing, not a covert, accidental proselytizer for the very local knowledge of our globalizing ethnos. The necessary tools are being created, but they are widely scattered and are often lost. The new information infrastructure for technoscience will be extremely powerful; with good bricolage we can make it just and effective as well.

## WORKS CITED

Braudel, F. 1986. *L'identité de la France: espace et histoire*. Paris: Arthaud-Flammarion.

Castells, M. 1996. *The Rise of the Network Society*. Cambridge, Mass.: Blackwell.

Coleridge, S. T. 1833. "Notebooks." In *British Museum Add. Mss. 47546*. London: British Museum.

Collins, H. M. 1985. *Changing Order: Replication and Induction in Scientific Practice*. London: Sage.

Détienne, M. 2003. *Comment Etre Autochtone: du pur Athénian au Français enraciné*. Paris: Seuil.

Latour, B. 1987. *Science in Action: How to Follow Scientists and Engineers through Society*. Milton Keynes, UK: Open University Press.

Leibniz, G. W., et al. 1994. *Writings on China*. Chicago: Open Court.

Loraux, N. 1996. *Né de la terre: mythe et politique à Athènes*. Paris: Seuil.

Padel, F. 1998. "Forest Knowledge: Tribal People, Their Environment, and the Structure of Power." In *Nature and the Orient: The Environmental History of South and Southeast Asia*, eds. R. Grove, V. Damodaran, and S. Sangwan, 891–917. Delhi: Oxford University Press.

Serres, M. 1980. *Le Passage du Nord-Ouest*. Paris: Editions de Minuit.

Tanaka, S. 2004. *New Times in Modern Japan*. Princeton, N.J.: Princeton University Press.

Toledo Maya Cultural Council and Toledo Alcaldes Association. 1997. *Maya Atlas: The Struggle to Preserve Maya Land in Southern Belize*. Berkeley, Calif.: North Atlantic Books.

Weschler, L. 1996. *Mr. Wilson's Cabinet of Wonder*. New York: Vintage Books.

Wolfram, H. 1988. *History of the Goths*. Berkeley: University of California Press.

# 18

# LAW, NATION, AND (IMAGINED) INTERNATIONAL COMMUNITIES

## Ruth Buchanan and Sundhya Pahuja

*If nationalisms in the rest of the world have to choose their imagined community from certain "modular" forms already made available to them by Europe and the Americas, what do they have left to imagine?*

—Partha Chatterjee, "Whose Imagined Community?"

It is difficult to approach the subject of nation without invoking Benedict Anderson's *Imagined Communities*. For although many disagree with Anderson's analysis that "from the start, nation was conceived in language not in blood" (Anderson 1991, 133), it is, in the wake of his book, difficult to consider nation and its relation to community without also considering the modern discursive and cultural forms through which they are each conjured and connected. What Anderson failed to take sufficient notice of, however, is the extent to which the very boundaries of the imaginable for "most of the world"[1] are already determined by a particular form of the nation-state prescribed by the West. Embedded within that form, according to Partha Chatterjee, is a predetermined relationship between community and the state, in which community must take the form of nation: "[t]he modern state, embedded as it is within the universal narrative of capital, cannot recognize within its jurisdiction any form of community except the single, determinate, demographically enumerable form of nation" (Chatterjee 1993, 238).

This chapter will begin from the perception of this straitened relation between community and nation produced by the nation-state form (Chatterjee 1993; Buchanan and Pahuja 2004) but will seek to extend this insight in two ways. First, we will shift from the purely "domestic" production of nation to consider the way in which notions of an international community operate to cohere and normalize the modern nation-state as the axiomatic form of social organization. Second, we will introduce a more explicit consideration of the role of law as an essential medium, both discursive and institutional, through which communities and nations are constituted and legitimated. Thus we frame our problematic not in terms of an oscillation between two poles, nation and community, but rather as a stabilizing triangular arrangement in which the third element is law. Law, as we will elaborate, is fundamental to the constitution of the nation-state, the paradigmatic form taken by nation in modernity. These two strands of analysis are brought together in the argument that some notion of an international community, that is, an authentic community located beyond or outside of nation, is more and more frequently invoked as a panacea to all manner of "global" crises. This invocation has been occurring in various ways in a number of different contexts.

In this chapter, we will identify three such contexts: U.S. unilateral action in relation to the war in Iraq; responses to the crisis of legitimacy of the World Trade Organization; and changes in the discourse of development emanating from the World Bank. We argue that recent developments in each of these sites reflect an emerging tendency for a conception of international community to play the crucial legitimating role as the stabilizing "ground" of law that the community as nation has traditionally provided and that the "community as nation" has traditionally played. In addition, using our three cases as illustrations, we will suggest that the concept of international community is deeply implicated in legitimizing the juridical processes by which contemporary hierarchical orderings between nations are (at least partly) maintained.

It is worth noting at this juncture that a significant element of our analysis in this chapter cuts against at least one recurrent tendency in contemporary debates over the governance implications of globalization. This is the assertion that the economic and social processes of convergence and integration associated with globalization are causing a diminution, or at least a radical transformation, in the capacities of the nation-state to govern. For legal scholars especially, this "withering away" is mostly understood in terms of a diminution of sovereignty, or the ability of particular nation-states effectively to govern their own territories and populations. The political corollary to this argument about governance is the suggestion that nation has become less salient as the imagined vehicle for the aspirations and identities of publics. If globalization is understood as undermining the capacity of nation-states to govern, then it may consequently be seen also as posing a challenge to their legitimacy and accountability to their own populations or constitutive communities. This challenge to legitimacy can be described as "the crisis of the hyphen" (Anderson 1996, 8) between nation and state: States continue to make laws and sign treaties that have ever more immediate effects, but the uncertainty lies in whether or not they are taken to do these things on behalf of and for the benefit of their entire population, understood as a whole and indivisible "community." This perceived crisis might explain why so many scholars and policymakers, in identifying and trying to remedy the potentially destabilizing effects of this delinking, have responded by seeking to locate "community" in another place and in a more inclusive public. Yet, this type of response all too frequently tends to perpetuate a belief in the demise of the nation-state. We believe this premise is fundamentally mistaken.

As the examples that follow will illustrate, it is our argument that the modern nation-state is in fact a crucial element in the maintenance of current structures of global governance. Indeed, far from withering away, nation-states persist in their current form because they are reinforced as such by international institutions, both political and economic. But in the turn to "international community" as a new source of popular legitimacy in the context of globalization, the dependence of the current order on the continued existence and conceptual unassailability of the nation-state is obscured. Indeed, it is our argument that unpacking the way in which the international community has increasingly become the rhetorical vehicle by which legitimacy is sought for the (nondemocratic) decisions of international institutions (and even the unilateral actions of a powerful state such as the United States) reveals how that concept functions *together with that of the nation-state* to reinforce the modern, unequal system of nation-states. This stands in sharp contrast to the panacea or promise of inclusion that the idea of international community would seem to invoke.

Many of the modern mechanisms of governance by which communities are made into nations—constitutions, representative democracy, even the traditional institutions of civil society—are to some extent defined and hence authored by law. It is also law, through the notion of sovereignty, which both author(ize)s and mediates the universal and particular dimensions of the modern nation-state. Law assumed this central yet problematic role in the Enlightenment thinking that gave shape to these institutions. However, this also means that law is implicated, less virtuously, in the modernist discourses of development. Ultimately, it is this entanglement and its resonances within contemporary international law that we seek to analyze and understand in this chapter.

## THE MODERN LOGIC OF LAW AND NATION

Both law and nation first need to be understood in terms of their peculiarly modern natures. One key shift that heralds modernity as a distinct period is, of course, the loss of external foundations or what is sometimes shorthanded as the "death of God." This existential bereavement has provoked a crisis of authority such that institutions in modernity face the need to become self-founding, to posit their sources of authority within the modern world (and often within themselves) rather than beyond the world in some transcendent source. But of course, for any gesture of self-founding to be definitive would be impossible—the proverbial pulling oneself up by one's own bootstraps. We can trace the paradox of this necessary but impossible act of self-founding through each of the subjects of our inquiry. Law and nation each hold themselves out to be autonomous, legitimate, and authoritative. But the question then arises: From where do they draw the source of this authority? The short answer is that they narrate, or author, it themselves. Law's narratives assert that the law is what the law says it is. And nations, too, must create themselves by narrating their own stories of origin that are always imagined, never "real" (Bhabha 1990, 291–322). In order to secure the legitimacy of this authority, it is necessary for both nation and law to conceal these acts of self-authorization. One way this concealment happens is through deferral, that is, by reference to some source of authority outside the particular entity whose foundation is in question. So, for example, to secure its authority, law gestures towards the legitimacy granted it by a sovereign nation. In turn, nation coheres as an entity through its claim to being endowed with sovereign (i.e., legal) authority. Usually this takes the form of a constitution that constitutes the specific nation as a juridical entity but whose authority depends on some notion of the community-as-nation pre-existing the constitution. Similarly, international law classically obtains legitimacy through its claim to being the consensual product of sovereign and putatively equal nation-states. The criteria that determine the existence of nation-states, however, are themselves products of international law. Alternatively, when the effect of international law is clearly nonconsensual in relation to some, international law's own assertion is that it embodies and is implementing the "values" of the international community. In that instance though, the boundaries of that community are themselves constituted by international law, as are the values that the law supposedly reflects.

Overall, the effect of these reciprocally deferred foundations is not only to produce the sought-after legitimacy or authority of that which is being founded, but also to render each concept coextensive with the other. Thus, we can see that the modern concepts of nation and law, rather than being conceptually distinct, are mutually constitutive. Similarly, international law and international community each bound and found the other. But in addition to the reciprocity of foundations, law shares another compelling characteristic with nation: the twin dimensions of universality and particularity. Both law and nation face the challenge of reconciling the determinate with that which is beyond determination. For law, this takes the form of a tension between the necessary qualities of determinacy and responsiveness (Fitzpatrick 2001).[2] The law must be made up of rules that are, by definition, fixed and certain. But at the same time, the law also needs to be capable of doing justice, that is, of responding to everything that lies beyond the rule.

Further, we know that nations can only exist in the world attached to determined people and territories. But every nation must also narrate itself in general terms as the best possible container for the realization of the needs and capacities of human beings. Given this duality, it is not surprising that it is through a juridical form—the nation-state—that nations have been able to combine their universalist aspirations with particular instantiations in "blood and soil" (Fitzpatrick 2001, 159; Fitzpatrick 2004; Chatterjee 2004, 29).

Turning again to the world imagined in international legal discourse, we can see that one necessary implication of this "combining" within the form of the nation-state is that the earth eventually had to be covered by a patchwork of nation-states, all imagined as equals because all participated in the same "universalist" form. This putative equality, however, sat uneasily with the evident inequalities of the time: colonialism and imperialism. And so it was that this Enlightenment idea of "comity," or the sovereign equality of nations, became dangerously emancipatory. Although the universal promise of nation gave rise to the possibility of an emancipation to which colonized peoples could themselves lay claim through self-determination, the inclusion of putatively sovereign equals into the international order could not overcome the way in which the "universal nation" was still instantiated in the very particular European form. The explanation was that some "nations" were simply fuller or more complete realizations of the "universal" form of the nation-state than others (see Fitzpatrick 2004). These latter were automatically assumed to aspire to, though not yet embody, the same ideal. And so the world of nations became "organized and classified along a spectrum ranging from the most 'advanced' or exemplary nations to barely coherent nations always about to slip into the abyss of an ultimate savage alterity" (Fitzpatrick 2001, 127–28). It is a key theme of this chapter that this spectrum is still clearly evident within the structures and institutions of international law and, indeed, is cohered rather than contradicted in the contemporary developments relating to "international community" to which we will now turn. In our first example, we consider the manner in which the space of the exemplary or universal nation must be occupied by one state or group of states, whereas in the second and third, we discuss how evident and persistent inequalities among sovereign nations are legitimated within international institutions and "authorized" by international law.

## The Exemplary Nation-State or the U.S. Occupation of Iraq

One instance in which "international community" has recently been invoked as a curative is the case of U. S. unilateralism. As readers will know all too well, the willingness of the United States to engage in the unilateral use of force in the name of the war on terror has frequently been met with calls to the United States to have regard to the international community and its laws—that is, to international law.[3] The idea of "coalitions of the willing" in which "the mission determines the coalition" rather than the other way around is anathema to understandings embedded in international law, that body of rules being a product of a coherent community reflecting and upholding an agreed set of values. If neither the coalition nor the mission may be determined in advance, such action cannot logically be seen as taking place pursuant to a rule of law. Yet, upholding the rule of law is precisely what the United States is claiming to be doing in Iraq. In order to understand this paradoxical positioning, we need to explore further the mutually constitutive relation between international law and international community, and the position occupied by the United States in relation to each. We will argue that in the context of the debates over the legality of the war in Iraq, the United States situated itself both inside and outside the international community and international law. Rather than simply viewing this as a cynical and transparent cover for power politics, we argue that the United States is inserting itself into a space made available to it by the logic of the international nation-state system: the space of the exemplary or universal nation. The position of exemplarity here assumed by the United States is the means by which claims to arbitrate the boundaries of both international law and international community can be made. The perennial difficulties faced by other, less "exemplary" nations in occupying their own rightful places in the international community flow from their persistent "failure" fully to embody the nation-state form as currently represented by the United States.[4] The way in which the United States casts itself in relation to the international community is illustrated by a press release issued by U.S. Secretary of State General Colin Powell on August 19, 2003, immediately after the bombing of the UN headquarters in Iraq: "The terrorist bombing that occurred today at the UN headquarters in Baghdad is a heinous crime against the international community and against the Iraqi people. I condemn the bombing unequivocally. I spoke to UN Secretary-General Kofi Annan earlier today to convey my deepest sympathy. We extend our sympathies also to the victims of this vicious attack and to their families, colleagues, and the international community. At the UN headquarters in Baghdad, the international community has been working with the Iraqi people to build a better future for Iraq. The United States strongly supports the vital role of the UN in Iraq's reconstruction. We will not be deterred by such immoral acts. The international community must renew its commitment to working with the majority of the Iraqi people who seek to build a free and stable country." As banal as this statement might seem at first glance, we think it is quite suggestive of certain ways in which "international community" functions as a concept in relation to international law. The first thing to note is the repetitive invocation of the international community itself: a discrete incident targeting an international organization becomes a "crime against the international community"; sympathy is extended beyond the victims and their families to the entire international community; the controversial and coercively patched together coalition of the willing occupying Iraq becomes the international community engaged in a nation-building exercise. This repetitive invocation seems to be almost incantatory in effect—directed at bringing into being the very international community to which it refers. So when General Powell asserts that "a crime" has been committed against the international community, those responsible are being placed firmly outside both law and the community. Arguably, in this equation, what is being brought into being is not just a community, but a community of law. The effect of this dual origin is to underpin the foundations of (international) law by locating its impelling authority in a community that would appear to give it legitimacy, and simultaneously to legitimize the community by equating it with that which is lawful. Furthermore, in one breath, the United States is expressing its sympathy to the international community, thus placing itself outside it, while in the next breath, it is implicitly including itself within the international community that must respond to such "heinous crimes." This oscillation is a tellingly ambivalent "borderland" positioning that replicates the United States' relationship to international law itself.

International lawyers are endlessly trying to explain the United States' vexatious relationship with international law. The relationship is obviously not one of wholehearted compliance, but nor can it be explained as complete disdain. It is rather a more complex engagement with international law, even as the United States breaches it. One way to explain this might be to say that rather than allowing its conduct to become involved in questions of legality and illegality, the United States attempts to inhabit the place between law and nonlaw. In other words, it seeks to occupy the space of law itself, which is, as we now understand, also to determine the borders of community. This attitude is tellingly illustrated in Robert Kagan's *Of Paradise and Power*, an influential book in foreign-policy circles. In drawing the central contrast that impels the book—between American unilateralism and European support for a rule of law—Kagan implicitly acknowledges that unilateral action stands in contrast to law. But it is not illegal. Indeed, the subtext is that unilateral action is the sovereign act par excellence (though he does not put it in these terms). From this it follows that the United States is the sovereign that inhabits the borderline between law and nonlaw as well as the entity that ensures the safety of the international community inside that border and governed by law. Indeed, in one particularly telling quote, Kagan suggests that the United States "mans the walls [of the European Kantian paradise] but cannot walk through the gate" because it has to stay outside "to deal with the Saddams and ayatollahs . . ." (Kagan 2003, 76). In this "manning of the walls," the United States, for the time being, is arguably occupying the space of both law and community by virtue of its assumed role as exemplary nation.

In General Powell's previously quoted statement, we also see a clue about the way in which the international community operates to secure the modern nation-state as the only way to "enter the world" (Fitzpatrick 2001, 126) and take a place in it. The general refers more than once to the role of the international community in helping to "build a better future" for Iraqis and to "build a stable country." The suggestion is that working together with the people of Iraq, the international community will create a modern nation-state. This will ostensibly enable the people of Iraq—who are evidently currently outside the international community (even though sovereignty has officially now been "handed over")—to join that coveted clique. This notion, of tutelage leading to inclusion is a common—and possibly the only—result of the interventions, both military and economic, that we see unfolding at the moment. Indeed, as we will explore further, the only choice being offered to the new and developing subjects of international law—such as East Timor, Kosovo, Afghanistan, and Iraq—"is to be governed by economically rational governments under the tutelage of the international economic organizations [who follow the military] as representatives of the international community" (Orford 2003, 27). The challenge this poses to the competing foundational principle of international law—that of sovereign equality—is contained in part by the way the international community operates to cohere the disparate dimensions of nation (universality and particularity) and enabling that concept to, in a sense, cover the earth. This cohesion happens through the way the international community can encompass a scalar progression from the "obdurate particularity" of the (reforming) state of Iraq to the universality of its most exemplary members, here the United States. But if the international community stands on higher ground, it is also highly contested ground. As we will discuss in the further examples, international financial institutions, themselves comprised of nation-states, are having their claim to occupy the space of international community challenged by other imagined collectivities. We will consider two manifestations of this: first in the form of challenges to the World Trade Organization by "global civil society," and second, in the recent move made by the World Bank to embrace social concerns, including human rights.


## "GLOBAL CIVIL SOCIETY" AND THE WTO'S CRISIS OF LEGITIMACY

*Global civil society* is a term that has become widely, if not always precisely, deployed to describe the growth of both new types of transnational actors and a new realm of advocacy in and around international institutions over the past several decades (de Búrca and Walker 2003). Growing interest in the realm of global civil society has paralleled the increase in concern over the perceived crisis of the nation-state (Strange 1996; Boyer and Drache 1996). Indeed, global civil society has become a preferred vehicle for the very types of arguments that seek to compensate for the perceived diminution of popularly endorsed sovereignty caused by globalization by refounding the impugned legitimacy of nation-states in some more "authentic" form of community. Invocations of global civil society often operate as the same sort of panacea as the notion of international community discussed in the previous example. Advocates of global civil society have described it as "a crucial agent for limiting authoritarian governments, strengthening popular empowerment, reducing the social effects of market forces, improving the quality of governance, and the role of civic organizations in the delivery of public goods" (Harvard Institute for Development Studies 1998) as well as a sign of "the evolution of a new global consciousness" (Pearson 2004, 85).[5]

We argue, however, that this ideal of global civil society emerges from the same set of rather older, ostensibly universalist ideals previously described that are deeply embedded in both our international legal order and the nation-state form.[6] Both the appeal and the difficulty of the notion of global civil society reside in the way in which it appears to sweep away the multiplicity and conflict that are a necessary part of interactions among actors situated in different parts of the world. Because of the universalist aspirations underpinning the notion of global civil society, activists working within the messy particularities of international networks can imagine that they are working towards a common purpose. As such, global civil society operates effectively and seductively as yet another incarnation of the imagined international community.

The increased attention paid to global civil society is a response to the perceived challenges presented by globalization. Indirectly, however, global civil society also presents a challenge to the self-founded nature of nation; that is, to the claim that nation corresponds to community. To put it another way, the belief that nation-states are passé and "can't cope" with globalization gives rise to the need for a new site for "global" politics. But because of the link between the foundations of law and nation, this also presents a challenge to law. In this way, global civil society seems to challenge the deferral we've described: the way that nation locates its ground in sovereign law, or the claim that a nation's sovereignty cannot be inquired into. In part, this challenge becomes plausible at certain historical moments because the general population becomes aware of the deep incursions into the affairs of sovereign nations already effected by international financial institutions. This was the case throughout the 1980s and into the 1990s. This was also the moment at which we saw a dramatic expansion of non-governmental organizations (NGOs) focused on issues and topics that cross national borders. People sought to influence decisions where they were being made, which increasingly appeared to be somewhere other than in national capitals. Thus, whether right or wrong, the challenge to nation represented by global civil society was, and is, the claim that at the international level, gatherings of the representatives of individual nation-states do not adequately represent the global community. Rather, community at the international level must be imagined to include the "people," which means global or transnational civil society.

The dynamic set into motion by global civil society's claim to occupy the space of international community in the current juncture can be illustrated by reference to the efforts of global civil society in relation to one international institution, the World Trade Organization. After the upheavals at the Seattle Ministerial in 1999, it was widely acknowledged that the WTO was experiencing a "crisis of legitimacy." That crisis had its source in two distinct challenges to the institution, which might be described as the "internal transparency" and "external transparency" critiques.[7] We are concerned here with the "external" challenge to the WTO, articulated by a range of networks and organizations that we are here taking to be the representatives of global civil society.[8] The critique of external transparency argues that the WTO should become more open and accessible to the civil society representatives of the world community directly, and not only via the representatives of member states. Implicitly, the argument is that the laws that are negotiated at the WTO lack a legitimate "ground" because the institution is not representative of the global community. Arguments made by the defenders of the WTO that it is itself a community of nations are rejected for the reasons we have already considered. Ironically, it was in part the incursions into sovereignty effected by WTO rules themselves that created the space for other challenges to national sovereignty, including that mounted by global civil society. And following our earlier argument, if law may no longer claim to found itself in a community, or if that community is no longer understood to be authentic, so must law's claim to authority and legitimacy fail. It is in the solution proposed by global civil society to this dilemma that we see its inability to escape the encompassing modern frame of law and nation. For global civil society itself proposes to occupy the space of the "cohering community" that seems legitimately to found authority. For many of the WTO's civil society critics, what will fix the external transparency problem is simply the greater inclusion of global civil society into the twin processes of the negotiation of trade rules and the adjudication of disputes arising from the application of those rules. In other words, the problem is not the groundlessness of law or community per se; the critique is limited to the inauthenticity of the "grounding" of the World Trade Organization as currently constituted.[9] This argument thus prioritizes the critique of formal, procedural matters such as accountability and transparency. In its embrace of such arguments, global civil society is participating in the circular logic of the self-constitution of law and community and therefore unwittingly undermining the potentially radical politics unleashed by the crisis of legitimacy.[10]

But perhaps we should not be surprised that "global civil society," in seeking to relocate politics to another level, has shown itself to be incapable of grasping the foundations of modern law and nation by their tangled roots. For we count ourselves among those scholars who seek to cut against the grain of currently fashionable postnational theory in arguing for the continuing need for analyses that grapple with the historical particularity of the nation-state form as a crucial building block of our contemporary international order (Balakrishnan 1996; Fitzpatrick 2001; Pahuja forthcoming; Buchanan forthcoming). In a similar vein, Chatterjee argues that we should look first within the nation, rather than beyond it, for the sources of what we have called the current crisis of the hyphen between nation and state (Chatterjee 1998, 57). In so doing, he proposes that an important distinction be drawn between the notion of "civil society" and that of "political society."

Civil society represents "those characteristic institutions of modern associational life originating in Western societies that are based on equality, autonomy, freedom of entry and exit, contract, deliberative procedures of decision making, recognized rights and duties of members and other such principles" (Chatterjee 1998, 60). In contrast, political society is a term that represents a much wider domain of institutions and activities concerning the "rest of society" that is reached by the legal bureaucratic apparatus of the state in the colonial and postcolonial period, a domain that has more in common with Foucault's notion of "governmentality" (Foucault 1991). For Chatterjee, civil society is the (restricted) domain of citizens, whereas political society operates within the much wider realm of populations. Civil society is the product of modernity, whereas political society is a product of democracy. So in countries such as India, in his example, civil society is most accurately used to describe "those institutions of modern associational life set up by nationalist elites in the era of colonial modernity, though often as part of their anticolonial struggle" (Chatterjee 1998, 62). In other words, for "most of the world" civil society represents a political project that is elitist and exclusive, not one that is inclusive and nonhierarchical, as contemporary advocates of global civil society would have us believe. In response, one might point to an alternative tradition that focuses on the political potential of "disorganized" civil society (Hardt and Negri 2000; Christodoulidis 2003). However, our view is that the evidence of recent civil society engagement with the WTO is much more closely reflected by Chatterjee's account. For most of the world, these types of interventions are likely to read as confined and elitist. In order for a critique of the WTO to resonate more widely with political society, it would be necessary to connect it directly to those "legal bureaucratic apparatuses" that have real and immediate consequences for populations.

## MAKING THE INTERNATIONAL COMMUNITY: THE WORLD BANK AND NATION-STATE BUILDING

In our final example, we want to turn to the way in which contestations over the nature and authenticity of the meaning of international community have provoked shifts in the practice of the World Bank. These shifts have engaged the Bank in practices of what is commonly known as "nation building." In our view what the Bank is actually engaged in should be described more precisely as "nation-state building," with the hyphen accorded as much importance as each of the terms it unites. What this example illustrates is first the way in which the nation-state remains a crucial part of contemporary global configurations, and second, the way in which, in the context of development, the notion of international community operates to stabilize the hierarchical nature of those configurations.

It must be some time ago—indeed, if ever it was—that the World Bank was seen as a representative of the international community charged with the task of helping newly independent nation-states grasp the promise of development. But whether that version of the Bank is nostalgia or fiction, it is certainly true that in the past decade or so there has been a widespread acknowledgment that the institutions of international economic governance, including the World Bank (and indeed, the WTO), have faced a "crisis of legitimacy." The crisis manifested at the World Bank in the early 1990s as it became clear that structural adjustment policies had not delivered what they promised. Many of the Bank's critics charged that the Bank policies reflected in those structural adjustment packages were antithetical to the values of the wider international community. In response to the crisis, the World Bank underwent a significant shift in its personnel, policies, and programs, towards what became known as the "post-Washington" consensus. To simplify the story, in this shift the Bank became increasingly aware that the programs it had been engaged in—of stripping back or paring down the state in order to facilitate the expansion of global markets, and so to promote economic development—could no longer be sustained. This was because of a growing awareness that markets could not function adequately without law, and that law was, in turn, an institution reliant on the state (Buchanan and Pahuja 2004). The shift can be traced through the publications of the Bank from the mid-1990s onwards, including its annual World Development Reports (e.g., Orford and Beard 1998). This evolution could be said to have culminated in the 2002 report, *Building Institutions for Markets*, which is overtly directed at strengthening state institutions, now proclaimed by the Bank to be necessary to the functioning of efficient and effective markets. Instructively, most of the exemplars of such institutions are legal (World Bank 2002, iii). But this recognition of the necessity of the existence of state institutions (especially law) was happening at the same time as multilateral economic institutions were suffering the more generalized crisis of legitimacy. There was a widespread perception that the version of the international community being represented in such organizations was not sufficiently inclusive, or authentic. Those who considered themselves to be the excluded elements of this community began to urge the Bank to take on board a collection of values endorsed by what was understood as the wider international community. These values are principally those embodied in human rights norms, environmental standards, labor rights, and gender equality.

The effect of this clamor, and indeed of concerted action by many activists, human rights lawyers, and development practitioners among others, was to provoke another shift in Bank practice that is still occurring, this time to "bring the social on board." Once again, this shift can be traced through a chronology of Bank publications, but in this case, one document does stand out. The Comprehensive Development Framework (CDF), first circulated in 1999, is an important indicator of the expansion of the Bank's concerns toward "the social." In the CDF, Bank President James D. Wolfensohn explicitly states that the development agenda must have two sides. The Bank's traditional preoccupation with the macroeconomic and financial aspects of development was to be complemented by an attention to its "social, structural, and human" dimensions (Wolfensohn 1999).[11] In the CDF, the Bank is embracing human rights, good governance, and the rule of law as explicit development goals (in addition to economic growth). This would have been hard to imagine a decade ago. This shift has had the desired effect of bolstering the legitimacy of World Bank interventions, extending even to human rights standards, for example. The increased legitimacy has also had the effect of enabling the World Bank to be perceived (perhaps once again) as a representative of the international community and bearer of its values in its interventions in "most of the world."

The two-fold move by the Bank toward "good governance" and the "social" has also facilitated a dramatic expansion of the Bank's capacity to intervene in the domestic affairs of ostensibly sovereign nations. Initially, the Bank's lending practices aimed to identify and isolate "economic" issues from the wider zone of politics not only to insulate reforms from political "interference" but also to comply with the Bank's own prohibition on interfering in the domestic affairs of nation-states.[12] But the recognition of the importance to a nation's economic performance of laws and institutions, as well as social policies such as human rights and gender equality, meant that trying to keep the Bank's interventions out of the realm of domestic politics, even for the sake of appearances, became increasingly untenable. Instead, the Bank simply redefined the line between the economic and political in terms of the new thinking on governance. Indeed, the Bank's legal counsel simply issued a legal opinion authorizing the shift (Shihata 2000, 245). This is a bold example of the self-authorizing nature of (international) law daring to reveal itself.

Besides illustrating the way law and community can each found and delimit the other, what is interesting about this example is that it is suggestive of the way in which populations must be rendered into nation-states in order to be commensurable with this "community of law" on which the global order depends. This rendering happens through "global technologies of governmentality," in particular those "that claim to ensure that the benefits of development are spread more evenly and that the poor and the underprivileged do not become its victims" (Chatterjee 2004, 67–68). The shift in bank practice toward holistic development has thus also included an increased emphasis on "participation," the creation of "social capital," and a focus on developing local "capabilities,"[13] emphasizing what Foucault has called the "pastoral" functions of government (Foucault 1991, 104), or in this instance, the pastoral functions of the institutions of global governance. Through these pastoral functions, heterogeneous populations are reshaped and categorized, at least for the purposes of governmental administration, into homogenous socialities.[14] These socialities are "convenient instruments for the administration of welfare to marginal and underprivileged groups" (Chatterjee 2004, 40) and so provide a way for agencies to deal with unruly people other than as bodies of citizens who might make demands outside the confines of dominant forms of social, political, and indeed legal, organization, in other words, outside the bounds of civil society. For this latter grouping supports the nation-state form through its connection to the nation-state's now-mandatory foundation on popular sovereignty and the formal granting of equal rights to citizens (Chatterjee 2004, 27). In contrast, other forms of (political) community such as Chatterjee's "political society" threaten the stability of the law-nation-community triangle on which the nation-state is balanced. But of course, if nation-state formation is the goal of the Bank's interventions, we are then led to the myth of the sovereign equality of nation-states on which the international legal order, at least, is said to be founded. And it is here that the notion of international community—with the Bank as its vehicle—performs its dual role. That is, the Bank in this example seeks to occupy a space similar to that of the United States in our first example, holding together the universal promise of the community of sovereign nations and the patent inequality of the present order. And it does so by prescribing a certain idea of development from poor ethnic, religious, particular nations to rich liberal, secular, and universal nations. Nation-states are therefore perceived not to coexist equally in their heterogeneity in the same time-space, but rather are conceptually captured and arranged in a hierarchical progression from past to present to future. The present moment in time of the exemplary, universal nation represents the future for the particular, ethnic nation. The threat to this hierarchy apparently posed by the foundational principle of sovereign equality would seem thereby to be averted.

The increased legitimacy promoted by the putative adoption of the values of the international community only reinforces World Bank tutelage as the proper way in which those who are currently outside (or only marginally within) the international community may enter the world (Fitzpatrick 2001, 126) and capture the elusive promise of membership. That the international community can encompass this progression, from the particularity of its reforming members to the universality of its most exemplary members, illustrates that it operates to cohere within it the nation and its universal and particular dimensions.

## CONCLUSION

We suggested at the outset that our argument in this chapter would cut against the tendency in current globalization debates to look "beyond the nation" for both effective institutions of governance and their sources of legitimacy.[15] We have argued that nation, far from withering away, is firmly at the center of a conceptual framework through which the modern world and its subjects continues to be produced and hierarchically ordered. Further, we have sought to consider the extent to which this modern conceptual frame depends integrally upon law to hold itself together. Moreover, we maintain that in the shift to the international triggered by globalization, this basic architecture has not altered, but intensified.

Through each of three examples, we have explored the way in which international law "founds" itself through a characteristically repeated gesture towards some notion of "community," replicating at the international level what we think of as a foundational logic of modern law and nation. That is, the manner in which international community can combine a promise of universality with the particularity of its constitution is what enables it to conceal the self-groundedness of international law. This concealment makes the particular ways of being and knowing of modernity—effected in part through modern law—appear to be both grounded (in the world) and universal. By revealing the logic of this interplay, we hope to have illustrated why the comfort that seems to be offered by the idea of international community is illusory. For in the tempting move embraced by many contemporary resistance movements to redefine international community and then to refound the institutions of international law in those communities, we wonder whether the radical potential offered by questioning those foundations is lost. In our view, any pathway towards more equitable and inclusive governance at the international level must lead directly into a critique of its modernist paving stones: law—nation, and community—and not pronounce us already beyond them.

## NOTES

This chapter is based on a talk given in the "Challenging Nation" series at the University of British Columbia in January 2004. The authors would like to thank Catherine Dauvergne and Wes Pue for their generous invitation to participate. This chapter also forms part of an ongoing collaborative project undertaken by the authors funded by the Social Sciences and Humanities Research Council of Canada. The authors also gratefully acknowledge the research assistance of Pooja Parma in the final stages of preparation of the manuscript.

1. In a remarkable new work, Chatterjee rejects loaded terms such as the "East," the "third world," or "developing countries" to describe the roughly "three-fourths of humanity" to whom those terms are habitually applied and instead coins the term "most of the world" to describe those who "were not direct participants in the history of the evolution of the institutions of modern capitalist democracy" (Chatterjee 2004, 3).
2. See generally, Fitzpatrick (2004).
3. See, for example, the comments by then UN Secretary General Kofi Annan made to the BBC on

September 16, 2004, available at: http://news.bbc.co.uk/go/pr/fr/-/2/hi/middle_east/3661134.stm (accessed November 1, 2004).

4. See, for example, the preamble at page v, as well as pages 6 and 19, in which the United States alternately narrates itself as protector and member of the international community: National Security Strategy of the United States 2002.

5. See also sources cited therein.

6. According to de Búrca and Walker, "civil society" was resurrected by John Locke and the Scottish Enlightenment in the late seventeenth and eighteenth centuries for the immodest purpose of accounting for and justifying the very foundations of social and political order in an age where the certainties of an external or transcendent referent . . . God, King, or even the givenness of traditional norms and behavior itself were disappearing (2003, 388). See also Buchanan (2003).

7. The internal challenge, not at issue in this article, is the one mounted by and on behalf of developing states against processes such as the widely critiqued "Green Room" negotiations, which are seen as heavily weighted in favor of the rich nations, particularly the United States and the European Union. For a full account of the internal transparency critique, see Kwa (2003).

8. There is a further distinction to be drawn between the role of "organized" and "disorganized" civil society, and debate over which might be taken to be the "real" representative of global community. See the *European Law Journal* 9/4 Special Issue: "Law, Civil Society, and Transnational Economic Governance" (2003) in general and the article by Christodoulidis for further consideration of this question. We are here confining our analysis of the WTO context to the arguments of representatives of "organized" civil society. For rationale, see Buchanan (2003).

9. We note that a similar limitation could be observed of the internal transparency critique, which does not, in most formulations, fundamentally challenge the modern forms of law and nation, but only the processes by which nations appear to be differentially empowered within the institution.

10. Of course, this is by no means the only political stance taken by civil society in relation to the WTO. However, it has arguably come to represent a dominant strand of argument because it is an issue around which a large number of otherwise disparate groups seem to be able to converge. See Buchanan (2003). For a contrasting account of civil society politics in relation to the WTO, see Said and Desai (2003).

11. See also Rittich (2006) for a discussion of CDF.

12. For example, the International Bank for Reconstruction and Development Articles of agreement, Article IV Section 10, say under the heading Political Activity Prohibited: "The Bank and its officers shall not interfere in the political affairs of any member; nor shall they be influenced in their decisions by the political character of the member or members concerned. Only economic considerations shall be relevant to their decisions, and these considerations shall be weighed impartially in order to achieve the purposes stated in Article I." At: http://web.worldbank.org/WBSITE/EXTERNAL/EXTABOUTUS/0, contentMDK:20049603~pagePK:43912~piPK:36602,00.html#I11 (accessed November 1, 2004).

13. The capabilities approach is inspired by the Nobel-Prize-winning economist Amartya Sen. See Sen (1999). For a good example of participation, see World Bank, Voices of the Poor at www.worldbank.org/poverty/voices/index.htm (accessed November 1, 2004).

14. This doesn't mean that the groups do not resist or are not political. Indeed, Chatterjee's thesis in *The Politics of the Governed* is precisely that "the line connecting populations to governmental agencies pursuing multiple policies of security and welfare . . . points to a different domain of politics" to the domain of civil society. He calls this domain "political society" (Chatterjee 2004, 37–38).

15. This is a reference to the declaration made by Arjun Appadurai, "We need to think ourselves beyond the nation" (Appadurai 1993, 411).

## Works Cited

Anderson, Benedict. 1991. *Imagined Communities: Reflections on the Origin and Spread of Nationalism.* London: Verso.

———. 1996. "Introduction." *Balakrishnan* 1996: 1–16.

Appadurai, Arjun. 1993. Patriotism and Its Futures." *Public Culture* 5, no. 3: 411–29.

Balakrishnan, Gopal, ed. 1996. *Mapping the Nation*. London: Verso.

Bhabha, Homi K., ed. 1990. *Nation and Narration*. London: Routledge.

Boyer, Robert, and Daniel Drache, eds. 1996. *States against Markets: The Limits of Globalization*. New York: Routledge.

Buchanan, R. 2003. "Perpetual Peace or Perpetual Process: Global Civil Society and Cosmopolitan Legality at the World Trade Organization." *Leiden Journal of International Law* 16, no. 4: 673–99.

———. forthcoming. "Reconceptualizing Law and Politics in the Transnational: Constitutional and Legal Pluralist Approaches." *Acta Sociologica Mexico*.

Buchanan R., and S. Pahuja. 2004. "Legal Imperialism: Empire's Invisible Hand?" In *Empire's New Clothes: Reading Hardt and Negri*, eds. Paul A. Passavant and Jodi Dean, 73–94. New York: Routledge.

Burchell, Graham, Colin Gordon, and Peter Miller, eds. 1991. *The Foucault Effect: Studies in Governmentality: With Two Lectures by and an Interview with Michel Foucault*. Chicago: University of Chicago Press.

Chakrabarty, Dipesh. 2000. *Provincializing Europe*. Princeton, N.J.: Princeton University Press.

Chatterjee, Partha. 1993. *The Nation and Its Fragments: Colonial and Postcolonial Histories*. Princeton, N.J.: Princeton University Press.

———. 1996. "Whose Imagined Community?" *Balakrishnan 1996*: 214–25.

———. 1998. "Beyond the Nation? Or Within?" *Social Text* 56: 57–69.

———. 2004. *The Politics of the Governed: Reflections on Popular Politics in Most of the World*. New York: Columbia University Press.

Christodoulidis, E. 2003. "Constitutional Irresolution: Law and the Framing of Civil Society." *European Law Journal* 9, no. 4: 401–32.

de Búrca, G., and N. Walker. 2003. "Law and Transnational Civil Society: Upsetting the Agenda?" *European Law Journal* 9, no. 4: 387–400.

Escobar, Arturo. 1995. *Encountering Development: The Making and Unmaking of the Third World*. Princeton, N.J.: Princeton University Press.

Fitzpatrick, P. 2001. *Modernism and the Grounds of Law*. Cambridge: Cambridge University Press.

———. 2003. " 'Gods Would be Needed . . . ': American Empire and the Rule of (International) Law." *Leiden Journal of International Law* 16, no. 3: 429–66.

———. 2004. "We Know What It Is When You Do Not Ask Us: The Unchallengeable Nation." *Finnish Yearbook of International Law* 15: 129–47.

Foucault, M. 1991. "Governmentality." In *The Foucault Effect: Studies in Governmentality: With Two Lectures by and an Interview with Michel Foucault*, eds. Graham Burchell, Colin Gordon, and Peter Miller, 87–104. Chicago: University of Chicago Press.

Hardt, M., and A. Negri. 2000. *Empire*. Cambridge, Mass.: Harvard University Press.

Harvard Institute for Development Studies. 1998. Web site description of civil society project. At: www.ids.ac.uk/ids/.

Kagan, Robert 2003. *Of Paradise and Power: America and Europe in the New World Order*. New York: Knopf.

Kaldor, Mary, Helmut Anheier, and Marlies Glasius, eds. 2003. *Global Civil Society*. Oxford: Oxford University Press.

Kwa, A. 2003. "Power and Politics at the WTO." In *Focus on the Global South*, 2nd ed., ed. Alec Bamford. At: www.focusweb.org.

Orford, Anne. 2003. *Reading Humanitarian Intervention: Human Rights and the Use of Force in International Law*. Cambridge: Cambridge University Press.

Orford, A., and J. L. Beard. 1998. "Making the State Safe for the Market: The World Bank's World Development Report 1997." *Melbourne University Law Review* 22: 195–216.

Pahuja, S. forthcoming. "The Necessary Inclusion of the Excluded: The Inherent Plurality of IMF Conditionality." *Acta Sociologica Mexico*.

Passavant, Paul A., and Jodi Dean, eds. 2004. *Empire's New Clothes: Reading Hardt and Negri*. New York: Routledge.

Pearson, Z. 2004. "Non-Governmental Organizations and International Law: Mapping New Mechanisms for Governance." *Australian Yearbook of International Law* 73

Powell, General C. 2003. Press Release August 19. At: http://usinfo.state.gov/is/ Archive_Index/Powell_Condemns_Bombing_at_UN_Headquarters_in_Iraq.html (accessed November 1, 2004).

Rittich, Kerry. 2006. "The Future of Law and Development: Second-Generation Reforms and the Incorporation of the Social." In *The New Law and Economic Development: A Critical Appraisal*, eds. David M. Trubek and Alvaro Santos, 203. Cambridge, UK: Cambridge University Press.

Sen, Amartya. 1999. *Development as Freedom*. Oxford: Oxford University Press.

Shihata, Ibrahim F. I. 2000. *The World Bank Legal Papers*. The Hague: Martinus Nijhoff.

Strange, Susan. 1996. *The Retreat of the State: The Diffusion of Power in the World Economy*. Cambridge: Cambridge University Press.

Wolfensohn, J. 1999. "A Proposal for a Comprehensive Development Framework." Discussion draft at: http://www.worldbank.org/cdf/cdftext.htm.

World Bank. 2002. *World Development Report: Building Institutions for Markets*. Oxford: Oxford University Press.

# 19

# GLOBALIZATION AS NEO-, POSTCOLONIALISM: POLITICS OF RESENTMENT AND GOVERNANCE OF THE WORLD'S RES PUBLICA

*Ileana Rodríguez*

*Ours, I submit, is not an age of postcolonialism but of intensified colonialism, even though it is under an unfamiliar guise.*

—Maso Miyoshi, "A Borderless World? From Colonialism to Transnationalism and the Decline of the Nation-State"

On the morning of September 11, 2001, at 9 o'clock a.m., one of my colleagues came to pick me up to work on a promotion and tenure case. I opened the door and after polite greetings, I believe I heard him mutter something about losing patience. Determined not to be distracted from the task at hand, I brushed aside the comment and asked him to focus on the case. When we came to the office, I felt a tension in the air, something like the fluttering of wings. Two members of the staff looked at me as if asking for comments. Comments about what? I thought to myself, and I proceeded to dismiss their startled gaze, which I attributed to "drama" in the office, and moved on. But for some fortuitous reason I had to come back to the office to fetch something and then I was either coaxed into or persuaded to go to another room—perhaps a TV set had been brought to our own central office—in any event, the case is that the mesmerizing image that was to cause so much consternation worldwide was right there, in front of me on the screen.

A plane going through a tower is a familiar scene in insurgency and counterinsurgency films. That and a car chase, people that are never hit by machine guns, people who escape the blast of powerful bombs, are all ordinary tricks of the trade, part of the genre. For a split second my brain downloaded postmodern aesthetics before politics hit full blast. But immediately, in one single blow, a deeper understanding of the epoch-making event came to me. The adrenaline rush gave this awareness the aspect, character, and tone of a revelation. I was stunned! We had crossed the threshold. There was no point of return. After that, I calmly went to the phone to call my husband and ask him to turn the TV on. Then I could see the university buildings under custody. The internal mobilization had begun. I shall therefore speak about globalization from the sudden realization of world politics that instantaneously came to me that day.

In this piece I propose to treat the over- and the under- side of globalization as a neo- and post- form of colonialism. My aim is to underscore the common thread that runs through the scholarship on this concept at an academic, as well as "development" and Nongovernmental Organization (NGO) agencies, level. My basic texts come from both these venues. I define globalization as the name used to define the logic of high capitalism and the effect transnational corporations have in the governance of the world. My central thesis is that whereas the intellectuals hired by "development" agencies and NGOs address globalization by coming to terms with the effects of policies such as fiscal responsibility and its effects in administration, governability, and democracy, academics in the central nations analyze commodity circuits and their effects in human consciousness that give rise to theories of postmodernism and postcolonialism with emphasis on multiculturalism, neo- and post- ethnicity, racism, and feminism. These approaches are complementary and together make up the face of the res publica of the world at large. My end point is criminality, a by-product or underside of globalization, defined as the politics of resentment expressed in terror, terrorizing, and terrorism.

I do not quite remember when I heard the word *globalization* for the first time or in what context. Perhaps it was at the University of Mona, Jamaica, at a conference on commonwealth literature—*The Empire Writes Back*, one of the most talked-about books on postcolonialism, was a very celebrated text at that conference (Ashcroft, Griffiths, and Tiffin 1989). Perhaps I heard it from my friend Robert Carr who was then a graduate student at Maryland and a student of globalization. But whenever and wherever it was, my first impression and feeling of the word was modernistic and poetic. Globalization is a very euphonic word; it is sonorous! To grasp the real meaning intended by the term, however, I had to radically veer away from aesthetics into an altogether different set of texts, another genealogy. What first came to mind were the works of the classics—works such as Fernand Braudel's and Pierre Vilar's, whose research thoroughly instructed us on capitalism as one world system (Braudel 1973; Vilar 1962, 1976). I also thought of Vladimir Ilyich Lenin's work on imperialism as a higher stage of capitalism, and about how popular this pamphlet was in the 1960s (Lenin 1996). Also came to mind the work of Immanuel Wallerstein on capitalism and his breakdown of the system in stages or moments and the terminologies in use—colonialism, mercantilism, laissez-faire; or colonial, neocolonial, postcolonial; or premodern, modern, postmodern (Wallerstein 1984). Not far off were the works of André Gunder Frank on dependency theory and his provocative concepts of lumpen proletariat and lumpen bourgeoisie that so much resonated in my Marxist universe (Frank 1972). But globalization also brought to mind low and high modernity and cosmopolitanism and tied the word very definitely to markets, to economies, and yes, to aesthetics. In this respect the work of Fredric Jameson (1991) seemed to me to be an indispensable reference.[1]

By the 1990s, globalization was an unavoidable term, a new way of naming a different stage in the development of capitalism. Not by chance I bought three of the most quoted books on the subject in Washington D.C. the same afternoon. I am referring here to Robert Reich's *The Work of Nations*, Immanuel Wallerstein's *Geoculture and Geopolitics: Essays on the Changing World-System*, and Kenishi Ohmae's *The Borderless World* (Reich 1991; Wallerstein 1991; Ohmae 1990). That was one of the first lessons I learned on my way to reintegrating myself into the academic world of the United States after my earlier immersion in the Sandinista Revolution. It is not my task here to rehearse the vast bibliography on the subject but to underscore what for me were the most insightful pieces—those mentioned above, plus the work of Jacques Attali's *Millennium: Winners and Losers in the Coming World Order*, Giovanni Arrighi's *The Long Twentieth Century*, Samir Amin's *Empire of Chaos*, Michael Hardt and Antonio Negri's *Empire*, and lately, Josefina Saldaña's *The Revolutionary Imagination in the Americas and the Age of Development* (Attali 1991; Arrighi 1994; Amin 1992; Hardt and Negri 2000; Saldaña 2003). So much has been produced in an effort to fill the concept with context that there is plenty to chew on. The real task for us now is to examine the conditions of possibility of current economic ideas and to forecast the use, function, and utility of intellectual work. What kind of service or purpose does this knowledge render to globalization? What new wealth does it bring into the world?

It is clear that to speak about globalization after September 11, 2001, we must determine if we are to define it negatively, as the obliteration of concepts, forms of life, disarticulation of meaning, loss, nostalgia, melancholia, or if we are to privilege the multiple challenges globalization poses to the theory of knowledge, the redefinition of fields of inquiry, the understanding of alternative and contradictory logics, or, a third option, if we shall be completely celebratory of the multifarious interfaces globalization brings to us. Reading the work on the subject, I realize that in the great centers of intellectual production in the West (the United States and Europe), the discussion on globalization tends to favor the market approach; it favors the *economic* side of productivity, whereas in the rest of the world, in my field for example, the discussion dwells on governance and governability: it favors the *political* effects of productivity.[2] I will argue that these two aspects are complementary. The economic emphasis draws on the circulation of technologies, commodities, and peoples; it docks at the harbors of multiculturalisms, hybridity, and the in-between spaces (postcolonial and postmodern theories); we consider migration and labor and have a rich discussion of liberalism. The political emphasis underscores the precarious nature of the nation-state and foregrounds a multiplicity of issues concerning governance, administration, and democracy. One hopes such a bifurcation enables us next to establish the connection between the two and to untangle the new rules of engagement that globalization brings to bear in the governance of the res publica.

Globalization subtends everything we know and everything we do. It pervades all our social practices. This is what scholars mean by modeling society and subjectivity after its own norms. Some of the most visible effects of globalization in our lives are the process of subsumption of industry into services and information, the changes in the patterns and places of labor—be it the migration of labor from industry to services or the transfer of manufacture abroad—and the dismantling of the welfare state, fiscal responsibility, deregulations, and privatization of all productive sectors.[3] Globalization has thus changed the parameters of everything including the meaning of development and modernization, the notion of structure, the world juridical system, and the idea of self-regulating nation-states. Trying to make the world fit the new structural paradigm of globalization results in today's cluster of world organizations. But what is structurally embedded is of major consequence for humanity, and thus to square the goals of universalism and the festive impulse and desires for a belle epoque behind the idea of one "global village" looks simply chimerical. The latest analyses on the subject, north and south, east and west, waver between celebrating the virtues of integration and chastising the vices of marginalization. For the hard-core believers of market economies, the world has become the biggest fair. For those who believe otherwise, the world has become apocalyptic. In one case, overnight millionaires; in the other, starving, benighted, and bedeviled masses—the promise of delivery both over- and underachieved.

Just to provide one example, economic and sociological research some decades ago forecasted the polarization of society when they studied the transition from Taylorism to Fordism, to Post-Fordism, to Toyotism in what they called the postwork societies.[4] They took to task the celebration of the closure of one type of workers' discipline and the inauguration of the flexible work schedules by pointing out that this was just the effect of new production policies. But these production policies brought to a halt the close communication between production and consumption and shifted over from full to zero stocks and commodities, producing just-in-time to supply demand. This shift totally reformatted the idea of full employment and seniority, workers' rights, the struggle to expand the social power of labor and to increase the value of labor power and redesigned the set of workers' needs and desires. All these desires were grossly compromised when not altogether foreclosed.

In tune with this trend, but taking it to its extreme, world banker Jacques Attali drew a panorama we all must take stock of (Attali 1991). The core of his rereading of world economies is the exclusion of the great masses—he called them nomads—and the deepening of profound sociocultural heterogeneities—what others and I call globalization from below. His point of reference was Africa, but a recent book by Martin Hopenhayn speaks about a parallel phenomenon in Latin America. Hopenhayn describes three crises of globalization, namely: the crisis of utopia, the crisis of state modernization and development discourse, and the crisis of intelligibility and organicity (Hopenhayn 2001).[5] The first set points in the direction of losing all the creative energies of human beings who turn to popular religion, grassroots movements, diversified consumption, esoteric doctrines, programs of personal development, aerobics, Buddhism, or retribalization. The second set is visible in the famines created by development discourse, in the end of subsistence economies and in the street terror of gangs, crime, and terrorism, due in part to the closure of the welfare state. The third set is evident in the difficulties we intellectuals face in grasping the new political, cultural, and social scenarios that have emerged across the global map.

Massive violence coupled with massive emmiseration recalls Marx's dictum on the falling rate of profit—the larger the profits, the smaller the employement; ideal absolute profit and unwelcoming absolute unemployement dovetail—whose dynamism is right before our eyes. Faced with this type of social and economic entropy and with a kind of fundamentalism that cannot be easily done away with, the larger issue hovering in the shadows is: what must be done? The great prophet of doom, Michel Foucault, already triggered all the censors when he provided us with his metaphor of the panopticon, a structure of vigilance and discipline that surveys all spheres of life, from subsistence economies to genes, and puts them under the light of market economies, making the final threshold of capital only nature itself. If he is right, we must follow his lead: we must continue exercising the power of what Theodor Adorno called negative dialectics; we must take Ranajit Guha's advice of reading against the grain; we must consider Antonio Gramsci's thoughts on the difficulties of building national popular blocs; we must note Louis Althusser's multiple articulations, and we must heed Enrique Dussel's return to ethics. We must contribute what we can to put a halt to thinking about populations as surplus people—sufferers, nomads, sicarios, "murderers not martyrs"—and to begin having some respect for their demands, lest we truly transit to posthuman societies.

To service the story of globalization well, we must begin by acknowledging a double theoretical injunction. The first refers to the vocabulary we employ in speaking of the object; the second, to thinking of the totality as a nonabsolute absolute. We cannot access previous vocabularies, for they have become empty signifiers; we cannot access new ones, because they fall short of fitting the object. And although there is no dearth of theoretical knowledge available, the name of the object is characterized by a lack. It doesn't approximate, let alone meet, the challenges of globalization. Thus, our knowledge of the world can no longer be anchored in either a liberal or a Marxist conception of the world, be circumscribed to geographies and populations, or be understood by accessing single disciplines. The system must be thought of as a nontotalitarian totality, the absolute one and only system, a system without fissures or oppositions—the notion of "outside" having been erased (Wilson and Dissanayake 1996).

The prohibition to use older vocabulary amounts to deactivating concepts such as nation and national, comprador bourgeoisies and intelligentsia, development and underdevelopment, center and periphery. These are all terms to think the nontotalizable converted into empty signifiers; they point to ways of thinking of the system's past. Today, the preferred terms are more generic, beginning with localities, globalities, and spaces, and followed by flows, fluctuations, configurations, interfacing, fractal and webbing—that is, they are the *unstable cyber*, that which Amin (1992) claims is impossible to analyze, to predict, to forecast.[6] To think of the totality in absolute terms, we must start by conceding that the core aspect of globalization is global capitalism, whose aim is twofold: first, to convert all the sensorial and extrasensorial into a commodity, or worse, into commodity fetishism; and secondly, to make as efficient, secure, and absolute as possible the siphon that channels the surplus from everywhere to the upper strata or elite of the military-industrial-cyber complex. If one makes these dubious concessions, then it is easy to conclude that anything that encumbers or curtails the system, everything that doesn't groom it, must be immediately and mercilessly cut out.[7]

One of the prerequisites to thinking the system as an absolute totality is to facilitate the withering away of the nation-state. Today that is not a difficult task, given that the nation-states (at the local level—that is, what is actually called "non-national" states) cannot be relied upon because their role is limited to ensuring the terms and conditions of trade and economic transactions of the transnational corporate. Slavoj Žižek (1994, 2) states it in its most dramatic form when he says that two reasons for the limitation of nation-state sovereignty are "the transnational character of ecological crisis and nuclear threat."[8] However, in the new theoretical configuration, the withdrawal of nation-states from the picture is tantamount to the withdrawal of their functions as gatekeepers of citizenship, local law and security, precarious forms of identities as well as control of currency, public health, and education—all that which has been already severely compromised and disabled.

One of the gravest and most immediate effects of the withdrawal of the concept of the nation-state as a stable category, however, is a change in the notion of subjectivity. The logic of globalization looked at from below brings about "chronic" and "structural" poverty, which in turn feeds all forms of ungovernability and social chaos. Intellectuals at NGOs amply and obsessively speak about it. Testimonial literature documents that poverty engenders all kinds of desperate subjects. Their designations as indigents, sufferers, and mendicants are sufficient indicators to fill the idea of the zero degree of telos and end of history with content, not precisely of the brand Francis Fukuyama envisioned.[9] I will speak about this in detail further on.

If, in order to preserve the absoluteness of the system, all the nontotalizing categories of thought (representing opposition) have been thrown overboard, then so have been all of those standing for liberalism. With one hit, democracy, civil society, and the public sphere were swept under the rug and became empty epistemes—the end of all ideologies, to round out Fukuyama's idea. Thus, Žižek claims that the "eroding of state authority . . . is mirrored in the fact that today the basic political antagonism is that between the universalist 'cosmopolitical' liberal democracy (standing for the force corroding the state from above) and the new 'organic' populism-communitarianism (standing for the force corroding the state from below)" (1994, 3). To put it in an abstract manner, the "zero level" of ideology for him "consists in (mis)perceiving a discursive formation as an extra-discursive fact" (10).

Now, if it is true that globalization represents total economic control, if there has been a progressive and effective withering away of the nation-state as the main unit of governance, the question that looms large is the political form of its representation. Does globalization require an imperial, neo- and postcolonial, form of governance—that is, a single political system, a megastate? Scholars working across multiple developmental financial agencies respond to this question by claiming that that form of governance is already in place, that we know it under the name of governability.[10] Scholars in academia are still debating the regulatory structure that will make it possible to govern all types of "localities" (the new name for demobilized former nation-states) and putting their efforts into imagining the form and content of the constitution of *empire*—the megastate. Their model is the familiar tripolar constellation composed of the United States, Japan, and the European Community.

On the other side of the divide, Samir Amin (1992) contests this idea by reading the system, as Ranajit Guha (Spivak 1988) recommends, in reverse. The megastructure he envisions is not the like of any of the present megastructures. For Amin, reports and analyses coming from multinational agencies such as the World Bank offer a picture of the world similar to those the newspapers *Pravda* (Soviet Union) or *Gramma* (Cuba) offered of Socialism during the Cold War years. This type of mental configuration locates the analysts within a "saccharine" type of fascism. Thinking in reverse, within a chimerical type of Dusselian humanism if you will, Amin imagines possible patterns of regional states or continental governance. This should not surprise us, for Amin's point of departure is the analysis of capitalism as a system based on the logic of accumulation through the expansion of markets. He knows that to the increment in accumulation there is a direct proportion of polarization of forces (i.e., a falling rate of profit effect). The nature and importance of such polarization is political; namely, it tends to enlarge the gap between the over- and under- sides of globalization, making the situation of the world "unbearable." *Unbearable* is Amin's favorite adjective to define the world's present governance of the res publica. The situation is unbearable, he explains, because that is the way it feels subjectively. It is unbearable at all levels, for those who suffer from it as much as for those who cannot grasp it or for those who cannot govern it. Thus the adjective has an emotional, subjective, ethical side, but it also has an analytical and political one.[11]

So, what does Amin propose? He proposes a very unviable reformatting of the economic system: to substitute the criterion of profit for one based on a redistributive social justice; to construct a polycentrist state where all the nations and regions of the world can discuss their problems—a kind of public megasphere. He attempts "to defeminize the periphery" and treat it as equal, with respect. He entertains the possibility of thinking in terms of redistribution logic, one that pays attention to social services, full employment, training, food, and culture. This new model of governance would eliminate the problems brought about by adjustment and supplement and would turn all thinking about the system into something truly structural and global. However, if this does not occur, his prognosis is lethal: the abyss between the active and passive labor reserve will become wider, making the situation even *more* unbearable. Unfulfilled needs will further strain all forms of subjectivities and will bring about unedited and unexpected forms of struggle—not precisely of a Leninist type. It will bring about, alongside the abject, that which is out of proportion and measurement—horror, the uncanny, *worldwide*.

Once again, these observations take us directly to the discussion of the public sphere and recall the ominous forecasting by Foucault and Deleuze of the intervention of mass media in it.[12] As it is, social democracy has abandoned the public sphere and created a simulacrum of discussion in which public discourse is engineered by mass media. Left and right seem to have reached consensus and are indistinguishable one from the other—such is the case of the Democratic and Republican Parties in the United States. The abyss between a conservative social democracy at the center and a radical and disparate periphery at its borders will increase geometrically until the two of them become dissociated and all types of anarchisms and autarchisms break loose. Terrorism qualifies as an instance of this desperate attempt to mobilize the disaffected. The point made is that of limit or threshold. Is there a way out of this apocalyptic predicament?

Giovanni Arrighi doesn't think so. In his book *The Long Twentieth Century* he had already offered an apocalyptic vision stating with force that within the present conjunctures, "[e]ntire communities, countries, even continents . . . have been declared 'redundant,' superfluous to the changing economy of capital accumulation on a world scale" (330); that "[c]lass struggle and the polarization of the world-economy in core and peripheral locales . . . have almost completely dropped out of the picture" (xii), and that the "equality of courage and force which, by inspiring mutual fear, can alone overawe the injustice of independent nations into some sort of respect for the rights of one another" (21) is also dead (Arrighi 1994).

To be sure, his is not a simple manner of speaking, but a very profound and systemic analysis of capitalism. For Arrighi, what we are going through is not a crisis but simply a structural trait of the system, its logic.[13] Capitalism works through cycles: there is a regulative phase, characterized by governability and a clear normativity (a belle epoque), followed by an eclectic phase, characterized by chaos and ungovernability. The eclectic moment—our present stage—is the moment of freedom and experimentation in which the system dislocates and flies over all the regulations and restrictions of the previous phase. However much this is the condition of the life of capitalism, this dynamic obviously triggers fear.

If in the past, as Étienne Balibar and Immanuel Wallerstein (1991) argue, the development of European capitalism is intimately linked to the development of the nation-state and to the accumulation of its force; now the nation-state can be subtracted from the equation, leaving sheer force alone.[14] By *force* these analysts mean first the supply of variable accumulated capital, which strong nation-states can move freely during the eclectic period, and second, armies. Both forces regulate the different moments of the cycle—hence the motto that strong nations act like gangsters whereas weak nations act as prostitutes.

In consonance with this analysis is Miyoshi's (1996) idea of a refurbished type of colonialism. In his article on globalization as "a borderless world . . ." he explains the difference between "multi" and "trans" in corporations. *Multi* and *trans* refer to giant, megaenterprises/megacorporations that combine all the elements of trade and marketing—import, export, manufacture, wire transfer capital, factories, sales, workers, and sale outlets across borders. Their domination of the world has been unchallenged, he tells us, since the 1950s. Although the distinction between them is not quite clear, in multinationals the accent is on national, whereas in transnationals the blurring of borders is emphasized. The move from noun, in the first term, to prefix, in the second, corresponds to lesser national and greater corporate identification and sufficiency—the accentuation of the virtual, invisible space where movement occurs. Deprived of national determination, the policy and logic of companies is to maximize profit regardless of consequences. Space is now judged on the basis of availability of cheap labor, tax inducement, feeble environmental rules, flexible governance structures, fixable political stability, adequate infrastructure, low civil rights awareness, and underdeveloped feminism.

Furthermore, the recruitment of local workers in different global spaces gives the corporate world a range and variety of nationalities and ethnicities, unseen and unheard of before. This means corporate employers must develop a feeling of familiarity with local cultures, rules, and social connections—a most welcomed and deceitful type of multiculturalism. At the level of high management, the model configurations of employment are provided by the local selection of workers done by international agencies such as the United Nations and all the corresponding "development" agencies affiliated to European embassies. These institutions choose their workers among the members of the local elites who, in turn, recommend their friends, family, and colleagues; they serve as a filter for the selection process that ensures loyalty to the organization, the company, and the local elites. English is their lingua franca and social vehicle of communication and understanding. The result is the creation of a transnational class of professionals who understand each other very well and partake of the same values. These cadres are cosmopolitan in nature. They know how to manage a variety of codes, and to speak about the local/provincial is considered to be in bad taste unless it refers to folklore or idiosyncratic forms of local performances. They belong to and practice the "universal chic" and are decadent, postethnic, and neoracist. They usually elude the past and privilege the present where the common themes are shopping malls, traveling, performances, and cable TV. Viewers of the world, unite! It is the world of the instant, the subjectivity of electronics. Tomorrow, there will be new forms of automated labor, new machines, new migrants, that may well render them individually obsolete.

These people must be differentiated from those workers who need to migrate to the central nations—Attali's nomads—to constitute the servant classes—a very problematic kind of multiculturalism for liberalism, as the works of Charles Taylor (1991) and Will Kymlicka (1991) testify. And then, there are the local workers and those who cannot and will never integrate or migrate, the "chronic poor" and the mendicant classes of all demobilized humans.

From this we can gather that Miyoshi's article underwrites Balibar's thesis that nation-states and capital accumulation are the two forces that constitute the foundation of European colonialism and European racism. The difference is that Miyoshi calls it neoracism and links it to the discussion on multiculturalism, which for him "is a luxury largely irrelevant to those who live under the most wretched condition" (Miyoshi 1996, 95). Multiculturalism is merely an "important strategy of the TNC [Transnational Corporations] managers. . . . In fact, it may very well turn out to be the other side of the coin of neoethnicism and neoracism" (95). Actually, if Kenishi Ohmae (1990) had absolutely demonstrated the workings of globalization by offering us unarguable data, and Robert Reich (1991) had done a superb job in dismantling the notion of nation and national allegiance and affect in favor of corporate citizenship, Miyoshi does a superb job in viewing globalization as the new form of colonialism. His thesis is that "The liberated citizen of a colony now [has] to renegotiate the conditions of a nation-state in which they [are] to reside thereafter. . . . [O]nce dragged out of their precolonial state, the indigenes of the peripheries have to deal with the knowledge of the outside world. . . . [P]eaceful progress has been structurally denied to them. Alliances amongst Third World states against First World domination have all performed poorly, ultimately surrendering to the Bretton Woods system" (Miyoshi 1996, 81).

Miyoshi's prognosis is ominous but coincides with all of those mentioned previously. It is also my sense of the world. The feeling is one of absolute darkness, closure, and sorrow. Hence, the turn to the abject, the other side of which is frivolity, decadence, and triviality. The question now is: what to do with the poor?

Throughout this paper, I have been arguing, together with the theoreticians mentioned, the uselessness of the category of nation-state to the analysis of capitalism in its present form; I have noted how globalization demands, among other things, new forms of imagination. Now, one of the conceptual devices that accompany fiscal reform is that of the "chronic poor." By definition these are people who cannot integrate themselves into the new economic model. To all appearances, reform programs definitively weaken all but the position of larger social groups. This occurs in spite of the fact that funding agencies maintain that the correct articulation of the economic model will reduce poverty. On paper, the projects favor development and give the poor access to all the material opportunities: they speak of equity, public investments, markets, credits, services, and claims to prioritize the institutional frames and sectorial policies that offer assistance to the poor and that listen to their plight. But, why is it that in spite of the "goodwill" of the developing agencies, there continue to be so many chronic poor?

In principle, developmental models for the poor are proposals presented by qualified intellectuals in the social sciences hired by the funding agencies to solve the problem of poverty. Often, the results are theoretical models—fiction as the structure of truth, as Lacan would have it—that, when inserted within the realities and logic of globalization and the historical distinctiveness of people at the local level, turn sour within a couple of years. It is axiomatic that the macroeconomics of globalization constitute a core hegemonic regulation, and hence local governments find it difficult to gather political support alongside a sufficient technical capacity to vigorously tackle the problem of poverty at a large enough scale. There is a structural impediment to truly implement a pro-poor type of governability. The new fiscal reforms terminally, it seems, hinder the possibility of integrating them by means of a political and institutional medium. Gone are the days of Keynesian economics that harbored the illusion of regulated growth and benefits; gone the days of Bandung (1955–75) when the idea of national development created the illusion that the poor areas of the world could be developed and that the world-system was predicated on the advantages of interdependence.

For Angel Saldomando (2002), who has written extensively and intelligently on the subject, macroeconomic factors leave no space to local, autonomous, independent forms of governance. Economic growth, development, and democracy are terms defined by the core nations and their institutions. The effect is that local governments disengage themselves from the responsibilities of coordinating the economic and the social. They administer the reform and transfer the responsibility of the social to civil society and the private sector. This brings us to the question of liberalism and the celebrated transition to democracy—or to ideology as the naturalization of the symbolic order, as Barthes would have it. Those who partake of the idea of liberal reform believe that the social costs of the reform are transitory and that growth will progressively absorb poverty as the regional economies find themselves in shape to apply healthy, nonpopulist, economic measures. Those who disbelieve liberal reforms hold that the cost is structurally permanent. What reality demonstrates is that the latter is a truer explanation. Liberal reforms do not raise the issue of the content of growth, or what are the institutional and political spaces most favorable to the poor. They forbid making explicit the hidden necessity of what appears contingent. Forbidding thoughts from being inscribed into their objects does not preclude the increment of poverty to be directly proportionate to the contents of the economic model, oriented towards deregulation, and a liberalization that favors transnationalization. By now, it is an incontrovertible fact that fiscal reforms systematically destroy the social tissue, the capacity for organizing and mobilizing the poor.

Furthermore, reform programs have never demonstrated their capacity to create consensus or the conditions of an expanded social coalition. Rather, the coalitions they foster are those of corrupt minorities that favor old and new power groups. The members of this new national and social coalition come from the propertied classes, emergent financial and commercial groups, and high-ranking officials of government and armies—old and new money. Their administration of the res publica is reduced to administrative procedures. Government officials are proconsuls whose job is to implement the reforms that debilitate the state and favor the macro. Parliamentary structures are solely engineered to serve fiscal reform. In these hands, the role of the state is that of administrator. The state administers the fiscal reforms and the social programs financed by the international agencies. Governability is a transregional and transcontinental pact with no possibility of alternative construction.

I have stated that development proposals ignore, and to a certain point prohibit, the contextualization of the problem and that local historical variables are excluded. The economic model is never made part of the frame. In the periphery, globalization all but deepens the asymmetries of power, brings the political space to a close, overdetermines the role of the international institutions, and engineers the systemic exclusion of social groups. And worse! It is not only that the fiscal reforms drastically curtail the possibilities of social organization that could bring some form of redress in the guise of social justice. It is that now any form of social struggle is proscribed. Hence, any mobilization on the part of the chronic poor against the unbearable is immediately called terrorism and hence surgically treated. All legitimacy has been withdrawn from the concept of social conflict as the central problem of all democracies. The chronic poor have been fused with common delinquency, criminality, and organized terrorism. The institutionalization and recognition of the participative process were historically the product of social pacts produced by successful social mobilizations. But now, conflicts such as unemployment and chronic poverty are no longer seen to be the legitimate expression of social problems but rather as examples of a politics of resentment, the resources of the nonadaptables, of the nostalgic, those suffering from the illness of melancholia, the abject.

In this predicament, the poor have no medium to express themselves. Their vulnerability is total. They have no possibility of transforming themselves into political subjects because they cannot construct their identity around social problems and there is no point of just calling attention to their lacks, their fragmented individualities. The elites favorable to fiscal reforms are the only ones visible in the public space. There is no social movement that represents the masses or the diversity of social identities. The chronic poor—women, children, peasants, youth, Indians, blacks, workers, inhabitant of marginalized and poor communities—are circumscribed to their local spaces. There is a total disconnection between their place in the world and the national and global space.

In the meantime, NGOs have come to play the role formerly played by social organizations— a "lobby" in favor of participation and against poverty. However, in their hands, governability in favor of the poor is a joke. Their pledge of social justice ends by financing social expenses without a plan to reconstruct the social tissue. They always lack a growth or redistribution strategy. The construction of nations rests at the hands of the international cooperation that pays legions of technical assistants to monopolize the public space and make decisions with an absolute lack of transparency. They also pay for the implementation of the reforms sometimes by providing the salaries of government officials, sometimes by supporting the social structures and institutions that would make the reforms viable; in the process they create temporary structures to provisionally eliminate high levels of conflict and impede grave crisis or the immediate polarization of forces.

Ironically enough, the main battle is to reconstruct the state. The state—that is, a state conceived as a welfare state—is viewed as the sole structure that can reactivate the process of political recognition, open up the political space, and stimulate anew the organization and mobilization processes. The state is the only force capable of controlling and implementing reforms, the sole instance of regulation and intermediation between the local and the global that could be construed as a protective nucleus, a rampart against theft, greed, and denationalization. There is a need of revitalizing the civil society so that citizens can express themselves as consumers and as social agents. Two steps forwards, one backwards, Lenin (1996) claimed!

A space for public participation, where political parties, social organizations, and the corporate structures could vent their differences, is a dream. Actually, it is *Samir Amin's* (1992) dream: a polycentrist government organization, a state of legality that would legitimize local administration and channel social demands. But that space is closed. The urgent necessity to redefine the nature of the reforms and their fit into the local situation is part of the double and triple daring of developing an economic model that would have as one of its variables the ending of poverty. This is at least the humanist plight. Naturally, under the present regime of accumulation, this is only a chimerical illusion, a true aporia. The progressive emptying of the political spaces has, in my view, all but reached a point of entropy, of no return.

Coming from a utopian vision of the world and from an experience where change was not only a possibility but also the conditions of the "real," my conclusions are all but apocalyptic. Žižek has accurately framed things as they are when he ironically claims that "today, as Fredric Jameson perspicaciously remarked, nobody seriously considers possible alternatives to capitalism any longer, whereas popular imagination is persecuted by the visions of the forthcoming 'breakdown of nature', of the stoppage of all life on earth—it seems easier to imagine the 'end of the world' than a far more modest change in the mode of production, as if liberal capitalism is the 'real' that will somehow survive even under conditions of a global ecological catastrophe" (Žižek 1994, 1). Žižek is clearly being facetious. Only in the most extreme forms of psychotic delusion could capitalism be thought of as the surviving 'real' of a global ecological catastrophe. By the same token and using the same allegory, neither could intelligent situation analysis be conceived within the dominant epistemes. Under the current conditions, no matter how smart, well honed, and structurally tight the analysis is, no matter how innovative, avant-garde, postcolonial, or Derridean it is, the problem of poverty remains outstanding. Poverty begets violence, and violence shakes up Western structures of thought. It throws prevalent schemas and models into disarray. If Arrighi is right and we are no longer in a situation of crisis but within the logic of capital, this logic has placed us face to face with the unbearable—Amin's sense of limit, border, threshold.

Therefore, what of intellectuals? What of knowledge? Insofar as the intellectual is concerned, there is, at best, a sense of a true aporetic impasse, undecidability, no leading edge or clear sense of a path to follow out from this swamp. This unquestionably takes us not towards the enriched human life of liberal or Marxist utopia but to an unthinkable terminus and irrationality. Under these circumstances, the role of intellectuals, the role of knowledge, has moved away from the illusion of organicity. Former public intellectuals have become the demobilized prophets of doom.

## NOTES

1. Here the work of Fredric Jameson is an unavoidable reference. See Jameson (1991), Jameson and Miyoshi (1998), and Hardt and Weeks (2000).

2. Privileging markets over politics partially explains the large bibliographical corpus on postmodernism. Understood as the new cultural logic of late capitalism, postmodernism is defined as a prodigious expansion into yet uncommodified areas—the unconscious first, the human DNA lately. Some of its characteristics are the ascendancy of popular culture over high arts; the dominance of the image, appearance, and surface effect over depth; preference for parody, nostalgia, kitsch, and pastiche over realism or naturalism; a preference for the popular or decorative over the brutal or functional in architecture and design; the erasure of a strong sense of history; the slippage of hitherto stable meaning; the proliferation of difference and cultural diversity related to the multiplication of social worlds and logics available through consumption; and the end of deterministic rationalism and the grand narrative of progress, development, Enlightenment, rationality, truth, and Western political philosophies. In postmodernism, the paradoxes of modernity are no longer occult; the double-edged and problematic character of modernity that Adorno called negative dialectics (coexisting opposite poles) is visible. These stark paradoxes project uncertainty into any secure judgment or assessment of the trends and tendencies of new times. There is a sense of being permanently impaled on the horns of extremes. There is the urgency to keep in mind the idea of different temporalities; not to be duped by the naturalization the Right makes of the ascendancy of capital, the hegemony of the new right, and the headlong commodification of hitherto uncommodified areas. They are not necessarily indissoluble or locked together. We must not take our bearings from the idea of empty, homogenous time.

3. This is the main argument of Michael Hardt and Antonio Negri (2000). For them, at the heart of globalization is the question of a one-world system, the capitalist system, the logic of which is maximizing profits; the fear of which is Marx's phantom prediction of the falling rate of profit. Under globalization, capitalism can be understood as a process of subsumption of agriculture into industry and of industry into service and informatics. At each one of the junctures of this subsumption, society and subjectivities are modeled after the new organizing principle. Thus in the first subsumption we move from the pastoral to the factory. In the second, as society becomes industrialized, it becomes the analogue of a factory. In the third, it becomes a service industry. There are always residualities and unevenness in this process. The logic of the global implies there are poles of development, growth, and modernization that always produce underdevelopment, stagnation, and subordination. In the current stage, the idea of subsumption moves from the formal to the real. Expansion is intensive rather than extensive and not directed towards the noncapitalist environment, because there is no outside but towards the capitalist terrain itself. Subsumption is going from machine-made goods to machine-made machines to machine-made raw materials. When mechanical and industrial technologies have expanded to invest the entire world; when the modernization process is complete and the formal subsumption has reached its limit and all nature has become capital, the following visible effects are noticed: changes in the pattern and places of labor, be it the migration from industry to services or of industry to other geographical areas; the transfer of manufacture abroad, creating workers' colonies and factory countries (China)—this curtails migration, modernizes traditions, demobilizes labor, and preempts the accumulation of struggle; the creation of zones excluded from capital flow and new technologies—countries and city areas metaphorized as debris in names such

as the sufferers, the undesirable, the untouchable, disposable people, and areas of starvation and high crime; and finally a move from Taylorism and Fordism to Post-Fordism and Toyotism—here is the definition of Toyotism from high discipline to flexible schedules and from full to zero stock and commodities, establishing close communication between production and consumption and producing just-in-time to supply demand. The opposite logic is that of the workers whose aim is to expand the social power of labor, increase the value of labor power, and redesign the set of needs and desires. Their aim is a transformation of labor itself, a proposal for a new regime of the production of subjectivities. From a political and judicial standpoint, globalization is modeled on the nation-state, but the aim is to have a single overdetermined power to construct, legalize, and legitimize one imperial sovereignty. "EMPIRE is the political subject that effectively regulates these global exchanges, the sovereign power that governs the world" (Hardt and Negri 2000, 1). The UN Charter is the center for normative production, planted squarely within the old framework of nations. The United Nations is a way of obtaining consensus to preserve order, security, and economic balance ("justice") for the central or hegemonic nations and to regulate corporate competition ascertaining the corporate character of the dominant group—a civil society for those on top. The two models, the Hobessian and Lockean, underscoring global security or global constitutionality run parallel to each other. In the first case, the proposal is to create a third element in discord concentrated in the hands of the military; and in the second, the existence of a global civil society. Looking now at globalization from below, it has come at the cost of traditional beliefs and norms, what the UN documents called the disintegration of old social institutions, caste bonds, creeds and race, and ancient philosophies. Globalization is a thwarted modernization—forever interrupted and never achieved; it is the subordination of politics to economy, the dismantling of the welfare state and of anything that has to do with state control of the economy, be it in the form of ownership or co-ownership of production or services. Fiscal responsibility, deregulation (i.e., intervening in price control), and privatization mean to bring all and every sphere of life into visibility and subject it to market regulations.

4. Post-Fordism is the name given to the shifting social and technical landscapes of modern industry, a shift to new productive regimes: a new epoch distinct from the era of mass production, with its standardized products, concentrations of capital, and its Taylorist form of work organization and discipline. There is a shift to new information technologies, new ways of thinking, a constant negotiation and articulation, a shift towards a more flexible, specialized, and decentralized form of labor process and work organization—hiring-off or contracting-out of contracts or services formerly provided "in-house" on a corporate basis. There is a leading role for consumption, marketing, packaging, designing, and targeting and a decline in the proportion of male, skilled, manual workers and rise of the services and white-collar classes. There is an increase in the proportion of flextime, part-time, female, and ethnic workers. It is an economy dominated by the multinationals, globalization of the new financial markets, emergence of new patterns of social division (especially those between private and public), greater social fragmentation, and a weakening of older solidarities and communal identities. There is no commitment to any prior determinism. The subject is no longer the whole individual, centered, stable, and complete, ego or autonomous rational self but one that is fragmented and incomplete with multiple selves or identities according to distinct social milieus. It is differently placed and positioned in discourse. Toyotism is a model described above.

5. Also see Andrew Lakoff on related topics at http://sociology.ucsd.edu/faculty/anxieties.pdf.

6. As an example of the velocity of change, between 1989, the hiatus that marks the fall of the Berlin Wall and the defeat of Sandinismo, and 2001, the hiatus that marks the destruction of the Twin Towers in New York and the collapse of Argentinean economy, are only eleven years, not even the fifteen years Dilthey prescribed for the transition between one generation and the next.

7. For a discussion of a transformation of everything encompassing human life, consciousness, and values, see Lauren Berlant (1997).

8. See Slavoj Žižek (1994).

9. A clear example is the work of Angel Saldomando (2002).

10. As an example of the type of the work produced by these agencies, see Angel Saldomando (2002) and Silvio Prado (1999).

11. That is the reason why studies on alternative development, like those of the Colombian school—I am thinking here of works such as Arturo Escobar's and Cristina Rojas's—turn the analysis radically

from things to people. See Arturo Escobar (1995), Cristina Rojas (2002), Josefina Saldaña (2003), and Kevin Healy (2001).

12. For an insightful discussion of this topic, see Michael Hardt (1998).

13. Arrighi's (1994) thesis is that "finance capital is not a particular stage of world capitalism, let alone its latest and highest stage. Rather, it is a recurrent phenomenon, which has marked the capitalism era from its earliest beginning in late medieval and early modern Europe. Throughout the capitalist era financial expansions have signaled the transition from one regime of accumulation on a world scale to another. They are integral aspects of the recurrent destruction of 'old' regimes and the simultaneous creation of 'new' ones" (ix–x).

14. "The capitalist world-economy is a system built on the endless accumulation of capital. One of the primary mechanisms that make this possible is the commodification of everything. . . . [All capitalist social relations must be] 'universally solvent', working to reduce everything to a homogeneous commodity form denoted by a single measure of money. . . . But if one wants to maximize the accumulation of capital, it is necessary simultaneously to minimize the costs of production (hence the costs of labor-power) and minimize the costs of political disruption (hence minimize—not eliminate, because one cannot eliminate—the protests of the labor force). Racism is the magic formula that reconciles these objectives" (Balibar and Wallerstein 1991, 231–32).

## Works Cited

Amin, Samir. 1992. *Empire of Chaos*. New York: Monthly Review.

Arrighi, Giovanni. 1994. *The Long Twentieth Century*. London: Verso.

Ashcroft, Bill, Gareth Griffiths, and Helen Tiffin. 1989. *The Empire Writes Back: Theory and Practice in Post-Colonial Literatures*. New York: Routledge.

Attali, Jacques. 1991. *Millennium: Winners and Losers in the Coming World Order*. New York: Times Books.

Balibar, Étienne, and Immanuel Wallerstein. 1991. *Race, Nation, Class: Ambiguous Identities*. London: Verso.

Berlant, Lauren. 1997. *The Queen of America goes to Washington City: Essays on Sex and Citizenship*. Durham, N.C.: Duke University Press.

Braudel, Fernand. 1973. *The Mediterranean and the Mediterranean World in the Age of Philip II*. New York: Harper & Row.

Escobar, Arturo. 1995. *Encountering Development: The Making and Unmaking of the Third World*. Princeton, N.J.: Princeton University Press.

Frank, André Gunder. 1972. *Lumpenbourgeoisie: Lumpendevelopment; Dependence, Class, and Politics in Latin America*. New York: Monthly Review.

Hardt, Michael. 1998. "The Withering of Civil Society." In *Deleuze & Guattari: New Mappings in Politics, Philosophy, and Culture*, eds. Eleanor Kaufman and Kevin Jon Séller, 23–39. Minneapolis: University of Minnesota Press.

Hardt, Michael, and Antonio Negri. 2000. *Empire*. Cambridge, Mass.: Harvard University Press.

Hardt, Michael, and Kathi Weeks, eds. 2000. *The Jameson Reader*. Oxford: Blackwell.

Healy, Kevin. 2001. *Llamas, Weavings, and Organic Chocolate: Multicultural Grassroots Development in the Andes and Amazon of Bolivia*. South Bend, Ind.: University of Notre Dame Press.

Hopenhayn, Martin. 2001. *No Apocalypse, No Integration: Modernism and Postmodernism in Latin America*. Durham, N.C.: Duke University Press.

Jameson, Fredric. 1991. *Postmodernism, or the Cultural Logic of Late Capitalism*. London: Verso.

———. 1998. *The Cultural Turn: Selected Writings on the Postmodern, 1983–1998*. London: Verso.

Jameson, Fredric, and Masao Miyoshi, eds. 1998. *The Cultures of Globalization*. Durham, N.C.: Duke University Press.

Kymlicka, Will. 1991. *Liberalism, Community, and Culture*. Oxford: Clarendon Press.

Lakoff, Andrew. 2001. "The Anxieties of Globalization: Antidepressent Sales and Economic Crisis in Argentina." At: http://sociology.ucsd.edu/faculty/anxieties.pdf.

Lenin, Vladimir Ilyich. 1996. *Imperialism: The Highest Stage of Capitalism*. London: Junious.

Miyoshi, Maso. 1996. "A Borderless World? From Colonialism to Transnationalism and the Decline of the Nation-State." In *GLOBAL/LOCAL: Cultural Production and the Transnational Imaginary*, eds. Rob Wilson and Wimal Dissanayake, 78–106. Durham, N.C.: Duke University Press.

Ohmae, Kenishi. 1990. *The Borderless World: Power and Strategy in the Interlinked Economy*. New York: Harper Business.

Prado, Silvio. 1999. *Descentralización y Participación Ciudadana en Centroamérica*. Managua, Nicaragua: Ediciones Heinrich Boll.

Reich, Robert B. 1991. *The Work of Nations*. New York: Vintage.

Rojas, Cristina. 2002. *Civilization and Violence: Regimes of Representation in Nineteenth-Century Colombia*. Minneapolis: University of Minnesota Press.

Saldaña, Josefina. 2003. *The Revolutionary Imagination in the Americas and the Age of Development*. Durham, N.C.: Duke University Press.

Saldomando, Angel. 2002. *Gobernabilidad: Entre la democracia y el Mercado*. Managua, Nicaragua: Programa de Gobernabilidad de COSUDE y el Secretariado Suizo para Centroamérica.

Spivak, Gayatri Chakravorty, and Ranajit Guha, eds. 1988. *Selected Subaltern Studies*. New York: Oxford University Press.

Taylor, Charles. 1991. *Multiculturalism*. Princeton, N.J.: Princeton University Press.

Vilar, Pierre. 1962. *La Catalogne dans l'Espagne moderne: recherches sur les fundaments économiques des structures nationals*. Paris: S.E.V.P.E.N.

———. 1976. *A History of Gold and Money*. London: Humanities Press.

Wallerstein, Immanuel. 1984. *The Modern World System*. New York: Academic Press.

———. 1991. *Geoculture and Geopolitics: Essays on the Changing World-System*. Cambridge, Mass.: Cambridge University Press.

Wilson, Rob, and Wimal Dissanayake, eds. 1996. *Global/Local: Cultural Production and the Transnational Imaginary*. Durham, N.C.: Duke University Press.

Žižek Slavoj, ed. 1994. *Mapping Ideology*. London: Verso.

# POSTSCRIPT

## An Interview with Arjun Appadurai

### John C. Hawley

I conducted this interview on June 21, 2004, at New School University, where Arjun Appadurai had recently been appointed provost. That was the year that the National Commission on Terrorist Attacks upon the United States (the 9/11 Commission) held public hearings at the school. Founded in 1919 by historian Charles Beard and economists Thorstein Veblen and John Dewey, the school's early reputation for research into the social sciences seemed a fitting environment to suggest our volume's desire to wed the humanistic bent of postcolonial studies with what some would argue are the more pragmatic interests of globalization theory.    —J.C.H.

HAWLEY: In *Globalization*, your book of collected essays, you propose that globalization is not simply the name for a new epoch in the history of capital or in the biography of the nation-state but rather is marked by a new role for the imagination and social life. And in your elaboration of those ideas, you speak about the need for a deparochialization of the research ethic and include in that a kind of distinction between theoria and praxis: those in the academy, moving in the direction of theoria oftentimes, those in the actual parts of the world that are under study dealing more immediately with practical matters. Is that a good place to begin our discussion?

APPADURAI: Sure. Let me put it this way: it's my view that the postcolonial period, both in the countries that were actually colonies and those that were either colonizing countries or simply outside of this process, still is an era that affected everybody and created a set of aspirations (which is why we associate postcolonialism with nationalism, for example, the wish to be free, the wish to be somehow not under the colonial yolk, and so on and so forth)—aspirations are a part of it. And where aspirations are at war, the imagination cannot be far behind. The other thing is that the postcolonial also created a whole series of interests in different parts of the world in *other* people with similar experiences. So, for example, the Bandung Conference of 1956 brought together what were then called the newly independent nations: Indonesia, India, Egypt, and others in a very important event, but part of what was at issue was a kind of globalizing of the imagination, that is looking out to *other* postcolonial countries, so, even at its very beginnings, especially among the avant-garde of the postcolonial work—people like Nehru, Nasser, Sukarno, and Nkrumah, and so on, major leaders, their postcolonial aspirations and roadmaps for their own people were intimately tied up with their understanding of their place in the world, in history, in relation to each other—they never talk just as national voices.

HAWLEY: So, you're saying they were seeing themselves as being in a conversation with each *other* immediately, before a conversation with what we used to call the first world.

APPADURAI: The two are connected, so if you take Nehru as an example, which I know better than the others, he saw his place in the world as something very important to articulate. So, in other words, from the start, what I mean to say is that the postcolonial vision was always, in some sense, a global vision. It was never a vision just for the liberation of a certain people from a certain ruler.

HAWLEY: Right.

APPADURAI: From the beginning, that word might not have been exhaustive but it always included other, let's say newly freed countries, populations, societies, but also included the rulers—the ex-rulers.

HAWLEY: And this would include the nonaligned movement?

APPADURAI: It's centrally about that. So, the Bandung example is key in the formation of our life. And so, the reason I bring up this is to say that from the start, the postcolonial moment is a kind of a global moment in its own right. It's not the globalization of the '70s, '80s, '90s, but is also a moment in which people conceived of their interests and aspirations in a world framework.

HAWLEY: So, it never was the Eurocentric movement that it has generally been described as being?

APPADURAI: Right, and you can certainly say it was never restricted to a confrontation between one ruled colony and its rulers. It's always about *other* colonies and as well as *other* rulers. It is always about the new world that was coming into place as these countries became free, and that was a world of *ex*-rulers and ex-*ruled*. So, in a way everybody was involved. And, so, two points, then. One, as I said, the postcolonial moment itself has a kind of globalized feeling to it. And secondly, imagination is important because postcolonial leaders, intellectuals, and avant-gardes always formulated their visions not just as "freedom *from* certain kinds of oppressions" (external), but also freedom *to*—from a vision of equality, a vision of justice— and that's where the imagination kicks in. So, the imagination from the *start* is central—it's not just ending something, its starting something. So, the future.

HAWLEY: A certain amount of experimentation, even in how they might conceive of the nation-state?

APPADURAI: Sure, because the national project was itself something new. It had to be. This way you may say slightly *against* the image of nationalism, say in Benedict Anderson's work, which suggests that there is a kind of modular form that once it emerges circulates in the world—it just gets picked up. I would say the practical experience of nationalism, is that it is *built* up, and it is built up by, indeed, experiments, by efforts to link the future to *specific* pasts, not just some generic past or oppression, whether the Indian past or the Egyptian past, and so on. And, indeed, to formulate what it means to be Indian or Indonesian or Egyptian, or so on, is necessarily in some way a localized effort. It can never be generic and never was.

HAWLEY: Do you see that playing itself out in Iraq these days?

APPADURAI: Iraq is a very interesting and complicated situation because it is a case of . . . rather than creating democracy or some ideal democracy as the postcolonial period did by the departure, forced or unforced . . . In Iraq, rather, it is democracy created by the arrival. It's an inversion of the relation with democracy and empire. So, in Iraq, what we're witnessing is a kind of imperial action to produce democracy. So many people have commented on this, of course, but it raises a deep question of can you produce democracy by some kind of forcible act of intervention? Now of course today the Iraq story we're starting to see . . . we watch the United States trying to detach, but we see the strange paradox of "we're leaving but we're not leaving." You know, Iraq is going to be sovereign, but really we're still staying there. So, it's very mysterious what this kind of sovereignty is. But, in the postcolonial period there was a simpler sense: "you leave" and we begin to rule ourselves. It was a more *innocent* narrative.

HAWLEY: And yet, in so many of the countries that are now dealing with nationalism in various ways, their history with the colonizer has been one in which they did not necessarily imagine themselves as a nation until the colonizer by imperialist moves imposes that upon them, right?

APPADURAI: Yes, these nationalisms were often born in the crucible of colonial rule, but I think the difference here is the rapidity, in other words, that that happened. Furthermore, Iraq was most decidedly a nation before the U.S. invasion. There's a strongly developed Iraqi nationalism. It may be Baathist, it may be this, it may be that, but no one doubts that there was a very powerful national project—was it a *democratic* project, that's the question. But, there was no question it was a nationalist project. So, you might say, yes, the nationalism that was produced over the long durée of the past hundred or four hundred years in the Middle East—the nationalisms that were produced, which included African nationalism, departed from this U.S. intervention.

HAWLEY: What in general do you see as the interplay between democracy and globalizing forces?

APPADURAI: It's clearly a kind of contradiction that we're in the midst of. The contradiction is that as large numbers of people find themselves at *risk* in gaining any of the benefits of globalization—that is we don't know whether they're going to be winners or losers, and in some cases feel that they have become losers and are likely to remain losers in the commerce of globalization—they certainly open the door to the seas of other messages and approaches. Including messages that lean them towards violence or towards extreme political or religious positions or other forms of extreme action. Or, when people feel that they have nothing to gain, you also have what Albert O. Hirschman called the "exit solution"—"we don't care—we're out." Recent Indian elections are a very interesting counterexample, because there you have a people who are decidedly not saying, "we're out." They are saying we are going to exercise what Hirschman called "voice" not "exit." In other words, we are going to get you out by voting you out. In probably the most remarkable democratic election that we have seen, I would say maybe this century, maybe ever.

HAWLEY: And Sonia Ghandi's decision not to run for prime minister, or accept prime minister, is also quite interesting.

APPADURAI: Very interesting and by all accounts quite brilliant because she is going to be a very powerful force and yet not attackable for being a usurper, an outsider, a foreigner, and so on and so forth. So she has both ways—it is both statesmanlike and a very brilliant political move. The question how the new government will better mobilize people's energies and better forestall their frustrations and give them a different sense of globalization, that remains to be seen. But a much more intolerant vision has been dimissised by the voter. So the Indian election certainly seems to me to say that globalization both sparks very intense worries as it clearly has done for the rural population of India, but it doesn't take them outside the democratic globe; in other words, it brings them into the elections as a way of saying we want a better deal.

HAWLEY: Right.

APPADURAI: So, on the whole, I feel that in the vast array of grassroots movements we have now seen throughout the world, on hundreds of issues ranging from housing, to alcohol, to environment, to health—around the world (and, again, India is a big place for all these movements) in the most out-of-the-way, small rural places, we have small civil-society movements that mobilize against debt or against money lending or for microcredit; very humble issues. Many of these movements also consciously build on global possibilities; build on possibilities of linking up to other like-minded movements, and so on and so on. I see direct connections between democracy and globalization, positively speaking, as people leveraging connections and networks. Just as we have the same syndrome going on with terrorisms that are very worrisome, in a democracy we also have very interesting efforts, and so on, that work outside the framework of the nation-state to foster democratic methods of inclusion.

HAWLEY: And do you hear echoes in these movements from the nonaligned political movements of the earlier generation?

APPADURAI: I would not normally have thought of them in the same frame or in the same breath, because nonaligned movements seemed to be much more top heavy, driven by certain intellectuals and avant-gardes, not so much grassroots, very much dominated by the Cold War and the desire to stay outside of it—so, if you like, produced by some grand narratives and their question of how we should relate to them, then it's these grassroots movements very often, very localized, very specific on issues, *not* into, if you like, grand narratives of what brings us together or apart. They're much more pragmatic. They're much more sensory in what they want to do; they're much more modest in what they aspire to in many ways. I'm not talking about big antiglobalization focus; I'm talking about the efforts to act on specific issues. But, that said, I *do* think there is a feeling that poor people, and people who are advocates, their advocates—who want greater justice, greater inclusion, greater tolerance, and so on, greater rule for human expression, human rights, in addition to economic benefits, greater security in the sense of everyday security as opposed to high-level political security have something in common with the nonaligned movement in the sense that in both cases there is a feeling that the big battles are not our battles. In other words, the United States is fighting with Iraq, or China is fighting Russia, or something. "It's not our issue. We want to be outside of that because we're about building up peace, we're about prosperity, we're about justice, and what do we care about these 'epic' struggles?"

HAWLEY: And related to that, do you think that there is a kind of implied master narrative connecting these grassroots movements that suggests the need for a raising of consciousness of those that are involved in these supposedly larger issues? That those who are involved, for example in environmental questions in India, or in Africa, maybe suggesting in how they're working on their local issues that those who are in government in the United States, or China, or Russia may need to learn from them—learn, that is, something that is ultimately going to come around and bite them if they don't.

APPADURAI: Yes, I think there is that. Yes, that is a very interesting question. Perhaps we [now] more than during the period of the nonaligned movement when I think, since that also was during the heyday of the modernization period, where the feeling was, even among people who didn't like it so much, that the question worked; let's say that the developed world really already had *accomplished* certain things, had achieved certain levels of education and public health and technological advancement—all the things that everyone in the world desired. The feeling was that the *newly* developed countries hadn't gotten there, so I think there was *not* as much of a sense that, we, let's say, now speaking for India and the nonaligned, had much to teach. There were exceptions of course—people like Gandhi and others who knew that India had something to teach the world and it did; nonviolence and things like that. But on the whole, I think there was not that sense. Now, I think there is a profound sense that, let's say the degradation of the environment, or let's say the abuse of women, physical or otherwise, are two examples of hugely widespread problems that are not only problems of the poorer countries. I think there is a much bigger sense that solutions can come from anywhere. And that anyone and everyone can learn if there is a good solution about jobs, or a good solution about family structures—and that it's a level playing field.

HAWLEY: And that that is one of the benefits of globalization in the sense that we're all in the same boat.

APPADURAI: One, we're all in the same boat. Secondly, smaller solutions can be amplified and made available really fast to anybody and everybody.

HAWLEY: So, you see speed as one of the central factors here?

APPADURAI: Yes, I see two things. I see speed as a factor in two ways. One is that when there are solutions to the problem of everyday life, they can be made available to a wider population than was originally possible, and more quickly through the Internet, through other kinds of media, through word of mouth; through travel and through all the methods available through technology. Speed is also a *problem*, in the sense that things arrive so fast it makes societies, many groups, and many individuals have a tremendously hard time coping with the assault of the movement. For example, the speed at which, let's say, foreign capital, investment capital, came to places like Thailand, creating the Asian economic crisis—that's what's wrong with speed. It's not just that there was money that the economy couldn't handle, but that it came in too quickly, and sort of broke the back of the banking and other institutions of these countries, as is now widely appreciated. Yes; I think, you know, I'm now in a university where my own president is very actively involved in the 9/11 Commission. We hosted in this very building some of the important hearings with New York officials and the commission. So, it's premature: on the one hand, I'm torn between the temptation to say, you know, 9/11 is not only a *focal* event in the sense that it's not only that there's a history before 9/11, and there's a history after 9/11; but it's especially sitting in the United States—it's difficult to deny that it transformed the nature of politics and, as far as the world is concerned, created, you know, an understanding, created a set of conditions that reminded the world both of American power and of American vulnerability. And to me, that's what 9/11 most brings to my mind—is that that event, the reactions to that event, and all the aftermath of that event, right up until now, in the political realm, in the cultural realm, differently than say the common realm, points out the paradox that this is both an extraordinarily powerful country and in some ways a very weak and vulnerable country. Now, recently, Lawrence Summers, the President of Harvard, has written a piece based on lectures in the journal *Foreign Policy*, saying that American debt, the way-low levels of savings, the high deficit, all of these are very weakening, that this makes the strongest of economies actually rather hollow. And it's not an entirely new argument. I'm not talking in politics here. What 9/11 did is both remind people that this very powerful country is also very vulnerable and second, and this is the sadder part, produce the conditions in which the current administration could create the climate of profound fear that it still seems to be doing a great deal to fortify; which, in turn then means that as fear is produced successfully here, the American public is mobilized to be hostile to outsiders, to people different than themselves, to Muslims in particular, and so on. And that has a weird effect, which has a kind of odd mirroring of fundamentalists, extreme fundamentalist messages coming out of the Islamic world. So, we're producing some extreme fears of outsiders and the unknown, which then feeds the parallel fears and the angers on the other side. There *is*, I think, a very dangerous cycle involving fear and vulnerability. So the question for me on 9/11 is, given the reality of that event, given the reality that those kinds of things can happen, how can America—the United States to be more precise—more fully and deeply understand both its special power and the limitations on that power—the fact that it indeed—an image I've used, it's like Gulliver—it's a very large creature in world politics but it's also held by those little gossamer threads—hundreds of them. One set of which has to do with the vulnerability to new forms of attack, and that requires both some very smart global diplomatic solutions and some very wise internal social policies so we don't ratchet up the fear industry.

HAWLEY: Thank you very much.

# Publication History

CHAPTER 1 originally appeared as "From Development to Globalisation: Postcolonial Studies and Globalisation Theory," in *The Cambridge Companion to Postcolonial Literary Studies*, ed. Neil Lazarus (Cambridge: Cambridge University Press, 2004). Reprinted with permission of Cambridge University Press.

CHAPTER 2 first appeared in *Traces: A Multilingual Journal of Culture Theory and Translation* 1 (2001): 37–70, published in English by Traces, Inc., 2001; in Japanese by Iwanami Shoten; in Korean by Moonkwa Kwahaksa; and in Chinese by Jiangsu Education Publishing House. Reprinted with the acknowledgment and permission of Traces, Inc.

CHAPTER 4 was originally published in *Critical Globalization Studies*, eds. Richard P. Appelbaum and William I. Robinson (New York: Taylor and Francis, 2005). Copyright 2005. Reprinted by permission of Routledge/Taylor and Francis Group, LLC.

CHAPTER 11 first appeared as a chapter in Inderpal Grewal, *Transnational America: Feminisms, Diasporas, Neoliberalism* (Durham, N.C.: Duke University Press, 2005). Reprinted with permission of Duke University Press.

CHAPTER 18 originally appeared as "Law, Nation, and (Imagined) International Communities," *Law Text Culture* 8 (2004): 1–30. Reprinted with the permission of the journal.

# CONTRIBUTORS

PAL AHLUWALIA is professor of ethnic studies at University of California, San Diego and Research SA Chair and professor of postcolonial studies at the University of South Australia. His recent books include *Politics and Postcolonial Theory* and *Edward Said*. He is currently working on a book titled *Out Of Africa: Post-structuralism's Colonial Roots* and is the coeditor of three Routledge journals, *Social Identities, African Identities,* and *Sikh Formations*.

GEOFFREY C. BOWKER is executive director of the Center for Science, Technology, and Society at Santa Clara University, where he is the Regis and Dianne McKenna Professor. He is the author of *Sorting Things Out: Classification and Its Consequences* and *Memory Practices in the Sciences*.

TIMOTHY BRENNAN is professor of English, comparative literature, and cultural studies at the University of Minnesota. His essays on literature, cultural politics, American intellectuals, and colonialism have appeared in numerous publications, including *The Nation,* the *Times Literary Supplement, New Left Review, Critical Inquiry,* and the *London Review of Books*. He is the author, most recently, of *Wars of Position: The Cultural Politics of Left and Right* (2006), *At Home in the World: Cosmopolitanism Now* (1997), and the forthcoming *Secular Devotion: Afro-Latin Music and Imperial Jazz*.

RUTH BUCHANAN is associate professor at Osgoode Hall Law School, York University in Toronto, Ontario, Canada. She has also taught at the Law Schools of the University of British Columbia and the University of New Brunswick and has been a visiting research associate at Birkbeck College, University of London. She teaches and publishes in the areas of globalization, international economic law, law and development, and political and social theory. She has also held faculty appointments at the University of British Columbia and the University of New Brunswick. Her recent publications include "The *Unforgiven* Sources of International Law: Nation-building, Violence, and Gender in the West(ern)" (with Rebecca Johnson) in *International Law: Modern Feminist Perspectives* (2005) and "Global Civil Society and Cosmopolitan Legality at the WTO: Perpetual Peace or Perpetual Process?" in *Leiden Journal of International Law,* 2003.

VERITY BURGMANN is professor of political science at the University of Melbourne. Her publications include *Power, Profit, and Protest; Unions and the Environment; Green Bans, Red Union; Revolutionary Industrial Unionism; Power and Protest; A People's History of Australia*; and *'In Our Time': Socialism and the Rise of Labor*.

PHENG CHEAH is professor of rhetoric at the University of California at Berkeley. He is the author of *Spectral Nationality: Passages of Freedom from Kant to Postcolonial Literatures of Liberation*, and *Inhuman Conditions: On Cosmopolitanism and Human Rights*, and coeditor of *Cosmopolitics: Thinking and Feeling beyond the Nation* (Minnesota, 1998). He is currently completing a book on world literature and a book on the concept of instrumentality.

INDERPAL GREWAL is professor of women's studies at the University of California, Irvine, and director of the PhD program in Culture and Theory. She is the author of *Home and Harem: Nation, Gender, Empire, and the Culture of Travel and, Transnational America: Feminisms, Diasporas, Neoliberalisms,* and coeditor (with Caren Kaplan) of *Scattered Hegemonies: Postmodernity and Transnational Feminist Practices* (Minnesota, 1996).

RAMÓN GROSFOGUEL is professor of ethnic studies at the University of California, Berkeley, and a senior research associate of the Maison des Science de l'Homme in Paris. He has published on the political economy of the world-system and on Caribbean migrations to Western Europe and the United States. His most recent book is *Colonial Subjects*.

BARBARA HARLOW teaches English at the University of Texas at Austin. She has also taught in Egypt, Ireland, and South Africa. She is author of *Resistance Literature, Barred: Women and Political Detention* and *After Lives: Legacies of Revolutionary Writing*, and she is coeditor (with Mia Carter) of *Imperialism and Orientalism: A Documentary Sourcebook* and *Archives of Empire*. She is working on an intellectual biography of the South African activist Ruth First.

JOHN C. HAWLEY is professor and chair of English at Santa Clara University. He is author of *Amitav Ghosh: An Introduction,* and editor of *Encyclopedia of Postcolonial Studies* and *Postcolonial, Queer*. He is associate editor of *South Asian Review*.

REVATHI KRISHNASWAMY is associate professor of English at San Jose State University. She is author of *Effeminism: The Economy of Colonial Desire*. She has published in *Interventions, Diacritics, Journal of Postcolonial Writing, Ariel*, and other journals.

ANOUAR MAJID is founding chair and professor of English at the University of New England in Maine. He has written and lectured widely on the nexus of postcolonial theory, globalization, and Islam. His most recent books are *A Call for Heresy: Why Dissent Is Vital to Islam and America* (Minnesota, 2007) and *Freedom and Orthodoxy: Islam and Difference in the Post-Andalusian Age*.

JOHN MCMURTRY is professor of philosophy and University Professor Emeritus at the University of Guelph, and a Fellow of the Royal Society of Canada. His work has been internationally published in philosophy and social science journals, and his most recent books are *Unequal Freedoms: The Global Market as an Ethical System, The Cancer Stage of Capitalism,* and *Value Wars: The Global Market versus the Life Economy*. He has been selected by the United Nations/UNESCO as the director of philosophy and world problems for its *Encyclopedia of Life Support Systems*.

WALTER D. MIGNOLO is William H. Wannamaker Professor at Duke University and director of the Center for Global Studies and the Humanities. Among his recent publications are *Local Histories/Global Designs: Coloniality, Subaltern Knowledges, and Border Thinking* (2000) and *The Idea of Latin America* (2005), which received the Frantz Fanon Award from the Caribbean Philosophical Association (2006). He coedited with Madina V. Tlostanova *Double Critique: Knowledges and Scholars at Risk in Post-Soviet Societies* (2006). In collaboration with Arturo Escobar, he edited *Globalization and the Decolonial Option* (2007). He coedited with Margaret Greer and Maureen Quilligan, *The Black Legend: Discourses of Race in the European Renaissance* (2007).

SUNDHYA PAHUJA is an associate professor and codirector of the Law and Development research program at the Institute for International Law and the Humanities at the University of Melbourne. She has taught at the London School of Economics, Birkbeck, and New York University. Her research interests center on law and development, international law, legal philosophy, and globalization. Her recent publications are on the postcolonial/global intersection and include *Divining the Source: Law's Foundation and the Question of Authority* (edited with Jennifer Beard), "Postcoloniality of International Law" (*Harvard Journal of International Law*, 2005), and "Rights as Regulation: The Integration of Development and Human Rights," in *The Intersection of Rights and Regulation*, edited by Bronwen Morgan (2007).

R. RADHAKRISHNAN is professor of Asian American studies, English, and comparative Literature at the University of California, Irvine. He is author of *Diasporic Mediations: Between Home and Location* (Minnesota, 1996), *Theory in an Uneven World* (2003), *Between Identity and Location: The Cultural Politics of Theory* (2007), and *History, The Human, and the World Between* (2008) He is the editor of *Theory as Variation* (2006), and coeditor (with Susan Koshy) of *Desi Diasporas* (2008) and (with Kailash Baral) of *Theory after Derrida* (2008). His essays have appeared in a wide variety of journals and collections. He is also the translator of contemporary Tamil fiction into English and author of a volume of Tamil poems, *Moved, I but not in Time*.

ILEANA RODRÍGUEZ is Humanities Distinguished Professor of Latin American literatures and cultures at Ohio State University. She has published extensively on the literatures, cultures, and politics of Central America and the Caribbean and has authored several books, including *Transatlantic Topographies: Islands, Highlands, Jungles* (Minnesota, 2004); *Women, Guerrillas, and Love: Understanding War in Central America* (Minnesota, 1999); and *House, Garden, Nation*. She has edited *The Latin American Subaltern Studies Reader* (2001), and coedited *The Process of Unity in Caribbean Society* and *Marxism and New Left Ideology*.

E. SAN JUAN JR. is codirector of the Board of the Philippine Forum in New York and officer-in-charge of the Philippines Cultural Studies Center in Storrs, Connecticut. He was recently Fulbright Professor of American Studies at Katholieke Universiteit Leuven, Belgium, and visiting professor of English at Wesleyan University. His recent books are *Beyond Postcolonial Theory, Racism, and Cultural Studies*, and *Working through the Contradictions: From Cultural Theory to Critical Practice*. Forthcoming works are *In the Wake of Terror* and *U.S. Imperialism and Revolution in the Philippines*.

SASKIA SASSEN is now at Columbia University's Committee on Global Thought, after a decade at the University of Chicago and London School of Economics. Her recent books are *Territory, Authority, Rights: From Medieval to Global Assemblages* (2006) and *A Sociology of Globalization* (2007). She has now completed for UNESCO a five-year project on sustainable human settlement for which she set up a network of researchers and activists in more than thirty countries; it is published as one of the volumes of the *Encyclopedia of Life Support Systems* (EOLSS). Her books are translated into sixteen languages. Her comments have appeared in *The Guardian, The New York Times, Le Monde Diplomatique*, the *International Herald Tribune, Newsweek International*, the *Financial Times*, among others.

ELLA SHOHAT is professor of cultural studies at New York University. She has lectured and published extensively on the intersection of gender, post/colonialism, and multiculturalism as well as on Zionist discourse and the Arab-Jewish and Mizrahi question. Her publications include *Israeli Cinema: East/West and the Politics of Representation, Unthinking Eurocentrism: Multiculturalism and the Media* (with Robert Stam), *Talking Visions: Multicultural Feminism in a Transnational Age*, and *Forbidden Reminiscences*. She has coedited *Dangerous Liaisons: Gender,*

*Nation, and Postcolonial Perspectives* (Minnesota, 1997) and *Multiculturalism, Postcoloniality, and Transnational Media*. She is the recipient of a Rockefeller Fellowship and has served on the editorial boards of *Social Text, Public Culture, Jouvert*, and *Critique*. Her writing has been translated into French, Spanish, Portuguese, Arabic, Hebrew, German, Polish, and Turkish.

**LESLIE SKLAIR** is professor emeritus of sociology at the London School of Economics and Political Science. He has researched transnational corporations throughout the world and is author of *The Transnational Capitalist Class*, excerpts of which has been translated into Chinese and German. He is also author of *Sociology of the Global System*, which has been widely excerpted and translated into Japanese, Portuguese, Persian, Korean, and Spanish; a new edition of this book was recently published as *Globalization: Capitalism and Its Alternatives*, with an Arabic translation forthcoming. His latest research project connects capitalist globalization and iconic architecture. Sklair is currently president of the Global Studies Association.

**ROBERT STAM** Is University Professor at New York University. He is the author of more than fifteen books on cinema and popular culture, including *Film Theory: An Introduction; Literature through Film: Realism, Magic, and Adaptation; Subversive Pleasures: Bakhtin, Cultural Criticism, and Film; Tropical Multiculturalism: A Comparative History of Race in Brazilian Cinema and Culture; François Truffaut and Friends: Modernism, Sexuality, and Adaptation*; and (with Ella Shohat) *Unthinking Eurocentrism: Multiculturalism and the Media* and *Flagging Patriotism: Crises of Narcissism and Anti-Americanism*. He has won Fulbright, Guggenheim, and Rockefellers Awards, and has taught in France, Brazil, and Tunisia. His work is translated into fifteen languages.

**MADINA TLOSTANOVA** is professor at the department of Comparative Politics at the Peoples' Friendship University of Russia in Moscow and visiting research fellow at Duke University. Her scholarly interests include postnational, transcultural, and global studies. She has authored two books in Russian and two in English. The most recent are *Postsoviet Literature and the Aesthetics of Trans-culturation* (2004) and *The Sublime of Globalization? Sketches on Trans-cultural Subjectivity and Aesthetics* (2005). Presently she is writing a new book on gender and race discourses in the non-European Soviet ex-colonies.

**HARISH TRIVEDI** is professor of English at the University of Delhi and was visiting professor at the University of Chicago and at the School of Oriental and African Studies at the University of London. He is the author of *Colonial Transactions: English Literature and India* and has coedited *Post-Colonial Translation: Theory and Practice*.

# INDEX

Brown, E. L., 242
Brown, Paul, 145
Brown, Peter, 193
Bruce-Novoa, Juan, 10
Bruckner, Pascal, 124–26, 132n.1
Brundtland Report, 223–24
Bryson, J. R., 86
Buchanan, Pat, 127
Buchanan, Ruth, 5, 12, 15, 17n.16, 213, 261, 268, 269, 272n.6, 272n.8, 272n.10
Buck, Pearl S., 208
Buck-Morss, Susan, 22, 172–73, 174–75, 176n.8
Buda, Mario, 142
Buechler, Simone, 86, 91n.1
*Building Bridges: The Emerging Grassroots Coalition of Labor and Community* (Brecher and Costello), 246
Building Institutions for Markets (2002), 269
Buncombe, Andrew, 140
Bunzl, Matti, 16n.3
*Burger's Daughter* (Gordimer), 79
Burgmann, Verity, 14, 15, 24, 212, 246
Burke, Anthony, 169
Burton, Antoinette, 16n.3
Buruma, Ian, 144
Buru quartet (Toer), 63–65, 67n.20; four volumes of, 67n.17
Bush, George H. W., 127
Bush, George W., 130, 132, 138, 141, 159, 164, 164n.4, 173; State of the Union address (2002), 160
Business Charter for Sustainable Development, 223
Business Council for Sustainable Development, 224
business education with global focus, growth in, 218
Butler, Judith, 80n.16
Bystydzienski, Jill M., and Steven P. Schacht, 244

Cabral, Amilcar, 112, 158
Caliban, 158
Callinicos, Alex, 15, 17n.23
Caltex Petroleum Corporation, 196
Calvocoressi, Peter, 194
Camus, Albert, 71, 79n.8
Canadian Union of Postal Workers, 246
capabilities approach, 270, 272n.13
*Capital* (Marx), 238
capital accumulation, 89, 102, 281–82
capital: autonomy of working class vis-à-vis, 238–39; exteriority to, 13–14; global, 82; globalization of, 226n.7; labor transnationalism vs. capital mobility, 241–43; limits of, 13; network of global cities as strategic infrastructure for

constituting of global corporate, 86–87; symbolic, 95; traditional Marxist emphasis on power of, 238, 239; transnational movements of finance, 189
capitalism: children as casualty of, 145; complicit with materialization of Atlantic economy, with Catholicism and Protestantism, 115–16; contradictions of, 149–50; cycles of, 280–81; differences between capitalist globalization and previous phases of, 215–16; financial expansions signaling transition from one regime of accumulation to another, 287n.13; foundation of, 110; fundamental flaw in, 150; under globalization, process of subsumptions in, 277, 285n.3; maximizing profits as logic of, 281, 285n.3; multiculturalism criticized as ideal ideological form of global, 128–29; phase of decline and crisis reflected in global social and cultural breakdowns, 149; reactive history of, 239; in Russia, transmuted nature of, 117; social movements against, 225–26; social relations defined by, 135; systemic analysis of, 280–81; transnational capitalist class, 215, 216–26; twofold goal of global, 279
capitalist nihilism, 163
capitalist societies, as presentist and modernist, 38
capitalist world-system: accumulation of capital entangled with racist, homophobic, and sexist global ideologies, 102; core-peripheral zones of, 94, 96, 102–3, 283; developmentalist illusion of eliminating inequalities of, from nation-state level, 101–2; first modernity, 97–98; formation in sixteenth century, 97; postcolonialists vs. world-system scholars on, 100; second modernity, 98–99
capital mobility, labor transnationalism vs., 241–43
car bombs, 142; *See also* suicide bombers/bombing
Cardoso, F. H., 218
Caribbean diaspora, 184
Carr, Robert, 276
Carty, Victoria, 242–43
Casanova, Pascale, 29
Castells, Manuel, 253
Castro, Fidel, 140
Caucasus, 115
Cavallo, D., 218
Cavanagh, John, 141
centrality, new geography of, 86, 87
Cervantes Saavedra, Miguel de, 118
Cesaire, Aimé, 103, 109, 112

modern imperial discourses founded on basis of, 110; in Russia and Soviet Union, 115

colonialism, 95; binary logic of, 77–78; coloniality in contemporary world-system stemming from long history of European, 95, 96; defined, 135; difference between imperialism and, 47–48; globalization as new form of, 282; modern sovereignty spread through, 168; refurbished type of, 281; subjugation entailed in, 46–47; usability of past by colonized man in name of future, 78–79; violent resistance entailed in, 173

coloniality (colonial matrix of power), 5–6, 94–96, 109–12, 122n.1; ascribed superiority of European knowledge and, 103; as constitutive of modernity, 112–14; culture versus economy dilemma and, 101; defining, 109–10; dependency on modernity, 113; distinction between colonialism and, 95; founded as consequence of Christian and Castilian colonization of Americas, 111; four levels of, 111; implication for world-system and postcolonial paradigms, 99–103; international division of labor and, 95, 96, 102; invisibility of global, in process of building modern, 98–99; logic of, 118–19; power to, 113; racism, colonial difference built upon, 111–12

colonial situations, 95, 96

colonial wounds, 112, 120

colonization: European, nationalism emerging in context of, 186–87; European, of the Americas, 97, 111; external, of space in external history of Europe, 114; formation of global racial/ethnic hierarchy, 97–98; internal, of time in internal history of Europe, 114; Russian, 116; time/space of modernity distinguished from time/space of premodern Europe and premodern America, Asia, and Africa by, 113–14; U.S. expansion, 98

colony, as site of exception, 172

Columbus, Christopher, 113, 132

commodification of everything, 222, 287n.14

communal socialism, 138

community unionism vs. marketization, 245–46

comparativity, 4–5, 16n.4

competitive advantages, 221

"Competitiveness: A Dangerous Obsession" (Krugman), 218

competitiveness: benchmarking systems to measure, 219–22; national, as discourse of capitalist globalization, 218–22

Comprehensive Development Framework (CDF), 269

computer technology, e-waste and, 145

Comte, Auguste, 252

Condé, Maryse, 22

Confucianism, 61, 63

Congress of Democrats (South Africa), 193

Conlon, Justin, 195

Connolly, William E., 30n.14

Conrad, Joseph, 143

Constable, Nicole, 164n.2

consumer capitalism, multiculturalism and, 128

consumer class, 145; credit card debt among, 146–47

consumerism, culture-ideology of, 178, 217, 222, 225; electronic revolution and emergence of global, 215–16

consumption: insatiable desire in postcolonial world for Western consumer goods, 169–70; maintenance of borders/boundaries between nations and different levels of, 170; politics of, 175; subversive, 14, 17n.23; sustainable, 224, 225

continental governance, 280

continuous improvement, idea of, 220

control of knowledge, 255–56

Convention on Biological Diversity, 257

conventions of practice, infrastructure links with, 254

co-operation between area research and the disciplines, 57

Cordero-Guzmán, Héctor R., 86, 91n.2

core zones of capitalist world-economy, 96; ideological/symbolic strategies developed by, 102–3

Cornevin, Chistophe, 151n.8

Coronil, Fernando, 44

corporate citizenship, 282

corporate control of new technology, cybertariat vs., 247–49

corporations: benchmarking and "world best practice" strategies for globalizing, 219–22; corporate capture of sustainable development, 222–25; denial of human subject by global corporate system, 232; difference between "multi" and "trans" in, 281; multinational, 242, 281; privileges given "foreign," 219; transnational (TNCs), 40, 41, 215, 225–26, 234, 281

Correa, Rafael, 140

cosmopolitanism, 107, 178–89: and ability to produce comparative knowledge, 179; colonial, of English-educated Bengali middle classes, 180–81, 182; defined, 44; discrepant, 179, 188; European colonial aggression antithetical to, 186; in Ghosh's texts, 180–89; international literature and, 181–82; key aspects of, 178; opposition between nationalism and, 178, 179, 185; postcolonial, 179–81, 184–87; as proper ethical basis of global identity, 8; technopols and, 218, 219; trade and, 184–85, 187, 188, 189; transnational connectivities circulating knowledge and, 183; as "world of accommodations," 187

Costa, Mariarosa Dalla, 238

Costa Rica, parataxonomists cataloging botanical species richness in, 255

Costello, Tom, 226n.8, 246

Counter-Empire, 240

countergeographies of globalization, 35, 82

counterhegemonic globalization, 131

counterrevolution, neoconservative, 158, 159–60, 163n.1

Cousteau, Jacques, 71

Cox, Oliver Cromwell, 38, 45–46, 90

Craft, J., 245

Crapanzano, Vincent, 162

Crawford, Jeff, 196

credit card debt, 146–47

Crespo, Luis, 139

Crichlow, Michaeline A., 91n.1

crime: criminality as byproduct of globalization, 276; income inequality and, 136–38; *See also* violence

crisis of hyphen between nation and state, 262, 268

*Critical Globalization Studies* (Appelbaum and Robinson), 28

Cronkite, Walter, 41

cross-border networks of activists, as subnational sites for globalization, 83–84

cross-border politics, 89–90

*Cry the Beloved Country* (Paton), 196

Cuba, suicide as tool of resistance in, 143

cultural agency, bottom-up, 130

cultural citizenship, 130, 132

cultural hegemony, 158

culturalism, 9, 16n.7

culturalist ethnocentrism, 7

cultural relativism, 61

Cultural Studies as disciplinary practice, 163

culture(s): colonialism and creation of new and "familiar," 47; of disengagement, discontinuity and forgetting, 27; mass, 38; national, 106; of "planned obsolescence," 146

*Culture and Imperialism* (Said), 158

culture-ideology of consumerism, 178, 217, 225; commodification of everything closely connected with, 222, 287n.14; electronic revolution and global, 215–16

culture versus economy dichotomy: as false dilemma, 100; notion of coloniality of power in thinking about, 101

Cunhambebe (Tupinamba rebel), 132

Cunningham, S., 245

cybertariat vs. corporate control of new technology, 247–49

cycles of struggle, autonomist concept of, 239, 247

damnes, 14

Danielewski, Tad, 208

Daniels, P. W., 86

Darfur, 199

Darwin, Charles, 27, 146

data abuse, 256

data repatriation, calls for, 255

Datz, Giselle, 84

Davis, Mike, 142, 151n.6

Davos Forum (1996), 23

De, Esha Niyogi, 16n.1

*Death of Discipline* (Spivak), 106

death worlds, 174, 175; sovereignty in, 171–72

debt, credit card, 146–47

de Búrca, G., 266, 272n.6

decoding the national, 83

decolonial attitude/thinking, 112, 120–21, 122n.8

decolonization: coloniality as independence without, 99; first, as incomplete, 103; limitations of, 94–99; mythology about, 96, 99; second, need for, 103

decolonization of knowledge (decoloniality), 112, 120–21: two simultaneous moved implied by, 121

Deleuze, Gilles, 79n.6, 158, 236, 280

Delp, L., 244

Deming, William Edwards, 220

Deming Prize, 220, 221

democracy: as central to social movements against capitalism, 226; equation of Europe and, 124–25; interplay between globalizing forces and, 291, 292; in Iraq, imperial action to produce, 290–91; liberalism and transition to, 283; neoliberal philosophy of, 119; of pluralist polyarchy, technopols and, 218, 219; political society as product of, 268

demographic transition in global cities, less legible localizations of globalization embedded in, 88

denegation of the West, 61

dependency theory, 9, 38, 46

dependentista school in Latin America, 101, 102–3

deregulation, 234; informalization as low-cost equivalent of, 88

film. *See* Hindi cinema, globalization of
*Filmfare* (magazine), 207
finance, globalization and development of, 41
Finance Sector Union (Australia), 246
financial markets, global electronic, 82
Finley, Karen, 130
firearms, deaths in U.S. by, 151n.2
First, Ruth, 107, 191–92, 193, 194, 196–98
First Nation people, legal claims of, 89
fiscal and monetary policies, as subnational sites
    for globalization, 83
fiscal reforms, chronic poverty and, 282–83
Fisher, William F., 23–25
fishing industry, 146
Fitzpatrick, Peter, 175n.5, 263, 264, 266, 268,
    271, 271n.2
flag and American patriotism, 176n.10
food fascism, 30n.13
Food First/Institute for Food and Development
    Policy, 137
*Food Magazine,* 147
foods, luxury, 145
Fordism, shift to Post-Fordism and Toyotism
    from, 277, 286n.3
*Foreign Policy* (journal), 293
Forero, Juan, 138, 139, 140
Foster, John Bellamy, 39
Foucault, Michel, 55, 76, 79n.1, 80n.20, 112,
    122n.8, 163, 171, 175n.4, 235, 268, 270,
    278, 280
Fox, Jonathan, 86
Foxley, A., 218
Frake, Charles, 162, 163
framework agreement, 242
France: discrimination in, 132; gratuitous
    violence in, 144; rejection of
    multiculturalism in, 127; strikes
    in (1995), 245
Frank, André Gunder, 38, 46, 101, 276
Frank, T., 240
freedom: in Hegel's teleology of world history, 59;
    of individual, global market system
    commands masquerading as, 234–35; as
    self-determining consciousness, 55, 59; as
    transcendence of particularity and
    finitude, 60
Freeman, Simon, 152n.9
free markets, technopol support for, 218, 219;
    *See also* capitalism
Freer-Hunt, J.L., 208
free trade, international institutional
    emphasis on, 217
free will, Hegel on, 62, 63
Frege, C. M., 240
French Revolution, 63–64
Friedman, Thomas L., 4, 14, 16n.9, 16n.11,
    22–23, 24, 25, 30n.7, 39, 42, 131, 141–42

Fukuyama, Francis, 16n.11, 59, 114,
    176n.7, 279
Fuller, Graham, 90
Fuller, Melissa, 90
fundamentalism: Christian, 148–49; post-9/11
    climate of fear in U.S. mirroring Islamic
    fundamentalist messages, 293–94

Gabardi, Wayne, 27
Gaia, 146
*Gandhi* (film), 208
Gandhi, Indira, 167
Gandhi, Mahatma, 112, 120, 173, 203, 293
Gaonkar, Dilip Parameshwar, 6
García Canclini, Néstor, 4, 22, 26, 30n.12
Garcia Marquez, Gabriel, 22
Gasparov, B., 119
gated communities, transnational capitalist class
    living in, 218
Gautney, Heather, 16n.9, 17n.13
Geertz, Clifford, 162
gender: colonization of Americas and control of,
    111; international division of
    labor and, 243
General Electric Company, 196
General Motors, 196
genocide, 164n.3
geo- and body-politics epistemic shift, 121
geoculture, in world-system approach, 99
*Geoculture and Geopolitics: Essays on the
    Changing World-System*
    (Wallerstein), 276
geopolitics of knowledge, 96–99,
    112, 120–21
Georgia, 122n.4
Germanic *Volksgeist* vs. Oriental *Volksgeist,* 60
Germany, rise of Hitlerism and rejection of
    globalization in, 144
*Gestaltung,* 59
Ghandi, Sonia, 291
Ghosh, Amitav, 77, 80n.14, 80n.19, 180–89,
    189n.1, 208; anticolonial nationalism and
    cosmopolitanism of, 181, 184;
    contradictions in text of, 187–88; English-
    educated middle class background of,
    180–81; new cartography proposed by,
    184–85; nostalgia for nonnational
    perspective cosmopolitanism of, 185
Giddens, Anthony, 2, 5, 11, 14, 40, 118, 166
Gikandi, Simon, 3, 4, 7–8
Gillette, King Camp, 146
Gills, Barry, 84
Gilpin, Robert, 43
Gilroy, Paul, 4, 8, 172, 184
*Glass House (Rumah Kaca),* 63–64, 67n.17,
    67n.19
Glazer, Nathan, 135

global capital, 82; global cities network as strategic infrastructure for global corporate capital, 86–87

global-city model, 85

global-city studies, 83–84

global civil society, 15, 266–68: ideal of, 266; universalist aspirations underpinning notion of, 267; WTO crisis of legitimacy and, 267–68

global climate change, 146

global electronic financial markets, 82

Global Environmental Management Initiative (GEMI), 223

global inequality, 170

globalist conception of globalization, 216

*Globalization* (Appadurai), 289

globalization: from below, 278, 279, 286n.3; benefits of, 293; countergeographies of, 35, 82; counterhegemonic, 131; criminality as byproduct or underside of, 276; crises of, 212, 278; critical mapping of spaces and actors of, 82–93; defined, 276; discussion on, after September 11, 2001, 277; distribution of benefits of, 16; as dual function of increased migration and rise of new electronic media, 8–9; economic vs. political emphasis in, 277; Empire as, 168–69; evidence of, 166; of extreme violence, 172; the global as partly endogenous to the national, 82, 84; of Hindi cinema, 200–210; Hitlerism and Germany's rejection of, 144; insatiable desire for Western consumer goods illustrated by, 169–70; interplay between democracy and, 291, 292; as main producer of extremism and violence in world today, 144–51; national competitiveness as discourse of capitalist, 218–22; need to evaluate, 174–75; as new form of colonialism, 282; new role for imagination and social life, 289; in 1960s and 1970s, neocolonialism as name for, 200; parallelism between national state formation and, 49; policies associated with, 239–40; political activism in developing world against, 138–41; political form of its representation, 279–80; preferred terms in discussing, 278; process started with "discovery" of America, 122n.3, 122n.5; as proliferation of modernities, 6; similarity and overlap between postcolonialism and, 3,200; as strategy and rhetoric pursued by capital to control labor, 239; subnational as site for, 83–84; suicide in protest against antisocial policies of, 137; support for through world, 26, 29n.5; terrorism and, 136,

141–42; thinking the totality in absolute terms, 278–79; three distinct conceptions of, 216; undermining capacity of nation-states to govern, 262; universalization of areas in contemporary, 65; visible effects of, 277; weakening of Western hegemony by, 11–12; working-class responses to, 238–51

globalization theory/studies, 2–20: ancestors of, 37–38; central features summoned by, 40; confusion around use of term, 37; dissociation of globalization from features of colonialism/imperialism, 48; evolution in social sciences, 2; focus of, 2; forerunners of, 45–46; fundamental ambiguity of, 39; imperiality and, 10–13; as its own explanation, 39–40; mobility and, 8–10; modernity and, 5–8; "new" dynamic, 40; paradigmatic tone and style of, 40; postcolonial content of, 3; relationship between postcolonialism and, questions about, 3–4; relevance to global justice movement, 28; representative positions arising from literature on, 41–43; resistance and, 13–15; style of thinking informing, 39; teleology of shared mores linking postcolonial studies and, 45, 46, 49; tension between process and policy in, 39; terms of, 3, 43–44; world reconstituted as single social space in, 39

globalizing politician, role of, 219–20

globalizing practice, "world best practice" (WBP) as, 220–22

globalizing professionals, role of, 220

globalizing vs. localizing state agencies and actors, 216

global market: absolutist universals of, 233–36; image and reality in postmodern, 228–29; inner logic of command, 234–35; as total obligatory system, 230

global system theory, 215–27: building blocks of, 216; corporate capture of sustainable development, 222–25; national competitiveness as discourse of capitalist globalization, 218–22; transnational capitalist class in, 215, 216–18, 225–26

global technoscience/global infrastructure, 253–55: features defining infrastructure, 253–54; international technoscience, promise of, 254–55

Global Union Federations, 241–42

Global Unions web site, 242

global works councils, 242

Goethe, Johann Wolfgang von, 182

Goffman, Erving, 44

Goitein, S. D., 187

Goldsmith, Edward, 226n.2

labor movement revitalization, 240; *See also* unionism

labor transnationalism vs. capital mobility, 241–43

*Labour Monthly* (journal), 198

Lacan, Jacques, 282

Laclau, Ernesto, 17n.26

*Lagaan* (film), 203

Lahiri, Jhumpa, 208

Lahr, John, 207

Lakoff, Andrew, 286n.5

Lal, Vinay, 187

Lambert, Rob, 243

land appropriation, colonization of Americas and, 111

Lander, Edgardo, 96, 122n.1

Landes, David, 46

language of Hindi cinema, 202–5

Lapham, Lewis H, 42

Lapping, Brian, 196

Larsen, Janet, 145

Las Casas, Bartolomé de, 37, 132

Lasswell, Harold D., 29n.1

Latin America, 137; class disparities and poverty levels in, 137–38; dependentista school in, 101, 102–3; hegemony of Euro-American elites in Latin American periphery, 98–99; miners and indigenous people exploited in, 137–41; political dynamism in, 138–40; rise of indigenous people in, 138–39; technopols in, 218–19

Latour, Bruno, 258

law(s): hierarchical progression of, 271; international, 263, 264–66, 270, 271; made to comply with or merely replicate U.S./"international" law, 17n.16; modern logic of, 263–64, 271; nation-state and, 261, 262–63; tension between determinacy and responsiveness, 263

Lazarus, Neil, 9, 14, 16n.9, 17n.14, 17n.18, 44, 49n.3

leadership role in quest for continuous improvement, 220

Lebanese Communist Party, 142

Lechner, Frank J., 226n.1

*Lectures on the Philosophy of World History* (Hegel), 59

Left, critiques of multiculturalism from the, 126–31

legitimation crisis, 73

Legum, Colin and Margaret, 194

Leibniz, G. W., 259

Leisink, P., 239, 241, 243

Lemoine, Maurice, 139

*Le Monde* (newspaper), 132

Lenin, Vladimir Ilyich, 37, 198, 276, 284

Lentschner, Keren, 147

Le Pen, Jean-Marie, 132

Leroi-Ponant, Alexandre, 151n.4

Lewis, P. G., 16n.9

liberalism, legacy of nineteenth-century, 100

liberal reform, 283

liberal subject as possessor of rights, 178

*Liberation* (newspaper), 127

Liberation Philosophy, 29n.2

Lieven, Dominic, 115, 122n.7

life-ground, postmodern denial of responsibility to, 229, 230–33

life-serving function, disconnection of global market and the postmodern from, 230–32

lifestyle of transnational capitalist class, 218

Lim, Linda, 65

*Limits to Growth, The* (Club of Rome), 222

Lipsig-Mummé, Carla, 245–46

Lipsitz, George, 129

literature: globalization of publishing industry and, 181; international, emergence of, 181–82; with a national identity, 182; Nobel Prize for, 181, 182; postcolonial Indian writing in English, 207–9

Little Englanders, 195

living dead, status of, 171–72

Livingstone, David, 200

Lloyd, David, 16n.1, 17n.25, 100, 131

local, reconceptualization of the, 89

localizations of the global: less-visible, 88; as multiscalar, 85, 88–90

localizing global technoscience, 252–60

localizing state agencies and actors, globalizing vs., 216

local knowledge, 257–59

Locke, John, 130, 272n.6

*Long Twentieth Century, The* (Arrighi), 276, 280

Loomba, Ania, 2, 16n.3, 28

Loraux, N., 252

Lorde, Audre, 14

Los Angeles public hospital system, union-led campaign in defense of, 246

Lovelock, James, 146

Low, Setha M, 86

Lowe, Lisa, 16n.1, 17n.25, 100, 131, 184

Lowell, T., 240, 244

Lowy, Michael, 163

Lucas, Linda, 86

Luddism, 249

Luhrmann, Baz, 204

Lumumba, Patrice, 38

Lungo, Mario, 86

Lutuli, Albert, 193

luxury foods, 145

Lyotard, Jean-François, 235

Macaulay, Thomas Babington, 180

*Mahabharata* (Sanskrit epic), 201

concept, 5; defined, 43; first (from 1492 to 1650), 97–98; Giddens concept of, 118–19; as justification for continuing colonization of time and space, 114; multiple, hybrid, or alternative, 6–7; non-European models of, 63–64; paradoxes of, 285n.2; paradox of self-founding by institutions in, 263; rhetoric of, 114, 117; second (1650-1945), 98–99; as structural relationship, 6; subalternist critique of, 6; ubiquitousness of, 5, 11

*Modernity at Large* (Appadurai), 6

modernization theory, 46

Mohn, Tonya, 147

monetary and fiscal policies, as subnational sites for globalization, 83

*Monsoon Wedding* (film), 204, 205, 206–7

Montaigne, Michel de, 37

Moody, K., 241, 243

Morales, Evo, 138–39, 140

Morgan, J. P., 142

Morgenthau, H. J., 57–58, 66n.5

Morita, Akio, 218

Moro Islamic Liberation Front (MILF), 161

Moro National Liberation Front (MLNF), 161

Moro people in Philippines, 161–62, 163, 164n.2

Morrill, Richard, 89

Morris, William, 37

Morrison, Toni, 129

Morris-Suzuki, T., 89

Mouffe, Chantal, 17n.23

*Moulin Rouge* (film), 204

Movement toward Socialism, 138

Mudimbe-Boyi, Elisabeth, 31n.17

Mukherjee, Bharati, 30n.11, 181, 183, 208

Mukherjee, Meenakshi, 29n.3

multiculturalism, 281, 282; as apolitical, 130; as constellation of discourses, 127; critique from the Right, 124–26, 129; critiques from the Left, 126–31; in large cities, as constitutive of globalization, 86; narcissisms at root of some international opposition to, 132; origins in minoritian and revolutionary movements of 1960s, 129; radical, 128–29; source ideas of, 128; transnational relationalities, 131–32

multinational corporations, 281; framework agreements between global union federations and, 242

Munck, R., 249

Muppidi, Himadeep, 16n.2, 16n.10, 26, 27

murdercide, 143

murder-suicides in U.S., 151n.2

Murdoch, Rupert, 218

Murphy, Brian, 151n.4

Muscovite principality, 116

Muskal, Michael, 151n.2

*Muslim Rulers and Rebels* (McKenna), 164n.2

Muslims in Philippines, 161–62: *See also* Islam

Myconas, George, 240, 241–42, 243–44, 246

Mydans, Seth, 151n.3

myths: in Rich's "Diving into the Wreck," 70–71; right-wing, about multiculturalism, 124

NAFTA, 242–43

Naicker, G. M., 193

Naidu, Sarojini, 183

Nair, Mira, 204, 205, 206–7, 209

Namibia, 198

Nandy, Ashis, 6, 203

Narayan, R. K., 202, 208

narcissisms at root of some international opposition to multiculturalism, 132

Nasrallah, Sheikh Hassan, 142, 151n.6

Nasser, Gamal Abdel, 289

nation, modern logic of, 263–64

national, endogeneity of the global to the, 82, 84

National Commission on Terrorist Attacks upon the United States (9/11 Commission), 289, 293

national competitiveness: as discourse of capitalist globalization, 218–22; world best practice in service of, 220–22

national cultures, 106

*National Geographic* (magazine), 147

*National Identity in Indian Popular Cinema: 1947–1987* (Chakravarty), 201

National Institute for Standardization, Metrology, and Industrial Quality (Inmetro) of Brazil, 221

nationalism: emerging in context of European colonization, 186–87; Hindi cinema and, 201–2; methodological, 84; opposition between cosmopolitanism and, 178, 179, 185; postcolonial, 78, 79; practical experience of, built up by experiments, 290

nation-state(s), 16n.9; antagonism toward, 8; community-nation relation produced by, 261; crisis of hyphen, 262, 268; current crisis of, 169; decomposed into variety of subnational components, 86; exemplary, 264–66; experimentation in conception of, 290; globalization and challenge to legitimacy of, 262; hierarchical progression of, 270–71; impossibility of transforming capitalist world-system by privileging control/administration of, 101–2; insertion into global capitalist system, discourse of national competitiveness and, 219–22; invisibility of global coloniality in process of building modern, 98–99; law as fundamental to constitution of, 261;

race, constitutive role in shaping modern world-system, 6
"race to the bottom," 217, 226n.8, 243
racism, 117–19, 287n.14; colonial matrix of power and, 111–12; colonization and formation of global racial/ethnic hierarchy, 97–98; entangled with international division of labor and capitalist accumulation at a world scale, 102; institutional, 132; migrants from the South and, 94–95; multiculturalism as indirectly racist, Žižek's charge of, 128, 129–30; as pan-European disease, 128; in U.S. colonial expansion and colonial regimes, 98
Radhakrishnan, R, 2, 5, 14, 17n.15, 35, 79n.5
radical ecologists, 225
radical multiculturalism, 128–29
*Radical Regeneration: Protest, Direct Action and Community Politics* (Hain), 196
Rafsanjani, Ayatollah Ali Akbar Hashemi, 140
Rai, Aishwarya, 206, 207
Rai, Himansu, 208
Rajadhyaksha, Ashish, 208
*Raja Harishchandra* (film), 201
Raleigh, Sir Walter, 37
Ramirez, Silene, 140
Ranciere, Jacques, 17n.26
Ranger, Terence, 49
Rani, Devika, 208
Rao, Raja, 208
Raoni (Kayapo activist), 132
Rau, B., 245
Raynal, Abbé Guillaume-Thomas-François, 37
reach or scope of infrastructure, 254
Readings, Bill, 164n.3
Reagan, Ronald, 44, 223
reality: and image in postmodern global market, 228–29; postmodern denial of access to, 230–32
"Rebuilding America's Defenses: Strategy, Forces and Resources for New Century" (2000), 159–60
reciprocal accountability, 107
Reddy, E. S. (Enuga Sreenivasulu), 193
Redeemed Christian Church of God, 149
Ree, Jonathan, 185
Reel, Monte, 139
reform programs: chronic poverty and, 282–84; coalitions fostered by, 283
refugee camp, 10
refugees, perceived influx of, 175n.1
regional labor collaborations, 242
regional states, 280
*Reich,* 59
Reich, Robert B, 276, 282

religion(s): of Asia, treatment of, 59; clash between secularism and, 148–49; as refuge of oppressed, 144; suicide bombings and, 142, 143; *See also* Christianity; Islam
remote manipulation of scientific equipment, 255
Renaissance University, 111
Renan, E., 77
rentiers, transnational capitalist class as, 217
resentment, politics of, 276, 283
*Reservoir Dogs* (film), 205
resistance, 13–15: agencies for, 22–32; community-based, 245–46; globalization and conditions conducive to intensified, 169; in imperiality, subjects and sites of, 13–15; "necropolitics" and politics of, 171–72; political violence and, 172–75; subaltern knowledges as forms of, 103; *See also* working-class responses to globalization
responsibility: imperialism of, 195; international, developing definition of, 26; to life-ground, postmodern denial of, 229, 230–33
Responsible Care Program, CMA, 223
res publica of world, 276
reverse postcoloniality, 13, 17n.21
revisionism, historical, 35, 69–81: of Fanon, 76–79; motivation for, 71; as perspective vs. as guaranteed truth, 76; as return, 70; Rich's "Diving into the Wreck" and, 70–76, 77, 78; semantics of, 76; usability of past in name of future, 78–79
*Revolutionary Imagination in Americas and the Age of Development, The* (Sandaña), 276
Reynolds, David, 246
rhizome, 158
Rhodes, Cecil, 195, 197
Ribas-Matteos, Natalia, 86
Rich, Adrienne, 35, 70–76, 77, 78
Rieder, Ross, 248
Rieff, David, 133n.3–3
Rifkin, Jeremy, 145
rights: human, 83, 91n.3, 195, 269–70; indigenous, 138–39; liberal subject as possessor of, 178
right wing critique of multiculturalism, 124–26, 129
Rimmer, P. J., 89
Rio Tinto-Zinc, 196
Rittich, Kerry, 272n.11
Rizal, José, 158
Robbins, Bruce, 30n.11, 179
Robertson, Bruce, 2, 258
Robertson, Roland, 9
Robinson, William I., 16n.2, 28, 31n.18
*Rockford* (film), 204
Rodney, Walter, 38, 46

Spinoza, B., 120
spiritual crisis of our era, 225
Spivak, Gayatri Chakravorty, 4, 6, 16n.4, 30n.17, 45, 76, 80n.17, 99, 106, 116, 157, 202
sports boycott, 196
Srivastava, Jayati, 15
Stahl, Lesley, 192
Stalin, Josef, 117
Stam, Robert, 4, 5, 27, 106, 133n.5
standards: infrastructure as embodiment of, 254; quality, 219–22
Star, Susan Leigh, 253
Starr, A., 242
state agencies and corporations, links in creation of benchmarking and best practice systems between, 221–22
state: as administrator of fiscal reforms, 283; battle to reconstruct, 284; *See also* nation-state(s)
state-centrist conception of globalization, 216
*State of World 2004,* 145, 146, 147
*State of World 2006,* 146
Stauffer, Robert, 164n.2
Stavrianos, Leften Stavros, 38
Stead, W. T., 195
Steele, Jonathan, 107, 191, 193, 196, 197, 198–99
Stevenson, Nick, 178
Stiglitz, Joseph, 17n.15, 142
Stock, Richard, 22
Stockwell, Jaime, 151n.2
Stone, Sharon, 206
Stop the Seventy Tour (STST), 196
Strange, Susan, 266
Stratton, Jon, 3
Strauss, Andrew, 41
Striker, Jeff, 147
strikes: of IT workers, 247; against marketization (neoliberal austerity), 245; *See also* working-class responses to globalization
Strong, Maurice, 224
Strope, Leigh, 145
structural adjustment policies, 269
Structural Adjustment Programs, 245
structural heterogeneity, 102
subaltern, the, 6, 13, 14
subaltern knowledges, 103
subjectivity, colonization of the Americas and control of, 111, 112
subjugation, 46–47
subnational as site for globalization, 83–84
subnational scales, 85
subsumption, capitalism under globalization as process of, 277, 285n.3
subversive consumption, 14, 17n.23
suicide bombers/bombing, 151n.6; as effective weapon in war, 173–74; history of, 142–43; jihadi forms of, 151n.7; liberation

of territory from foreign occupation as goal of, 142; Palestinian, 174; proliferating cult of, 136; religion and, 142, 143; as taboo subject in post-9/11 world, 173
suicide: by cop, 143; death as representative of, 172; global death toll of (2001), 136; of Kyung Hae (South Korean farmer), 136–37
Sukarno, 289
Suleiman the Magnificent, 110
Sullivan, Michael, 176n.11
Summers, Lawrence, 293
Sundaram, Jomo, 67n.10
supranational scales, 85
sustainable development: corporate capture of, 222–25; global capitalist theory of, 223–24
sustainable development historical bloc, 224
sustainable models of development, 146
Sutherland, P., 243
Swyngedouw, Erik, 90
symbolic capital, 95
symbolic violence, 174
Szeman, Imre, 16n.1

*Taal* (Musical Beat), 203–4
Tabak, Faruk, 91n.1
Tagore, Rabindranath, 182
Tambo, Oliver, 191, 193, 194
Tamil Tigers in Sri Lanka, 142
Tanaka, Stefan, 252
Tardanico, Richard, 86
Tattersall, Amanda, 246
Taylor, Charles, 7, 281
Taylor, G., 248
Taylor, George E., 57
Taylor, Peter J., 84, 86, 249
Taylorism, shift to Post-Fordism and Toyotism from, 286n.3–4
technology(ies): computer, e-waste from, 145; cybertariat vs. corporate control of new, 247–49; development of more efficient, impact of, 146; enabling transnational connectivities, 183; interactive, 84, 89; role in globalization, 212–13
technopols, political trajectories of, 218–19
technoscience: information infrastructure for, 253–55, 259; localizing global, 252–60; promise of international, 254–55
Teeuw, A., 67n.20
telecommunications, multiscalar transactions facilitated by, 89
temporal difference, 179
temporality: Fanon's definition of, 79; space/place and overcoming of, 44
10-40 window, missionary territory of future as, 148–49

associated with, 99; as forerunner of globalization theory, 45–46; geoculture in, 99; heterarchical thinking and, 101; from perspective of colonial difference, 94–96; postcolonialism compared to, 99, 100; from subaltern side of colonial difference, 103; Wallerstein on, 100

World Trade Organization (WTO), 213; crisis of legitimacy, 267–68; external transparency problem of, 267–68; failure of 2003 summit, 141

Worldwatch Institute, 145, 146

Worth, Robert F., 152n.9

*Wretched of Earth, The* (Fanon), 76

Wright, S., 247

*Writings on China* (Leibnitz2,) invention of, 259

Yanov, A., 119

Yeats, William Butler, 38, 228

Yerofejev, Victor, 115, 120

Yeung, Yue-Man, 86

Yevtukhov, K., 119

Young, Iris, 237n.3

Yúdice, George, 130, 133n.4

Zapatistas, 91n.3

Zernike, Kare, 151n.8

Zhen, Zhang, 14

Žižek, Slavoj, 80n.15, 128–30, 279, 284, 286n.8

Zlolniski, Christian, 88

Zupnick, Elliot, 196